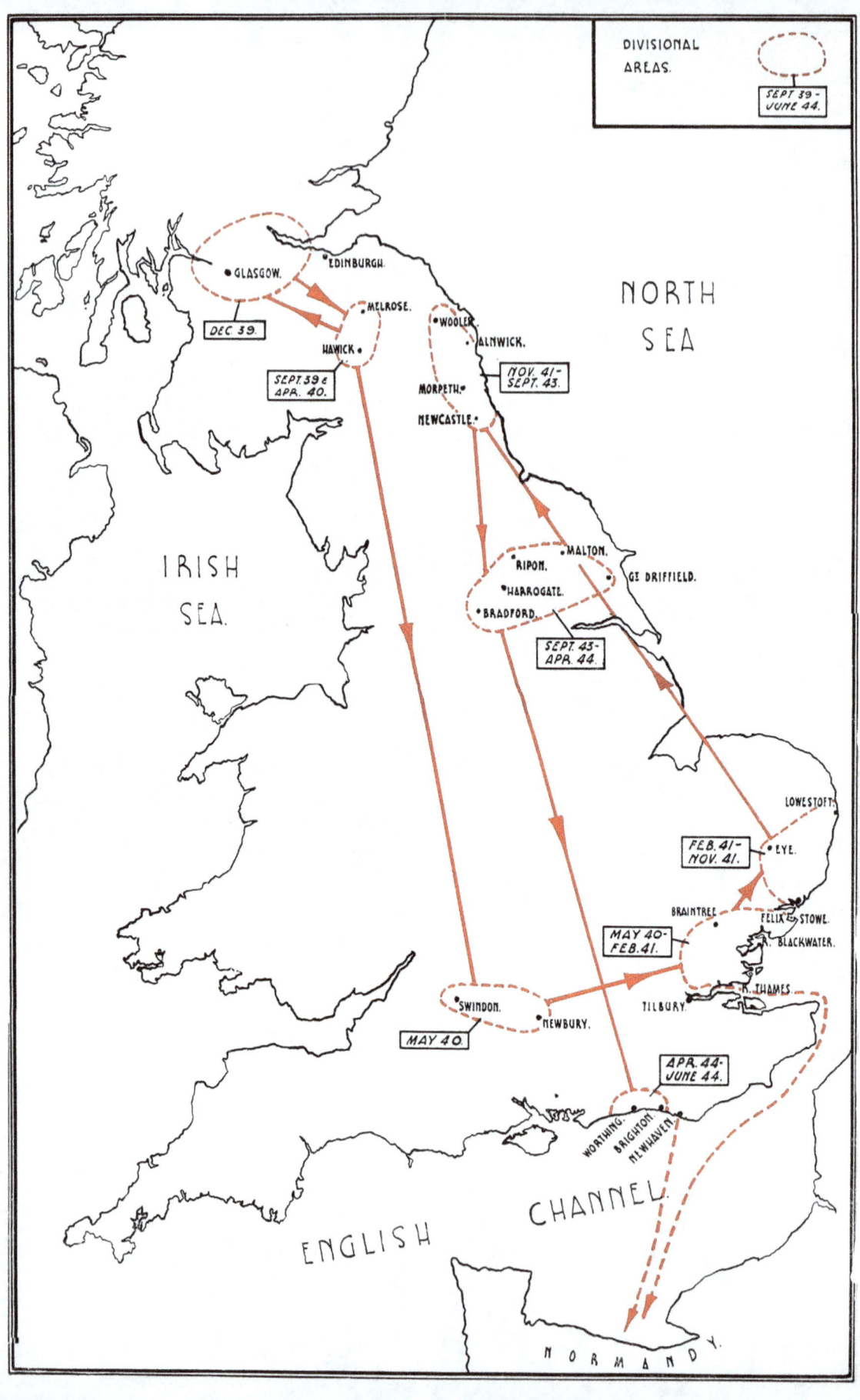

THE HISTORY OF
THE FIFTEENTH SCOTTISH DIVISION
1939-1945

This book is dedicated to the glorious memory of those who, while serving with the 15th Scottish Division, gave their lives in the Service of their King and their Country, 1939-1945.

THE HISTORY OF
THE FIFTEENTH SCOTTISH DIVISION
1939-1945

BY LIEUTENANT-GENERAL H. G. MARTIN
C.B., D.S.O., O.B.E.

WITH MAPS AND ILLUSTRATIONS

The Naval & Military Press Ltd

Published by

The Naval & Military Press Ltd
Unit 10 Ridgewood Industrial Park,
Uckfield, East Sussex,
TN22 5QE England

Tel: +44 (0) 1825 749494
Fax: +44 (0) 1825 765701

www.naval-military-press.com
www.military-genealogy.com

In reprinting in facsimile from the original, any imperfections are inevitably reproduced and the quality may fall short of modern type and cartographic standards.

FOREWORD.

This is the history of a Division which played a very gallant and outstanding part in the campaign in North-West Europe.

Landing soon after D Day, their arrival delayed a little by the high winds which were blowing in the Channel, they went straight into battle near Caen; and from that day until the German surrender found them on the shores of the Baltic they were always in the van.

They have many hard-won battle honours, the memory of which will live for ever, and of one in particular, the break-out at Caumont, they may truly say that they led the way for the Second Army.

No one who knew the Division will ever forget their individuality, their great fighting qualities, and their steadfast courage until the war was won.

Those who were privileged to be members of the 15th Scottish Division have set an example and founded a tradition of which they may well be proud.

Dempsey

General.

January 1948.

ACKNOWLEDGMENT.

ALL who served with the 15th Scottish Division, 1939-1945, will wish to record their gratitude to our historian, Lieutenant-General H. G. Martin, C.B., D.S.O., O.B.E., for the very great care and immense trouble he has taken in the preparation of this history.

Without his hard work, and much research on his part, the history could hardly have been started, much less completed.

We thank him for the very great interest he has taken and all he has done for us.

PREFACE.

THIS history has been written by Lieutenant-General H. G. Martin from all available brigade and regimental histories so far published. The thanks of the Division are due to all those who have prepared these or helped in other ways, and above all to Major-General C. M. Barber, whose enthusiasm and encouragement made the work of production both possible and pleasant.

A history such as this must necessarily deal mainly with the actions of its infantry battalions, but they would be the first to acknowledge that but for the team work provided by the supporting Arms and the Services in the Division, no history would have been made.

We realise, too, the help and support ever forthcoming from units and formations outside the Division who fought with us in all our main actions, but who are too numerous to record. Mention must, however, be made of the 6th Guards Tank Brigade, who were for a short time part of this Division, with whom we trained so hard, and who, when the time came, ably supported us in most of our main actions, and to whose gallantry and devotion we owe so much.

INTRODUCTION.

THE writer, who has tried to describe events which he did not see, offers his thanks to all those whose descriptions of what they saw have gone to make his tale. To the authors of histories, whether brigade or regimental, battalion or battery, to the writers also of personal narratives and of diaries—to all these, too numerous to name, he offers thanks. If they should think that, here and there, he has followed their text too closely, he asks their forgiveness for such plagiarisms. It is so hard to improve on the *mot juste*.

Two names, however, the writer must mention. To Brigadier Harry Clark and to Captain C. G. Lawton he owes especial debts. It was Brigadier Clark who, from the first day in Normandy, set to work to gather material for the history to be. Without these records the history could never have been written. And it is Brigadier Clark who has given the writer the story of the Division's years of preparation —the story which makes the first three chapters which follow.

Captain Lawton's part was to complete that labour of love, 'The Path of the Lion.' His was a detailed chronicle of the campaign in North-West Europe in general and of the 15th Scottish Division's part in it in particular, compiled with infinite care by an officer who served on Divisional Headquarters throughout the campaign. As a work of reference it is beyond price.

Finally, there are the maps. For these Brigadier Dick Villiers relieved the writer of all responsibility. To him and his draughtsman all credit is due for these superb maps which elucidate the story.

H. G. MARTIN.

LONDON, S.W.1,
    January 1948.

CONTENTS.

	PAGE
FOREWORD BY GENERAL SIR MILES DEMPSEY, K.C.B., K.B.E., D.S.O., M.C.	v
ACKNOWLEDGMENT	vii
PREFACE	ix
INTRODUCTION BY LIEUTENANT-GENERAL H. G. MARTIN, C.B., D.S.O., O.B.E.	xi

CHAPTER

I.	THE BIRTH OF A DIVISION	1
II.	DECLINE AND RESURGENCE	13
III.	PRELUDE TO BATTLE	19
IV.	THE BRIDGEHEAD BATTLE: THE ODON BATTLE—ETERVILLE—ADVANCE TO EVRECY—BREAK-OUT AT CAUMONT	29
V.	THE CROSSING OF THE SEINE AND ADVANCE INTO BELGIUM	108
VI.	THE GHEEL BRIDGEHEAD AND BEST	129
VII.	TILBURG—MEIJEL—BLERICK AND THE MAAS	171
VIII.	THE RHINELAND BATTLE	224
IX.	THE RHINE CROSSING	274
X.	THE ADVANCE TO THE ELBE	305
XI.	THE ELBE CROSSING AND THE FINAL ADVANCE TO THE BALTIC	321
XII.	DISSOLUTION	338

APPENDICES—

A.	CASUALTIES OF UNITS BY BATTLES	347
B.	LIST OF COMMANDERS	355
C.	ORDER OF BATTLE	359
D.	SOME STATISTICS	363
E	HONOURS AND AWARDS	365

INDEX 367

ILLUSTRATIONS.

(By courtesy of Imperial War Museum, Crown Copyright.)

SENIOR OFFICERS AT EXERCISE "PETER," YORK, DECEMBER 1943 . . . . *Facing p.*	20
2ND ARGYLLS DURING OPERATION "GREENLINE" . . ,,	71
2ND GLASGOW HIGHLANDERS ADVANCING AT CAUMONT . ,,	87
8TH ROYAL SCOTS CROSSING THE SEINE AT PORT JOIE . ,,	115
7TH SEAFORTH AT LES ANDELYS . . . . ,,	117
190TH FIELD REGIMENT CROSSING THE ALBERT CANAL PRIOR TO GHEEL BATTLE . . . . . . ,,	130
1ST MIDDLESEX IN ACTION NEAR MEIJEL . . . ,,	193
278TH FIELD COMPANY BRIDGING AT HELENAVEEN . ,,	207
1ST CANADIAN ROCKET PROJECTORS FIRING AT BLERICK . ,,	215
6TH ROYAL SCOTS FUSILIERS IN ACTION AT BLERICK . ,,	219
ASSAULT ON GOCH BY 44TH LOWLAND INFANTRY BRIGADE . ,,	260
(Drawing by Captain Bryan de Grineau. Reproduced by courtesy of 'The Illustrated London News.')	
MASSED PIPES AND DRUMS PLAYING "RETREAT" IN TILBURG, 4TH MARCH 1945 . . . . ,,	273
BUFFALOES CROSSING THE RHINE . . . . ,,	283
2ND GORDON HIGHLANDERS CROSSING THE RHINE FLOODBANK ,,	289
10TH HIGHLAND LIGHT INFANTRY CARRIED BY TANKS OF 3RD SCOTS GUARDS DURING ADVANCE TO UELZEN . . ,,	310
(Standing by Staff car are: Brigadier E. C. Colville, D.S.O., Commander, 227th Brigade, and Lieutenant-Colonel C. I. H. Dunbar, D.S.O., Commander, 3rd Scots Guards.)	
RIVER ELBE AT ARTLENBURG . . . . . ,,	322

MAPS.

COLOURED.

1. THE ODON BATTLE AND ETERVILLE	*Facing p.* 64
2. ADVANCE TO EVRECY	,, 78
3. BREAK-OUT AT CAUMONT I.	,, 92
4. BREAK-OUT AT CAUMONT II.	,, 106
5. CROSSING RIVER SEINE	,, 118
6. ADVANCE INTO BELGIUM	,, 128
7. BEST	,, 170
8. LIBERATION OF TILBURG	,, 184
9. ASTEN-MEIJEL	,, 206
10. CLOSING TO RIVER MAAS	,, 222
11. THE RHINELAND BATTLE	,, 240
12. CAPTURE OF CLEVE	,, 244
13. MOYLAND	,, 254
14. SCHLOSS CALBECK	,, 272
15. CROSSING RIVER RHINE	,, 304
16. ADVANCE TO CELLE	,, 310
17. UELZEN	,, 320
18. CROSSING RIVER ELBE	,, 336

BLACK AND WHITE.

	PAGE
1. THE GHEEL BRIDGEHEAD	133
2. THE AART BRIDGEHEAD	139
3. THE VILLAGE OF BEST	161
4. MEIJEL	203
5. BLERICK	217
6. GOCH	257

MOVES OF DIVISION, 1939 TO D DAY . . . *Front End-Papers*
PICTORIAL CHART OF DIVISION'S MOVES IN NORTH-WEST EUROPE . . . . . . *Back End-Papers*
(By courtesy of 'The Scottish Field.')

The History of the Fifteenth Scottish Division in the World War of 1939-1945.

CHAPTER I.

THE BIRTH OF A DIVISION.

On 2nd September 1939 the 15th Scottish Division was born. It had been begotten by national necessity out of the 52nd Lowland Division.

The business had started that spring, when, with a wave of his magician's wand, the then Secretary of State for War, Mr Hore Belisha, had duplicated the Territorial Army. The international situation had looked ugly enough. Unfortunately, Mr Belisha had omitted to duplicate with the same gesture the Territorial Army's equipment, accommodation, and training facilities. In consequence there was, during that summer of 1939, a good deal of confusion. On paper, the army as a whole had been recently mechanised. New vehicles and equipment had not yet reached the Territorial Army, however, and it had to be content with fleeting glimpses of these rarities at demonstrations held at the summer camps of 1939. At the same time permanent staff instructors, those mainstays of the Territorial Army, were far short of requirements, while even arms and ammunition were available only on the lowest of scales.

The units of the 52nd Lowland Division had adopted different methods to reproduce themselves. Some blended old hands with new throughout old and new sub-units alike; others formed new sub-units composed almost wholly of new hands. Both methods worked equally well. Fortunately, many of these new hands were, in fact, old soldiers, officers and men of the Territorial Army Reserve, or ex-Regulars or veterans of the first World War. What they might lack in recent experience, these old soldiers more than made up for by that priceless possession, an understanding of the ways of army life.

Fortunately, too, in those difficult days of every sort of material shortage, the embryo Division could draw on two unfailing sources of spiritual strength. First and above all, it drew its spiritual strength in ample measure from the 52nd Lowland Division, its parent. No Division was ever more richly endowed than the 52nd with the Territorial Army's spirit of voluntary service to country and of pride in regiment. The 15th Scottish Division-to-be inherited that great and precious tradition in full measure.

Its second source of spiritual strength the 15th Scottish Division found in its proud ancestry. It traced back directly to that other and illustrious 15th Scottish Division of the first World War. The new Division and its infantry brigades—all had inherited the old numbers. The new battalions all belonged to Scottish regiments, though they were not, it is true, identical with the old. Devotion to place and community and reverence for one's forebears are clannish characteristics of the Scot himself which tend to infect all those who come in contact with him. Thus it was noticeable how quickly units and drafts which joined the 15th Scottish Division from beyond the Border would absorb its community spirit and enthusiasms. In illustration of this point the story goes that, when two Lancashire lads in a unit of the Division found themselves in disagreement on a military matter, one of them clinched his argument with the striking words, " Ah've been a Jock longer than thou."

As its Divisional sign the new Division took the letter " O," the fifteenth letter of the alphabet. But the " triangular Scotch " within the circle of the " O " which had marked its predecessor, that emblem the new Division did not take. For more than a year the circle was to remain empty.

The march of events in August 1939 precipitated the 15th Scottish Division's birth. The accouchement presented Major-General James Drew, Commander of the 52nd Lowland Division, who was responsible for the delivery of the child, with quite a problem. The only staff officers of the new Division whom he had to hand were three infantry brigade majors—and these three could not muster a single clerk or manual among them. The first arrival of the Divisional staff was the G.2, who reported on 26th August. The Divisional Commander, Major-General R. Le Fanu, appeared two days later, followed closely by Brigadier John Scott, the C.R.A. Then thick and fast they came at last, until on 2nd September the 15th Scottish Division was able to begin its independent career. The relief to Major-General Drew and his staff must have been immense. They had spared no pains to ensure that their child should have the best possible start in the world, but now at last they could turn their minds to their own troubles for a change.

The 15th Scottish Division began life scattered all over the south of Scotland. Headquarters and the 46th (H.L.I.) Infantry Brigade were in Glasgow; the 45th Infantry Brigade was in and around Hamilton, extending into Ayrshire; the 44th Lowland Brigade was in the Lothians and the Border counties. The Divisional troops, very much in embryo, were forming in the West and in Edinburgh. In those days there were neither M.M.G. Battalion, Reconnaissance Regiment, nor R.E.M.E. Quartering and general administration, these were the two fundamental problems—and their solution was far beyond the professional knowledge then to be found in the Division. Few of the 52nd Division's drill halls were available, so the 15th Scottish Division had to make do with what requisitioned quarters it could find in halls, houses, or even schools.

The C.R.A. was the man with perhaps the biggest problem of all. He had to train his gunners in the use of guns and vehicles, of which they possessed not even samples. The 64th (Queen's Own Royal Glasgow Yeomanry) Anti-Tank Regiment, for instance, whose parent unit was itself only recently formed, may have heard of the 2-pounder A.Tk. gun—then the very latest—but had certainly never seen it. It was to be two months before they acquired their first specimen.

The progress which the 15th Scottish Division, and other second-line Territorial Army Divisions with it, made in the months that followed, when everything of necessity was going to the Regular Army and to the first-line, was nothing short of amazing. To those officers and men whose unquenchable enthusiasm overcame the difficulties of these days the Division owes an immeasurable debt of gratitude. Unfortunately, many of them for one reason or another were not destined to see the war through in its ranks.

The Divisional Commander was quick to realise that the Division must cut adrift from the scattered towns where it had begun life and come together in the country, where it could get down to individual and collective training. His plan was to move the Division by road and rail to training areas in the Borders. Setting 30th September as the date by which the move must be completed, the Divisional Commander left his subordinate commanders to get on with it. Despite lack of experience, the inadequacy of hired or requisitioned transport, and the idiosyncrasies of supply by local contract, the move, to the surprise of all concerned, was finished on time. Divisional Headquarters went to Jedburgh; the 44th Brigade to Melrose, St Boswells, Earlston; the 45th Brigade to Hawick; the 46th Brigade to Galashiels; the artillery to Selkirk and Jedburgh.

The Division settled in well in those pleasant and autumn-tinted surroundings. Lack of experience led to difficulties, however. Respect for the property of others was not inherent in many newcomers to army life, so powers of requisition were sometimes abused. Infringements of black-out regulations, too, were a sore trial to the local Civil Defence authorities, who quite properly took the danger of enemy air-attack very seriously. The trouble was that the vast, old, multi-windowed mills in Galashiels and Hawick in which the troops were quartered were almost impossible to black-out.

The Division was to stay in the Border country for three months or so. Here for the first time it met the warm welcome which ever after it was to receive wherever it went, not only in Scotland but also in England, and later in the liberated countries. There was no lack of kind friends to look after welfare and entertainment. In particular, the troops appreciated the concerts given by Sir Harry Lauder. It was during this first winter, too, that the Divisional Concert Party was formed, called the "Tam-o'-Shanters" after the "Cap T.O.S." or Scottish bonnet, which is the traditional headgear of Scottish troops. The "Tam-o'-Shanters," recruited from artists serving in the Division, soon grew into an excellent travelling party, which played a big part in the life of the Division.

In those days the Division lost many of its best men filched from it by the Ministry of Labour as essential workers, while the nineteen-year-olds were posted away and a severer medical standard removed many more as unfits. In October much-needed reinforcements arrived, among them an excellent infantry draft from the Midlands of England, which was soon to become as Scottish as the Scots.

Before the year was out the Division changed places with the 52nd Lowland Division. The return journey, which took place in mid-December, was carried out a good deal more tidily and with a better understanding of road discipline, work tickets, and traffic accident reports than the outward move in September. The Division was finding itself.

1939.

The layout of the Division in winter quarters was in part tactical, designed to meet the requirements of the defence of the Forth and Clyde approaches. The 44th Brigade, with the 129th Field Regiment in support, was disposed astride the Forth; while the 46th Brigade was disposed astride the Clyde in Kilsyth and Kirkintilloch and Johnstone. The 45th Brigade—less the 6th R.S.F., which had gone off to Northern Command—went back to Hamilton. The 130th Field Regiment went to Kilmarnock, the 131st into the south-western suburbs of Glasgow, and the 64th Anti-Tank Regiment to Strathaven. Divisional Headquarters took up its quarters in Park Terrace, Glasgow. So the Division settled down to face what turned out to be the severest winter in years. The clearing of blocked roads and railways was very often the order of the day. Individual training, technical and non-technical, progressed apace. In particular, motor engineering firms in Glasgow ran courses for motor mechanics and drivers, greatly to their benefit and to the benefit of the vehicles which they looked after. Officers, warrant officers, and N.C.O.s went off to attend all manner of courses of instruction. Some officers indeed even went so far afield as to do short attachments to their regular units in the B.E.F. Junior leaders generally were gaining confidence with growing experience and were acquiring a better understanding of the principles of man-management.

Early in April the Division got orders to return to the Borders in relief of the 52nd Lowland Division once more. On this occasion the 44th Brigade was allocated to the 46th Brigade's old quarters in Galashiels, with its affiliated field regiment, the 129th, in Selkirk; the 45th Brigade moved again to Hawick, with its field regiment, the 130th, in Stobs Camp close by; the 46th Brigade was allocated to Dumfries, with its field regiment, the 131st, in Annan. The 64th Anti-Tank Regiment was to go to Jedburgh, and Divisional Headquarters to Melrose.

1940.

Somewhat to the consternation of Scottish Command, who pictured frozen corpses by the way, the Divisional Commander determined that the Division should march, bivouacking *en route*. It would be, he considered, the best possible pick-me-up, physical and psychological. At once all units began intensive marching practice. In the event the Divisional Commander was amply justified in his decision. The 44th Brigade marched over the hills from the Forth to St Boswells; the 45th Brigade marched by way of Peebles to Hawick; the 46th Brigade trained to Douglas and marched thence to Dumfries, bivouacking at Abington and Moffat. The Division thus gained invaluable experience in march discipline and in living in the open; the sappers learnt how to provide water-points; staffs learnt how to handle the supply of marching columns; the troops gained new confidence in themselves and in their officers. Apart from one frosty night, which "iced-up" a number of the sleepers in their bivouacs, weather conditions were good. There were very few casualties, and the troops marched in bravely at the finish with their tails well up.

Weapons and ammunition were still woefully short and the Division was still dependent on a heterogeneous collection of requisitioned transport. None the less, all reckoned that they were now entering upon a settled period of collective training which would make of the Division an instrument fit for war. But it was not to be. Already the Norwegian campaign was in full swing, and the 46th Brigade was called on to staff a transit camp in Dumfries for transport units of the Norwegian Expeditionary Force. Soon after, the withdrawal from Norway followed. This withdrawal had major repercussions on the 15th Scottish Division. Within a fortnight of its arrival in its training areas on the Borders it was ordered south at very short notice in order to make room for the returning Norwegian Expeditionary Force.

The Division's new destination was Wiltshire, where it was to take over the quarters in Swindon, Newbury, Hungerford, and Marlborough recently quitted by the 42nd Division. The move by rail and road went smoothly. For many it was their first visit to England, and, as events were to prove, the 15th Scottish Division had said a last good-bye to Scotland. In the warmth of the English spring units settled down to resume their interrupted training amidst the unfamiliar thatch and chalk of the Wiltshire downs. There was news at last of the Divisional R.A.S.C., which was forming in Surrey. Again everything seemed to point to an orderly progress till at last the Division should be ready to the last button.

Hitler disposed otherwise. On 10th May he invaded the Low Countries. So fast did the German armies advance that on 14th May orders reached Divisional Headquarters at Hungerford to set the Division on the move once more.

The first to go was the 46th Brigade from Swindon—at less than twenty-four hours' notice. On 15th May it set out under sealed orders for an unknown destination, which turned out to be south-east Essex. There the 46th Brigade came under the 2nd London Division and took over a sector between the Rivers Thames and Blackwater, recently vacated by Brigadier C. Nicholson's Motorised Brigade of Riflemen. In a few days news was to come from France that these Riflemen had fought to the last in their gallant defence of Calais.

In its change of allegiance to an English Division the 46th Brigade found certain compensations in that it was ordered to indent on Ordnance forthwith to complete its equipment and transport to war establishment scale. Battalions suffered something of an emotional shock when they found their Bren guns increased from eight to thirty-two, but their triumph was short-lived. The 15th Scottish Division soon arrived on the scene to relieve the 2nd London Division and to resume command of the 46th Brigade, whereupon the latter lost its right to be equipped on the higher scale. So back went the new issues to Ordnance, bonny Bren guns and all. It was a bitter moment.

What had happened back in Wiltshire after the departure of the 46th Brigade was this. On 16th May the 44th Brigade had left to come under command of London District at Leatherhead. Next day the 15th Scottish Division (less the 46th and 44th Brigades) had been ordered to the Hertford district on the northern fringe of London, where it had arrived by 23rd May. It was on 26th May, after a pause to allow the 2nd London Division to pull out, that the 15th Scottish Division (less the 44th Brigade) took over the defence of Essex other than that part of it which belonged to London District. The Division found itself in the 11th Corps, commanded by Lieutenant-General H. R. S. Massy, who had first come to visit it in Scotland when he was Deputy Chief of the Imperial General Staff. The Divisional area formed part of No. 2 Sector of Eastern Command. Divisional Headquarters opened at Great Dunmow, moving thence on 7th June to Hatfield Peveril. The 45th Brigade took over the coastal area north of the River Blackwater and on the left of the 46th Brigade. After a couple of weeks the 44th Brigade, now under command of Brigadier J. A. Campbell, returned to the Division and went into reserve round Braintree.

Forward infantry brigade commanders found themselves responsible for their respective areas in their every aspect, right back to Dagenham and Epping. Yet these unfortunate Brigadiers, who expected to see the Germans landing on their beaches in a short time, were given no extra staffs to help them to cope with all the other problems of their wide realms.

The guns had the stupendous task of covering from static positions the whole forty miles of the Divisional front from Southend along the Essex coast to Harwich. And what guns! The field regiments averaged eight museum pieces per regiment—18-pounders, Marks I. and II. bearing the ominous markings "Drill purposes only," and 4.5's no less antique. The pride of the C.R.A.'s flock was the 56th Medium Regiment, which he superimposed over the whole front. Its armament showed a pleasing variety, consisting of four 6-inch howitzers, six 6-inch mortars, two 4·7-inch Q.F. naval guns, two 4-inch B.L. naval guns, one 75 mm. (French) gun taken off a ship, two 12-pounders on fixed mountings, and four 6-pounders. The rumour that Mons Meg was on her way south to join the party proved unfounded.

While the Division was taking up its defensive positions the B.E.F. was withdrawing from Dunkirk. Thus by early June the 15th Scottish, painfully conscious of its many deficiencies, found itself responsible for the defence of an English county which stood full in the path of seemingly imminent invasion. It was all rather bewildering.

The training and administrative units scattered through the Divisional area had to be brought into the defence plans, together with that grand body of men, the Local Defence Volunteers, forerunners of the Home Guard. The primary rôle of the L.D.V.s, whose arms were shot-guns, hay-forks, and such-like, was to guard road-blocks and to provide an intelligence service and guides.

Operational instructions poured in thick and fast. Wire and mines were to be laid on vulnerable beaches—but the type of mines and the means of laying were left unspecified. Obstacles against parachute and glider landings were to be erected in open spaces. An Engineer mission arrived to drive an anti-tank ditch over hill and dale, through countless miles of fair countryside behind the coastal front. Farmers saw their precious fields gashed by this fatuous exhibition of misplaced zeal, and as often as not found their stock cut off from the entry gates and dew-ponds on which they depended. In fact, however, these defensive beginnings all amounted to pitifully little. If the Germans had landed in these early months the resistance they would have met would have come more from the fighting spirit of the defenders than from the strength of their defences.

During this vigil in Essex there were many changes in the Division. Major-General R. C. Money replaced Major-General Le Fanu as Divisional Commander. It was Major-General Le Fanu's insistence on a high standard of turn-out, saluting, and conduct in the Division's infancy that had created the sure foundation on which were built up the discipline and steadfastness of maturer years. Brigadier Joe Beckett arrived to replace Brigadier John Scott as C.R.A., and the 1/7th Middlesex joined as the Divisional M.M.G. Battalion. Divisional signals were deployed for the first time, and with limited resources and a lot of very inferior equipment developed and maintained an extensive and vitally important system of wireless and cable communications—a most notable achievement. It was at this time that the brigade Signal Sections identified themselves with their brigades in that spirit of selfless co-operation which was to distinguish them in the years ahead. The Services, too—the R.A.S.C., the R.A.O.C., under its diminutive but big-hearted A.D.O.S., and the R.A.M.C.—were now playing their proper parts in the administration of the troops in the Divisional area. At this time, too, the first special service unit of Commando type was attached for training in raiding over beaches. It was composed of picked men, Guardsmen and men from English county regiments, and its Commander, Lieutenant-Colonel Laycock, was in course of time and much brave experience to rise to be Chief of Combined Operations. The unit took part in a mobile exercise along with the 46th Brigade.

The operational requirements these days brought home the need for some form of motorised unit in the Division for reconnaissance. A reconnaissance unit, to which every infantry brigade in the Division contributed, was duly formed. At first the unit was mounted in heavy motor-vans, but later these were changed for Bren carriers. This unit was the progenitor of the Divisional Reconnaissance Regiment of 1944.

The Division received many visitors in those days, most distinguished of whom was H.M. the King, who inspected the 8th Royal Scots at Colchester on 9th July and returned to visit Divisional Headquarters on 31st October. It was on the latter occasion that His Majesty gave permission for the Lion Rampant, the Royal Emblem of Scotland, to

1940.

be incorporated in the " O " of the Divisional sign—a distinction which was a source of immense pride to all ranks.

The Battle of Britain gave the Division its baptism of fire. London itself and the fighter aerodromes attracted most of the bombing, but towns like Chelmsford and Colchester and the oil-tank farm at Thameshaven also got their share. Watching the battle overhead, the men of the Division could sense with admiration and sympathy the strain under which the R.A.F. was fighting back against such odds. With the triumph of the R.A.F. overhead, there came as the months passed more and better weapons for the troops below, more and better training and better defences. In winter, too, the muddy Essex coast was no place for an invasion, so the close watch on the beaches could be relaxed. Gradually the danger of invasion receded, until in 1941 the emphasis in Divisional training was to shift from defence to mobile operations.

With the stand-down on the coast there began the phase of Divisional exercises directed by the Corps Commander. The first of these was a Command and Staff exercise, in which Divisional Headquarters moved with indescribable creaks and groans from Bramford, near Ipswich, to Sudbury. Everything went wrong that could go wrong. There followed a succession of similar exercises, which are thus described in retrospect by a participant: "These endless winter tests of endurance were more like the early wanderings of the Children of Israel than the moves of formations ready for battle with the *Wehrmacht*." None the less these exercises were of undoubted value to commanders and staffs, though they may have seemed sometimes a waste of precious time to regimental officers who might otherwise have been training their men.

1941.

The Division had prepared to bring in the New Year in the traditional Scottish fashion, so it suffered a considerable set-back when it got notice from 11th Corps that another Command and Staff exercise would start on 1st January. The Sassenach Higher Command was moved by suitable reminders of Scottish tradition to postpone the start of the exercise at least till the afternoon of New Year's Day. The Division accepted the concession and the challenge to Scottish custom in the best of spirits. All felt, however, that justice had been done when a snowstorm intervened to cause the exercise to be abandoned a day early.

On 1st February Major-General Sir Oliver Leese arrived to take over command of the Division from Major-General Money. Three weeks later, in bitter weather, the Division moved from Essex to Suffolk to replace the 42nd Division. The new coastal front was so long that even with three infantry brigades up the Division could not hold it. Indeed a fourth brigade, the 37th Independent Infantry Brigade, under Brigadier R. S. P. Wyatt, was soon put under the Division to help.

From south to north the infantry brigades formed up in the following order along the coast: the 46th Brigade between Felixstowe and Orford; the 45th Brigade between Aldeburgh and Dunwick; the 37th Independent Brigade between Southwold and South Lowestoft; the 44th Brigade in much-bombed Lowestoft itself. By this time the 131st Field Regiment was proud possessor of four 25-pounders, but it was not till September that all field regiments were to receive their full complement. Divisional Headquarters opened at Thornham Park to westward of Eye.

General Leese was to stay with the Division only five weeks before he went to command the Guards Armoured Division. Under his inspiring leadership the Division carried out exercises in river-crossing over the Lark and mobile exercises with the medium tanks and R.A.S.C. troop-carrying transport, which now became available for the first time. Major-General A. F. P. Christison succeeded him.

So the summer of 1941 passed. In September the Divisional Games at Saxmundham made a memorable climax to the Unit and Brigade Games which had preceded them. Amid intense enthusiasm and rivalry the 44th Lowland Brigade gained a well-deserved victory, with the 37th Independent Brigade in second place. The playing of the Retreat by the Massed Pipers and Drummers of the Division made a most impressive ending.

In October Brigadier C. M. Barber came from the 45th Division to relieve Brigadier Harry Clark in command of the 46th Brigade. Brigadier "Tiny" Barber thus began a continuous period of service with the Division which would not end until the Division ceased to exist in 1946.

So we come to the autumn of 1941. The Division could count itself fortunate that it had kept its original shape through two years of war. Within its solid framework of Scottish Territorial Army units, it had been able to incorporate all the units and drafts and Services which had joined it from without and yet to keep its character

1941. unchanged. It was largely due to its family spirit of co-operation that, despite repeated interruptions in training and highly inconvenient dispositions imposed by the threat of invasion and despite grievous shortages of weapons, equipment and transport, the Division had attained at last so high a standard of efficiency. Such, then, was the position when in November there fell a grievous blow. The 15th Scottish Division was placed on the Lower Establishment.

CHAPTER II.

DECLINE AND RESURGENCE.

THE 15th Scottish Division was now entering on the grimmest period of its career—its period of "banishment" to Lower Establishment. It was the victim of a change in British strategy. By autumn 1941 the danger of invasion had receded, while the call for reinforcements in the Middle East—and particularly for armoured reinforcements—had grown beyond all bounds. In consequence there had to be a general reorganisation of our military resources. In the process, unfortunately, the 15th Scottish Division had not only to lose many of its original units and a host of its original officers and men, but also to accept a lower status. Now after two years of war, when despite all difficulties and interruptions by the way the Division had climbed at last to the peak of efficiency, it was hard indeed for it to be cast back into the depths. Though perhaps the 15th Scottish was lucky after all. Things might have been worse: it might have been disbanded, or renumbered like its Highland contemporary, the 9th Division.

The 15th Scottish Division was ordered to relieve the 59th Division in Northumberland. Before it moved north in the third week of November it had already parted with the 10th and 11th H.L.I. from the 46th Brigade, which had thus lost its H.L.I. character. Gone, too, were a field regiment, a field company, a field ambulance, and an R.A.S.C. company, all of which other than the last had mobilised with the Division in September 1939. And gone were the 1/7th Middlesex to join the 51st Highland Division in Scotland, taking with them the high regard and good wishes of all in the 15th Scottish. The 10th H.L.I. were to come back to the Division in time for the invasion of Normandy, and the 11th H.L.I. the Division was to meet in an armoured rôle in Normandy; but the rest were to go farther afield.

Grieving that all that had been built up so laboriously over two long years should thus be thrown down, the Scotsmen set out to retrace their steps northward as far as Northumberland. At least there was comfort in the thought that home would be so much the nearer and home leave so much the less costly.

1941.

In Northumberland the Division found itself under the 9th Corps, which was able to give it at least this much good news that its rôle would be a mobile one. In the weeks that followed, the little town of Amble on the coast south-east of Alnwick was developed *à la* Tobruk as a defended pivot of manœuvre, while the main body of the Division was disposed as follows: in the south round Newcastle, the 45th Brigade; in the centre round Alnwick, the 46th Brigade, with the 131st Field Regiment and the 278th Field Company in support; in the north round Wooler, the 44th Brigade, with the 129th Field Regiment and the 279th Field Company in support. Divisional Headquarters opened at Hexham, but soon moved to Morpeth, where it stayed. So ended 1941.

1942.

1942 opened with the Division's fortunes at their nadir. Units were being bled white to meet the incessant demands for drafts for overseas. In face of these losses of officers and other ranks, commanding officers struggled unceasingly to maintain the team-spirit in their sub-units. Everybody and everything were being upset by constant change.

Nor were these changes confined to individuals only: many units were affected. In place of its lost H.L.I. battalions the 46th Brigade received the 7th Seaforth, who stayed with it to the end, and the 7th Camerons, who left in March to join the Parachute Regiment. The 7th Camerons were replaced by the 4th Camerons from the West Indies, where Brigadier Barber himself had previously commanded them. They in turn were replaced in November by the 9th Cameronians from the 45th Brigade. From the 45th Brigade, too, the 6th R.S.F. went to the 44th Brigade. As for the Gunners, the new C.R.A., Brigadier R. Hilton, who had joined the Division shortly before it left Suffolk, lost two of his old-timers during 1942—the 129th Field Regiment and the 64th Anti-Tank Regiment. Brigadier "Bosun" Hilton was one of those in key positions who were to see the Division through its bad times and to stay to see it launched against the enemy.

It was under these trying conditions that the regimental spirit of the Scottish units was to prove its worth. Men might come and men might go, but loyalties and traditions persisted. A leaven of devoted and indomitable officers and men, to whom the survival of these verities meant everything, remained in the Division, many of them right through to the end of its career. Inspired and encouraged by their commander, himself a Cameron Highlander, and by their senior officers, they saw to it that the Scottish characteristics and enthusiasms were preserved. A small example of what this spirit could achieve was the winning of the " Battle for the Bonnet." In this memorable engagement all " nationalities " combined in defence of the wearing of the traditional Scottish headdress, the " tam-o'-shanter," and so overcame official opposition to the extension of this honourable custom to all " Allied " units serving in the Division.

1942.

All ranks had their interest kept alive by intensive training, which took the form of exercises with a competitive motive. Samples of these were brigade exercises to study an opposed crossing over the River Tweed, a study period devoted to assault landings, and Exercise " Cheviot," in which artillerymen proved that they could find their way on foot over many miles of pathless hills. No. 20 Motor Coach Company was hardly ever off the road during its attachment to the Division, and could not have given better service. To vary the training there were social distractions in plenty.

In these activities the Padres of the Division played their Christian part. The succession of Chief Padres who served the 15th Scottish Division throughout its war-time existence saw to it that religious needs were satisfied and that unit Chaplains gained the confidence and respect of officers and men. All ranks owed a great deal to these sincere and understanding men of God.

In May Major-General Christison left the Division to go to a command in India. All who had come under his wise and understanding leadership regretted his going. They were to watch with satisfaction his subsequent career as a Corps Commander in the victorious Burma campaign. He was succeeded by Major-General D. C. Bullen-Smith, a King's Own Scottish Borderer. General Bullen-Smith continued his predecessor's policy of " work hard and play hard," and he was to see that policy triumph with the return of the Division to first-line status.

In October Northumbrian Headquarters took the place of 9th Corps District Headquarters. This change removed a future commander of the 15th Scottish Division from his staff association with it. Brigadier G. H. A. MacMillan, the B.G.S. at 9th Corps Headquarters, accompanied it to North Africa, and went on to command an infantry brigade of the 51st Highland Division before returning home in the autumn of 1943 to command the 15th Scottish.

The year ended on a note of hope. The Division heard on 7th December that it was to be restored to Higher Establishment in the near future. This new hope, however, was naturally tempered by

1942. the fear that a wayward War Office in its winsome way might yet change its mind.

1943. 1943 opened with a severe loss to the family life of the Division. The 45th Brigade was ordered off in January to the 80th Division in Western Command. The 45th was a "founder member" of the Division, though its original Cameronian–Royal Scots Fusiliers composition was much changed. It was a sad day for its Brigadier, Jimmy Russell, and for his faithful Scotsmen when they were exiled, especially now that the Division's hopes of qualifying for a fighting front were mounting. Report had it that the 45th Brigade's place was to be taken by the 6th Guards Tank Brigade. Regret at the loss of the 45th was softened by the prospects opened up by this new association with armour. The building-up of the 15th Divisional Reconnaissance Regiment by the posting to it of the 45th and 54th Reconnaissance Squadrons was another encouraging sign of activities to come. The 6th Guards Tank Brigade was to remain in Yorkshire, where it could continue to train more effectively. When the 45th Brigade left, therefore, the 44th Brigade moved down from Wooler to take its place in the south. About this time the 4th Northumberland Fusiliers joined the Division as its support battalion.

On 28th March the Division's hopes were confirmed that the promise of a return to Higher Establishment would be fulfilled. From that date the tide of its fortunes remained at the flood right up to its ultimate triumph in Germany.

Things now began to happen quickly, though the results may not have been immediately apparent to officers and men. In April the Division became part of the 1st Corps. In May came the order to mobilise to full establishment by 7th June, but without unit first reinforcements. By now the final Order of Battle of the Division as a "mixed formation" was beginning to take shape. The 181st and 190th Field Regiments came to join the 131st, and so to complete the field regiments of the Divisional Artillery. The 97th Anti-Tank Regiment had already joined, and the 119th Light Anti-Aircraft Regiment came soon after. The 20th Field Company and the 624th Field Park Company came to complete the Divisional Engineers. The Services gained the 62nd and 399th R.A.S.C. Companies, the 153rd Field Ambulance and the 20th and 22nd F.D.S., the Ordnance Field Park and the 305th Mobile Laundry, the R.E.M.E. Workshops, and the 39th Field Security Section.

All this time training was going on, with special emphasis on the tactical co-operation of infantry and tanks. The majority of officers and men lacked battle experience—were not "battle inoculated," to use the current phrase. In consequence, the lessons of battle in the Desert and in Tunisia were carefully studied for guidance. The friendships and understanding now forged between Tank Guardsmen and Scottish infantry bred a mutual confidence in each other and knowledge of each other's methods, which were to prove invaluable in the operations ahead.

In May the Division heard that its partners in the 1st Corps were the 43rd and the 61st Divisions and that the Corps had an assault rôle. In the latter half of June, however, the Division suddenly found itself transferred to the 8th Corps. To add to the curiosity which these high-level adjustments caused came the news in July that the 227th Infantry Brigade, an all-Highland formation from the north of Scotland, would come under command of the Division, though not in substitution for the 6th Guards Tank Brigade. The 227th Brigade comprised the 10th H.L.I., the 2nd Gordons, and the 2nd Argylls, the first making a welcome return to the fold. The Brigade Commander was Brigadier Ronnie Mackintosh-Walker, a Seaforth Highlander.

Next there came a most significant order, on 16th August, for the Division to move to a training area in Yorkshire in September. The move, which was to bear the shining title Exercise "Brasso," confirmed the Division's place in the 8th Corps. Soon after another "flash" announced that Major-General Bullen-Smith was to hand over command to Major-General G. H. A. MacMillan on 27th August and to go to Sicily to command the 51st Highland Division. The outgoing Divisional Commander had done much to hearten the Division in the dark days of its "banishment." He had maintained the interest of all ranks in their training and kept the administration and staff work at a high level. Now that the time had come for the Division to expand again, the ease and smoothness with which it grew to full stature testified to the soundness of its constitution.

An Assault-at-Arms at Rothbury on 2nd September was the occasion for a Divisional farewell to Northumberland and an opportunity for the new Divisional Commander to speak to the entire assembled Division. Major-General MacMillan introduced himself in words which carried conviction and inspiration.

On 5th September came the news that the Division was to include the 227th Infantry Brigade in its establishment and to release the 6th Guards Tank Brigade, thus reverting to the status of an infantry Division. Though all felt pleasure at the return of the Division to its original shape, it was pleasure tempered by regret at the loss of those good friends, the 6th Guards Brigade. The Divisional Commander sent a message to Brigadier G. L. Verney expressing that regret, and received the following reply :—

"Many thanks for your message. In spite of official separation we look forward to serving constantly together. On behalf of all ranks I send best wishes for the future."

Advanced parties left for the new locations in the West Riding of Yorkshire on 7th September. The main body moved on the 11th; Exercise "Brasso" was duly polished off by the 16th. Divisional Headquarters opened in Rawdon on the outskirts of Bradford; the 44th Brigade went to Ripon, Knaresborough, Boroughbridge; the 46th Brigade to Bradford, Keighley, Baildon; the 227th Brigade to Great Driffield, Malton; the Divisional Artillery to Bradford, Leeds, Harrogate, and Tadcaster. The 1st Middlesex, which had now taken the place of the 4th Northumberland Fusiliers as support battalion, went to Otley.

The 8th was what was known as a "mixed" Corps, containing two armoured Divisions. The 15th Scottish Division was privileged to be the only infantry Division in it. Thus it behoved the Scotsmen to make a close study of the tactics of armoured Divisions. Time was short. If they were to be ready for active operations by the summer of 1944, they would have to make the best possible use of the approaching winter weather, fair or foul.

The good people of the West Riding gave to officers and men a welcome as warm as any they had received elsewhere. All in the Division remember with gratitude the many who, often at great inconvenience or even hardship, entertained the strangers in their midst so well and provided so many comforts for them. The drafts which the Division had been receiving throughout the years had brought many Yorkshire men and men from the Midlands into its ranks. Meeting the stock from which these drafts had come, their Scottish comrades were left in no doubt as to whence they inherited their fine qualities.

CHAPTER III.

PRELUDE TO BATTLE.

THE Division's training under the 8th Corps began with Exercise "Blackcock," which opened on 25th September and lasted six days. The exercise was designed to practise the Division in an attack to breach a minefield and to clear the way for the passage of an armoured Division. Thereafter the 15th Scottish was to advance to the River Derwent, to cross it, and to establish a bridgehead on the far bank—in prophetic anticipation of happenings to come on the banks of the Seine, the Meuse-Escaut Junction Canal, the Rhine, and the Elbe.

1943.

The exercise provided precisely the wider experience that the Division, training on its own, had hitherto lacked. Units new to the Division were run in; the Divisional Commander was able to make his number with all ranks in the field; and the 15th Scottish and Guards Armoured Divisions—both as yet unblooded—had a chance to make each other's acquaintance. The exercise went off to the normal accompaniment of traffic congestion and mud—features inseparably connected with the mass moves of armour over the English countryside. During the exercise an aircraft photographed some of the naughtier examples of traffic indiscipline, and these were shown later in glorious Technicolor—to the confusion of the perpetrators.

With "Blackcock" over, the Division settled down to study the lessons learnt. The School of Military Engineering at Ripon was now giving demonstrations to show how to waterproof vehicles. There were also local demonstrations in "wading" vehicles through water. And the Divisional Battle School, acting as agent of Barnard Castle, was busy broadcasting the infantry school's doctrines. There was plenty to do.

As the November days closed in, a series of more restricted exercises began. An infantry brigade group series known as "Glaxo" and a Divisional artillery exercise bearing the significant title "Heretic" were put on regardless of what the weather might do. Then there was an exercise called "Oyster 1," held near Goole on the River Ouse,

1943.

which was the first of a succession of exercises to study and practise the technique of crossing a tidal river.

About this time the Divisional Staff Officer for Education produced a 'Short History of the 15th Scottish Division in the 1914-18 War,' compiled from the original War History by Lieutenant-Colonel J. Stewart and John Buchan. This short history served to strengthen the Division's bonds with its historic past.

December opened with a gathering of all available officers at the Odeon Cinema, Harrogate, to hear an address on training and fitness for battle by the 8th Corps Commander, Lieutenant-General John Harding, who came fresh from the Eighth Army in the field. For the rest the month produced a couple of cloth model exercises, one run by the 44th Brigade as the basis for a discussion between the Guards Tank Brigade and the Division on infantry co-operation with army tanks; the other run by the Division itself to study a Divisional breakout in the follow-up stage from a bridgehead previously established by an assault corps.

During the month a representative of 2nd Echelon, G.H.Q., arrived to explain to the headquarters of formations and units how to work the army system of overseas documentation, which, significantly, they were to adopt on 1st January.

There was also held at Harrogate a Confirmation School for all ranks to discuss the purposes of the Churches of Scotland and England and to encourage membership. The Bishop of Knaresborough led the Church of England discussion, Dr Jarvis of Glasgow that of the Church of Scotland. Over 500 attended the School, with encouraging results: nearly all joined one or other of the Churches at the end of the five-day course.

1944.

The first major event of 1944 was Exercise "Clansman," a Divisional exercise with troops designed to practise the passage of river obstacles and a minefield. The 44th Brigade, with the Inns of Court Regiment under command, acted as "enemy." There thus began the association of the regiment with the Division which was to continue so happily in Normandy. The remainder of the Division, starting from an assembly area west of Bradford, advanced northward across successively the Rivers Aire, Wharfe, and Nidd. The ground was frozen; the roads icy; snow fell at intervals; on the Upper Wharfe near Bolton Abbey the sappers had to do a pretty considerable job of bridging. Exercise

SENIOR OFFICERS AT EXERCISE "PETER," YORK, DECEMBER 1943

BACK ROW

LAWTON	LOCHORE	JOHNSTONE		LAWSON		CHITTOCK	HARDWICK		BROWN	JACKSON	EDMEADES	COPPLE
(G.S.O. 3 O.P.S.)	(B.M. 227th)	(2nd i/c K.O.S.B.)	BUCHER	(B.M. 46th)	WOOD	(A.P.M.)	(A.D.C.)	DELACOMBE	(2nd i/c R.A.S.C.)	(B.M. 44th)	(B.M. R.A.)	(46th Bde. Workshops)
			(Div. School)		(279th Fd. Coy.)		GILLINGTON	(8th R.S.)	BROOME			
							(20th Fd. Coy.)		(278th Fd. Coy.)			

MIDDLE ROW

WARREN	CAMPBELL	WHITWORTH	BUCHANAN	WALKER	WALKER	M'GRATH	CAMPBELL	GRANT-PETERKIN	GRAHAM	MACKINTOSH-WALKER	YOUNG	STREATFIELD	COLVILLE
(193rd Fd. Amb.)	(2nd Glas. H.)	(C.R.A.S.C.)	(6th R.S.F.)	(A.D.O.S.)	(2nd i/c 9th Cameronians)	(A.D.M.S.)	(153rd Fd. Amb.)	(Recce Regt.)	(97th A.Tk.)	(227th Bde.)	(10th H.L.I.)	(190th Fd.)	(2nd Gordons)
	YOUNG		TWEEDIE		GRANT			BUCHANAN			ATTLEE	WALDRON	
	(119th L.A.A.)		(2nd A. & S.H.)		(7th Seaforth)			(194th Fd. Amb.)			(G.S.O. 3 (I.))	(1st Mx.)	

FRONT ROW

GRANT	DEVEREUX	BARBER	HILTON	CLARK		MILLAR			MONEY		TYLER	HAILEY	KINGSFORD-LETHBRIDGE
(D.A.Q.M.G.)	(181st Fd.)	(46th Bde.)	(C.R.A.)	(G.S.O. 1 (L.))	GARDINER	(C.R.E.)	SEELEY		(44th Bde.)	MACMILLAN	(G.S.O. 1)	(131st Fd.)	(A.A. & Q.M.G.)
					(C.R.E.M.E.)		(C., R. Sigs.)			(G.O.C.)		BURNETT	
												(G.S.O. 2)	

[To face p. 20

"Clansman" was a real endurance test—and an appropriate beginning to the Division's "hardening process."

Close on the heels of "Clansman" came the 8th Corps' Signals Exercise "Tally-ho," which, true to its name, moved by bounds over a wide stretch of fair hunting country to the east and north of Leeds.

About this time there was an exchange of officers and men with those of the 28th U.S. Infantry Division, which was the American Division then affiliated to the 15th Scottish. The Commanding General of the 28th Division, Major-General Lloyd D. Brown, visited the 15th Scottish, and was guest of honour at a Guest Night with its proper accompaniment of pipe music. As an account written later by an American officer testified, these exchanges did a great deal to foster inter-Allied interest, understanding, and goodwill.

At the beginning of February there came two notable visitors—General Sir B. L. Montgomery, Commander of the 21st Army Group, and Lieutenant-General Sir Richard O'Connor, the new Commander of the 8th Corps. For General Montgomery's visit the Division was divided into four groups, each of which he addressed in turn, speaking from a raised stance on the bonnet of a jeep. He radiated confidence. General O'Connor was a Cameronian and one famed for that series of brilliant victories won against great odds in Libya during the winter of 1940-41—the victories which put the British Army back on the map. All remembered how, after he had had the misfortune later to be taken prisoner when trying to restore a situation which he himself had not created, he had made his escape from Italy. General O'Connor found the 15th Scottish Division very much to his liking and gained its affection from the start.

Of the pre-invasion period of preparation Exercise "Eagle," which ran for twelve days in mid-February, was the outstanding event. It was the 8th Corps' one opportunity to practise its armoured rôle at full strength: the next and only other occasion on which it would take the field similarly constituted would be in the break-out battle at Caumont at the end of July. The Divisions in the Corps were the 15th Scottish, the Guards Armoured, and the 11th Armoured. G.H.Q., Home Forces, ran Exercise "Eagle" and controlled the "enemy," who were made up from the 38th and 47th Infantry Divisions and the 9th Armoured Division—none of which was included in the army of invasion. The field of battle was the Yorkshire Wolds.

"Eagle" was designed primarily as a test of the control and supply of armour in battle. In consequence, the 15th Scottish spent much of its time in moving between bivouac areas, and was committed to action only during the minefield-breaching stage. The exercise, however, was an excellent test of the soundness of the Division's battle drill and administration, which latter had a full-dress rehearsal in every detail, down to the submission of recommendations for honours and awards and a trial run for the Mobile Laundry and Bath Unit—that apple of A.D.O.S.'s eye.

"Eagle," too, served to introduce the Division to the thrill of armoured movement in mass and the sense of invincibility which it can bring. In the unavoidable absence of German 88-mm. gunners, however, "Eagle" could not bring a counter-balancing awareness of what contact with a determined enemy really means: that knowledge could be driven home only by bitter experience in battle. As was to be expected at the time of year, mud, bogged vehicles, and congested roads revealed many weaknesses in driving, traffic control, and anti-aircraft defence. The exercise resulted in the issue of more powerful types of vehicles for cross-country movement.

After a rest period, during which the Division received a consignment of Wasps or flame-throwing carriers for trial, there followed two brigade exercises in rapid succession. The first was Exercise "Tatler," staged by the 44th and 6th Guards Armoured Brigades in a rather restricted area suitable for tanks which had been found near Nottingham. The exercise grew out of a series of attachments which the battalions of the Division were then making in turn to their affiliated battalions of the 6th Guards Tank Brigade at Welbeck Abbey. The second exercise was another in the "Oyster" series, a five-day bridging exercise carried out by the 46th Brigade over the Ouse at Goole, where there is a big rise and fall of tide. The exercise taught both the Engineers and the 46th Brigade a lot which was to be extremely useful later on. The Higher Command, too, profited by the lessons learnt.

Even in these strenuous pre-invasion days, however, life was not all soldiering. The Chaplains were now holding their second Confirmation School at Farnley Park, near Otley. About 630 of all ranks attended, with the same good results. The Bishop of Knaresborough again led for the Church of England; for the Church of Scotland, however, on this occasion the leader was Dr E. J. Hagan, the Moderator himself, who was paying the Division a very welcome visit.

About this time, too, the Divisional Commander was interesting himself keenly in the formation of a Divisional Piping Society, as President of which he appointed his Chief Umpire, Colonel H. J. D. Clark, with Major Iain Grant, the D.A.Q.M.G., as Honorary Secretary. The object of the Society was to improve the standard of playing, not only of unit pipers but also of the Massed Pipes and Drums of the Division. The Society started a piping school for young pipers at Divisional Headquarters. There they had the benefit of instruction from two famous Scottish pipers, Pipe-Majors MacLeod of the Seaforth and Nichol of the Gordons.

The issue of equipment and stores and the practice of vehicle waterproofing—which latter pastime involved welcome trips to an establishment in Scarborough—occupied the Division till well into April. About this time the British Army found itself short of officers, whereas the Canadian Army had a surplus. So, under a scheme called "Canloan," a number of Canadian officers were posted to units of the Division. These Canadians generally were first-class officers, and were to prove welcome reinforcements to their units throughout the campaign.

It was at this time, too, that Their Majesties the King and Queen with the Princess Elizabeth honoured the Division with a visit. The Division paraded in three groups, each of an infantry brigade with its affiliated arms, and the Royal party walked along the ranks and saw everyone. During an interval for tea and buns—the responsibility of the C.R.A.S.C.—all officers of Divisional Headquarters were presented to Their Majesties. None who was present will forget that heartening visit on the eve of battle. Later, Mr Winston Churchill, our great war leader, came to see the Division.

When in the middle of April the Division received orders to move to a concentration area in Sussex, everything was "on the top line." As a farewell to Yorkshire the "Tam-o'-Shanters," with a party of pipers and drummers, gave two performances on the ample platform of the Sheffield Town Hall. With the whole-hearted encouragement of the Divisional Commander, the "Tam-o'-Shanters" had now fully recovered from the lean times they had suffered when the Division was on Lower Establishment. The people of Sheffield gave such enthusiastic support to these performances that a large profit for the Divisional Welfare Fund accrued.

On arrival in Sussex the Division found to its satisfaction that its concentration area had that strongest of attractions to offer—comfortable quarters within reach of light entertainment. This fact,

1944.

in combination with mild weather and a lovely countryside, persuade⟨d⟩ even the critical Scotsmen to take a favourable view of their surround⟨-⟩ings. Littlehamption, Worthing, Brighton and Hove were all within easy reach. There was still an air about these famous watering-places, shorn though they were of their peace-time glories and cluttered up with beach obstacles and barbed-wire. It was something of a shock to find the tanks of the Guards Armoured Division in firm possession of Brighton's more fashionable thoroughfares. The harbours, too, on the Sussex coast were packed with a miscellany of multi-coloured landing-craft, while overhead there passed an unending stream of aircraft formations gleaming in the sun. Strangely enough, no enemy aircraft came to invade this idyllic scene. The Luftwaffe's failure to reconnoitre the concentration area and invasion ports during these weeks is unaccountable.

A blend of work and play calculated to keep the Division mentally and physically fit was the order of the day. The Divisional Senior Chaplain led a third Confirmation School; the Bishop of Chichester conducted the Confirmation Service. Her Royal Highness the Princess Mary, Colonel-in-Chief of the Royal Scots, honoured the 8th Battalion by visiting them in Worthing. On 20th May all officers of the rank of Lieutenant-Colonel and above went off to Chichester to hear General Montgomery speak on the subject of the invasion. They returned marvelling at the certainty of success which he had inspired. At a parade of the 227th Brigade General Eisenhower met the commanding officers of the Division. All felt that here was a man and a soldier whom they could trust. The 1st Middlesex won the Northern Command Association Football Cup, beating the 535th Guards R.A.S.C. Company, and the 6th K.O.S.B. overwhelmed the Welsh Guards in a Rugby football final. Unit 1st Reinforcements went off to 105th Reinforcement Group at Bordon. Fortunately, the Divisional Commander paid them a visit not long after—in time to save a number of them from being whisked off, to their dire consternation, to join other formations which, it appeared, were short of men. This incident revealed what seemed to be a strange disregard on the part of the A.G.'s Branch for the regimental spirit.

It now began to seem probable that it would fall, not to the 6th Guards Tank Brigade but to the 31st Brigade Royal Tank Corps to support the Division in its earliest battle. In consequence there was held at the headquarters of the 44th Brigade an exercise called

"Tatler 2," which was attended by brigade commanders and commanding officers of all arms of the Division, and also by officers of the 31st Tank Brigade. The lessons of "Tatler 1" formed the basis of the discussion whereat a common doctrine was evolved. About this time, too, a new appointment was created at Divisional Headquarters, that of G.1 (Liaison), which, to the great delight of all, went to Colonel Harry Clark, the original commander of the 46th Brigade and afterwards Divisional Chief Umpire, thus enabling him to accompany the Division overseas.

A memorable event of these last days was the Divisional Games held at the Greyhound Stadium at Brighton on 24th May. Those who had borne the burden of the past five years could look around them on that day with quiet pride. The Division had come to maturity at last. The matchless spirit of the 15th Scottish radiated from these poised, fit, smart, enthusiastic, self-reliant men who met thus in a spirit of friendly rivalry. In retrospect these old-stagers could recall the mob of boys, uncouth and untidy, but dauntless of spirit, who had come crowding in to begin their struggle for knowledge under instructors only little more instructed than themselves and with nothing but a mockery of equipment on which to learn. Despite temporary banishment to Lower Establishment which had sapped the Division's strength for a time, that mob was now transformed: the 15th Scottish was a Division second to none and trained to the moment—though most of its fine soldiers still lacked fighting experience and asked themselves, as soldiers will, what that unknown experience would bring.

The Division was a peculiarly happy one. Among the officers the use of Christian and nicknames was an accepted custom on military no less than on social occasions. The Games brought all officers and men together for one last gathering, social and competitive, before they set off into the unknown. It is an opportunity, therefore, to say a word or two about the more prominent personalities.

First and foremost there was the Divisional Commander, Major-General MacMillan. To him indeed war was already familiar. In the first World War he was a distinguished front-line regimental officer, and his recent experience in the second World War has already been mentioned. His powers as trainer, leader, and driver of men were evidenced by the way in which the Division had come on since he had taken command. There, too, was Brigadier Douglas Money, commander of the 44th Lowland Brigade and himself a Royal Scot. In 1940 as a battalion commander he had been wounded in France. A shrewd, experienced commander he was, proud of his Lowlanders and convinced of their ability to show the way to the two Highland brigades leagued against them. Then there was Brigadier "Tiny" Barber of the 46th Highland Brigade, himself a Cameron Highlander, well known alike for his great height and dry sense of humour. When Major-General MacMillan was wounded later, after two months in Normandy, Brigadier Barber was to succeed to the command of the Division and to lead it to the end. His tactical sense, resolution, and cool self-reliance were to prove a very present help in time of trouble. Last of the infantry brigade commanders, there was Brigadier Ronnie Mackintosh-Walker of the 227th Highland Brigade. A Seaforth Highlander, he had been taken at St Valerie and had afterwards escaped. It was thanks mainly to his capacity as trainer and to his humorous outlook and understanding insight into his men's interest and problems that the 227th Brigade had been able to take its place in the Division so quickly and so well. Last of the Brigadiers there was the C.R.A., Brigadier "Bosun" Hilton, that apostle of physical fitness who had been a flyer in the first World War. In the realms of gunnery he was ever in search of some new thing. The grand teams of gunners that he produced were sufficient testimony to the quality of his leadership.

The C.R.E., Colonel "Jock" Millar, had been a Scottish Rugger Internationalist in his youth. He still showed those qualities of anticipation, quick decision, and determination which had got him his "Cap." Colonel D. L. Kerr, the A.D.M.S., had not been long with the Division, but he had cause for well-merited pride in the high standard of his medical units. The other heads of Services were Lieutenant-Colonel Ken Whitworth, the C.R.A.S.C.; Lieutenant-Colonel Syd Walker, the A.D.O.S., who had been with the Division from the beginning; and Lieutenant-Colonel Gardiner, the C.R.E.M.E.—all of them what the Americans call "Can-Do" boys. Then there was Lieutenant-Colonel Frank Seely, O.C. Divisional Signals, without whose participation no battle could be fought. And at Divisional Headquarters there was the G.1, Lieutenant-Colonel Desmond Tyler, and the A.Q., Lieutenant-Colonel Kingsford-Lethbridge, or "K. L." for short. And last but not least, there was Colonel Harry Clark, the new G.1 (Liaison). "In sooth a goodly company." The Games had brought them all together.

It was a lovely day: the Lowland Brigade defeated its Highland rivals; the 8th Royal Scots Tug-of-War Team pulled its serene way to victory; a young sapper won the Piping Championship; the Massed Pipers and Drummers of the Division played and marched and counter-marched in perfect rhythm, sending the gathering home with the strains of the Divisional March, "Scotland the Brave," ringing in their ears.

So June came, with suspense in the air. On 6th June came news of the assault, so long awaited. Soon it would be the turn of the 8th Corps in the follow-up. Advanced parties and transport were all to go by way of Tilbury; all marching troops, on the other hand, were to cross by L.C.I. from Southampton and Newhaven. On 8th and 9th June the advanced parties slipped away to the Port of London, and with them went the Divisional Commander. Four days later they reached Normandy. Major J. F. Marnan, Irish Guards—then G.3 and afterwards G.2 of the Division—thus describes the scene:—

"At 6 o'clock on the morning of 13th June the steamer carrying the advanced parties of the 15th Scottish Division collided gently with a troopship which was at anchor off Courseulles. A mere brushing of cheeks it was, and with the tide which was running against a fresh breeze all agreed that nobody was to blame. Nor was anybody hurt, though some of the troopship's boats which had been hanging outboard on their davits were crushed like hazel-nuts, with much the same cracking noises. To the soldiers in the steamer the trivial accident was the first unexpected happening of a great adventure. Three hundred yards away a cruiser was firing inland over the beaches. Less than a mile away was the coast of France, white surf and yellow sand against a green countryside.

"It was a brilliant morning. In every direction, even astern and out to sea, ships at anchor were dotted across the dancing water in a close pattern. They reminded one of skaters grouped in an old Flemish painting or the elegant crowd in a piazza by Guardi. Close at hand small craft fussed about. A huge Rhino ferry—a raft powered by four outboard engines—manœuvred miraculously at the speed of a heavy rowing-boat. Farther down the coast two battleships, grey shimmering pyramids in the early sun, gave focal height to the pattern. There was joy in the air, something more and deeper than the mere exhilaration of a fine morning at sea. A great achievement lay spread out in the sunlight before our eyes."

On 11th June main Divisional Headquarters went to a marshalling area at Southampton, where they remained cabined and confined till 13th June. So one by one all units of the Division passed over. The last to leave home saw something of the first V.1's. Indeed a medical unit had one of its trucks blown up in London Docks.

The Division landed for the most part on the eastern beaches between "Queen" and "Rodger." As a general rule there was to have been a two-day interval between the landing of advanced parties and main bodies. The weather, however, began to deteriorate about 16th June, and by 19th June had reached gale force, so upsetting all time-tables; in fact, some transport arrived only on 24th June, just in time to move up that night direct to assembly areas for Operation "Epsom," the Division's first battle.

The years of preparation were over: the year of action had begun.

CHAPTER IV.

THE BRIDGEHEAD BATTLE.

PART I.—THE ODON BATTLE.

15th to 25th June.

No such summer gale as that which blew from 19th to 22nd June across or directly into the British and American beaches had been known in living memory. The whole shipping programme was thrown into confusion; rafts and landing-craft were sunk or smashed, equipment lost or its disembarkation delayed. The 8th Corps' landing was so much behind schedule that Dempsey had to postpone the Second Army's new offensive, planned for 22nd June, till 25th June. And even then many units of the 15th Scottish Division were still short of their transport or had received it only just before the battle was to begin.

Briefly, the story of the preceding eighteen days in the bridgehead had been this. When the Allies had landed on 6th June, Rommel had promptly committed all the armoured reserves he had locally available—that is, the 21st Panzer Division, the 12th S.S. Division, and the Panzer Lehr—in a series of fierce but rather disjointed counter-attacks. When these attacks had failed to wipe out the bridgehead, however, Rommel had changed his tactics. His new plan was to cordon off the bridgehead and so to gain time to collect a really powerful armoured reserve for a deliberate counter-attack.

Montgomery for his part, having gained the initiative, had no intention whatever to lose it. His object, therefore, had been to give Rommel no respite to build up his armour. To this end Montgomery had put in one limited offensive after another, and had thus contrived to use up Rommel's reinforcements piecemeal as they arrived. Meanwhile Montgomery had been doing his utmost to develop his bridgehead in readiness for the master-stroke which he had planned from the beginning—the break-out southward by the 1st U.S. Army on the right.

The plans maturing when the 15th Scottish Division arrived in the bridgehead were these. As soon as the necessary American

15th to 25th June.

reinforcements had landed, the 1st U.S. Army on the extreme right was to break out southward, directed on Grainville, Avranches, and Vire. This was to be the master-stroke. Meanwhile, however, the Americans were to capture and open the port of Cherbourg. At the same time the Second British Army on the left was to take Caen and so to attract towards itself the maximum of enemy reserves, especially of armour, whilst providing a strong left pivot of manœuvre for the whole of the 21st Army Group.

These operations against Caen were to take the form of a double envelopment—a thrust, that is, on the right across the Odon and Orne south-west of Caen, and on the left another thrust from the Orne bridgehead to northward of it. It had been Dempsey's original intention that the 8th Corps should deliver this latter thrust north of Caen. In consequence, on 17th June, the reconnaissance parties of the 15th Scottish Division had gone off, along with those of the rest of the Corps, to reconnoitre the 51st Highland Division's sector north of Caen, on the extreme left of the 1st Corps' front. They had soon found, however, that the Orne bridgehead was far too cramped, exposed to enemy fire, and lacking in approach roads, to be suitable for a corps forming-up area. The plan, therefore, had had to be changed —much to the relief of all concerned.

Thus the Second Army was now to regroup for the coming operation with the 30th Corps on the right, the 8th Corps in the centre, and the 1st Corps on the left. The right thrust, across the Odon and the Orne, was now to be delivered jointly by the 30th Corps and the 8th Corps—with the 8th Corps playing the leading part; the left thrust —much scaled down—was to be delivered by the 51st Division of the 1st Corps.

Originally scheduled to begin on 18th June, the operation had had to be postponed for a week on account of the shipping hold-up. The attack was to open on the left of the 30th Corps' front on 25th June, when the 49th West Riding Division was to advance to seize the high ground around Rauray in order to give flank protection to the subsequent advance of the 8th Corps on its left.

The fighting was then to spread from right to left. Thus on 26th June the 8th Corps in turn was to take up the attack. It was to break out through the front held by the 8th Canadian Brigade of the 3rd Canadian Division on the right of the 1st Corps, was to force the crossings of Odon and Orne, and was to seize the high ground north-east of Bretteville-sur-Laize in order to command the exits from Caen towards the south. Such was to be the 8th Corps' Operation "Epsom," its baptism of fire in North-west Europe. It was to be the largest operation yet mounted in Normandy.

<small>15th to 25th June.</small>

Finally, on 28th June, the fighting was to extend still farther left or eastward. The 3rd Canadian and 3rd British Divisions of the 1st Corps were then to close on Caen and to clear the city.

It was on 19th June at the 15th Scottish Divisional Headquarters at St Gabriel that the Divisional Commander first gave out the plan of Operation "Epsom." The Division, with the 31st Tank Brigade under command, was to have the honour of spear-heading the operation. Attacking south of Bretteville l'Orgueilleuse, it was to seize the crossings of the Odon.

Briefly, the plan of attack as it finally took shape was this. H-hour was to be 7.30 A.M. on 26th June. The Division was to attack on a two-brigade front: on the right, the 46th Highland Brigade with the 9th Cameronians and the 2nd Glasgow Highlanders up; on the left, the 44th Lowland Brigade with the 8th Royal Scots and the 6th R.S.F. up.

For armoured support the 46th Brigade had the Churchills of the 7th Royal Tanks; the 44th Brigade those of the 9th Royal Tanks. There was, too, a contingent of the 79th Armoured Division's invaluable "Funnies"—to wit, two squadrons of Flail tanks for making passages through minefields and one squadron of Armoured Vehicles R.E. (A.V.R.E.s), which either launched petards of great explosive effect but rather short range or else laid bridges over gaps. These "Funnies" were divided about equally between the two brigades. In addition, two companies of medium machine-guns of the 1st Middlesex went to the 46th Brigade, one company to the 44th Brigade.

A word must here be said about the system of liaison between the infantry and their guns—the system which was to shoot the infantry on to their objectives and hold their front in countless critical situations all the way from Normandy to the Elbe. Of the three Divisional field regiments, the 181st worked always with the 44th Brigade, the 190th with the 46th Brigade, the 131st with the 227th Brigade. Thus these field regiments were soon to become part and parcel of the brigades which they served. The regimental commanders lived and worked in the pockets of the respective brigade commanders, the battery commanders in the pockets of their respective battalion

15th to 25th June.

commanders, while an F.O.O. and O.P. party went with every forward company. Soon there was to grow up between battalion and battery an intense feeling of mutual trust, affection, and esteem. Of the many shining examples of this perfect relationship I need cite one only: that which was to grow up between the Seaforth and the 531st Field Battery, which latter was to have a Major and three Captains killed alongside the Jocks.

The Divisional start-line ran from a point just north of Le Mesnil Patry eastward along the road to Norrey-en-Bessin. The first objective was to be the ridge which runs from Le Haut du Bosq to pass southward of Cheux and La Gaule. This was to be the O.P. ridge for the further advance. On this objective the 227th Highland Brigade was to pass through the 46th Brigade and was to secure the crossings of the Odon some five miles from the start-line. The 11th Armoured Division was then to pass through in its turn and to exploit to south-eastward.

The attack was to be supported by close on 900 guns, which included the guns of three cruisers and a monitor. In the barrage alone 344 field and medium guns were to be employed.

There was also an extensive programme of air support, which, dependent on weather and other conditions, provided for attacks by heavy, medium, and fighter bombers on enemy rear areas, gun positions, and headquarters.

With such support the 15th Scottish Division could feel confident that, as a formation new to battle, it was to be committed for the first time under conditions which, so far as was possible, would ensure success—success, however, to be won only by bitterly hard fighting.

During the next few days reconnaissance parties from the 15th Scottish Division spent up to forty-eight hours in the line with forward Canadian units to familiarise themselves with the ground over which they were to assault. Here in Le Mesnil Patry and Norrey the Canadians had been dug in since D + 1. The villages were now mere heaps of rubble and stones, swept by violent gusts of enemy mortar and machine-gun fire from the slope a few hundred yards to southward. The Division owes the Canadians an immense debt of gratitude for all the help they gave, not only over the reconnaissance but in a score of ways besides, such as the lifting of their own defensive minefields for us.

The ground over which the attack was to go was typical of the rich farmland of Normandy. It was close, blind country, where O.P.s were difficult to find—a land of ridge and hollow, farmstead and small village, high-standing corn and pasture, copse and orchard and hedgerow. These Normandy hedges—thick, strong, old, and so often concealing dry ditches at their foot—made perfect cover for resolute defenders. And the resolute defenders were there. The front was held by the 12th S.S. Panzer or Hitler Youth Division—young fanatical troops who had earned a bad reputation with the Canadians for the shooting of prisoners.

15th to 25th June.

Ahead, the ground to the south sloped gently down at first to an insignificant stream, the Muc, beyond which it rose again to a commanding ridge which, from the Rauray spur in the 49th Division's sector on the right to the hump known as the "ring contour 100" on the left, ran more or less east and west across the 15th Scottish Division's front some 4000 to 5000 yards south of the start-line. Visible below this ridge lay Le Haut du Bosq and Cheux. The ridge concealed the country beyond, which sloped gently down once more to the Odon. The observation from the ridge was very necessary in order to support a further advance.

The Divisional reconnaissance parties found great difficulty in identifying their objectives by the map in the close and undulating country ahead. In particular, St Mauvieu was almost entirely hidden in the bed of the Muc. The start-line, too, was under observation and fire and difficult to reconnoitre thoroughly. Le Mesnil Patry, with its narrow, sunken lanes, turned out to be a perfect tank obstacle, so the Cameronians' rifle companies and supporting tanks would have to move up by different routes. On the left, the flank towards Carpiquet airfield was open and swept by enemy fire.

The destruction already wrought in that fair countryside was sad to see. Bretteville l'Orgueilleuse—Bretteville the Proud—was nothing more than a pitiful heap of ruins, while a shattered stump was all that marked where Norrey Church had stood for 800 years—Norrey, described on a neighbouring road-sign as "Merveille du XII. Siècle."

After dark on 24th June the bulk of the guns moved up to the gun area, there to remain concealed in barns and coppices throughout daylight next day. At the same time the infantry of the 15th Scottish Division moved up to its forward assembly area behind the line. On 25th June the Divisional Commander held a last briefing conference.

During the night of 25th June battalions moved up to their forming-

26th June.

26th June.　up places; artillery ammunition was brought up; gun-pits were dug and occupied. A miserable morning of low cloud and drizzle dawned. Indeed, visibility was so bad that the bombing programme had to be cancelled. Moreover, the 49th Division had failed to take the Rauray spur, so the 15th Scottish Division would lack right-flank protection in its advance.

As H-hour approached the suspense was extreme. At 7.29 A.M. the orders came over the Tanoy speakers to the waiting guns: " Stand by to fire Serial 1—one minute to go—30 seconds—20 seconds—10 seconds—5, 4, 3, 2, 1, FIRE." As with an ear-splitting crack several hundred guns hurled their shells overhead, the infantry and tanks advanced to close up to the opening barrage-line, where our shells were bursting some 500 to 1000 yards ahead. It was the moment for which the 15th Scottish Division had been preparing for five years.

The barrage stood for ten minutes on the opening line while the infantry closed. It then advanced at 100 yards every three minutes, with the infantry at first well closed up behind it. Before long the first prisoners were beginning to trickle back—tough, arrogant boys most of them, in camouflaged smocks.

On the right the 46th Brigade had to make its way through large fields of standing corn. Both forward battalions soon found that enemy snipers had survived the barrage in plenty in the high corn, not only on the Brigade's direct front but also on its right flank in the area for which the 49th Divisional Reconnaissance Regiment was responsible. Light machine-guns, too, and mortars kept coming to life everywhere. The right forward company of the Cameronians ran into particularly stiff opposition and had all its officers hit but one. That day the mopping-up of snipers had been made the responsibility of reserve platoons and companies, who were thus diverted from their main job of maintaining the momentum of the attack. Subsequently this arrangement was to be changed.

Within a quarter of a mile of the start-line, too, the forward battalions ran into a minefield. Despite casualties from anti-personnel mines, the rifle companies went on, but the advance of the carriers and supporting Churchills and A.V.R.E.s was held up. Another trouble was the poor communications between tanks and infantry, for the No. 38 sets provided for this purpose were at best an unsatisfactory medium and did not work well on that day.

In consequence of these delays the pause of fifteen minutes which the barrage made after an advance of about a mile and a half—on the highway, that is, from Caumont to Caen—proved too short for the leap-frogging of companies and the reorganisation of the further advance. From this point the forward battalions of the 46th Brigade lost the barrage. None the less they pushed on to secure their objectives. By 11.30 the Cameronians had reached and mopped up Le Haut du Bosq; the Glasgow Highlanders had occupied the ruins of Cheux. The enemy was all around—in the standing corn behind, on the right flank, on the ridge in front, in the ruins of Cheux itself. Tired out but very proud, the two battalions consolidated under a ceaseless rain of shells, mortar-bombs, and Nebelwerfer rockets, which last the Jocks soon came to know as " Moaning Minnies " or the " Sobbing Sisters." At once a squadron of the 2nd Northamptonshire Yeomanry appeared, trying to find its way through Cheux and on to the Odon. It was the Reconnaissance Regiment of the 11th Armoured Division.

Losses had been very heavy. On the right the Cameronians had lost 6 officers and 120 men. The Glasgow Highlanders on the left had lost 12 officers and nearly 200 men.

About 2 P.M. the Seaforth—the reserve battalion of the 46th Brigade—advanced southward, by-passing Cheux to the eastward, with the task of establishing a firm base on the hump aforesaid—known as the " ring contour 100 "—about 2000 yards to the south-east of Cheux on the left of the road to Colleville. The Seaforth, who had been delayed by snipers and mines on their way up, found the reverse slope of the hump strongly held and failed to take it. After suffering 50 casualties, including 4 officers, and losing several tanks, the Seaforth dug in north of the hump, leaving the crest as a no-man's-land between themselves and the Germans. Thus by afternoon the 46th Brigade had all but completed the whole task allotted to it in phase I. of the operation. But time was getting on, and a firm base on the O.P. ridge still remained to be established.

Meanwhile the 44th Lowland Brigade on the left had also gone in at 7.30 A.M. The only start-line which the R.S.F. could find was a sunken road which ran diagonally to, and only 125 yards short of, the barrage opening line. Unfortunately they had a number of casualties from our own guns.

Here, too, the assault took place over large fields of standing corn which were full of snipers, who took a heavy toll. After the early rain it was a damp, still day, and the smoke of our barrage hung motionless,

26th June.

creating conditions almost of a fog-bank. Enemy observers on the rising ground towards Carpiquet were quick to take advantage of this and to put their own defensive fire down behind our barrage as it advanced. In particular, the R.S.F. on the left suffered heavily in consequence.

Both forward battalions pushed on, however. By 10.30 A.M. they were astride the highway Caumont-Caen, and half an hour later the Royal Scots on the right had taken and cleared their objective, La Gaule. There the Royal Scots remained till they were relieved by the 129th Brigade of the 43rd Wessex Division before last light. They then withdrew to the 44th Brigade's assembly area round Le Mesnil Patry.

The R.S.F. meanwhile had closed on St Mauvieu, their objective, a straggling village among orchards on the far bank of the Muc. By the time the leading companies had reached the village their casualties had been so heavy that their capacity for mopping-up was sadly diminished. Very confused fighting in the village went on throughout the day. In the afternoon the enemy counter-attacked the R.S.F. with elements of the 12th S.S. and 21st Panzer Divisions, putting in their attack from Marcelet, about 2000 yards to eastward of St Mauvieu in the direction of the airfield. The R.S.F. met and broke the attack with the help of their medium machine-guns and of their supporting field regiment, the 181st, which had not yet moved. It was on this occasion that the F.O.O. with the R.S.F. gave the surprising order—a map reference—Scale 40 Fire, whereupon every gun fired forty rounds as fast as its crew could load it. Under this brusque treatment the very ugly counter-attack died almost at birth.

Realising the difficult situation at St Mauvieu, the Brigade Commander, Brigadier H. D. K. Money, sent up in support of the R.S.F. his reserve battalion, the K.O.S.B. (less one company, which he had already sent to support the Royal Scots). At about 6 P.M., in torrents of rain, the K.O.S.B. passed through the R.S.F. to occupy St Mauvieu. The 44th Brigade thus completed its allotted task. The R.S.F. were then withdrawn to the Brigade assembly area. They had had four officers killed, among them two company commanders. The K.O.S.B. subsequently beat off another counter-attack on St Mauvieu about 8.30 P.M. They were relieved by the 129th Brigade before dawn on 27th June. They, too, had lost a company commander killed.

THE ODON BATTLE

So ended the first phase of the operations—almost entirely successful, but a good deal behind schedule. In the next phase, it will be remembered, the 227th Brigade was to pass through the 46th Brigade and to secure the Odon crossings.

According to plan, the 227th Brigade was to have done this in two stages. In the first stage the H.L.I. on the right and the Gordons on the left were to have passed through the 46th Brigade's firm base to occupy Grainville and Tourville respectively, both of which lie on the farther slopes of the O.P. ridge. In the second stage the Argylls, operating as two half-battalions, were to have passed through the H.L.I. and the Gordons and to have secured the Odon bridges on the right at Gavrus, on the left of Tourmauville. The hope was that the Argylls would get these bridges by dark on the opening day, 26th June.

All day, therefore, the 227th Brigade had been moving up slowly behind the attack to its forming-up place just north of Cheux. The Jocks had found it a tedious business in periodical drenching showers. It was not till about 6 P.M. that the H.L.I. on the right and the Gordons on the left formed up with their tanks at last in a torrential downpour which ruled out all hope of air support. From the forming-up place they set out southward through Cheux by the two roads that lead to the Odon.

Cheux they found a heap of ruins—its streets flooded and cumbered with fallen masonry. In it was the most appalling traffic jam. Vehicles were trying vainly to go in every direction at once, and no one seemed to be in charge. Moreover, the place was in the grip of an intense sniper scare, and indiscriminate firing was going on up and down the streets. To get through the jam was bad enough for the rifle companies: it was pretty well impossible for carriers and tanks. So the infantry parted company with their transport, and the H.L.I. lost touch also with their tanks.

In pouring rain and growing darkness the H.L.I. on the right pushed on towards their start-line, which lay south of Le Haut du Bosq on the road to Grainville. Short of their start-line, however, they ran into German tanks, dug in. Finding that a further advance was impossible in such conditions, Lieutenant-Colonel J. D. S. Young concentrated the H.L.I. in the southern outskirts of Cheux preparatory to a renewed advance at daylight.

On the left, meanwhile, the Gordons, with a troop of the 9th Royal

26th June. Tanks in support, had been pushing on on a two-company front astride the more easterly road towards their objectives, Colleville and Tourville. As they approached the col through which the road runs across the O.P. ridge south of Cheux, they came under very heavy tank and machine-gun fire. Several of their supporting tanks were knocked out; they had a lot of casualties; and Battalion Headquarters lost all touch with the left forward company, which in fact had broken through into Colleville, where it was temporarily surrounded. Our tanks withdrew, and there was some confusion in the darkness. Lieutenant-Colonel Colville collected what he could of the battalion and set to work to form a tight perimeter beside the Cheux-Colleville road, about a mile south of Cheux. There their transport joined the Gordons, and they spent a thoroughly unpleasant night, digging in as best they could. In this engagement they had lost four officers killed and one missing. All night the medical officer and stretcher-bearers worked devotedly.

So ended the opening day of Operation "Epsom." In this its first engagement with the picked troops of a war-hardened enemy, the 15th Scottish Division had added fresh lustre to the laurels which, thirty years before, it had won in a previous incarnation at Loos and on the Somme. The 30th Corps on the right had not yet succeeded in occupying Rauray spur—and would not do so till next day. Already, with the 49th Division held up near Fontenay-le-Pesnil to westward and with the enemy to eastward still in Marcelet and Carpiquet, the 15th Scottish Division was creating a salient, the flanks of which would become increasingly exposed. "Scottish Corridor" was in the making.

27th June. Throughout the night of the 26th the battalions of the 46th Brigade continued to hold their firm base in Le Haut du Bosq, Cheux, and on the northern slopes of "ring contour 100," under incessant sniping and mortar-fire. No counter-attack developed, though enemy tanks had been reported in Rauray and to the south-west of Le Haut du Bosq.

At 5 A.M. the relief of the 46th Brigade by the 214th Brigade of the 43rd Wessex Division began. The 46th Brigade (less the Seaforth) then withdrew to an assembly area about a mile north of Cheux.

About 10 A.M. the Seaforth put in an attack over the crest of "ring contour 100," to find that the advance of the Argylls—which I have yet to describe—followed by that of the 11th Armoured Division down the road to the west, had made the enemy clear out. The Seaforth thereupon occupied the ring contour. Later they relieved the Gordons nearby, who had by then occupied Colleville. Still later, the Seaforth were relieved in their turn by the 7th Battalion the Somerset Light Infantry, of the 214th Brigade, and went back to rejoin the 46th Brigade.

27th June.

The 44th Brigade, too, was now in, or moving to, its assembly area. Thus on the morning of this second day of battle both the 44th and the 46th Brigades (less the Seaforth) were temporarily withdrawn from action.

Of the 227th Brigade the H.L.I. were on the move again at first light out of Cheux. As we shall see, however, the Argylls of the 227th Brigade were also passing through Cheux at the same time, headed for Colleville and the Odon. The axes of the two battalions crossed. Moreover, what little space there was left in the lanes of Cheux seemed to be filled by our own tanks, closed down and deaf to all appeals. None who was in Cheux that morning is likely to forget the confusion.

Having extricated themselves at last, the H.L.I. pushed on towards their start-line south of Le Haut du Bosq. Before they could reach it, however, they once more ran into the enemy's dug-in tanks. By 8.30 A.M. they were again held up. Presently four enemy tanks appeared in a farm close to Battalion Headquarters. Handling his anti-tank platoon with the utmost gallantry, Captain Scott knocked out all four. All day the H.L.I. remained pinned under intense mortar-fire. Casualties were heavy, and no praise can be too great for the work of the stretcher-bearers. That night the H.L.I. dug in once more round Cheux. Towards nightfall the 2nd Fife and Forfar Yeomanry of the 29th Armoured Brigade passed through on the road to Grainville.

The Argylls, it will be remembered, had been originally scheduled to take the Odon crossings the previous evening. Instead, the first day of battle had been for them a day of moves by fits and starts interspersed with much weary waiting. At 5.30 A.M. on that second morning, however, Lieutenant-Colonel Tweedie was called to the headquarters of the 227th Brigade for orders, and weary waiting gave place to a mad scramble—such is war. The objective for his whole battalion was now to be Tourmauville bridge; the start-line given him was just north of Cheux; H-hour was to be 7.30 A.M. It says a lot for their battle procedure that the Argylls got off to time.

After their difficult passage through Cheux, of which mention has already been made, the Argylls went through the Gordons still in

27th June. position beside the road to Colleville. Colleville itself they mopped up after house-to-house fighting. Pushing on from Colleville regardless of open flanks, the Argylls next reached the twin villages of Mondrainville and Tourville, which stand on the highway which runs across the front straight as a die from Caen to Villers Bocage. These villages, too, they quickly mopped up, after driving off some armoured cars which were patrolling the highway and knocking out one of two tanks which tried to intervene from eastward.

All this, however, was only a prelude to what was to follow—the further advance by "B" and "C" Companies, covered by "D," down the road towards Tourmauville for another 1200 yards or so beyond the highway, culminating in the assault by "C" Company, led by Major Fyfe, to seize the Odon bridge itself. The whole affair was a tactical masterpiece. About 5 P.M. "C" Company took the bridge intact.

Lieutenant-Colonel J. Tweedie, commanding the Argylls, pushed "B" and "D" Companies across after "C," and so established a small bridgehead, little more than 200 yards in diameter. Here, then, were the Argylls, across the Odon and deep in enemy-held country, but as yet unsupported. Ahead rose that historic ridge between the Odon and the Orne that the Division was to get to know so well in the days to come.

Presently a company of the 8th Rifle Brigade—the motorised battalion of the 11th Armoured Division—reached the bridge and crossed it to reinforce the Jocks in the bridgehead. Behind was following the 29th Armoured Brigade, also of the 11th Armoured Division. Loudly cheered by the Jocks, tanks of the 29th Brigade crossed the bridge in their turn and passed on towards the high ground beyond —in the direction, that is, of Point 112, soon to earn so evil a repute. Thus the Argylls had won a crossing of the Odon for our armour. By so doing they had performed for the 15th Scottish Division its main task in Operation "Epsom." For this fine action the Argylls won the proud title of the "Crossing Sweepers."

During the morning the lost company of the Gordons had rejoined them. In the early afternoon the Gordons moved up to Colleville. About this time "snipers' fever" was raging in Colleville, as indeed everywhere else. It was an infectious disease. Promiscuous firing in one area would cause casualties in the next, where more firing would then break out. Thus false alarms spread. These false alarms in all likelihood caused more casualties to our troops than did the enemy snipers themselves. On the other hand, persistent sniping was undoubtedly taking place. For instance, about that very time the R.S.F. in their concentration area behind St Mauvieu were rounding up twenty-five snipers in a wood which had supposedly been cleared twenty-four hours earlier.

Later, on relief by the Seaforth in Colleville, the Gordons moved up to Tourville. There they found the surviving German tank of the pair that earlier had worried the Argylls, still in position on the straight highway about half a mile to the east of Tourville, whence it was shooting down the main street. In this manner it was knocking out one after another of our tanks.

In Tourville the Gordons relieved the headquarters and "A" Company of the Argylls. By 7 P.M. the whole of the Argylls were reorganising beyond the bridge, where their transport and a hot meal duly reached them.

Meanwhile the 46th Brigade, after a brief pause to refit in its assembly area north of Cheux, had begun the relief of the rear elements of the 227th Brigade. At 2 P.M. on 27th June the Glasgow Highlanders had set out for Colleville. By this time the armour of the 29th Armoured Brigade was streaming over the Colleville crossing and down the road to Tourmauville. By 3 P.M. the Glasgow Highlanders were established in Colleville.

Mounted on tanks, the Cameronians followed the Glasgow Highlanders with the task of clearing Grainville. From the Colleville crossing the Cameronians turned off west along the railway towards Grainville. On arrival outside Grainville Lieutenant-Colonel Villiers, commanding the Cameronians, found a single tank of the Fife and Forfar Yeomanry of the 29th Armoured Brigade. The tank commander reported a few enemy at the far end of the village. Lieutenant-Colonel Villiers sent in his leading company, supported by his Churchills. They found the far side of the village firmly held by enemy infantry, with about four tanks skilfully concealed. When darkness fell, the enemy still held the church and main street, so Lieutenant-Colonel Villiers decided to withdraw his men and to remain in observation for the night outside the village.

So ended the fighting of 27th June. The Division had suffered a sad loss that day in its C.R.A., Brigadier R. Hilton, who had been badly wounded. On his way from Divisional Headquarters

27th June. to visit his F.O.O.s, "Bosun" Hilton had met the surviving German tank which was still enfilading the highway through Tourville. He might easily have made a detour and gone on his way. Instead he had manned a 17-pounder A.Tk. gun which he had found in the offing and had taken on the tank. Unfortunately, the tank had been the quicker on the draw.

The night of 27th June found the Division disposed as follows. The 44th Brigade and the 7th Royal Tanks were reorganising around Le Mesnil Patry; the 9th Royal Tanks were reorganising west of St Mauvieu. Of the 46th Brigade, the Glasgow Highlanders were in Colleville, the Cameronians were taking over from the 2nd Fife and Forfar Yeomanry outside Grainville; and the Seaforth were reorganising near Cheux. Of the 227th Brigade, the H.L.I. were still in the south-western outskirts of Cheux; the Gordons had moved forward into the close, built-up area Mondrainville-Tourville; and the Argylls were holding their bridgehead near Tourmauville.

On the right of the 15th Scottish Division the 49th West Riding Division was now in Rauray, but the enemy still held Le Manoir and the country to westward of it. Armoured elements of the 12th S.S. Panzer and 2nd Panzer Divisions had been met. Operation "Epsom" had already cost the enemy about sixty tanks lost on the fronts of the 15th Scottish Division and of the 49th West Riding Division.

28th June. Next day, 28th June, the Divisional Commander's main object was to extend and consolidate the bridgehead across the Odon which the Division had won. To do this he had to secure the two bridges at Gavrus, to broaden and strengthen the corridor which led to the river, and to establish firm and close control over the area between the 15th Scottish Division and the 49th West Riding Division, where things were not yet tied up. In consequence, this day's fighting developed as a series of operations directed, on the right, to the opening of the road through Grainville to the Odon at Gavrus, and, on the left, to the strengthening of our hold on the road through Colleville to Tourmauville.

Early that morning, 28th June, the 159th Infantry Brigade of the 11th Armoured Division took over the Tourmauville bridgehead from the Argylls and left Lieutenant-Colonel Tweedie free to turn his thoughts to the two bridges at Gavrus, a mile or more upstream, on the 15th Scottish Division's other or western axis of advance.

These bridges, it will be remembered, had been part of his original objective. At once he sent off two officers' patrols to investigate. About 4 P.M. these patrols reached the Gavrus bridges, which they found intact and unguarded—proof sufficient that the Argylls were now clean through the enemy's original front. The rest of the battalion followed along the banks of the Odon over extremely difficult going. Before dark the Argylls had arrived complete at Gavrus. The Odon runs here in two channels about 150 yards apart; the road crosses these channels by the two bridges. Three companies dug in south of the river, Battalion Headquarters and "D" Company on the north bank. The Argylls were here almost completely isolated, for the westerly Divisional axis through Grainville to Gavrus was still interrupted.

28th June.

Fighting to clear this westerly axis had started early. At 5.30 A.M. the Cameronians had renewed their attack on Grainville. At the second attempt they took the village in style, with strong artillery support. In the process they flushed three enemy tanks, two of which our own tanks knocked out in the open as they tried to get away. The Cameronians then consolidated in Grainville, where they were to remain until their relief on the morning of 1st July. The enemy had excellent observation over Grainville and kept it almost continuously under extremely accurate fire; so, apart from losses due to counter-attacks, the Cameronians were to suffer a constant drain of casualties.

At the same time, with the intention of linking up Grainville with the Gavrus bridges over the Odon, which the Argylls' patrols were now approaching on the farther side, Brigadier Barber put in his reserve battalion, the Seaforth, against Le Valtru, 1000 yards or so south of Grainville. Since the enemy might appear in any quarter, Lieutenant-Colonel E. H. G. Grant decided to deploy the Seaforth in a wide diamond, with the command post, his S.P. guns and most of his Churchills in the centre, and his soft vehicles in the tail. Soon after dawn the battalion crossed " ring contour 100 " in this formation and headed south-west for Colleville. There, at the only crossing-place over the railway for tracks, the Seaforth had also to cross the axis of the 11th Armoured Division, so some delay ensued. Having made touch with the Cameronians on the right and the Glasgow Highlanders on the left, the Seaforth continued their advance on Le Valtru, astride the highway from Mondrainville. Very confused

28th June. fighting followed, during which the supporting Churchills more than once put down the forward companies by firing their Besas across their front and hitting a number of the Jocks. As the tank liaison officer's wireless had broken down, Lieutenant-Colonel Grant had no means of communicating with the Churchills. The leading company of the Seaforth reached Le Valtru after stiff fighting and heavy casualties. The rest of the battalion followed just in time to stop the Germans from infiltrating back into the village. The Seaforth consolidated and pushed out one company to hold the ridge overlooking, and 500 yards westward of, the Le Valtru cross-roads. Towards evening they also sent a carrier patrol south which managed to contact the Argylls at the Gavrus bridges.

Meanwhile, about 10 A.M., the Divisional Commander had ordered up the 44th Brigade from reserve to clear the area through which the northern section of the same road passed between Le Haut du Bosq and Grainville. At 2 P.M. the K.O.S.B. moved up through Cheux to relieve the H.L.I., who were still dug in southward of Cheux and west of the Grainville road. Cheux was still a bottleneck. The K.O.S.B. found their forward assembly area in the valley to the northward of it packed with tanks and soft-skinned vehicles, which were milling round like the traffic in Piccadilly Circus. By this time Cheux itself presented a scene of incredible destruction, with every house in ruins, orchards blasted, trees and telephone poles across the roads, derelict carriers, burnt-out 25-pounders and quads, and knocked-out Panthers and Shermans in the offing. It was an anxious moment, for enemy tanks and infantry were infiltrating westward from the direction of Colleville, where the Glasgow Highlanders were busy beating off a counter-attack. The Churchills of the 9th Royal Tanks were massed in the eastern outskirts of Cheux, where many A.Tk. guns were in action.

The K.O.S.B. relieved the H.L.I. without incident. Later, about 7 P.M., the Royal Scots came up on the right of the K.O.S.B. Both battalions then advanced southward, and by 9 P.M. were abreast of one another, about half a mile short of the Cameronians in Grainville. There they remained for the night, under harassing mortar-fire. The 2nd Northamptonshire Yeomanry—the Reconnaissance Regiment of the 11th Armoured Division—had covered the left flank of the K.O.S.B. throughout this operation.

When the day's fighting ended, the enemy still controlled two stretches of the right-hand or westerly road—north of Grainville and north of Gavrus—but the Argylls now held the Gavrus bridges.

28th June.

We return now to the left-hand or easterly road. There, dawn on 28th June had found the Glasgow Highlanders in Colleville. In the course of the morning Brigadier Barber had ordered them south to Tourville to relieve the Gordons. As they were about to move off, however, they were attacked from the east by enemy infantry and tanks—some of whom, as we have seen, infiltrated westward towards the Grainville road. At that, the Glasgow Highlanders resumed the defence of Colleville, and with the help of elements of the 11th Armoured Division successfully beat off the attack. Afterwards they were ordered to stay where they were and to hold on.

Towards evening the H.L.I., after their relief by the K.O.S.B. at Cheux, came across to this left flank. On arrival they were ordered, in co-operation with the 4th King's Shropshire Light Infantry of the 159th Infantry Brigade (11th Armoured Division), to clear the area beyond Colleville up to Mouen, a village on the railway about 1000 yards farther east. This the H.L.I. did successfully, after a fierce fight in the darkness which cost them twenty-one killed, among whom was the commander of "D" Company. It was here, too, that they lost their Quartermaster, Captain Bain, "father of the battalion," who ran into the enemy on his way back to "B" Echelon in the darkness and was killed. Tired and rather lonely, the H.L.I. spent an anxious night out on their own by Mouen.

By nightfall on 28th June the situation on the front and flanks of the 15th Scottish Division was this. In the course of the day the whole of the 29th Armoured Brigade had crossed the Odon by the bridge near Tourmauville. Our armour was now fanning out on the rising ground beyond, but resistance here was fierce.

On the right of the Division the 49th Division now held Le Manoir and the commanding wood of Tessel west of it. On the left the 8th Canadian Brigade had taken La Byude and Marcelet.

Despite these gains in the flanks, the Scottish Corridor in its extension south of Cheux was still only some 2500 yards wide and remained completely open to attack from either flank. It was served by one road only, and that a bad one, which was under enemy observation in many places. Moreover, enemy formations were gathering round the corridor like wasps. True, after the beating it had taken, the 12th S.S. Panzer Division was now down to about twenty-five men

28th June.

per company and under fifty tanks. But elements of the 1st and 2nd S.S. Panzer Divisions and of the 2nd and 21st Panzer Divisions had been identified. And there were reports, too, that the 9th S.S. Panzer Division had arrived from Russia. That night the Divisional Commander sent out a warning order to all brigades that they must expect strong enemy counter-attacks by infantry and tanks to come in eastward along the road and railway from the direction of Noyers. The bottleneck at Cheux was likely to be the enemy's obvious objective.

29th June.

Next day, 29th June, the fighting developed as the Divisional Commander had foreseen; it was to be characterised by the fierce and co-ordinated counter-attacks which the enemy put in throughout the afternoon against the whole right or westerly flank of the corridor south of Le Haut du Bosq.

During the morning of the 29th, however, things remained fairly quiet. On the right, west of the Grainville road, the Royal Scots of the 44th Brigade continued their attack of the previous evening and took their final objective—the wood round the Château of Grainville.

Farther south the headquarters of the 46th Brigade had moved to Colleville. The Cameronians were still in Grainville, the Seaforth in Le Valtru; the road to Gavrus was not yet open. On the other road the Glasgow Highlanders, on relief by the H.L.I. in Colleville about 10 A.M., moved south to Mondrainville, where they dug in.

Of the 227th Brigade the H.L.I., as we have seen, had been pulled in early from Mouen to Colleville; the Gordons were in Tourville; the Argylls were still holding the Gavrus bridges, but with the enemy still to the westward and northward of them, separating them from the 46th Brigade.

Still farther south, elements of the 4th and 29th Armoured Brigades had reached the high ground beyond the Odon. By mid-day the 44th Royal Tanks of the 4th Armoured Brigade on the right were approaching Evrecy; the 8th Rifle Brigade were north of Esquay. The 159th Infantry Brigade of the 11th Armoured Division was moving into the area astride the Odon round Baron.

On the left, farther east, the 129th Brigade of the 43rd Division had moved up from St Mauvieu to cross the Odon with the task of clearing the densely wooded area on its south bank north of Baron. The timely arrival of these two Brigades, the 159th and the

129th, here in the Odon valley to the eastward was to relieve the Divisional Commander of much anxiety about his left during the afternoon's critical fighting on his right.

This fighting began about mid-day, whereafter counter-attacks continued more or less concurrently along the whole right face of the corridor from Grainville to Gavrus throughout the afternoon. For the sake of clarity, I shall deal with the doings of each Brigade in turn, starting with the 44th Brigade in the north.

During the course of the morning, it will be remembered, the Royal Scots had taken their final objective—the wood by Grainville Château. Hardly had they done so when they were pushed out of it by an immediate counter-attack. Back they came again, however, and retook the wood, whereafter they held their front despite severe enemy pressure. The Royal Scots here captured an officer of the 19th S.S. Panzer Grenadiers, thus confirming the report that the 9th S.S. Panzer Division had arrived.

Later, Brigadier Money ordered the R.S.F. to relieve the Royal Scots. As this relief was in progress about 6.30 P.M. the enemy put in a particularly heavy counter-attack, which caught the forward companies on the wrong leg. First, enemy tanks lay off hull-down and picked off the Royal Scots' forward A.Tk. guns. Then two flame-throwing tanks charged home into the two forward company areas, where they milled round and killed a lot of men in a particularly unpleasant manner before they withdrew.

For a time there was great confusion. Profiting by this, a number of enemy tanks penetrated deeply into our forward positions. Enemy infantry was following. It was a very critical moment. At his headquarters almost in the front-line, Brigadier Money held a memorable " O " Group, and a plan was made. Responding magnificently, our infantry counter-attacked in their turn and halted the enemy infantry, thus depriving the enemy tanks of their infantry support. Meanwhile the Divisional Commander had managed to get hold of tanks of the 4th Armoured Brigade and S.P. guns of the Corps Anti-Tank Regiment, the 91st, and had lined these up in depth behind our infantry. This backstop held. The enemy tanks tried vainly to penetrate it—only to be destroyed in detail for lack of infantry support. Thus late that night the situation was stabilised.

Brigadier Money then ordered up the K.O.S.B. to take over the whole Brigade front. By dawn next day, 30th June, the K.O.S.B.,

29th June. with a 17-pounder troop of the 97th Anti-Tank Regiment under command, had dug in on a line through the Château of Grainville, between the Noyers road and the railway, with the Royal Scots and the R.S.F. disposed in depth behind them. The 15th Scottish Divisional Reconnaissance Regiment on the right formed a link between the Royal Scots and the 49th Division. The 44th Brigade, in conjunction with the 49th Division in Rauray, thus effectually commanded the approaches to Le Haut du Bosq and Cheux from the south-west.

Next we come to the 46th Brigade, whose three battalions in Grainville, Mondrainville, and Le Valtru now formed a fairly compact triangle. The morning passed quietly. About 2 P.M., however, the enemy began to put down heavy concentrations on the Seaforth in Le Valtru and to infiltrate between them and the Glasgow Highlanders in Mondrainville. During one of these concentrations two German tanks approached the outlying Seaforth company west of the cross-roads, knocked out its two A.Tk. guns, and proceeded to shoot up the forward platoons at close range. After a fierce fight these platoons were overrun, and the rear platoon withdrew to the main position.

German infantry then attacked Le Valtru itself. They were beaten back, thanks largely to the magnificent support given by the 531st Field Battery, which never failed the Seaforth in any emergency throughout the campaign.

Next, after a further bombardment, four enemy tanks charged down the hill, past the cross-roads, and through the main street of Le Valtru. Every anti-tank weapon was let loose, and all four were destroyed. It was a great moment. These four "flamers," however, acted as an aiming mark, on which every gun and mortar within range seemed to concentrate throughout the rest of the day and night which followed. At the same time snipers and spandaus opened up from all sides. The Seaforth lost six officers killed and four wounded in this bitter fighting in and around Le Valtru.

Soon after the fighting on the Seaforth front had begun, the enemy also attacked the central forward company of the Cameronians in Grainville. Unfortunately the only lookout, a Bren-gunner, on the enemy's line of approach, had been killed by a shell before he could give warning. In consequence, the Germans came in unseen and penetrated to company headquarters. For a time pandemonium reigned in Grainville. Hand-to-hand fighting raged; bullets streamed up every lane; the place was in flames; the wireless rear link with

Brigade had been knocked out; the telephone wires had been cut by shelling; casualties were heavy. At length, however, the enemy were driven out—and a strange silence fell. A liaison officer who got through from Brigade was able to return with a reassuring report.

Meanwhile German tanks and infantry had also penetrated eastward between Grainville and Le Valtru into the orchards towards Mondrainville. There, however, they were counter-attacked in their turn by the Glasgow Highlanders, supported by a squadron of the 7th Royal Tanks. After severe fighting the enemy here, too, was driven back. At 11 P.M. Brigadier Barber was able to report that all the 46th Brigade's positions were intact.

That evening the Divisional Commander, realising how vitally important was the 46th Brigade sector at Grainville-Le Valtru-Mondrainville, put the following additional troops under Brigadier Barber's command: the 7th Royal Tanks, the H.L.I. in Colleville, and the Gordons now on the move from Tourville to Colleville, there to take up a counter-attack rôle on Grainville in case of need. The Gordons took up a position near the Colleville railway crossing, where they came under heavy mortar-fire.

Brigadier Mackintosh-Walker, whose headquarters was in Colleville, was thus left with only one battalion of the 227th Brigade, the Argylls, under his command. The Argylls had spent a fairly quiet day in the Gavrus bridgehead. Their mortar platoon on the north bank had been busy with some spandaus firing from positions west of Gavrus; but it had been impossible to get up any mortar ammunition by the western axis Cheux-Grainville-Gavrus, on which the Argylls were now wholly dependent and which was under enemy small-arms fire throughout.

Soon after three that afternoon the scene at Gavrus changed abruptly. The 9th S.S. Panzer Division had arrived on the front. It announced its arrival by a sudden and vicious counter-attack from the direction of Bougy against the three companies in the bridgehead. For the next five and a half hours confused and heavy fighting continued on the south bank, during which the enemy's artillery and mortar-fire never let up. In order to shorten the front, "B" and "C" Companies moved over in the course of the fight to join "A" Company in its locality in the wood overlooking the bridges. The enemy drew off about 8 P.M., leaving the Argylls still in firm possession of the bridges. Many parties isolated in the fighting afterwards joined up in the wood. A carrier with ammunition also got through from Battalion Headquarters and medical jeeps to evacuate the wounded. Casualties had been heavy.

Throughout the night mortar-fire was intense on all parts of the Divisional front, causing even more casualties than the day's fighting. Even the H.L.I. in Colleville, who had been out of that day's action, had many casualties, among them their Commanding Officer, Lieutenant-Colonel J. D. S. Young, and their Second-in-Command, Major Colwill, both of whom were wounded. Major J. R. Sinclair, Second-in-Command of the Gordons, took over temporary command of the H.L.I.

Such, then, was the fighting, mainly defensive, throughout 29th June on the Divisional front. The guns had played a great part. For this the Division owed much to its new C.R.A., Brigadier Lyndon Bolton. Arriving straight from two sleepless nights on the stormy Channel just in time for the enemy counter-attack from the west, he had done a magnificent job in organising the artillery support.

The situation had radically changed. In addition to the many new enemy identifications of the preceding day, the 9th S.S. Panzer Division had now been identified on the right flank. Almost certainly, therefore, the 10th S.S. Panzer Division—which together with the 9th constituted the 2nd S.S. Panzer Corps—must also have arrived from the Russian front. Clearly, then, the hopes of an immediate break-through to Bretteville-sur-Laize had gone. Rather, it was a question now of holding what had been won. The 8th Corps must change its rôle from the offensive to the defensive.

As Lieutenant-General Sir Richard O'Connor, the Corps Commander, saw the situation, the area round Point 112 and Point 113—though excellent for an armoured offensive if it could have gone through with a bang—was no place for the 11th Armoured Division, with its insecure communications across the Odon, to wait about in. Consequently he now issued the following orders, to take effect on the night 29th-30th June. The 11th Armoured Division (less the 159th Infantry Brigade) and the 4th Armoured Brigade, both of which had already suffered severely in heavy fighting round Points 113 and 112, were to withdraw northward across the Odon into Corps reserve, beginning their move at 3 A.M. on 30th June. The 159th Infantry Brigade w to take over from the armour on and beyond the Odon, where it would come under command of the 15th Scottish Division.

29th June.

Furthermore, in order to relieve the 15th Scottish Division of superfluous commitments and to permit its commander to concentrate on essentials—on holding, that is, the vital key points Le Haut du Bosq, Cheux, Grainville, Le Valtru, Gavrus—the 43rd Division was now to take over the left or eastern portion of the Scottish Corridor. Thus the 214th Brigade of the 43rd Division was to move up from Cheux to occupy Mouen, Mondrainville, and Colleville, relieving the H.L.I. and the Gordons in Colleville during the night; while the 129th Brigade was to continue to hold the south bank of the Odon on the left of the 159th Brigade, and the 130th Brigade was to remain to westward of St Mauvieu.

Finally, the Corps Commander had ordered the 32nd Guards Infantry Brigade of the Guards Armoured Division up to the area Cheux-St Mauvieu and the leading group of the 53rd Welsh Division up to Le Mesnil Patry. The 53rd Division had not yet been in contact with the enemy, so its movements were top secret. It was destined to relieve the 15th Scottish Division in due course.

By daylight next morning, 30th June, the withdrawal of our armour from beyond the Odon was well under way. It was a day for ever memorable for the congestion which now reached its climax on that narrow cross-country track through Colleville, which was still the sole axis of movement between our original front-line and the Odon crossing at Tourmauville. All day long the traffic moved nose to tail, past the burnt-out hulks of carriers and trucks and tanks and the swollen carcasses of cattle.

30th June.

Almost everywhere the track was under observation from enemy O.P.s on Points 112 and 113 on the south bank of the Odon, and was being shelled and mortared accordingly. The intermittent downpours of the past grey days had reduced sections of it to a quagmire. That, despite all these difficulties, reliefs were still carried out according to plan and that supplies were delivered, reflects the greatest possible credit on the organisation of traffic control. The organisation was never more highly tested than on this day.

For the Brigades north of the Odon the day was otherwise remarkable chiefly for incessant enemy mortar-fire and frequent probings by single tanks accompanied by small detachments of

30th June. infantry. It was not that the enemy had given up his designs against the Cheux bottleneck: it was merely that he needed a day to regroup.

During that day the 44th Brigade had nothing to report.

On the 46th Brigade front the enemy made a more serious thrust at the Seaforth in Le Valtru during the morning, and in the afternoon managed to infiltrate between the Seaforth and the Cameronians in Grainville. Meanwhile the H.L.I., who had spent the night in Colleville under command of the 46th Brigade, reverted to the 227th Brigade and moved south into a particularly unpleasant position, half wood, half swamp, between Mondrainville and the Odon, where they came under heavy mortar-fire.

The Gordons, too, had reverted to the 227th Brigade and had been ordered by way of the Tourmauville bridge to Monceaux, the next crossing of the Odon a mile or so west of Gavrus. The congestion on the road was unbelievable. Beyond Tourville the road came under a crescendo of mortar-fire from the hills south of the Odon. Here Major John Lochore, Brigade-Major of the 227th Brigade, was killed. On reaching the Odon the Gordons were ordered back to Tourville. There they were to remain under continual mortaring until their relief on the night of 1st July. It was to be a costly twenty-four hours.

At 11 P.M. that night the relief of the 46th Brigade by the 160th Brigade of the 53rd Division began. It was finished by first light on 1st July. The 46th Brigade then withdrew to Le Mesnil Patry under command of the 53rd Division. There it remained to rest and refit, reverting on 2nd July to the command of the 15th Scottish Division in Corps reserve.

Turning now to events south of the Odon during 30th June, we find a different picture. On this southern front the 10th S.S. Panzer Division had now made its expected appearance. During the day the 159th Brigade had to beat off several determined attacks to the north of Esquay. Much enemy movement, too, was reported on the high ground farther west.

It was against the Argylls at Gavrus, however, that the enemy made his principal effort. After their fierce fighting of the previous evening the Argylls had spent a fairly quiet night in their bridgehead The respite was too good to last. About noon on 30th June the enemy put down a neat box-barrage round the three-company locality in the

THE ODON BATTLE

wood on the south bank and at the same time opened a most accurate and intense artillery and mortar bombardment of Battalion Headquarters and "D" Company on the north bank. Major Cornwall, the artillery F.O.O., was wounded, and his wireless to the 131st Field Regiment—which had done such splendid work the day before—was knocked out, as was the wireless from battalion to infantry brigade. Much of the transport was destroyed. Lieutenant-Colonel Tweedie ordered Battalion Headquarters and "D" Company to take up alternative positions, but the bombardment followed them up. Casualties were very high; there was some confusion; contact with forward companies was lost.

30th June.

Meanwhile Brigadier Mackintosh-Walker had issued orders to withdraw the Argylls and had sent up tanks to cover the withdrawal. Acting on these orders, "D" Company found its way back by way of Tourmauville to Colleville, and took much of Battalion Headquarters with it. Nothing was then known of Lieutenant-Colonel Tweedie and Major D. R. Morgan, both of whom had gone off to try to contact "A," "B," and "C" Companies on the south bank.

That day these three companies, dug-in in the wood on a reverse slope, had escaped the enemy's fire fairly lightly. When about 3 P.M. the enemy formed up to counter-attack from the south, they were ready for him. With the help of extremely effective fire from the 131st Field Regiment—another F.O.O. had now come up—and from machine-guns of the Middlesex and 17-pounders of the 97th Anti-Tank Regiment on the north bank, the Argylls smashed the counter-attack. Later a carrier got through to them with Brigadier Mackintosh-Walker's orders to withdraw. At 9.30 P.M. Major M'Elwee, now the senior officer present, withdrew the three companies across both bridges without further loss and took them back by way of Le Valtru—where the Seaforth were busy repelling a counter-attack—and Mondrainville to Colleville, where they found the headquarters of the 227th Brigade. Next day, 1st July, Lieutenant-Colonel Tweedie and Major Morgan both rejoined the Argylls at Colleville. Of the many missing a surprising number finally turned up.

Gavrus alone had been lost. For the rest, at the close of the fighting on 30th June the Division held all its positions firmly.

1st July was another day of repeated enemy attacks, both south and north of the Odon. It was in the south that the battle began.

1st July.

1st July.
Before dawn the enemy put in a heavy attack from the south-west against the right of the 159th Infantry Brigade, whom they pushed out of Baron. At first light, therefore, the Divisional Commander sent off the 31st Tank Brigade across the Odon to the 159th Brigade's aid. By mid-day the 159th Brigade was able to report that it had retaken Baron. Meanwhile the battle had flared up to the north-west, where both the 44th and the 160th Brigades had become heavily engaged. The 31st Tank Brigade, therefore, was recalled to the right flank north of the Odon. It was an unfortunate necessity. Later, the 159th Brigade was again heavily attacked, from south-west, south and east, and suffered heavy casualties.

North of the Odon the battle began at about 7 A.M., when the 9th S.S. Panzer Division and elements of the 2nd S.S. Panzer Division attacked north-east astride the road Noyers-Le Haut du Bosq—that is, against the junction of the 8th and 30th Corps. On the right the German front of attack extended to the 160th Brigade, which, it will be remembered, had now relieved the 46th Brigade in Grainville and Le Valtru. In the centre it struck the K.O.S.B., the forward battalion of the 44th Brigade, round Grainville Château. On the left it struck the 70th Infantry Brigade of the 49th Division on the Rauray spur —and particularly the Tyneside Scottish, who were here in touch with the K.O.S.B. on the inter-corps boundary.

It was on the front of the K.O.S.B. and the Tyneside Scottish that the pressure was heaviest. On the K.O.S.B. front the German tanks at first lay off, hull-down, to pick off the A.Tk. guns one by one. Fierce and confused fighting followed for many hours. By mid-day Captain Rollo's " C " Company, the right forward company, of the K.O.S.B. was nearly surrounded and reduced to the strength of a platoon. Though its A.Tk. guns had been knocked out, " C " Company still held on, till Lieutenant-Colonel Shillington, after a personal reconnaissance, obtained authority to withdraw what was left of its forward platoons. Nowhere else did the K.O.S.B. yield ground. The 181st Field Regiment, too, played a great part in the fight, putting down particularly effective defensive fire. In the late afternoon a company of the R.S.F. reinforced the open flank of the K.O.S.B., and another unit at the same time reinforced the Tyneside Scottish. The fight was won. In it the 9th S.S. Panzer Division had lost many tanks. Three of these—Mark IV.s—were left behind in " C " Company's front-line.

Of this day's fighting Field-Marshal Montgomery has this to say on page 89 of his 'Normandy to the Baltic':— 1st July.

"On 1st July the S.S. formations made their last and strongest attempt against the 2nd Army salient. Nos. 1, 2, 9, 10, and 12 S.S. Divisions formed up with their infantry and tanks and made repeated though not simultaneous attacks against our positions. All of these attacks were engaged by our massed artillery with devastating effect, and all but one were dispersed before reaching our forward infantry positions."

Next day, 2nd July, enemy pressure on the 44th Brigade had slackened. During the day the Brigade's relief by the 71st Brigade of the 53rd Division took place. After dark the K.O.S.B. went out— the last to go. The 44th Brigade withdrew to rest and refit at Secqueville-en-Bessin, where it was to spend five wet and unpleasant days under canvas. 2nd July.

It remains to recount the happenings on the 227th Brigade front since the evening of 30th June, when the 2nd Argylls were withdrawn to Colleville. On arrival at Colleville the Argylls became the counter-attack force for Grainville. The Gordons were still in Tourville; the H.L.I. in their swampy wood south of Mondrainville. In these positions both Gordons and H.L.I. found themselves very thoroughly overlooked by enemy O.P.s on the hills south of the Odon and under incessant and galling artillery and mortar fire in consequence.

On 1st July advanced parties from the 158th Brigade of the 53rd Division arrived. The relief of the 227th Brigade was completed during the night of 1st-2nd July. The Brigade then withdrew to refit at and around Norrey-en-Bessin.

This, the first, battle of the 15th Scottish Division was over— the five-day battle of the Scottish Corridor. In retrospect there is no doubt that it was the fiercest fighting that the Division was to know in the whole war.

In the first two days the Division had driven home its thrust five and a half miles deep into the enemy's vitals and had taken ten square miles of territory. For the next three days it held its ground against all comers.

At the beginning of the battle the Division had been faced by the 12th S.S. Panzer Division alone. Before the battle ended, however, the 12th S.S. Division had been reinforced by the 1st, 2nd, 9th, and 10th S.S. Panzer Divisions and the 21st Panzer Division—by all of

2nd July. these or by elements of them. These enemy troops, too, were seasoned, battle-hardened formations, whereas the Scottish infantry had come to the fight with no collective experience beyond that learnt on exercises and at the battle school. The Scot had proved himself the better man.

But at no small cost. The Division's casualties amounted to 31 officers and 257 other ranks killed, 91 officers and 1547 other ranks wounded, 8 officers and 786 other ranks missing—a total of 130 officers and 2590 other ranks. The losses of the three infantry brigades were very evenly divided. Of the total casualties that it was to suffer up to VE-Day, the Division had lost one-quarter in these five days.

From senior commanders at all levels came recognition of the Division's splendid achievements and of its sacrifices.

From the Divisional Commander, 15th Scottish Divisional Order of the Day, 3rd July :—

"All ranks of the 15th Scottish Division may well look back with satisfaction on their first action in France between 26th June and 1st July 1944.

"It has been no mean trial for troops, who have never before fought against the Germans, to advance 4000 yards under a barrage, capture all their objectives in the course of which severe street and wood fighting was necessary, and then exploit their success for a further two and a half miles.

"I am proud indeed of all officers and men of this Division : of the infantry for their coolness and courage in attack and counter-attack and steadfastness in defence under intense mortar-fire and sniping ; of the artillery for their unfailing support at all critical times ; and of the sappers and provost who made the indifferent communications work so well. Thanks are also due to all the services who have maintained us so well in this period, and perhaps especially to the devoted work of the Medical Services.

"As an indication that the work of the Division is appreciated by the general public, the following extract from a B.B.C. announcement on 1st July is reprinted for information :—

"'The weight of the German attacks has fallen on the troops of a famous Scottish Infantry Division, most of whom have never been under fire before, but nevertheless they stood up to the ordeal with amazing coolness and courage.'

"I hope that many of those who have been wounded will soon be back with us and that we shall in a day or two be as fit as ever for the next battle, as well as seasoned by our practical experience.

"I wish all ranks the very best of luck in our future operations.

(Signed) G. H. A. MACMILLAN."

THE ODON BATTLE

From Corps Commander, 8th Corps, 3rd July 1944 :—

"I wish to congratulate all most heartily on your recent successful operations.

"Greatly hampered by weather conditions, which prevented the full employment of our supporting aircraft, you reached your final objectives in the face of fierce opposition.

"In the subsequent difficult fighting you maintained your positions intact, defeating many enemy counter-attacks. Your courage, tenacity, and general fighting qualities have confirmed in battle the high opinion I have always held of you. You have well upheld the highest fighting traditions of Scotland.

(Signed) R. N. O'CONNOR."

From the Commander, Second Army, on 4th July 1944 :—

"I want to tell you in writing how much I admire the splendid way in which your Division has fought during the past week.

"It has been a great start, and you have every right to be proud of yourselves.

"I would be glad if you gave them all my sincere congratulations.

(Signed) M. C. DEMPSEY."

From the Commander-in-Chief, 21st Army Group :—

"I would like to congratulate the 15th Division as a whole on the very fine performance put up during the past week's fighting. The Division went into battle for the first time in this war; but it fought with great gallantry and displayed a grand offensive spirit. Scotland can well feel proud of the 15th Scottish Division, and the whole Division can be proud of itself. Please congratulate the Division from me and tell all officers and men that I am delighted at what they have done.

(Signed) B. L. MONTGOMERY."

With proud hearts the men of the Division set about preparing for their next action.

CHAPTER IV.

PART II.—ETERVILLE.

2nd to 6th July.

AT the beginning of July the broader picture in Normandy was this. On 27th June Bradley's First U.S. Army had taken the port of Cherbourg, with many prisoners; by 1st July it had cleared the enemy out of the whole of the Cotentin Peninsula. At the same time Montgomery had urged once more on Bradley the necessity to speed up his break-out from the bridgehead. So far, Von Rundstedt, still anticipating an allied landing in the Pas de Calais, had kept his 15th Army beyond the Seine intact. Montgomery felt sure, however, that this state of affairs was too good to last: at any moment Von Rundstedt might realise his mistake and send a stream of infantry reinforcements across the Seine to fight on the decisive front in Normandy. Before this could happen the Americans must break out. When they did, they were first to drive south across the base of the Cotentin Peninsula, whereafter they were to swing east by way of Le Mans and Alençon to block the German bolt-hole between Orleans and Paris. Montgomery's ultimate aim was to destroy the enemy against the Lower Seine.

Meanwhile it was the task of Dempsey's Second British Army to continue to hold all possible enemy strength on the front Villers-Bocage-Caen. With this object in view Montgomery had ordered Dempsey to mount two new offensives against Caen.

The first, a preliminary operation called "Windsor," began on 4th July, when the 3rd Canadian Division of the 1st Corps attacked Carpiquet. The 43rd Division of the 8th Corps co-operated by attacking north-eastward out of the Scottish Corridor. The 15th Divisional Artillery was in support—an instance, by no means unusual, of the guns having to remain in the line when the Division went out to rest. The Canadians took Carpiquet, but were unable to clear the buildings on the south edge of the airfield till six days later. At the same time the 214th Brigade of the 43rd Division occupied Verson.

The main attack on Caen, Operation "Charnwood," was put in by the 1st Corps on 8th July. Five hours after a devastating bombardment by heavy bombers—the first of its kind in North-West Europe—three Divisions, supported by two armoured brigades, made a direct attack from the north. By 10th July they had cleared Caen up to the Orne. So far, so good.

2nd to 6th July.

On the First U.S. Army front meanwhile the 7th Corps on 4th July had begun an attack directed on Periers. Farther east, too, the 19th Corps was nearing St Lo. If the Americans could secure the road Periers-St Lo, they would be positioned for their break-out. Montgomery had now realised, however, that the enemy was almost as interested in this part of the front as he was. During the first week in July, Von Rundstedt—or Von Kluge, perhaps, who had replaced Von Rundstedt about this time—had withdrawn the 1st and 2nd S.S. Panzer Divisions, the Lehr, and the 21st Panzer Division into reserve, replacing them on the British front by the 16th G.A.F. (Air Force) Division brought up from Evreux, and the 276th and 277th Infantry Divisions brought from the south beyond the Loire. And now, on 8th July, the 2nd S.S. Panzer Division had reappeared far to the west in a counter-attack against the Americans. More of the enemy armour might well follow westward, unless Dempsey's Second Army could increase its pressure forthwith and so force the enemy to re-engage his armour against it once more, and unless, too, it could keep up its pressure till Bradley had staged his break-out much later in the month. How was the Second Army to do this?

For answer, Montgomery set Dempsey two tasks. First, he was to drive south-east from Caen into the good tank country round Falaise. The fear of a break-through here would be sure to bring the German armour hurrying back. Secondly, he was to open up the lateral communications south of Caen. Later on, when the Americans had broken out, the Second Army would need these lateral communications; for Montgomery then meant to left-wheel its whole front eastward against the enemy, who, he hoped, would by that time be cooped up against the Lower Seine.

Of these two tasks, Dempsey was able to set about the second—that of opening the lateral communications south of Caen—the earlier. On 10th June, therefore, the Second Army began a new offensive directed southward between the Odon and the Orne and designed to secure the general line Le Beny Bocage-Mont Pinçon-Thury Harcourt—a line,

2nd to 6th July.

that is, deep in the Normandy Highlands, athwart the upper waters of the Odon and the Orne. This series of operations went on till 18th July.

We are concerned with three of these operations—" Jupiter," " Greenline," and " Bluecoat." The first of these, Operation " Jupiter," was primarily the 43rd Division's affair. In it the 44th and 46th Brigades both took part, but the 15th Scottish Division as such remained in Corps reserve.

7th July.

On 7th July the 44th and 46th Brigades were warned for Operation " Jupiter " and put under the 43rd Division. By that time the units of the 15th Scottish Division had been made up in officers, equipment and transport, and almost made up in men.

The Second Army's dispositions in and around the former Scottish Corridor were then as follows: in the east, the 3rd Canadian Division was still fighting around Carpiquet airfield; of the 43rd Division, the 129th Brigade was in the woods on the south bank of the Odon north-east of Baron, the 130th Brigade was in the Odon bridgehead at and north of Baron, the 214th Brigade was in Mouen and Verson; of the 53rd Division, the 71st Brigade was in front of Le Haut du Bosq, the 158th Brigade in Rauray, the 160th Brigade in Grainville and Gavrus; still farther west was the 49th Division of the 30th Corps.

On 10th July the 43rd Division was to attack south-eastward and to occupy Point 112, Maltot, and Eterville as the first step in the Second Army's subsequent drive southward through the corridor between the Odon and the Orne.

In order to free the 43rd Division for this attack the 44th Brigade relieved the 130th Brigade in the Odon bridgehead on the night of 7th-8th July. The Royal Scots went into Tourmauville and the woods towards Gavrus, where they were in touch with the enemy on the higher ground west of Point 113; the R.S.F. went into Baron itself, where they, too, were in touch with the enemy on the high ground north of Point 112; the K.O.S.B. were in reserve in Mondrainville; Brigade Headquarters was in Tourville. Thus the 44th Brigade found itself in the shadow of the hills south of the Odon precisely in the area where the 227th Brigade had suffered so severely from enemy mortar fire during the closing days of Operation " Epsom." Conditions had not improved meanwhile.

At noon on 8th July the 44th Brigade passed from the command of the 43rd Division to that of the 53rd Division, which latter Division then became responsible for the protection of the whole western flank from Gavrus to Le Haut du Bosq. This change of command, however, left the 44th Brigade's position unaltered.

8th July.

The weather was fine and hot. Every movement along the old Divisional main artery from Colleville up to the Odon crossing at Tourmauville now raised clouds of dust, which were clearly visible to enemy O.P.s perched up on Point 112. "No dust, no shells" was the slogan along the road—but it was hard indeed to implement. The 44th Brigade found itself exposed for the first time to accurate, sustained, and concentrated mortar-fire. It was a most trying experience. Air bursts, especially in the trees by the Odon crossing and round Baron, were particularly deadly. As protection against these, the troops here began to put head-cover over their slit-trenches.

It was about this time that the C.R.A., Brigadier Lyndon Bolton, set-to to create an effective counter-mortar organisation. Under the direct control of that rare enthusiast, Lieutenant-Colonel "Sailor" Young of the 119th L.A.A. Regiment, this organisation first took shape at Divisional Headquarters, where it was based on the communications of the 1st Middlesex, the Divisional machine-gun battalion. Soon, however, the organisation was extended to Brigade Headquarters, and additional communications were provided. Lieutenant-Colonel Young aimed to provide immediate retaliation—at Divisional level by the counter-mortar group of medium artillery and 4·2-inch mortars, at brigade level by 3-inch mortars, supporting field artillery and machine-gun companies—against suspected enemy mortar areas opposite any part of our front where enemy mortar-fire was reported. This immediate retaliation was to be followed by deliberate retaliation as soon as the exact locations of enemy mortars could be confirmed. As time went by, this counter-mortar organisation steadily improved, and finally an establishment was sanctioned which provided a counter-mortar officer with two radar sets, listening-posts, and communications. By that time the worst of the mortar menace was past.

The 46th Brigade had the more active part in Operation "Jupiter." Its task was to give left flank protection to the 43rd Division's attack and to clear the apex formed by the Odon and the Orne east of Eterville. There, towards Bretteville-sur-Odon, the 46th Brigade was to make contact with the 8th Canadian Brigade.

10th July.

After carrying out reconnaissance on the 8th and 9th, the 46th Brigade moved up to its forward assembly area at Mouen on the night of 9th July. At 5 A.M. on 10th July the 43rd Division attacked on a two-brigade front, the 129th Brigade on the right against Point 112, the 130th Brigade on the left against Eterville.

The Cameronians followed up the 130th Brigade with orders to relieve the 4th Dorsets in Eterville as soon as they had taken it. In the second phase of the attack the 130th Brigade was to push on down the forward slope to Maltot and the Orne.

Lieutenant-Colonel Villiers halted the Cameronians in Fontaine Étoupefour, about 1000 yards from Eterville, while he went forward to contact the 4th Dorsets. On arrival in Eterville he found it a most uninviting spot. It is a large, straggling village, much overgrown with trees and orchards. There was practically no observation. The only approach for vehicles was by a sunken lane, which at the time was blocked by several of the Dorsets' carriers, all of which were in flames. The Dorsets were still fighting for possession of the far side of the village itself, which was being continually mortared by the enemy. The Dorsets' regimental aid-post was overflowing with wounded, who could not be evacuated because no ambulance could reach the village. As a defensive position, Eterville was a tactical nightmare. Lieutenant-Colonel Villiers decided none the less that the Cameronians must start taking over immediately in order to relieve the Dorsets for their next operation.

The Cameronians had already suffered casualties from shell-fire when the rifle companies started to move forward about 8 A.M. The intense and persistent shelling and mortaring ruled out detailed reconnaissance. It was mid-day before the Cameronians were in position at Eterville, with " C " Company in an isolated wood in the centre and the remaining companies on the perimeter of the village itself.

The 130th Brigade went on towards the Orne and into Maltot; but with the heights beyond the Orne still in German hands, nothing could live on those forward slopes. Elements of the 9th and 10th S.S. Panzer Divisions counter-attacked fiercely. The 130th Brigade lost Maltot and was driven back to the crest behind.

Farther to the south-west the 129th Brigade had won Point 112 after a fierce struggle. For days to come, however, Point 112 was to remain bitterly disputed; for here, too, the forward slope toward the Orne remained in German hands, while the summit was a no-man's-land which neither side could call its own.

10th July.

Meanwhile, at 9.45 A.M., the Seaforth and the Glasgow Highlanders, starting from Trette Poux on the south bank and Verson on the north bank respectively, had begun a sweep north-eastward astride the Odon.

On the right the Seaforth ran into stiff opposition in Rocrenil and in the orchards to the eastward. After hard fighting they reached their objective, Le Mesnil, about 7 P.M.

On the left the Glasgow Highlanders met neither enemy nor mines. By mid-day they had contacted the 8th Canadian Brigade south of Bretteville-sur-Odon and were consolidating on their objective. At 2 P.M. they handed over to the Canadians and withdrew through Verson into reserve in the woods on the south bank near Rocrenil. Unfortunately the dust of their withdrawal was seen by the enemy, who still held the commanding spur that runs north-eastward from Eterville to Louvigny. "No dust, no shells." The Glasgow Highlanders had a number of casualties from mortar-fire.

In the afternoon the left flank company of the Cameronians sent a platoon patrol down the Eterville-Louvigny spur towards Rocrenil to contact the Seaforths. The patrol did not get far, for an enemy strong-point was very much on the alert between Eterville and the Seaforth's position. The patrol brought back information, however, which afterwards was of great use to the Seaforth.

That evening the Cameronians had plenty on their hands in Eterville. Soon after dark the enemy managed to work his way in between "D" and "B" Companies on the perimeter, and, overrunning "D" Company Headquarters, got away with a number of prisoners. Battalion Headquarters lost all touch with "D" Company, and their efforts to contact it only led to further heavy casualties. In the ensuing dog-fight the enemy very nearly got into Battalion Headquarters itself, where every available man was standing-to at his alarm-post throughout the night.

All this time the enemy was mortaring Eterville like nobody's business. Lieutenant-Colonel Villiers was knocked out—though only temporarily—by a mortar-bomb, which had burst practically on his helmet, and the Second-in-Command and three company commanders were also casualties, so Major J. C. Davies, Second-in-Command of the Glasgow Highlanders, came up and took over. Later that

10th July.

night " C " Company of the Glasgow Highlanders, under Major Lambie, also came up in support and at first light was put in east of the church to fill the gap where the enemy had broken in. Unfortunately " C " Company was caught by mortar-fire while it was getting into position and had a lot of men hit.

11th July.

Soon after, the enemy again attacked Eterville in strength. This time about two hundred infantry, supported by two or three tanks, attacked " C " Company in its isolated wood. Major Bingley, the company commander, had been wounded, so Lieutenant Quinn was in command. " C " Company fought a great fight. A party of the enemy got a footing in the corner of the wood, but they were killed to a man in a bayonet charge led by Corporal Lorrimer. When the enemy finally withdrew at about 8 A.M., they left over a hundred dead in and around " C " Company's position.

In the afternoon of 11th July the rest of the Glasgow Highlanders came up to relieve the Cameronians in Eterville. So accurate was the enemy mortar-fire that their few hours in Eterville that day were to cost the Glasgow Highlanders eighty-five casualties.

Meanwhile the 7th Seaforth, who had been worried by the enemy strong-point on the Eterville-Louvigny spur, had sent a company against it. The company wiped out the post successfully, but afterwards ran into two dug-in tanks and lost a lot of men.

On the night of 11th July the 46th Brigade was relieved by the 4th Canadian Infantry Brigade of the 2nd Canadian Division, newly arrived in Normandy. The 46th Brigade then withdrew to refit in the area south-east of Secqueville-en-Bessin.

Already the relief of the 44th Brigade by the 160th Brigade of the 53rd Division had begun on the night of 10th July when the Royal Scots had gone back to refit at Ste. Croix-Grand-Tonne. On this, and the following night, the rest of the 44th Brigade was relieved in its turn.

So ended Operation " Jupiter." Three very busy days of preparation for Operation " Greenline " were to follow.

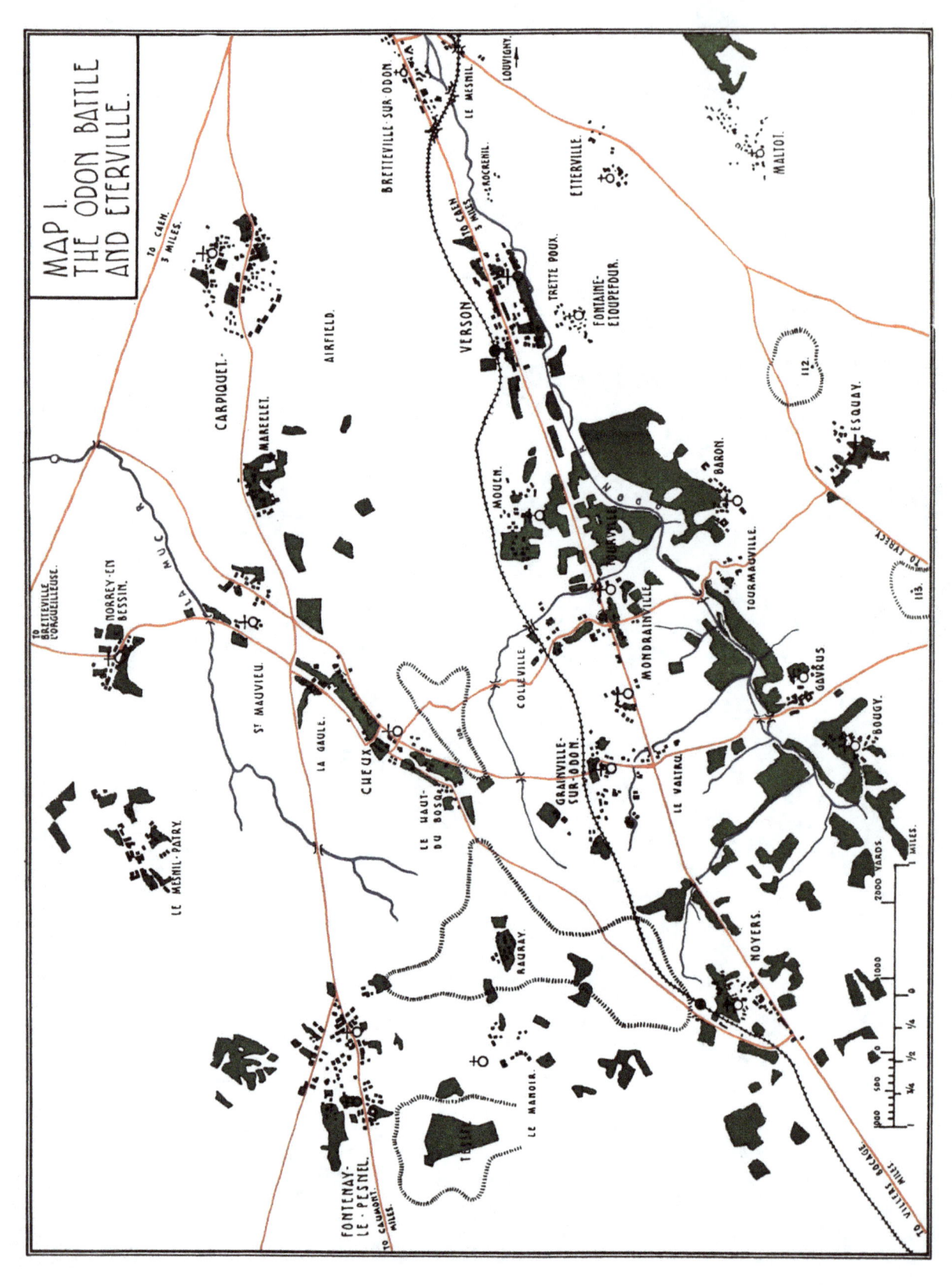

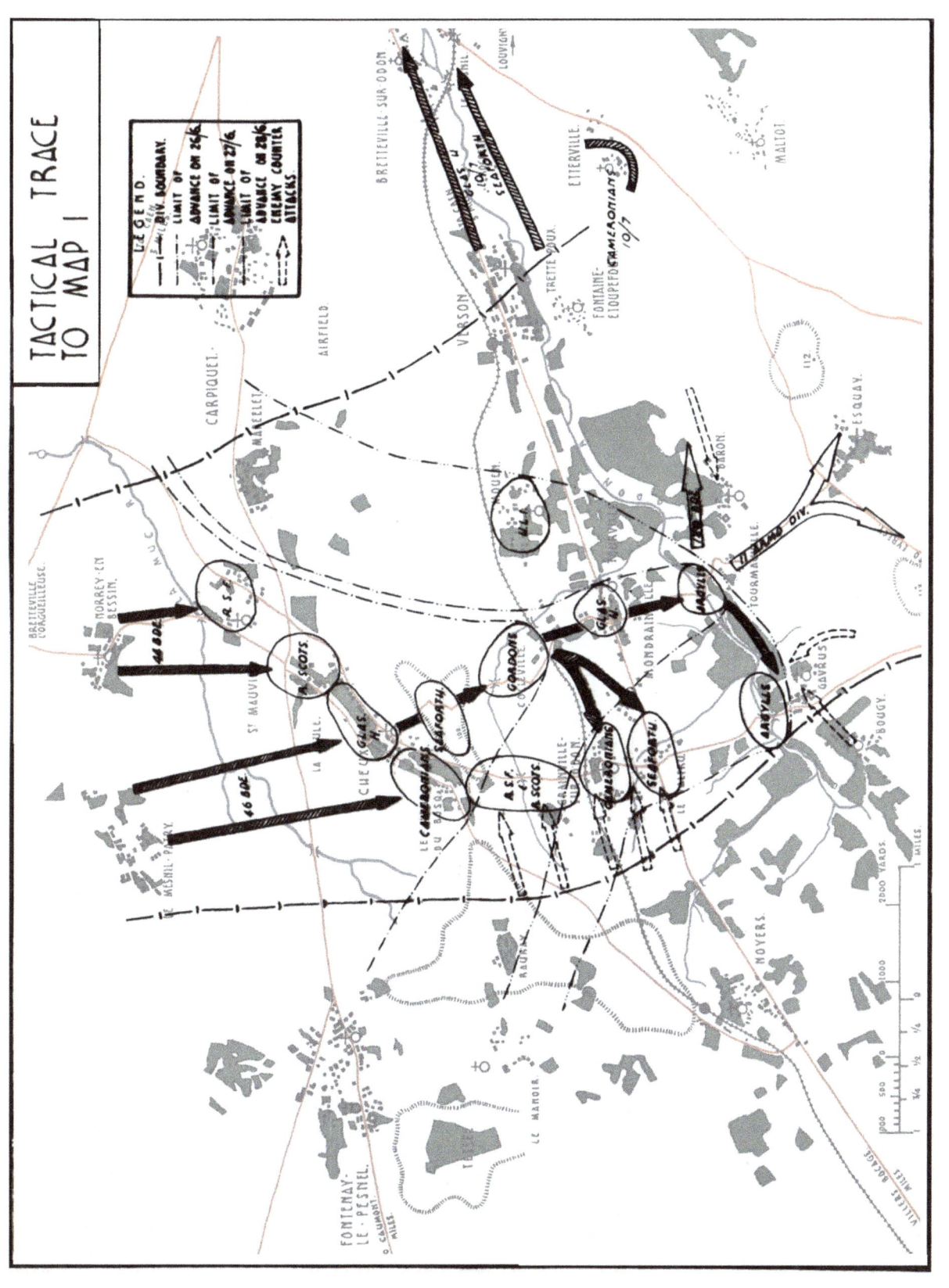

CHAPTER IV.

PART III.—ADVANCE TO EVRECY.

12TH JULY found the 15th Scottish Division resting in the area Secqueville-en-Bessin – Putot-en-Bessin – Ste. Croix. On the night of 12th July extensive regrouping took place in the Second Army. The 12th Corps Headquarters, which had now arrived in Normandy under Lieutenant-General Neil Ritchie, took over the 8th Corps' sector, thus releasing Lieutenant-General Sir Richard O'Connor and his 8th Corps Headquarters to carry out the second of the two tasks which Montgomery had assigned to the Second Army—the armoured thrust, that is, to be directed south-eastward through the 1st Corps' front north-east of Caen. At the same time the 2nd Canadian Corps, consisting of the 2nd and 3rd Canadian Divisions, became operational on the left of the 12th Corps, between it and the 1st Corps. Thus, from right to left, the Corps now in the line were the 30th, 12th, 2nd Canadian, and 1st.

According to Montgomery's plan, the 30th and 12th Corps were now to renew the thrust southward directed on Thury Harcourt through the corridor between the Odon and the Orne. On the night of 15th July the 12th Corps, spearheaded once more by the 15th Scottish Division, was to open the attack, directed on Bougy, Evrecy, and Maizet. The 15th Scottish Division, with the 158th Brigade of the 53rd Welsh Division and the 34th Tank Brigade under command, was to advance southward in its old sector on the Odon, through the front now held by the 160th Brigade of the 53rd Division, and was to take Evrecy and the dominating high ground beyond, which is crowned by the Ferme de Mondeville. There was to be no barrage. Instead, the attack would be supported by concentrations fired by about 400 guns.

At the same time the 71st Brigade of the 53rd Division, on the right, was to pass through the 160th Brigade farther to the west, directed on Cahier, and was to clear the 12th Corps' area north of the Odon as far as the boundary with the 30th Corps; while, on the left,

12th July.

the 43rd Division carried out the all-important task of " dominating " the enemy on the commanding ground by Point 112.

Next morning, 16th July, the 30th Corps was to take up the attack, directed on Noyers, whence it was to exploit to the high ground north-east of Villers Bocage.

13th to 14th July.

On 13th July reconnaissances began. These proved difficult. In its bridgehead beyond the Odon the 214th Brigade of the 43rd Division had only a precarious hold on the plateau to the northward of Point 112. The corpses and burnt-out tanks and other wreckage of war which littered the foreground spoke plainly of the bitter fighting that had taken our troops so far. The enemy—elements of the 21st and 22nd S.S. Panzer Grenadier Regiments, and as tough as they come—were still firmly dug in close at hand on the reverse slopes round the Croix des Filandriers and Point 112 itself. Baron Church was about as far as our reconnaissance parties could go, so they could see nothing of the dead ground round Esquay village or in the valley of the River Guigne, over which the attack would go. Nor did any of the reconnoitring patrols which were sent out manage to get through. The 15th Scottish Division, moreover, had no previous acquaintanceship with the 34th Tank Brigade—a disadvantage which was remedied as far as possible by numerous conferences and meticulous joint planning.

15th July.

On the night of 14th July and by daylight next day the 15th Scottish Division moved up to its forward assembly areas. The 44th Brigade on the right followed the old road through Cheux and Colleville, past " Dead Cow Corner," with its unrivalled stenches. The 46th Brigade in the centre—which, with the 158th Brigade, was to be in Divisional reserve—moved up to Mouen; the 227th Brigade on the left, with the Glasgow Highlanders under command, to the banks of the Odon by Haut de Verson and Miebord. The weather was still hot and hazy, the dust terrible. The move was watched by German reconnaissance aircraft, which at night dropped flares, evoking some very wild anti-aircraft fire at dangerously low angles. In the outcome the assembly area got some unpleasantly accurate shelling During the dark hours of the move, searchlights were practising with Movement Light (diffused searchlight beams), which they were soon to use for the first time to illuminate the battlefield. Drivers found

ADVANCE TO EVRECY

the light a great help to them in finding their way up the pot-holed track through the blinding dust.

15th July.

It was over the Odon in Operation " Greenline " that the 15th Scottish Divisional Engineers built their first bridge—a small one, it is true, but the forerunner of the many bridges that they were to build thereafter. During this operation, too, the Division first made use of its traffic control system—repeatedly practised during training—whereby the Divisional Reconnaissance Regiment controlled all traffic up to and over the Odon bridges.

The general " lie " of the enemy's defences faced the River Odon. The Divisional Commander proposed to attack south-westward, more or less parallel with its farther bank. In this manner he hoped to catch the enemy off balance. His plan for the opening phase of Operation " Greenline " was to build up his attack from left to right. The 43rd Division at or near Point 112 would cover the left flank of our initial attack on Esquay. Once they were established in Esquay our troops there would cover in their turn the left flank of our attack on Point 113. And once established on the ridge between Point 113 and Gavrus our troops there would cover the flank of our attack on Gavrus and Bougy in the Odon valley below, and would also form a firm base for the final advance on Evrecy and the Ferme de Mondeville. Clearly, everything depended on the security of the left flank. If the 43rd Division could look after the enemy on the reverse slopes round Point 112, all should go well. The alternatives open to the 43rd Division were to push the enemy off these reverse slopes or to try to dominate him by fire. Unfortunately, the 43rd Division chose the latter course—and failed.

It fell to the Glasgow Highlanders—temporarily under the 227th Brigade—to begin Operation " Greenline." Their rôle was to take Esquay and the important cross-roads nearby at Le Bon Repos, and so to secure the left flank of the subsequent and main attack directed against the high ground to northward of Evrecy. For this battle the Glasgow Highlanders, still under strength, could " field " three companies only. In support, they had the 157th Regiment R.A.C. (Churchills), one squadron of A.V.R.E.s, one squadron of Crocodiles (flame-throwers), and one company of the 1st Middlesex (medium machine-guns).

At last light on 15th July the Glasgow Highlanders moved up from Miebord towards their start-line north of Baron, preparatory to

15th July. attacking southward over the saddle between Baron and Esquay. As they emerged into the open with "A" and "B" Companies leading, each preceded by a troop of Churchills and a troop of Crocodiles, the Glasgow Highlanders were greeted by a storm of mortar-fire which temporarily threw the battalion out of control. To make matters worse, the very welcome smoke-screen which our guns were putting down on Point 112 and the slopes to south-west of it had turned into a fog which was obscuring the whole area. In consequence there was a proper mix-up on the start-line. None the less, "A" and "B" Companies managed to cross it on time at 9.30 P.M.

From that point the attack went without a hitch. First, the Crocodiles did their stuff, quickly burning the enemy garrison out of the entrenchments dug along the road between Le Bon Repos and the Croix des Filandriers. The survivors surrendered, and Esquay was reached. There it was the turn of the Churchills. With their help the Glasgow Highlanders had cleared Esquay by 11 P.M. They had no intention of occupying it, however. Down in the bottom of a saucer, Esquay was nothing but a shell-trap. Companies at once moved out to consolidate the areas on the surrounding slopes, which Lieutenant-Colonel Campbell had already allotted to them on air photographs. Thus the Glasgow Highlanders were now positioned for their task of protecting the left flank of the main attack.

It was at this stage that the main attack went in farther west. In it both the 227th Brigade and the 44th Brigade were taking part. The attack opened at 11.30 P.M. when the Gordons, moving up under heavy mortar-fire from their forming-up place in Baron, crossed their start-line on its southern outskirts. At the same time the K.O.S.B., moving up from Tourmauville on the right of the Gordons, formed up on the road from Mondrainville to Esquay—an awkward enough start-line since part of it was still in enemy territory. Though the K.O.S.B. had reduced their time in the forward assembly area to the minimum, they had had, none the less, a rough passage from mortar-fire on the way up. Battalion Headquarters, in particular, had been badly shot up by "Minnies." In order that they might move as noiselessly as possible, both battalions had left their "F" Echelon transport behind. The Gordons left also their A.Tk. guns.

It was a dark night. The country ahead was unreconnoitred and ill-defined hillside, extremely confusing in darkness. In such conditions the operation would have been quite impossible but for the use of the diffused searchlight beams. For the successful use of this Movement Light two conditions must be fulfilled: the troops to be employed must be practised with it beforehand, and its use must come as a surprise to the enemy. Here both these conditions were fulfilled.

15th July.

At 11.30 P.M., then, the two battalions moved off, each on a two-company front, into enemy territory in darkness only faintly illuminated by Movement Light. An hour later they were in touch on their intermediate objective, which was the track from Gavrus to Le Bon Repos, where it crosses the ridge—the water-parting between the Odon and the Orne—north of Point 113. So far they had met only slight opposition and had taken a few prisoners.

Meanwhile the Tactical Headquarters of both Brigades had been having a very tough time. Both were near the front-line—the 44th Brigade Headquarters by the bridge near Tourmauville, made famous by the Argylls, the 227th Brigade Headquarters in an orchard in Baron, already notorious as a target for enemy bombing and shelling. The enemy had both headquarters taped: they shelled, mortared, and sniped them unmercifully. In addition, enemy aircraft bombed the Odon crossings repeatedly. About 1 A.M. the inevitable happened—the 227th Brigade suddenly went off the air. A direct hit on the scout car which was being used as Brigade Tactical Headquarters had almost wiped out the headquarters and had killed Brigadier Mackintosh-Walker. The Division thus lost a most gallant officer, whose amazing escape from the Germans after he had been taken at St Valerie will long be remembered. Lieutenant-Colonel J. M. Hailey of the 131st Field Regiment, who was at Tactical Headquarters, at once took command and proceeded to fight the battle until Lieutenant-Colonel E. C. Colville of the Gordons could arrive to take over permanently. Inevitably, however, there was temporary loss of control, which could not fail to have an unfortunate effect on the development of the battle.

At 1.35 A.M., after leap-frogging companies on their intermediate objective, the K.O.S.B. and the Gordons were due to go forward once more into the darkness, again on a two-company front. Their objective was now the high ground overlooking Evrecy from the north. The right forward company of the K.O.S.B. was directed on that part of the ridge that overlooks Bougy from the south-east, the left forward company on the crest of the ridge; while the Gordons, still farther

16th July.

16th July. to the left, were to have continued their advance astride the track from Baron Church to Point 113. It was of the utmost importance that the K.O.S.B. and the Gordons should keep touch throughout.

By 2.30 A.M. both forward companies of the K.O.S.B. had reached their objectives, where they began to consolidate. Soon after, the A.Tk. guns arrived, but without the four 17-pounders destined for the left forward company. These four, with Captain Meredith, the F.O.O. from the 181st Field Regiment, had gone temporarily astray. Finding himself in the outskirts of an unknown village, Captain Meredith bethought him to call for a D.F. task on Evrecy in order to get his bearings. He certainly got them, for the shells landed all round him. Realising that he was in Evrecy—an Evrecy full of German tanks—Captain Meredith withdrew gracefully, taking his 17-pounders with him, and duly rejoined the K.O.S.B.

With the Gordons, however, the K.O.S.B. had lost all touch. What had happened was this. When the Gordons had come to leap-frog their reserve companies on the first objective, these companies had found themselves pinned by very heavy and accurate machine-gun fire from the left flank. Enemy machine-guns, perfectly sited on the reverse slopes round Point 112 in the 43rd Division's area, were raking their front on well-chosen fixed lines. In these circumstances, Major Sinclair, who had now taken over command, ordered the two original forward companies to continue to advance. These companies seem to have lost direction somewhat and to have veered too far left. By dawn they had reached a point a bit short of their final objective, where an order from Brigade reached them to dig in. This they did under heavy fire from the enemy posted along the road from Evrecy to Le Bon Repos. Thus two awkward gaps had appeared, one between the Gordons and the left forward company of the K.O.S.B. near Point 113, and another between the forward companies of the Gordons and their rear companies still pinned near the first objective. The situation on the open flank of the K.O.S.B. round Point 113 soon became difficult.

About 4.30 A.M. there was a report that the Gordons were on their objective, but farther to the east. There was still no definite news of them, however, for the 227th Brigade was not yet in communication either with the Gordons or with Division. Meanwhile, difficult fighting on the K.O.S.B. front had continued. By this time the enemy had pinned the left forward company by fire and had isolated it.

2ND ARGYLLS DURING OPERATION "GREENLINE"

While these events had been happening, the Argylls and the H.L.I. 16th July. had been moving up from their forming-up places in Baron and Gourney respectively—where both of them had been shelled and mortared unceasingly—to carry out their parts in the final phase of the battle. At 5.30 A.M. next morning they were to attack through the Gordons, who by then should have been firmly established on the high ground overlooking Evrecy from the north. The objective of the Argylls was the Ferme de Mondeville; that of the H.L.I. was Evrecy itself.

Immediately behind the Gordons and temporarily under command there moved two companies of the Argylls. These companies were to come up on the left of the Gordons on the first objective and so fill the gap between the Gordons and the Glasgow Highlanders round Esquay. As the Argylls subsequently passed through, these companies were to revert under command.

Behind these leading companies moved the rest of the Argylls. Behind them again came the H.L.I. Harassed by mortar-fire, this whole densely packed column of infantry and supporting Churchills, Crocodiles, A.V.R.E.s, and machine-guns slowly progressed by fits and starts down the forward slope from Baron and through the ill-defined gap in our own minefield, about quarter of a mile southward of Baron Church, only to come to a full stop as the Gordons ahead were checked on their first objective. Inevitably the troops behind, continuing to press on in the darkness, piled up on those in front. The leading companies of the Argylls tried to deploy to the left, clear of the Gordons, but could find no way through. In these circumstances the Movement Light was anything but blessed. Every man in that traffic jam imagined himself silhouetted, a perfect target for the enemy.

When dawn came it found all three battalions of the 227th Brigade and their supporting arms packed in an area less than a thousand yards deep and three hundred yards wide. Mist and smoke shrouded the heights to the left towards Hill 112. The Germans had been offered the ideal opportunity for a counter-attack, but for once they missed their chance. Lieutenant-Colonel Tweedie of the Argylls and Lieutenant-Colonel Young of the H.L.I. discussed the situation. They were still out of touch with Brigade. Lieutenant-Colonel Young, whose supporting tanks had been held up in our own minefield, decided to withdraw the H.L.I. up the slope towards Baron and to dig in on its southern outskirts. The Argylls dug in where they stood. Thus our dawn attack on Evrecy and the Ferme de Mondeville did not

16th July. take place. Later that day the Argylls were withdrawn to Tourmauville and Les Vilains. Both the H.L.I. and the Argylls had lost a lot of men without ever being in contact with the enemy.

The K.O.S.B., on the other hand, were firmly dug in by dawn on top of their hill, a little north of the Evrecy-Bougy road. They had re-established contact with their own left forward company, but they were still out of touch with the Gordons. At 7.15 A.M., and again about 8 A.M., Lieutenant-Colonel Shillington went out on personal reconnaissance to try to find them. On the second occasion he was severely wounded—a great loss to the K.O.S.B., whom he had trained for three years. He was succeeded in command by Major C. W. P. Richardson. In an attempt to fill the gap where the Gordons should have been, Richardson soon after extended his left eastward to the spur above the Esquay-Evrecy road.

The Gordons were still spread-eagled under heavy fire, with Battalion Headquarters and two companies dug in just south of where the track from Baron Church to Point 113 crosses the road from Tourmauville to Esquay, and with their two original forward companies also dug in some hundreds of yards farther south. Not till afternoon was Major Sinclair able to get any A.Tk. guns up to those forward companies. As things turned out, however, he was to be very glad to have the guns back at Battalion Headquarters, for about mid-day five German Mark IV. tanks, followed by infantry, bore down on him from the direction of Le Bon Repos. His anti-tank platoon, in action close by, promptly knocked out all five Mark IV.s at almost point-blank range, while the 131st Field Regiment dispersed the infantry. Battalion Headquarters breathed again. While all this was going on, the forward companies were dealing successfully with a succession of counter-attacks.

On the extreme right of the 44th Brigade, meanwhile, the Royal Scots, with 153rd Regiment R.A.C. in support, had advanced at 5.30 A.M. along the south bank of the Odon from Les Vilains on Gavrus and Bougy. Lieutenant-Colonel Delacombe of the Royal Scots and Lieutenant-Colonel Wood of the 153rd Regiment R.A.C. had been instructors together at the Staff College, and they made a joint plan which would have done credit to any Directing Staff. Moving along the slopes to the south, the tanks were to by-pass Gavrus and attack it from the rear while the Royal Scots attacked it from the front. Here the advantages of the Divisional build-up from left to right became fully apparent. Already the K.O.S.B. held the crest above, so the left or uphill flank of the tanks was secure.

The plan worked like a charm, first at Gavrus and then at Bougy. By 8 A.M. Gavrus had fallen to the joint attack, yielding seventy prisoners; by 10 A.M. Bougy also had fallen, yielding a hundred more. Throughout, however, enemy mortar-fire never slackened. Moreover, from 8.30 A.M. onwards Focke-Wulfs had been coming over in lots of twenty or so. Unluckily, both Lieutenant-Colonel Delacombe and Lieutenant-Colonel Wood were among the wounded. Casualties among more junior leaders, too, were particularly heavy. So good had been the initial briefing, however, that the operation went through to the end without a hitch. Major P. R. Lane Joynt succeeded Lieutenant-Colonel Delacombe in command of the Royal Scots.

Thus by 10 A.M. the 44th Brigade had successfully completed its allotted task—a fine achievement in one of the fiercest battles of the campaign. That evening the 44th Brigade received a special message of congratulation from the Corps Commander, Lieutenant-General Neil Ritchie.

Throughout the day enemy mortars continued to plaster the Divisional front; and in the afternoon the invariable counter-attacks began. At about 2.30 P.M. the Royal Scots were heavily attacked from the south-west and had part of their position overrun at Bougy. This they managed to restore by 4 P.M. Meanwhile, Brigadier Money had moved the R.S.F. up to Gavrus in support.

Later, these counter-attacks extended eastward to the K.O.S.B. and beyond. On the top of the hill things were now in better shape to meet them, for the K.O.S.B. and the Gordons had made firm contact at last about 5 P.M. The enemy repeatedly counter-attacked the junction of the two battalions, and at one moment had penetrated to a depth of 500 yards north of Point 113. By 8 P.M. the front was everywhere restored, with the help of some very effective artillery fire.

North of the Odon, too, progress had been made throughout the day. By 9 A.M. the 71st Brigade of the 53rd Division had taken Cahier and the woods between it and the Odon. It was evening, however, before the Royal Scots in Bougy could make contact with the 2nd Monmouthshires across the Odon. About noon the 59th Division, attacking in the 30th Corps' sector Tessel-Rauray, took Brettevillette and, later, Noyers; while the 49th Division, still farther west, took Vendes.

We must now return to the Glasgow Highlanders, whom we left

16th July.

16th July. doing their best to dig in on the stony slopes round Esquay the night before. According to the 227th Brigade plan, the Argylls were to have linked up with them at Le Bon Repos during the night. The link-up, however, could not take place, so Lieutenant-Colonel Campbell had put "A" Company into Le Bon Repos and the houses and orchards immediately south of it. It was a strange position in which the Glasgow Highlanders found themselves that morning—their three companies deployed, as it were, round the curve of a saucer, with Esquay, unoccupied, lying below them at the bottom, and the enemy in position above them on the rim, both at Point 112 to the eastward, only 600 yards away, and, to the westward, on the slopes near Point 113. Despite the fact that Point 112 was kept continually blinded by a smoke-screen, it was impossible to move unseen. Till evening, however, the enemy failed to locate "B" and "D" Companies, and wasted untold ammunition on Esquay in consequence.

At first "A" Company on the cross-roads bore the brunt of repeated attacks by enemy tanks and infantry which came up the road from Evrecy. The fighting was fierce. Several times the platoon in the orchard beyond the cross-roads had to be withdrawn to allow medium artillery defensive fire to come down on the attacking tanks. On the cross-roads itself Sergeant Blair's 6-pounder knocked out two tanks almost at its muzzle.

In the evening the counter-attacks extended to all three companies. It was at this time, too, that the Gordons farther west were under heavy attack; thus the 227th Brigade found itself hard pressed all along its front. The front held, however. After dark "B" and "D" Companies of the Glasgow Highlanders, whose positions the enemy had now located, slipped away into alternative positions.

All this time the Divisional Commander had been making new plans for the taking of Evrecy. When his original plan broke down, which had provided for the taking of Evrecy on the morning of 16th July, he had ordered up the 158th Brigade, which had been in reserve north of the Odon. Originally he had not intended to use the 158th Brigade till the morning of 17th July, when it was to have exploited south-east from Evrecy to Maizet. He now planned that the 158th Brigade should attack Evrecy after dark on the 16th, with the help of Movement Light.

At 11.30 P.M. the 158th Brigade passed through the 227th Brigade in the Gordons' sector between Point 113 and Esquay, and advanced south on Evrecy. One of the two fundamental conditions for the successful use of Movement Light could not be fulfilled, however: there was no cover plan and the enemy was ready. At the precise moment when the attack went in the enemy released a great cloud of smoke, which rolled across the battlefield from the direction of Point 113, creating a fog impenetrable to Movement Light. The Royal Welch—the 158th Brigade consisted of three battalions of them —thus found themselves advancing down the steep forward slope into the glen of the River Guigne in complete darkness. Lying as it does deep down in this glen between Point 113 and the Ferme de Mondeville, Evrecy was to prove a most awkward place to attack.

16th July.

By 2 A.M. next morning the 7th Royal Welch Fusiliers had crossed the Guigne and were advancing uphill on the Ferme de Mondeville. Their A.Tk. guns, however, were unable to follow across the Guigne. A thick, hazy morning dawned, with the Royal Welch beyond support and out of touch with the 158th Brigade. It was in these circumstances that, about 6 A.M., Major-General MacMillan ordered the 158th Brigade to halt its advance and to clear the Guigne valley on both flanks, with the object of finding crossings for carriers. Soon after, however, it became clear that it would be impossible to maintain the momentum of the attack. Thereupon he ordered the 158th Brigade to withdraw.

17th July.

That morning there was thick mist everywhere till about 6.30 A.M. On the right beyond the Odon the enemy had counter-attacked the 59th Division in Noyers during the night and had driven it back northward as far as Noyers railway station. On the 15th Scottish Divisional front enemy mortar-fire went on unceasingly, but there was a temporary let-up in counter-attacks. As the mist cleared, the Glasgow Highlanders round Esquay saw revealed below them many marvellous targets in the valley of the Guigne, which their F.O.O.s engaged with great effect. By this time, however, enemy snipers had worked their way into Esquay itself and were giving the Glasgow Highlanders some trouble in their positions around the village.

Later in the morning the enemy began to counter-attack the K.O.S.B. and the Gordons once more, but on a smaller scale than on the previous day. Indeed, the fighting here is a good example of the enemy's strange practice of delivering an endless succession of small and costly local counter-attacks which achieved little or nothing. By

76 THE FIFTEENTH SCOTTISH DIVISION

17th July.   this time the understanding between our own infantry and guns was so good that few of these counter-attacks got far enough to bother the infantry. At about 7 P.M. the enemy did put in a heavier attack with infantry and tanks against the junction of the K.O.S.B. and the Gordons, but with no more success.

About 9.30 P.M. that evening the 158th Brigade again went through to renew its attack on Evrecy. At first all went well. The Royal Welch caught the enemy forming up for yet another counter-attack, and took a number of prisoners of the 276th Infantry Division.

Later, however, the Royal Welch ran into enemy tanks in the growing darkness and were caught simultaneously by intense enemy mortar and artillery fire. All the officers in the forward companies were hit, and the advance was brought to a standstill. Soon after 11 P.M. the forward companies had again to be withdrawn. This time the enemy followed up on the heels of the Royal Welch as they fell back through the K.O.S.B. and the Gordons, and some very confused fighting followed.

Behind the front meanwhile there had been some regrouping. The Corps Commander had ordered the relief of the forward brigades of the 15th Scottish Division by the 53rd Division to begin that night, 17th July. As a preliminary move, the 46th Brigade (less the Glasgow Highlanders), which was concentrated at Mondrainville in Divisional reserve, was to relieve the 160th Brigade of the 53rd Division. In accordance with these orders the Seaforth took over from the 2nd Monmouthshires in the line between Cahier and the Odon, while the Cameronians found themselves back in Grainville once more, in relief of the 1st East Lancashire Regiment.

On the night of 17th July the 160th Brigade duly relieved the 227th Brigade (less the Gordons, who remained in the line temporarily under the 160th Brigade). The 227th Brigade then withdrew to its concentration area at Le Mesnil Patry, where it was to remain till 23rd July, while the Glasgow Highlanders rejoined the 46th Brigade at Mondrainville.

18th July.   At 2 A.M. on the morning of 18th July the 44th Brigade, together with the 34th Tank Brigade and the 158th Infantry Brigade, came under command of the 53rd Division. Throughout the early hours the enemy continued to jab at the 44th Brigade front, ending up with a savage punch at about 6 A.M. At the same time the enemy aircraft were busy behind the lines, bombing the headquarters of the 46th, 160th, and 214th Brigades.

Later in the morning the 44th Brigade had to beat off four more counter-attacks, but by afternoon enemy pressure was slackening.

After dark on 18th July the 160th Brigade relieved the Gordons, who then went back to join the 227th Brigade.

By the morning of 19th July fire had died down on the 44th Brigade front, and it was evident that the enemy had thinned out. Indeed, Lieutenant-Colonel Richardson was able to send forward fighting patrols of the K.O.S.B. south-west along the ridge and across the road from Bougy to Evrecy.

After dark the 71st Brigade of the 53rd Division relieved the 44th Brigade, which withdrew to its concentration area at Le Haut du Bosq, where it reverted to the command of the 15th Scottish Division. Unfortunately an enemy patrol had seen and reported the relief of the K.O.S.B., so they were badly shelled on their way back.

So ended Operation "Greenline," and with it the second battle of the Odon. Nothing the 15th Scottish Division was afterwards to experience throughout the campaign was to equal these two battles in intensity. The Division could have undergone no more searching test of its tactical efficiency and skill at arms. The standard set had been the standard of the enemy's best troops. That the Division had passed the test so well is sufficient testimony to the soundness of its training.

This second battle of the Odon Field-Marshal Viscount Montgomery sums up thus :—

"The 12th and 30th Corps attacks had thus not made much ground by 18th July, but the fighting had been severe, and above all we were attaining our object by pulling the enemy armour back into the line. 1st S.S. Panzer Division was identified in counter-attacks round Esquay, where 10th S.S. Panzer Division was also heavily engaged ; 9th S.S. Panzer Division was committed at Evrecy and Maltot ; . . . To sum up, the enemy had now only 12th S.S. Panzer Division out of the line in the woods north of Falaise . . ."

Thus the success or failure of this battle was not to be measured by the progress on the ground. The First U.S. Army had now taken St Lô, and the time was near for the break-out in the west. It was vitally important to the success of this break-out that the German

19th July.   armour should be kept busy in the east. Operation "Greenline" had achieved that object. The bitter fighting in which the 15th Scottish Division had played so leading a part had indeed served its purpose.

Meanwhile, on 18th July, the 8th Corps had launched its armoured offensive through the 1st Corps' front east of Caen and beyond the Orne. By 20th July the southward advance of our armour was to be brought to a standstill at Bourguebus; other long-drawn offensives would be needed before Falaise could be reached. The 8th Corps' operation had had the effect, however, of drawing a strong force of enemy armour still farther east across the Orne.

20th to 22nd July.   Of the 15th Scottish Division during the next three days, 20th to 22nd July, only the 46th Brigade was still in contact with the enemy, between Grainville and the Odon; the rest of the Division was resting.

On the afternoon of 20th July Brigadier Barber ordered the Seaforth to probe the enemy defences in their Cahier sector as far as the road from Missy to Monceaux. The Seaforth soon ran into stiff opposition. As Brigadier Barber had thus got the information he required, he then ordered the Seaforth to withdraw.

That day the long spell of fine weather broke; drenching rain filled the 46th Brigade slit-trenches, making life a misery.

23rd July.   On 23rd July the 15th Scottish Division made a sudden and secret move westward to the Caumont area. The circumstances were these: the break-out of Bradley's First Army was now timed to begin on 24th July, by which date the weather was expected to have mended sufficiently to permit of the use of heavy bombers. In order to release another U.S. Division for this operation Montgomery now ordered Dempsey to take over the left Divisional sector of the 1st U.S. Army on 24th July. To carry out this task Dempsey chose the 15th Scottish Division.

Accordingly, on 23rd July, the 15th Scottish Division (less the 46th Brigade) moved through Bayeux and Balleroy to Caumont, preparatory to relieving the 5th U.S. Division that night, while the 46th Brigade—after the relief of the Seaforth in Cahier by the 176th Brigade of the 59th Division—moved up by bus direct to St Paul de Vernay, where it came into Divisional reserve. The Division now passed under the 30th Corps.

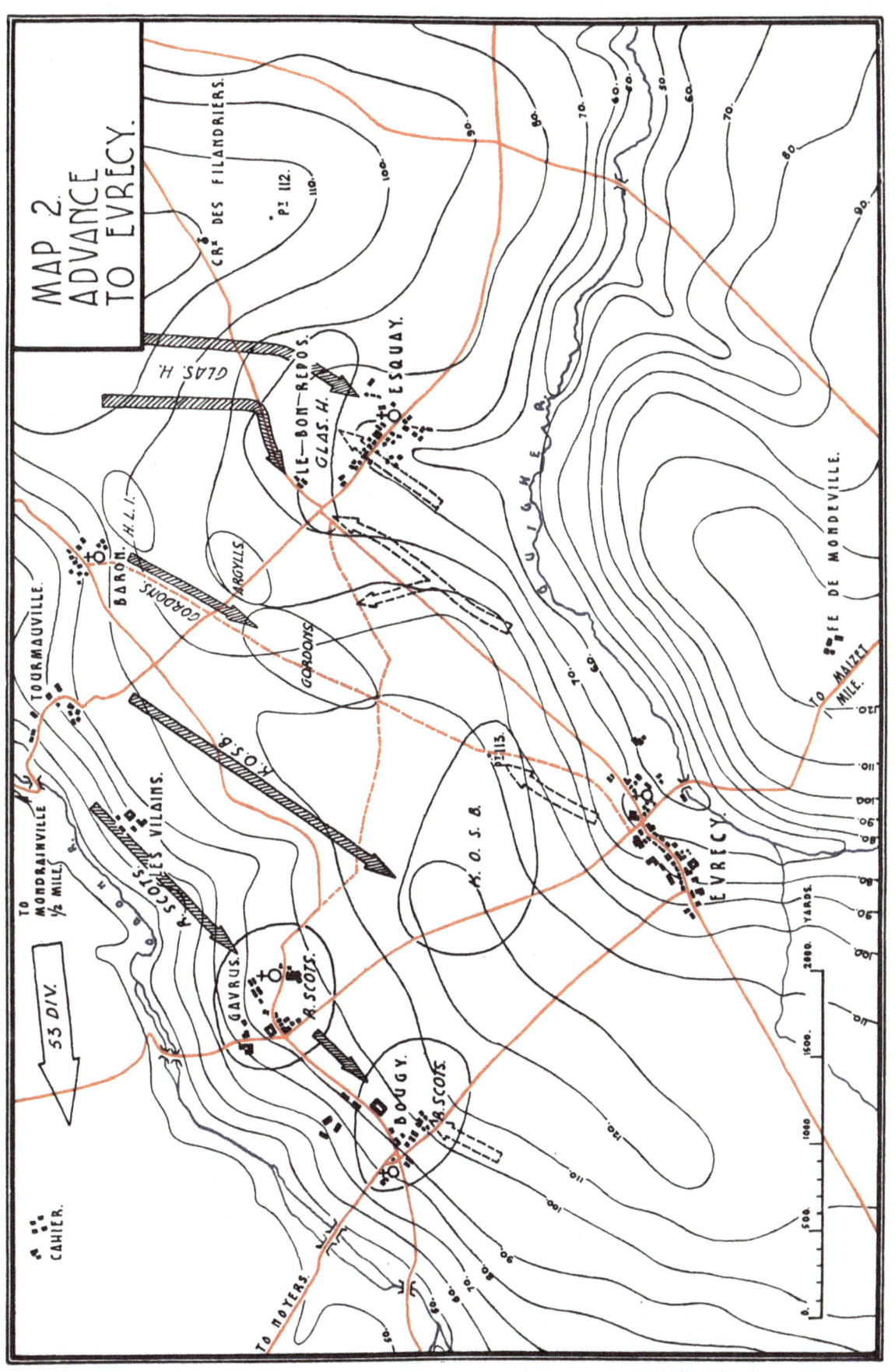

After dark on 23rd July the 44th Brigade relieved the 10th U.S. Regimental Group in the right sector between La Vacquerie and Caumont (exclusive); the 227th Brigade relieved the 11th U.S. Regimental Group in the left sector between Caumont (inclusive) and Le Repas. The men of the 5th U.S. Division were fine material—many of them of German stock; they were obviously well trained. Their ample establishments and their excellent rations, equipment, and welfare service—all these made a great impression on the Scots.

24th July.

Here in the Caumont sector the 15th Scottish Division found itself in the *Bocage*—in the tract, that is, of close, intricate country which stretches southward to Le Beny Bocage and Mount Pinçon in the Normandy Highlands. There had been little fighting in these parts, so the country was still unspoilt, in startling contrast with the Odon valley. It was a beautiful and bounteous land, flowing with milk and honey, where there were eggs and butter in plenty and where the cows were still alive.

The enemy, too, was little in evidence. The Division's opposite number here was the 326th Division. It was holding a wide front and seemed quite content to leave well alone. In these idyllic surroundings the 15th Scottish Division found life very pleasant. The broad belt of no-man's-land between themselves and the enemy gave the troops in the line their first occasion to practise active patrolling.

On 25th July Bradley's break-out operations west of St Lô, which had been postponed from the 24th on account of bad visibility, began. In order to maintain the pressure in the east, the 2nd Canadian Corps attacked southward along the road from Caen to Falaise on the same day.

25th July.

On the night of 26th July the 46th Brigade relieved the 44th Brigade in the line. There were still no signs of impending operations on the 15th Scottish Division's front. None the less the peaceful interlude was ending.

26th July.

CHAPTER IV.

PART IV.—BREAK-OUT AT CAUMONT.

27th July.   BRADLEY's break-out was now going well, both east and west of St Lô. Montgomery suddenly saw a golden opportunity to make it go even better. On 27th July he ordered Dempsey to mount a new offensive at the shortest notice with the Second British Army in the Caumont sector, while the enemy's armour was still concentrated opposite Caen.

The 8th and 30th Corps, after some extremely rapid regrouping, were to attack southward on 30th July on a narrow front. On the left the 30th Corps was to wheel south-eastward up to the line Villers Bocage–Aunay-sur-Odon. On the right the 8th Corps was to wheel more widely by way of Beny Bocage to occupy the area Vire-Tinchebray-Condé. At the same time the 5th U.S. Corps, still farther to the right, would advance southward on the west bank of the River Drome in conformity. These three corps would thus insert themselves behind any enemy forces which Rommel might have swung back to face west against Bradley's irrupting avalanche. Such was the bold conception of Operation "Bluecoat."

28th July.   Time was everything: Dempsey could give his troops only the briefest warning. The repercussions on the 15th Scottish Division were immediate. On the night of 28th July the 44th Brigade took over the whole Divisional front, thus relieving the 46th and 227th Brigades, which marched straight to their forward assembly areas in preparation for "Bluecoat." The 44th Brigade put all three battalions in the line, the K.O.S.B. taking over the whole of the 227th Brigade sector.

It was at this juncture that Brigadier Money, on completion of his three-years' tenure of command, went home to another appointment. His successor in command of the 44th Brigade was Brigadier J. C. Cockburn of the Argylls, who, as commander of the 8th Corps Anti-Tank Regiment, the 91st, was already well known to the Division.

From 6 p.m. on 29th July the 15th Scottish Division passed once more under the command of the 8th Corps, which now took over the right-hand or western portion of the 30th Corps' sector.

In addition, the 8th Corps had under its command for Operation "Bluecoat" the Guards Armoured Division, the 11th Armoured Division, the 6th Guards Tank Brigade, the 2nd Household Cavalry Regiment, and the Inns of Court Armoured Car Regiment. In fact, for the first and last time in its history, the composition of the 8th Corps in battle was going to be identical with that at its formation and during its training in the United Kingdom, and, in the opinion of its Commander, Lieutenant-General Sir Richard O'Connor, "Bluecoat" was probably the 8th Corps' best battle.

The Corps' immediate task on 30th July was to punch a hole through the enemy's prepared defences south of Caumont and to establish itself on the dominating feature Quarry Hill (Point 309), immediately west of the Bois du Homme; by so doing it would protect the right flank of the 30th Corps and open the way for its own armour. This task the Corps Commander allotted to the 15th Scottish Division, under the command of which he placed the 6th Guards Tank Brigade, a squadron of the Household Cavalry Regiment, and a squadron of the Lothian and Border Yeomanry.

At the same time on the right of the 15th Scottish Division the 11th Armoured Division was to advance south, directed on Dampierre, while on the left the 43rd Division—on the right of the 30th Corps—was to take successively Cahagnes and Point 361, to the east of the Bois du Homme.

About the forthcoming operation there was one feature that was particularly noteworthy. It would be the 15th Scottish Division's first action with its old friends, the 6th Guards Tank Brigade, under Brigadier G. L. Verney. For a time in 1943 the Brigade had actually formed part of the Division, and with it the Division had done all its infantry-cum-tank training. Now in the fighting ahead the 6th Guards Tank Brigade was to give the Division the fullest measure of support. The great success the two were to achieve together was the result largely of their previous and intimate co-operation in the United Kingdom.

What with "O" Groups, joint tank and infantry reconnaissances and other preparations, 29th July was a strenuous day. During its course the Divisional Commander visited as many of his troops as

29th July.

he could to explain to them the necessity of so impromptu an attack and to tell them how completely unaware the enemy was of the impending blow. To meet this blow the enemy would have to move two Armoured Divisions complete from his extreme right opposite Caen to his left opposite Caumont, all in two nights. So if an early attack was going to be difficult for the 15th Scottish Division, it was going to be much worse for the enemy. The immediate opposition would come from the 326th German Infantry Division alone, which was holding a nine-mile front with two of its three regiments fully committed.

To understand the Divisional plan for 30th July it is necessary to form a rough picture of the main features of the battlefield. Caumont stands on a high ridge which runs east and west. In the valley a mile or so to southward the enemy held two strong-points, on the right the village of Sept Vents and on the left Lutain Wood—known to the local people as the "Bois Mondant"—a thick covert which crowns a slight rise. Some thousand yards beyond and to southward of these two enemy strong-points was the army start-line, which the troops must cross at 9.55 A.M. if their advance was to synchronise with the bombing programme and the artillery time-table. It is hard to understand why Army had chosen so ill-defined and awkward a start-line. The explanation seems to be that it was an arbitrary line on the map which had been intended originally to be merely the safety line for the first heavy bomber attack, but which, in the rush of events, came to be accepted also as the start-line.

The Divisional Commander at once appreciated that, if his troops were to cross the start-line to schedule, he must take Sept Vents and Lutain Wood by a preliminary operation in good time and so secure the Division's jumping-off place. This precaution he considered all the more necessary because of the existence of an awkward-looking stream—the brook of Briquessard—which rose on the 15th Scottish Division's front, not far from Lutain Wood, to run thence eastward across the 43rd and the 50th Divisions' fronts in the 30th Corps' sector. To reach the army start-line all three Divisions must cross this brook.

The Divisional Commander therefore decided on the following plan. At 7 A.M. on 30th July the 227th Brigade, with the Cameronians under command and supported by the 4th Tank Grenadier Guards, would put in a two-battalion attack from Caumont ridge to take Sept Vents and Lutain Wood. Their jumping-off place thus secured, the other two battalions of the 227th Brigade, supported by the 4th Tank Coldstream Guards and the 3rd Tank Scots Guards, would at once pass through and, crossing the army start-line at 9.55 A.M., would advance some two and a half miles southward astride the Caumont-Vire main axis to take La Fouquerie on the right and, on the left, Les Loges and the prominent hill at Point 226, which looks down on the northern salient of the Bois du Homme. That done, the 46th Brigade would pass through in its turn from a forward assembly area in the neighbourhood of Point 226 and would advance still farther south to secure Quarry Hill (Point 309), an advance in all of about five and a half miles from Caumont.

29th July.

Such was the plan. As for the country, it was typical *bocage*—a close and intricate patchwork of tiny fields, of sudden wooded hills and boggy streams, of high banks and thick hedges, woodlands and orchards, white stone farmsteads and narrow winding lanes. There are only two good roads: the one which runs south from Caumont through St Martin des Besaces to Vire was the main axis of advance; the other, which runs south-east from Caumont to Cahagnes, was not much help, for it passed out of the Divisional sector to enter that of the 43rd Division within the first two miles.

Long before dawn on Sunday, 30th July, troops were beginning to arrive at their forming-up places north of Caumont ridge. Dawn revealed a milling crowd of tanks, carriers, half-tracks, Crocodiles, Flails, Infantry, all struggling to sort themselves out on the reverse slopes preparatory to the attack. It was a grey and sultry day, with the cloud base at about eight hundred feet. The 227th Brigade start-line was the main east and west road through Caumont, which follows the crest of the ridge; the enemy artillery had this road thoroughly taped. H-hour for the preliminary attack was 6.55 A.M.; there was to be no preparatory bombardment.

30th July.

At 6.55 A.M. the Cameronians (under the 227th Brigade) on the right and the Gordons on the left, each supported by tanks of the 4th Grenadier Guards together with some Crocodiles and Flails, topped the ridge to pass through the outpost line and drop down the forward slopes into the valley. No sooner had they gone than the two other battalions of the 227th Brigade with their own tanks and other supporting arms edged forward over the crest in their turn to form up in full view on the forward slopes. Tanks and still more tanks, scout cars and

30th July. carriers, there they waited in serried ranks three deep along the hedgerows till those ahead of them should have secured their jumping-off place for them. Presently the waiting multitude saw a heartening sight. The air was filled with a great fleet of heavy and medium bombers—over 1300 of them. They came, those Lancasters, Halifaxes, and Mitchells; they dropped their bombs; in twos and threes they roared homeward only some two hundred feet above Caumont ridge.

All this time down in the smoke and mist of the valley the fight for the jumping-off place was continuing. On the right the Cameronians attacked astride a narrow, sunken lane which leads south from Villeneuve, a suburb of Caumont, to Sept Vents, clearly visible ahead. This lane was the battalion axis, along which all transport had to move. A last-minute change of orders nearly caused confusion; for Major Clark of the left forward company, "D" Company, was hit at the start-line—which the enemy was shelling at rapid rate—before he had time to point out the new objective. However, Major Shearer, whose "A" Company was following up, luckily grasped the situation and took his own company through. Here on the battalion's left the supporting tanks, having found themselves stopped by the steep banks, tried to get forward along the sunken lane. The lane, however, was very thoroughly mined, and it was soon blocked to all comers, battalion transport and Flails alike, by a Churchill minus its tracks. None the less "A" Company reached the final objective.

Meanwhile the right forward company of the Cameronians was heading for Sept Vents itself. By the time it reached the village, about 8.30 A.M., however, all its supporting tanks but one had been disabled by mines. Delayed action mines, too, in the sunken lane were repeatedly blocking it as soon as it was cleared, so the battalion transport could not get forward. The Cameronians, therefore, found the clearing of the village a slow job until tank reinforcements got up to them from the reserve squadron. By 3 P.M., however, Lieutenant-Colonel Villiers was able to report that the Corps' main axis through Sept Vents was open. The Cameronians reverted soon after to the 46th Brigade and were ordered south by the main axis to La Morichesse les Mares.

On the left of the Divisional front the Gordons, advancing on a two-company front astride the road from Caumont to Cahagnes, had gone down the steep forward slope at 7 A.M., through the little fields and passed the scattered cottages. Ahead, they saw Lutain

Wood crowning a rise down in the valley. Mortar and spandau-fire was heavy and delayed the advance. Leaving a company to mop up the scattered houses of Le Lieu Mondant on the left of the road, the Gordons crossed the brook of Briquessard and by 8.30 A.M. had reached the wood, in the near or northern edge of which they found the enemy heavily entrenched. While the Crocodiles were burning the hedges which led up to the wood—a bank prevented them from reaching the forward edge of the wood itself—a troop of the Grenadier Guards' Churchills, circling the wood to the right, came in on the garrison's dug-outs from the rear. At once the garrison, two or three companies of a battalion of the 752nd Grenadier Regiment, began to surrender. Two companies of the Gordons then swept the wood under intense mortar-fire, made all the more galling by air-bursts in the trees. By noon they had cleared the wood. Lieutenant-Colonel Sinclair then ordered his companies to dig in around it.

We come now to the second phase of the operation. As laid down by Army, the start-line for this phase ran east and west about a thousand yards to the southward of Sept Vents and Lutain Wood. In order to conform with the artillery barrage (75 per cent air-burst), the H.L.I. on the right and the Argylls on the left must pass this start-line at 9.55 A.M. Despite the fact, therefore, that the operations by the Cameronians and the Gordons were taking longer than had been expected, the H.L.I. and the Argylls, who were formed up on the forward slopes at Caumont, could not afford to wait. As soon as the heavy and medium bombers had passed, off they went heading for the start-line with all speed. Major Russell Morgan of the 2nd Argylls had now succeeded Lieutenant-Colonel Young in command of the H.L.I., the latter having been evacuated on account of his wound.

Down in the valley the forward companies of both battalions at once ran into mortar and machine-gun fire. Very soon, too, the rifle companies were parted from their transport, for the lanes were blocked by all manner of vehicles, and half-tracks and carriers could make no progress across country through the maze of high banks and hedges and thick woods. Trying to by-pass Lutain Wood to the westward, the Argylls ran into an anti-personnel minefield east of Le Bourg; and they found that, far from stopping at Lutain Wood, the enemy's defences extended in depth southward right back to the start-line. Through all this the H.L.I. and the Argylls had to fight their way. In consequence they were quite unable to reach the start-line to schedule.

30th July.

The 4th Tank Coldstream Guards and the 3rd Tank Scots Guards, on the other hand, who were in support of the H.L.I. and the Argylls respectively, had managed meanwhile to crash through to the start-line more or less on time, doing considerable execution with their Besas and high-explosive against machine-gun posts and strong-points on the way. On learning that the infantry were temporarily out of touch, Brigadier Verney ordered these two tank battalions to push on from the start-line about 9.30 A.M. in order to get the benefit of the artillery barrage. The advance of the tanks was slowed down by difficult country, but by 11.30 A.M. the Coldstream on the right had reached the important cross-roads of Hervieux; the Scots Guards on the left were in La Recussonniere. Half an hour later the H.L.I. caught up with the Coldstream in Hervieux and they went on together to take their final objective, the high ground about eight hundred yards farther south, by about 3 P.M.

Following in the wake of the Scots Guards, the Argylls were carrying out a fighting advance in a methodical manner and were taking a number of prisoners in the process. After pausing to leap-frog companies, they reached the start-line about 1 P.M. There they were ordered to halt till 1.30 P.M. while a revised programme of artillery support was laid on. Meanwhile the forward squadrons of the Scots Guards had gone on alone once more, and by 2.30 P.M. had occupied the all-important Hill 226, which formed the left of the objective. Soon after, the leading company of the Argylls came up and cleared the village of Les Loges, which lies farther to the right. By 3.30 P.M. two more companies of the Argylls had arrived to occupy Hill 226 itself. The Argylls, however, were still without their transport and A.Tk. guns. Instead, therefore, of withdrawing from Hill 226 to rally, the Scots Guards kept their tanks lined up in a hull-down position on the crest, while the Argylls held a reverse slope position. The situation here was extremely precarious. By this time the 43rd Division on the left should have been closing on the Bois du Homme. Instead it was far behind, still fighting for the crossings of the brook of Briquessard. In consequence, the eastern flank of the 15th Scottish Division was left entirely open. To meet this danger the Divisional Commander now ordered the 44th Brigade to move up behind this exposed flank.

While this second phase was in progress the 11th Armoured Division on the right passed through La Vallée. The 46th Brigade,

2ND GLASGOW HIGHLANDERS ADVANCING AT CAUMONT

too—still without the Cameronians—had been moving up to its forward assembly area on the low ground north-east of Hervieux cross-roads in readiness to pass through the 227th Brigade in the third and final phase. The Glasgow Highlanders and the Seaforth had reckoned to reach their forward assembly area by noon. On the way up, however, they soon ran into much the same trouble with mines and transport blocks as had so delayed the H.L.I. and the Argylls. It was only by striking across country that they managed to reach the forward assembly area by about 3 P.M.

30th July.

Around 4 P.M. two waves of Marauders passed over, glistening in the sun, to bomb Quarry Hill. That was the signal for the third phase to begin: according to plan the 46th Brigade, supported by the Tank Coldstream and the Tank Scots Guards, should now have advanced to take the hill. The Divisional Commander, however, decided that, with the 43rd Division still far behind and the 44th Brigade not yet closed up, he was getting too strung out; so he cancelled the 46th Brigade's advance and, after consultation with Brigadier Verney at Caumont, sent on instead the 4th Tank Coldstream Guards to occupy Quarry Hill alone. This vitally important decision and the bold way in which it was put into effect were to be two of the major factors in the winning of the battle. At the same time, since it was obviously necessary to get infantry to Quarry Hill as soon as any could be spared, the Divisional Commander arranged to send the 4th Tank Grenadier Guards south to pick up the Glasgow Highlanders at a rendezvous on the main axis north of the Hervieux cross-roads, to which the Highlanders were now to move from their forward assembly area close by. The Grenadier Guards were to lift the Glasgow Highlanders to Quarry Hill in order that they might take over from the Coldstream before dark.

In accordance with these orders the Coldstream set off along the main axis headed for Quarry Hill. At La Morichesse les Mares, however, they found the enemy in possession, so they by-passed the village to the eastward and headed across country for the great conical mass of Quarry Hill, about one and a half miles away to the south-east. They had trouble with the bogs and springs at the foot of the hill, where the River Drome has its source, but they met no opposition. Soon they were established on the crest above the quarry, looking down into the expanse of the Bois du Homme to the eastward of them and across to the twin Hill 361 beyond the wood where, if all had gone

30th July. well on the left, the 43rd Division would now have been arriving. As it was, the Coldstream were alone, nearly six miles deep in the enemy lines.

Meanwhile the Glasgow Highlanders, complete with all their transport, had reached their rendezvous on the main axis north of Hervieux, where they joined forces with the 4th Tank Grenadier Guards coming from Sept Vents. The next few hours must surely have been a nightmare for all concerned. The main axis was chock-a-block with transport, much of it belonging to the 11th Armoured Division, which had strayed there from farther west. First, the tanks got stuck in a traffic jam in Hervieux. Next, they were held up by the enemy in La Morichesse, who had there one well-concealed 88 mm. in action. Then some M.E. 109's appeared to enliven the proceedings with cannon-fire. And all the time the Coldstream were calling up on the wireless for infantry help, and dusk was getting nearer.

Gradually it became clear that this was an occasion when the man on foot does best. The leading company of the Glasgow Highlanders were the first to dismount; they by-passed La Morichesse on foot and headed for Quarry Hill unaccompanied. Later, the three remaining rifle companies also dismounted and made their way through La Morichesse; by this time they had lost their transport, separated from them by a traffic block. "S" Company had struck out on a line of their own through La Ferriere au Doyen by lanes impassable to tanks. In La Ferriere they ran into the enemy, but managed to fight their way through in the dark. It was not till 2.30 A.M. next morning that the last of the rifle companies and the A.Tk. guns reached Quarry Hill; the command post using the tracks made by the Coldstream tanks had arrived a little before; "S" Company arrived soon after. Lieutenant-Colonel Campbell at once held an "O" Group and took over the defence of the hill, whereupon the Coldstream formed close squadron harbours about three hundred yards below the crest.

All this time the Seaforth, too, were on their way up to Quarry Hill, for Brigadier Barber had ordered them to make their way up across country after dark. After an extremely difficult night advance in intricate enemy country, they arrived before dawn and linked up with the Glasgow Highlanders. Quarry Hill was secure.

That evening there had been a tragic mishap on Hill 226. At the end of the second phase, it will be remembered, the Argylls and the

Scots Guards had been left there very much "in the blue," the Argylls still without their A.Tk. guns. Exactly at 6 P.M. enemy mortars in the northern salient of the Bois du Homme to the left front put down a very heavy "stonk" on the hill. Immediately after, what was evidently an out-sized high-velocity gun opened rapid fire from a wood about three hundred yards to the left rear, a wholly unexpected quarter. The first three shots demolished three Churchills. Then two enormous S.P. guns emerged from the wood and, covered by a third, lumbered deliberately up the hill and through the position. They were Jagd Panthers, mounting 128-mm. guns, 55 calibres or about 23 feet long, the largest things of the kind in existence, and they had destroyed eight more Churchills at point-blank range before they disappeared over the crest to the front, leaving eleven demolished tanks and many dead and wounded behind them. An artillery F.O.O., who found himself almost in the path of one of them, had a close-up of its commander, who was standing up in his vest, visible from the waist up, and laughing. Indeed the whole affair as far as it went had been a model of minor tactics, for the Jagd Panthers had made most skilful use of the cover of a cottage and a hedge in their surprise approach. No infantry attack followed, however, and Hill 226 remained firmly in our hands.

During the day the 11th Armoured Division on the right made good progress. In fact, it had cut the main road through St Martin at a point to the westward of the village, and was thus up level with the 46th Brigade on Quarry Hill. The 43rd Division on the left, however, was still far behind. Thus the 8th Corps had driven a sharply pointed wedge, nearly six miles deep, completely through the enemy's defences. In the process the Corps had inflicted very heavy losses on the 326th Division, which, consisting mainly of seasoned troops from twenty to thirty years old, had fought most stubbornly. The Divisional Commander himself, General-Lieutenant Von Drabich-Waechter, had been killed by a shell. Operation "Bluecoat," undertaken at such short notice and with so many misgivings, had paid handsomely.

In his plan for the next day the Corps Commander gave first priority to the clearing and securing of the Corps' main axis from Caumont southward to Vire. To this end he ordered the 11th Armoured Division to clear La Morichesse and St Martin, and the 15th Scottish Division to push their Divisional Reconnaissance Regiment and the Inns of Court Regiment through to seize the crossings of the River Soulevre.

30th July.

Far to the west the armour of the 1st U.S. Army had now broken through north of Ville Dieu on its way to Avranches.

31st July.

Dawn on 31st July found a pretty involved situation on the Divisional front. The enemy were still in the Bois du Homme and on the high ground to the north and north-west of it, where they interposed between the 46th Brigade on Quarry Hill and the Argylls in Les Loges. Indeed the troops on Quarry Hill had the enemy east, west, north, and south of them, for German S.P. guns were now active in La Ferriere directly in their rear, and the enemy were also in strength in St Martin and along the railway line which runs east and west through it.

With daylight the Coldstream resumed their hull-down positions on the crest of Quarry Hill and began the difficult process of re-arming and refuelling by half-track. The balance of the Glasgow Highlanders' transport, which had been benighted, also struggled in, and the Glasgow Highlanders and the Seaforth completed their consolidation of the hill.

Early that morning the 15th Divisional Reconnaissance Regiment started south towards the Soulevre, only to be held up by the enemy in and near St Martin. By 11 A.M., however, the 11th Armoured Division had cleared St Martin, whereupon the Inns of Court Regiment got through. Soon after, the Cameronians relieved the 8th Battalion, the Rifle Brigade, in St Martin.

The Corps Commander now switched the 11th Armoured Division to a more westerly axis of advance by the main road from Tortigni to Le Beny Bocage. At the same time he launched the Guards Armoured Division south along the original axis of advance, the road from Caumont through St Martin to Vire. By 5 P.M. the Guards Armoured Division was streaming through St Martin, and at dusk it had occupied Le Tourneur.

In the afternoon the 44th Brigade was ordered to take the high ground north-west of the Bois du Homme and so to link up the 46th Brigade on Quarry Hill with the Argylls in Les Loges. The Royal Scots, supported by one squadron of the Grenadier Guards, advanced to the attack at 6.45 P.M. By this time the 43rd Division on the left was through Cahagnes at last and was fighting in the eastern outskirts of the Bois du Homme round Pierre du Fresnes and Jurques. In their attack on the spur that rises south-east of La Ferriere, the Royal Scots and their supporting tanks had to run the gauntlet, not only of smoking and shelling by the 30th Corps' artillery but also of several Typhoon attacks. However, there was little harm done and they took their objective by 10 P.M.

31st July.

During the day the 15th Scottish Division's old enemy, the 21st Panzer Division, had made its expected reappearance from Caen. Ever since D Day it had been flicking like a shuttlecock back and forward across the beach-head. Elements of it had now been identified in the Bois du Homme and on the high ground west of Le Beny Bocage, where they checked the advance of the 11th Armoured Division.

Farther north the 5th U.S. Corps had taken Tortigni.

Next day, 1st August, was a day of counter-attacks, during which the 15th Scottish Division held a firm base for the 8th Corps' armour, which was operating on or beyond the Soulevre.

1st Aug.

It had been a quiet night at Quarry Hill. About 5.30 A.M., however, the enemy put down a heavy concentration of artillery and mortar-fire which lasted half an hour, and at the same time tried repeatedly to infiltrate, particularly into the Seaforth's position on the southern slopes of the hill. Infantry and tanks of the 21st Panzer Division then attempted to counter-attack both from the south and from La Ferriere to the north-east, but were dispersed by our artillery. Though the Royal Scots were now in position south-east of La Ferriere, the enemy were very much still there, and their S.P. guns hit two of the Coldstream tanks on Quarry Hill. Between 11 A.M. and noon the enemy's shelling rose in a new crescendo, and it continued all afternoon. Again and again, however, his attempts to counter-attack were broken up by our fire. At last, about 4 P.M., enemy tanks and infantry appeared in strength, both out of the Bois du Homme to the eastward and from the north-east along the road to its northern edge. They were met by everything we had got—medium and field artillery, 4.2 and 3-inch mortars, medium machine-guns. Some were taken prisoner, some came in under a white flag, the rest broke. By 6 P.M. the enemy, who had lost six Tiger tanks in this fighting, could be seen withdrawing from La Ferriere, pursued by our artillery fire. Throughout, the response of our guns had been magnificent. Our own losses had been severe, the Seaforth in particular losing three company commanders wounded—Majors Blair, M'Kenzie Mair, and Harrison.

Brigadier Barber now ordered the Cameronians, who were in and around St Martin, to counter-attack in their turn and to clear Galet and La Mancelliere. Attacking in the afternoon, with support from the Coldstream and the Divisional Reconnaissance Regiment, the Cameronians took their objectives in face of slight opposition.

In order finally to consolidate this eastern flank it was necessary also to fill the gap between Quarry Hill and the Royal Scots, the more so since there were reports that a large force of enemy armour was advancing into the gap from the Bois du Homme. In the late afternoon, therefore, the K.O.S.B., with support from the Grenadier Guards, advanced through the Royal Scots and up the spur of La Ferriere. It was Minden Day and the K.O.S.B. attacked with roses in their hats. After a stiff fight in the wood they reached their objective, the road from St Martin to Villers Bocage, thus clearing the awkward northern annexe of the Bois du Homme and linking up at last with the 43rd Division.

The K.O.S.B. took prisoners of the 125th Panzer Grenadier Regiment of the 21st Panzer Division, and from them learnt that four companies of their regiment and four tanks were concealed behind the railway line in the Bois du Homme, with the two other battalions of the regiment in support. In answer to the K.O.S.B.'s call, a concentration by seven or eight artillery regiments was put down in the area. Typhoons also attacked. The enemy were scattered. Next day the K.O.S.B. buried forty-one dead in the area and found four or five Panthers either knocked out or abandoned for lack of fuel.

All this time the Guards Armoured Division on its way south to Estry had been meeting unexpectedly strong opposition from dug-in tanks and mortar-fire. Its flank guard on the commanding Hill 238/244, two miles south-east of St Martin, was being heavily counter-attacked by tanks of the 21st Panzer Division; and its forward elements, which had now passed through Le Tourneur, had been stopped short in the steep hills and narrow glens beyond Catheolles. The 11th Armoured Division, which had now taken Le Beny Bocage, was also up against determined resistance on the road to Vire. By evening, however, the Household Cavalry Regiment had got a foothold in Vire itself.

According to the Corps Commander's plan for the next day, 2nd August, the 227th Brigade, with the 3rd Tank Scots Guards in support, was to take over Hill 238/244 from the 5th Coldstream and the 2nd Armoured Irish Guards of the Guards Armoured Division. The Guards Armoured Division itself was to continue its advance on Vassy. The

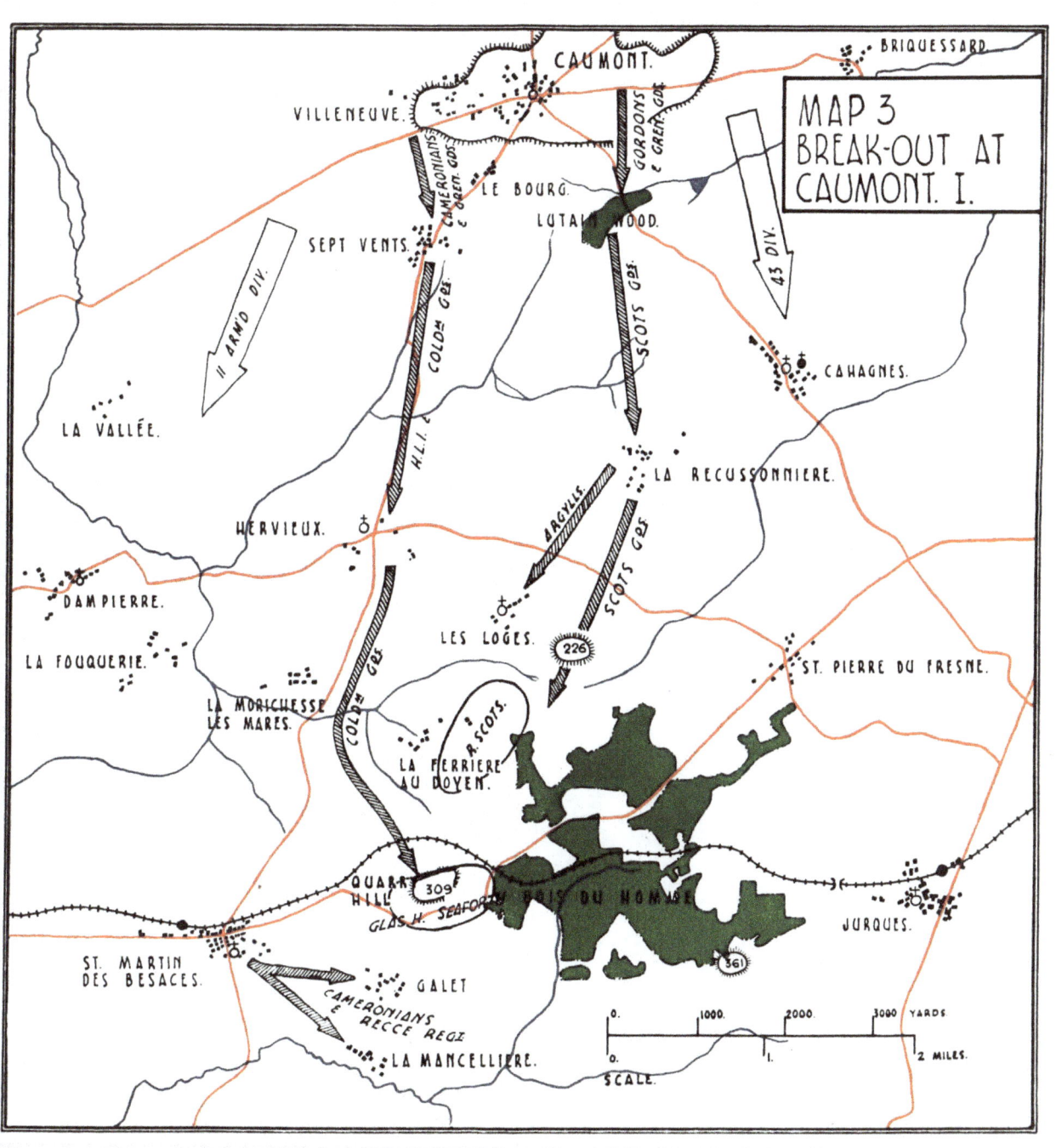

15th Divisional Reconnaissance Regiment was to follow and to watch the left flank.

1st Aug.

The 9th and 10th S.S. Panzer Divisions were now arriving fast on the heels of the 21st Panzer Division. Resistance on this front was stiffening accordingly. The bulk of the 11th Armoured Division was still about five miles short of Vire, though elements of it had crossed the Vire-Vassy road. The Guards Armoured Division was still fighting in the glens east and south of Catheolles towards Montcharival and Montchamps; the main axis from St Martin to Le Tourneur was crowded with its vehicles. The 15th Scottish Division held a firm base on Quarry Hill and Hill 238/244. On the far side of the Bois du Homme the 43rd Division had occupied Hill 361.

2nd Aug.

By 3rd August the British armour had begun its wheel south-eastward, so the 5th U.S. Corps took over the responsibility for occupying Vire, from which the Household Cavalry Regiment was withdrawn. The 11th Armoured Division, advancing on Tinchebray in two groups, was heavily engaged south of the Vire-Vassy road; the Guards Armoured Division was equally heavily engaged near Estry. The 3rd Division, which had come under command of the 8th Corps, was backing up the 11th Armoured Division on the right; the 15th Scottish Division was similarly backing up the Guards Armoured Division on the left.

3rd Aug.

In fulfilment of this rôle the 44th Brigade with the Seaforth under command moved up during the day to a forward assembly area near Le Tourneur, where it came under command of the Guards Armoured Division. The Seaforth went to Le Beny Bocage, where they, too, passed under command of the Guards. When the Seaforth went forward, the Glasgow Highlanders took over the whole of the 46th Brigade front round Quarry Hill. Later, the Cameronians took over the original Seaforth's sector.

The 44th Brigade's new task was to clear the two parallel ridges on the north and south banks of the Souleuvre east of Catheolles. That morning the Guards Armoured Division had been fighting a tank and infantry battle round Arclais, on the crest that overhangs Catheolles, while farther north the enemy had stopped the 15th Divisional Reconnaissance Regiment outside St Pierre Tarentaine, and they still held Montamy and Brimoy in the same quarter. Brigadier Cockburn's

3rd Aug. plan was to take the northern ridge of Arclais that afternoon, the southern ridge at dawn on 4th August. In fulfilment of this plan the R.S.F., lifted by the 4th Tank Grenadier Guards, came up early to Le Tourneur across country.

Arclais ridge is long, narrow, steep-sided, wooded, and scored with ravines. It may best be likened to a battleship on a westerly course, bow-on to Catheolles. Advancing from Catheolles, the R.S.F. were to board the battleship by way of its bows and then to fight their way east along its decks. To do this they must first cross a tributary stream which, flowing round the foot of the hill from the north, joins the Soulevre a little to the east of Catheolles. The bridges across this tributary stream were broken.

At 9 P.M. the R.S.F. attacked, accompanied by a squadron of the 4th Tank Grenadier Guards. It is noteworthy that this attack was supported not only by artillery but also by the fire of the 1st and 2nd Grenadier Guards, who were then in the neighbourhood—a unique conjunction of Grenadiers. In the fading light all but four of the accompanying tanks were bogged at the outset in the tributary stream. The R.S.F. went on, however, up the precipitous slopes beyond and across the plateau to Les Haies. By 10.30 P.M. they were on their objective on the high ground overlooking Montcharival—or Montchauvet as some maps call it.

That day the 15th Scottish Division suffered a grievous loss: Major-General G. H. A. MacMillan, when returning to his own headquarters at Sept Vents from a conference at the headquarters of the Guards Armoured Division at Le Tourneur, was wounded by a shell splinter. He was succeeded in command of the Division by Brigadier C. M. Barber. Lieutenant-Colonel R. M. Villiers of the Cameronians thereupon took command of the 46th Brigade.

4th Aug. Next morning Brigadier Cockburn turned his attention to the opposing ridge on the south bank of the Soulevre. On the ridge there were four or five large rectangular coverts, in which the enemy guns and mortars had been active.

At 6.30 A.M. the Royal Scots and the K.O.S.B. advanced east through the front held by the 1st Welsh Guards, who had come temporarily under command of the 44th Brigade. The first obstacle which the attackers met was an almost perpendicular bluff, which stopped even carriers and was difficult enough climbing for laden infantry on foot.

There was little or no opposition, however. The two battalions swept eastward along the ridge, the Royal Scots along the crest, the K.O.S.B. along the northern slopes. By 9 A.M. they were on their objective—the road from Montchamp to Montcharival where it tops the ridge. They had taken a number of prisoners of the Ausbild Regiment of the 9th S.S. Panzer Division. The 44th Brigade here reverted to the command of the 15th Scottish Division.

4th Aug.

In the early afternoon the Seaforth came up from Le Beny Bocage to relieve the R.S.F. on the northern ridge near Les Haies. The R.S.F. were thus freed for the task of clearing Montcharival in the valley of the Soulevre below. A squadron of the 4th Tank Grenadier Guards had been ordered up in their support. Together they took Montcharival, where they made contact with the 43rd Division coming down from the north.

In the afternoon, too, the 1st Welsh Guards attacked and took Montchamp after a hard fight. Using a number of Tiger tanks, the 9th S.S. Panzer Division counter-attacked Montchamp repeatedly, but without success. Here the Welsh Guards reverted to the 32nd Guards Brigade.

The 46th Brigade (less the Seaforth) now came up from St Martin des Besaces to relieve the 44th Brigade. The Glasgow Highlanders relieved the Royal Scots on the crest of the ridge above Montchamp; the Cameronians came into reserve farther north about Drouet; the Seaforth moved to Arclais, where they reverted to the 46th Brigade. The 46th Brigade was to remain here for two days, out of touch with the enemy.

On relief by the 46th Brigade the Royal Scots and the K.O.S.B. continued their advance eastward to clear the remainder of the southern ridge up to La Motte at its eastern extremity. Their attack went in after dark in the glare of the blazing houses and hayricks of Montcharival and Montchamp down in the valleys on either hand. The problem was to move all the paraphernalia of the attack—F.O.O.'s carriers, command posts, the S.P. guns of the 91st Anti-Tank Regiment—along the worst of hill-tracks in darkness and under intense mortar-fire. It was an all-night job that did not finish till after daylight next morning, when a morning mist fortunately hid the later stages of the advance.

During the day the 5th U.S. Corps on the right had closed on Vire from the north, to link up with the 11th Armoured Division a mile or

4th Aug. two to the northward of the town. On the left the 43rd Division, coming down the main road from Villers Bocage to Vire, had made contact with the 15th Division Reconnaissance Regiment in Montamy. Far to the north the enemy had now evacuated Esquay and Evrecy, and the 30th Corps had taken Villers Bocage. On the more immediate front, however, the enemy was still holding the line Vire – Estry – La Caverie – Mount Pinçon – Aunay-sur-Odon with the utmost determination as a pivot on which to swing back his forces farther to the south-west. For the time being both the 11th Armoured Division and the Guards Armoured Division were fought to a standstill.

Far to the south-west the American spearheads were beginning to turn east. At the other end of the battlefield the 1st Canadian Army was now to resume its attack south-eastward from Caen upon Falaise. There was news at last that reinforcing German Divisions had now begun to arrive in Normandy from the 15th Army beyond the Seine.

5th Aug. For 5th August Major-General Barber's plan was to break through the German front at La Caverie in the direction of Lassy, which was one of the 8th Corps' original objectives. With this object in view he decided to leap-frog the 227th Brigade through the 44th Brigade.

At that time the 227th Brigade was concentrated round Mancelliere, on the southern slopes of Quarry Hill. Early that morning it moved up, riding on the tanks of the Scots Guards. By noon all three battalions were through Montcharival. The advance continued eastward, the Argylls on the right along the Montchamp – La Caverie road, the 10th H.L.I. and the Gordons on the left directed on Au Cornu. The Argylls made no contact with the enemy; they halted for the night, covering the important bridge about a mile short of La Caverie. The H.L.I. reached Au Cornu, where they came under very heavy shelling and suffered a number of casualties. The Gordons occupied the cross-roads south of Au Cornu, where they, too, were shelled. The Divisional Reconnaissance Regiment meanwhile had located troops of the 9th S.S. Panzer Division in strength to the eastward in the wooded hills round St Jean le Blanc and Danvou.

That night the 46th Brigade moved up from reserve through the 44th Brigade round Montcharival and into a forward assembly area a little farther east. The 44th Brigade did not move.

During the day the 19th U.S. Corps on the right had entered Vire from the south-west. The 11th Armoured Division and the 5th U.S.

Corps were still fighting a little way to the northward of Vire. On the left the 43rd Division was now attacking Mount Pinçon. 5th Aug

For the next day the Divisional Commander planned two operations. Driving south and south-west from La Caverie cross-roads the 227th Brigade was to establish a firm base in and around Estry, while, farther to the north-east, the 46th Brigade was to attack eastward to cover the northern flank towards Mount Pinçon.

On Sunday morning, 6th August, the 46th Brigade opened the day's operations. The enemy, it was believed, was in full retreat: little opposition was expected. At 6 A.M. the Cameronians, supported by the Coldstream, advanced south-east from La Bruyère against the steep hill crowned by the Bois des Monts, which rises a thousand yards or so to the southward of the village of Le Codmet. There was a very thick morning mist which delayed the advance. But for that the advance went smoothly, and the forward company occupied the Bois des Monts without much difficulty. 6th Aug.

On the farther edge of the Bois des Monts the ground drops almost sheer to the tributary of the Orne that runs in the bottom of the glen two hundred feet below. The other three rifle companies of the Cameronians now went through, directed against the opposing hill across the glen, which is crowned by the orchards and fields of Gourney village. The approach to Gourney up the far side of the glen is thickly wooded, and it was soon evident that the enemy was holding these slopes and Gourney itself in strength. As the attackers went down the steep forward slopes, they ran into intense artillery and machine-gun fire. The going was so bad that tanks could not leave the road, which was under accurate shell-fire and blocked by burning vehicles. There was no way round. In the outcome these three Cameronian companies found themselves pinned by fire in the bottom of the glen, near the bridge which is known as "La Pont Soffrey," where they had a great many men hit. Battalion Headquarters suffered particularly severely. For the Cameronians this was indeed "Black Sunday."

Meanwhile, after a longish delay caused by the blocking of the track from their forward assembly area at La Bruyère by a disabled Cameronian carrier, the Glasgow Highlanders had come up to the Bois des Monts by about 10 A.M. to take over from the original company of the Cameronians. The Glasgow Highlanders took up position in the Bois des Monts under heavy mortar-fire.

G

6th Aug.

In the third phase of the operation the Seaforth, with a squadron of the Coldstream in support, were to pass through the Glasgow Highlanders and to occupy Lassy, a small village which lies in the valley to the south of the Bois des Monts. The Seaforth expected to meet no enemy short of Lassy.

At about 3 P.M. the Seaforth went through in advanced guard formation, headed by their carrier platoon. No sooner had the leading company topped the crest to go down into the glen, however, than it ran into a hail of fire. Its forward platoons attacked and wiped out the nearer of the German outposts, but the company could make no further headway. Pinned to the ground on the open forward slopes, it was soon reduced to about forty men under one officer. At the same time the supporting Coldstream had a number of their tanks knocked out by well-concealed 88-mm. guns; and Lieutenant-Colonel Robertson, who had recently succeeded Lieutenant-Colonel Grant in command of the Seaforth, was mortally wounded.

Major Brander, the senior company commander, then took charge and organised a battalion attack. At about 5 P.M. he sent two fresh companies through the original forward company, which he withdrew into reserve. Artillery and small-arms fire were so intense, however, that these fresh companies could gain no more than about a hundred and fifty yards—and that at the cost of heavy casualties, among whom were both company commanders. There the two companies dug in—a thoroughly unpleasant business, since they were completely overlooked by the high ground close ahead. At about 7.30 P.M. permission was received to withdraw them, which was done under cover of a smoke-screen.

In conditions so difficult a further advance down the fire-swept forward slopes was clearly impossible. The Divisional Commander, therefore, ordered Brigadier Villiers to withdraw his three battalions under cover of darkness to the area La Caverie-Au Cornu-La Druerie. The Glasgow Highlanders in the Bois des Monts covered the withdrawal of the Cameronians and the Seaforth. The last of the Seaforth passed the Brigade check-point about midnight. Then the Glasgow Highlanders themselves withdrew through a screen formed by their own carrier platoon. So completely was the enemy deceived that he continued to mortar the Bois des Monts till the following afternoon.

Meanwhile the 227th Brigade farther to the south-west were also meeting with extremely tough resistance. The 227th Brigade's opera tions for the day hinged on the cross-roads of La Caverie. First, the Gordons, supported by a squadron of the Grenadier Guards, were to advance south-west from La Caverie astride the road to Estry: their objective was the important cross-roads on the ridge at Estry, some two miles away. Next, the Argylls, supported by a squadron of the Scots Guards, were to attack south from La Caverie astride the road to Vassy: their objective was the Hill 208 overlooking Canteloup. Finally, the H.L.I., also supported by a squadron of the Scots Guards, were to follow the Gordons to Estry and, as soon as the Gordons had secured the Estry cross-roads, were to attack thence south-eastward astride the road to Le Theil: their objective was Le Theil ridge, on which they would link up with the Argylls, who would be on the same ridge to the eastward of them. Here, too, little resistance was expected.

The Gordons and Grenadiers moved off from La Caverie about 9.30 A.M. Two more battalions were to use these cross-roads, so La Caverie was already packed with armour waiting to join forces with its infantry. All went well till the Gordons were no more than half a mile from the Estry cross-roads: close ahead on either hand were the village orchards; beyond and to the left lay the village itself, clustered round its church. Here the Gordons ran into a minefield, and the action began. The leading company attacked and reached the cross-roads, but it could get no farther. It soon became clear that the 9th S.S. Panzer Division had turned Estry into a strong-point, which it meant to hold at all costs. Two or three companies of an S.S. Regiment, a dug-in tank, 88-mm. guns, bazookas, mortars, Nebelwerfers, machine-gun nests, mines—all were there, and the garrison had a call on powerful artillery farther back.

Lieutenant-Colonel Sinclair now put in another company, this time astride the sunken lane which, taking off from the road on the left half a mile short of the cross-roads, runs parallel to the road and directly into Estry village. After losing four of its supporting tanks, this company was stopped short of the village.

Next, Lieutenant-Colonel Sinclair sent one of his two remaining companies to turn the right flank of the village and the other to turn the left, each accompanied by two S.P. guns. Both these attempts failed. In the maze of walls and lanes and ditches there was little room to manœuvre, and the field of fire was seldom as much as fifty yards. In this type of fighting almost everything depended

6th Aug. on the initiative of the commanders of infantry platoons or sections and of individual tanks. Here at Estry the 15th Scottish Division was to feel the absence of the many grand junior leaders that it had lost since its arrival in Normandy. Moreover, the fact that the Churchill, even with its reinforced hull and turret, could not stand up to a direct hit from the Tiger's 88 mm., whereas the Tiger—so long at least as it faced the foe—could afford to ignore the Churchill's 6-pounder or 75 mm., inevitably had a discouraging effect on our tanks in close fighting of this nature. From this fact, too, sprang the very natural tendency to magnify all enemy tanks into Tigers.

By afternoon No. 2 Squadron of the Grenadiers had lost its squadron commander killed and four other officers wounded, and had had all its tanks disabled but five. The enemy was shelling the road heavily and casualties were mounting fast, not only in the Gordons but also in the H.L.I., who, with their supporting squadron of Scots Guards, were halted behind the Gordons about where the sunken lane takes off.

At this stage Lieutenant-Colonel Russell Morgan came up from the H.L.I. to discuss matters with Lieutenant-Colonel Sinclair. Together they made a plan. Pulling back his leading company from the crossroads, Lieutenant-Colonel Sinclair dug in on the eastern outskirts of Estry; the remnants of No. 2 Squadron of the Grenadiers withdrew. The mediums put down a concentration on Estry; thereafter, about 7 P.M., the H.L.I. and the Scots Guards attacked through the Gordons.

By late evening the H.L.I. had fought their way beyond the crossroads on the right and, on the left, to the neighbourhood of the church. But resistance was now stronger than ever, and casualties had been heavy; clearly, if they were to avoid piecemeal destruction, the H.L.I. must concentrate before nightfall. As darkness closed in, Lieutenant-Colonel Russell Morgan withdrew his men to the orchards on either side of the cross-roads. There beside the Gordons they dug in, supported by Scots Guards tanks which formed close squadron harbour. Lieutenant-Colonel Morgan and Lieutenant-Colonel Sinclair set up a joint command post. Hardly were the H.L.I. dug in when the enemy swept the orchards with a heavy concentration of medium artillery.

In their advance down the Vassy road the Argylls had also run into difficulties. The road was mined; machine-gun and mortar-fire were heavy; dug-in tanks and S.P. 88-mm. guns on the high ground on the left towards Lassy—which had been part of the

46th Brigade's objective—caused a lot of trouble. By evening the Argylls, with their supporting squadron of Scots Guards, had taken most of the near side of Hill 208. There on the slopes the Argylls were forced to dig in for the night, still about three hundred yards short of the main German positions on the crest.

6th Aug.

So ended a day of bitter and inconclusive fighting, which had come as a wholly unexpected surprise at a time when the enemy had been thought to be in full retreat. In fact, as we have since learned, Hitler had by this time ordered his suicidal Mortain counter-offensive, which was designed to drive through to the sea at Avranches and so cut off the Third U.S. Army. And it was an essential part of the plan to stand firm here along the north-western face of the Falaise Pocket while the counter-offensive developed. To this end the German defences had been organised as a system of "hedgehog" positions on the Estry pattern, garrisoned by troops who were ready to fight to the last, and supported by mobile forces for local counter-attack.

During the day the 44th Brigade moved up into reserve between Montchamp and Estry. Coming down from the north-west, the Guards Armoured Division, too, had advanced through Montchamp; its forward elements were now about a mile to the north-west of Estry. To the north-east the 43rd Division had taken Mount Pinçon after extremely hard fighting.

Throughout 7th August the Gordons and the H.L.I. remained in Estry, and Estry remained a very hot spot. Enemy machine-guns and 88 mm.s commanded the cross-roads. Spandaus swept the roads; artillery exchanges were incessant; our mortars plastered the enemy defences concentrated round the church; enemy mortars plastered the orchards and the road up from La Caverie. Yet up that road unfailingly the infantry carriers brought supplies three times a day.

7th Aug.

Over on the Vassy road meanwhile Lieutenant-Colonel Tweedie had renewed the Argylls' attack soon after dawn in a final attempt to get the crest of Hill 208. It was a most gallant effort, but it failed. A number of wounded men were left out in the open, among them Major Alan Fyfe of "B" Company, who was mortally wounded. The stretcher-bearers could not reach them, so Major Moreton of "C" Company went out with a Red Cross flag to where they lay. Almost immediately a German officer joined him; they arranged a half-hour's suspension of hostilities; the wounded were brought in.

102 THE FIFTEENTH SCOTTISH DIVISION

7th Aug.   For a day and a half more the Argylls were to remain out on the slopes of Hill 208. The position in which they found themselves was precarious enough. The enemy were dug in all around; their fire swept the road up from Au Cornu. During the night of 7th August they even put in an attack against Au Cornu itself, which was beaten off, with the loss of two tanks, by the machine-guns of the Middlesex and the 17-pounders of the 97th Anti-Tank Regiment.

Throughout the day the 44th and 46th Brigades remained in their defensive positions north-west of Estry and round Au Cornu respectively. Away to the south-west the 30th U.S. Division was bearing the brunt of the German armoured counter-offensive at Mortain. Fortunately the lovely summer weather gave the Allies every chance to use their vast air superiority to break the German attack. That night the First Canadian Army renewed its drive on Falaise, designed to close the mouth of the Pocket in conjunction with the 12th U.S. Army Group, whose right was to swing up through Alençon to Argentan. Victory was in the making.

8th Aug.   Estry still remained to be taken. The Divisional Commander's plan for 8th August was to take it with the 44th Brigade, after an hour's bombardment by every available gun.

During the morning the Gordons and the H.L.I. thinned out from Estry accordingly, withdrawing northward into reserve towards La Caverie. The last to leave, however, were caught by the Corps artillery preparation for the 44th Brigade's attack, which came down on Estry about 11 A.M. Fortunately this rear party got out before much harm had been done.

Approaching from the north-west, the 44th Brigade attacked at noon. The road from Montchamp was its axis of advance. The K.O.S.B. were on the right, the R.S.F. on the left; a squadron of the Grenadiers and a large contingent of Crocodiles and A.V.R.E.s were in support. The first job of the infantry and the Churchill tanks was to manœuvre the Crocodiles and A.V.R.E.s into position where they could blast and burn out the garrison at close range. Once more, however, the banks and narrow sunken lanes round Estry proved impassable obstacles: so much so that not one of these "Funnies" seems to have got near enough to use its weapon.

It was soon evident that Estry was still as much of a hornets' nest as ever. On the right, things at first went well. Both forward companies of the K.O.S.B. fought their way across the road from Vire to Estry. Beyond the road the right forward company, which was advancing clear of the village, managed to work forward up to its objective. The left forward company, on the other hand, was at once involved in a fierce struggle in backyards and gardens—made all the more difficult because the R.S.F. had been unable to come up into the key area of the church still farther to the left. It was here that C.S.M. A. Millar stalked an enemy tank, hit it five or six times with a P.I.A.T., and destroyed it. For this very brave act C.S.M. Millar was awarded the Military Cross.

8th Aug.

The R.S.F. meanwhile had been having a very rough time. Their supporting tanks never reached the start-line. Ahead were open orchards swept by the fire of a determined enemy strongly posted in thick hedges and other cover. Repeatedly the R.S.F. tried to work their way forward: progress was impossible. At about 1 P.M. German infantry, led by three Mark IV. tanks, counter-attacked and pushed the R.S.F. back over the cross-roads. The R.S.F. pointed out these tanks to their supporting troop commander of the 97th Anti-Tank Regiment, who promptly engaged them with the single gun he had available. His second and third shots destroyed two of the tanks; the third made off, followed by the infantry. The R.S.F. then occupied the positions recently vacated by the H.L.I. There they held their ground. In this fighting Lieutenant-Colonel Buchanan was wounded, whereupon Major I. Mackenzie took command.

By 3 P.M. the attack was entirely held up everywhere. A couple of hours later the enemy began to close on the K.O.S.B.'s right forward company, which was still alone and isolated on the objective. The situation of the left forward company was scarcely less precarious. The Brigade Commander, therefore, gave permission for the withdrawal of both these companies of the K.O.S.B. to the 227th Brigade's positions in the north-eastern outskirts. There the K.O.S.B. and the R.S.F. spent an anxious night under incessant mortar-fire and in close contact with the enemy, whose tanks ranged the orchards only a few yards away. Casualties had been heavy.

That night the Argylls, who had remained out on the slope of Hill 208, also in close contact with the enemy, were pulled back into reserve in the gap between the Seaforth in La Caverie and the H.L.I. on the road from La Caverie to Estry. The Argylls, too, had lost heavily in their thankless fight.

9th Aug.

The final issue of the battle of Normandy was now being decided at Mortain and on the approaches to Falaise. As his part in this final phase the Corps Commander was about to launch an armoured drive against Flers. The 15th Scottish Division was to form a firm base on which he could pivot his forthcoming drive. In accordance with this plan the Divisional Commander ordered the following dispositions: the 44th Brigade, with the 4th Tank Grenadier Guards in support, was to continue to hold the Estry ridge and cross-roads; the 227th Brigade, echeloned along the road from Estry to La Caverie, was to have a counter-attack rôle; the 46th Brigade was to remain in La Caverie, Au Cornu and La Druerie and to "watch" eastward; on the left of the 46th Brigade the 15th Divisional Reconnaissance Regiment was to link up with the 43rd Division. The enemy was still holding Gourney and the Bois des Monts.

In execution of these orders the Royal Scots moved up in support behind the K.O.S.B. and the R.S.F. in Estry. In Estry itself two counter-attacks were beaten off. The fire fight went on incessantly; no advance was possible. Casualties continued to mount, the K.O.S.B. losing two of their old officers killed, Major Waters and Captain Young. Repeated rumours of the enemy's withdrawal proved quite unfounded. On the rest of the front patrolling was the order of the day. There was some mortaring and artillery fire, but there were no counter-attacks. Enemy mortaring was now being dealt with most efficiently by the Divisional Counter-Mortar Organisation: the enemy had only to fire a round to get a return packet of ten or more—on suspected mortar positions on his front.

10th and 11th Aug.

On the morning of 11th August the 3rd Division and the Guards Armoured Division, then in the neighbourhood of Vire, began the drive south-eastward on Flers, keeping south and north respectively of the railway from Vire to Flers. The 15th Scottish Division was to be in readiness to follow up any withdrawal on its front. Though the progress of the 3rd Division and the Guards Armoured Division was slow, rumours of enemy withdrawals were rife; patrolling was intensified; the enemy did not budge.

The close fighting in Estry continued; on the 10th the enemy made another counter-attack; on the night of the 11th the Royal Scots relieved the R.S.F.

By 12th August Von Kluge had shot his bolt at Mortain and was now clearly doing his utmost to pull back his armour through the Falaise gap. To close the gap the 12th Corps was fighting its way to Falaise from the north-west, the First Canadian Army from the north; while on the other side of the gap the 15th U.S. Corps was nearing Argentan from the south. The extent of the victory would depend on how soon and how effectually the gap could be closed. It was at this stage, therefore, that the 15th Scottish Division was ordered east to help the 12th Corps in its drive on Falaise. The 46th Brigade was to be relieved by the 11th Armoured Division on the night of 12th August, the rest of the 15th Scottish Division on the night of 13th August. As cover for the move, the 15th Scottish Divisional Signals prepared a wireless deception plan, designed to make the enemy believe that the Division had gone to Vire. *12th Aug.*

On 12th August the Royal Scots took over the whole of the 44th Brigade front in Estry, relieving the K.O.S.B. That night the enemy withdrew at last from Estry, while in and around Au Cornu the 29th Armoured Brigade duly relieved the 46th Brigade.

On the morning of 13th August the Royal Scots found that the enemy had gone, whereupon they occupied Estry and pushed on to Le Theil. *13th Aug.*

Meanwhile the battalions of the 46th Brigade had marched to their concentration area after their relief: it was a long and exhausting march on an intensely hot morning. About 2 P.M. they embussed for Feuguerolles, a village on the Orne about ten miles south of Caen. They went by the road they knew so well, through Villers Bocage, most bombed of towns, and past Evrecy and Hill 113, Hill 112, and Esquay. Feuguerolles itself they found a shattered ruin which stank of war; every field and orchard around was a minefield. There the 46th Brigade came under the 12th Corps.

On the night of 13th August the 159th Brigade of the 11th Armoured Division relieved the rest of the 15th Scottish Division.

On the morning of 14th August the Division (less the 46th Brigade) concentrated in the lovely unspoilt country round St Pierre Tarentaine, where all heard General Eisenhower's broadcast that decisive victory was within the Allies' grasp. There was no elation. The price had *14th Aug.*

14th Aug.

been high, and all were too tired to rejoice. Out of the fifty days since the Division first went into action on 26th June it had been in action or in contact on thirty-seven days; on the other thirteen it had been within shelling distance of the enemy. Its losses had been heavy, particularly among battalion and company commanders and senior N.C.O.s. That those promoted had filled the gaps so worthily reflects immense credit on the Division's training.

Later in the day the Division embussed for Amaye-sur-Orne, where, after a hot and dusty ride, it rejoined the 46th Brigade.

So ended Operation "Bluecoat," and with it the 15th Scottish Division's fighting in Normandy; for, despite sundry plans to the contrary, the Division was not to be employed in the Falaise fighting after all.

During or after Operation "Bluecoat" the Division received the following congratulatory messages :—

From Lieutenant-General Sir Miles Dempsey, Commander, Second Army, on 2nd August 1944—

"It was the 15th Scottish Division which broke through the enemy's main defence line south of Caumont on 30th July and opened the way for the Armoured Divisions to pass through.

"The result of your great action on that day can now be seen by everyone.

"You have set the very highest standard since the day you landed in Normandy, and I hope you are as proud of your achievements as I am to have you under my command.

(Signed)   M. C. DEMPSEY."

From Lieutenant-General Sir Richard O'Connor, Commander, 8th Corps, on 3rd August 1944—

"I want again to congratulate you all on a magnificent achievement in the recent operations south of Caumont.

"Your capture of the high ground in the area of the Bois du Homme was vital to the success of the whole 2nd Army plan.

"This was carried out in most difficult country and in the face of stiff enemy opposition. Furthermore, you held your ground against all enemy counter-attacks.

"I am very glad to know how much the excellent co-operation between you and the 6th Guards Tank Brigade helped to make this operation such a success. It is a tribute to the training carried out between you, and has produced a state of mutual confidence which will go far to ensure further successes in the future.

(Signed)   R. N. O'CONNOR."

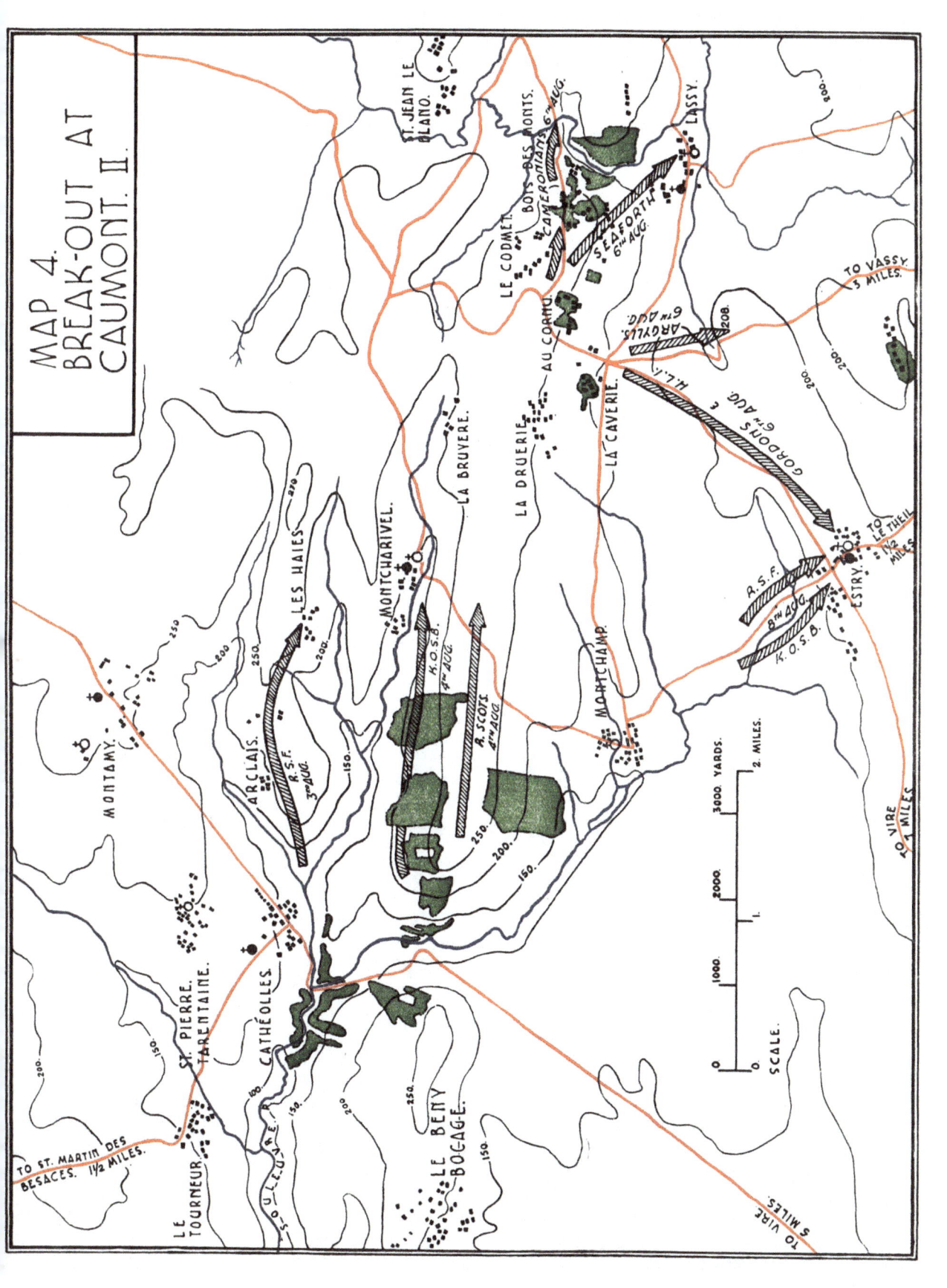

From Major-General G. H. A. MacMillan, Commander, 15th Scottish Infantry Division, on 2nd August—   14th Aug.

"I am indeed proud of the Division and I wish to include in my congratulations and thanks the 6th Guards Armoured Brigade, whose splendid co-operation made our latest success possible.

(Signed)   G. H. A. MACMILLAN."

From Major-General C. M. Barber, Commander, 15th Scottish Infantry Division, on 23rd August—

"On assuming command of the 15th Scottish Division I know I am expressing the feelings of all ranks in saying with what regret we learned that Major-General G. H. A. MacMillan, C.B.E., D.S.O., M.C., had been wounded. I am glad to be able to tell you that his wound is not serious, and, on your behalf, I wish him a speedy recovery.

"It was as much due to his inspiring leadership as to your fine fighting qualities that the Division has earned the great reputation it now holds.

"I assume command with a great sense of pride and of the honour done me, and with your help I shall endeavour to maintain our reputation.

(Signed)   C. M. BARBER."

CHAPTER V.

PART I.—THE CROSSING OF THE SEINE.

16th to 17th Aug.
THROUGHOUT 16th and 17th August the 15th Scottish Division remained echeloned along the Orne south of Caen. Eterville, Maltot, Point 112, Evrecy, Maizet—for the first time it was possible to appreciate how these looked from the enemy's side. The Divisional Commander conducted a tour of the Odon battlefield to discuss various episodes, with particular reference to the enemy's use of ground. The battle-field seemed strangely silent and empty, save where an occasional supply dump or prisoners' cage had sprung up since fighting had ceased. Everywhere around lay the wreckage of the German army. The Scotsmen spent these brilliant summer days resting, refitting, bathing in the Orne, and battling with the grievous plague of mosquitoes and wasps. All the while allied aircraft in endless succession droned overhead, their wings glistening in the sun. Later the Division was to see something of the work these aircraft had done in the " Killing Ground " of Falaise.

18th Aug.
On 18th August the Division moved south out of the dismal wilderness of the Odon battlefield into the delightful valley of the Bois Halbout, a few miles east of Thury Harcourt. Here the Division (less the 46th Brigade) was to spend three more restful days devoted to tidying up generally. Left abandoned in the Pocket close by there was German transport in plenty, so the provident were able to improve the shining hour by scrounging invaluable additions to their transport echelons, which ever after had a somewhat Teutonic air in consequence.

19th Aug.
On 19th August the 46th Brigade relieved the 160th Brigade of the 53rd Division in a defensive position west of Falaise. Patrols went out and contacted the enemy, who showed every inclination to surrender. Brigadier Villiers made plans for a brigade attack next afternoon, directed south-west on Bazoches, with the object of putting a further squeeze on the fast vanishing Pocket.

THE CROSSING OF THE SEINE

On this day the 5th U.S. Corps linked up with the Polish Armoured Division at Chambois, about seventeen miles east of Falaise, thus closing the mouth of the Pocket at last. Montgomery in consequence now turned his attention to a still wider envelopment of the fleeing Germans along the Seine. *19th Aug.*

Next morning the 46th Brigade's patrols found the front clear of the enemy. Soon after, the 53rd Division itself took Bazoches, so the 46th Brigade's attack laid on for that afternoon was unnecessary. *20th Aug.*

That night the idyllic peace of the Bois Halbout was rudely shattered. In the bright moonlight German dive-bombers attacked the headquarters of the Argylls. The high fragmentation anti-personnel bombs arrived before the Argylls could reach their slit-trenches. In the outcome the Commanding Officer, Major Kenneth—who had just taken over from Lieutenant-Colonel Tweedie—two other officers and twenty-six other ranks were wounded. Major Ferguson took over temporary command.

Another sad loss to the Division about this time was Colonel Harry Clark. His appointment as G.1 (Liaison) was abolished and he was relegated to Home Forces. He had been with the Division from its birth.

On 21st August, in a tropical downpour of rain, the 46th Brigade withdrew from its defensive position and concentrated south-west of Falaise. For the next three days reorganisation, maintenance, and ceremonial were to be the order of the day. *21st Aug.*

Montgomery's plan for a wider envelopment on the Seine had now taken shape. The Second Army, following in direct pursuit, was to advance eastward on a two-corps front, 30th Corps on the right, 12th Corps on the left, directed on the Seine between Les Andelys and Louviers. In order to provide the transport for this move the 8th Corps had been grounded. The First Canadian Army on the left was to advance to the lower Seine in conformity. Meanwhile the sweep by the Americans to head off the Germans from the Seine was proceeding. Thus the 19th U.S. Corps by 23rd August had moved up from the south into Evreux, while the 15th U.S. Corps was wheeling north-westward along the Seine towards Louviers. In consequence both these U.S. Corps were now crossing what would be the front of the Second *23rd Aug.*

23rd Aug.   Army. This crossing of axes was to cause the Second Army a lot of trouble in its advance, but it was an indispensable feature of the plan for a wider envelopment.

On 23rd August the 15th Scottish Division (less the 46th Brigade) moved through Falaise to a concentration area to the south-westward in preparation for the Second Army's move up to the Seine. Falaise, once lovely and gracious, was now nothing more than a squalid ruin, to which its townsfolk were creeping back in dumb despair.

The Division, which now had the 4th Armoured Brigade under command, was to lead the 12th Corps' advance to the Seine. For its move next day, therefore, the Division had been allotted all three Corps routes, known from right to left as " Moon," " Sun," and " Star." As yet none of these was completely open, however, so diversions would be necessary. In particular, the important road junction of Vimoutiers was reported to be badly congested.

It was on this day that Patton crossed the Seine south-east of Paris, between Fontainebleu and Mélun.

24th Aug.   On 24th August the Division made a short but extremely slow and tedious move by motor transport. Short of Vimoutiers there were diversions to be made by difficult and intricate hills through the woods. The transport of other formations was crowding the roads. Traffic discipline had been forgotten. In consequence, columns of vehicles stood head to tail for hours together. Everywhere around there was the slaughter, destruction, and stench of war. Upturned tanks, smashed armoured cars, burnt-out transport lined every road. For miles together paths for single-line traffic had been bulldozed through the mess of stranded vehicles and corpses. Noteworthy even in this museum of the macabre was " Dead Horse Alley," where for seven miles the carcasses of horses and mules were piled high in the ditches—and the stench was unbelievable. Such was the " Killing Ground " of Falaise. Never again would any who saw it lightly question the R.A.F.'s claims.

By 9 P.M. the 44th Brigade was in harbour on " Star " route east of Vimoutiers, the 46th and 227th Brigades in harbour on " Moon " route west and east of Trun respectively. The Royals (armoured cars) were on ahead. The 4th Armoured Brigade was in Monnai. The Division was leaving behind it at last the battlefield of Normandy. There the fighting had brought with it almost universal destruction.

Inevitably, therefore, the Allies had found the warmth of their welcome tempered by this sombre fact. Ahead now lay a France unravaged by war. There and in Belgium there would be another tale to tell. There joy would be unconfined.

24th Aug.

By 25th August the position ahead on the banks of the Seine was this. The enemy remnants were still struggling to break the Allies' wider envelopment. The climax of the struggle was taking place on the 15th Scottish Division's left front, where the 19th U.S. Corps had driven north through Louviers to Elbeuf in an effort to cut off the enemy rearguards who were fighting to keep open their escape routes to the Rouen ferries. All the while our aircraft were keeping these ferries under continuous attack. In the outcome the enemy was to lose on the Seine practically all the equipment that he had saved from the Pocket, but was to get most of his men away.

25th Aug.

According to Montgomery's plan for the subsequent development of the campaign, the 21st Army Group was now to drive north-eastward in pursuit, in order to destroy the enemy in north-east France, to clear the Pas de Calais of V-bomb sites, to capture the Belgian airfields, and to open the port of Antwerp—all as preliminaries to the isolation of the Ruhr. The first step was to cross the Seine all along the front. To this end the 43rd Division was to establish a bridgehead in the 30th Corps' sector, the 15th Scottish Division a bridgehead in the 12th Corps' sector. Before all else, however, the 19th U.S. Corps must pull out southward to make way for the Second Army.

Soon after dawn on 25th August the 15th Scottish Division moved off once more towards the Seine. It was a triumphal march in clean air and through glorious country. There were enemy stragglers about, and there was always the possibility that roads or bridges might be mined, but for the rest there was no likelihood of resistance.

The 44th Brigade went by way of Orbec and Bernay, heading for Le Neubourg. On the River Charentenne at Bernay the Brigade had to halt for some hours to allow the 4th Canadian Armoured Division to clear "Star" route. Farther on, at the crossings of the Risle —famous in happier times as one of the best trout streams in France— the 44th Brigade found all the bridges blown. The Royal Scots, who were leading battalion, thereupon dismounted and went on eastward into Le Neubourg on foot, where they found the Americans already

25th Aug. in possession. The rest of the Brigade made a detour southward, crossed by a small bridge which was still standing, and entered Le Neubourg from the south.

The 227th Brigade on "Moon" route crossed the Risle without difficulty. By 7 P.M. the Brigade had reached Emanville, six miles south of Le Neubourg. During the night Brigadier Colville sent the Gordons and the H.L.I. fifteen miles on into Louviers to relieve the U.S. troops there. The Gordons were now under the command of Lieutenant-Colonel R. W. de Winton, for Lieutenant-Colonel Sinclair had gone off to command a brigade in the 51st Highland Division on 15th August.

The 46th Brigade halted that night on "Sun" route, west of Beaumont le Roger.

It was on this march that the Division had its first and unforgettable experience of the welcome which was awaiting it in the days ahead—a crescendo of welcome which would reach its delirious peak in Belgium. On every cross-roads, in every village, crowds had gathered —to shout themselves hoarse in paroxysms of joy, to embrace their deliverers, and to load them with gifts of wine, fruit, and flowers. Pandemonium reigned. If there were any in the Division who had had their doubts about what the Allies were fighting for, they can have doubted no longer, now that they had seen for themselves what liberation meant to Occupied Europe. It was here, too, that the Division heard for the first time that invariable refrain on the tongues of all French children in those days, "Cigarette pour papa!"

That evening the 43rd Division began its crossing of the Seine in the 30th Corps' sector, immediately on the 15th Scottish Division's right. It was on that day, too, that French troops entered Paris.

26th Aug. Soon after dawn on 26th August Brigadier Colville sent up the Argylls from Emanville through Louviers to occupy a covering position on the escarpment overlooking the Seine at St Pierre du Vauvray. At the same time the 46th Brigade moved south-eastward from Beaumont le Roger to Emanville to take up a defensive position to cover the southward withdrawal of the Americans. For the rest, the day was devoted to preparations for the crossing.

The character of the country was this. The Seine here follows a meandering course in a sunken bed between steep escarpments some three or four miles apart. East of Louviers the river forms two tight loops which together resemble a letter "S" laid horizontally. At the outer curves of these loops the river runs beneath the cliffs of the escarpments, which are in places as much as four hundred feet high. The peninsulas within the loops are wooded and comparatively low-lying, but at the bases of the loops the ground rises steeply to escarpment level. The river itself averages about three hundred yards in width.

26th Aug.

For reconnaissance purposes the Divisional Commander divided this stretch of the Seine into two sections, giving the right section from Gaillon to Portjoie to the 227th Brigade, the left section from Portjoie to Poses to the 44th Brigade.

To cross a river obstacle such as the Seine against any form of opposition must always be a formidable operation. Moreover, the necessary build-up of storm-boats and close support rafts, and of material for the Class 9 and Class 40 bridges which come after, must at best present a major administrative problem. Here, however, the problem of the build-up as it presented itself to the R.E. and Provost was complicated by two further factors: first, time was very short; and, secondly, all roads other than that from Conches through Le Neubourg to Louviers had been allocated to the 19th U.S. Corps as it pulled back southward. Indeed, even the road from Le Neubourg to Louviers the 15th Scottish Division had to share with the Americans, the traffic moving smoothly enough in two parallel streams—with back-traffic barred. Immense credit is due to Provost for the way they handled the traffic on this and on succeeding days. To help matters as far as possible, priority was given to the move of bridging materials to the build-up area at Louviers, other forms of Divisional traffic being kept off the roads.

In the evening the Divisional Commander held an "O" Group to discuss the plan for the crossing: in view of the disorganisation of the enemy, he had determined to assault on the following night.

The wider picture was now this. The Second Army's immediate objective beyond the Seine was to be the area Arras-Amiens-St Pol. As soon as the Seine bridgehead could be established, armoured spearheads were to push through and, by-passing enemy centres of resistance, were to penetrate far ahead. On the Second Army's right the First U.S. Army would advance north-eastward in conformity. On its left, the First Canadian Army would clear the Channel ports. That evening the 4th Canadian Armoured Division began its crossing of the Seine at Pont de l'Arche, immediately to the left of the 12th Corps' sector.

27th Aug.

By the next morning the plan for the 15th Scottish Division's assault crossings had taken shape. The assault was to take place round the more westerly loop of the "S," where the Seine forms a salient into what was then our territory. Briefly the plan was this: first, before dark that same evening, the 227th Brigade was to assault in the centre at St Pierre du Vauvray, near the outer curve of the loop; secondly, the 44th Brigade was to assault after dark at Portjoie on the left flank of the loop; finally, the 46th Brigade was to assault opposite Muids on the right flank of the loop. In accordance with this plan the 44th Brigade moved up from Le Neubourg to a forward assembly area in the woods near Louviers that morning; the 46th Brigade from Emanville to a forward assembly area near Venables.

About 11 A.M. Lieutenant-General Neil Ritchie, the Corps Commander, arrived by plane at the headquarters of the 227th Brigade in the outskirts of Louviers. In view of the enemy's disorganisation he confirmed the decision to assault that night. This decision meant that the leading Brigades, the 227th and the 44th, would have to finish their reconnaissances and planning, the allocation and distribution of their boats, and their moves to their forming-up places all within the next few hours. It seemed an impossible task, but the decision turned out to be a very wise one.

To relieve—or perhaps to increase—these feverish activities, there were other and less serious happenings that morning. There was, for instance, the "Liberation" reception held by the citizens of Louviers —a reception embarrassing in its fervour. There is the story, too, which is told of the Brigade Commander of one of the assaulting brigades who, having left the jeeps and drivers of his reconnaissance party in a village half a mile back from the Seine, went down to the bank opposite Muids to have a quiet close-up of his intended crossing-place. As he and his party neared the bank with all the stealth of Red Indians they were greeted by these striking words in a female voice, "Oh, boys, am I glad to see you!" The speaker, a vision in the brightest of summer wear, was standing for all to see on the river's edge. Having shoo-ed the radiant lady away, the Brigadier carried out his reconnaissance—and returned to find high carnival on the village green, where his drivers, garlanded with flowers, were dancing to the strains of a gramophone.

About 4 P.M. a patrol of the Divisional Reconnaissance Regiment

8TH ROYAL SCOTS CROSSING THE SEINE AT PORT JOIE

crossed the Seine at Portjoie and made its way into Herqueville. It met no organised resistance. 27th Aug.

In accordance with the final plan, the 227th Brigade in the centre assaulted at St Pierre at 7 P.M.—that is, in broad daylight. The Divisional Commander chose this time partly in order to obtain surprise and partly because he did not expect serious resistance. The Gordons went in on the right, the H.L.I. on the left. The Argylls, in reserve, found working parties for the boats.

In front of St Pierre the Île du Bac divides the Seine into two channels. Over the farther channel the road-bridge was still undestroyed—this was the H.L.I.'s objective. Lieutenant-Colonel Russell Morgan sent one platoon ahead, which crossed to the island with few casualties. The rifle companies of the H.L.I. followed without difficulty and secured the bridge. They were soon established on the farther bank.

On the Gordons' front, things did not go so well. All three leading boats were sunk by machine-gun fire, and any who managed to land on the far bank were captured. Brigadier Colville thereupon decided to stop the attack here and to reinforce success. Switching the Gordons to the left in D.U.K.W.s, he sent their rifle companies across behind the H.L.I. Soon after, the H.L.I. dispersed the enemy detachment who had been opposing the Gordons and released most of the prisoners.

By 10 P.M. the rifle companies of the Argylls had also crossed in the wake of the Gordons. The Argylls went through to take up their position across the loop between Le Mesnil Andé and Andé. As yet, of course, they went without their supporting weapons, for the 227th Brigade was not to be complete with all its A.Tk. guns and 3-inch mortars till noon on 29th August; but fortunately the enemy was in no condition to counter-attack. All night long the untiring sappers worked in Class 9 ferry from St Pierre to get essential transport over.

On the left at Portjoie, H-hour for the 44th Brigade was 12.30 A.M. next morning. The Brigade had made a long approach march from Louviers. The R.S.F. led the assault in assault-boats. They met light machine-gun fire and had a few casualties. By 2 A.M. their rifle companies were across; by 5 A.M. they had established the bridgehead; by dawn the R.E. were beginning to raft over the vehicles; by 8 A.M. the rifle companies of the Royal Scots had followed across; 28th Aug.

28th Aug. by 11 A.M. the K.O.S.B., too, were over, and the 44th Brigade had linked up with the 227th Brigade near Andé.

Meanwhile the Gordons had been advancing across the tip of the peninsula from Le Mesnil Andé towards Muids, thus securing the 46th Brigade's crossing-place from the flank. At 9.15 A.M., therefore, the Divisional Commander ordered the 46th Brigade to start its crossing west of Muids in storm-boats and Class 9 rafts as a peaceful operation. By 4.30 P.M. the Brigade had crossed complete with essential transport. By this time the R.E. had finished the Class 9 bridge at Muids and were well under way with the Class 40 bridge at St Pierre du Vauvray.

During the afternoon the 227th Brigade had continued operations to clear the peninsula and to enlarge the bridgehead. In face of scattered resistance the Gordons, heading for Le Thuit, pushed along the right side of the peninsula to Fretteville, where they had a sharpish fight. On the left of the Gordons the Argylls moved through the central woodland of the peninsula to seize the high ground crowned by the Château des Buspins, where they found some enemy on the reverse slopes. In the evening the H.L.I. on the left took the high, steep bluff of the escarpment north of Connelles.

That night the 46th Brigade advanced in its turn to relieve the Gordons and Argylls and to establish itself on the top of the escarpment at the base of the peninsula. The Seaforth, now under the command of Lieutenant-Colonel P. M. Hunt, led the advance. Their objective was Grand Roncherolles, which stands on a steep bluff above extensive woodland in very broken ground. The Glasgow Highlanders followed the Seaforth; their objectives were Petit Roncherolles and Couverville, about a thousand yards farther on across the plateau. About the same time the Cameronians, now under the command of Lieutenant-Colonel Sir E. M. A. Bradford, set off to relieve the Gordons in Le Thuit, but there they found the Germans still in possession.

The Seaforth, followed by the Glasgow Highlanders, went by a narrow path, through thick woods, in growing darkness. There were many long checks during which the Glasgow Highlanders had the ill-luck to run into a heavy mortar concentration and to suffer about twenty-five casualties. The din of battle on the left told where the Gordons were still busy clearing Fretteville. The Seaforth duly took Grand Roncherolles in inky darkness, but in view of the difficulties of the entirely unknown country ahead Brigadier Villiers postponed the subsequent attack by the Glasgow Highlanders till dawn next day.

7TH SEAFORTH AT LES ANDELYS

THE CROSSING OF THE SEINE

That night, too, the R.S.F., temporarily under command of the 227th Brigade, went through the H.L.I., who were already on the escarpment on the extreme left, and occupied Senneville, a couple of miles farther north, where they found some Germans. Thus the 15th Scottish Division had now occupied nearly the whole of the loop from the outskirts of Le Thuit to Senneville and had secured the bridgehead.

28th Aug.

By this time the 43rd Division on the right had also established its bridgehead. There the 11th Armoured Division had begun to cross, and the Guards Armoured Division was moving up behind it.

Next morning the Cameronians on the extreme right advanced through Le Thuit and crossed the sheer-sided gorge of La Vacherie to reach Noyers on the bluff that overlooks Les Andelys from the northwest. Early that morning, too, the Glasgow Highlanders completed the operation of the night before by clearing Petit Roncherolles and establishing themselves in Couverville. Thus the 46th Brigade was now firmly established above the escarpment at the right shoulder of the loop. The Class 40 bridge at St Pierre was open. The 147th Regiment R.A.C. of the 34th Tank Brigade was the first to cross; it moved up to support the Cameronians at Noyers.

29th Aug.

About 2.30 p.m. patrols of the 15th Divisional Reconnaissance egiment entered Les Andelys to find the Germans gone and the F.F.I. control. Beyond, the patrols contacted the 43rd Division to southward. Later, the Seaforth passed through the Cameronians and occupied Les Andelys.

In the early afternoon the 44th Brigade moved up on the left of the 46th Brigade. Passing through the 227th Brigade and mounting the escarpment, the K.O.S.B.s occupied Houville and the Royal Scots Le Londe. The 44th Brigade had thus filled the gap between the Glasgow Highlanders in Couverville and the R.S.F. in Senneville. The R.S.F. here reverted to the command of the 44th Brigade. The 15th Scottish Division was now firmly established on all the high ground which commanded the bridgehead.

Patrols of the Divisional Reconnaissance Regiment operating beyond the front reported the country clear of the enemy between the Corps boundaries up to the Paris-Rouen highway. Pushing five or six miles east of the highway at Ecuis, however, the patrols drew machine-gun and anti-tank fire from a number of enemy strong-points and also sighted enemy tanks in the offing.

29th Aug.   As yet the 7th Armoured Division was not ready to take the lead in the 12th Corps' sector. Next day, therefore, the 53rd Division, with the 4th Armoured Brigade and the Royals under command, was to push through the bridgehead and to continue the advance. The 4th Armoured Brigade, which was to spearhead this advance, had already begun to cross. To make way for this movement the 15th Scottish Division was to keep its transport off the roads.

So ended the assault crossing of the Seine and the establishment of the 12th Corps' bridgehead. The crossing, carried out without sufficient time for planning or reconnaissance and without any build-up whatever of ammunition or other reserves, had been a gamble.

The gamble had come off. The 15th Scottish Division had bounced the enemy off the Seine with complete success. R.E. and Provost services in particular had worked against time and under difficult conditions. They had worked wonders. So far, fortunately, the weather had favoured them. Now it broke. The continuous downpour of the next three days was seriously to complicate the traffic problems of the bridgehead.

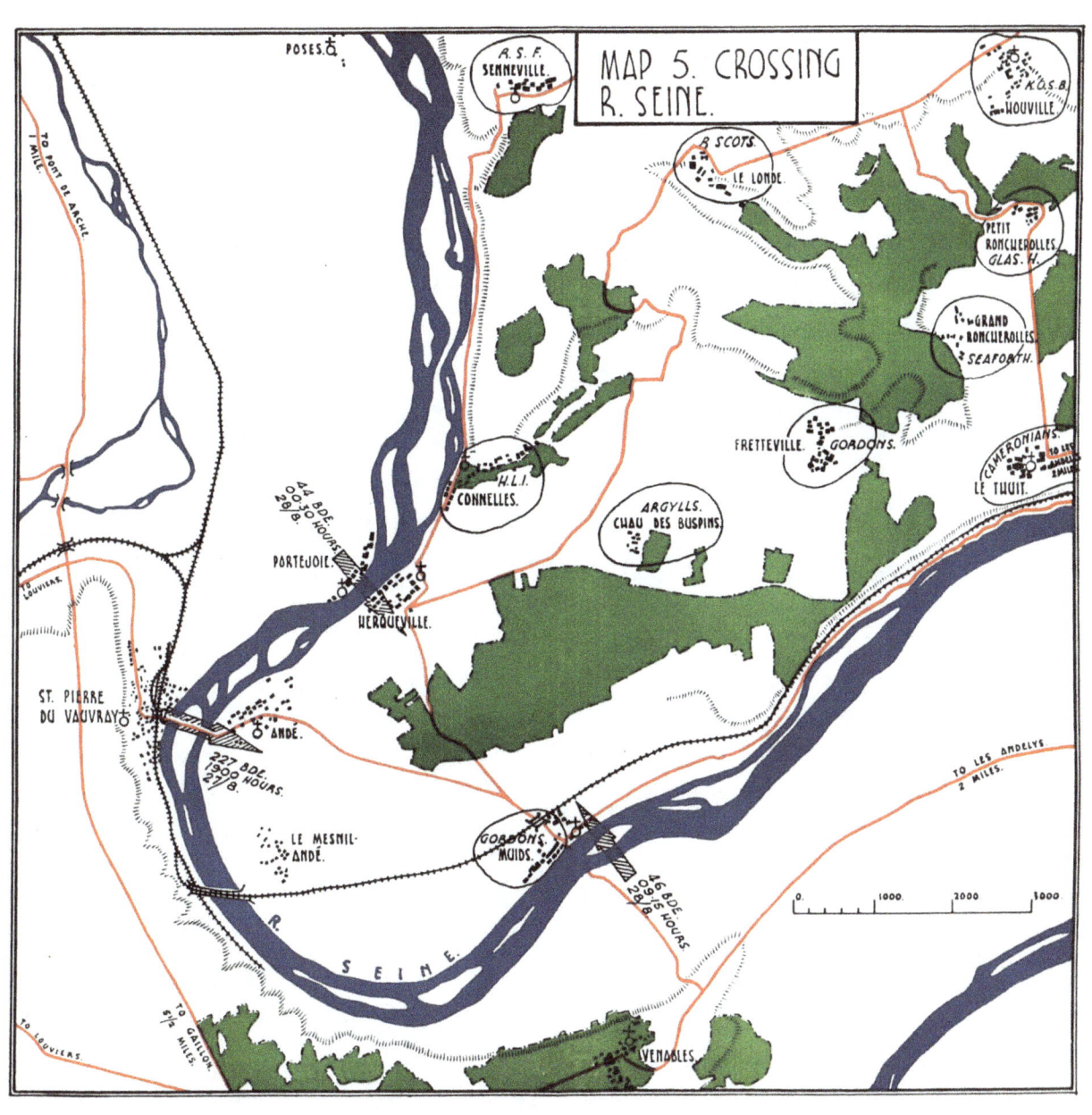

CHAPTER V.

PART II.—ADVANCE INTO BELGIUM.

THROUGHOUT 30th August the rain descended and the long columns of tanks and guns of the 4th Armoured Brigade and the 53rd Division poured across the river at St Pierre and through the 46th Brigade's front heading north-east for Gourney, which was occupied that evening. 30th Aug. to 2nd Sep

During the day the 15th Scottish Divisional Reconnaissance Regiment contacted the 2nd Canadian Corps on the left at Fleury. Thus all three Corps' bridgeheads—30th, 12th, and 2nd Canadian—had now coalesced.

The great move into Belgium had begun. On 31st August the 11th Armoured Division, advancing from the 30th Corps' bridgehead, entered Amiens. On the same day the 7th Armoured Division followed up the 53rd Division through the 12th Corps' bridgehead. This great advance strained our transport resources to the limit. For four days, therefore, the 15th Scottish Division was to remain in the bridgehead inactive. These were pleasant enough days. The country was lovely; the fruit was ripe; there was bathing and there were dances; there were the F.F.I. to be contacted—F.F.I. with exultant tales to tell of the S.S. who had passed through such a little while ago, grim and dispirited, with little equipment left but their own personal arms. At Divisional Headquarters in Monsieur Renault's charming house in Herqueville the Divisional Commander was "At Home" to the leading citizens, who danced eightsome reels and drank to the "Auld Alliance."

On 1st September the Greys of the 4th Armoured Brigade secured the Somme bridge at Bernaville, between Amiens and Abbeville. Next day, 2nd September, the Argylls went off at three hours' notice on a 120-mile ride in troop-carrying vehicles (T.C.V.s) to take over the defence of these Somme crossings. For the next twenty-four hours the Argylls were to alternate under command of the 4th Armoured Brigade and the 22nd Armoured Brigade. By this time Lieutenant-

30th Aug. to 2nd Sept.

Colonel Russell Morgan had returned from the H.L.I. to command his old battalion, the Argylls.

On 2nd September the 15th Scottish Division at last got its orders to start next day on its north-eastward progress into Belgium. The first few marches, however, would have to be carried out with Divisional transport, for T.C.V.s were not yet available. Harbour parties went out that day to the Forêt du Lyons, west of Gourney.

3rd Sept.

On 3rd September the Division set out at 7 A.M. in two columns. On the right the 46th Brigade led on "Star" route, followed by Divisional Headquarters. On the left the 44th Brigade led, followed by the 227th Brigade (less the Argylls). For the ferrying of the troops fifty 30-tonners had been allocated per brigade in addition to unit transport. These vehicles went to the harbours loaded and, having dumped their loads, returned to pick up the marching columns. By this means the Division was in harbour before dark, having covered about twenty-five miles. Again there had been scenes of wild enthusiasm by the way.

On ahead in the 12th Corps' sector the 53rd Division and the 4th Armoured Brigade had now run into stiff resistance round La Bassée and Bethune and northward of St Pol. According to plan, the 7th Armoured Division was to by-pass this resistance and continue its way north, leaving the 53rd Division to mop up.

That evening the Guards Armoured Division entered Brussels, and Montgomery ordered the Second Army to push on to the Rhine. Dempsey's plan was to drive ahead with the 30th Corps, while the First U.S. Army guarded the right flank and the 12th Corps the left. Thus was conceived the operation that led to Arnhem.

4th Sept.

On 4th September the 15th Scottish Division did another short march of fifteen miles to the area of Formerie, again ferrying the troops with Divisional and unit transport. That day the transport lifted the troops at the start, returning to pick up its normal loads which had been left in the original bivouac area under guard.

During the day the Argylls moved up from the Somme crossings at Bernaville to St Pol, where they were to await the arrival of the 227th Brigade. In the evening the 11th Armoured Division entered Antwerp. Thus the Second Army's spearheads had covered 250 miles in six days.

ADVANCE INTO BELGIUM

By this time some T.C.V.s had returned at last from lifting the 53rd Division to St Pol. Consequently on 5th September the 15th Scottish Division was able to make its first full-scale move of seventy to eighty miles. Its way took it over the Somme and on by the straight poplar-lined roads that cross the rolling chalk-lands of Picardy and Artois to Frevent and St Pol. All the way it was a triumphal procession. There were many bands of German prisoners in evidence who had been caught in the woods by the F.F.I. That day, too, the Division saw flying-bomb sites for the first time.

5th Sept.

The general situation was now this. On the Second Army's right the First U.S. Army was on the line Namur-Tirlemont; on its left the First Canadian Army was far behind, closing on Le Havre and on the lower Somme. Immediately ahead lay Flanders. The 7th Armoured Division had reached Ghent at the junction of the Escaut and the Lys, and had occupied that part of the town south of the canal. In the area westward of a line Antwerp-Ghent-Lille-Bethune-Hesdin (thirteen miles west of St Pol) a heterogeneous collection of some 150,000 Germans were cooped up. This rabble had three courses open to it: to go to ground in the Channel fortresses; to break out northward across the Scheldt estuary; or to break out eastward across the Lys south-west of Ghent. It was the 12th Corps' concern to guard against this last possibility.

That evening, therefore, a 46th Brigade battle-group called "Lys Force" was formed with the task of establishing a firm base on the Lys south-west of Ghent and of destroying the enemy in the area Thielt-Deynse-Courtrai-Menin-Roulers up to the Corps' boundary beyond the Lys. This group consisted of the 46th Brigade (less the Glasgow Highlanders and the Cameronians), the Royals, the 15th Divisional Reconnaissance Regiment, and a medium machine-gun company of the Middlesex, together with field, medium, and heavy regiments R.A. The Glasgow Highlanders were put temporarily under the 227th Brigade, the Cameronians under the 44th Brigade.

Next morning the 15th Scottish Division (less the 227th Brigade) did another long forward move by T.C.V. over the *pavé* and roads of the "Black Country" by Bethune and La Bassée, past the slag heaps of Loos, where in a previous incarnation it had won eternal fame in the Kaiser's war, past Lille, and on through the gaunt industrial towns of the Belgian frontier region. The Germans had pulled out of

6th Sept.

6th Sept.

Lille for Ypres only a few hours before. No British troops had been through this area since May 1940. The welcome the 15th Scottish received was indescribable. Everywhere hysterical crowds, delirious with joy, blocked the roads, showering our troops with flowers, fruit, and kisses, loading them with brandy and beer.

On its arrival at Courtrai, Lys Force set about its task. Brigadier Villiers put one company of the Seaforth into Courtrai to hold it as a firm base. Despite the fact that Courtrai had been badly knocked about by the R.A.F., the welcome was beyond all bounds. At the same time Brigadier Villiers sent forward the Royals and the 15th Divisional Reconnaissance Regiment, each with a company of the Seaforth under command, to secure the crossings of the Lys. They soon found, however, that the 7th Armoured Division, anticipating that the enemy would try to break out across the Lys in force, had blown all the bridges. Moreover, any attempts they made to advance north-west across the Lys met very strong resistance. They could make no progress.

In the afternoon the Divisional Commander himself reached Courtrai and took over command of Lys Force, which he ordered to hold the line of the Courtrai-Bossuyt Canal in order to "refuse" the right flank of the Division.

At about 7 P.M., however, the 7th Armoured Division withdrew to the line of the Escaut, whereupon Lys Force was dissolved and the 46th Brigade (still less the Cameronians) came under command of the 7th Armoured Division with the task of holding the line of the Escaut south of Audenarde. By this time the Glasgow Highlanders had moved up to the neighbourhood of Courtrai. There they had reverted to the command of the 46th Brigade and had taken up a position on the Courtrai-Bossuyt Canal.

Meanwhile the 44th Brigade had also been moving up through scenes of wild enthusiasm. On their way through Lille to their rendezvous with the 44th Brigade the Cameronians had run into a solid mass of frenzied humanity, who had brought their T.C.V.s to an abrupt halt. Not till 2 A.M. next morning had they managed to break through to the rendezvous. Again, when the K.O.S.B., the leading battalion of the Brigade, reached the Belgian frontier at Halluin on the road to Menin, they found the town hung with the black, yellow, and red of the Belgian tricolour, and the street ahead of them jam-packed by tens of thousands of citizens similarly bedecked. Yet the

German rearguard was still exchanging shots with the "White Brigade" or Belgian Maquis across the Lys River Canal only a mile or so away on the road to Menin. It was warfare under peculiar difficulties.

6th Sept.

The bridge on the Menin road had been blown. The 44th Brigade, however, found another bridge over the Lys River Canal intact three miles to eastward at Lauwe. The K.O.S.B. deployed and went through into the bridgehead, after surviving a welcome in Lauwe that outdid even that at Halluin. Later, Brigadier Cockburn sent the 8th Royal Scots and the 6th R.S.F. still farther eastward to relieve the 46th Brigade in and around Courtrai.

During the day the 227th Brigade closed up in the St Pol area, where the Argylls reverted under command.

Next day the 44th Brigade reached Courtrai early. The Royal Scots took over from the Seaforth in Courtrai, the R.S.F. from the Glasgow Highlanders on the Courtrai-Bossuyt Canal. The Divisional Reconnaissance Regiment, patrolling three or four miles north of this canal, found enemy infantry dug in, with S.P. guns, at a number of points in the neighbourhood of Kerkhove on the Escaut.

7th Sept.

That morning the Royals crossed the Lys River Canal west of Courtrai and fought their way almost to Roulers, taking many prisoners. The Royal Scots followed up to Nederbeke. The K.O.S.B. went southwest from Courtrai to Weyelghem. In the evening the R.S.F. crossed the Courtrai-Bossuyt Canal east of Courtrai, took Deerlyck, ambushed some embussed columns, and returned with seventy-five prisoners.

Meanwhile the 181st Field Regiment, who were supporting the 44th Brigade, had been having a party of their own. That morning Captain J. S. Cunis, the F.O.O. from the 177th Battery, arrived in Courtrai wet and cold, to be greeted by a captain of the Belgian Resistance, who led him to a tall block of flats known as the White Residence. The Belgian ushered Cunis and his O.P. party into the lift and mounted with them to the roof-garden. There Cunis established his O.P. complete with wireless. It was a misty morning, but a hot bath, followed by eggs and bacon, served to pass the time. After breakfast the mist conveniently lifted. "Look!" said the Belgian captain. "What did I tell you?" There, drawn up nose to tail on three roads not more than a mile away, stood revealed long columns of German transport—a strange array of stolen country carts piled high with loot. It was a target such as generations of gunners had dreamed of. No sooner had

7th Sept. Cunis dealt faithfully with this target than another presented itself. And so it went on throughout the day. The news spread. The lift worked unceasingly. Soon the roof-garden became a grandstand where the assembled beauty and fashion of Courtrai watched the fun and applauded the higher flights of gunnery. Later, the more enterprising spirits went out to round up prisoners and to cut steaks off dead horses. A good day was had by all.

During the day the 227th Brigade moved up by T.C.V. from St Pol via Lille, Tourcoing, and Rubaix to cross the frontier at Moscrun. Everywhere pandemonium reigned once more. The H.L.I.—now under the command of Lieutenant-Colonel Mackley—and the Argylls went to St Genois, a couple of miles south of the Courtrai-Bossuyt Canal.

The 46th Brigade meanwhile had moved east under command of the 7th Armoured Division to hold the line of the Escaut from Audenarde to Avelgham inclusive—that is, nearly to Bossuyt. At Avelgham the Cameronians reverted to the command of the 46th Brigade. Brigade Headquarters went to Quarement, where they found a V.1 assembly plant complete with a number of flying bombs ready for use.

In the afternoon the 4th Armoured Brigade, with the Seaforth and Cameronians under command, carried out a sweep. The Cameronians met stiffish resistance from an enemy strong-point and had to put in three companies with Sherman support before they took it. Both battalions, however, were back on the Escaut before dark, having taken 200 prisoners at a cost of 25 casualties. The Glasgow Highlanders meanwhile had moved by T.C.V. to Audenarde, where they came under command of the 131st Brigade. By 3 P.M. they had relieved the 1/7th Queens in Audenarde.

Out ahead the enemy front had begun to harden. The Guards Armoured Division on the right and the 11th Armoured Division on the left were now meeting strong enemy resistance on the line of the Albert Canal.

For 8th September the plan was this. After the relief of the 44th Brigade by the 53rd Division, the 15th Scottish Division (less the 46th Brigade) was to clear the country between Escaut and the Lys as far north as Ghent in an "advance-to-contact" move.

8th Sept. The 53rd Division moved up as follows: during the morning of 8th September the 71st Brigade duly relieved the 44th Brigade in

ADVANCE INTO BELGIUM

Courtrai; by noon the 160th Brigade had reached the Roulers area; the 158th Brigade was coming up to relieve the 131st Brigade in Ghent.

8th Sept.

After the relief the 15th Scottish Division began its sweep as planned. On the left the 44th Brigade, preceded by the Divisional Reconnaissance Regiment, leap-frogged battalions north-eastward along the southern bank of the Lys River Canal. The enemy withdrew across the Lys and blew the bridge at Harlebeke as our patrols approached. By evening the R.S.F. had reached Deynse—they had taken 335 prisoners in two days; the K.O.S.B. had reached Zulte; the Royal Scots were in Harlebeke. Thus the Brigade was now echeloned along about fourteen miles of the Lys against any possible excursions of the enemy. There it was to remain until 10th September.

On the right meanwhile the 227th Brigade, starting from the Escaut between Kerkhove and Bossuyt, was sweeping northward simultaneously into the area St Denis-Nazareth-Machelen, immediately south of Ghent, where it was to remain till 11th September.

Of the 46th Brigade the Glasgow Highlanders remained in Audenarde while the rest of the Brigade side-stepped northward along the Escaut to relieve the 131st Brigade, which now had the job of clearing that part of Ghent still occupied by the enemy. The Cameronians went into Gavere, the Seaforth into Scheldrode. Owing to lack of T.C.V.s, together with road congestion, they did not finish their moves till midnight. The 46th Brigade was then echeloned along the Escaut for about eleven miles to northward of Audenarde. There, less the Glasgow Highlanders, it reverted under command of the 15th Scottish Division. And there it was to remain till 10th September. It was at this stage that the 4th Armoured Brigade moved away north-eastward to clear the area between Ghent and Antwerp.

Out in front on the Albert Canal the Guards Armoured Division on the right had now established a bridgehead at Beeringen, the 50th Division on the left a small bridgehead south-west of Gheel.

For the next two days the Glasgow Highlanders were to have a monopoly of the fighting done by the 15th Scottish Division. At 5.30 A.M. on 9th September a liaison officer brought orders to the battalion in Audenarde to move by T.C.V. two hours later to a concentration area south of Ghent, there to carry out a task under the 131st Brigade. At the same time the 7th Armoured Division (less the 131st Brigade) was withdrawn into reserve.

9th Sept.

9th Sept.

The situation as the Glasgow Highlanders found it in and around Ghent was this. The Canal de Ghent here forms three sides of a rectangle, which projects southward to encompass the northern or industrial section of the town. The southern section of Ghent itself up to the canal had been in the possession of the 7th Armoured Division for the past four days. Not so the northern section. This northern section within the canal the Germans were still holding most stubbornly as a pivot of resistance against our efforts to squeeze out their pocket south of the Scheldt estuary.

After picking up guides in their concentration area the Glasgow Highlanders did not finally debus in their forward assembly area in Ghent till 6 P.M. that evening. Lieutenant-Colonel Campbell, who had gone on ahead with his reconnaissance party, had carried out a reconnaissance as best he could from the south bank. H-hour for the Glasgow Highlanders' attack he had fixed at 7.5 P.M., so there was going to be desperately little time. Already the 5th and 6th Queens of the 131st Brigade had managed to establish precarious footholds on the farther bank. Three rifle companies of the Glasgow Highlanders were to assault across a partly demolished bridge in the 5th Queens' sector and to relieve a platoon of the Queens which was isolated on the far bank. The fourth company of the Glasgow Highlanders was to hold a firm base on the south bank of the canal.

All three companies of the Glasgow Highlanders crossed according to plan. The Germans fought back fiercely. They had no tanks in action, but they had spandaus, bazookas, and 88 mm.s in plenty in the forward area and heavier artillery, including railway guns, farther back. The Glasgow Highlanders for their part were supported from the south bank of the canal by four S.P. M.10's, a squadron of Shermans, a platoon of medium machine-guns, a field regiment, and some mediums. Support, however, was difficult. Neither O.P.s nor satisfactory maps were available, and the municipality had urged that material damage to the industrial quarter be kept to a minimum. Houses were locked and shuttered, and had to be searched from cellar to garret. The asylum in particular proved to be an immense rabbit-warren. None the less the Glasgow Highlanders managed to clear that evening a largish area north of the canal—so large in fact relative to their own strength that they could not prevent the enemy from infiltrating back into it under cover of darkness.

The rest of the 15th Scottish Division spent a quiet day. From 9 P.M. that evening all anti-aircraft fire in the Divisional area was forbidden. This was a precautionary measure connected with the great airborne operation on the 30th Corps' front which was now imminent.

9th Sept.

Next morning the Glasgow Highlanders' first task was to clear once more the area that they had already cleared the previous evening. Throughout the day it was a platoon commanders' battle, in which higher control was impossible. Among many gallant deeds, two incidents in particular stand out. There was No. 17 platoon's clearing of the factory building on the right—where " D " Company had such hard fighting. No. 17 platoon itself took 200 prisoners. And there was No. 18 platoon's fight in the square, where they were rushed by about eighty Germans from three directions. Sergeant M'Laren dropped Private Albert Evans with a Bren gun to cover the approaches. Almost immediately Evans was mortally wounded in the stomach, but refused to leave his post. Afterwards ten Germans lay dead in front of his post and many more had been wounded.

10th Sept.

By afternoon the R.E. had built a bridge over the canal, and the tanks crossed at last to co-operate at close quarters in clearing the vast cemetery. At night the Glasgow Highlanders withdrew once more to the line held by them on the previous evening. They had contacted the 6th Queens and had taken 6 officers and 233 prisoners at a cost of 66 casualties.

During the day the 15th Scottish moved to a concentration area south and west of Malines. The burghers of Malines celebrated the arrival of the Division by playing a recital of Scottish tunes on the famous carillon. This Divisional move was preparatory to a crossing of the Albert Canal north-east of Lierre. This crossing was planned as cover for another crossing which the 53rd Division was to make north of Antwerp. That afternoon the 15th Scottish sent out combined infantry and R.E. patrols from Lierre to reconnoitre the Albert Canal. Late in the evening, however, the orders were changed: the Division was now to relieve the 50th Division in the Gheel bridgehead over the Albert Canal farther east. Still farther east on the Albert Canal at Beeringen the Guards Armoured Division had broken through to the next great water-obstacle, the Meuse-Escaut Junction Canal, and had taken the De Groot bridge.

11th Sept.
Next morning all three companies of the Glasgow Highlanders searched the ground in front of them up to the railway, their final objective; they found that the enemy had left Ghent during the night. Thus Ghent was free at last.

In the afternoon the Polish Armoured Division relieved the 131st Brigade and the Glasgow Highlanders in Ghent; this relief was part of the general relief now in progress of the 12th Corps by the First Canadian Army. The 12th Corps was thus freed to concentrate in the area Gheel-Diest-Malines-Antwerp in conformity with Montgomery's plan to break through to the Rhine with the 30th Corps and the Airborne Army.

On 12th and 13th September the Glasgow Highlanders moved by way of Lipperloo into the Gheel bridgehead, where they came once more under command of the 46th Brigade.

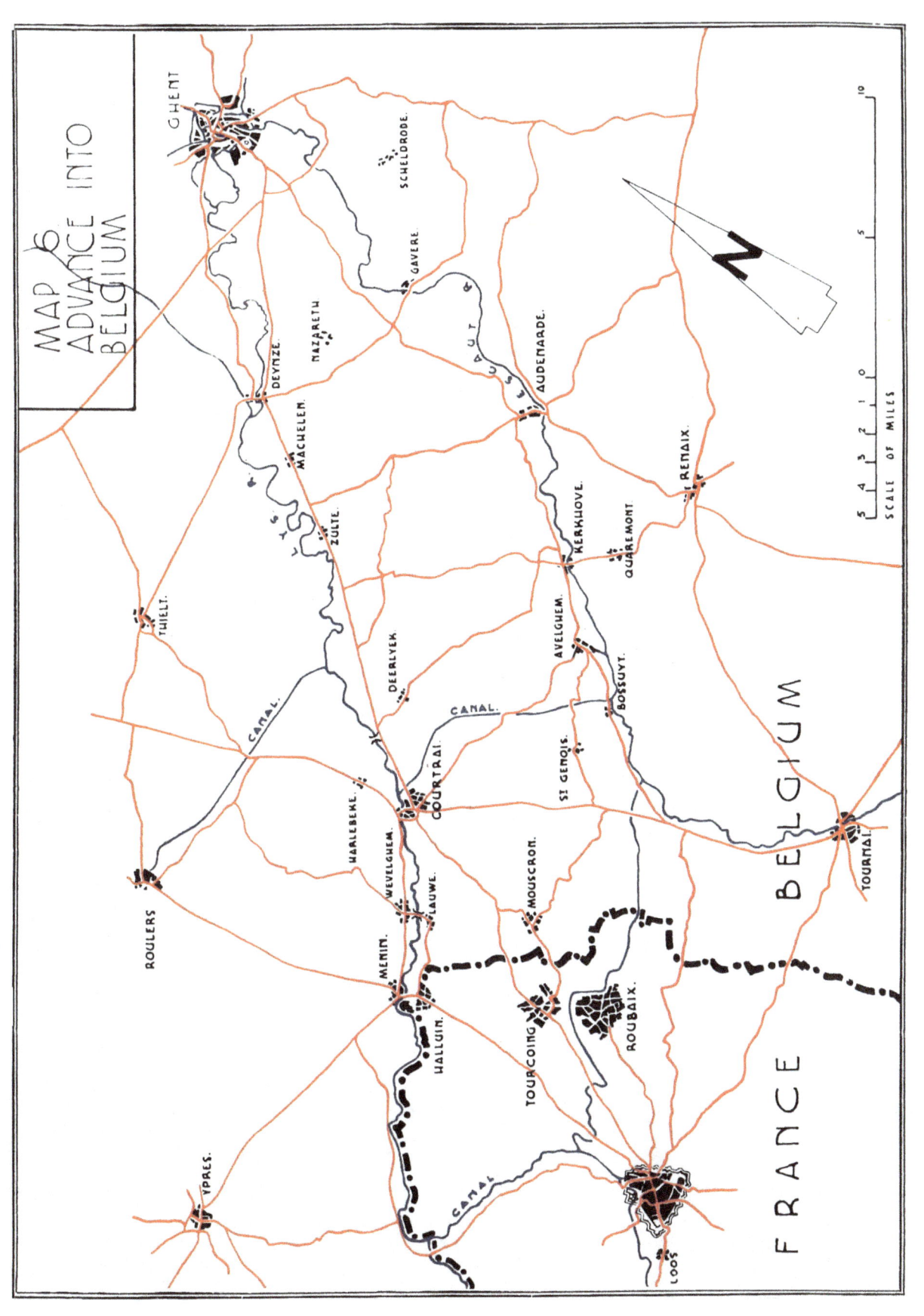

CHAPTER VI.

PART I.—THE GHEEL BRIDGEHEAD.

On 12th September the general situation in the 21st Army Group was this. Montgomery had decided that he could be ready by 17th September to make his thrust for the Rhine crossings which would open the way to Germany. Breaking out of the De Groot bridgehead beyond the Meuse-Escaut Junction Canal, the 30th Corps was to advance north to Arnhem over a carpet of airborne troops which the 1st Airborne Army would lay across the intervening water-obstacles, among which were the Maas and the lower Rhine. Such was to be Operation "Market Garden." Simultaneously, the 8th Corps on the 30th Corps' right and the 12th Corps on its left were also to break out on their own bridgeheads across the Junction Canal in order to broaden the base of the 30th Corps' salient and so to strengthen its flanks.

As a preliminary to Operation "Market Garden," the 15th Scottish Division was to relieve the 50th Division in the Gheel bridgehead beyond the Albert Canal. The 50th Division, thus relieved, would move east into the De Groot bridgehead, where it in turn would relieve the Guards Armoured Division and so free the latter to spearhead the 30th Corps' advance. At Gheel, moreover, the 15th Scottish Division would be positioned to make the 12th Corps' break-out across the Junction Canal, which, as we have seen, was an essential feature of the plan.

On the afternoon of 12th September, therefore, the 15th Scottish Division (less the 227th Brigade) moved up embussed from the neighbourhood of Malines to debus south of the Albert Canal and to cross it into the Gheel bridgehead. The Division found the crossings under pretty continuous shell-fire and suffered casualties. The 50th Division, which had been recently pushed out of Gheel itself by a counter-attack by G.A.F. troops, was holding its bridgehead with two brigades up. The 44th Brigade relieved the 151st Brigade on the right, the 46th

12th Sept.

12th Sept. Brigade the 69th Brigade on the left. A tank counter-attack, which came in at last light from the direction of Poyel, somewhat delayed the Cameronians' take-over from the Green Howards. That night German gun and mortar-fire were heavy, and our patrols contacted the enemy all round the perimeter.

The 15th Scottish Division's task was to clear the country between the Albert and Junction Canals and to establish a bridgehead over the latter. For this task it had under command the 3/4th County of London Yeomanry. The plan for next day was this. The 44th Brigade was to clear Gheel itself up to the railway and was then to advance north to the Junction Canal. The 46th Brigade was to extend the bridgehead north-west towards Herenthals, which was still strongly held. The 227th Brigade, which would come up from Malines during the day, was to extend the bridgehead north-eastward and was to take Moll. At Donck, due north of Moll, there was a bridge on the main road over the Junction Canal which was reported to be still standing. That bridge was to be the 227th Brigade's final objective.

13th Sept. Dawn patrols on 13th September found that the enemy had withdrawn from the perimeter during the night. Thereupon the K.O.S.B. and the Royal Scots sent their patrols out to the Junction Canal, while the Reconnaissance Regiment fanned out north-eastward of Gheel and northward of Moll. By 8 A.M. the Royal Scots had occupied Gheel; they learnt that about two hundred Germans had cleared out shortly before.

The Divisional Commander's intention was to close on the Junction Canal immediately and to rush it on a wide front, beginning the assault that same night before the enemy could be ready for him—in fact, to repeat the tactics which had paid so well on the Seine. To this end he was prepared once more to dispense not only with detailed daylight reconnaissance but also with the build-up of shells, mortar-bombs, and other stores which would normally precede an assault of this nature. In arriving at this decision he was taking what was a deliberately calculated risk.

In accordance with this plan Lieutenant-Colonel R. K. Millar, the C.R.E., had allocated his field companies as follows : the 20th Field Company in support of the 227th Brigade ; the 279th Field Company (with one platoon of the 278th under command) in support of the 44th Brigade ; the 278th (less one platoon) to the maintenance of the

190TH FIELD REGIMENT CROSSING THE ALBERT CANAL PRIOR TO GHEEL BATTLE

THE GHEEL BRIDGEHEAD

Albert Canal bridges. Colonel Millar's intention was to build one 13th Sept.
Class 9 and one Class 40 bridge over the Junction Canal as soon as
possible. The 280th Field Company of the 12th Corps Engineers had
been placed under his command with the special task of building the
Class 40 Bailey bridge. Colonel Millar had been warned that he would
have to be frugal with bridging material because he would get no
more for the present—in fact, all reserves were earmarked for the
30th Corps' impending Operation "Market Garden" with its three
major water-crossings.

Two roads run through Gheel to the Junction Canal. On the right
is the road to Rethy, which crosses the Junction Canal four miles
north-east of Gheel; astride this road the K.O.S.B. now advanced.
On the left is the road to Turnhout, which crosses the Junction Canal
at Aart two and three-quarter miles due north of Gheel; along this
road went the Royal Scots. Late in the afternoon both battalions
were nearing the Junction Canal. On the Rethy road the K.O.S.B.
were held up for some time by a road-block in the large wood just
short of the canal; their patrols finally reached the south bank about
11 P.M. They found the main road-bridge blown, but the lockgates
only partially destroyed and a small bridge over the gates still standing.
First reports suggested that this small bridge would take not only
the battalion's supporting weapons but also the Yeomanry's Sherman
tanks.

On the Turnhout road the Royal Scots reached the canal in the
late afternoon; at Aart both the road-bridge and the by-pass bridge
had been destroyed. Forward companies halted about five hundred
yards short of the canal. Lieutenant-Colonel Lane Joynt decided
to cross in assault-boats on a two-company front at points about
five hundred and a thousand yards west of the demolished road-
bridge at Aart. At dusk reconnaissance parties went forward in
pairs to the canal. They found the bank steep, with a drop of about
six feet to water-level, which was then low. Mud banks were showing
on the farther side, on which some barges were stranded. All that
they could see of the opposite bank some fifty yards away was the
outline of the towpath and the tops of the trees beyond.

On the left of the 44th Brigade, the 46th Brigade also closed up
to the Junction Canal on a two-battalion front. The 46th Brigade's
rôle was defensive. The Cameronians on the right were responsible
that no Germans crossed the Junction Canal on the left of the 44th

13th Sept. Brigade; the Seaforth on the left were responsible for checking any enemy movement eastward out of Herenthals between the two canals; the Glasgow Highlanders remained in Brigade reserve.

Meanwhile the 227th Brigade had also come into the Gheel bridgehead to extend it north-eastward. The H.L.I. were advanced guard battalion, and they passed through Meerhout, heading for Moll, where the Reconnaissance Regiment had reported scattered opposition.

In the gap between the advanced guard and the main body was moving the 131st Field Regiment. About 4 P.M. there came from in front a call for fire. There followed that rare event reminiscent of Exercise "Gallop"—a "regimental quick action" on an advance to contact move. Unfortunately, to-day there were no umpires about to admire, for 319th—the advanced guard battery—got its first round off in two minutes, while the whole regiment was ready, with survey done, in about a quarter of an hour. Indeed the 131st Field Regiment was answering a Divisional Artillery call on the 44th Brigade's front very soon after.

By the time the H.L.I. had deployed and entered Moll—amid scenes of wild enthusiasm—the enemy had gone. Thereupon the H.L.I. established themselves in Moll to hold it as a firm base while the Argylls, riding on the Yeomanry's tanks, passed through at top speed headed for the precious road-bridge at Donck, some three miles farther on. Their efforts were vain, however; the bridge had now been blown. That night the Argylls dug in on the south bank of the Junction Canal at Donck; the H.L.I. were in Moll, where they were royally fêted; the Gordons were in Zittaart and Meerhout.

Such, then, was the situation on the night of 13th September. In readiness for the assault-crossing, the Divisional Commander had his Division closed up to the Junction Canal on about a nine-mile front from Donck to the Binneneinde bridge west of Gheel.

14th Sept By 2 A.M. on a very dark night "A" Company of the K.O.S.B. reached the south bank of the canal by the damaged lock on the Rethy road. There was considerable mortar and machine-gun fire. During a pause in this fire Lieutenant Lountain crossed the bridge and returned to report no enemy close by. Sergeant M'Queen then began to take his platoon over. As soon, however, as the leading section had crossed, it was engaged by two 20-mm. guns and a number of riflemen at point-blank range. At the same time the enemy opened

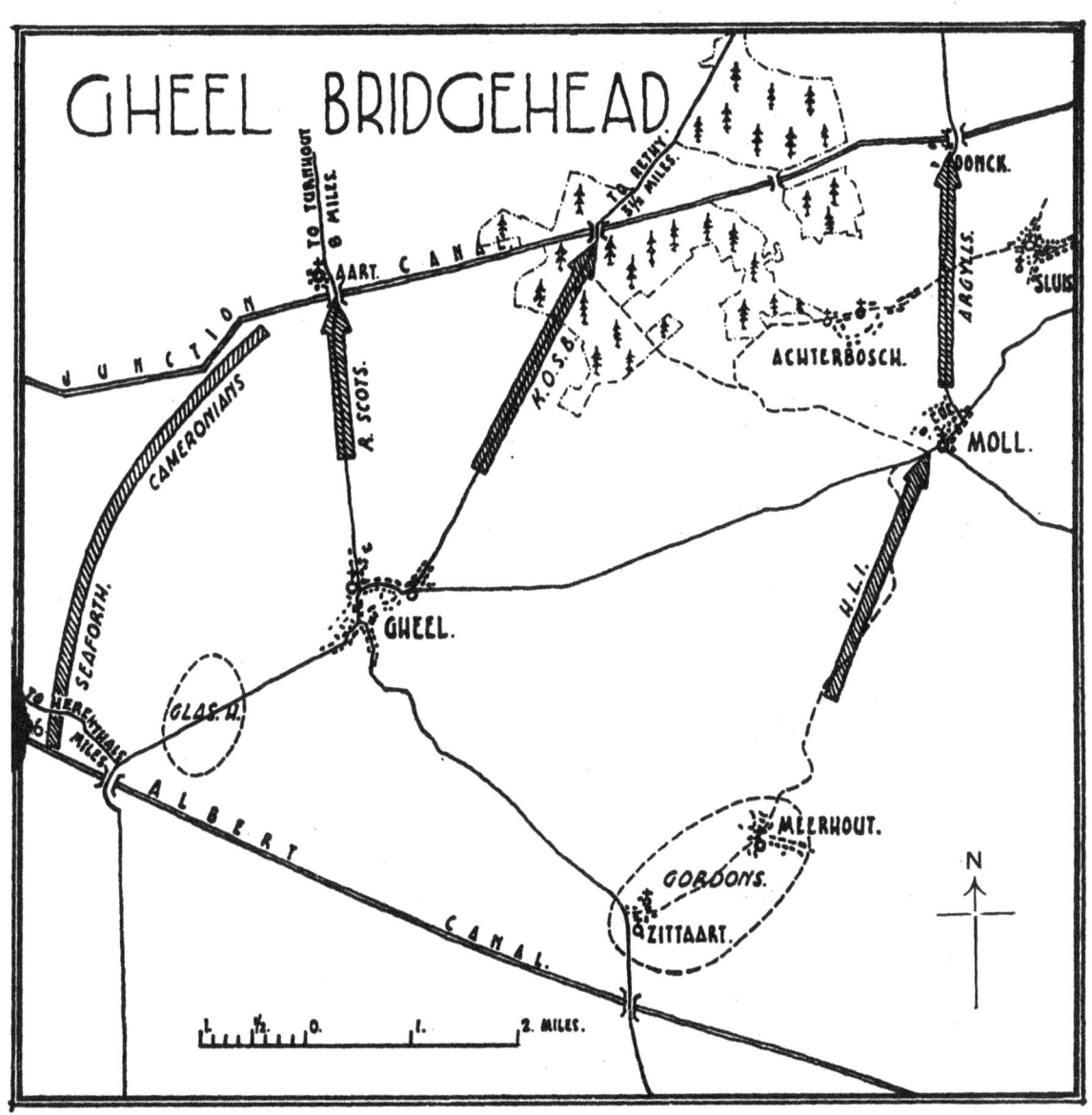

14th Sept.

up intense mortar-fire on those behind and swept the canal with the enfilade fire of 88-mm. guns, thus effectually preventing any help from reaching the isolated section. Clearly, the enemy had been ready for the K.O.S.B. at this somewhat obvious crossing-place. The Engineers now had a look at the bridge and reported that it would take neither tanks nor other supporting weapons. The K.O.S.B. remained pinned on the south bank—their section lost to them. Here, too, Major Rollo, who had won so gallant an M.C. at Grainville Château, was mortally wounded.

By morning it was clear that the K.O.S.B. crossing had failed. Nor was this all. The Germans meanwhile had manipulated the canal locks to flood the battlefield. By 10 A.M. there was two feet of water across the Rethy road south of the canal, and the flood was spreading westward. An hour and a half later Lieutenant-Colonel Richardson had to order his forward companies to withdraw about a mile south of the canal—through three feet of water.

Meanwhile the Royal Scots had been more successful farther west. Before midnight Lieutenant-Colonel Lane Joynt had held a final " O " Group. At about 4 A.M. the 279th Field Company had delivered two lorry-loads of assault-boats per forward company; forward companies had sub-allotted these at two boats per forward platoon, keeping two in reserve. Beginning at 5.30 A.M. the two leading companies, " A " and " B," crossed in face of some rifle and spandau-fire and established an initial bridgehead to westward of Aart as planned. At 8 A.M. " D " Company had followed, with the task of clearing the farms and houses eastward up to the main street of Aart and then of clearing the big square factory building which dominates Aart itself. This task " D " Company had carried out successfully. So far all had gone well, though one or two 88-mm.s were giving trouble.

The tiny village of Aart consists of little more than a single street that runs north from the road-bridge for 400 yards to the church at the cross-roads. The factory is about half-way up this street on its right-hand or east side. In the area to the eastward of the street there are many more houses than are shown on the map. Beyond the church, about another 450 yards northwards along the Turnhout road, a by-pass takes off to pass to eastward of Aart and over the by-pass bridge, 200 yards east of the road-bridge. The Royal Scots' next step was to extend their bridgehead, originally established in the open country west of Aart, to include Aart itself. To this end " A "

Company now went east through "D." East of the main street "A" Company ran into heavy fire from two-barrelled flak guns and suffered severely. However, by 10 A.M. all four companies were over the canal and "A" and "B" Companies were in position east of the by-pass. The Aart bridgehead had been established.

The 44th Brigade's supporting Field Company R.E., the 279th, had been getting busy meanwhile with the Class 9 bridge to be built of close support raft or Bailey equipment. The building of this bridge was all the more urgent now that the small bridge on the K.O.S.B. front was out of the reckoning. Major P. T. Wood chose as his bridging site a lock on the Canal, Number 8, which is situated about three hundred yards to eastward of the by-pass bridge, and which was thus outside the bridgehead. The enemy had booby-trapped the vicinity of the lock and was keeping it under spandau, 20-mm., and mortar-fire. Major Wood proceeded none the less to bring up his bridging equipment under the high south bank and to bulldoze a ramp up it. Next he set to work to measure the gap. Under the covering fire of some of his Brens which he had put in the lock-keeper's cottage, Major Wood clambered along outside the handrail of the footbridge over the lockgates—the footbridge itself was blocked with barbed-wire hung with booby-traps—to hold the tape on the far side whilst Sergeant Parr held it at the near side. They measured the gap as 23 feet.

At this stage, however, Major Wood noted that the water east of the lockgates was rising fast: he saw that an overflow accompanied by a collapse of the banks was imminent. At once, therefore, he had charges prepared with which to blow the lockgates. Lighting the fuse, he made a dash from cover to place the charge, and blew a good hole in the more easterly of the gates. The water swirled through, and so made the blowing of the second gate a more difficult job. Three charges had to be used, and that wasted a lot of time. Sapper Davis placed one of the charges; Major Wood himself placed the other two—the first and third. At the third explosion the water poured through the second gate—but too late: at that moment the bank collapsed, drowning bulldozer and bridging equipment under four feet of water. Working chest-deep, the sappers salvaged their gear and removed it by lorry.

The only alternative now left was to make a bridge or ferry of folding-boat equipment. Major Wood decided to get this going beside

14th Sept. the wreck of the main road-bridge in the centre of the Aart bridgehead. The enemy was not only shelling the site heavily but also had it under small-arms fire. Regardless of mounting losses of men and equipment, the 279th Field Company worked on. Between 7.30 and 10.30 P.M. they ferried the Royal Scots' 6-pounder A.Tk. guns across to them. After dark they managed to get some more rafts built.

It had been Brigadier Cockburn's intention to pass the R.S.F. over to the eastward of the Royal Scots about mid-day. The flooding of the area, however, caused him to postpone the R.S.F.'s crossing. A company of the Glasgow Highlanders had now come under his command. He used it to hold the south bank of the Canal west of the bridgehead and to link up with the Cameronians.

In the bridgehead the Royal Scots were involved in confused fighting throughout the afternoon, in which they took about a hundred prisoners belonging mainly to the 51st and 53rd Air Force Regiments. Some of our own tanks and S.P. guns were giving the Royal Scots supporting fire from the south bank. The enemy, who were in a wood immediately north of Aart and in the scattered houses north-eastward of it, made repeated but half-hearted counter-attacks. Flak guns firing air-bursts were troublesome, and two S.P. guns worked forward within a hundred and fifty yards of our forward positions before they were seen off by our own artillery. The day ended satisfactorily enough, however, with every hope that the bridge would be built that night and that the 44th Brigade would cross complete on the following day.

It was at about 10 P.M. that night that serious trouble first developed. As we know now, General Student of the 1st Parachute Army, who was responsible for this sector of the German front, had made up his mind to prevent at all costs the 15th Scottish Division's break-out over the Junction Canal. In proof of his intention he had sent up the Hermann Goering Training Regiment post-haste from Rotterdam; he had formed a collecting centre at Turnhout, where all German troops arriving from the west were to be reorganised, provided with S.S. officers and N.C.O.s, and hurried south to Aart; and he had sent into action on the canal guns of every type from the artillery school close by at Bourg Leopold, manned by the school's crack N.C.O. instructors.

About 10 P.M., then, a heavy attack by Air Force troops led by

S.S. came in from the east under covering fire both from the east and from the canal bank. The enemy overran "C" Company Headquarters of the Royal Scots north-east of the by-pass, capturing all the officers, and went on to cut up both "C" and "A" companies pretty badly.

14th Sept.

Soon after, two companies of the Hermann Goering Training Regiment drove up by bus to a point about a hundred yards north of the road and by-pass junction, debussed, and went straight into action. Killing or capturing a platoon in their path, they swept yelling and firing past the church and straight down the main street to the canal crossing. So near did they come to the crossing itself that they were able to open spandau-fire on the rafting site at close range. Here on the south bank there was no infantry other than rear Battalion Headquarters of the Royal Scots, so the sappers downed tools and manned their bank. At this stage, however, the attack was first held and then driven back by "D" Company of the Royal Scots posted on the north bank.

Finally, about 11 P.M., an attack of two-platoon strength, supported by two S.P. guns very boldly handled, came in against a farm west of the main street, which was held by a platoon of "D" Company. In the bright light of burning houses and stacks, the platoon put up a grim hand-to-hand fight before it was overcome. Afterwards the corpses of friend and foe littered the ground round the farm, many of them locked together in death.

For the rest of the night confused fighting in the bridgehead continued. One company of the Royal Scots had been partially surrounded, and the situation generally was most obscure.

When next morning came the bridgehead was found to be exceedingly small. It was now only about two hundred and fifty yards wide on the canal bank and very much less in depth. The Royal Scots, sadly reduced in strength, were clinging to a number of platoon posts in houses or gardens or slit-trenches on both sides of the main street from the crossing to a point short of the factory. The enemy were not only up against the bridgehead in large numbers, but they also held posts in the bridgehead itself intermingled with those of the Royal Scots. At about 10 A.M., however, the enemy disengaged somewhat in order the better to bombard the tiny bridgehead.

15th Sept.

Soon after dawn the leading elements of the R.S.F. came up to

15th Sept. the south bank at Aart in preparation for their own crossing; the R.S.F. had handed over their anti-infiltration rôle in the central sector of the south bank to the Reconnaissance Regiment. The sappers then withdrew. By this time large areas on the south bank east of the Gheel-Turnhout road were under water. Moreover, the floods were spreading westward under the road, and it was raining.

Delayed by the floods, the R.S.F. did not begin to cross till noon. They made their crossing by assault-boat between road and by-pass, to the eastward of and just outside the Royal Scots' bridgehead. Their task was to expand the bridgehead eastward and northward. About the same time the sappers were able to resume their rafting.

One company of the R.S.F. cleared the west side of the main street right up to the by-pass junction. Another company cleared the east side of the main street. Thus by 2.30 P.M. the R.S.F. had reoccupied Aart itself, the "core" of the bridgehead, and had made it once more reasonably secure. Beginning a couple of hours later, however, the Hermann Goering Regiment put in two more heavy counter-attacks straight down the road against the R.S.F. West of the road the enemy went through till they were finally stopped by a company of the Royal Scots who had followed up in support. East of the road the enemy made less headway. The R.S.F. had to pull back, however, so the bridgehead was once more tightly compressed.

About 6 P.M. the K.O.S.B. in their turn began to cross into the bridgehead, with the task of expanding it northward and westward. Two hours later two companies had crossed and a third was crossing. They arrived, however, to find the garrison of the bridgehead under heavy attack and fighting for their lives in a scene of some confusion. In the circumstances, the K.O.S.B. and the R.S.F. were unable to put in a co-ordinated attack according to plan—far less to reach their objectives; instead, the K.O.S.B. got themselves into company areas as best they could round the village, preparatory to a break-out which was now planned for eight o'clock next morning.

At about 4 P.M. the Glasgow Highlanders, the whole of whom had now come under the 44th Brigade, had also moved up towards Aart preparatory to crossing. In view of the fact, however, that the bridgehead had remained so congested, the move of the Glasgow Highlanders was stopped. They now concentrated astride the road north of Gheel.

By this time the ammunition situation was beginning to cause

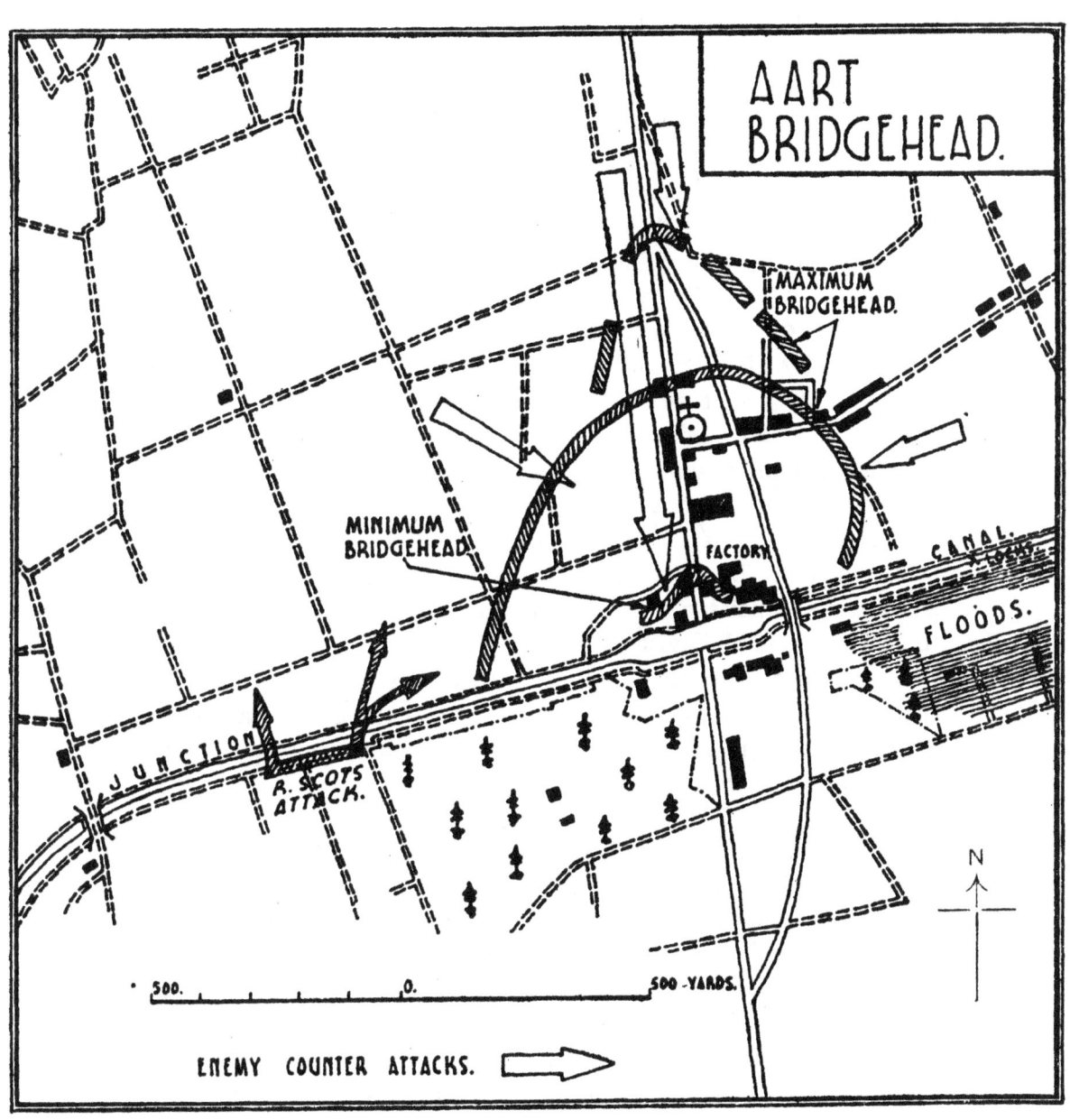

15th Sept. anxiety. The shortage of shells, which was due in the first instance to the length of the lines of communication, coupled with the anticipated requirements of Operation "Market Garden," was now such that the 44th Brigade had to restrict its calls for fire to defensive fire tasks only—put down solely to meet enemy counter-attacks.

All afternoon the sappers had been working feverishly to ferry the essential vehicles of the R.S.F. and the K.O.S.B. across. The ferry site was no longer under small-arms fire, so Major Wood decided to expand his raft of folding-boat equipment into a bridge. Unfortunately, however, the enemy guns had got the ferry taped, and they now scored direct hit after direct hit on the raft, first reducing its length bit by bit, and finally sinking it altogether. Undismayed by the losses they were suffering, the sappers set about the salvaging of their folding-boat equipment.

That day the situation on the flanks of the 15th Scottish Division was this. To the eastward on the Hasselt Branch Canal the H.L.I. had contacted the 231st Brigade of the 50th Division, which had come up through the Beeringen bridgehead over the Albert Canal. On the left the Reconnaissance Regiment had made contact at Oelen with the 7th Armoured Division.

During the night the Gordons and the H.L.I. moved up to a concentration area near Donck, preparatory to making an assault-crossing very early next morning with the object of expanding the bridgehead and of relieving pressure on the 44th Brigade.

16th Sept. At 4 A.M. the Gordons began their crossing of the Junction Canal near Donck. When only part of the battalion had got across, however, they were pinned by intense and accurate machine-gun fire. After some hours of indecisive fighting, it was clear that the crossing had failed. Brigadier Colville therefore called off the attempt, with the approval of the Divisional Commander. They decided instead that the H.L.I. should try again later on at a point farther west. In the afternoon the Gordons and the H.L.I. withdrew from Donck, leaving the Argylls to carry on with their patrolling of the south bank. The H.L.I. went by way of Moll to a new concentration area north-east of Gheel, where they were to spend the next day and a half reconnoitring and taping a new crossing east of the existing Aart bridgehead. In the event this particular crossing did not take place.

In the Aart bridgehead the night had been notable chiefly for the heavy shelling of the ferry site. The plan for the morning was 16th Sept. this. The R.S.F. on the right and the K.O.S.B. on the left were to make a joint attack at 8 A.M. to enlarge the bridgehead. The Glasgow Highlanders were then to pass through, directed on the bridge over the River Neth on the Gheel-Turnhout road one and a quarter miles short of Casterle. This bridge secured, the 46th Brigade would have a clear run to Turnhout.

In the event, unfortunately, it was the enemy who still held the initiative and they forestalled the 44th Brigade's attack. As usual, they tried their hardest to smash through at the road junction by the church. The R.S.F. were so heavily counter-attacked that they could not reach their start-line, while at 7.10 A.M. the K.O.S.B. reported that they were under heavy shell-fire and ringed by enemy riflemen at close range. The situation was such as to make the plan impossible.

Fighting never ceased all day—and all the time the water-level was rising. The R.S.F.'s positions on the south-east side of Aart were below bank-level, and by about 4 P.M. the water was bank high. Already these positions were water-logged. It was at this critical moment that the water ceased to rise—but it had been touch and go.

Meanwhile the 279th Field Company had salvaged much of its folding-boat equipment. There was no immediate need of it, however, for by mid-day the sappers had put most of the essential vehicles across. The traffic with which they would afterwards have to deal would consist for the most part of casualties, rations, ammunition, prisoners. To handle these Major Wood had organised six assault-boat ferries, manned by sappers dug in on the banks. At each ferry a rope was stretched across the canal. Passengers crossed under their own power. At 6 P.M. the 279th Field Company handed over to the 278th: no relief has ever been better earned.

At about 8 P.M. the enemy counter-attacked from the north-east at battalion strength, first hitting the R.S.F. in the " Red House " and then extending their pressure along the whole eastern face of the bridgehead. The enemy pushed home their attack with the greatest courage, but our infantry held off the leading waves while our guns dealt faithfully with those in rear. After an hour's fighting the enemy were repulsed with very heavy losses. They next turned their attention to the western face of the salient. Our guns followed them up, however, to punish them as they were forming up. Indeed, no praise can do justice to the work of the guns throughout all this bridgehead fighting.

16th Sept. Their fire was directed by an intrepid band of F.O.O.s of the 181st Field Regiment, who from their O.P. high in the factory building kept an unending vigil under a ceaseless rain of high velocity shells.

By this time the Royal Scots were no more than a shadow battalion. Brigadier Cockburn had decided, therefore, to get them back out of the bridgehead that night. Things were happening so fast in the bridgehead, however, that the three battalion commanders of the 44th Brigade jointly recommended to him that the Royal Scots should stay put. And stay they did. During the night the enemy once more concentrated their guns of all types on the bridgehead.

Long afterwards this day's situation report of the German 1st Parachute Army was found. It runs :—

"Lock machinery at Wineghen blown by 719th Infantry Division. Indecisive fighting in the Aart bridgehead. The 15th Scottish Infantry Division identified in this area fights toughly and stubbornly."

"Tough" is the *mot juste*.

17th Sept. At dawn next morning the enemy made a minor penetration into the bridgehead, which—once more greatly compressed—now extended barely four hundred yards inland to the church. At about 6.30 A.M. the Royal Scots were pulled out successfully and ferried across the canal. In their unforgettable three-day battle they had lost 230 officers and men. They went back to reorganise in Gheel.

This was to be a day of many plans. The first of these was Operation "Flood," which was designed to enlarge the Aart bridgehead. Division sent out an order to warn the 227th Brigade and the Glasgow Highlanders—still under the 44th Brigade—to be in readiness to cross the canal, right and left of the Aart bridgehead respectively, at any time after 6 A.M. next day, 18th September.

Happenings elsewhere, however, were to give events a different course. This was the day appointed for the opening of Operation "Market Garden"; the initial "drops" were planned for 1 P.M. Sure enough, in the early afternoon the sky became black with aircraft: wave after wave of Dakotas and gliders passed over, their escort fighters darting round them like destroyers round a convoy. It was an uplifting sight. Yet German flak was heavy and took its toll.

On the De Groot-Eindhoven road to the eastward the Guards Armoured Division was waiting for a sign. As the leading waves of this great air fleet appeared, the sign was given to it and the Irish

Guards moved off: Operation "Market Garden" had begun. That afternoon the 30th Corps broke out of its bridgehead as planned. In consequence new orders reached the 12th Corps and, in due course, the 15th Scottish Division.

17th Sept.

In view of the 30th Corps' break-out and of the enemy's fierce resistance at Aart, the Commander of the 12th Corps now determined to develop his main axis of advance from a new bridgehead farther east. Operation "Flood" was cancelled. Instead, the 53rd Division was to make two crossings of the Junction Canal—the one north of Lommel, fifteen miles east of Aart, early the next morning, the other at De Maat, nine miles east of Aart, the following night. The 15th Scottish Division was to maintain its Aart bridgehead the while, and was to enlarge it sufficiently to permit of the building of a Class 9 bridge. The Division was also to remain responsible for holding the line of the Junction Canal from the Hasselt Branch Canal to a point near Herenthals, and for containing the enemy on its front, who might otherwise have opposed the crossing at De Maat.

In execution of this plan the Reconnaissance Regiment, with the Royal Scots under command, took over the line of the Junction Canal from the Hasselt Branch Canal to the Gheel-Rethy road; the 227th Brigade took over between the Gheel-Rethy and the Gheel-Turnhout roads; the 46th Brigade, with the Glasgow Highlanders again under command, remained responsible farther west. The 227th Brigade was ordered to relieve one battalion of the 44th Brigade in the bridgehead that night, the other on the night following.

For this relief the 278th Field Company was to prepare one Class 5 and one Class 9 raft, to raft across the vehicles and guns. The sappers duly completed their salvaging of the folding-boat equipment accordingly. Later, however, the 44th Brigade agreed to leave its vehicles and guns in the bridgehead for the 227th Brigade, so the rafts were not required; the assault-boat ferries would suffice.

During the day the bridgehead was slightly extended eastward. In the late afternoon another counter-attack from the north-east was smashed with the help of our guns. Enemy artillery—and big stuff particularly—was more active than ever, mostly against targets south of the canal. In the evening the Argylls sent reconnaissance parties into the bridgehead. The congestion was so great, and the R.S.F. and the K.O.S.B. so intermingled, that these parties had a job to sort out their company areas. After dark the Argylls crossed success-

17th Sept. fully in the assault-boat ferries without losing a man, though five boats were sunk and the cables cut eight times. It was just as well that there was no question of rafting vehicles and guns, for by the time the Argylls were across nearly all the salvaged folding-boat equipment had again been hit and damaged. Arrived in the bridgehead, the Argylls came under command of the 44th Brigade and relieved the R.S.F. on the right.

18th Sept. At 7.30 A.M. next morning the R.S.F. began their withdrawal from the bridgehead. They went to a concentration area east of Gheel. Thus the Argylls and the K.O.S.B. were now left in the bridgehead; while on the south bank of the canal, from right to left, were the Reconnaissance Regiment, with the Royal Scots under command, the H.L.I., and the 46th Brigade. The Gordons were in Gheel.

Throughout the day the enemy kept up the harassing fire of their heavy and medium artillery on the road from Gheel to Aart and on the site of the road-bridge. Evidently they still feared a break-out from Aart. South of the canal the 131st Brigade of the 7th Armoured Division relieved the Seaforth, together with a company of the Cameronians. The Seaforth thereupon side-stepped eastward to relieve the H.L.I., who then joined the Gordons in Gheel preparatory to going into the bridgehead. Unfortunately that night three heavy shells hit the billets of "A" Company of the H.L.I. and killed or wounded every sergeant in the company.

At about 6 P.M. that evening the enemy put down an intensive bombardment on Aart itself, which lasted for about half an hour. At the same time a single enemy tank, closely followed by infantry and other tanks, advanced along the track which enters Aart from the west, about two hundred yards from the canal. No sooner had the K.O.S.B. repulsed this attack than another attack from the west followed, this time synchronised with an even heavier attack on the Argylls, which came in at battalion strength from the north. The attack from the north the Germans pushed with the utmost determination straight down the main street, handling their supporting S.P. guns with great boldness. Confused fighting went on till about 10 P.M., when all was over. With the help of our guns, the enemy had been driven back once more with very heavy losses. Already the F.O.O.s of the 131st Field Regiment had shown themselves every bit as much at home in the factory O.P. as had their predecessors of the

181st Field Regiment. Indeed the story goes that an F.O.O. was seen that evening erect on the roof observing the fire of his guns with earnest concentration while a stream of 88-mm. shells, fired point-blank, sped between his legs.

During the night the Gordons were ferried across the canal to relieve the K.O.S.B. Such was the congestion prevailing in the bridgehead that the Argylls and the Gordons shared a common command post.

18th Sept.

At 3.40 A.M. the K.O.S.B. handed over to the Gordons in the bridgehead and crossed the canal. Thus ended the responsibility of the 44th Brigade for the bridgehead which it had won and which it had held for five days and nights—held under the ceaseless rain of shells and mortar-bombs that had beaten down on that tortured patch of ground. The 44th Brigade had met and broken no less than thirteen counter-attacks, not a few of these at battalion strength and supported by tanks. It had lost 24 officers and 513 other ranks, of whom 9 officers and 134 other ranks had been killed. As has well been said, at Aart the 44th Brigade had had its Arnhem.

19th Sept.

Yet it was as victor that the 44th Brigade had withdrawn at last: the enemy had not dislodged it. Far from it: the enemy had lost 200 prisoners to it, and the long tale of the enemy dead may be counted still in the German cemetery outside Aart.

The day passed more quietly in the bridgehead. Enemy shelling was only intermittent. This improvement was particularly fortunate, since all our tactical air force was now busy on the 30th Corps' front, so there could have been no typhooning of targets even if it had been called for. That afternoon the 30th Corps reached Nijmegen.

During the morning the 44th Brigade moved eastward to take over the canal line from the Reconnaissance Regiment in the afternoon. The Royal Scots went into Achterbosch, the R.S.F. into Sluis.

The Corps and Divisional Commanders were now considering two alternative plans for the future employment of the 15th Scottish Division: either an advance to Turnhout through the Aart bridgehead, or else an advance to Boxtel and s'Hertogenbosch through the bridgehead at Lommel, which the 53rd Division had established on the previous day. It was the latter plan, Operation "Box," which they were finally to adopt.

That afternoon the 20th Field Company relieved the 278th at Aart. At the same time the H.L.I. moved up from Gheel to a wood

19th Sept. short of the canal at Aart in readiness to cross. Enemy S.P. guns on the far bank shelled them in their wood with unpleasant accuracy. After dark they crossed without difficulty, however, and immediately put in an attack to enlarge the bridgehead. At first all went well. "A" Company and the carriers, however, having overshot the mark, were heavily counter-attacked, so some of the gains were lost. During the night the 20th Field Company made yet another gallant but fruitless attempt to build a Class 9 bridge.

20th Sept. The 53rd Division, pushing out of its Lommel bridgehead, had now reached the Turnhout-Eindhoven road. The enemy's resistance was much less strenuous here than at Aart. Orders had come from the 12th Corps, therefore, that the 15th Scottish Division was to hand over at Gheel to the 7th Armoured Division and was to drive northward through the 53rd Division in order to push forward the 12th Corps' axis of advance to the westward of Eindhoven. It was urgently necessary thus to widen and strengthen the narrow and precarious corridor through Eindhoven by which the 30th Corps had advanced towards the lower Rhine. The full reasons which underlay this change of plan are best summed up in the following letter, dated 19th September, from Lieutenant-General Neil Ritchie, the 12th Corps Commander, to the Divisional Commander :—

"I know that you would like to know that General Horrocks, commanding the 30th Corps, told me yesterday that he had had grave doubts as to the possibility of his being able reasonably quickly to break out of his bridgehead in Operation 'Market Garden.' The fact that he has been able to do so with such speed he attributes very largely to the fact that a very great proportion of the enemy's available reserves in this part of the theatre have been drawn against the 15th Scottish Division front to counter the offensive operations carried out by your Division between the Albert Canal and Junction Canal and the establishment by you of a bridgehead across the latter north of Gheel. You know that it was the original intention to develop the main axis of advance via that bridgehead, but that in view of the enemy's strength now opposing you it has been impossible for me to stick to this plan, and I have therefore decided to develop the main axis farther to the east. The Division has had some very tough fighting and has as well suffered casualties. It is small consolation, I know, but the initial success of the 'Market Garden' operation does, I think, owe a lot to what the 15th Scottish Division has achieved and the threat that you have developed against the enemy, thus forcing him to move his reserves from the vital place."

The 15th Scottish Division's sacrifice at Aart had not been in vain. 20th Sept.

In accordance with this change of plan the 46th Brigade passed under command of the 53rd Division in the early afternoon, and that night the 44th Brigade was relieved by the 131st Brigade.

The enemy continued to shell and mortar the Aart bridgehead all day, but the bridgehead was now secure. That evening the 227th Brigade began to withdraw; the 279th Field Company had built a raft for the withdrawal of as many vehicles as was possible in the time; by the early hours of the morning the Brigade was all out. It was bitterly hard to go like this—and to leave behind the dead unburied and so much equipment that could not be removed; all the harder in that the enemy, too, as was soon to appear, had shot his bolt and was about to pull out. On leaving the bridgehead the 227th Brigade came temporarily under command of the 7th Armoured Division.

The long ordeal of the Aart bridgehead was over. What had been endured by all in it can never be adequately described. Packed together in that tiny patch of ground barely four hundred yards in depth, pounded by a ceaseless bombardment, and assailed by swiftly recurring counter-attacks pushed home with fanatical courage, the 44th Brigade and then the 227th Brigade in its turn had known no respite in this inferno. They had lost over 700 men within six days. Yet they had never failed. The heroism of the gunner O.P. parties must be mentioned once more. Nothing could drive them from their O.P.s. And nothing could exceed the confidence of the infantry in their guns. Nor must the ration parties be forgotten. Whatever the conditions, they had fulfilled their nightly task of ferrying rations and ammunition across and of delivering these to their units—the garrison had never gone short. The doctors, too, who had tended the wounded in a house just south of the canal, had won the respect and admiration of all.

Yet, when all is said and done, it was the Field Companies who had made the bridgehead possible. The Germans had had command of the canal. They had swept it with machine-guns and 20-mm.s; they had plastered the crossing-place with 88-mm. shells. Yet day and night the sappers had worked on devotedly. Men, equipment, vehicles, ammunition, rations—they had ferried all these across without fail. At the end they had only 30 assault-boats left serviceable out of 154, and they had 200 feet of folding-boat equipment sunk or damaged. Here at Aart these Field Companies—and especially the

20th Sept. 279th—had added another and memorable page to the glorious annals of the Royal Engineers.

The crux of the whole operation had been the building of the Class 9 bridge. The bridgehead had been too small to afford the necessary minimum of cover for the building of the bridge. For the sappers, therefore, the task had not been humanly possible. But without the Class 9 bridge it had been impossible to expand the bridgehead. The vicious circle had remained unbreakable.

There is one other memorable incident to be mentioned. On 15th September, at the height of the fighting at Aart, Field-Marshal Sir Bernard Montgomery had paid a visit to the Division to present medals. He had then spoken as follows :—

" In the present operations we have employed some Divisions that had already done a great deal of fighting and were very experienced. There were others with no experience at all. The Divisions without any experience have made good use of their training. They have done every bit as well as the old-stagers, and I can say that there is no one to beat the 15th Scottish Division to-day.

" I hope that all units will get to know what I have said about the Division. I hope, too, that this news will get home to Scotland (although I know that you have some Englishmen with you, and that is a good thing), and I came here to-day and told you that the 15th Scottish Division had done magnificently."

CHAPTER VI.

PART II.—BEST.

During the later stages of the fighting in the Aart bridgehead, the situation farther east round Eindhoven had been this. On 17th September the 102nd U.S. Airborne Division had dropped in the Eindhoven area. The 102nd had gone on to do an extremely good job of work. The 506th Parachute Regiment had occupied Eindhoven itself and had secured the crossing of the Wilhelmina Canal at Zon—though not the bridge itself, which had been destroyed. The 502nd Parachute Regiment had secured intact the bridge over the River Dommel at St Oedenrode, while the 501st Parachute Regiment had secured the bridge over the Willems Waart Canal at Veghel. Thus the 102nd U.S. Airborne Division had given a lead to the 30th Corps over the first three fences.

17th Sept.

On 18th September the 53rd Division had established its bridgehead over the Junction Canal at Lommel, but had failed to make a crossing at De Maat. The 53rd Division, therefore, had built both its bridges, Class 9 and Class 40, at Lommel. Pushing north through the Lommel bridgehead, the 71st Brigade of the 53rd Division had crossed the Eindhoven-Turnhout road to the westward of Eindhoven by midnight on 19th September.

18th Sept.

Out in front the 30th Corps in its race to the Rhine had reached Nijmegen by 20th September. That evening, in conjunction with the 82nd U.S. Airborne Division, it took the great Nijmegen bridge over the Maas. Von Rundstedt, however, who had been reappointed Commander-in-Chief in the west earlier in September, had now reacted to the stimulus of this attack. That morning, between Eindhoven and St Oedenrode, the Germans had counter-attacked and had cut the 30th Corps' axis for the first time. The axis had been soon restored, but the situation remained anxious. Eastward of the axis there

20th Sept.

20th Sept. was the German 1st Parachute Army; westward of it there was the German 15th Army with about fifty tanks. True, neither of these armies was as yet fully formed, but the cohesion of both was growing fast. To give left flank protection to the 30th Corps' axis against the 15th Army's attack from the west, therefore, was now more than ever the urgent task of the 12th Corps. That day the 7th Armoured Division, with the 227th Brigade temporarily under command, took over the Aart bridgehead, while the 46th Brigade was placed under command of the 53rd Division preparatory to the advance of the 15th Scottish Division through the 53rd Division bridgehead at Lommel. The 9th Cameronians moved at once to Lommel to take over the close defence of the Class 40 bridge.

21st Sept. On the morning of 21st September the 1st Oxfordshire and Buckinghamshire Light Infantry of the 71st Brigade sent patrols across the Wilhelmina Canal south of Oirschot, which lies about eight miles west of Zon, where, it will be remembered, the 30th Corps' axis crossed the canal. These patrols met stiff opposition and later withdrew.

At this stage the 12th Corps made the 53rd Division responsible for the left flank protection of the 30th Corps' axis as far north as the Wilhelmina Canal; the 15th Scottish Division responsible for its protection north of the Wilhelmina Canal towards s'Hertogenbosch. The first and urgent task of the 15th Scottish Division, therefore, was to cross the Wilhelmina Canal.

On 21st September the 46th Brigade (less the Cameronians) moved early by 3-tonner over the Junction Canal at Lommel and across the Dutch frontier to Veldhoven, five miles west of Eindhoven. There the 46th Brigade picked up the Cameronians. In the afternoon the Cameronians went on about eight miles north-westward to relieve the 1st Oxfordshire and Buckinghamshire Light Infantry in a god-forsaken waste of rough moorland on the south bank of the Wilhelmina Canal opposite Oirschot. It had been the original intention that the 46th Brigade should make a crossing here. The nearest metalled road was miles away, however; vehicles could scarcely move over the sandy tracks, and the enemy in strength on the north bank dominated the approaches and greeted every movement with heavy mortar-fire. Altogether it was a thoroughly unpropitious spot. The crossing, therefore, was first postponed and then abandoned.

Meanwhile the 46th Brigade (less the Cameronians) was moving on again to a forward assembly area north of Eindhoven and south of the Wilhelmina Canal, while reconnaissance groups went forward to reconnoitre the crossing over the canal on the road to Best and Boxtel, which crossing lies about half-way between the crossing at Zon and that at Oirschot.

To their great surprise the reconnaissance parties found the crossing undefended—a piece of good fortune, all the more unaccountable since the Wilhelmina Canal was here a formidable obstacle with steep twenty-foot banks. Both road and railway bridge had been destroyed. Men on foot, however, could still cross the sagging structure of the road-bridge by wading. By 6 P.M. Seaforth patrols had crossed. But for a little desultory shelling, the crossing had been ours for the asking.

Ahead the country was dead flat. On the right front, about a quarter of a mile away beyond the canal, was visible the dark edge of a big wood. This was the wood of Zonche, in and around which the 506th U.S. Parachute Regiment had dropped four days before. Where the Americans were now, none quite knew. They had left evidence behind them, however, of the job they had done. The Seaforth patrols reported plenty of German corpses, some of them headless, littering the ditches on the farther side, and one or two derelict 88-mm.s —but of live Germans, not a sign.

Looking from the canal one sees, straight ahead, leading slightly west of north, the main road to Boxtel stretching to infinity through a medley of orchards and scrub and scattered houses. Less than a mile and a half along it is the main cross-roads, where a lateral road takes off right-handed for St Oedenrode, and another left-handed for Best and Oirschot.

On the left front the foreground stretches in an expanse of flat and desolate heath to the railway, which crosses the canal at a point three-quarters of a mile to westward of the road-crossing, to run northwestward parallel with the main road to Boxtel.

Between road and railway, straggling along the lateral road from the main cross-roads to the level-crossing, is the village of Best, dominated by its two landmarks—the church steeple and the monastery close by. Beyond the level-crossing and westward of it is the village of Naastebest, so long to be an unattainable goal.

The first half-mile or so of the railway beyond the canal runs on an embankment across the open heath. Farther on, the railway, too, disappears into the medley of scrub and ditches and scattered houses, which extends all the way to where Best has developed ribbon-like along its complex of roads and lanes. On the east side of the railway and about 1400 yards up it from the canal, there stand the two long rows of parallel sheds known as the cement factory—to be the scene of so much bitter fighting. Beyond the factory scattered houses and farms and the station buildings form a continuous chain on both sides of the line. To sum up, then : save for the open foreground up to the railway embankment on the left, the whole battlefield of Best was a patrol leader's paradise.

At 9.15 P.M. that evening the Seaforth moved off from their forward assembly area, followed by the Glasgow Highlanders. The plan was this : that night the Seaforth would cross the canal and establish a bridgehead ; the Glasgow Highlanders would then form up behind them in the darkness and would attack northward on Best. The Glasgow Highlanders had laid on guides and forming-up places with the Seaforth accordingly.

Three companies of the Seaforth waded in turn across the submerged road-bridge. The leading company went straight on astride the main road ; the second headed left-handed across the open ground for the railway embankment and, after some close fighting, pushed the enemy back to it ; the third company went right-handed to the lock in the direction of Zonche wood. By 10.30 P.M. the Seaforth had established their bridgehead—which, however, did not extend as far westward as the railway. Lieutenant-Colonel Hunt had sent his patrols on towards the cross-roads and into Best itself. Rafting material had arrived ; the Seaforth's pioneer platoon had built a Class 9 raft ; already their essential fighting vehicles were crossing smoothly. The Glasgow Highlanders were closing up behind the Seaforth in readiness to cross. The R.E. had chosen a site for their Class 9 bridge some distance to the eastward of the demolished road-bridge. All was going well.

So much for the 46th Brigade ; now for the 44th. After relief by the 7th Armoured Division in and around Moll, the 44th Brigade had started that afternoon on its move into Holland. Less than forty-eight hours before, it had emerged from its fiery ordeal at Aart. All ranks knew, however, how pressing was the emergency in the north which called them into action again. There was great confusion on the road through the Lommel bridgehead that day, and the 44th Brigade had to endure many disheartening delays in consequence. By dusk it had entered Holland.

21st Sept.

By dawn next morning the Seaforth up on the Wilhelmina Canal had rafted all their A.Tk. guns across, together with a sufficiency of jeeps. It was now the turn of the Glasgow Highlanders. Unfortunately, before they could raft any of their essential transport across, the raft sank. At that, Brigadier Villiers postponed the Glasgow Highlanders' crossing till after daylight, when they would be able to pass their "F" Echelon across the sappers' Class 9 bridge, which was now nearing completion.

22nd Sept.

Meanwhile the Seaforth patrols had reported Best to be unoccupied, and Brigadier Villiers had ordered Lieutenant-Colonel Hunt to occupy the place. This Lieutenant-Colonel Hunt decided to do after daylight. At 8 A.M. he sent "D" Company of the Seaforth into Best.

At first "D" Company found no trace of the enemy. The Jocks seem to have been standing around at street corners in section groups when suddenly a German soldier bicycled into their ken. He did not stop when challenged, so the nearest section commander opened up on him with his Sten. At that, German soldiers came tumbling out of every house. Surprise was mutual—but the Germans recovered the quicker. "D" Company had to pull out with the loss of thirty-three officers and men, including the F.O.O. killed. Brigadier Villiers then decided to send the Glasgow Highlanders through to make a battalion attack.

At first light the Glasgow Highlanders' reconnaissance group and company commanders had been out to have another look at the scene of action. By 9 A.M. the R.E. had finished the Class 9 bridge. Less than an hour later the rifle companies of the Glasgow Highlanders crossed and reached their forming-up places in the Seaforth Company areas, where essential "F" Echelon vehicles joined them soon afterwards.

Briefing was difficult, for the Glasgow Highlanders had only one air photograph—and that did not show the whole area—while their 1/25,000 maps were extremely inaccurate and in such short supply that platoon commanders—the very men who would want them most in this close country—had to go without. Moreover, there was no supporting armour—and this was to prove a dire deficiency throughout all the house-to-house fighting round Best. Many a time and oft in

22nd Sept. the week of frustration ahead the 15th Scottish Division was to long for just an hour or two's help from the 6th Guards Tank Brigade, not to mention the Crocodiles and other " Funnies " of the 79th Division. All would then have been so easy. Even a quota of flame-throwing Wasps in the carrier platoons of infantry battalions would have made all the difference here, but the Wasps had not yet arrived. The Jocks were to do their house-clearing unaided.

At 11.40 A.M. the Glasgow Highlanders crossed their start-line about two hundred yards beyond the Canal on a three-company front, to attack Best from the south. " C " Company on the right advanced straight up the main road, with the main cross-roads as its objective; " B " Company in the centre headed for the church and monastery; " A " Company on the left for the level-crossing between Best and Naastebest.

As soon as " A " Company had left the start-line it came under intense mortar-fire from the neighbourhood of the railway, which followed up its every movement. Through the smoke and dust of what seemed to be countless direct hits, the Jocks could be seen plodding grimly on. Then heavy spandau-fire opened up in enfilade from the railway line—and that did pin " A " Company down with many casualties.

Seeing " A " Company in difficulties, Lieutenant-Colonel Campbell gave " A's " objective, the level-crossing, to " B " and put in his reserve company, " D," giving it " B's " original objective, the church. Not till after dark, however, was he able to withdraw " A " into reserve from its exposed position.

As soon as " B " Company got level with the cement factory sheds, it, too, was pinned by withering machine-gun fire from the left flank, and so failed in its turn to reach the level-crossing. Indeed, it became increasingly obvious that both " A " and " B " Company had been trying to move across what was in fact a strongly held enemy front facing east along the railway line and in the cement factory—a movement all the more impossible since, in view of the negative patrol reports on the previous night, no covering fire had been put down along this western flank. It seems that the enemy, firmly dug in along the railway or snug in the factory cellars, had escaped the notice of our patrols in the darkness.

Meanwhile " C " Company on the right had been making almost equally slow progress up the main road. House-clearing, always difficult without armoured support, was here further complicated by the old " Ghent difficulty " : the inhabitants were still in their cellars, so the Jocks were loth to make free use of their grenades. Like every other infantry company, moreover, " C " was now largely composed of inexperienced drafts who knew little about house-clearing. " C " Company was finally stopped by machine-gun fire in the southern outskirts of Best.

Only " D " Company in the centre reached its objective, the church and monastery, both of which it cleared.

Towards dusk Lieutenant-Colonel Campbell realised that further progress was impossible. He therefore ordered " B," " C," and " D " Companies to consolidate, facing west, where they were—" C " Company, that is, in an orchard south of the main road junction ; " D " Company in the church and monastery ; " B " Company in a group of houses by the complex of roads five or six hundred yards north-east of the cement factory. That night the link-up between companies was far from firm. Two sections of the carrier platoon did their best to keep touch between " B " Company and the Seaforth. After dark the rather scattered bits and pieces of " A " Company withdrew—to coalesce into a company once more.

That morning the 44th Brigade had moved up into a harbour on the north-western outskirts of Eindhoven. The Dutch gave the Low-landers a welcome no less warm if less hysterical than those they had been receiving farther south.

Late in the afternoon the K.O.S.B., who had been the leading battalion of the 44th Brigade, were placed under command of the 46th Brigade and followed a squadron of the Reconnaissance Regiment across the Class 9 bridge.

Beyond the bridge the K.O.S.B. went on right-handed through the Zonche wood, which the paratroopers had cleared a few days before. The countryside around was still littered with their parachutes. Before dark the K.O.S.B. had reached the north-western edge of the wood, whence they continued north-westward on the village of Steenweg. This village, which lies on the Boxtel road about six hundred yards beyond the main cross-roads, they had occupied before 9 P.M. Thus by nightfall the K.O.S.B. had outflanked the enemy position in Best and were positioned beyond and to the north-east of it.

That afternoon the enemy had cut the 30th Corps' axis once more, this time between Veghel and Uden, while the 43rd Division, fighting its way to link up with the 1st Airborne Division, had been held up

22nd Sept. at Elst, four miles short of Arnhem. The situation was critical. In consequence, the 44th Brigade was put for a time under Army command and at one hour's notice to move north to reopen the road. Later, however, the 227th Brigade (less the H.L.I., who were still back in the Gheel area under command of the 7th Armoured Division) also moved up to a harbour north of Eindhoven. On arrival there the 227th Brigade was put at one hour's notice in place of the 44th Brigade.

At about four that afternoon the R.E. began work on the Class 40 bridge. Originally they had intended to build it beside the Class 9 bridge and east of the demolished road-bridge. In consequence they had been involved in much heavy work on the approaches— usually the most difficult part of a field bridging job. Now, however, they had decided to build the Class 40 bridge on the exact site of the demolished road-bridge, where they could use the old approaches. So well was this plan to work that the R.E. were to complete their Class 40 bridge in eighteen hours.

23rd Sept. At first light the Reconnaissance Regiment pushed up the main Boxtel road in an attempt to find a way out of the bridgehead and towards s'Hertogenbosch. They bumped a road-block about half a mile beyond Steenweg, however, and, though they fanned out wide on either side of the road, they were unable to find a way through.

In the Best bridgehead the night of the 22nd had been spent in making plans to renew the fight. The enemy garrison of Best and its environs was now put at about two battalions, extremely well dug in and amply provided with machine-guns and mortars. The enemy also had a few S.P. guns, but handled these poorly, wasting their fire power on the indirect shelling of road junctions and the bridge site, using rather ineffectual air-bursts.

Brigadier Villiers decided on a three-battalion attack. In the early morning the K.O.S.B. were to clear the houses along both sides of the side-road which curves south-westward from Steenweg towards Best and the railway. By 9 A.M. the K.O.S.B. were to reach the cross-roads in Best, level with the right-hand company, " C," of the Glasgow Highlanders. There the K.O.S.B. and the Glasgow Highlanders would link up. Later, the Glasgow Highlanders on the right and the Seaforth on the left were to put in a two-battalion attack westward, with the railway line as their general objective.

South of Oirschot the 1st Oxfordshire and Buckinghamshire Light 23rd Sept. Infantry had relieved the Cameronians during the night, whereupon the Cameronians had moved in pouring rain to a concentration area at Acht, one and a half miles south of the Best crossing, where they had arrived by 10 A.M. Soon after, the Cameronians relieved the Seaforth in the bridgehead, in order to free the Seaforth to take part in the impending attack on Best.

Starting from Steenweg at about 5.30 A.M., the K.O.S.B. fought their way all day from house to house down the lane towards the Glasgow Highlanders. It was a desperately slow and costly business. By nightfall they had gained only four hundred yards.

When he realised that the K.O.S.B. could not link up with the Glasgow Highlanders, Brigadier Villiers confirmed H-hour for the Glasgow Highlanders and Seaforth as 3.30 P.M. At that hour, then, the two battalions attacked west, after twenty minutes' preparation, with the Zonsche Steeg—the lane which runs west from the main road to cut the railway a hundred and fifty yards north of the cement factory—as the inter-battalion boundary. They were supported by two field and one medium regiment R.A., some 4.2-inch mortars, and two platoons of the Middlesex medium machine-guns.

A machine-gun position more ideal than that in which these two platoons came into action that day would be hard to find. On the south bank of the canal, immediately west of the railway, there stands a large group of factory buildings. It is the Bata Shoe Factory. Viewing this factory from afar, Major Waller, M.C., commanding "A" Company of the Middlesex, had decided that it looked promising. Closer investigation had revealed that from the upper story of the Bata Factory it would be possible to bring enfilade fire to bear right across the enemy front, absolutely at right angles to the direction of the attack. So into the factory with infinite stealth had crept these two platoons that morning. Presently, unperceived by the Germans, the muzzles of their guns were peeping through the upper windows. When the time came they opened up with a will—to the confusion of these same Germans who, a moment earlier, had been strolling unconcernedly in the open.

On several more occasions the machine-gunners were to use the Bata Shoe Factory to good purpose. Artillery O.P. parties were likewise to haunt it. The view was invariably magnificent, but the climate sometimes unhealthy.

23rd Sept.   The Glasgow Highlanders went in on a three-company front, with their right resting on the main lateral road that leads to the level-crossing between Best and Naastebest; both sides of this road they had to clear. For the rest they had also to clear the station—about four hundred yards south of the level-crossing—and other buildings along the railway and to link up with the Seaforth in the cement factory. "A" Company of the Glasgow Highlanders, still in reserve, had fought its way to the school-house by the first cross-roads on the lateral road west of the main cross-roads, where it remained.

After clearing all the houses north of the lateral road, "C" Company of the Glasgow Highlanders on the right reached the level-crossing. The enemy were still close by on the other side of the line and in the houses beyond. At dusk "C" pulled back a few yards and dug in.

"D" Company in the centre was the first to reach its objective, the station, to find the enemy here, too, in strength across the line. After the company commander and the only other officer had both been wounded, the company consolidated under the C.S.M. in a house overlooking the line. On the left "B" Company—only two platoons strong—had been held off till dark by fire from the cement factory. After dark both platoons worked forward independently, to establish themselves in the same isolated farm building which abuts on the railway line about four hundred yards north of the factory.

All three forward companies of the Glasgow Highlanders spent the night within twenty-five yards of the enemy, listening to the sounds of digging and of shoring of houses that came from the other side of the line, and of transport, both horsed and tracked, on the move through Naastebest.

That afternoon Brigadier Villiers had given "C" Company of the Cameronians as a temporary reinforcement to the Glasgow Highlanders. This Cameronian company went into "B" Company's former area at the track junction south of Best, where it took over contact duties from the Glasgow Highlanders' carrier platoon.

During the night wireless inter-communication throughout the Glasgow Highlanders' area was poor owing to the built-up nature of the neighbourhood. Nor did contact patrols work too well.

On the left of the Glasgow Highlanders, the Seaforth, too, had gone in on a three-company front. They, too, had their troubles. Their right company, "B," was directed on the cement factory; "C" and "A" against the railway line and embankment towards the canal.

The enemy, they soon found, had turned the factory into a fortress and were dug deep into the railway embankment and under the railway wagons in the sidings, whence they enjoyed an excellent field of fire in the gaps between the houses. About four hundred yards short of the railway line, the Seaforth were pinned by mortar and machine-gun fire, though one platoon of "C" did reach the railway, to be subsequently withdrawn under a smoke-screen. About 6.45 P.M. the Seaforth set to work to dig in as best they could in the open. They had lost six killed and thirty-three wounded.

23rd Sept.

So much for the 46th Brigade. Turning now to the 44th Brigade, we find that during the afternoon the R.S.F. had crossed the Wilhelmina Canal on foot to go on north through the K.O.S.B. around Steenweg, who then reverted under command of the 44th Brigade. The R.S.F.'s rôle was to strengthen the 44th Brigade's hold on the main cross-roads. Advancing north-east from these cross-roads and astride the road to St Oedenrode, they occupied a position for the night a little short of Vleut, a village a mile and a quarter from Steenweg. The Royal Scots, too, closed up to the Wilhelmina Canal.

That day the H.L.I. rejoined the 227th Brigade in its concentration area north of Eindhoven. The evening before the H.L.I. had had a strange experience. They had gone up to patrol the Junction Canal south of Aart. Aart itself they had found empty and the enemy gone; the way to Turnhout, so bitterly contested, stood open at last.

During all this fighting around Best the weather generally was to remain foul. On this afternoon, however, there was a break in the low cloud, and once more a great air fleet passed over. It was flying in the Glider Regiment of the 82nd Airborne Division and the Polish Brigade to reinforce the 30th Corps. But things were not going well Arnhem way. There was no hope left of preparing air-strips north of Arnhem as had been intended, so the plan for flying in the 52nd Lowland Division had now to be abandoned.

24th September dawned pouring wet. The Glasgow Highlanders, it will be remembered, had spent the previous night with three companies —from right to left, "C," "D," and "B"—strung out along the railway line within grenade-throwing range of the enemy. The whole of "B" Company's two platoons had concentrated in one isolated farm building beside the line. At 6.30 A.M. "B's" wireless went off the air, and soon things began to happen.

24th Sept.

24th Sept.

At 7 A.M. the C.S.M. of " B " Company arrived wounded at Battalion Headquarters near the school-house. He reported that Major Millar, the company commander, had been wounded; that " B " Company had been overrun; and that the enemy had broken in behind " D " and " C " Companies. Almost immediately afterwards " C " Company of the Cameronians, which was still backing up in " B " Company's former area five hundred yards farther back, confirmed the bad news. Thereupon Lieutenant-Colonel Campbell sent up his carrier platoon towards the cemetery in an attempt to seal off the penetration: he had no call on the Cameronians. Before it could get far, however, the carrier platoon was stopped by spandau-fire.

Next, " D " and " C " Companies of the Glasgow Highlanders reported that they, too, were under close spandau-fire. At 7.45 A.M. the C.S.M. in command of " D " Company reported his left under a three-way attack and his position untenable. He then withdrew his company northward through " C " Company, whereupon Major Briggs, now in command of " C," took charge of both companies. Having got Lieutenant-Colonel Campbell's approval to his withdrawal to the church and monastery, where his front would be back in line with that of the Seaforth, Major Briggs took both companies back. By 9.15 A.M. the Glasgow Highlanders had the situation once more under control.

A few minutes later Brigadier Villiers held an " O " Group at the school-house. He ordered the Cameronians to relieve the Glasgow Highlanders at once: a squadron of the Reconnaissance Regiment would take over the close defence of the bridgehead from the Cameronians. In the early afternoon the Cameronians came up. Lieutenant-Colonel Sir E. Bradford put " D " Company into the school-house and " A " Company through to clear up to the level-crossing. North of the station, " A " Company had little trouble. Farther south, however, heavy fire from both sides of the line stopped any attempt by " C " Company to advance. South of the station, the Cameronians and Seaforth, keeping close touch, remained holding a line about four hundred yards east of the railway. Seaforth patrols at dusk found the cement factory and the railway line south of it still strongly held.

The Glasgow Highlanders withdrew into Brigade reserve astride the main road south-east of Best, where they were to remain for three days. They had lost 9 officers and 138 men, of whom 1 officer and 50 men were missing. Of " B " Company only 6 were left. The

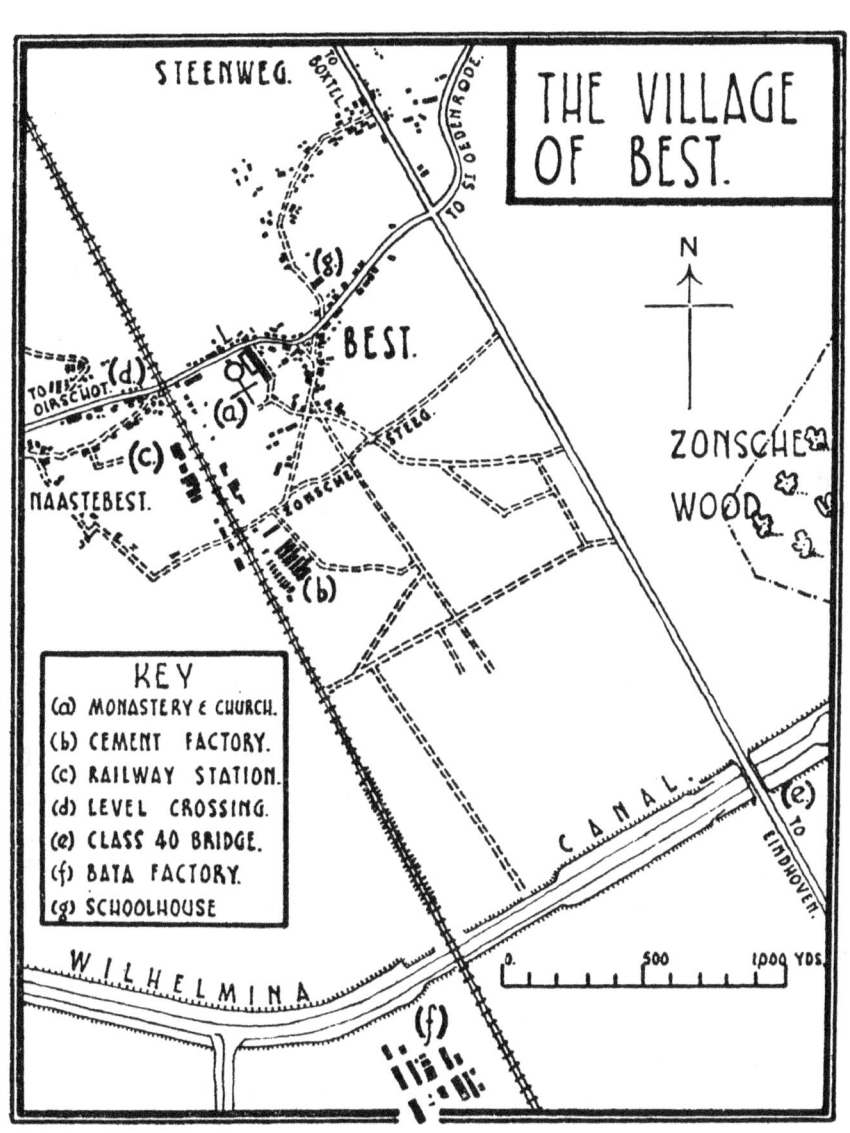

24th Sept.   Glasgow Highlanders reorganised as three rifle companies of two platoons each, with only four officers in all.

The story of "B" Company's disaster, so far as it can be pieced together, seems to be this. On the previous night the Germans, close by on the other side of the railway line, had heard the noise made by the two platoons as they entered the farm building in the darkness. They had thus been able to locate the platoons exactly and to perfect their dispositions for rushing them. The platoons had occupied only one building, and only the ground floor of that. They were out of touch altogether with the Seaforth on the left, who were four hundred yards farther back; they were in scarcely better touch with "D" Company on their right. Before dawn the Germans had closed in on the building. As daylight came they opened up a surprise burst of bazooka and spandau-fire on it, which momentarily put down the heads of the defenders. With that, a sudden rush and a few grenades tossed in at the windows finished the business.

While this fighting had been going on in Best itself, the 44th Brigade had been trying to break out northwards. At 7.30 A.M. the Royal Scots went through the K.O.S.B. and straight up the main road, with the din of the counter-attack on the Glasgow Highlanders ringing in their ears. Their objective was the strip of woodland which crosses the road about a mile beyond the cross-roads. They took it, but not before they had had an unpleasant foretaste of the difficulties of fighting in that close scrub country between the Wilhelmina Canal and the River Dommel—difficulties of which both the 44th and the 227th Brigades were to have a bellyful before they were done. It was fighting at close quarters, in conditions which made direction keeping most difficult, and which offered every advantage to a resolute enemy who was prepared to lie hidden and to hold his fire. To make matters worse, most of the so-called roads in those parts were mere sandy tracks passable only by infantry.

Simultaneously with the Royal Scots' advance, the R.S.F. had sent fighting patrols into Vleut, which they shortly afterwards occupied.

The Reconnaissance Regiment had already contacted the 502nd U.S. Parachute Regiment a couple of miles south-west of St Oedenrode, and also the 506th Parachute Regiment a couple of miles west of Zon. In the next stage of the 44th Brigade's operation, the K.O.S.B., riding the tanks of the 5th Royal Inniskilling Dragoon Guards (of the 22nd Armoured Brigade), were to have gone through the R.S.F. and to have broken out north-eastward towards St Oedenrode. This afternoon, however, the enemy once more cut the 30th Corps' axis, this time south of Veghel, so the 5th Dragoon Guards were ordered off at short notice to reinforce the 131st Infantry Brigade between Veghel and St Oedenrode. The K.O.S.B.'s break-out, therefore, had to be cancelled. Instead, the Divisional Commander ordered Brigadier Cockburn to consolidate the positions won—the R.S.F. in Vleut, the K.O.S.B. round the main cross-roads, the Royal Scots a mile or so farther up the Boxtel road.

24th Sept.

Back in its concentration area north of Eindhoven, the 227th Brigade spent a wet Sunday of " organised rest." The hospitality of the Dutch was boundless, and the pastor of the Baptist Church held a special service for the Brigade.

Early next morning the 227th Brigade moved up to cross the Wilhelmina Canal. Brigadier Colville's plan was this. First, the Gordons were to attack westward out of the bridgehead and along the north bank of the canal, while the Argylls and the H.L.I. remained in readiness in a forward assembly area to the eastward of Best. When the Gordons had secured sufficient elbow-room west of the railway line, the Argylls and the H.L.I. were to go through in their turn and to attack Naastebest from the south.

25th Sept.

At 10 A.M. the Gordons began their advance through the Seaforth and across the desolate, open heath. At the same time the three forward companies of the Cameronians on the Gordons' right tried to infiltrate forward to the railway and the houses beyond, using all available cover.

Coming out into the open, the Gordons at once ran into heavy fire, which came mainly from the cement factory. Typhoons were called up and they knocked the factory about very thoroughly. The enemy's fire was little abated, however, and it brought the Gordons to a standstill with heavy casualties. At about 4.30 P.M. Brigadier Colville had to call off the attack. The Gordons withdrew to the 227th Brigade's forward assembly area, where the Brigade spent an unpleasant night in a damp and burnt-out wood. The Cameronians, however, had made some progress and were now up to the railway in several places.

The 44th Brigade spent the day in carrying out local clearing operations. Having finished the clearing of Vleut and Hoefke, Lieutenant-Colonel MacKenzie sent a company of the R.S.F. on foot north-

25th Sept. eastward along the road to St Oedenrode. That evening, too late to attack, it came up against a strong company locality in the woods at Donderdonk. Later that night the Divisional Intelligence Officer came up to the R.S.F. with a loud-speaker to broadcast a surrender message in German to the enemy. Rocket-firing Typhoons lent an added force to his arguments. It was an amusing but rather fruitless effort: German officers and N.C.O.s were on the watch for would-be deserters.

It was on that morning that Montgomery decided to withdraw the remnants of the 1st Airborne Division from Arnhem. Operation "Market Garden" was thus drawing to its tragic but glorious close. Rundstedt now turned his attention to the Nijmegen bridge—"the gateway to the Reich"—which he was determined to retake or destroy. The safety of the 30th Corps' axis to Nijmegen, therefore, was to remain a matter of supreme importance.

26th Sept. By this time it was evident that our offensive at Best was bogging down into something very like position warfare. It was on this day that the 46th Brigade made its last set-piece attack to take the cement factory and the railway.

It was mainly the Seaforth's battle, and a most gallant one. Soon after seven that morning Lieutenant-Colonel Hunt held an "O" Group. While the Cameronians farther north cleared the isolated houses on their front between Best and the railway, the Seaforth—sadly reduced in strength—were to take the factory and the railway south of it. The whole of the Divisional artillery were to be in support. Four S.P. 17-pounders were to accompany the Seaforth.

At four that afternoon the Seaforth attacked on a two-company front in face of the invariable and deadly machine-gun and mortar-fire. To-day nothing could stop "B" Company on the right. "B" broke into the range of sheds which make the factory and cleared the enemy out of them at last. "D" Company on the left, however, was held up by cross machine-gun fire from the railway wagons south of the factory before it could reach the line. While "B" Company organised the factory as a firm base, "C" Company tried to go through as planned in order to take the buildings on the far side of the line. At the railway line, however, "C" Company ran into enfilade fire from houses on the right of the factory and was able to get only one platoon over. At the end of this bitter fighting the position was this: "B" and "C" Companies, each only about twenty strong, were in and around the factory; "D" Company half-way between the factory and "A" Company, which last was still giving flank protection in its original position on the left. The Seaforth had lost four officers and thirty-eight men killed, wounded, and missing, but the factory was theirs at last, while their S.P. guns commanded the railway wagons, so long a thorn in their flesh.

Meanwhile "D" Company of the Cameronians had cleared the scattered houses on the right up to the line—but not without considerable losses. Thus the Cameronians and the Seaforth were now along the railway line from the level-crossing to the cement factory, and there were no enemy left anywhere east of the railway line. The two battalions established touch by contact patrol. Their positions here were to remain practically unchanged for the next six days.

In view of the enemy's prolonged resistance in Best, the Divisional Commander had determined to by-pass the place and to extend the Divisional front northward to the River Dommel. With this object in view, the 227th Brigade, with the R.S.F. under command, had also put in an attack that same morning, 26th September. At 10.30 A.M. the H.L.I. on the right, Argylls in the centre, and the R.S.F. on the left had formed up on the general line of the Best-St Oedenrode road for an "advance-to-contact" move northward with Typhoon support. The belt of thick woods south of Liemde was to be the limit of their advance. The Gordons were in reserve.

At first all three forward battalions made good progress through the thick scrub. There the enemy offered little resistance, and the keeping of contact and direction were the main difficulties. The Jocks and Fusiliers took a number of prisoners. In the early afternoon, however, when they had entered the dense woodland south of Liemde, the Argylls in the centre got involved in murderous fighting at very close range. Three officers were killed, "B" Company losing two more company commanders in a few minutes. The body of Major H. C. Robinson, who had been killed by a burst of point-blank spandau-fire, lay in a clearing. On it were some marked maps which were in danger of falling into the enemy's hands. C.S.M. Davies, who had already distinguished himself in Normandy, risked almost certain death to crawl out and bring back the maps. He afterwards got the D.C.M.

The H.L.I. on the right and the R.S.F. on the left were up against much less stiff resistance. They took eighty and seventy-three prisoners

26th Sept. respectively at the cost of slight losses. Before dusk all three battalions had finished their job of wood-clearing. Brigadier Colville then pulled them out and ordered them to dig in on the south edge of the woods from a point a little to the westward of Donderdonk to the square wood on the east of the Boxtel road, about a mile and three-quarters beyond the cross-roads. Their task here was to block any enemy thrust from the west against the 30th Corps' axis. Here the H.L.I. and the Argylls were to stay for the next week, their time fully occupied by continuous patrolling punctuated by skirmishes and false alarms.

On the right the H.L.I. were in touch with the 502nd Parachute Regiment near Donderdonk, so the road from Best to St Oedenrode was open at last. Patrols of the Reconnaissance Regiment went through to Boschkant and Gasthuishoef, villages near the south bank of the River Dommel, a mile and a half or so short of St Oedenrode. Soon after, the Divisional Commander ordered Brigadier Cockburn to send up his reserve battalion, the K.O.S.B. (less one company, which had been ordered off for the close protection of the bridge at Zon), to take over the area from the Reconnaissance Regiment. The Glasgow Highlanders, now reorganised, replaced the K.O.S.B. in Steenweg and round the main cross-roads nearby. Going by way of Vleut and Donderdonk, the K.O.S.B. got into the little villages of Kremsel and Boschkant soon after dark. Patrols reported the enemy close by in Gasthuishoef and in the farm buildings on a slight rise to the north of it.

27th Sept. It was the Divisional Commander's intention to get the rest of the 44th Brigade up to the Dommel to join the K.O.S.B. as soon as possible. Next morning, therefore, the R.S.F., who had reverted under command of the 44th Brigade, and the Royal Scots followed the K.O.S.B. by the road to St Oedenrode round the right flank of the 227th Brigade. The Gordons came up from 227th Brigade reserve to take over the battalion area vacated by the Royal Scots at the first wood, three-quarters of a mile up the Boxtel road from the cross-roads. Thus all three battalions of the 227th Brigade were now in defensive positions between Donderdonk and the Boxtel road, where they were to remain until relief.

Forward on the Dommel things began to happen early. At 9 A.M. Lieutenant-Colonel Richardson sent " C " Company of the K.O.S.B. against Gasthuishoef, which it took under cover of an artillery concentration. About 10.15 A.M. "D" Company went through to take the farm buildings on the hillock to the northward, close by the bank of the Dommel. Half an hour later "D" had closed to assaulting distance. At that point, however, the enemy suddenly opened up a devastating fire. "D" Company was pinned to its ground with the company commander and the C.S.M. killed, while many wounded were left lying out beyond reach.

27th Sept.

Here followed one of those chivalrous episodes which adorn the annals of war. Captain H. R. Thomson, the battalion medical officer, was determined to get these wounded in. Taking a couple of stripped Bren carriers distinguished by Red Cross flags, he went out to fetch them. In his search, however, Captain Thomson strayed too far; the enemy picked him up. Fortunately, he spoke German. Taken to platoon headquarters, he explained what he was about and gave his word as an officer to tell nothing of what he might have seen behind the enemy lines. At that the enemy let him go to get on with the job.

For the moment the K.O.S.B., who were very weak, could do no more, particularly as villagers had warned them that enemy reinforcements had arrived in Fratershoef, half a mile farther on, the night before. By this time the R.S.F. were coming up, but Brigadier Cockburn decided to postpone their attack till after dark.

In the afternoon the enemy laid a smoke-screen in front of "C" Company of the K.O.S.B. in Gasthuishoef and counter-attacked from the north-west. Difficult fighting went on till about 8 P.M., by which time the K.O.S.B. had beaten off the attack. Soon after, "A" Company rejoined them from Zon and the tension was eased.

At 11 P.M. the R.S.F. put in their attack against the hillock crowned by the farm building, where they found a reinforced enemy company well dug in. After losing a number of men, the R.S.F. took the hill with forty-five prisoners. There on the bank of the Dommel the R.S.F. dug in.

That night the Seaforth back at Best sent a fighting patrol to the railway wagons south of the cement factory. The patrol found that the enemy had gone.

At first light next morning the Royal Scots went through the K.O.S.B. at Gasthuishoef to attack north-westward on Fratershoef, which they took with forty prisoners after an hour's fighting. The Royal

28th Sept.

28th Sept. Scots dug in at Fratershoef, with the R.S.F. to the east and the K.O.S.B. to the south-east of them. The north flank of the Division up to the Dommel was thus secured. The 44th Brigade was not to move again till its relief on 1st October.

The enemy, however, had no intention of leaving the 44th Brigade in peace. At about 4.30 P.M. they put in a heavy counter-attack from two quarters, directed against the Royal Scots and also against the junction of the Royal Scots and the K.O.S.B. During the subsequent fighting one German unit—it was a training unit of young airmen—seemed to have lost its bearings, for it tried to form up in the open close to battalion headquarters of the Royal Scots. Every rifle and automatic that could be brought to bear opened up on them, and down on them, too, came our artillery defensive fire. By 6 P.M. the enemy had had enough and they withdrew under a smoke-screen, leaving the ground littered with their wounded. Soon after, an emissary with a white flag came to the Royal Scots to ask them for one hour's cease-fire in order that the German stretcher-bearers might collect their casualties. In view of the enemy's generous behaviour to the K.O.S.B. on the previous day, Lieutenant-Colonel Lane Joynt granted the request.

That day the Cameronians back in Best staged a successful company operation to clear the goods-yard by the level-crossing and some houses close by. Such was the enemy's vigilance, however, that patrolling across the railway line was still impossible by day and remained strictly limited to the hours of darkness.

After dark the Divisional Intelligence Officer repeated his loud-speaker appeal for surrender, speaking from the H.L.I.'s front-line near Donderdonk. His bag, however, was no bigger this time than on the occasion of his previous effort.

29th Sept. Next day, in accordance with the Corps Commander's orders, the Divisional Commander took over from the 7th Armoured Division responsibility for the front up to the road from Eerde to Schijndel, about three and a half miles beyond the Dommel. The object of this extension was to relieve the 131st Brigade of the 7th Armoured Division for operations still farther north beyond the Willems Waart Canal. The Corps Commander gave Major-General Barber for his task beyond the Dommel the 158th Infantry Brigade of the 53rd Division, the 8th Hussars, and one battalion of the 131st Brigade. The 158th

Brigade was in touch with the 44th Brigade near Fratershoef on the Dommel, whence it held a line north-eastward towards Schijndel. *29th Sept.*

On the 44th Brigade's and 227th Brigade's fronts 29th September passed quietly. On the 46th Brigade's front there was intermittent shelling and mortaring.

The next morning, too, passed quietly on the 44th Brigade's front. In the early afternoon, however, the enemy put in a small counter-attack from the north-west, which was easily repulsed. There was more to follow. Soon after 6 P.M. the enemy's shelling increased ominously. Sure enough, half an hour later a strong counter-attack came in against all three battalions. After an hour's fight the Germans were again repulsed, this time with heavy losses. It was their last effort against the Lowland Brigade in this fighting. *30th Sept.*

On this day the enemy at Best pulled back a bit. The Cameronians got their patrols right into Naastebest, half a mile beyond the level-crossing. The Seaforth, too, got their patrols well across the railway farther south.

A word now as to the general situation. Even before the Second Army entered Holland the impetus of its great offensive was already petering out. The army had outrun its supplies. It lacked artillery and shells, tank bridges and tank brigades. Above all, its men were tired. In all the fighting in Holland that followed, the exhaustion of the army, both physical and material, became absolute. The enemy, on the other hand, falling back on their reinforcements and supplies, had been steadily regaining cohesion and poise.

By now the 15th Scottish Division in particular was long overdue for relief. For a hundred days it had never been out of range of the enemy's guns. In that time it had had only one week's rest. From the Bois Halbout to the Dommel it had come four hundred miles with no rest at all. It had had no time whatever to assimilate the countless small drafts that it had received. Exhausted, weak in numbers, and inadequately supported, the 15th Scottish Division had found itself pitted once more against young and fanatical troops in extremely strong, defensive positions. It had fought on devotedly. So long as it was called upon to do so, it would still fight on—but to ever-lessening purpose. Soon its fighting would serve merely to lengthen its casualty lists still further.

Such were the views on the state of his Division which the Divisional

30th Sept. Commander had already put before the Corps Commander, who had satisfied himself that these views were sound. The 15th Scottish Division was to be relieved at last.

1st Oct. Up to the very end Best was to maintain its reputation as a scene of frustration and misadventure. On 1st October a fighting patrol of the Cameronians crossed the level-crossing, where no enemy had been seen on the previous day. To-day the enemy were there. They ambushed the patrol, killing five and wounding eight.

There were other and more propitious happenings that day, however. The advanced parties of the 51st Highland Division (less those of the 154th Brigade, which was left behind outside Dunkirk) arrived from the 1st Corps' area. The 51st Division was fresh; it had taken no part in the pursuit into the Low Countries. On arrival it came under the 12th Corps for Operation "Haggis"—the relief of the 15th Scottish Division. That night the 153rd Brigade—now commanded by Brigadier R. Sinclair, formerly of the 2nd Gordons—relieved the 44th Brigade. 44th Brigade Headquarters, the Royal Scots, and the R.S.F. then moved about ten miles eastward across the 30th Corps' axis into rest-billets in Gemert, six miles north of Helmond; the K.O.S.B. to Boekel, three miles farther north. At the same time the 152nd Brigade began its relief of the 227th Brigade, the H.L.I. going out to rest-billets in Milheeze, near Bakel, two and a half miles north of Helmond.

2nd to 4th Oct. On 2nd and 3rd October the 152nd Brigade completed the relief of the 227th Brigade, which went to the Bakel area. On 3rd October the 152nd Brigade relieved the 46th Brigade in its turn, the 46th going to rest-billets in and round Helmond. Thus by 4th October the whole of the 15th Scottish Division was out at rest in the 8th Corps' area. At first only five days of rest were promised. Eventually, however, the period was extended to a welcome and much-needed three weeks.

CHAPTER VII.

PART I.—TILBURG.

THOUGH the weather was generally bad, life around Helmond in those days was very pleasant. The troops needed rest, baths, reinforcements, training. Most of them found billets in Dutch homes; all found hospitality and a welcome; many made lasting friendships. In Helmond there was that most welcome of institutions, a Mobile Bath Unit. There were football matches, cinemas, theatres. The Massed Pipes and Drums of the Division marched through the streets of Helmond to the Town Hall, where the Burgomaster took the salute. At this time, too, all units got their Dutch interpreters, mostly enthusiastic young members of the Dutch Resistance who were to do invaluable work in days to come. And there were excellent training areas in the country round about.

4th to 18th Oct.

All was not plain sailing, however. In an ideal world units would have received their much-needed reinforcements promptly; would have drawn up programmes of reorganisation and training at the start to cover the complete rest period; and would have carried these out without interruption—the world forgetting and by the world forgot. But things never do happen like that. In fact, drafts came in slow and rather uncertain driblets, while the repeated departures of reconnaissance parties to study various operations believed to be impending interfered seriously with training programmes—for the few experienced instructors who were left were usually also reconnaissance party members. The study of each of these operations meant, too, an immense amount of work for Divisional, Brigade, and Battalion staffs. Nor had the period of three weeks' rest been ordained from the outset: the initial five days was gradually extended by more than one change of plan by the Higher Command. Still, thanks to N.C.O.s, cadre classes, and platoon and section training, commanding officers saw their units gradually take shape once more as the weeks went by. More than one battalion commander, however, had to be content to reorganise on only a three-company basis.

4th to 18th Oct.

It was at this time that the 46th Brigade established a rest-centre and brigade battle-school in Helmond, which was to do invaluable work throughout the five winter months ahead. And others did likewise.

At first it had been Montgomery's intention to carry on with his Rhineland battle without a pause. In consequence, when the 15th Scottish Division had been at rest only a couple of days, it was ordered to send off reconnaissance parties to prepare an attack on Gennep, east of the Maas, as a prelude to an invasion of the Rhineland south of the Reichswald forest in conjunction with the 3rd Division.

By 7th October, however, Montgomery had come perforce to the bleak conclusion that he had exploited the victory in Normandy to the limit: he would have to postpone his invasion of the Rhineland till the 21st Army Group could gather fresh impetus for another prolonged offensive. To the intense relief of all concerned, therefore, the Gennep operation was called off after the reconnaissance parties had been away only a day or so.

With its invasion of the Rhineland thus deferred, the 21st Army Group could now turn to three more immediate tasks: to open the Scheldt and so free the port of Antwerp; to reinforce the Nijmegen bridgehead; and to push the enemy over the Maas to the eastward and so establish an economical right flank.

On 12th October the 8th Corps embarked on the last-mentioned task, the drive eastward to the Maas. The 3rd Division, with the 6th Guards Tank Brigade (less the Scots Guards) under command, advanced on Venraij, while the 7th U.S. Armoured Division farther south attacked through Deurne. By 17th October the 3rd Division had occupied Venraij, about thirteen miles east of Helmond.

At the same time the 15th Scottish Division and the 3rd Tank Scots Guards were busy planning in great detail a parallel operation south of Weert, which would have involved an assault crossing of the Wessem Canal and the clearance of south-eastern Holland up to Roermond on the Maas. 15th Scottish Divisional reconnaissance parties went off to spend several days with the 7th U.S. Armoured Division near Weert, fifteen miles or so due south of Helmond; while the 15th Scottish Division itself carried out an exercise in canal crossing by assault-boat and also, in conjunction with the Scots Guards, trained with armoured troop-carrying Kangaroos—Canadian ram tanks with their turrets removed.

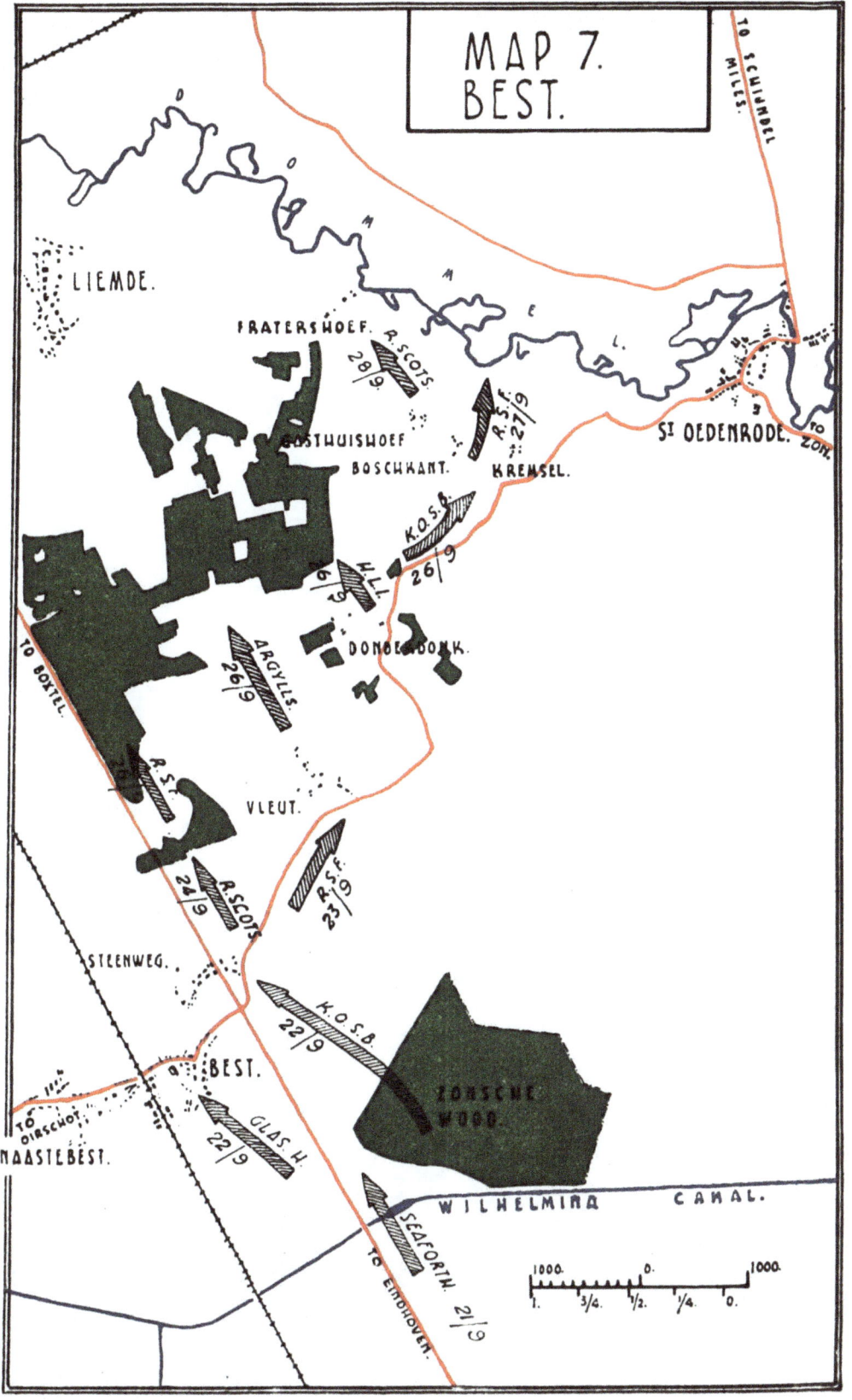

By about the middle of October, however, the insatiable demand for supplies and still more supplies—a demand which came not only from the 21st Army Group but also from the First U.S. Army, which now found itself threatened by a stalemate in the Siegfried Line—had necessitated yet another change of plan. The only way to meet this demand was to open the port of Antwerp. Montgomery, therefore, had now resolved to subordinate everything to this task. In pursuance of this new plan, Dempsey had to order the 8th Corps to release the 15th Scottish Division and the 6th Guards Tank Brigade for a joint operation to clear the Scheldt. Thus it was that the 15th Scottish Division found itself back under the 12th Corps on 17th October and about to go into battle once more in company with its old friends, the 6th Guards Tank Brigade. *(4th to 18th Oct.)*

Briefly the plan of operations was this. The 12th Corps was to advance west from the line Oss-Veghel-St Oedenrode-Best, with its right on the Maas and its axis through s'Hertogenbosch to Breda. On 22nd October the 7th Armoured Division and the 53rd Division would attack in the north between Oss and Veghel, directed on s'Hertogenbosch. Next day the 51st Division farther south would attack from Veghel directed through Schijndel on Vucht, Esch, and Boxtel. Finally, the 15th Scottish Division still farther south would clear the triangle Best-St Oedenrode-Boxtel and would advance thence on Tilburg, supported by the 6th Guards Tank Brigade. Such was to be the 12th Corps' Operation " Pheasant." On 18th October intense preparations for Operation " Pheasant " began.

On 19th October the 227th Brigade began its return move from Bakel. The H.L.I. and the Gordons came back into the dripping woods by Donderdonk and Vleut, where they relieved the 152nd Brigade, which would be taking part in the earlier phases of Operation " Pheasant." The 227th Brigade found the mud increased beyond belief, and the trenches, which had been dry and comfortable less than three weeks before, now brimful of autumn rain. *(19th to 22nd Oct.)*

On the same day the Royal Scots of the 44th Brigade went to Dinther on the Willems Waart Canal north-east of Schijndel, where they took over part of the 131st Brigade's front in order to free the 131st Brigade to take part in the 7th Armoured Division's advance on s'Hertogenbosch.

Next day, 20th October, the Argylls came up into the 227th

19th to 22nd Oct.

Brigade reserve at Steenweg. At the same time the Cameronians of the 46th Brigade returned to Best, where they came under the 227th Brigade. There the Cameronians completed the relief of the 152nd Brigade. They found Best a bit quieter than formerly. The church steeple had gone—knocked down by enemy artillery fire—but the enemy themselves were still in their old place on the far side of the railway. Artillery and mortar exchanges and night patrolling were the main activities on the front of the 227th Brigade and the Cameronians during the three days that followed.

On 22nd October Operation " Pheasant " started as planned.

23rd Oct.

Operation " Pheasant " was going well, in better weather. By last light on 23rd October the 51st Division had taken Schijndel and Olland, had crossed the Dommel between Boxtel and s'Hertogenbosch, and was approaching Boxtel itself. Farther north the 53rd Division was approaching s'Hertogenbosch. There was not much German artillery fire; minefields were the main obstacle.

Meanwhile the enemy on the 15th Scottish Division's front had been looking nervously over their shoulders at the growing danger on their flank and rear. On the 227th Brigade's front the enemy had been holding a position in considerable strength in the woods south of Liemde. On the night of 23rd October the 227th Brigade's patrols found that the enemy had gone. The clearing of these woods by the 227th Brigade, with the 44th Brigade (less the Royal Scots) and the 6th Guards Tank Brigade (less the Scots Guards) under command, had been planned for 25th October. The Divisional Commander promptly cancelled this operation and ordered the 227th Brigade to start its wood-clearing not later than noon next day.

24th Oct.

During the course of the next morning Cameronian patrols discovered in their turn that the enemy had gone, too, from Naastebest and from behind the railway in the Best sector. The 46th Brigade (less the Cameronians) was due to come up from Helmond by T.C.V. that afternoon to concentrate behind the Cameronians; and on the following day, 25th October, the 46th Brigade was to have broken out of Best, preparatory to fighting an " advance-to-contact " battle westward along the axis Best-Oerschot. It now seemed likely, however, that Oerschot was to be had for the asking at any time. The 46th Brigade would arrive too late to do anything about it that day, but the 44th Brigade (less the Royal Scots) was also on its way up from Gemert, as was the 6th Guards Tank Brigade from Bakel: elements of these two brigades might be available in time. The Divisional Commander therefore issued urgent orders to Brigadier Cockburn to concentrate the 44th Brigade near Best cross-roads, with the Tank Grenadier Guards in support, as soon as possible.

24th Oct.

At noon the 227th Brigade advanced west, as ordered, on a three-battalion front from the line Donderdonk-Vleut to sweep through the woods towards the Best-Boxtel road. There was no opposition. Mud and innumerable flooded ditches made the going extremely difficult, however, and the two flank battalions ran into large belts of mines and booby-traps. On reaching the road, forward companies went on to consolidate on the railway line. Thus by nightfall the 227th Brigade was up abreast of the Cameronians on the railway line.

Meanwhile the 44th Brigade (less the Royal Scots) and the Tank Grenadier Guards had concentrated in great haste near the Best cross-roads by about 4 P.M. An hour and a half later the R.S.F., riding on the tanks of the Grenadiers, set out westward from Best to Oerschot. They found it a strange experience to advance across that familiar level-crossing and on through Naastebest—and not a shot fired. Oerschot they found already occupied by a squadron of the 15th Divisional Reconnaissance Regiment, which was also by now in Boxtel, where it had found the Dutch Resistance in charge. Lieutenant-Colonel Mackenzie at once sent on a company of the R.S.F. to a demolished bridge over the Groote Stroom at Spoordonk, about two miles beyond Oerschot on the Tilburg road. There the company gave cover to an R.E. working party which was building a Class 40 bridge. By 3.30 A.M. next morning the R.E. had finished their bridge successfully.

That evening the Royal Scots came in from Dinther to rejoin the 44th Brigade by the Best cross-roads. In the north, the 53rd Division had taken a large part of s'Hertogenbosch.

At seven next morning the Glasgow Highlanders and the Seaforth began to close up on Best from their forward assembly area south of the canal. These two battalions had had a busy night. Not till 9 P.M. the evening before had Brigadier Villiers been able to tell the battalion commanders that the original plan for the break-out on 25th October had been cancelled. Instead, the 46th Brigade, starting

25th Oct.

25th Oct. as early as possible, was now to make an "advance-to-contact" move along the axis Best-Oerschot-Moergestel. The 3rd Tank Scots Guards would be in support. The Glasgow Highlanders, riding on the tanks of the Scots Guards, were to form the advanced guard; the rest of the brigade would follow in Kangaroos. Battalion commanders in their turn had not held their "O" Groups much before midnight; orders had not reached platoons and sections till the early hours. Not till they reached the forming-up place that morning did sub-unit commanders of the Glasgow Highlanders meet their tank *vis-à-vis* to discuss matters.

A squadron of the Reconnaissance Regiment led. Next came the vanguard, which consisted of "D" Company of the Glasgow Highlanders, moving behind a point of two tank sections. By 9 A.M. the head of the vanguard was passing the starting-point at Best crossroads. All went well till the point reached the stream on the eastern outskirts of Moergestel about noon. There the tanks found the bridge demolished and the way barred to them. The assembled populace, however, led by a friar from a neighbouring monastery, set to work with a will to build a footbridge of planks and to hurl rocks into the stream to make a tank crossing. Having de-tanked, the Glasgow Highlanders were able to cross by the footbridge and so to enter Moergestel. Soon after 2 P.M. they were in position round the village.

Meanwhile the leading Churchill had got bogged while trying to cross the stream by the improvised causeway, so the Scots Guards had had to send for one of their bridge-laying tanks. The crowd greeted its arrival with immense enthusiasm. As the scissor-bridge reared itself to fall into position, however, there fell a sudden hush. Then the whole crowd began to sing. It was their National Anthem. They sang till the waiting tanks had started up their engines to cross the bridge.

The first site chosen proved too soft to bear the weight of Churchills, but the Glasgow Highlanders' "F" Echelon transport got over. When about 3 P.M. another bridge-laying tank had laid a second scissor-bridge on the site of the demolished road-bridge the Scots Guards were able to cross successfully.

About the same time the Seaforth and the Cameronians arrived in their Kangaroos. The Seaforth, with a squadron of the Scots Guards in support, were to go on northward through the Glasgow Highlanders and to seize the road-bridge over the Voorste Stroom, a tributary of the Aa, on the southern approach to Oisterwijk. Oisterwijk is a long, straggling village which extends east and west on commanding ground on the north bank of the Voorste Stroom. According to plan, the Seaforth were to secure Oisterwijk as a firm base through which the 46th Brigade would then swing left-handed down the main s'Hertogenbosch-Tilburg road into Tilburg itself.

That afternoon, as the Seaforth in their Kangaroos and their accompanying Churchills soon found, Moergestel was congested beyond measure. Traffic was struggling vainly to move in two opposing streams and everything was at a standstill. One troop of Churchills did get through at last, however, and headed north for the Voorste Stroom. Bursting through a road-block, the troop pressed on under mortar and machine-gun fire directed on them from the heights beyond the stream. Finding the road-bridge demolished, the troop engaged in a fire fight with the enemy dug in on the commanding ground and in the defended houses on the north bank. Later, the rest of the supporting Scots Guards squadron arrived, followed by the Seaforth. Under cover of the fire of the tanks and of the smoke of burning houses, the Seaforth were able to drive up in their Kangaroos and to dismount and close up to the Voorste Stroom with very few casualties. Clearly, however, the Seaforth were up against a strong enemy rearguard position. Moreover, the Voorste Stroom was unfordable and the main road-bridge blown. The Seaforth, therefore, made no further attempt to cross that evening.

Meanwhile back at Moergestel Brigadier Villiers had given fresh orders both to the Glasgow Highlanders and to the Cameronians. Coming to the headquarters of the Glasgow Highlanders about 3 P.M., he had ordered Major Davies, who was in temporary command, to take his battalion on with a supporting squadron of the Scots Guards and to dig in across the Moergestel-Tilburg road, about two miles west of Moergestel. By dusk, as the sounds of mortar and machine-gun fire reached them from Oisterwijk, the Glasgow Highlanders finished digging in in their new position. After dark their patrols went up to the Wilhelmina Canal, about a mile farther on, on the south-eastern outskirts of Tilburg: they found no enemy east of the canal.

Going on from the Glasgow Highlanders to the Cameronians, whom he found just about to settle down in their concentration area, Brigadier Villiers ordered Lieutenant-Colonel Sir E. Bradford to push on at once and to seize the main canal-bridge on the s'Hertogenbosch-Tilburg road which enters Tilburg from the east. Possession of this bridge was clearly of vital importance, not only in order to secure the left

25th Oct. flank of the Seaforth at Oisterwijk but also to ensure a clear run into Tilburg later on. "A" and "B" Companies of the Cameronians were well ahead of the rest, so Lieutenant-Colonel Bradford sent these on, led by the reconnaissance troop of the Scots Guards. By last light, however, the Kangaroos and their accompanying Honey tanks were still about a quarter of a mile short of the bridge and in the middle of what appeared to be an enemy company area, for they were under fire from the surrounding farms. Three of the Honeys got bogged. Two of these they pulled out that night under fire; the third they pulled out next morning. With an enemy attempt to counter-attack, the Cameronians dealt very effectively by Bren-gun fire. It was only darkness that had beaten them in their very gallant effort to seize the bridge. The Cameronians dug in short of the canal, facing the road and railway bridges into Tilburg, both of which the enemy now destroyed. There the Cameronians were to remain throughout the next day.

At about 8 P.M. that evening Brigadier Villiers held an "O" Group, at which he ordered the Glasgow Highlanders to move across early next morning to a forward assembly area behind the Seaforth outside Oisterwijk, in readiness to co-operate with the Seaforth in their attack next day.

Next we come to the 44th Brigade. The R.S.F. had started the day near Oerschot, the K.O.S.B. and the Royal Scots back by the Best cross-roads. Brigadier Cockburn's intention was to concentrate his brigade as far west as possible in the direction of Tilburg, avoiding wherever he could do so movement along the Divisional axis Best-Oerschot-Moergestel, which was likely to be hopelessly congested. The Royal Scots, therefore, moved off early by forest tracks north of the main axis; the K.O.S.B., preceded by a troop of the Reconnaissance Regiment, followed the canal bank south of the axis. By afternoon the Royal Scots had got no farther than Oerschot. There they stayed: ahead the traffic jam was impenetrable. The K.O.S.B. went on farther west along the canal to reach their objective, which was the crossing-place where the track from Moergestel to Biest crosses the canal. There the R.E. were to build a Class 40 bridge, by which the 44th Brigade would cross later on. About 3 P.M. the K.O.S.B. patrols contacted the Glasgow Highlanders at Moergestel.

The 227th Brigade also moved up during the day into the Oerschot area.

The Seaforth on the south bank of the Voorste Stroom had spent another busy night preparing for their attack. Lieutenant-Colonel Hunt had not held his final " O " Group till 10 P.M., in order that he might have in his possession the latest information given by the intensive patrolling which he had ordered for the early part of the night. There were two possible crossings over the Voorste Stroom — the one a footbridge still standing about a hundred yards east of the demolished road-bridge; the other a minor road-bridge, passable by battalion vehicles, which was also still standing about three-quarters of a mile farther east, towards the eastern end of the town. He proposed to send a rifle company over each of these bridges under the covering fire of the squadron of Scots Guards. His object was to establish a small bridgehead up to the line of the railway in order to cover the building of a Class 40 bridge. Till this bridge was built, tanks would be unable to cross the Voorste Stroom.

26th Oct.

At first light half a squadron of the Scots Guards closed up to each of these bridges to open a twenty minutes' bombardment of the hillside beyond the stream. The covering fire of the tanks was accurate and intense. At the same time an artillery concentration came down on Oisterwijk. During this preparation the forward companies of the Seaforth—" A " on the right, " B " on the left—were moving up towards the two bridges under enemy mortar and machine-gun fire as heavy as it had been the night before. By about 7 A.M. these forward companies had closed. Thereupon they rushed their respective bridges with the greatest boldness, killing or capturing all Germans nearby. " A " and " B " Companies went on at once to clear the areas assigned to them. By about 9 A.M. they linked up, thus establishing a continuous bridgehead with a depth of five hundred yards or so. Meanwhile essential " F " Echelon vehicles had followed " A " Company over the minor road-bridge on the right. " C " Company had crossed over the footbridge to secure the left flank; the carrier platoon had crossed the road-bridge to secure the right. The enemy was still shelling and mortaring the area fairly heavily. In this action the Seaforth lost 2 officers killed and 2 wounded, 3 other ranks killed and 35 wounded. They took 44 prisoners.

The Glasgow Highlanders, who had moved off from their position west of Moergestel about 6 A.M., had been coming up to a forward assembly area in the large woods about three-quarters of a mile south of Oisterwijk, which they reached about 8 A.M. Thence the

26th Oct.

Glasgow Highlanders followed up the Seaforth into Oisterwijk. Major Davies sent three of his rifle companies, "C," "A," and "B," across the footbridge, his essential fighting vehicles across the minor road-bridge farther east. "C" Company's task was to clear the formidable-looking factory area beyond the railway; "A" and "B" Companies' tasks were to advance eastward along the two main streets which run parallel to and south of the railway and to clear these up to the eastern limits of the town.

South of the railway "A" and "B" Companies met no resistance other than shelling and mortaring. North of the railway, however, "C" Company found a huge convent building, east of the main level-crossing, strongly held and could get no farther. Major Davies here put in his reserve company, "D," across the railway still farther east, with orders to push through the factory area to the northern edge of the village in order to bring cross-fire to bear on the convent. This "D" Company did with complete success, whereupon the enemy withdrew altogether from Oisterwijk about noon, at the same time greatly reducing the volume of their shelling and mortaring. As if by magic the Dutch appeared in the streets, bearing very welcome pots of tea. The enemy were still in the offing to the northward, but the 7th Armoured Division and the 51st Division were approaching them from the east and could be left to deal with them.

At about 4 P.M. that afternoon "B" Company of the Glasgow Highlanders and a section of their carrier platoon staged a small joint operation on the eastern outskirts of Oisterwijk, which is of considerable interest, since it was the first occasion on which a Wasp of the 15th Scottish Division went into action. The enemy were holding a strong-point about four hundred yards from the houses. Our guns put down a five minutes' concentration on the strong-point and then lifted to put down smoke farther back, which would screen any positions there might be in depth. As the gun-fire lifted, the carrier section, with its one flame-throwing Wasp and its three Bren carriers, closed on the strong-point under the covering fire of "B" Company. The Wasp scored two direct hits with two squirts on occupied slit-trenches, whereupon all enemy in sight, to the number of about fifty, took to their heels, throwing away their arms. The Brens of the other three carriers did great execution, as did also those of "B" and "A" Companies in turn.

At Oisterwijk the Glasgow Highlanders lost one officer, a company commander, killed, and sixteen other ranks wounded. They killed and wounded a great many Germans and took seven prisoners.

26th Oct.

The Seaforth and the Glasgow Highlanders spent the night in Oisterwijk, the Cameronians farther west on the canal facing Tilburg. Thus the 46th Brigade was positioned for a break-in next day to Tilburg from the east.

The Divisional Commander, however, was not content with a break-in only from the east: the 44th Brigade was to force an entry simultaneously from the south. With this end in view, the R.S.F. and the Royal Scots had moved up early from Oerschot to Moergestel, where they had turned south to join the K.O.S.B. at the canal-crossing on the road to Biest. In the afternoon the 44th Brigade had sent harbour parties across the canal to Voorst and Hilvarenbeek, about a mile beyond Biest. The brigade and its supporting Tank Grenadiers followed as soon as the Class 40 bridge had been built. They had trouble with mines, and it was late that night before they got into their harbours.

Arrived in its harbours, the 44th Brigade was positioned for a straight push into Tilburg, astride the road from the south. Not that this approach was likely to be easy. Indeed, the Princess Irene (Dutch) Brigade, which together with elements of the 4th Armoured Brigade was in observation in the woods between the 44th Brigade's harbours and Tilburg, had had a company very roughly handled in the outskirts of Tilburg that afternoon. The country on both sides of the main road was an unpromising waste of heather and scrub and bog, while the strong enemy defences, revealed by air photographs, effectually commanded the road itself. Moreover, the bridges over the two large drains or leys which cross the road had been blown.

During the day the 227th Brigade had moved up from Oerschot to Moergestel in readiness to go in on the left of the 44th Brigade against the large village of Goirle, two miles south of Tilburg.

The Divisional Commander's plan for 27th October was to deliver simultaneous assaults by the 44th and 46th Brigades as early as possible.

27th Oct.

On the 44th Brigade's front a patrol from the 4th Armoured Brigade found Broekhoven, the southern suburb of Tilburg, still occupied at 7 A.M. Brigadier Cockburn's plan was first to send the R.S.F. round to the right along the canal tow-path to cause a diversion and then to send in the K.O.S.B. with all possible support straight up the road. At 11.30 A.M. the R.S.F. moved by an excellent covered route which they had found across the moorland to the canal. Advancing north along the tow-path, they surprised and overran an enemy company which was entrenched facing east, in defence of the crossing where the main road from Oerschot and Moergestel crosses the canal. Branching left-handed along this main road, the R.S.F. pushed straight on into Tilburg. Soon after 2 P.M. they were in the suburbs, and Lieutenant-Colonel Mackenzie was able to report that he could hear sounds of jubilation coming from the town itself. A couple of hours later he added that Tilburg might be considered liberated.

Meanwhile the K.O.S.B., with their supporting Tank Grenadiers, had formed up in an orchard in the Princess Irene Brigade's area and had moved off up the main road a few minutes after 1 P.M. Taking with them A.V.R.E.s or "Funnies" of the 79th Division to bridge the two road-gaps, they advanced behind a barrage—which Brigadier Cockburn had preferred to concentrations, since he knew so little about the enemy's dispositions. The country on either side of the road they found to be cut up by countless flooded ditches, which made the going atrocious, and the Newe Ley or Drain proved too much for the A.V.R.E.s and effectually stopped the Tank Grenadiers. By 2.30 P.M., however, the K.O.S.B. were in Broekhoven, where the townsfolk told them that most of the Germans had gone the night before. Half an hour later the K.O.S.B. were streaming into Tilburg itself. Thus the whole of south-eastern Tilburg up to the railway had been liberated by the 44th Brigade. Sub-units moved straight to the vulnerable points, such as power-houses and railway workshops, which had been allotted to them. They found, however, that the Germans had destroyed these installations very effectively before leaving.

Back at Oisterwijk the Seaforth and the Glasgow Highlanders had found early that morning that the enemy had withdrawn from the neighbourhood that night, and a patrol from the 7th Armoured Division contacted the Glasgow Highlanders at about 7 A.M.

During the morning Brigadier Villiers had ordered the Seaforth and the Glasgow Highlanders to close up behind the Cameronians, while the Cameronians, who were still facing the demolished road and railway-bridge on the eastern side of Tilburg, forced a crossing. The Cameronians had reported that it was still possible to crawl across the débris of the railway-bridge. Indeed Lieutenant-Colonel Sir Edward Bradford had sent a patrol across and into Tilburg the day before, but the patrol had never returned.

In accordance with these orders "A" Company of the Cameronians assaulted across the demolished railway-bridge at mid-day. It met only slight opposition, which came mostly from Dutch S.S. who had remained hidden in Tilburg after the Germans had gone. The rest of the Cameronians followed in assault-boats. They found the town strangely quiet and deserted. For the moment the Dutch were wisely staying indoors. Here, too, sub-units went straight to the vulnerable points allotted to them.

27th Oct.

The Glasgow Highlanders followed the Cameronians across the canal by the bridge and by boat. By 5.30 P.M. the Glasgow Highlanders were on their objectives, having extended the Cameronians' bridgehead in depth and north of the railway. At dusk the Seaforth closed on the canal about one and a half miles farther north. Ahead they sent a patrol across by assault-boat, while a rifle company lined the bank ready to give covering fire. The patrol could be seen advancing delicately to the nearest houses. Suddenly it was immersed in a flood of humanity. When next the Seaforth saw their patrol it was being carried off shoulder-high by a mob of triumphant Dutchmen. At that the covering party applied their safety catches. The Seaforth soon followed their patrol by assault-boat. Their essential vehicles crossed on two Class 5 rafts built by their Pioneers. The Seaforth went on to occupy the north-east corner of Tilburg.

Meanwhile the 227th Brigade, too, had been moving up. Accompanied by the Tank Coldstream, it had left Moergestel by Kangaroo about 10 A.M., to follow the 44th Brigade across the canal by the Biest crossing and into Tilburg from the south. Mud, blown bridges, and box mines along the roads made it a desperately slow move. However, by 7 P.M. the marching troops of the 227th Brigade were well into Tilburg, all but the western edge of which had by then been occupied. The Brigade's tracks and wheels followed after dark. Of the 6th Guards Tank Brigade only the Coldstream managed to make their way into Tilburg.

Tilburg was divided into three brigade areas. As yet the town had not been cleared, so units had to maintain a high degree of alertness throughout the night. Not till next day, therefore, could they take part in the celebrations of the populace.

That afternoon disquieting news had come from the east. Rundstedt, it appeared, had counter-attacked the 8th Corps. Crossing the Noorder and Deurne Canals, the Germans had struck the 7th U.S. Armoured

27th Oct. Division near Meijel. That Division had been holding a very wide front and it had failed to stop them. The Germans were pushing on towards Second Army Headquarters at Helmond, only thirteen miles north-west of Meijel.

28th Oct.   Next morning each brigade made a methodical clearance of its own area in Tilburg. Early in the afternoon the Divisional Commander declared Tilburg officially "liberated." After that, 50 per cent of all ranks were allowed to walk out till 10 P.M. The non-stop celebrations which the people of Tilburg kept up for thirty-six hours are beyond any description. Ninety thousand men, women, and children were in the streets—laughing, dancing, and singing. It was, above all, their National Anthem that they sang—time and again. The Pipe Band of the R.S.F. went to the main square to play selections. The crowd smothered the Band with their welcome. None could see these sights unmoved. The 15th Scottish Division will never forget Tilburg.

    News from the east was growing graver. The Germans had attacked with two Panzer Divisions and one Parachute Division. They had taken Meijel and were pushing on to Helmond. Clearly, Rundstedt was making a spoiling attack designed to interrupt Montgomery's operations to clear the Scheldt. Fortunately, however, the task of the 15th Scottish Division and of the 6th Guards Tank Brigade at Tilburg was already done: they were about to be squeezed out between the 7th Armoured Division and the 1st Corps.

    About noon, Division issued a warning order to the 227th Brigade and the Tank Scots Guards to move as soon as possible, and to the rest of the Division to move early next morning, 29th October. The 227th Brigade and their accompanying tanks got off about 4 P.M. and went ultimately to Asten, where, after a weary night march, they arrived in the early hours next morning.

29th Oct.   At 2.30 A.M. the 44th Brigade set out for Deurne, where it arrived at first light. The rest of the Division, preceded by reconnaissance parties, set out later in the morning. Only the Seaforth and the Pipe Bands stayed behind temporarily at Tilburg to represent the 15th Scottish Division in the march past at the ceremonial thanksgiving.

    So ended the liberation of Tilburg.

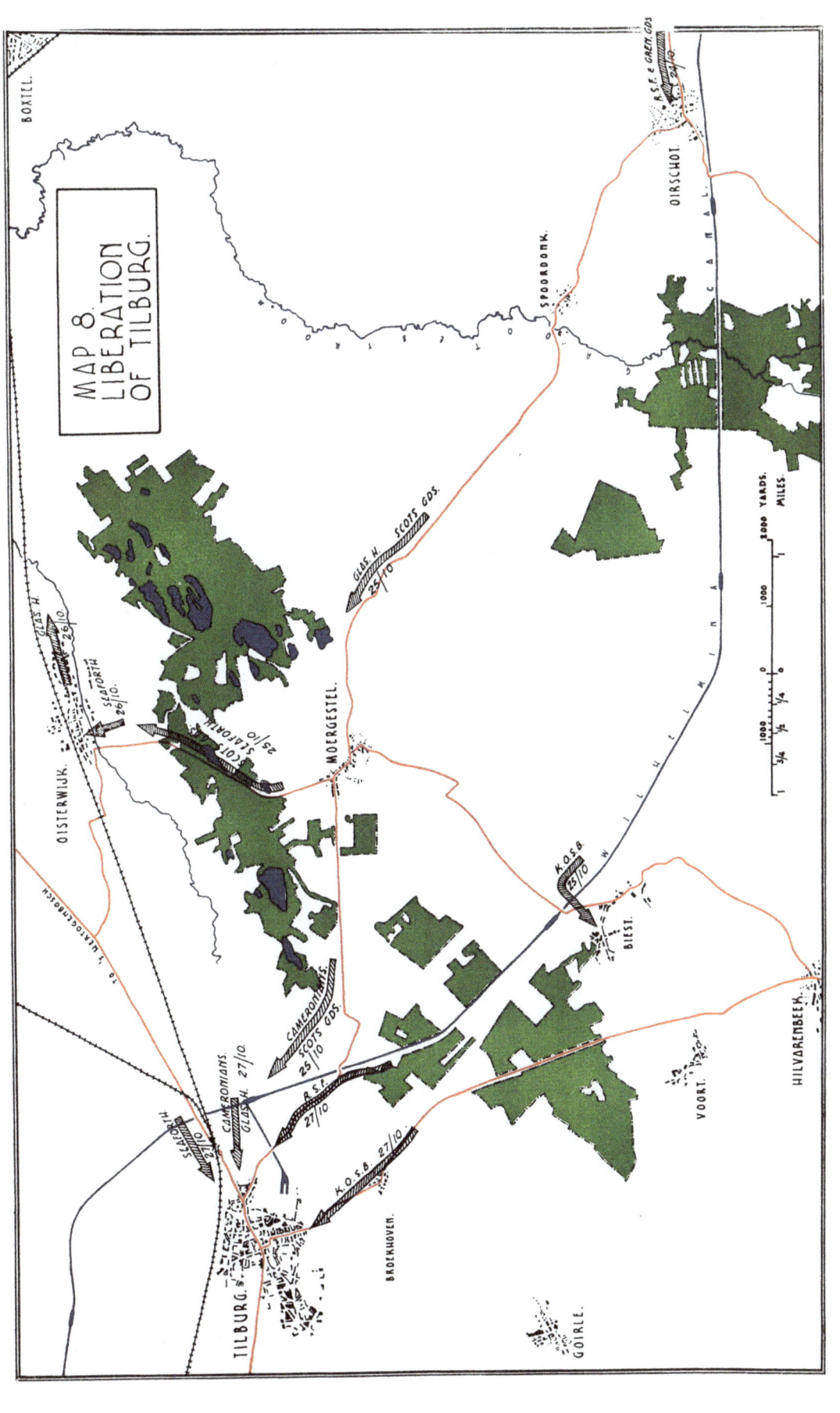

CHAPTER VII.

PART II.—MEIJEL.

How, it may be asked, had so critical a situation suddenly arisen on the 8th Corps' front ? We have to look back a couple of weeks for the answer.

27th and 28th Oct.

It will be remembered that, about the middle of October, Montgomery had found himself forced to halt the 8th Corps' drive eastward to the Maas in order to concentrate the 21st Army Group's whole offensive westward for the opening of the Scheldt. At that stage the 3rd Division had reached Venraij, with the 7th U.S. Armoured Division in the line to southward of it.

The 7th U.S. Armoured Division had thus found itself holding a " dog-leg " front some twenty-eight miles long, which extended from the Helmond-Venlo railway southward along the Deurne Canal to its junction with the Noorder Canal, thence south-west along the Noorder Canal to its junction with the Wessem Canal near Nederweert, and thence along the Wessem Canal south-eastward to the Maas at Wessem. All this immense front lies in the " Peel "—the vast, flat, desolate peat-bog of south-eastern Holland. It is an empty land of canals and dykes, heather and occasional vast woodlands that crown almost imperceptible eminences—a land where the movement of wheels and tracks is seldom possible off the roads and where the few poor villages and miserable crofts had already been more or less demolished in the fighting. In the winter months ahead the 15th Scottish Division was to have its bellyful of these peat-bogs of south-eastern Holland.

Opposite the 7th U.S. Armoured Division at this time had been the German 344th Division or " Division Walter," consisting of two parachute regiments—the Regiment Hubner along the Deurne Canal, the Regiment Hermann along the Noorder. It was through the front of the 344th Division that, towards the end of October, Rundstedt had decided to deliver with the 47th Panzer Corps his spoiling attack, which—or so he hoped—would interrupt the 21st Army Group's operations and so delay the opening of the Scheldt.

27th and 28th Oct.

Accordingly on 27th October the 9th Panzer Division and the 15th Panzer Grenadier Division had attacked across the Noorder Canal near Ospel and across the Deurne Canal at Meijel. Overextended as they were, the Americans had been unable to make any effective resistance. At the very outset the 47th Panzer Corps had taken not only Meijel itself but also the Hoogebrug bridge over the Deurne Canal farther north on the road from Helenaveen to Liesel. Thus the enemy had at once established a firm bridgehead in the angle formed by the Deurne and Noorder Canals.

Two roads run north-westward from this bridgehead towards Helmond, only thirteen miles away. The one runs through Liesel and Deurne, the other through the all-important cross-roads of Asten. Next day, 28th October, the Germans advanced along both roads, either pushing the Americans before them or else by-passing them. By evening the Germans were well beyond Liesel on the one road and were approaching Asten on the other. Despite very heavy losses of men and equipment, however, the remnants of the two U.S. Combat Commands on these roads fought on. In particular, the resistance of the party by-passed in Liesel was to be of immense value in delaying the enemy's progress. There was little enough left to stop the German advance, however, and Second Army Headquarters began to evacuate Helmond.

It was about mid-day on 28th October that the ripples caused by these disturbances spread to the 15th Scottish Division at Tilburg. The 227th Brigade had barely settled into its new brigade area when orders came to move east into 8th Corps reserve at Heeze, about nine miles west of Asten. Reconnaissance parties set out at once and reached Heeze in the late afternoon. Soon after, Brigadier Colville and his commanding officers went on to Asten. It was then that they realised something of the urgency of the situation. German aircraft were bombing Asten repeatedly, while sounds of heavy gunfire came from the south—ominously close at hand. Clearly, the 227th Brigade was needed much farther forward than Heeze.

The first unit to move up that evening was the 131st Field Regiment—still without orders to go into action. After various vicissitudes, Major Stewart, the Second-in-Command, was just getting the regiment into its new harbour about a mile west of Asten when two figures approached him in the moonlight and he heard a soft American voice ask, " Say, are you the field regiment we are expecting ? " The two Americans turned out to be the Brigade Major and Intelligence Officer of the 7th U.S. Armoured Divisional Artillery. How they had managed to find the 131st Field Regiment in the darkness and confusion remains a mystery. Quietly persistent, the Brigade Major urged that the 131st Field Regiment was needed in action then and there. He had everything laid on—the position reconnoitred, survey done, maps ready—and he was prepared to stay with the regiment throughout the night to see it in. And this indeed he did.

27th and 28th Oct.

Major Stewart at once got Lieutenant-Colonel John Hailey on the air, and the latter decided to put his regiment into action right away in the position reconnoitred by the Americans. The 131st Field Regiment advanced accordingly through Asten and thence nearly two miles southward down the Asten-Meijel road, to go into action about midnight east of the road and about level with Heusden. West of the road the 25th Field Regiment of the 8th Corps' A.G.R.A. had already been in action for a day or more, and it had an O.P. with the U.S. infantry still farther south. The 131st Field Regiment started shooting on this O.P.'s orders as soon as it was in, and it fired continuously for the rest of the night.

Meanwhile the remaining units of the 227th Brigade Group, together with the 3rd Tank Scots Guards, had also come up to the neighbourhood of Asten through the night. After giving his battalions a brief rest, Brigadier Colville towards morning put them into defensive positions in the southern outskirts of Asten for its close defence. Thus it came about that, when dawn broke, the 131st and 25th Field Regiments found themselves a good mile and a half in front of their own infantry.

29th Oct.

By this time the 131st Field Regiment was running very short of ammunition. Ranges, too, were growing shorter and shorter and expenditure was continuing at an alarming rate, while in answer to protests the 25th Field Regiment insisted that things out in front were much too critical to allow of any husbanding of ammunition. The situation was explained to all ranks, and all preparations were made for local defence. It was a fine morning and, though all knew that they might be engaging enemy tanks and infantry over open sights at any moment, spirits were high. The unexpected arrival of an anti-tank troop of 17-pounders raised them still higher.

It was about 11 a.m.—when the 131st Field Regiment was down

to about ten rounds per gun—that the full nakedness of the land was revealed. A party of American soldiers came straggling up the road towards Asten. These stragglers, it turned out, were almost the last of the Americans, amounting to two platoons, left in action on the Meijel road. Now that this party had packed up, there was only one platoon still fighting forward of the guns. Indeed, but for the fire of the guns the enemy might have walked into Asten at any time in the last twenty-four hours. Small wonder, then, that the Brigade Major of Artillery had been so anxious to see the 131st in action. Soon after, providentially, some ammunition reached the 131st from the 25th Field Regiment, and later in the day further supplies came up from the rear. Till evening these two field regiments continued to hold off the enemy on the Asten-Meijel road by their fire alone. This is perhaps the only instance of such an occurrence in the annals of the 21st Army Group.

So much, then, for the happenings on the Asten-Meijel road. Let us see what was happening on the other road—from Deurne to Meijel.

In the very early hours of 29th October the 44th Brigade had left Tilburg on its journey to Deurne, where, pending the arrival of Main Headquarters, 15th Scottish Division, it was to come temporarily under the command of the 11th Armoured Division. At about 4 A.M. that dark autumn morning Brigadier Cockburn reached 11th Armoured Division Headquarters in Deurne. There no one could tell him anything very definite. The U.S. Combat Command in the Liesel area was believed to have been overrun. The Germans were advancing northward on Deurne and might be no more than a mile or two away. Major-General G. B. P. Roberts, Commander of the 11th Armoured Division, had managed to collect the 14/18th Hussars of his own Division and the 1st East Yorks of the 3rd Division—no more units were available—and to deploy these astride the Deurne-Meijel road south of Deurne, but the 3rd Division farther east was urgent in its demands for the early return of the 1st East Yorks. Such was the picture. As his battalions arrived about first light, Brigadier Cockburn put them straight from the line of march into positions for the close defence of Deurne against attack from the south.

The hours that followed seemed like an eternity. The rest of the 15th Scottish Division, with the guns and the bulk of the 6th Guards Tank Brigade, was still far behind. Reports, each more alarmist than the last, kept coming in, to tell of the loss of Liesel, the approach of German troops, the appearance of German tanks here, there, and everywhere. But of the Americans there was no news at all—and, inevitably, no news appeared to be the worst of news.

29th Oct.

At about 6 A.M. that morning the Divisional Commander had met the Commanders of the 8th Corps and of the 7th U.S. Armoured Division at Zommern. They had agreed that he must get his three infantry brigade groups on the ground as quickly as possible. The Divisional Commander had then gone to find the two American Combat Commanders whom he had met in the fields beyond Asten. They had given him a clear and soldier-like picture of the situation, but it was clear that their commands were fast breaking up under the strain. He reached Deurne in the course of the morning. The real crisis, he had already realised, was likely to come not here but on the side-road from Liesel to Asten. The Germans held Liesel. If they were to advance west along this side-road they would soon be in possession of the vital cross-roads of Asten—and in rear of the 227th Brigade. It was a matter of the utmost urgency, therefore, to fill this gap. Readiest to the Divisional Commander's hand for this purpose was the 44th Brigade. He decided, therefore, to send it to Asten and to replace it outside Deurne as soon as possible by the 46th Brigade, which would be due up shortly in its turn. He issued orders to Brigadiers Cockburn and Villiers accordingly.

Preceded by their reconnaissance and command post parties, the battalions of the 46th Brigade had left Tilburg well after daylight that morning, heading for Helmond. *En route* they had been deflected to Deurne. At Deurne about noon Brigadier Villiers met his three commanding officers and told them to get on with the relief of the 44th Brigade as quickly as possible. Meanwhile, however—about 11.30 A.M. —German tanks had been reported only a mile or two south-east of Deurne. Thereupon Brigadier Cockburn had ordered the K.O.S.B. to advance through the 14/18th Hussars' screen and to take up a defensive position astride the Liesel road about a couple of miles south of Deurne. In view, therefore, of the move of the K.O.S.B. southward which was then taking place, coupled with the imminence of a German attack on Deurne itself, the Divisional Commander had to modify the plan : the K.O.S.B., he decided, would remain in their new position south of Deurne, coming under orders of the 46th Brigade ; while the Cameronians, who were leading battalion of the 46th Brigade, would replace the K.O.S.B. in the 44th Brigade for its move to Asten.

29th Oct.

It was a race against time, and in the outcome it was the Glasgow Highlanders who went in place of the Cameronians; for about 2 P.M. the Divisional Commander happened to meet Major Campbell Davies, commanding the Glasgow Highlanders, when he was looking for Lieutenant-Colonel Sir Edward Bradford of the Cameronians, whereupon he at once placed the Glasgow Highlanders under command of the 44th Brigade instead of the Cameronians.

During the afternoon Brigadier Villiers put the Seaforth and the Cameronians into position behind the K.O.S.B.—the Seaforth taking the place of the Royal Scots west of the Deurne-Meijel road, the Cameronians taking the place of the R.S.F. east of it. Here the 46th Brigade remained for the night. At dusk any Americans who were able to do so withdrew through it.

Meanwhile the 44th Brigade (less the K.O.S.B.) had gone off to Asten, Brigadier Cockburn having first ordered the Glasgow Highlanders to follow to a rendezvous north of the town. He had learnt that remnants of the U.S. Combat Command were still holding out in Liesel and also in Leensel, which is a village about a mile west of Liesel on the road to Asten. Brigadier Cockburn's plan was to send the R.S.F. through Asten to relieve the Americans in Leensel, while the Royal Scots held a back-stop position in Rinkveld and Voordeldonk on the road back to Asten, and the Glasgow Highlanders blocked the western exits of a very large wood which lies immediately to the southward of Leensel.

In accordance with this plan the R.S.F. and the Royal Scots were in position before 6 P.M. Not so the Glasgow Highlanders. Major Campbell Davies had got his orders at Voordeldonk only about 5 P.M., and had then set off on a hurried reconnaissance in fading light. Half an hour later new orders reached him. It had been found impossible to relieve the Americans; instead, they would withdraw between 6 and 8 P.M. through the 44th Brigade. The boundary between the 227th Brigade and the 44th Brigade would have to be moved northward. The positions of the R.S.F. and the Royal Scots would remain unchanged, but the Glasgow Highlanders would now have to occupy a defensive position in the north-east corner of the large wood aforesaid, where there were thought to be some American troops in close touch with the enemy.

This unavoidable change of plan presented the Glasgow Highlanders with an awkward problem. First, they would have to make their way in inky darkness through the depths of an unknown wood where they might or might not find the enemy, and then they would have to take up an unreconnoitred position exactly at the time when the Germans might be expected to be following up the Americans' withdrawal. Moreover, all this they must do without the help of tanks or medium machine-guns or an anti-tank troop, R.A., since none of these was available.

29th Oct.

Major Campbell Davies solved his problem in this wise: he assembled his battalion in the darkness behind the firm base provided by the R.S.F. in Leensel, while he sent fighting patrols forward through the wood to establish themselves, and to link up, on the objective. This, despite the manifold difficulties of direction-keeping through the wood, the patrols did successfully, whereupon the Glasgow Highlanders closed up behind them. By 10 P.M. the leading companies were on their objective; by midnight the battalion layout had been co-ordinated. The Glasgow Highlanders' position was extremely isolated. True, on their left rear there were the R.S.F. and the Royal Scots, but on their right there was the whole undefended area of the wood, which extended southward for a mile or more and offered a perfect covered approach to the Germans. The night passed quietly, however, but for intermittent shelling—sometimes extremely heavy. Patrols had contacted the enemy in a farm close by in the direction of Slot.

We must now return to the 227th Brigade, whose battalions had taken up defensive positions that morning on the southern outskirts of Asten. They remained there throughout the day. At dusk Brigadier Colville moved them southward, past his guns, along the road towards Meijel. On the south side of the road, about three miles out of Asten, there is a large wood on a slight rise. There the H.L.I. took up a position astride the road: they found soon enough that the wood had been carefully registered by the enemy. The Gordons dug in farther north, between the H.L.I. and that other wood south of Leensel, the north-east corner of which, as we have seen, the Glasgow Highlanders were to occupy. The Argylls were in Brigade reserve in the gun area, astride the road at Heusden and behind the H.L.I. In or near these positions the 227th Brigade was destined to remain till mid-November.

By the end of the day the tension generally was easing. The 15th Scottish Division had arrived and was firmly established on the ground. The dangerous gap had been closed between the 46th Brigade south of

29th Oct. Deurne and the 227th Brigade south of Asten. The task that now lay before the Division was to clear the country from the Helmond-Venlo railway in the north as far south as an east-and-west line through Meijel, and eastward up to the Deurne Canal.

Much farther south the 4th Armoured Brigade Group had also come up that day to reinforce the extreme right of the 7th U.S. Armoured Division's front in the Wessem Canal sector beyond the Noorder Canal. This reinforcement was intended to free the 7th U.S. Armoured Division to concentrate centrally preparatory to clearing the country on the 15th Scottish Division's right flank, between Meijel and the Noorder Canal.

That night the 15th Scottish Division had a foretaste of the bombardments it was to endure so often in the subsequent fighting on the approaches to Meijel. Three features of this fighting were to remain fixed in the memories of all who took part in it. First, there was the enemy's advantage of position. The 15th Scottish Division's main axis of advance on Meijel was down the road from Deurne, which runs parallel and ever nearer to the Deurne Canal. The farther bank of this canal was to remain throughout in the enemy's possession. In this dead flat country in consequence the enemy were to have perfect observation of the road and would be able to follow up the 15th Scottish Division's every move with accurate enfilade and reverse fire.

Secondly, there was the weight of guns and mortars that the enemy had contrived to deploy in support of this spoiling attack of theirs—a weight such as the Division had not encountered since the days of Eterville and Evrecy. These guns were massed beyond the Deurne Canal, mainly in the area to the southward of Amerika, and they seemed to have unlimited ammunition. In consequence, the 15th Scottish Division, which at first was the only Division operating in the area, was to find itself time and again the target of blistering gun and mortar concentrations. Liesel, Hutten, Heitrak, and the approaches to Meijel itself—all of these were to win a horrid notoriety.

Thirdly, there were the mines. Much of the country is impassable bog; all of it is intersected by ditches and waterways. The firmer areas between—the roads, verges, tracks, pull-ins—the enemy as they withdrew sowed with an assortment of every sort of mine—Teller, "R," "S," and the new and deadly Schu—in a profusion that the Division had never before encountered. These three factors and the rain conditioned all the fighting that followed. It was to be the wettest November on record.

1ST MIDDLESEX IN ACTION NEAR MEIJEL

Clearly, Liesel was now the key-point. On it next day the Divisional Commander proposed to make two converging attacks—from the west and from the north. The Tank Grenadiers and the Tank Coldstream were arriving and would be available for this operation.

29th Oct.

At an early hour the R.S.F. advanced from their defensive position in the defile between the two woods at Leensel to develop an attack on Liesel from the north-west. They had in support a squadron of the Tank Grenadier Guards.

30th Oct.

The enemy, however, had not yet realised that they were now up against the 15th Scottish Division, so they still had ideas of their own as to how the battle should progress. At about 8.15 A.M. the Glasgow Highlanders saw from their wood a force of Germans forming up in the direction of Slot. The whole affair was a lamentable exhibition, for the German officer in charge was smoking a large cigar while he let his men bunch unashamedly in the open. He must have got the shock of his life when our defensive fire descended to nip the attack.

That was only the beginning, however. About 9 A.M. the enemy began tapping all along the Glasgow Highlanders' front, while from Slot came sounds of tanks moving forward. An hour later the enemy put down on the Glasgow Highlanders' forward company areas a series of artillery and mortar concentrations reminiscent of the fiercest fighting in Normandy. The German infantry then closed, accompanied by one or two tanks or S.P. guns. Very close fighting along the whole battalion front followed. At the same time the enemy began to infiltrate round both flanks—along the edge of the wood to the northward and into the gap left by the R.S.F., which had not yet been filled by the Royal Scots, and into the undefended expanse of woodland to the southward.

By this time a M.M.G. platoon of the Middlesex had arrived under the command of Lieutenant Lloyd. He sited one of his sections to block the front edge of the wood, but the German tanks quickly knocked out both guns. After that the enemy poured unchecked into the wood to the southward. At the same time German tanks and infantry overran one of the Glasgow Highlanders' forward platoon localities. The wood was so thick that two S.P. A.Tk. guns which now came up were unable to get into position to engage the German tanks. Lieutenant Lloyd, however, got his other M.M.G. section into action with

30th Oct.

the utmost gallantry under close-range fire. Unfortunately he was to be killed later in the campaign, but not before he had been awarded the M.C. for his devotion to duty on this day.

Brigadier Cockburn had promised Major Campbell Davies a squadron of the Tank Grenadier Guards and also a company of the Royal Scots, to which he later added a second company. Meanwhile, however, the enemy had spread all through the wood, where they had immobilised all four rifle companies of the Glasgow Highlanders, and whence they emerged to open fire on the Royal Scots as they passed the north-western corner.

It was the arrival of the squadron of the Tank Grenadiers soon after mid-day that restored the situation. With the tanks moving along the broad rides in support, the Glasgow Highlanders very soon cleared the wood between their company areas and pushed the Germans back towards Slot. On the heels of the Grenadiers came the two reinforcing companies of the Royal Scots, whom Major Campbell Davies put in on the right to extend the Glasgow Highlanders' front southward. Later, one of these companies left to rejoin the remainder of the Royal Scots in Leensel, while the other completed the clearing of the wood with the help of the Tank Grenadiers. The Grenadiers then withdrew to harbour in Rinkveld, where they remained in support. So the grim fight ended. The Glasgow Highlanders and their supporting arms had suffered over eighty casualties; the machine-gunners in particular had only enough men left for two skeleton gun crews.

Meanwhile the R.S.F., with another squadron of Tank Grenadiers in support, had been pushing their attack on Liesel from the north-west. They had met intense fire from beyond the canal, however, and fierce resistance round the church, where the enemy was holding several pill-boxes, so their progress had been slow. At about 4.30 P.M. they reported that they were on the road on the north-western outskirts of Liesel, fully committed, and that they could not reach their final objectives. In the evening the R.S.F., with the help of the leading elements of the 46th Brigade which had come down from the north, repelled a violent counter-attack from the east.

Next we come to the 46th Brigade. At 9.30 A.M. that morning the Seaforth had passed through the K.O.S.B. to carry out an "advance-to-contact" move down the road from Deurne towards Loon and Liesel. The Tank Coldstream Guards were in support. The Cameronians moved wide on the east flank to protect the left towards the canal.

It was Brigadier Villiers's intention that, when the Seaforth had occupied Liesel, the K.O.S.B. should go through to Slot. 30th Oct.

The Seaforth took Loon without much difficulty, the Cameronians moving parallel with them to the east. At Loon, however, the Seaforth came under very heavy mortar-fire and every attempt they made to advance into Liesel was met by the short-range fire of S.P. 88-mm.s, so they dug-in in the northern outskirts of Liesel and made ready to clear the place next day. They had now made contact with the R.S.F. on their right front. In the evening the Seaforth helped the R.S.F. to beat off the enemy's counter-attack from the east.

By the end of this day's fighting the German Command had realised that they were up against strong reinforcements west of the Deurne Canal. Theirs had been a spoiling attack, the initial success of which they had been quick to exploit. Now, however, the fighting was getting too costly for them—already it had cost them twenty-five tanks and three S.P. guns—so it was time to call off the attack. That night, as afterwards became known, the 47th Panzer Corps was withdrawn across the Deurne Canal, while the Parachute Regiment Hubner took over the sector once more, still supported by some armour and by the full weight of artillery massed beyond the canal. Though the presence of Tiger tanks had been reported more than once, neither Tiger nor Panther had in fact been able to cross the Hoogebrug bridge, so throughout this fighting the enemy never used anything larger than a Mark IV. west of the Deurne Canal.

31st October dawned black and lowering. Low cloud and smoke limited visibility to about a hundred yards. 31st Oct.

The principal event of the day was the capture of Liesel and Slot by the 46th Brigade, with the support of the Tank Coldstream—and with the help of the R.S.F. at Liesel. At 8.30 A.M. the 46th Brigade advanced south from Loon on a two-battalion front. On the right the Seaforth attacked under a barrage and with two companies up. Their right company went in astride the main road, their left company over the open country immediately east of Liesel. Simultaneously the R.S.F., still farther to the right, advanced with Tank Grenadier support to clear the more westerly portion of Liesel.

Out on the left and abreast of the Seaforth, the Cameronians—also with two companies up—advanced southward across the open bog. Their task was to protect the left of the 46th Brigade, and their

31st Oct. objective was the Loonsche Bann or track, which runs eastward from the southern end of Liesel to the canal.

As they pushed on behind the barrage the Seaforth found the enemy's slit-trenches full of dead—satisfactory proof of the effectiveness of the guns. Over the open country to the eastward of the road their left forward company got on quickly enough and was on its objective within an hour. The right forward company, on the other hand, had to do some slow and difficult house-clearing along the main road through Liesel. Moreover, enemy shelling was extremely heavy, and the main road was soon blocked by burning vehicles. The Jocks, however, made such good use of their weapons that by about 1 P.M. they had taken the whole eastern portion of the village and over fifty prisoners with it. The R.S.F. meanwhile had cleared the western portion.

All this time the Cameronians out on the left had been pushing southward under accurate enemy observation from beyond the canal. "C" Company on the right had reached the Loonsche Bann of Liesel without much difficulty and had there linked up with the Seaforth. "D" Company on the left had had a much rougher passage. It had been directed on the cross-tracks on the Loonsche Bann, which lie about fourteen hundred yards east of the main road —less than half-way out, that is, along the track towards the Deurne Canal. Beyond "D" Company's left, in the two thousand yards or so between it and the canal, there was an enemy force going spare which the Cameronians reckoned at about three companies. The enemy was also holding localities round the cross-tracks and was in the farms that are strung out along the Loonsche Bann to the westward of them. "D" Company found itself under intense shelling and machine-gun fire. The company commander was killed; the second-in-command, two platoon commanders, and the C.S.M. wounded. None the less "D" Company, after reorganising under the command of Captain Carruthers who had been sent up from "A," went on to clear the farms to the westward of the cross-tracks. Throughout this action the carrier platoon under Captain Lisle—who later got an M.C. —did fine work clearing up pockets of enemy resistance between "D" and "C" Companies. Unfortunately the Cameronians lost Lieutenant-Colonel Sir Edward Bradford, who was wounded when his carrier struck a mine on its way from "C" to "D" Company. Major Hendriks took temporary command.

Both forward companies had to consolidate in ground too boggy for digging and under accurate enemy fire. After dark "D" Company managed to get a fighting patrol through to its objective, the crosstracks, where the patrol dug in. The Cameronians had lost one officer killed and three wounded, fourteen other ranks killed and fifty wounded —nearly all from "D" Company.

On the southern outskirts of Liesel itself the Seaforth had consolidated in the early afternoon, with the enemy still close in front of them. With their perfect observation from the east, the enemy was making Liesel itself an inferno. At about 3 P.M. the K.O.S.B., together with their supporting squadron of Tank Coldstream, formed up on a start-line behind the Seaforth's forward localities in preparation for an attack on Slot. Overlooking the whole proceedings, at very close range, there was a large windmill. Before the K.O.S.B. moved off one of the Churchills fired a round into the windmill just for luck. Thereupon out trooped a whole platoon of fully armed Germans—to be duly put in the bag.

The K.O.S.B. advanced on a two-company front astride the road. Both forward companies at once came under the inevitable mortar-fire. Soon after, the right forward company was stopped altogether by the fire of an enemy tank cleverly hidden in a house in Slot. Lieutenant Wood stalked it and destroyed it with a P.I.A.T.—an action for which he later got an M.C. About the same time the Churchills with the left-forward company knocked out a second Mark IV. tank. The K.O.S.B. leap-frogged companies in Slot and pushed on to a wood and farm farther south, where they consolidated. The reconnaissance troop of the Coldstream, pushing on another fifteen hundred yards or so through Hutten, ran into an enemy position that stretched from Kleine Heitrak across the road to Hoogebrug. Seeing that his troop was in trouble, the commanding officer of the Coldstream, Lieutenant-Colonel A. W. A. Smith, went forward in his own tank with an F.O.O. and extricated all but one Honey tank, the crew of which he brought back wounded. Night fell to the accompaniment of very heavy enemy concentrations, particularly on Liesel and Slot. The gathering darkness was lit by the glare of burning farms and stackyards.

Next we come to the 44th Brigade. The R.S.F., as we have seen, had taken the western portion of Liesel that morning. The Glasgow Highlanders were still in the north-eastern corner of their wood by Leensel. Just before 4 P.M. the Royal Scots, with Tank Grenadier

31st Oct. support, proceeded to sweep the southern and eastern portions of this wood once more. This action of theirs drew upon them a real tornado of gun and mortar-fire. The bursts in the trees were particularly deadly, and the Royal Scots had a lot of casualties before the job was done.

On the 227th Brigade's front, too, the H.L.I. had been having trouble with enemy parties which had been infiltrating into the large wood in their area, first on the night of 29th/30th October and again on the night of 30th/31st October. The first infiltration the H.L.I. had dealt with fairly easily by beating through the wood at daylight. The next infiltration on the night of 30th/31st October was a more serious affair, and it caused so critical a situation that Lieutenant-Colonel Mackley called on his accompanying battery commander, Major John Oliver, to put down an "Uncle"—Divisional artillery—concentration on the wood. Since the wood had not been registered and the H.L.I. had two companies immediately east of it and another immediately west, Major Oliver demurred, whereupon Lieutenant-Colonel Mackley accepted responsibility for any casualties that the concentration might cause. Down it came—on scale 5 from every gun in the Division—and it was repeated more than once. There was not a loose round or a British casualty, but the wood was so thoroughly plastered that the enemy ever after gave it a wide berth.

1st Nov. The 46th Brigade's first task next morning was to dispose of the three enemy companies believed still to be wide of the Cameronians' left. To this end the Cameronians changed direction east abreast of Liesel, while the Seaforth farther south changed direction east abreast of Slot. Then, at 8 A.M., both battalions advanced eastward towards the canal under intense covering fire from artillery and machine-guns. When they had gone half a mile or so, the supporting tanks could go no farther through the bottomless mud. The infantry went on, meeting little opposition other than mortar-fire: the enemy had already gone across the canal and in such haste that they had left a lot of their equipment behind. The Seaforth and Cameronians consolidated as best they could, facing east a little short of the canal. The ground was too boggy for digging.

At 10.30 A.M. the Glasgow Highlanders had reverted to the 46th Brigade and had moved to Liesel. According to plan, they were to have advanced through the K.O.S.B. in Slot and to have occupied

Hutten. Meanwhile, however, K.O.S.B. patrols had found Hutten unoccupied. About noon, therefore, Brigadier Villiers ordered the K.O.S.B. south through Hutten on Heitrak. A squadron of the Reconnaissance Regiment went ahead. Short of Heitrak the squadron found the enemy still in occupation of the position from Kleine Heitrak to the Hoogebrug bridge. In consequence the K.O.S.B. were ordered to halt for the night in Hutten and to revert to the 44th Brigade. It was at this stage that the 44th Brigade took over from the 46th Brigade responsibility for the advance on Meijel. For the next day's operation the Glasgow Highlanders also reverted once more to the command of the 44th Brigade. At 10 P.M. that night Brigadier Cockburn issued his orders for the attack southward next day, with Moostdijk as the final objective. *1st Nov.*

On 2nd November the 44th Brigade's four-day battle for Meijel began. It was a morning of thick mist with visibility down to thirty or forty yards. At 9.30 A.M. the Glasgow Highlanders on the right and the R.S.F. on the left passed the start-line—it was the front edge of the K.O.S.B. position in Hutten—and advanced southward with the Tank Grenadier Guards in support. There was little opposition, but one Churchill and three Flails were blown up by mines. By 10.30 A.M. both battalions were on their objective, which was Heitrak itself and the track that runs east from it. At Heitrak the Glasgow Highlanders again reverted to the 46th Brigade. *2nd Nov.*

In the afternoon the Royal Scots on the right and the K.O.S.B. on the left passed through, directed on Neerkant and Moostdijk. It was a difficult advance along narrow tracks through thick pine-woods. There were mines everywhere and the enemy's mortaring and shelling were merciless. The K.O.S.B. ended up as forward battalion in Moostdijk, with a dense belt of assorted mines just ahead of them on which a Churchill and an armoured car blew up. The accompanying squadron of Tank Grenadiers tried to push on beyond the minefield, but was stopped by heavy fire. Evidently Meijel itself and Vieruitersten or "Diamond Wood" to the north-east of it formed the core of the enemy's defensive position.

The 46th Brigade had now taken over responsibility for the protection of the east flank along the Deurne Canal. In the morning the Cameronians had come down to Slot, whence in the afternoon they drove eastward on a three-company front along the axis Slot-Hoogebrug

2nd Nov. bridge. But for one bit of cover within fifty yards of the bridge the bog was dead flat. The Cameronians maintained a standing patrol of one platoon in this cover. For the rest they dug in facing the bridge and about a thousand yards back from it. Here they found themselves on the right of the Seaforth, on whose left they had been the day before. Still farther to the right the Glasgow Highlanders advanced eastward to dig in to the southward of the Cameronians.

All this time the 227th Brigade had remained in its defensive positions at and south-east of Heusden. This day two companies of the Argylls and a squadron of the Tank Scots Guards staged an operation against the large wood on a hillock in the middle of the bog, about one and a half miles south of Heusden: harbouring in this wood was supposed to be a pool of enemy infantry who found all the patrols for the whole neighbourhood. The Argylls reached the wood and cleared the enemy out of it. The tanks, however, found the going impossible, and two of them were bogged short of the wood. The Scots Guards set to work to pull these out under cover of a smoke-screen, whereupon the Argylls mistook the smoke for the withdrawal signal and withdrew accordingly. The enemy followed up in the growing dusk. The brunt of a difficult rearguard action over dead flat country strewn with mines fell on "A" Company of the Argylls. The Scots Guards had to abandon one of their tanks, which they recovered intact next day.

Turning now to the wider picture, we find a new plan of campaign taking shape for the Second Army. The enemy's Meijel offensive had served to convince Montgomery that Rundstedt's bridgehead west of the Maas constituted a permanent threat to the Nijmegen salient. Before Montgomery could mount his battle of the Rhineland from that salient, therefore, he must eliminate Rundstedt's bridgehead. On 2nd November Montgomery ordered the Second Army to line up for a drive eastward to the Maas. In the north would be the 8th Corps, of which the 15th Scottish Division would still form part; in the centre would be the 12th Corps; in the south the 30th Corps. The target date for the beginning of the drive Montgomery gave as 12th November.

3rd Nov. During the night K.O.S.B. patrols had found no enemy within eight hundred yards of Moostdijk. The minefield was still very much there, however, and enemy fire was heavy. At 7.30 A.M. the three surviving Flails went on down the road with an escorting squadron of Tank Grenadiers. The Flails' job was to clear a passage through the minefield for the Reconnaissance Regiment. All three Flails were blown up and three of the Churchills were hit, but the passage was cleared. The Reconnaissance Regiment could not get much farther, however, either down the road or eastward towards the canal.

3rd Nov.

For the attack on Meijel next day Brigadier Cockburn's plan was this. By a preliminary operation the K.O.S.B. were to secure for the R.S.F. a start-line near Schelm. From this start-line the R.S.F., with Tank Grenadier support, were to advance southward and take Schans. At the same time another squadron of the Tank Grenadiers, crossing the start-line still farther east, was to swing wide to the eastward of Diamond Wood and come in on it from the rear. Finally, with the R.S.F. holding a firm base in Schans, the Royal Scots and the K.O.S.B. were to go through with tank support and take Meijel and Diamond Wood respectively.

A glance at the map will suffice to demonstrate one fact: the squadron of the Tank Grenadiers, whose rôle it would be to go round between Diamond Wood and the canal, was booked for a rough passage unless something could be done either to screen the canal bank or to neutralise the mass of enemy guns beyond it. Indeed, enemy shelling had now grown to such proportions that any movement along the main Divisional axis south of Liesel was becoming most difficult. At 10 P.M., therefore, 8th Corps sanctioned a postponement of the attack for twenty-four hours. The next day was to be devoted to bringing up plenty of smoke-shell and to methodical counter-battery work against the enemy's guns.

It was a wet night and enemy shelling was severe. During the night the K.O.S.B. took Schelm as a preliminary to the 44th Brigade's attack now scheduled for 5th November.

By this time conditions on the front of the 46th and 227th Brigades had become those of static warfare, so both Brigades instituted a system of reliefs whereby two battalions spent ten days in the line while the third spent five days out at rest. The 46th Brigade normally sent its battalions to rest in a comfortable camp in the woods half-way between Deurne and Liesel. The camp belonged to the Princess Irene (Dutch) Brigade, and here, for the first time in four and a half years, Dutchmen were training—within a few thousand yards of the front-line. The Commandant, Major Looringen van Beek, gave the 46th

3rd Nov.

Brigade every help and kindness. The 227th Brigade rested in Asten. The weather was atrocious. Back in Asten the men were able to get hot showers, dry clothes, rest, entertainment; while in the line the work of patrols, snipers, and O.P.s was brought to a very high pitch.

Immediately south of the 15th Scottish Division's sector, Combat Commands "A" and "R" of the 7th U.S. Armoured Division had now been in action for the past forty-eight hours. Having cleared the country that lies in the angle south-west of Ospel, between the Zuid Willems Vaart and Noorder Canals, these Combat Commands had now turned eastward along the north bank of the Noorder Canal. By midnight on 4th/5th November they were approaching Stokers Horst.

4th Nov.

During 4th November preparations for the 44th Brigade's attack were completed. Large quantities of smoke-shell were dumped.

5th Nov.

This was to be a day of sad mishaps. For once, however, it dawned crisp and clear, with excellent visibility. As the troops moved up to the start-line they could see the Germans bustling about like ants beyond the canal two thousand yards away.

First to cross the start-line was No. 2 Squadron of the Tank Grenadiers. It advanced from Schelm at 7.30 A.M., heading southeast towards Diamond Wood. At the same time the artillery put down their smoke to screen the wood from the canal.

All eyes were on the Grenadiers as they went ahead, through ever-deepening mud and a hail of fire. At the very start they had lost one of their tanks on a mine. After that it seemed that nothing could stop them. On they went till they had all but reached the northeast corner of the wood where they would have turned south to circle round it. Then there came disaster, sudden and complete. In their path was a bottomless bog liberally salted with mines—and they went right into it.

One after another tanks blew up whichever way they turned; tracks merely churned the mud, so manœuvre was impossible; all the while the enemy were putting down upon the bog everything they had got. If any tanks were to survive at all, the only course was to get the squadron out, so it was ordered to rally on the start-line eight hundred yards back. But only four tanks emerged from the bog, of which two were battle-worthy: the rest were stuck fast or disabled. For ten and a half hours that day the artillery kept up their

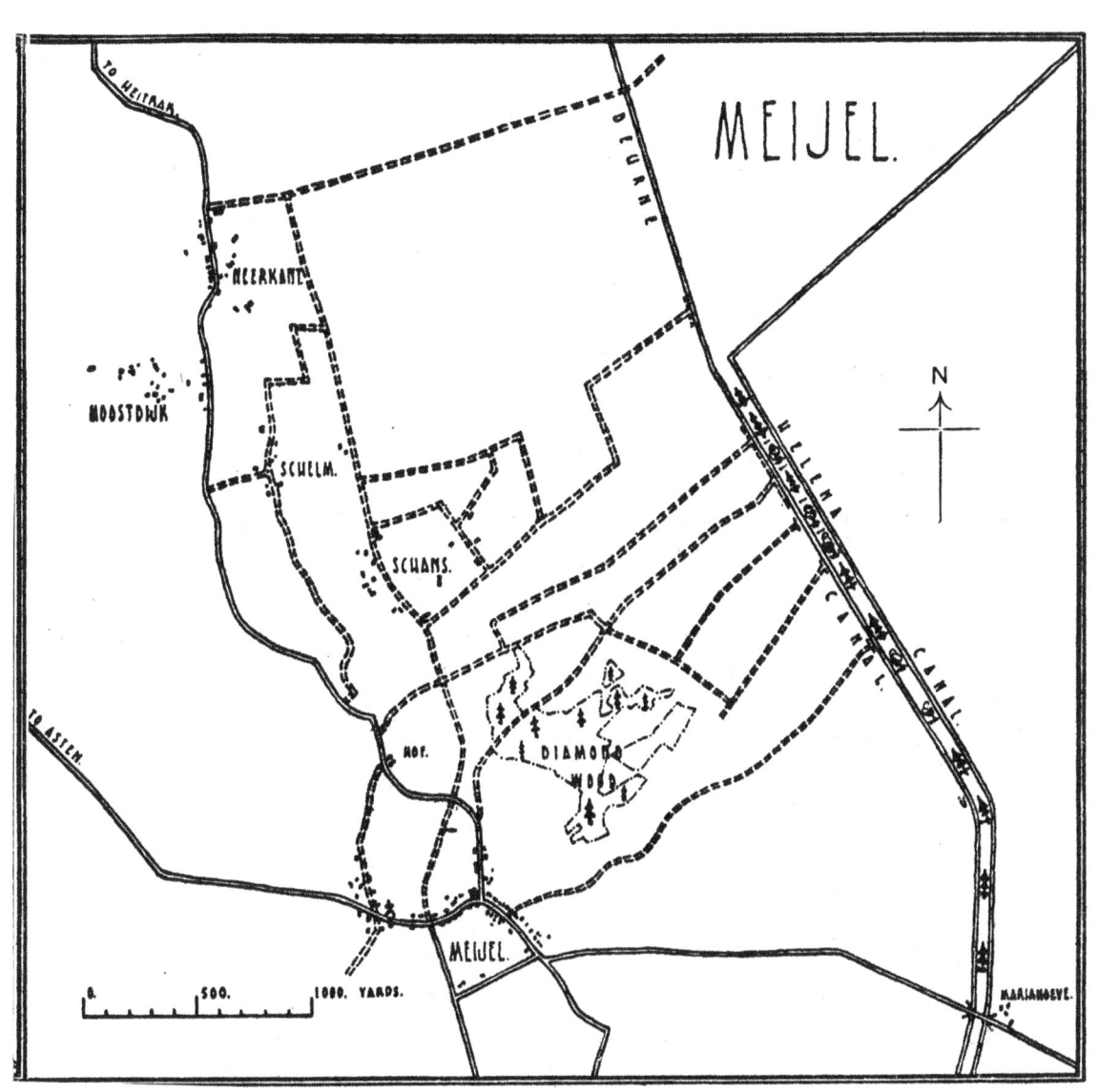

5th Nov. smoke-screen along six hundred yards of the canal bank. Under the cover of this screen the Grenadiers withdrew the crews and vital parts of these derelict tanks, together with their wounded and their codes.

Meanwhile at 8.45 A.M.—a quarter of an hour, that is, after No. 2 Squadron of the Tank Grenadiers had started on its gallant but disastrous venture—the R.S.F. on the right, supported by No. 1 Squadron, had advanced from Schelm in their turn and had headed south for Schans. Within twenty minutes of the start no less than five of No. 1 Squadron's tanks went up in the minefield: there was nothing for it but to halt the survivors. The R.S.F. went on. By 9 A.M. the forward platoons of their two forward companies had got as far as Schans. Not so the supporting platoons: they had been pinned in the open short of Schans by the enemy's fire from beyond the canal, which was now dominating the battle-field. Seeing the infantry's plight, No. 2 Squadron Commander ordered one of his troops to make its way up to Schans regardless of mines. The troop managed to break through the minefield, only to have all four of its tanks knocked out by A.Tk. gun-fire.

By this time it had become clear that to take Meijel from the north was not possible. On either hand were impassable bogs; the narrow isthmus of firm land between was barred by every sort of mine and swept by fire; on flank and rear beyond the canal the enemy had complete freedom of movement and observation. At about 12.30 P.M., therefore, the Divisional Commander called off the attack and ordered the R.S.F. to withdraw into Divisional reserve. The K.O.S.B. thus became the forward battalion once more. That night the Royal Scots came up on the left of the K.O.S.B.

6th Nov. For the next ten days or so static warfare conditions were to prevail in every sector of the Meijel front. In the 44th Brigade's sector the enemy were back in Schans and in Diamond Wood and to the northward of it. Any advance of the 227th Brigade from the north-west was barred by the great belt of marshland which lies athwart the road Asten-Meijel to the south-west of Moostdijk. West of Meijel the U.S. Combat Commands "A" and "R" had bogged down in the Peel about one and a half miles short of the main road that runs southward from Meijel to the Roggelsche bridge across the Noorder Canal.

On this day the R.S.F. came under the 227th Brigade and relieved the H.L.I., who went back to rest in Asten.

On 7th November the Tank Coldstream and Scots Guards pulled out to rest at Helmond, where they joined the Tank Grenadiers, who had already gone back on the night of 5th November.

On the same day the 152nd Brigade of the 51st Highland Division came up to relieve U.S. Combat Commands "A" and "R" in the Peel to the southward of the 15th Scottish Division. For this operation the 152nd Brigade came under the 15th Scottish Division, while the Argylls of the 227th Brigade came under the 152nd Brigade. That evening the Argylls relieved the 23rd U.S. Armoured Infantry Regiment in the flat marshland near Ospel—a most unpleasant business, for enemy observation made movement almost impossible by day, and the profusion of Schu mines made it equally difficult by night. The Argylls were to remain at Ospel for six days before their relief by the Gordons. Enemy patrolling was active and bold; enemy fire was heavy; such houses as there were—few and dilapidated—were accurately registered and regularly "stonked." At first only taped tracks were safe to use. Gradually by systematic mine-clearing the Argylls achieved some liberty of movement.

At 6 A.M. next morning the Americans pulled out and went south to rejoin their own 12th Army Group.

During the day the 227th Brigade relieved the 44th Brigade, which went out to the Asten area. The H.L.I. took over uneventfully from the K.O.S.B. and the Royal Scots in Moostdijk, Schelm, and Neerkant.

On 9th November the 12th Corps became operational to the southward of the 8th Corps. The 51st Highland Division had now come up behind the 152nd Brigade, so the latter reverted under its command.

Next day the 44th Brigade (less the R.S.F.) came back into the line north of Meijel. The K.O.S.B. went into Schelm.

11th November passed uneventfully. On the 12th there came reports of an enemy withdrawal from Meijel. At 10 P.M. that night Lieutenant Maconochie and Private Wood of the K.O.S.B. intelligence section set off from Schelm to investigate. All night they worked their way forward by way of Diamond Wood till, soon after 6 A.M. next morning, 13th November, they crept into a house in the centre of Meijel. All day they kept watch from an upper storey. After dark

11th to 13th Nov.	they returned to report that the Germans had left the night before—after blowing up the big windmill in Meijel.

On the 13th, too, the H.L.I. relieved the R.S.F. on the Asten-Meijel road, the R.S.F. reverting under command of the 44th Brigade. |
| 14th Nov. | Next morning the K.O.S.B. sent a fighting patrol by daylight into Meijel: it encountered no enemy and returned in the afternoon. At four that afternoon the sound of a tremendous barrage rolled up from the south, where the 51st Highland Division was attacking to establish a bridgehead over the Noorder and Wessem Canals. This attack marked the first phase of the Second Army's sweep eastward on a three-corps front to the Maas.

That night the H.L.I. sent a fighting patrol along the Asten-Meijel road and into Meijel. This patrol reported Meijel empty but for a few small German posts on the eastern outskirts. It was ordered to remain and to consolidate round the ruined church. |
| 15th Nov. | Next day, 15th November, the H.L.I. moved down methodically from the north-west to occupy the southern portion of Meijel together with its southerly extension, Donck. At the same time the K.O.S.B. came down through Hof to occupy the northern portion.

The H.L.I. and the K.O.S.B. sent patrols eastward up to the Deurne Canal. They found the Germans still holding positions at both ends of the Mariahoeve bridge on the road to Beringen and also in the wooded strip separating the Deurne and Helena Canals, which here run in parallel courses about a hundred yards apart. That evening the R.S.F. relieved the K.O.S.B., who went out to rest at Asten.

Meijel itself was in an indescribable mess. Every house in the village itself and every farm nearby was flat. Burnt-out tanks and half-tracks, American and German, littering the dreary peat-bog, gave silent testimony to the tough fight put up by the 7th U.S. Armoured Division. For the next three days the H.L.I. and the R.S.F. were to be busy clearing roads through the chaos of rubble, craters, felled trees, and mines of every sort sown in incredible numbers. |
| 16th Nov. | By 16th November the 51st Highland Division, advancing south of the Noorder Canal, was almost up to the Uitwaterings or Diversion Canal south of the junction of the Noorder and Deurne Canals. |

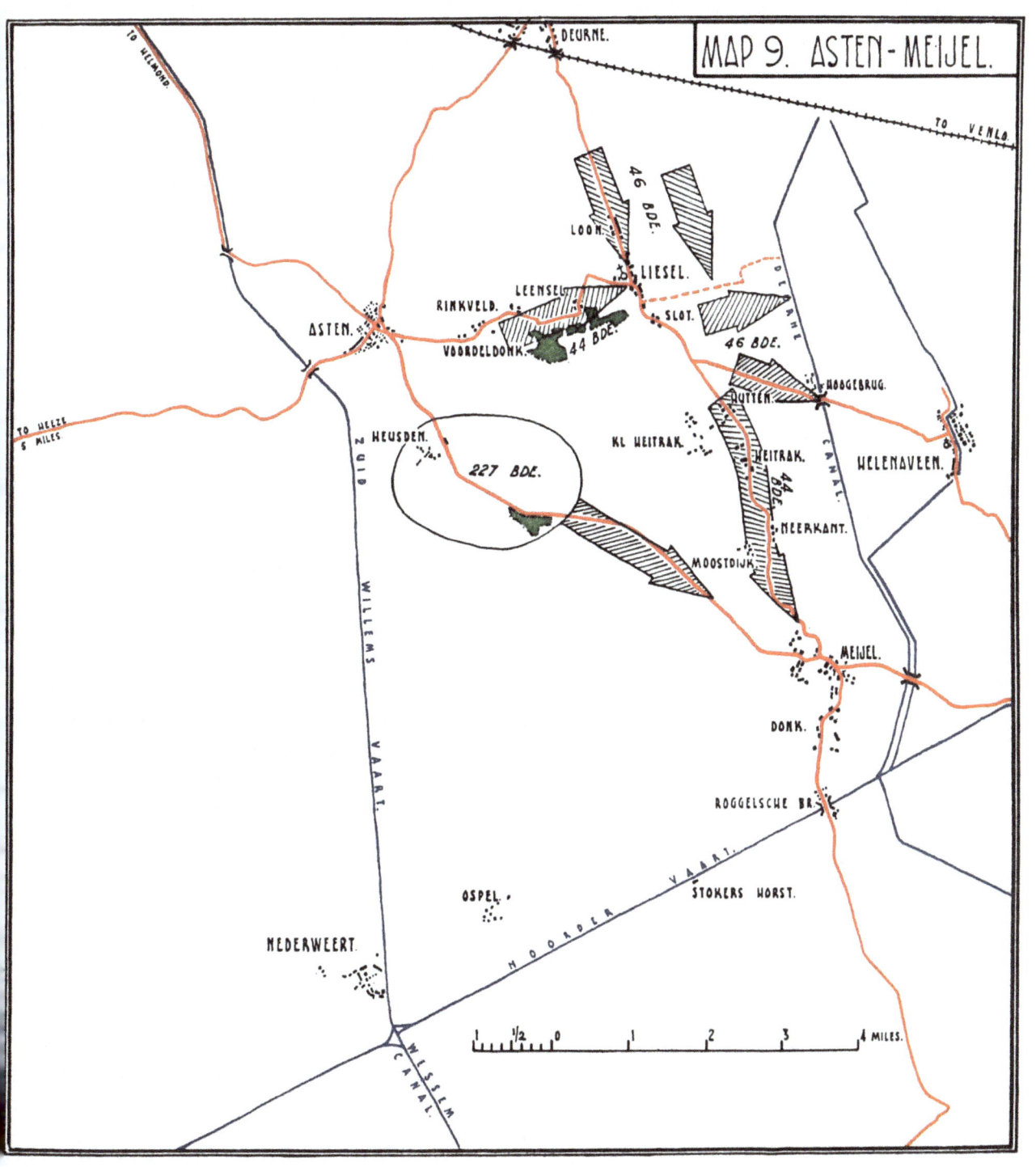

During the day the Gordons passed southward through the H.L.I. in Donck to the site of the Roggelsche bridge over the Noorder Canal, where they contacted the 5th Camerons of the 152nd Brigade. The 51st Division was already building a Class 40 bridge here to replace the demolished road-bridge. *16th Nov.*

That night the 15th Scottish Divisional patrols reported enemy posts still west of the Deurne Canal at Mariahoeve.

Next day, 17th November, the Argylls took over the close protection of the new Roggelsche bridge from the 51st Division, which had now crossed the Uitwaterings Canal. *17th Nov.*

On 18th November the 51st Division took Panningen—an advance which put them well on the flank of any enemy who might still be facing the 15th Scottish Division on the Deurne Canal. *18th Nov.*

By this time the K.O.S.B. were back in Neerkant. That evening one of their patrols swam the Deurne Canal to establish that the enemy had gone.

During the night a wireless intercept at 8th Corps' Headquarters confirmed that the enemy in the Hoogebrug sector were withdrawing eastward over the Helena Canal. Brigadier Villiers at once sent up an assault-boat and some Kapok to the Cameronians. At first light on 19th November a patrol crossed the Deurne Canal by boat without opposition. The remainder of the Brigade followed by Kapok to cover the building of a Class 40 bridge which was to replace the demolished Hoogebrug. In spite of losing men and equipment on mines at the bridge-site, the R.E. got the job done very quickly. *19th Nov.*

The H.L.I. also moved up to the Deurne Canal east of Meijel to cover the building of a Class 9 bridge on the road to Beringen. Here at the site of the demolished bridge at Mariahoeve they linked up with the 152nd Brigade, which had come up through Beringen. The enemy's Meijel salient was wiped out at last, and the 15th Scottish Division was all set for the drive eastward to the Maas.

The prospect ahead looked grim enough. Seen that evening through pouring rain and in the glare of fitful fires, the Peel was indeed the abomination of desolation.

278TH FIELD COMPANY BRIDGING AT HELENAVEEN

CHAPTER VII.

PART III.—BLERICK AND THE MAAS.

FOR the sweep eastward the 12th Corps on the right was to be responsible for clearing the country up to the Maas between Wessem and Blerick (opposite Venlo); the 8th Corps, on the left, for the clearing of the rest of the German bridgehead which lay to the northward of the Meijel-Venlo road.

The 15th Scottish Division was the right-hand formation of the 8th Corps. The Division's immediate task was to take over the Beringen area from the 12th Corps and to clear the country round Helenaveen and Sevenum. On its left the Division would have the 11th Armoured Division, which was to advance east along the Venlo railway by way of Amerika. Still farther north, the 3rd Division would advance eastward from Venraij.

When planning this operation the Divisional Commander had been quick to realise that rain and mud were likely to be his chief adversaries. The roads were no more than sandy tracks, the bottoms of which would surely fall out under heavy traffic. And the rain seemed everlasting.

With the help of air photographs, the Divisional Commander had chosen two axes of advance: the right hand, called "Skye," led from Meijel over the Class 9 bridge at Mariahoeve to Beringen and thence north-eastward to Sevenum; the left hand, called "Ayr," from Liesel over the Class 40 bridge at Hoogebrug to Helenaveen and thence eastward by way of Achterste Steeg to join "Skye" at Sevenum. Of these two roads Corps had selected "Ayr" to be the Corps' axis —hence the Class 40 bridge at Hoogebrug. So rather reluctantly the Divisional Commander had had to accept "Ayr" as his main Divisional axis as well. Along both these routes there was to be a carefully pre-arranged system of traffic control posts, and stringent orders were issued against double-banking. The R.E., too, had brought up immense stores of Sommerfeld track and double corduroy for road maintenance purposes. Last but not least there were the amphibian "Weasels," which had been provided on a scale of six per brigade. These Weasels were to be the salvation alike of the fighting troops and of the services.

On 19th November the Cameronians sent patrols along "Ayr" route from Hoogebrug towards Helenaveen; these patrols contacted the enemy west of the Helena Canal outside Helenaveen.

That night the H.L.I. on "Skye" route relieved the troops of the 49th Division in Beringen. The 49th Division had replaced the 51st Division on the left of the 12th Corps.

Next morning the Cameronians advanced eastward on Helenaveen. Short of the Helena Canal, however, their leading company ran into an anti-personnel minefield and suffered heavily. Resuming the advance in the afternoon, the Cameronians ran into another anti-personnel minefield which further delayed them. About 3 P.M. they at last reached the western bank of the Helena Canal, and there at dusk they dug in.

Meanwhile the Gordons, accompanied by a squadron of the Tank Scots Guards and followed by the Argylls, had passed through the H.L.I. in Beringen to head north-eastward for Sevenum. Within a mile the Gordons were held up by mortar and spandau-fire from scattered farms and woods. The Scots Guards pushed on to destroy the houses with gun-fire at close range. In the process they had three Churchills hit by S.P. 88's.

Here on "Skye" route was now beginning a three days' ordeal, which would not abate till the 227th Brigade was concentrated in Horst on the night of 23rd November. It was to be an ordeal such as had been familiar to so many of our troops in the winter conditions of the first World War—a stark agony of wet and cold, mud and exposure without surcease. Conditions over on "Ayr" route were to prove, if anything, even worse. By last light the Gordons had reached a point in the bog about three miles from Beringen. Ahead the Germans were burning farms and villages as they withdrew. At dusk fires flickered all along the eastern horizon. All day our troops had been meeting a pitiful army of refugees, who, with their few possessions stacked on perambulators or hand-carts or carried on their backs, trudged wearily westward through mud and rain—an unforgettable picture of abject human misery.

20th Nov.   In the afternoon the R.S.F., who were now temporarily under command of the 46th Brigade, had followed the Argylls through Beringen, whence they had headed northward preceded by a squadron of the Reconnaissance Regiment. The R.S.F.'s rôle was to deliver a concentric attack on Helenaveen in co-operation with the Cameronians. By evening the R.S.F. were approaching Helenaveen from the south, and were already in touch with the Cameronians across the Helena Canal. They had met no enemy.

21st Nov.   On 21st November the Gordons, ploughing their laborious way along the "Skye" route towards Sevenum, were nearing Voorste Steeg in face of weak enemy rearguards. On the Gordons' right were the Argylls, who were nearing Vorst. Mines, craters, blown bridges, mud—these were the real enemies. The H.L.I. were still in Beringen.

On the left of the Gordons the R.S.F. reached Helenaveen that morning from the south and cleared it, whereupon the 46th Brigade crossed the Helena Canal without opposition. After handing over Helenaveen to the Cameronians, the R.S.F. withdrew southward into the woods towards Beringen, where they reverted to the command of Brigadier the Hon. H. C. H. T. Cumming-Bruce, the new commander of the 44th Brigade. For the rest, Brigadier Cumming-Bruce had the Royal Scots still back in Meijel, the K.O.S.B. in Neerkant.

In the afternoon the Glasgow Highlanders and the Seaforth pushed on through Helenaveen and across the marshes to the eastward, at first against no opposition. At dusk the Glasgow Highlanders on the right were dug in on "Ayr" route about a thousand yards short of Achterste Steeg, whence the enemy was shelling them fairly heavily. The Seaforth on the left had their patrols in Achterste Hees.

All day weather conditions had been worsening. As night closed in, the skies opened. Supply routes to forward units melted away, to be transformed into rivers of glutinous mud a foot or more in depth and perhaps a hundred yards in width. Where traffic had tried to by-pass a peculiarly bad spot, the by-pass soon became merely another such mud-bath. The course of these nightmare rivers was marked by countless parties of exhausted men, who, knee-deep in trouble, struggled with bogged carriers or jeeps. Sometimes a passing Churchill would give a tow—on one occasion indeed a Churchill pulled the front right off a carrier without budging it. Sometimes the Churchills themselves were stuck. Even men on foot had to go warily; it took four men pulling on a rope to extricate a companion who had got himself bogged in a pot-hole.   *21st Nov.*

Division had ordered normal traffic off the axes by day to allow the R.E. to get down to road repair and to give light aid detachments a clear run on their lawful occasions. Into that bottomless bog the R.E. fed everything they had got—track, corduroy, even whole tree-trunks: the bog swallowed the lot and asked for more. Recovery vehicles and R.E.M.E. worked day and night—and still they could not catch up on their jobs. On " Ayr " route Weasels were the only vehicles that could reach forward battalions. That night the six Weasels of the 46th Brigade made fourteen trips apiece, carrying rations, cooking sets, and blankets. Battalions themselves were using all the carriers of their carrier platoons, together with any spares in the anti-tank platoons, exclusively for supply purposes. And all the while the pitiless rain descended to soak through everything. In all that bleak expanse there was no shelter—no hope of getting dry.

On 22nd November the weather was worse than ever.   *22nd Nov.*

On the right on " Skye " route the Gordons had reached Sevenum by last light; the Argylls had reached Vorst, a short way to the south-eastward. The Reconnaissance Regiment was three miles on in Horst, which they found clear. Moreover, Horst proved undamaged, thus offering prospects of shelter at last.

On the left on " Ayr " route the Seaforth were in Achterste Hees, where the Glasgow Highlanders had joined them. The Cameronians were farther west. All three battalions were thus east of the bog, while their transport and Brigade Headquarters and the guns were all still west of it. Weasels were the only means of supply across the bog. " Ayr " was now in such a hopeless mess that the Divisional Commander ordered Brigadier Villiers to send his transport and guns round to the northward by the 11th Armoured Division's axis through Amerika, on which route Division had obtained timings from Corps. In this manner the rest of the 46th Brigade Group was to close up on its battalions two days later. The 44th Brigade had not moved.

Next day the 227th Brigade, with an added quota of Weasels, pushed on along " Skye " to cross the railway north of Sevenum.   *23rd Nov.*

23rd Nov. By early afternoon all three battalions and the Tank Scots Guards were concentrated in Horst, where there was room for a complete brigade group under cover. Here the 227th Brigade contacted the 11th Armoured Division, while the Reconnaissance Regiment contacted the 3rd Division in Kastenraar, three miles to the north-west. The enemy, who were still in Tienraij, a few miles to the northward, were shelling Horst intermittently.

That day the 44th and 46th Brigades stayed put, while the R.E. performed prodigies of maintenance along " Ayr," but to little avail.

In the 12th Corps' area to the southward the 49th Division was approaching Hout Blerick.

24th Nov. On 24th November the infantry of all three brigades remained halted, while the R.E. and R.E.M.E. got on with their interminable jobs. In particular the R.E. had several bridges to repair on the canal system north of Horst.

The balance of the 46th Brigade Group came up by the 11th Armoured Division's axis through Amerika to join the battalions of the brigade, all three of which were still echeloned along " Ayr " to the westward of Sevenum.

The 227th Brigade also switched its supply route that day from Heusden to the Helmond-Deurne railway.

25th Nov. Next morning the weather showed signs of improvement. The 227th Brigade pushed northward from Horst in face of heavy shelling. The Gordons occupied Swolgen; the Argylls occupied Tienraij; the H.L.I. remained farther south in Eikelenbosch. Here the 227th Brigade found itself once more in an area of ruined houses, felled trees, mined roads, and booby-traps. Two miles south-east of Swolgen the Reconnaissance Regiment met fierce resistance outside Broekhuizervorst on the Maas, where the enemy were plying one of their few remaining ferries. Up here in the north the 227th Brigade was now side by side with the 3rd Division, for the 11th Armoured Division had been squeezed out.

The 46th Brigade moved up to replace the 227th Brigade in and around Horst. The 44th Brigade had not yet moved.

On the southern flank the 49th Division was now facing the defences of Blerick, which is the suburb of Venlo that lies on the west bank of the Maas.

BLERICK AND THE MAAS

26th Nov. The 227th Brigade and 46th Brigade now closed on the Maas on a nine-mile front from Blitterswijk in the north to Houthuizen in the south. At their several ferry sites the enemy at first resisted stubbornly. In the 227th Brigade's sector the H.L.I. on the left reached the Maas at Blitterswijk; but the Gordons had to fight hard by daylight for Broekhuizervorst, which they occupied only after dark when the enemy had gone.

In the 46th Brigade's sector the Cameronians were still fighting their way into Lottum at dark. The ferry site at Lottum they found heavily defended. All night long Cameronian patrols tried in vain to reach the bank and to destroy the ferry. The Seaforth entered Houthuizen that day. During the day the Glasgow Highlanders had cleared a wide stretch of woodland south-east of Horst.

27th Nov. Next day the 2nd Royal Ulster Rifles of the 3rd Division unexpectedly arrived to relieve the H.L.I. in Blitterswijk, whereupon the H.L.I. went back to rest at Asten. The Gordons were still having some trouble with a German post west of the Maas, in the flooded country between Broekhuizervorst and Lottum. The Argylls were still back in Tienraij.

At daylight the Cameronians occupied Lottum unopposed. The west bank of the Maas hereabouts overlooks the east bank, so the Germans on the farther side were in full view—digging like badgers. Our guns did not miss their chance.

28th Nov. This was to be a day of far-reaching changes.

The 3rd Division completed the relief of the 227th Brigade (less the Gordons), which pulled out to Asten. The Gordons remained in Broekhuizervorst under command of the 46th Brigade.

The 49th Division, too, was now pulling out to move northward into the "island" across the Nijmegen bridge. In consequence, the 11th Armoured Division was to come back into the line and to relieve the 15th Scottish Division that night, and the 15th Scottish Division was then to side-step southward to replace the 49th Division in the 12th Corps. In particular, the 46th Brigade was to relieve the 146th Brigade of the 49th Division in the line in front of Blerick. The fortress of Blerick was now the enemy's only considerable foothold west of the Maas, and the 49th Division had been planning its capture. This operation now became the responsibility of the 44th Brigade.

28th Nov. Before their relief by the 11th Armoured Division the Cameronians had sent a fighting patrol to clear the Germans out of the large house —the " Kasteel "—surrounded by a moat, which stands on the river bank in the direction of Broekhuizervorst. The plan of attack was carefully laid and provided for both covering fire and smoke. The castle, however, turned out to be unexpectedly strong. Its garrison held their fire until the leading sections had closed up to the wall and then opened up with deadly effect. In consequence, the attack failed with the loss of nearly half of the platoon. Next day the 11th Armoured Division staged a battalion attack and took the castle— but at a cost of about two hundred casualties.

29th Nov. By dawn on 29th November the 11th Armoured Division had completed the relief of the 46th Brigade and the Gordons. The 46th Brigade (less the Cameronians) then went south to Blerick, where the Seaforth took over from the right forward battalion of the 146th Brigade; the Glasgow Highlanders from the left forward battalion. The Reconnaissance Regiment held the line of the Maas to the northward of Blerick as far as Grubbenvorst—that is, for about four miles.

The Cameronians spent the day reorganising, while the Gordons went back to rejoin the 227th Brigade at Asten.

30th Nov. to 2nd Dec. On 30th November the Cameronians relieved the Seaforth in the line. The Seaforth then came under command of the 44th Brigade for the assault which had been fixed for 3rd December.

Brigadier Cumming-Bruce made his preparations with meticulous care. The Blerick defences were extremely formidable. The place stands in a shallow re-entrant of the Maas. Across the neck of this re-entrant, from bank to bank, the Germans had dug an anti-tank ditch over three miles long, and they had covered the ditch with a belt of wire and a minefield.

Into this re-entrant of the Maas the 44th Brigade would have to advance down a gentle glacis, bare of cover for the last two thousand yards or so. The glacis is overlooked not only by the tall buildings in Venlo across the Maas but also by the high ground still farther east. The attackers, therefore, would be exposed throughout their advance to the converging fire of the hundred or so guns and countless mortars which the enemy were believed to have massed beyond the Maas. And when the attackers had penetrated the wire and crossed the ditch, they would still have to fight their way through the intricate streets of Blerick. Such, then, was the debtor side of the balance-sheet.

30th Nov. to 2nd Dec.

There were, however, some very important entries on the credit side. The garrison of Blerick would have to fight with the Maas—an unbridged river one hundred and fifty yards wide—at their backs. The German Command, therefore, might well be reluctant to venture a large stake on Blerick. Yet the garrison would have to hold a three-mile perimeter—a task which they could not perform without adequate numbers.

At the same time, the 44th Brigade was to receive an ample scale of mechanical and fire support. The armoured support was to be provided by the 31st Tank Brigade Group under Brigadier Knight, whose brigade—then wholly equipped with Churchills—had supported the 15th Scottish Division in its first battle on the Odon. The 31st Tank Brigade now consisted of the 107th Regiment R.A.C. (Churchills) and the 22nd Dragoons (Flails), with one squadron of the 81st Assault Regiment R.E. (bridge-laying Churchills), two squadrons of the 49th Armoured Personnel Carrier Regiment (Kangaroos), and one squadron of the 1st Fife and Forfar Yeomanry (Crocodiles) attached.

As for fire support, the Divisional artillery was to be reinforced by no less than three A.G.R.A.s—the 3rd, 8th, and 59th—making a total of over four hundred guns, including super-heavies. Also in support there was the 1st Canadian Rocket Projector Unit equipped with six so-called " Mattresses," each capable of discharging over three hundred and fifty rockets simultaneously into an area two hundred yards square. These Mattresses were to be used here for the first time on land.

Brigadier Cumming-Bruce's plan was simple, and, by dint of exercises on a sand model, supplemented by ground reconnaissances during the next three days, he ensured that every man knew his job. The attack was to be preceded by a two-hour programme of bombardment and counter-battery on a vast scale. The attack itself, which was to come in from the west, was to be divided into two phases—the armoured phase and the infantry phase. In the armoured phase the Armoured Breaching Force was to advance behind a barrage and smoke-screens. First, the Churchill gun-tanks would take up position to give close covering fire; then the Flails would follow along six axes, to clear six lanes through the minefields and wire. When the Flails had reached the ditch, the bridge-laying Churchills would advance in their turn

1ST CANADIAN ROCKET PROJECTORS FIRING AT BLERICK

30th Nov. to 2nd Dec. down the six lanes and would bridge the ditch in six places. The Flails would then cross and would continue to clear their respective axes up to the outskirts of the town.

At this stage Brigadier Cumming-Bruce would take over from the armour and would order forward the infantry, who would be waiting in their Kangaroos. Along the three right-hand lanes the Royal Scots would advance, along the three left-hand lanes the R.S.F. They would drive in their Kangaroos right into the heart of Blerick.

The Kangaroos would then return to fetch the K.O.S.B. and the Seaforth and would decant them in their allotted areas, in support respectively of the Royal Scots and the R.S.F. In this manner the 44th Brigade would occupy the whole of Blerick.

Such, then, was the plan which, because of its signal success, was afterwards to become the sealed pattern for so many set-piece armoured attacks. As the '44th Brigade History' remarks :—

"Each time the recipe was the one learned at Blerick—meticulous preparation and planning, concentration of all available fire-power, use of the 'Funnies' (and not the infantry) to overcome the obstacles, and a quick, bold use of the infantry to exploit the advantage won by the success of the armour—if possible by moving straight into the heart of the enemy position. This recipe brought quick success at little cost."

On the nights of 1st December and 2nd December a cover plan was laid on in the Glasgow Highlanders' sector on the left or northern flank of the perimeter in order to mislead the enemy as to the real point of attack. This plan provided for the broadcasting of sonic effects to simulate the movement of tanks, the making of actual tank tracks, active patrolling by both fighting and reconnaissance patrols, and on the night of 2nd December the blowing of breaches in the wire with Bangalore torpedoes and the making of more sonic effects to simulate bridging operations. These deceptive measures paid a good dividend, for when, unexpectedly, the 44th Brigade attacked from the west, the defenders were looking north, and in the subsequent confusion put down the weight of their defensive fire on the northern sector during the opening phases of the attack.

In the afternoon of 2nd December, Tactical Headquarters, 44th Brigade, came up to Rooth. Brigadier Cumming-Bruce was most anxious to keep the assaulting infantry well back during the opening or armoured phase of the attack and then to send it straight through to the start-line without any long pauses. When they came to leave

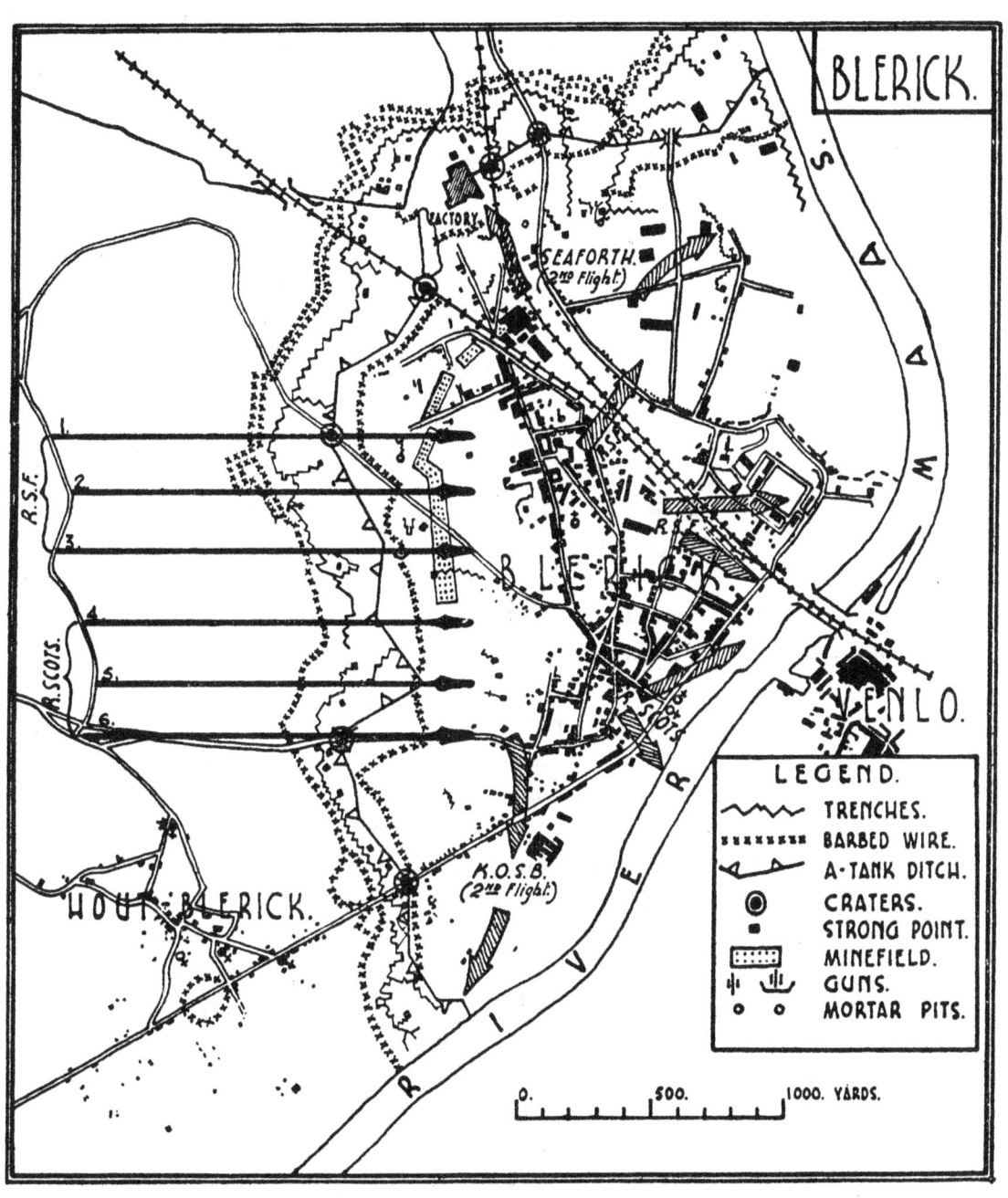

30th Nov. to 2nd Dec. their billets, therefore, forward battalions were to move straight up to Brigade Tactical Headquarters in their Kangaroos. Reserve battalions, on the other hand, were to move that night to forward assembly areas in the Blericksche Bergen.

All was going according to plan save for one unfortunate mishap. In the Cameronians' sector a medium gun had taken a wrong turning and, disregarding shouts and signals, had driven straight into the enemy's lines. The whole gun crew was missing, so it was possible that news of the impending attack had reached the enemy.

It was at this stage that another cause for far more serious anxiety manifested itself. Rain had again begun to fall heavily—on ground which was already soaking. By 6 P.M. Brigadier Knight could no longer guarantee that the Armoured Breaching Force would be able to move next morning. The question was whether or not the attack should stand. The Divisional Commander referred the decision to the Corps Commander, Lieutenant-General Neil Ritchie, who postponed his final ruling till midnight. Meanwhile, however, the rain stopped about 9 P.M., and Brigadier Knight, as the result of further reconnaissance, was able to give a reassuring report. Orders were given, therefore, that the attack should go in next morning as planned.

3rd Dec. At 5.25 A.M. the artillery programme began. Never before, perhaps, had so many guns been concentrated on so small an area. At once Blerick was blotted out by smoke and dust and sheets of flame. The tearing, rushing discharge and multiple explosion of the Mattresses sounded a new diapason in the orchestral music of the guns.

At 7.45 A.M. the Breaching Force advanced. On the way to the start-line no less than five of their Flails were bogged. Within an hour, however, the survivors were right through the minefield and the wire and up to the ditch on two of the lanes. And by 9.25 A.M. the A.V.R.E.s had laid their bridges successfully on lanes 1, 2, 5, and 6.

At this point Brigadier Cumming-Bruce ordered the Royal Scots and the R.S.F. forward from Brigade Headquarters in their Kangaroos. An hour later the Royal Scots had driven right through to dismount in the outskirts of Blerick. The R.S.F., on the other hand, who had found no shells falling in their sector but the ground extremely boggy, had decided to continue their advance on foot. If they had taken their Kangaroos any farther, these might never have got back to pick up the Seaforth. In consequence, the R.S.F. took a bit longer than the

6TH ROYAL SCOTS FUSILIERS IN ACTION AT BLERICK

Royal Scots, but by 1 P.M. both battalions were established in the heart of Blerick, and the K.O.S.B. on the right had driven through in support. The only hurt which the forward battalions had suffered between their billets and their objectives had befallen one section, who had "depouched" without orders.   *3rd Dec.*

In consequence of the bad going on the left, the Seaforth were about one and a half hours behind the K.O.S.B. Enemy shelling was now severe. A direct hit on Seaforth Battalion Headquarters miraculously claimed only one victim—but he was Major Sam Ginn of the 531st Field Battery, the Seaforth's well-beloved gunner-adviser. By 4 P.M. the battle was over but for the shelling. Blerick had fallen with 250 prisoners and large quantities of guns, equipment, and ammunition—all at a cost of only 50 casualties.

Blerick is a most confusing place of tortuous streets, where mapreading is a nightmare. There were many instances that day of parties who lost their way—to emerge unexpectedly on the water-front in embarrassing proximity to the Germans over the way in Venlo. In the cellars there had been two to three thousand Dutch, who now emerged, pale and shaken, to greet their liberators. As evening closed in, down came the rain again. All six lanes were soon impassable. For once Fortune had smiled.

Such, in brief, was the battle of Blerick—where everything went right and so much might have gone wrong. Later it was fittingly to become the theme of a War Office pamphlet. Of this skilfully planned and skilfully fought battle the psychological effect on the 44th Brigade was immense and lasting. Previously the Brigade had undergone a series of bitter and exhausting experiences, particularly in the Gheel bridgehead and at Meijel. Now it had got just the fillip it needed, and it was never to look back.

The day after the battle of Blerick the 15th Scottish Division began its winter watch on the Maas, which was to last till 21st January. At first only the 44th Brigade was in the line. On 4th December the 44th Brigade took over from the 46th Brigade its eleven-mile front astride Blerick. The 46th Brigade then went back to rest. The 44th Brigade held this front with a squadron of the Reconnaissance Regiment to the northward of Blerick, one battalion in Blerick itself, another battalion to the southward of Blerick, and the third in Brigade reserve at Rooth and Maasbree.   *4th Dec. to 28th Jan.*

4th Dec. to 28th Jan.

Next to come into the line was the 227th Brigade on 8th December, when it relieved the 160th Brigade of the 53rd Division in Baarlo and Kessel to the southward of the 44th Brigade. The 227th Brigade held its sector with two battalions up on the Maas at Baarlo and Kessel and the third in Brigade reserve at Helden. This relief left the 15th Scottish Division holding the Maas from a point just short of Grubbenvorst in the north to Kessel in the south. Next day the 8th Corps took over this front from the 12th Corps, which a few days later side-stepped south in its turn to take over the front of the 30th Corps. Headquarters, 30th Corps, was thus relieved for operations elsewhere.

Thus the 15th Scottish Division found itself back again in the 8th Corps. Lieutenant-General Sir Richard O'Connor, the former Corps Commander, had now gone to a command in India. Lieutenant-General Evelyn Barker, the new Corps Commander, soon came to visit the 15th Scottish on the Maas and inspected the front, often at a smart double, which left his entourage faint but pursuing.

It is necessary here to turn for a moment to the larger picture. Montgomery had never abandoned his intention to begin the battle of the Rhineland at the earliest possible moment. The battle was to be the responsibility of the First Canadian Army, of which the 30th Corps was to form a most important part. As soon as the 12th and 8th Corps had completed their drive to the Maas, therefore, Montgomery had set to work to assemble the constituents of the 30th Corps for this new battle—the Guards Armoured Division, that is, and the 15th, 43rd, and 53rd Divisions. While he was in the midst of these preliminaries, however—on 16th December, to be precise—Rundstedt had launched his Army Group " B " on its surprise offensive through the Ardennes towards the crossings of the Meuse. This offensive made such progress that, by 18th December, Montgomery realised that he must postpone his Rhineland battle once more. Instead, he decided to concentrate the 30th Corps with all possible speed between Brussels and Liege, ready to intervene if Army Group " B " should force the crossings of the Meuse. The 51st Division he found already out of the line and immediately available. Thus it came about that the 51st Division replaced the 15th Scottish Division in the 30th Corps and that the 15th Scottish Division was left to keep the winter watch on the Maas for seven rather dreary weeks.

On 17th December the 46th Brigade came into the line to

extend the 15th Scottish Division's front still farther south nearly to Roermond. The 53rd Division was pulling out to join the 30th Corps, so the 46th Brigade had to relieve the 158th Brigade in Haelen and Buggenum, making the total extent of the front held by the 15th Scottish Division between Grubbenvorst and Roermond over twenty miles. The 46th Brigade, too, held its sector with two battalions up on the Maas and the third in Brigade reserve at Roggel. All three brigades rang the changes on their three battalions at regular intervals.

4th Dec. to 28th Jan.

In general, the situation on the Maas was this. The Germans on the farther bank were first-class troops belonging to a Parachute Division, and they had been at pains to take over with them every boat to their own bank. In consequence, German patrols were able to cross the Maas nightly to our side, while the 15th Scottish Division was left with nothing more seaworthy than its assault-boats—craft quite unsuitable for crossing a rapid river a hundred and fifty yards wide. When real boats at last were forthcoming and the Division could get down to practising offensive patrols, it was too late. The enemy's tactics, therefore, were offensive throughout, while ours were of necessity wholly defensive. Inevitably, this state of affairs had a somewhat depressing effect on our troops. After all that had gone before, these seven weeks of comparative inaction came as an anti-climax. The feelings of all concerned are perhaps best described by the moving verse from an intelligence summary, which is quoted by Captain Baggaley in his delightful ' History of the K.O.S.B.' :—

> " As I sit on the banks of the Maas,
> I reflect it is really a farce,
> At my time of life,
> And miles from my wife,
> To be stuck in the mud on my ——"

At the same time everything possible was done to foster the offensive spirit. Our defensive tactics aimed at ambushing the German patrols on our bank, and above all at preventing them from " lifting " any of our own small posts. The German patrols, who were exceedingly bold, active, and elusive, were helped in their nightly crossings by the mist which usually hung over the water, and they often lay up on our side by day. The essence of the game was to deny them freedom of movement and reconnaissance. To this end our posts were well wired in ; linesmen were out continuously working on

4th Dec. to 28th Jan.

communications; minefields were laid; regularly at dusk our standing and reconnaissance patrols went down to the river bank; the locations, routes, and timings of these patrols were changed constantly. All night long the duel of wits would continue. On its front of twenty-odd miles, however, the Division was very thin on the ground, and the initiative was with the enemy. Despite our every precaution the German patrols had more than one minor success, whereas only once, towards the end of the watch on the Maas, did the Division manage to get its own back on a German patrol.

Topographically the different sectors along the Maas varied greatly in character. On some parts of the front, such as Blerick itself, the troops could find good billets in plenty in the front-line. There life was supportable enough. Elsewhere, as for instance between Blerick and Grubbenvorst, there was no shelter whatever along the banks. When therefore by mid-December the weather had turned bitterly cold and snow had fallen, the listening posts down on the river's edge spent miserable nights shivering in their slit-trenches with the temperature below zero. On some parts of the front, too—as at Baarlo, for instance—the Germans had ample cover from view on their bank, while our troops' every move was plain to see. Along most of the front, however, we had at least as good observation as the Germans. Intelligence O.P.s and snipers came into their own, and joint mortar and artillery shoots served to break the monotony. In return, enemy shelling and mortaring were intermittent. A new and unwelcome arrival was the 30-cm. Wurfkorper, which fired an outsize rocket with a 276-pound warhead.

During December the Division welcomed two notable visitors. The first was the Rev. E. J. Hagan, Moderator of the Church of Scotland, who had been a member of the Division in 1914-18. The second was Field-Marshal Montgomery, who visited the Division on 13th December to present medal ribbons. He then spoke as follows :—

"I remember very clearly visiting your Division in England when I came back from Italy, and I well remember your Division landing in Normandy when you came over just after D Day. You were untried then, though you had some veterans with you. I remember the first time your Division went into battle at the River Odon, and I remember feeling anxious that the Division should acquit itself well. One can't help feeling anxious at these times, though there is no need to. Your Division did very well indeed, and you have never looked back since. You have only to look at the Battle Honours on the stage behind me—I have noticed well-known names like Caumont—to realise how much you have done.

"I expect that to-day there are representatives here of every unit in the Division. When you go back I would like you to tell the others that I came here to-day and that I think this Division has done awfully well. In this fighting no Division has done better, and it is a first-class show. We did not expect anything else, but it is very creditable for all that."

Perhaps the most notable event of all, however, was the opening of the United Kingdom leave ballot on 16th December.

Christmas passed almost unnoticed. On New Year's Eve the first United Kingdom leave party set off. Next day the Luftwaffe appeared in force to interrupt the Hogmanay celebrations. It was the Luftwaffe's expiring effort—a vain effort to scotch the Allied airpower which, in the better weather that had prevailed during the previous week, had been smashing Army Group " B " in the defiles of the Ardennes. The German aircraft came over very low, and a number were shot down in the Divisional area.

By 16th January, what Montgomery called " the staunch fighting qualities of the American soldier " had reduced the German salient in the Ardennes to a bulge. His Ardennes offensive had cost Rundstedt 150,000 men and 600 tanks. Not only that, he had now to part with what was left of his 6th Panzer Army—which had been ordered off on a weary journey to the Eastern front. Thus Montgomery was able to turn his mind once more to the Rhineland battle. The 15th Scottish Division's watch on the Maas was nearing its end. On 19th January the 227th Brigade was relieved by Commando troops. On the next night the 227th Brigade in its turn relieved the 44th Brigade, which then went back to rest at Grammont. At the same time Montgomery issued his orders for Operation " Veritable," the Rhineland battle. This time there was to be no postponement.

For its preliminary organisation and training with the 30th Corps, the 15th Scottish Division was to assemble in and around Tilburg. On 22nd January the 46th and 227th Brigades were relieved on the Maas by the 6th Airborne Division and moved west to Tilburg, Merxplas, and Goirle. The cold had again become intense, making the icebound roads almost impassable. On 28th January the 44th Brigade arrived from Grammont to complete the concentration of the 15th Scottish Division. Great events were close ahead.

CHAPTER VIII.

THE RHINELAND BATTLE.

24th Jan. to 4th Feb.

As early as 21st January Montgomery had issued his orders for Operation "Veritable," though for reasons of security these orders did not percolate down to junior ranks until a fortnight later.

Montgomery's object was to destroy the German forces between the Maas and the Rhine and then to line up the three armies of the Allied left wing—from right to left, the Ninth U.S. Army, the Second British Army, and the First Canadian Army—along the west bank of the Rhine preparatory to the forcing of a crossing and the isolation of the Ruhr.

His plan was this. On target date, 8th February, Lieutenant-General Crerar's First Canadian Army, of which the 30th Corps would form the larger part, was to launch its offensive from the Nijmegen bridgehead south-eastward between the Maas and the Rhine, with the line Geldern-Xanten as its final objective. At the same time, or so Montgomery hoped, the Ninth U.S. Army, some sixty miles away to southward, would deliver a complementary offensive across the Roer —which is the tributary of the Maas that joins it on its east bank at Roermond—and would drive north-eastward to link up with the First Canadian Army on the Rhine south of Xanten. Meanwhile the Second British Army in the centre would hold the line of the Maas between the Ninth U.S. Army and the First Canadian Army. Finally, when the Germans between the rivers had been destroyed, the three armies would line up along the Rhine between Dusseldorf and Nijmegen.

Such, then, were the events which the immediate future had in store when the 15th Scottish Division concentrated in and around Tilburg between 23rd and 28th January. The people of Tilburg gave the Division—their own "Red Lion" Division—a welcome unforgettable for its genuine warmth and depth of feeling, showing plainly that they reckoned no kindness, no hospitality too great to offer to these men who had liberated them. Tilburg is a new and undamaged city, and it had become a second home to the 15th Scottish Division.

Despite the congestion, the kindly Dutch were eager in their offers of billets in their own homes and found room for all the " Red Lions." The peace of this pleasant interlude was marred only by the sinister droning of the flying bombs, which passed overhead in endless succession on their way to Antwerp.

24th Jan. to 4th Feb.

Training began at once—training in the breaching of heavily defended positions, carried out in co-operation with Kangaroos and other " Funnies." Planning, too, began, and gradually spread to ever-descending levels. Thus it was on 29th January that Brigade Commanders held their first " O " Groups. There followed at battalion level endless studies of aerial photographs and maps, endless conferences, and exercises on cloth models. It was not till 4th February, however, when the Division was on the point of moving up to Nijmegen, that Lieutenant-General Horrocks, Commander of the 30th Corps, briefed all officers of the Division in the tasks that awaited them. Put shortly, the 30th Corps' offensive was to emerge on a five-Divisional front from the Canadian positions between the Rhine and the Maas, with the 15th Scottish Division in the place of honour in the centre. The 15th Scottish Division's rôle in the opening phase would be to breach the Siegfried Line north of the Reichswald Forest and seize the high ground overlooking Cleve.

Throughout this period of preparation the most elaborate precautions were taken to ensure secrecy. Reconnaissance parties going up to Nijmegen had not only to remove their Divisional signs but also to travel in Canadian transport forward of the Grave bridge. At the same time a cover plan was put into effect to lead the enemy to believe that an attack was in preparation across the Maas, to be based on the area Breda-Tilburg and to be directed on Utrecht and Rotterdam. Bogus reconnaissances were carried out and bogus billets arranged—all with much ostentation and loud talk of the fictitious objectives.

For Operation " Veritable " the 30th Corps was to comprise one Armoured Division, six Infantry Divisions, three Armoured Brigades, eleven regiments of the 79th Armoured Division (" Funnies "), and five A.G.R.A.s—a total strength of over 200,000 men, 1500 assorted tanks, and 1000 guns. The First Canadian Army's build-up of stores for the operation was over 200,000 tons, and there was a dumping programme of half a million rounds of gun ammunition. At best, to pass this mass of men and vehicles and stores through the bottleneck formed by the two bridges over the Maas at Mook and Grave and into the restricted

24th Jan. to 4th Feb.

forming-up area around Nijmegen, all within the short time available, could not but be an extremely tricky business, necessitating the most meticulous movement tables; the more so since, on grounds of secrecy, no road movement other than that of reconnaissance parties could be allowed by day forward of the road Eindhoven-s'Hertogenbosch. Now, however, the task was further complicated by the fact that the hard frost had turned to thaw, with devastating effect on one of the two axial roads—that from Eindhoven to Nijmegen by way of Mook. Fortunately the other road, the two-way road from Tilburg to Nijmegen by way of s'Hertogenbosch and Grave, stood up to all the demands made on it. The railways, too, which had been greatly improved during the interlude of the Rundstedt offensive, now handled 10,000 tons of stores a day. In the outcome the whole force and its accompanying stores were assembled on time. It was a magnificent performance, for which the movement staffs and services concerned deserve immense credit. The 15th Divisional R.A.S.C., for instance, who had to dump 600 rounds a gun, were stretched to the limit.

4th Feb.

On the night of 4th February the 46th Brigade set off for Nijmegen in convoy without lights. In preparation for the move all Divisional signs had been removed. It was a nightmare journey over poor roads crowded with traffic and in pouring rain. In consequence of the thaw the original route was "out," so the convoy had to be diverted. But for some extremely efficient route-marking by the Canadian Provost, the convoy would never have made Nijmegen by the following morning.

5th Feb.

On the next night the 227th Brigade followed, and again had a long and difficult journey, getting into billets in Nijmegen in the early hours of 6th February. On the same night Main and Rear Headquarters, 15th Scottish Division, also moved up.

6th Feb.

Finally, on the night of 6th February, the 44th Brigade, which was to take no part in the opening phase of the operation, moved up to complete the Divisional concentration at Nijmegen.

Nijmegen was packed to overflowing with troops and vehicles, but the 30th Corps was taking every possible precaution to hide the concentration from the enemy. Thus all vehicles were meticulously camouflaged while troops were confined to billets, none but organised reconnaissance parties being allowed abroad. The infantry of the

46th Brigade shared their barracks with the Tank Coldstream, so joint planning was possible down to the level of tank crews and Jocks.

6th Feb.

As soon as each Brigade Group arrived, reconnaissances began on company and platoon levels. Canadian O.P.s on the high ground round the Nederriksche wood and Groesbeck gave excellent command over the country. On the right front flat ground extended eastward to the steep wooded hills of the Reichswald; on the left lay a seemingly limitless expanse of flood-water, filling the whole area between the Rhine and the road Nijmegen-Wyler-Kranenburg-Cleve, which was to be the northern axis of advance These floods, the legacy of the abnormal rains of November and December, were already three miles wide opposite Emmerich—and the Germans might yet manipulate sluice-gates or breach dykes to make them wider still. A little more and the floods would submerge the northern axis altogether. It was over the flat, rather featureless terrain south of the floods that the 15th Scottish Division would attack. Clearly, neither map-reading nor direction-keeping would be easy, and the going would be vile.

The German defence system which here faced the Canadians between the Maas and the Rhine was organised in three zones. First, there was the forward or outpost zone, two to three thousand yards in depth, which extended from the neighbourhood of the Canadian forward defended localities back to a line from Gennep in the south, by way of the western edge of the Reichswald, to Kranenburg. Through this zone the two main axes of advance were, in the south, the road Nijmegen-Mook-Gennep-Hekkens, and in the north the road Nijmegen-Wyler-Kranenburg-Cleve. To block the entries to these vitally important roads the Germans had constructed hedgehog defences in the Kiekberg woods and at Wyler. Also they had dug an anti-tank ditch that ran from Frasselt to pass in front of Kranenburg. In the flooded area north of the Nijmegen-Cleve road, however, they had considered elaborate defences to be superfluous.

A couple of miles or so farther east lay the second zone—that formed by the northern end of the Siegfried Line. The general lay-out of the Siegfried Line was as follows: from Roermond it followed the Maas to the neighbourhood of Geldern, where it turned north to the strongly defended town of Goch; from Goch it passed north-west across the River Niers and over the high ground in the central Reichswald north of Hekkens to terminate on the Nijmegen-Cleve road about

6th Feb. Tuthees, where there was another anti-tank ditch across the gap between the forest and the road.

These Siegfried Line defences consisted basically of pre-war concrete works, to which the Germans had since added an elaborate system of field works. In the north in particular the Germans had constructed subsidiary trench systems at Frasselt, Nutterden, Donsbreuggen, Materborn, and Cleve to give the main zone added depth. Moreover, to the main zone they had now appended a switch-line which ran from Goch to Cleve, behind the Reichswald, and gave the forest all-round defence.

Finally, six miles or so east of the Reichswald, there was the third zone, known as the Hochwald "lay-back," which consisted of a series of parallel trench systems.

This Reichswald sector opposite the Canadians was held by the 84th German Infantry Division reinforced by three parachute battalions —a total of thirteen battalions in all, with one hundred guns. In mobile reserve there were estimated to be three Panzer-type Divisions and two Parachute Divisions, all of which might reach the front within five or six days. Between Nijmegen and Wesel, east of Xanten, the Rhine was unbridged: the Germans had one or two ferries working in this stretch. Their railheads for the Reichswald front were believed to be at Goch and Cleve.

It has already been mentioned that on D Day, 8th February, the 30th Corps was to make its opening attack on a five-Divisional front. In more detail, these Divisions and their tasks were as follows:—

Outside Right—51st Highland Division :
    To seize the south-west corner of the Reichswald and to open the axis Mook-Gennep-Hekkens-Goch.

Inside Right—53rd Welsh Division :
    To seize the high ground at the north-west corner of the Reichswald and then to sweep east through the northern half of the forest.

Centre—15th Scottish Division :
    To break the Siegfried Line north of the Reichswald and to take Cleve.

Inside Left—2nd Canadian Division :
    To capture Wyler and so to open thus far the northern axis Nijmegen-Wyler-Kranenburg-Cleve.

Outside Left—3rd Canadian Division :
    To protect the left of the 15th Scottish Division and the 2nd Canadian Division and to clear the flooded area between the axis Nijmegen-Wyler-Kranenburg-Cleve and the Rhine.

Subsequently, when these five Divisions had thus broken the crust, the 43rd Wessex Division and the Guards Armoured Division were to pass through the 15th Scottish Division on the high ground overlooking Cleve and were to exploit—the former to Goch, the latter to Wesel, some twenty miles up the Rhine from Emmerich. The Corps Commander cherished great hopes that the Guards Armoured Division might " bounce " the Rhine bridge at Wesel. And indeed that might well have happened if only the frost had held and progress had not been so sorely impeded by mud and floods.

The 15th Scottish Division was to play its part in the break-in in four phases. In the first phase, which was to begin at 10.30 A.M. and end at 4 P.M. on D Day, 8th February, the 46th Brigade Group on the right and the 227th Brigade Group on the left were to secure the general line Frasselt-Kranenburg. In the second phase, which was to start by Movement Light at 9 P.M. on D Day, the 44th Brigade Group was to pass through the 46th Brigade and, repeating its Blerick operation, was to breach the Siegfried Line north of the Reichswald and penetrate to Nutterden. In the third phase, which was to continue by Movement Light at 1 A.M. on 9th February, the 46th Brigade Group on the right was to secure the high ground overlooking Cleve before daybreak; the 227th Brigade Group on the left was to open the northern axis Kranenburg-Cleve and to clear the wooded area to the north-west. Finally, in the fourth phase, which was to begin at first light on 9th February, the same two Brigade Groups were to clear Cleve itself up to the line of the canal. After all this, exploitation would follow.

Under command or in support, the 15th Scottish Division was to have the 6th Guards Tank Brigade, the 2nd Household Cavalry Regiment, the 22nd Dragoons (Flails), the 101st Regiment R.A.C. (Crocodiles) less one squadron, the 6th Assault Regiment R.E. (portable bridges and fascines) less two squadrons, the 1st Canadian A.P.C. Regiment less one squadron, and the 49th A.P.C. Regiment (Kangaroos), together with two S.P. field regiments and a medium regiment, two S.P. anti-tank batteries, and a searchlight company (Movement Light).

The artillery support for this operation calls for special mention, for it was to be on an unprecedented scale, greater even than that at El Alamein. Here in the Nijmegen bridgehead no less than 1334 guns had been concentrated, ranging from super-heavies to field-guns. Till 5 A.M. on 8th February, however, no artillery activity was to be

6th Feb. permitted other than the normal activity of the two Canadian Divisional Artilleries which had been holding the line. Thereafter the fire plan was to be as follows :—

(1)	5 A.M. to 7.30 A.M.	Destructive fire on enemy defences.
(2)	7.30 A.M. to 7.40 A.M.	Smoke-screens designed to draw enemy defensive fire and so to reveal his gun positions.
(3)	7.40 A.M. to 7.50 A.M.	Pause—to permit of sound ranging and flash spotting on gun-positions thus revealed.
(4)	7.50 A.M. to 9.20 A.M.	Renewed destructive fire.
(5)	9.20 A.M. to 10 A.M.	(a) Intensive counter-battery fire ; and (b) Opening line of barrage, to consist of mixed H.E. and smoke.
(6)	10 A.M. to 10.30 A.M.	Opening line of barrage thickened up in depth, as infantry close.
(7)	10.30 A.M.—H-hour	First lift of barrage.
(8)	4 P.M.	Last lift of barrage : 6000 yards from first lift. Artillery then to switch to front of 3rd Canadian Division.
(9)	5 P.M. to 9 P.M.	Support of 3rd Canadian Division.
(10)	9 P.M. to 1 A.M.	Support of second phase of 15th Scottish Division's and 53rd Welsh Division's attack.
(11)	1 A.M. to daylight	Support of third phase of 15th Scottish Division's attack.
(12)	Daylight	Prepare to support fourth phase of 15th Scottish Division's attack.

The barrage, which was to cover the front of the three centre Divisions only, was to move by a series of 300-yard lifts at intervals of twelve minutes. The end of each twelve-minute period was to be notified to the infantry by the firing of yellow smoke by one field-gun per troop.

For the artillery this programme was only the beginning of a fortnight of almost unceasing battle. The programme may serve, therefore, to convey some idea of the exacting nature of the gunners' task. When a Division is attacking, its C.R.A. becomes for the time being the senior partner and director of the artillery " combine," and he directs the fire not only of his own Divisional artillery but also of all other guns within range. In consequence, the man behind the gun —even when the infantry of his own Division is standing by—seldom gets any rest. And when his own Division is attacking, then of course the gunner gives each infantry brigade in turn the benefit of the full weight of all the guns of the Division. Repeated brigade attacks such as were to occur throughout Operation " Veritable " mean repeated moves for the guns, with more positions to be reconnoitred, more ammunition to be brought up, more survey to be done, more gun-pits to be dug, more calculations to be worked out and task-tables to be prepared—and prepared with an accuracy which, even in the uttermost depths of exhaustion, can yet admit of no error, for the lives of our own infantry are at stake. On one occasion during Operation " Veritable " no less than seven hundred guns answered a " Victor " call for all available guns. The artillery had changed a lot since those early days in May 1940 when the Division first deployed its gimcrack armoury in Essex. In the campaign in North-West Europe the artillery concentration was Britain's secret weapon—and it was never used better than in Operation " Veritable." *[6th Feb.]*

In addition to this artillery programme, each of the five forward Divisions had organised a " pepper-pot group," consisting of its medium machine-guns and 4.2-inch mortars, its light A.A. and A.Tk. guns. These pepper-pot groups, too, were to open up at 5 A.M., and their rôle was to deny all movement to the enemy in the forward area by a constant sweep of fire across the front.

Finally, the attack was to be supported by the whole weight of the 2nd Tactical Air Force, by Bomber Command, and by the 9th U.S. Bombardment Division. In the days prior to D Day these Air Forces had been busy attacking railways, bridges, and ferries in the enemy back areas. On the night of 7th February enemy railheads at Goch and Cleve, and road centres and billeting areas at Weeze, Udem, and Calcar were to be subjected to annihilating attack.

7th February was a day of intensive preparations. About 9 P.M. that night many hundreds of Lancasters and Halifaxes roared over on their way to Cleve and Goch; soon the glow of fires was turning the eastern sky to crimson. *[7th Feb.]*

In the early hours of D Day the move to forward assembly areas began. The eastern sky was still glowing red and shot with tracer. On the right the 46th Brigade, with the Tank Coldstream Guards and its share of " Funnies " in support, moved up to the woods by Groesbeek, where the forward battalions, the Glasgow Highlanders and the Cameronians, established their Regimental Aid Posts. The 227th Brigade on the left, with the Tank Scots Guards and more " Funnies " *[8th Feb.]*

8th Feb. in support, started rather earlier to move up to the Nederrijksche woods west of Hooge Hof. Already the roads—or tracks rather—to the front were packed with vehicles. At 5 A.M., as the 227th Brigade Group was passing through the gun area, the comparative quiet of the night was shattered by the earth-shaking roar of the bombardment's opening salvoes. Those who had forgotten their cotton-wool were to be deaf for many hours to come. In the forward assembly areas the forward troops ate their breakfasts—to the accompaniment of the pounding of the " pepper-pot " Bofors in action close by. Dawn came grey and miserable, with low cloud, heralding several days of almost continuous rain. So bad were the conditions that the medium bomber strikes which were to have been delivered that day on Nutterden and Materborn both had to be cancelled.

The 46th Brigade was to attack on a one-battalion front, with the Glasgow Highlanders leading. The Glasgow Highlanders were to advance with their right on the Lubertsche Straat, which was to become the 46th Brigade axis. Their objectives were the villages of Haus Kreuzfuhrt and Hettsteeg, about two thousand yards away. At about 10.10 A.M. the Glasgow Highlanders left their forming-up place in Groesbeek accordingly, to cross their start-line a short distance to the eastward. Here the enemy's front-line was only a few hundred yards away. The enemy's defensive fire was surprisingly light.

At the same time the two troops of Flails emerged accompanied by a squadron of the Coldstream ; their job was to clear a passage through the minefield as soon as the barrage had lifted at 10.30 A.M. On their way to the start-line, however, all the Flails were bogged except one on the right, which reached the minefield about 10.40 A.M. and flailed a passage through it. The tanks of the Coldstream then poured through to join the Glasgow Highlanders, who had already gone through on the tail of the barrage.

At Boersteeg at 11.50 A.M. the barrage paused for twenty-five minutes: here the Glasgow Highlanders leap-frogged companies. By 1.15 P.M. they had crossed the Dutch-German frontier to reach Haus Kreuzfuhrt and Hettsteeg, their final objectives, having taken 230 prisoners at the cost of very few casualties. The supporting Coldstream had had several of their tanks bogged by the way, but they had knocked out three 75-mm. A.Tk. guns. For the next forty-eight hours of continuous rain the Glasgow Highlanders were to be kept extremely busy in the neighbourhood, digging out countless vehicles of all sorts along the 46th Brigade's axis.

Meanwhile the Cameronians had been following up the Glasgow Highlanders to the woods at Haus Kreuzfuhrt, which Lieutenant-Colonel Remington Hobbs—now commanding the Cameronians—had chosen as his forming-up place and as the rendezvous with his supporting armour. There in the wood during the hour's pause in the barrage between 1.15 and 2.15 P.M. the Cameronians formed up, and as the barrage lifted at 2.15 their two forward companies crossed the start-line on time. Their accompanying tanks and transport, however, had great difficulty in finding a way through the wood, and were much delayed in consequence. The Cameronians could see troops of the 53rd Division abreast of them on their right, while reports from the left told that the 227th Brigade was also up in line.

By 3 P.M. the Cameronians' forward companies had reached the Galgensteeg spur or promontory which juts northward from the Reichswald south of Kranenburg. Here the left company, "B," ran into an anti-personnel minefield and suffered many casualties. Most of these wounded men had legs blown off: their evacuation was a most painful process, which they bore with the utmost courage.

On the spur and in the woods round Auf den Heovel the Cameronians found a most elaborate system of field defences, well sited and wired and mutually supporting. If the enemy had manned these defences, the attack would have been a very different story. Instead, it seems that what enemy there were had sought shelter from the bombardment in the cellars of Frasselt.

Here on the Galgensteeg spur " C " Company of the Cameronians was due to pass through from reserve with the last lift of the barrage at 4 P.M. and to clear Frasselt, which lay in the valley down below. When the time came, however, neither Churchills nor Crocodiles had yet arrived, so Lieutenant-Colonel Remington Hobbs postponed the attack till 5.15 P.M. Infantry, Churchills, and Crocodiles then advanced together over the eight hundred yards or so to Frasselt, and the Crocodiles burnt the houses. Many Germans were killed, and forty-eight prisoners and a battery of 88-mm. guns taken. By 6.30 P.M. the Cameronians had consolidated on a two-company front beyond Frasselt and had sent a patrol forward to investigate the bridges over the anti-tank ditch behind Tuthees.

On the right the Cameronians were now in touch with the 53rd

Division, which had occupied the Branden Berg, the culminating point of the Galgensteeg spur in the north-west corner of the Reichswald.

We now come to the 227th Brigade Group on the left. Its final objectives were Klinkenberg—that is, the northern extension of Frasselt—and the road and railway triangle east-south-east of Kranenburg. The 227th Brigade was to start on a one-battalion front, with the Argylls leading. At an early stage the H.L.I. were to come up on the left.

About 9 A.M. the Argylls climbed on the Scots Guards' tanks in their assembly area in the Nederrijksche woods and headed for their forming-up place. Their start-line was the track that runs south from Hooge Hof. Before they could reach it they had to pass through the old American minefield laid by the U.S. Airborne troops who had dropped in this area back in the previous September. The ground round about was still littered with their parachutes and with the skeletons of their gliders. Fortunately the Americans had laid their mines on top of the ground, plain to see, so the rifle companies and the accompanying Scots Guards found the gap, taped it, and passed through to reach the start-line safely. Not so the carriers and the " Funnies "—the mud was too much for them. Few of them ever reached the gap, far less the start-line. The rifle companies of the H.L.I. followed the Argylls through the gap.

From the outset the enemy's defensive fire on the 227th Brigade front was heavier than on the front of the 46th Brigade. Indeed the Argylls' left forward company, " A," had every one of its officers hit soon after the start. C.S.M. Green rallied the company and took it on, an act for which he was to get the D.C.M. from Field-Marshal Montgomery a few days later. Mines, too, took their toll, but the ample pauses in the barrage enabled the infantry to reconnect with it. By 11.40 A.M. the leading companies of the Argylls were up to the Dutch-German frontier on schedule.

Here on the frontier during the pause between 11.40 A.M. and 12.15 P.M. the H.L.I. passed through " A " Company of the Argylls, and the 227th Brigade thereafter continued its attack on a two-battalion front.

On the right the Argylls now advanced with one company up, " B," directed on Elsenhof and Hettsteeghof. " B " Company's taking of Elsenhof was a perfect example of how well it pays to keep well closed up to the barrage. Elsenhof was a special target for the

Mattresses super-imposed on the normal barrage. Yet " B " Company entered Elsenhof so close on the barrage lift that they took eighty prisoners before one of them could fire a shot, together with a whole battery of well-sited 88-mm.s still with their breach and muzzle covers on—all at the cost of one casualty caused by our own guns.

From Hettsteeghof, where the barrage paused again from 1.15 to 2.15 P.M., the Argylls continued on a two-company front against growing resistance and under increasing mortar-fire, evidently directed on them from the high ground in front of the Cameronians. " D " Company, coming up on the right of " B " through smoke and mud, had to go all out to close on the barrage before it lifted. Soon after, the last of the Scots Guards' Churchills supporting the Argylls bogged down just as it was shooting " B " Company into Kranenburg station. Close house-to-house fighting followed, both in the northern half of Galgensteeg, where the Argylls were in touch with the Cameronians, and along the railway beyond the station, where they were in touch with the H.L.I.

After the last lift at 4 P.M. the Argylls found themselves rather precariously positioned on their final objectives, painfully vulnerable to the counter-attack which did not come. An hour later they watched with satisfaction as the Cameronians and their Crocodiles swept over the Galgensteeg spur and into Frasselt. Thereupon the enemy's mortar-fire slackened greatly. By evening the Argylls had consolidated on their objectives, and the Scots Guards had extricated five of their Churchills. The Argylls too had sent patrols on to investigate the ditch.

Meanwhile the H.L.I., who had passed through the left of the Argylls on the frontier, had first pivoted left and had then swung up into line to the northward on a three-company front, to advance on Kranenburg with their left on the Wyler-Kranenburg-Cleve axis. Very soon the H.L.I. found themselves in an anti-personnel minefield. All their accompanying Flails were already bogged. In consequence they lost several men and were much slowed down. None the less they managed to recover their position behind the barrage soon after it had lifted at 12.15 P.M.—a very fine performance.

When an hour later the second pause in the barrage began, " C " and " A " Companies of the H.L.I. had reached the anti-tank ditch where it crossed the main road outside Kranenburg, while " B " Company was on the railway just short of the station. " C " Company

8th Feb. found the bridge over the anti-tank ditch on the main road still intact, and they rushed it with the help of the Scots Guards, eight of whose tanks bogged down just short of it. One only got across. With its help "C" Company went on into Kranenburg to clear the main street. South of the road, however, "A" Company found the ditch filled with water and swept by machine-gun fire. Major Merrifield, the company commander, was killed. After some confused fighting, "A" made its way, mostly by way of the railway station, to join "C" in Kranenburg, whereupon "C" and "A" jointly completed its clearance. "B" and "D" Companies meanwhile made their way round farther south along the railway. Having thus by-passed Kranenburg itself, these companies first cleared the factory area to the south-east and then came in on to the main road east of Kranenburg. By early evening the H.L.I. too had consolidated on their objectives. They were in touch with the Argylls on the railway. The Gordons were in reserve, still back in the Nederrijksche woods.

Thus by 6.30 P.M. the 15th Scottish Division had carried out the first phase of the operation with complete success. The weight of the artillery bombardment had now switched far away to the north across the floods, where the 3rd Canadian Division in its Buffaloes was busy taking Zyfflich and Zandpol on the banks of the Rhine. The next phase of the 15th Scottish Division's operation was scheduled to begin by Movement Light at 9 P.M., when the 44th Brigade, with the Gordons now under command, was to cross the anti-tank ditch east of Frasselt and, penetrating the Siegfried Line defences, seize the heavily defended areas of the Wolfs-Berg, the Hingst-Berg, and Nutterden, and thus open the northern axis Kranenburg-Nutterden. The 44th Brigade had sent reconnaissance parties forward behind the 46th Brigade, and had itself been waiting all day in Nijmegen, ready to move up along the 46th Brigade's axis in the Kangaroos of the 49th A.P.C. Regiment and of the 1st Canadian A.P.C. Regiment which had been allotted to it. The Armoured Breaching Force, which was to precede the infantry of the 44th Brigade, comprised the Tank Grenadiers, a section of Crocodiles, one and a half squadrons of Flails, a squadron of A.V.R.E.s with portable bridges and fascines, and a battery of S.P. guns.

A word must here be said about the traffic conditions prevailing by afternoon on the 46th Brigade's axis. Originally Division had allotted an axis to each of the two leading brigades, the 46th and the 227th. All day it had rained. The 227th Brigade's axis had been almost non-existent from the start, and by afternoon it had melted away altogether. The 227th Brigade—and much else besides —had been counting on using the main road Nijmegen-Wyler-Kranenburg by afternoon, since it was in fact the only real axis; but the 2nd Canadian Division on the left had found Wyler so hard a nut that it was unable to crack it till 6 P.M.—with the result that the main road remained closed till an hour later than had been reckoned on.

In consequence of these troubles farther north, the 46th Brigade's axis became that afternoon the 15th Scottish Division's only axis. It was a narrow, unmetalled track with deep ditches on either side. Along it had passed already " F " Echelon unit transport of the 46th Brigade, together with the tanks and lorries of the Coldstream and the " Funnies "—and they had done it no good. On to it was now thrown the extra load, not only of the 227th Brigade's transport but also of five field regiments, which, about 4 P.M., began their forward move into new positions from which they could cover the advance to Cleve. And there was still the 44th Brigade Group to follow. It was to be a nightmare night, throughout which every officer and man in the 46th Brigade was to be at work without a let-up on traffic control and vehicle recovery in an effort to produce some sort of order out of chaos—and this despite the fact that Division had made the most careful provision for traffic control. After that night the 46th Brigade axis, too, was finally finished : traffic had to go by the main road or not at all.

All afternoon, then, the 44th Brigade waited for the order to move. At last it came. The K.O.S.B., who were the leading battalion, set out from Nijmegen at 9 P.M., when according to plan they should already have been crossing the start-line at Frasselt. All night the 44th Brigade Group struggled forward through mud and rain and traffic jams, with repeated postponements of H-hour and changes of plan. The A.V.R.E.s in particular were a constant source of delay. The trees on either side of the narrow track fouled the bulky girder bridges which they carried and snapped the supports, with the result that the bridges fell forward into the lowered position in front of the A.V.R.E.s, making them almost unmanoeuvrable. Beyond Groesbeek the track became a shambles.

9th Feb.

Small wonder, then, that when the head of the Armoured Breaching Force at last reached the start-line about 4 A.M. it was in no sort of order; in the confusion several of its commanders could not even be found. About 5 A.M., without the formality of assembly area or forming-up place, the Armoured Breaching Force struggled into action somehow under the direction of Major Pike of the Grenadiers. The Flails and A.V.R.E.s advanced on the ditch along five of the numerous and more or less parallel tracks that led to it from the Frasselt road. At once Flails began to bog down, and soon three of the lanes were useless. On the other two, however, the A.V.R.E.s reached the ditch successfully, to lay a bridge on one of them and to make a fascine crossing on the other. As dawn was breaking, " C " Company of the K.O.S.B.—the only rifle company to make Frasselt across country—advanced over the bridge: a most memorable achievement. Almost at the outset, however, an A.Tk. gun towed by a Kangaroo fouled the bridge and blocked it. Switching to the very inferior fascine crossing, " C " Company completed its crossing and quickly established a bridgehead in Schottheide and Konigsheide, where it captured a bunch of very demoralised prisoners. The other three rifle companies of the K.O.S.B., which had been diverted north to the main road, soon found their way round by Kranenburg and over the fascines to join " C " in the bridgehead.

All night long the Gordons, too, with their supporting squadron of Scots Guards, had been moving up under orders of the 44th Brigade and directed on Kranenburg. The route allotted to them they had found obstructed by all manner of obstacles—mines, road-blocks, trenches—so it was almost dawn before they passed through the H.L.I. in the ruins of Kranenburg to force the Siegfried Line where it crossed the main road Kranenburg-Cleve. An hour later " A " Company reported that they had captured intact the road-bridge over the main anti-tank ditch. The large trees, too, which lined the road had not been felled, though they had all been prepared with charges ready for felling. Quite clearly the bombardment had completely disorganised the defence. Meeting little to stop them other than mud and a few " R " type mines, the Gordons reached Nutterden, which they cleared by 10 A.M., taking two hundred or so very " bomb-happy " prisoners in the large concrete bunkers.

According to the 44th Brigade's plan the R.S.F. should now have passed through the K.O.S.B. in their bridgehead to take the twin knolls, the Wolfs-Berg and the Hingst-Berg. In the existing conditions, however, the R.S.F. could not possibly have got forward in time. Brigadier Cumming-Bruce therefore ordered the K.O.S.B. to push on to the Wolfs-Berg and the Royal Scots, who were now coming up the main road to Nutterden, to take the Hingst-Berg. Thereupon Lieutenant-Colonel Richardson ordered "A" and "B" Companies of the K.O.S.B. to go for the Wolfs-Berg in their Kangaroos. This they did to great effect, taking the knoll by 11.15 A.M. together with 240 prisoners, of whom 10 were officers, and a battery of medium guns. Soon after, the Royal Scots occupied the Hingst-Berg half a mile away to the north-east, where they formed a link between the K.O.S.B. and the Gordons. Thus it was that by about noon on D + 1—unavoidably, that is, some eleven hours behind schedule—the 44th Brigade had successfully completed the second phase of the Division's attack.

In the third phase the 46th Brigade on the right and the 227th Brigade on the left should have passed through and advanced to the outskirts of Cleve. Again, however, conditions of weather and terrain compelled the Divisional Commander to modify his plan. Instead he ordered the 44th Brigade to remain in the lead and to push on.

Two hill features bar the way to Cleve from the south-west : both of these lie within a mile or so of Materborn, and so came to be known collectively as the "Materborn feature." The lower and more westerly of these features runs roughly north and south through Esperance. Against this Esperance feature Brigadier Cumming-Bruce now sent the Royal Scots from Nutterden with a supporting squadron of Grenadiers. The higher and more easterly feature runs north and south through Bresserberg. Against it Brigadier Cumming-Bruce sent the K.O.S.B. in their Kangaroos, supported by a second squadron of Grenadiers. At the same time the Gordons advanced from Nutterden along the main road towards Donsbreuggen.

Passing through the Gordons in Nutterden, the Royal Scots took the Class 3 road through the narrow neck of the Reichswald southeast of Nutterden and attacked the Esperance feature beyond, on which the defence over-print showed a formidable defence system. The enemy, however, offered very little resistance and the Royal Scots took about seventy prisoners, most of them still in the dug-outs. The trenches proved to be poor, shallow affairs of very recent construction. While they were consolidating about 4 P.M. the Royal

9th Feb. Scots came under a good deal of sniping and spandau-fire from the Bresserberg feature, half a mile on.

Meanwhile the K.O.S.B. had been driving east by forest tracks, heading with all haste for Bresserberg. The feature here was the obvious key to Cleve, and the K.O.S.B. reached it about 3 P.M., just in time to forestall elements of the 7th Parachute Division—the first of the German reinforcing Divisions—which had been sent to occupy it. After a sharp action on the slopes in the gathering dusk, the K.O.S.B. consolidated their position on the feature. They had won a decisive success.

The 44th Brigade's rapid progress showed plainly that the 15th Scottish Division had broken through the enemy's front and that the enemy had few local reserves available. The time seemed to have come for exploitation. In the late afternoon, therefore, the Divisional Commander ordered the 15th Divisional Reconnaissance Regiment up from Nijmegen to probe eastward. The Reconnaissance Regiment found a dense traffic block on the main axis Nijmegen-Kranenburg, and was greatly delayed in consequence. When at last its patrols were able to get through they found confusion reigning in Cleve itself, but met organised resistance on the by-pass road to the southward through Materborn. Another patrol got as far as the cross-roads at Bedburg on the way to Calcar before it was held up by S.P. 88-mm. guns.

Divisional orders for the next day were as follows: the 44th Brigade to remain on the Materborn feature; the 227th Brigade to clear Cleve in the morning; the 46th Brigade to assemble a mobile column, which was to consist of the Seaforth in Kangaroos, one squadron of the Coldstream, and one S.P. field battery, in readiness to exploit to Calcar; the 6th Guards Tank Brigade to assemble another mobile column, which was to consist of a tank battalion (less two squadrons), one infantry company in Kangaroos from the 46th Brigade, and one S.P. field battery, in readiness to seize the Emmerich ferry.

Floods, mud, and traffic congestion—these three were to defeat all plans. On the right the 53rd Division had cleared the northern Reichswald up to the Stoppel-Berg, but its axis too had now completely collapsed, with the result that its transport also had now come to swell the prevailing congestion on the 15th Scottish Divisional axis Nijmegen-Wyler-Kranenburg-Nutterden. Nor was this all. Corps had sent up two brigades of the 43rd Division along this same axis, with orders to turn right at Nutterden, by-pass Cleve, pass through

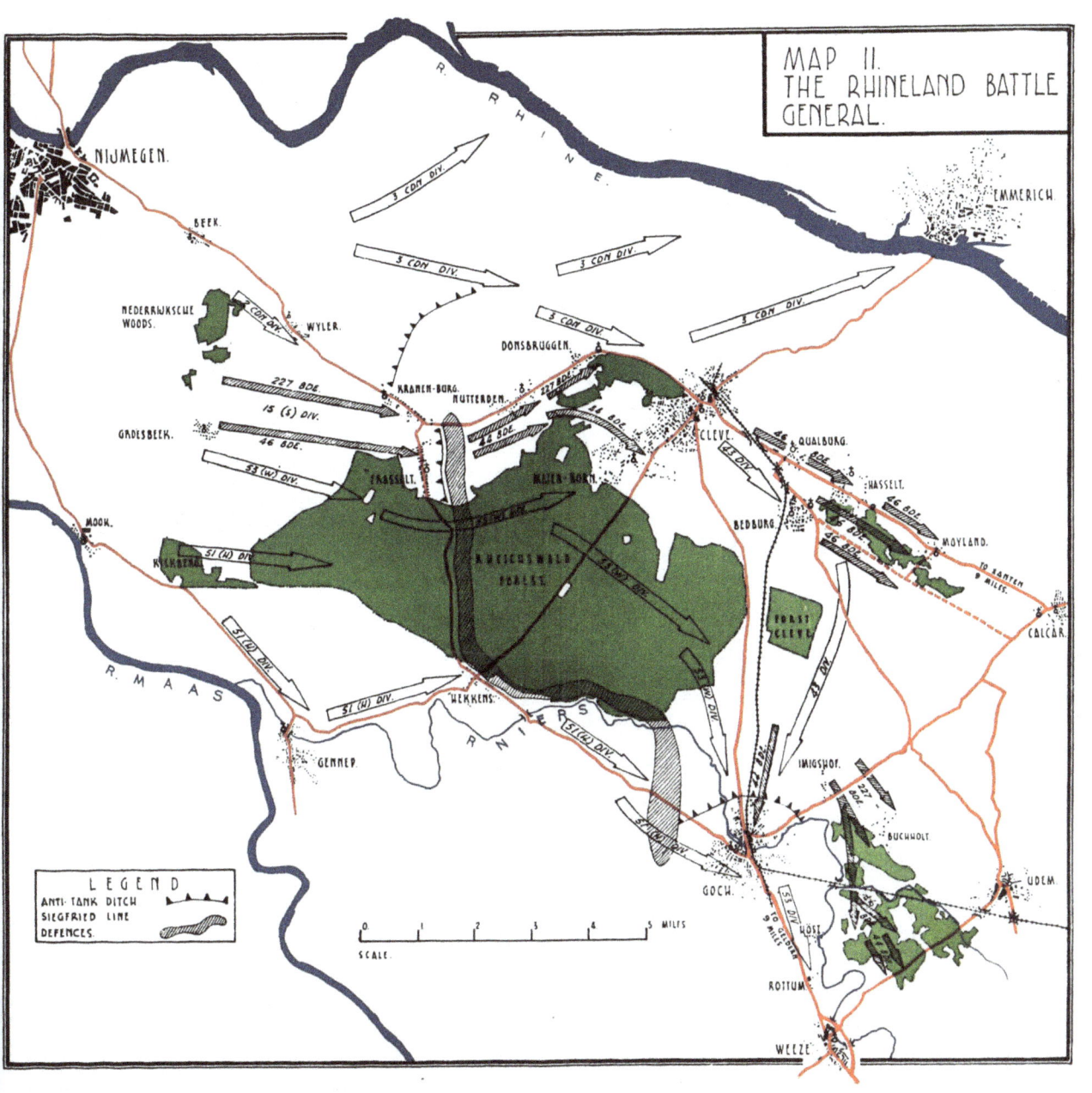

the 44th Brigade on the Materborn feature, and advance southward on Goch. Before midnight the leading brigade, the 129th, had reached Nutterden in Kangaroos, making confusion worse confounded.

9th Feb.

Moreover, most ominous fact of all, the flood level was steadily rising; already there were seventeen inches of water over this sole remaining axis at several points east of Wyler. Nor was this the only peril by flood: far away to the south, on the First U.S. Army front, the Germans had opened the locks of a large dam on the head-waters of the Roer, whereupon the Roer had overflowed its banks across the whole Ninth U.S. Army front. In consequence the offensive planned by that army for 10th February was now indefinitely postponed. This postponement was to leave the German Command free in the days immediately ahead to concentrate all their sector reserves against the First Canadian Army.

Driving on in darkness and rain by the intricate lanes south-east of Nutterden, the 129th Brigade missed its turning in the early hours of 10th February. Instead of by-passing Cleve, it drove straight on into the westerly suburbs of Cleve itself. There it was set on by newly arrived parachute troops full of fight. Attacked from all sides, the 129th Brigade formed a tight defensive laager, and there it remained stuck like a fly on a fly-paper. Its unexpected presence here in Cleve was to queer the pitch considerably for the 15th Scottish Division.

10th Feb.

Back in Nutterden, Brigadier Colville had ordered the Argylls and the Gordons—now back under his command—to entank on the Scots Guards' tanks at first light that morning and to make a quick move through the reconnaissance elements of the 43rd Division and into Cleve. Travelling by the third-class road which turns right beyond Nutterden, the Argylls were to go to an assembly area near the Clever-Berg or Lookout Tower Hill, while the Gordons were to push on by the main road through Donsbreuggen. The 43rd Division was to keep the 214th Brigade—following the 129th—off the road between 8 A.M. and 10 A.M. to facilitate this move. The H.L.I. were to remain in Brigade reserve south of Nutterden.

Unfortunately this move did not work out to plan. Coming up on to the main road from the south, the tanks and other vehicles with the Argylls found the 43rd Division's transport parked so closely along the road and in every side-lane that they almost despaired of

10th Feb. ever reaching the main road at all. When after endless delays and halts and about-turns the column did reach the road, it had lost all semblance of order and advanced on the enemy headed by an immense girder bridge. The reconnaissance troop of the Scots Guards managed to get through the jam and to push on to the Clever-Berg, where it met sharp resistance and had two Honeys knocked out. Soon after it had struggled through Nutterden, however, and turned right, the column itself was ordered to halt in the woods beyond and to clear the road. The traffic congestion had necessitated yet another change of plan. The Argylls were now to go up on foot to relieve the Royal Scots and K.O.S.B. on the Materborn feature, whereupon these two would advance into Cleve, extricate the 129th Brigade, and clear the place. At dusk the Argylls duly reached the Materborn feature and took over.

Meanwhile the Gordons had found the main road to Donsbreuggen scientifically blocked by countless fallen trees. All day they pushed laboriously along it. Not till nightfall did they reach Donsbreuggen, where they contacted the 3rd Canadian Division. Donsbreuggen had been very thoroughly destroyed: its ruins occupied the narrow fairway between the forest on the one hand and the wastes of flood-water on the other.

While the 227th Brigade had thus been struggling up to join him outside Cleve, Brigadier Cumming-Bruce had been busy consolidating the 44th Brigade's position. That afternoon he had ordered the R.S.F. to clear the two prominent hills astride the western approach to Cleve —the Clever-Berg and the Stern-Berg. Major Harrison, acting commanding officer of the R.S.F., thereupon sent off a mobile force of carriers, Wasps, and 3-inch mortars, under Major A. D. N. Hunter, to seize the Clever-Berg as a firm base. As it approached from the west, the mobile column drew fire from the hill. Dismounting his carrier crews, Major Hunter led an attack on the hill in the gathering dusk. After the Fusiliers had overrun several enemy slits, the Wasps closed on the tower itself and set it on fire. Unfortunately Major Hunter himself was mortally wounded, but the little force consolidated under Captain Sullivan. Despite subsequent enemy infiltrations into the woods round Lookout Tower, it continued to hold the hill till Cleve was finally cleared, accounting meanwhile for sixty or more of the enemy.

While this fight was going on round the Lookout Tower, the

remainder of the R.S.F. were advancing northward on a one-company front along the ride which runs through the forest just west of the Stern-Berg. It was at this stage that the guns supporting the 129th Brigade in Cleve opened fire on the Stern-Berg and the forest surrounding it, and unfortunately caused casualties in all four companies of the R.S.F. Throughout the night the R.S.F. remained in the wood round the Stern-Berg in contact with the enemy.

10th Feb.

We come next to the K.O.S.B. and the Royal Scots, who, according to the revised plan, should have gone down into Cleve that afternoon. By evening Brigadier Cumming-Bruce had decided that the operation was not on. Out in front the 129th Brigade, in close contact with the enemy, was still spread about over the southern part of the objective given to him—his own artillery therefore could not give him due support; on the other hand, the R.S.F. had already been persistently shelled by the 43rd Division's guns; and, finally, the relief of the K.O.S.B. and the Royal Scots could not arrive before dark. Brigadier Cumming-Bruce proposed, therefore, and the Divisional Commander agreed, that the 44th Brigade should relieve the 129th Brigade in an orderly manner next morning and that it should then set about clearing Cleve from the south.

That evening the Divisional Commander ordered the 46th Brigade (less the Seaforth, who had been detailed for mobile column) to take over the Materborn feature next morning, and the 227th Brigade to concentrate at Donsbreuggen preparatory to clearing Cleve from the north.

10th February had been a day of frustration. The weather was still shocking; the going deeper than ever. Despite the fact that all routes had been " frozen " to normal administrative traffic for twenty-four hours, traffic congestion had made troop movement almost impossible. Golden opportunities had slipped by in consequence—and all the time the enemy front was hardening. That day two more enemy Divisions had appeared, one of them the 6th Parachute Division.

But it was maintenance clearly that was going to be the biggest headache. The enemy had evidently breached the winter dykes on the Alter Rhine, for there was now two feet of water over the main road east of Wyler. That evening Divisional " Q " managed to get one day's supply sent forward under special authority along this " frozen " main axis.

11th Feb.   At 7 A.M. the K.O.S.B. sent reconnaissance parties into Cleve. Passing the Clever-Berg they ran into trouble with some enemy on its wooded slopes. Soon after, Captain Sullivan's detachment of R.S.F. on top of the Clever-Berg dealt with these with the help of tanks. An hour later the K.O.S.B. and the Royal Scots followed into Cleve. By 10.30 A.M. they had taken over the southern suburbs from the 129th Brigade, which then pulled out to concentrate farther east. At the same time the 214th Brigade was by-passing Cleve to the southward; in the afternoon it took Materborn village and after dark it entered Hau. The K.O.S.B. and the Royal Scots, with the Grenadiers in support, then set to work to clear the southern half of Cleve. They found hardly a house standing. Fortunately, however, in view of the critical supply situation, they found large stocks of food.

On their relief on the Materborn feature by the 46th Brigade the Argylls moved to Donsbreuggen. The Gordons meanwhile, with their supporting squadron of Scots Guards, had been ordered to push on from Donsbreuggen into Cleve along the main road. Where the densely wooded hills rise steeply on the right of the road the Gordons met some stiffish opposition, but Major J. P. Mann of the Scots Guards contrived somehow to get his tanks up on to the high ground, and with their support the Gordons in the afternoon reached Cleve, where Lieutenant-Colonel De Winton set up his headquarters in the cellars of a boot factory. Cleve had been bombed flat, so movement was difficult, but his forward companies soon reported not only that they had cleared the northern sector up to the Canal, but also that they had taken a bridge almost intact over the canal west of the railway station. By 3.30 P.M. they had established a bridgehead across the canal and the bridge itself had been repaired.

All day long the H.L.I. with another squadron of the Scots Guards had been halted in the rain by the northern road into Cleve. Their rôle was to pass through the Gordons and to clear that part of Cleve beyond the canal. At dusk orders came at last. With the minimum of preparation the H.L.I. went through the Gordons' bridgehead with tank and Crocodile support. At one moment there were all the makings of a promising battle between the H.L.I. and the Scots Guards on one side and the 44th Brigade and the Grenadiers coming up from the south. That difficulty resolved, the H.L.I. went on to clear the north-eastern half of the town. Thereupon the Reconnaissance Regiment managed to get patrols through along the road to Emmerich.

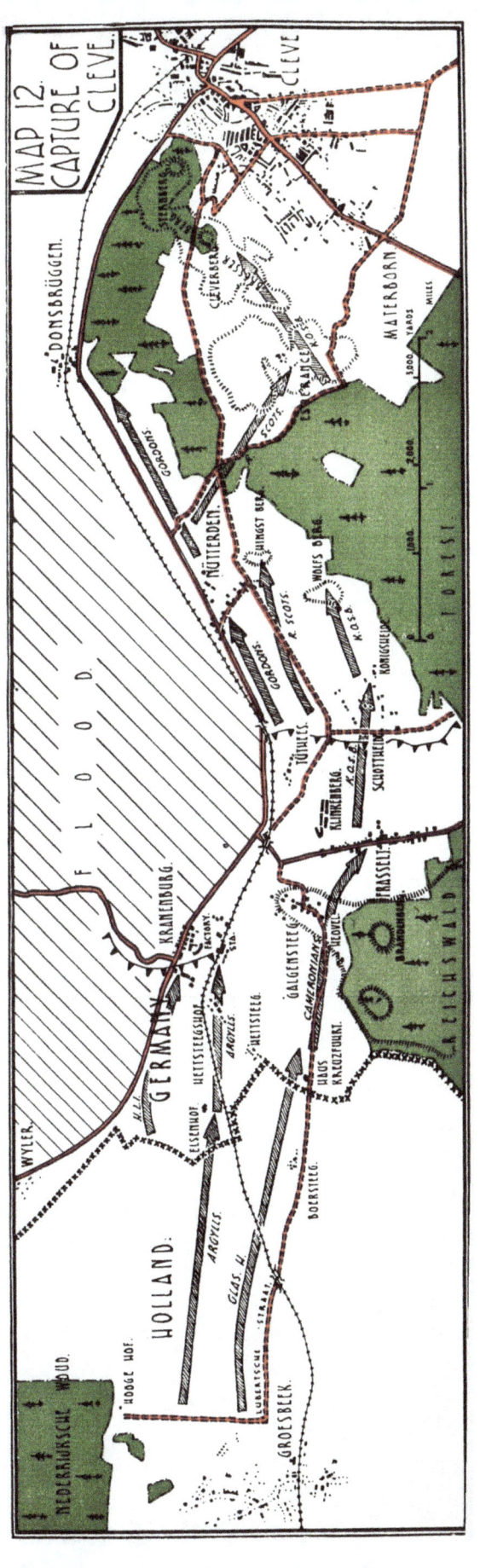

On this day the 15th Scottish Division Main Headquarters moved up from Nijmegen to the eastern outskirts of Nutterden. *11th Feb.*

The time had now come to release the 46th Brigade's mobile column, which, it will be remembered, was to consist of the Seaforth in Kangaroos, a squadron of the Coldstream, a battery of S.P. guns, and a platoon of sappers—all preceded by a squadron of the Reconnaissance Regiment and under command of Lieutenant-Colonel Hunt of the Seaforth. By 9 A.M. this column had formed up on the road from Materborn to Cleve. It then moved off through the town and past the station, leaving Cleve about mid-day by the road which leads south-east to Calcar. *12th Feb.*

Immediately the column met small groups of the enemy. At the same time reconnaissance patrols reported that the enemy in some strength were holding Qualburg, a village just beyond the level-crossing and less than a mile and a half from the station. "B" Company, the vanguard of the Seaforth, drove straight for Qualburg in their Kangaroos. The houses were full of the enemy, who blocked the road by knocking out four of the Kangaroos with the fire of their Bazookas and of an S.P. sited to fire down the road. Enemy shelling and mortaring, too, had now grown heavy. The Seaforth debussed in the middle of the enemy position, while the Coldstream reopened the road by towing the crippled Kangaroos out of the fairway. Then, while the Coldstream knocked out the S.P., "B" Company cleared the houses after a sharp fight at very close quarters, killing twenty-five Germans, wounding many more, and taking sixty-five prisoners. In this brilliant action "B" Company lost two officers and twenty-three other ranks.

Leap-frogging companies, the Seaforth passed on to reach Hasselt, a mile farther east, in the late afternoon, where they again found the enemy in some strength and the shell-fire heavy. Here on the high ground to the south they made contact with the 129th Brigade, which was about to take Bedburg that same evening. While the Seaforth were closing on Hasselt in the failing light and the Coldstream were engaging the enemy S.P.s, a report, which subsequently proved to be unfounded, reached Lieutenant-Colonel Hunt to the effect that enemy infantry and armour were heavily counter-attacking the 43rd Division on his right. In view of this report, Brigadier Villiers approved the disengagement of the forward companies and their withdrawal to

12th Feb. Qualburg, where the column consolidated for the night. The total bag of prisoners for the day was now eighty-five.

In the evening the 7th Canadian Brigade of the 3rd Canadian Division took over Cleve from the 44th and 227th Brigades. The Canadians were now across the whole length of the Cleve Canal from Cleve to the Rhine.

The 44th Brigade was to remain at rest in or near Cleve till 18th February. The rest, however, was to be qualified by fairly persistent enemy shelling, occasional bombing, and the incessant din of our own guns—for the Materborn feature had now become a 5.5-inch area.

Of the 46th Brigade (less the Seaforth) the Cameronians were still on the Materborn feature; the Glasgow Highlanders had gone into a temporary rest area in Cleve itself.

Of the 227th Brigade the H.L.I. and the Gordons were reorganising in Cleve; the Argylls were in Donsbreuggen.

The supply situation was growing worse. The axis between Beek, west of Wyler, and Kranenburg was now flooded to such a depth that the only supply vehicles which could get through were 3-tonners. With these "Q" managed to organise two forward supply points—one at Nutterden, the other at Kranenburg.

On this day elements of two new enemy Divisions, the 15th Panzer Grenadiers and the 116th Panzer, made their appearance farther south.

13th Feb. During the night the Seaforth's patrols reported that the enemy were withdrawing from Hasselt. Next morning the Seaforth occupied the village without opposition other than observed artillery fire, both heavy and well directed. The floods had now submerged most of the countryside on either side of the main Cleve-Calcar road, which here runs on a narrow ridge of slightly higher ground. Nevertheless patrols managed to get through from Hasselt some way towards Moyland. They reported that the enemy in strength were holding a position in the woods astride the road three-quarters of a mile or so east of Hasselt.

In these circumstances Brigadier Villiers decided that he would have to put in a brigade attack on Moyland the next day. He planned to bring up the Cameronians on the left and the Glasgow Highlanders on the right of the Seaforth in Hasselt. With the Seaforth and the Cameronians he would then attack east on Moyland, while he sent

THE RHINELAND BATTLE

the Glasgow Highlanders to secure his right flank by occupying the pine-clad ridge parallel to and about five hundred yards south of the road—the ridge which was soon to win so evil a notoriety. 13th Feb.

During the day the 129th Brigade, still farther to the right, took the Esels-Berg, a prominent hill a mile or so south-east of Bedburg, against determined opposition.

On the other side of Cleve the floods, which had now submerged five miles of the road between Beek and Nutterden up to a depth of four feet, had completely closed the main axis to all traffic. Unit transport which had taken refuge on the platforms of Kranenburg station and elsewhere was to be marooned for days. Twelve thousand rounds of 25-pounder ammunition which had been stacked at Kranenburg for early use slowly disappeared from view; the ammunition could not be saved, for the approaches to the dump were impassable. Telephone communication between 15th Scottish Division rear in Nijmegen and Main Headquarters near Nutterden broke down almost completely. One artillery headquarters had to move four times in thirty-six hours. The 130th Brigade—the third brigade of the 43rd Division—had been stranded for two days back in Nijmegen. These were only a few of the consequences.

Yet the machine continued to work. 15th Scottish Divisional "Q" organised a D.U.K.W.s service to bring up supplies for all units forward of Wyler, while Corps, who had a small forward dump in Nutterden, took over responsibility for the supply of ammunition and petrol. Miraculously, no unit was to go short throughout all the fighting ahead.

When reconnaissance parties of the Cameronians and Glasgow Highlanders moved up from Cleve towards the Hasselt cross-roads next morning they found that the water had now risen to hedge-top height south-east of the level-crossing and that the Seaforth at Hasselt were marooned on a small island in the encircling floods. Brigadier Villiers decided, therefore, that he must again change his plan. The Cameronians and the Glasgow Highlanders he diverted southward to assembly areas near Bedburg behind the 43rd Division front, and there at a hasty "O" Group he ordered them to advance south-eastward—the Cameronians on the right, the Glasgow Highlanders in the centre. At the same time the Seaforth on the left were to push forward along the main road as opportunity offered. 14th Feb.

14th Feb.

About 1.30 P.M. the Cameronians on the right, supported by a squadron of the Coldstream, set off in "advance-to-contact" formation along the track that leads south-east from Bedburg, to pass immediately north of the Esels-Berg, in the neighbourhood of which the 129th Brigade had been busy beating off a series of violent counter-attacks. The Cameronians themselves met very little opposition other than shelling, though they could hear sounds of heavy fighting on the Glasgow Highlanders' front in the pine-woods on their left. At 4.30 P.M., when they had advanced about one and a half miles from Bedburg and were already some six hundred yards ahead of any other troops, the Cameronians were ordered to halt and consolidate for the night. They had taken about thirty prisoners.

Meanwhile "D" Company of the Glasgow Highlanders, supported by another squadron of the Coldstream, had passed through the 130th Brigade, which had come up to Bedburg to relieve the 129th Brigade and had advanced on Rosendahl, a small village in a clearing about fifteen hundred yards east of Bedburg. "D" Company met little opposition other than heavy defensive fire, which caused a number of casualties.

"A" and "C" Companies now entered the pine-woods immediately south of Rosendahl to continue the advance south-eastward along the wooded ridge, using the central ride as their centre-line. Their objectives were the two twin knolls astride the sunken lane that runs south from the cluster of houses called Tillemanskath on the north edge of the wood a thousand yards or so from Rosendahl.

"A" Company on the right reached and took its objective, the more southerly knoll short of the lane. There it consolidated under heavy shell-fire and in touch with the enemy.

"C" Company on the left was much less fortunate. Its troubles began early. On the way to the start-line it took heavy casualties from enemy shelling, losing its jeep and company wireless set. In consequence, the company commander failed to learn that H-hour had been postponed, with the result that the company advanced prematurely into the wood and ran into our own fire.

At the same time the enemy's defensive fire again caught it. Thus by the time H-hour had in fact arrived, "C" Company's strength had already been reduced to about forty men.

Thereafter "C" Company met no ground opposition until it was nearing the sunken lane. Here the Highlanders found the enemy both in the houses of Tillemanskath, which were clear of the wood on their left flank, and on the knoll in the wood beyond the lane. Close and bitter fighting ensued, into which " B " Company, following in support, soon got drawn. First, " B " took over responsibility for watching Tillemanskath while " C " went on to take the knoll. By this time, however, " C " was pitifully weak. Counter-attacking, the enemy pinned part of " C " beyond the lane and drove the rest of the company back on company headquarters.

14th Feb.

The two company commanders next made a plan : " C " Company would withdraw its forward platoon under smoke to be provided by " A " Company ; " C " would then hold a firm base while " B," with the support of a Wasp, made simultaneous attacks on Tillemanskath and on the knoll.

Attacking with great determination in face of fierce resistance, " B " Company got a few survivors of No. 11 Platoon into the outlying houses of Tillemanskath on the left. The attack on the knoll, however, could not progress beyond the lane on account of the withering fire which now came from positions outside the wood on the left. Here the P.I.A.T. of No. 10 Platoon knocked out an enemy S.P. which tried to lead a counter-attack. By this time dusk had fallen, and " B " Company too had been greatly reduced in strength, not only in this action but also by the enemy's incessant artillery and mortar-fire. Lieutenant-Colonel Baker-Baker, therefore, ordered " B " to concentrate and consolidate. Under cover of darkness No. 10 Platoon withdrew from the lane, No. 11 Platoon from the houses. " B " Company consolidated as best it could in the maze of wooded gullies, watching Tillemanskath on its left and the lane to its front, and in close touch with " A " Company on its right. The Coldstream squadron, whose tanks could do little in this sort of country, withdrew into harbour, having lost one Honey knocked out by the S.P.

Meanwhile the Seaforth on the left had been able to start operations much earlier in the day than had the Cameronians or the Glasgow Highlanders. At 9.30 A.M., supported by another squadron of Coldstream and a heavy concentration of artillery, they had advanced from Hasselt through the water on a two-company front. Their objectives were the houses and the wood astride the road immediately north-east of Rosendahl. The tanks, which were unable to leave the road, were soon held up by mines, whereupon the leading companies,

14th Feb.　pushing on unsupported, took heavy casualties, which included Major Henderson, " D " Company Commander, killed.

At this stage Lieutenant-Colonel Hunt put " C " Company through, while the Seaforth pioneers, working under heavy fire, cleared a passage through the mines. With the support, not only of the tanks but also of extremely accurate artillery fire, " C " then took the houses and wood, and with them no less than twenty-three machine-guns. At dusk " C " Company consolidated here north-east of Rosendahl. Patrols reported enemy in strength in the small wood south of the road five hundred yards north-east of Tillemanskath and also in the grounds of the Schloss Moyland.

On the rest of the Divisional front 14th February passed without incident, save that the 227th Brigade stood to at short notice for the second day in succession to take part in the fighting for Moyland. Main Divisional Headquarters moved up into Cleve. The weather had now mended: day was to follow day of lovely spring sunshine.

The flood situation on the main axis was still most difficult. The heavy programme of artillery support had created demands for 25-pounder H.E. far in excess of what could be delivered by the few 3-tonners forward of the floods. In consequence D.U.K.W.s had to be used to off-load on gun-sites. Fortunately, however, flood-level had reached its peak. By evening, too, sixty 3-tonners loaded with 25-pounder ammunition had succeeded in getting round by the circuitous southern route through Malden and Ottersum to Hekkens, on the south edge of the Reichswald, where the 51st and 53rd Divisions had linked up after very severe fighting, and from Hekkens through the Reichswald to Cleve. The arrival of these 3-tonners eased the situation.

On the First Canadian Army's front there were now nine enemy Divisions in all, among them four Parachute Divisions, all of whom were fighting particularly savagely.

15th Feb.　Brigadier Villiers' orders to the Cameronians for the next day were to advance north and eliminate the opposition on the Glasgow Highlanders' front. Lieutenant-Colonel Remington Hobbs' plan was to seize a second pair of twin knolls—here to be called " East " and " West Knoll "—which form the spine of the wooded ridge immediately west of the road that runs north to Moyland across the ridge. " D " Company was to take West Knoll ; " C " Company was then to pass through and take East Knoll.

On its way to the start-line "D" Company ran into heavy enemy counter-preparation. Of company headquarters only the company commander survived, and one platoon was almost annihilated. In the ensuing confusion only one platoon reached the start-line by H-hour; up the hill and into the forest it went alone in order to take advantage of the artillery support. Only a few yards from the start-line, however, this forward platoon was pinned by fire, while mortar-bombs rained thick and fast on the remainder of the company behind. For the time being "D" Company was all in.

15th Feb.

At this stage Lieutenant-Colonel Remington Hobbs put in "C" Company with orders to take "D's" original objective, West Knoll. "C" Company, too, had had a rough passage. That morning its carrier, with the C.S.M., the C.Q.M.S., and the breakfasts, had driven straight into the enemy's lines, where the C.S.M. and the driver had been killed and the C.Q.M.S. captured. In consequence "C" Company had to go into action with nothing inside them but a few bites of cold compo rations. Attacking uphill against a well-dug-in enemy, "C" reached a point about fifty yards short of the crest. Here the company commander called for Coldstream's support. Though the tanks bedded down in the mud only a short way up the slope, they were able to shoot up the enemy on West Knoll to such effect that twenty-five Germans surrendered. By 5 P.M. "C" Company—no more than fifty-five strong—was digging in in the only small clearing on West Knoll.

There about half an hour later it was counter-attacked by some thirty Germans. A thick mist had now come down; dusk had fallen; visibility was down to twenty yards or less; "C's" wireless had faded; "D" Company was unable to break through in support. In an endeavour to open the battalion axis, Lieutenant-Colonel Remington Hobbs sent "A" Company to clear a small square wood on his right front. The leading platoon of "A" reached the small wood in the darkness immediately after a German company had occupied it. In the ensuing dog-fight "A" Company was repulsed. Isolated and without food or greatcoats, "C" Company hung on grimly on the knoll throughout the night.

On the ridge about three-quarters of a mile west of these happenings, the Glasgow Highlanders spent the day without any material change of position. Our guns were busy with counter-battery work and with shoots on targets on the Seaforth's front beyond the inter-

15th Feb.—battalion boundary which ran along the north edge of the wood. Enemy shelling and mortaring increased in violence all day, and towards evening opened up with a new multiple-rocket weapon of the Mattress type. About the same time, however, a company of the Seaforth managed to work forward to Killemanskath, on the left of the Glasgow Highlanders, who were then able to straighten their whole front through the wood.

After dark " D " Company of the Glasgow Highlanders passed through to occupy the farther knoll beyond the lane. Working along a taped approach through the under-brush in darkness and dense mist, " D " had established itself on the knoll by 2.30 A.M. next morning.

That afternoon the H.L.I. came under command of the 46th Brigade, originally with orders to push through in Kangaroos south of the Cameronians in order to secure the southern flank of the 46th Brigade and to occupy the high ground overlooking Calcar. In view of the enemy's very tough resistance, however, Brigadier Villiers modified the plan, postponing the attack till the night of the 15th and reducing its scope.

Coming up after dark as far as the Esels-Berg by the track that the Cameronians had followed, the H.L.I. there diverged southward to a forming-up place below its eastern slopes. Thence after dark they advanced eastward, parallel to and to the southward of the Cameronians' track. Here, too, the mist was thick. Having sent back their tanks in consequence, the H.L.I. relied solely on artillery support. Passing the Cameronians on their left, the two forward companies of the H.L.I.—" B " on the right, " D " on the left—pushed on another fourteen hundred yards or so and presently reached their objectives, two clusters of houses about a thousand yards apart. They had taken eighty prisoners. Their accompanying A.Tk. and S.P. guns had bogged down on the way, so they set to work to consolidate without them. Before they could do so, however, they were heavily counter-attacked by enemy infantry and S.P.s. " D " on the left dispersed its attackers. " B " on the right, on the other hand, was caught off balance with a number of men engaged in clearing cellars and the covering party silhouetted against the glare of burning houses. The covering party was overrun and the rest of the company thrown back. The area thus lost was not a vital one, however, so long as " D " Company held firm with " A " and " C " disposed in depth behind it.

On this day the 2nd Canadian Corps took over the left sector of the First Canadian Army's front, and the 46th Brigade came under command of the 3rd Canadian Division. *15th Feb.*

At 7.30 next morning Lieutenant-Colonel Bramwell Davis, who had been given "A" Company of the Glasgow Highlanders as a reserve, sent "C," his own reserve company of the H.L.I., to clear the wood on the right of the Cameronians—the large terminal covert, that is, which lies east of the road that leads north to Moyland. The H.L.I., however, found the enemy's machine-gun fire so intense that they failed even to reach the track which runs along the southern boundary of the covert. *16th Feb.*

A little later "D" Company of the H.L.I. was again counter-attacked, but again it dispersed its attackers by fire. For three more days "D" Company was to remain here out in front, exposed to incessant shelling and open to counter-attack, before the H.L.I. could be withdrawn at last.

Next we come to the Cameronians. "C" Company had spent a miserable night isolated on West Knoll. Lieutenant-Colonel Remington Hobbs ordered "B" Company to pass through them at first light and to take East Knoll, which lies about five hundred yards to eastward, overlooking the road to Moyland.

By 7 A.M. "B" Company had reached "C" on West Knoll. Only two hundred yards on, "B" met the Germans. After a fierce fight among the trees "B" took East Knoll and held it. There, a sadly depleted band, the survivors held on despite savage mortaring and repeated counter-attacks. For "B" and "C" Companies on their knolls these were hungry and thirsty days, for almost no food or water could reach them.

In the thick morning mist meanwhile "A" Company had resumed its attack on the small square wood. First, it met intense small-arms fire, and then it was counter-attacked. Now no more than forty strong, it was thrown back to its original position. In the afternoon, however, "A" staged yet a third attack on the wood—this time supported by tanks and Wasps. The Wasps did it. At the sight of the flames the Germans fled, throwing away a large number of automatic weapons. Thereupon "A" Company occupied its wood at last, and thus made things much easier for "B" and "C" out in front.

So heavy was the enemy's fire, however, that swept the Moyland road immediately east of their position that the Cameronians were quite unable to push patrols across the road and into the terminal covert beyond—a goal which, as we have seen, had proved equally unattainable to the H.L.I.

In the Glasgow Highlanders' area farther west the morning had found "D" and "B" Companies dug in on the two knolls east and west respectively of the sunken lane. "A" Company had now gone off to join the H.L.I. The enemy was still mortaring and machine-gunning the area unmercifully.

Later, orders reached the Glasgow Highlanders that they were to be prepared to pass through the Cameronians next day and to attack the village and Schloss of Moyland from the south. The news evoked no enthusiasm. The Schloss, which had been a seat of Frederick the Great, was a mediæval affair with immensely thick walls surrounded by two moats, one of which was twenty-five yards wide and spanned by a single narrow bridge. Moreover the whole countryside was flooded, so all movement would be canalised to the roads.

A preliminary to the Glasgow Highlanders' assault on the Schloss was to be the clearing of the terminal covert by the 7th Canadian Brigade, which, with the Tank Scots Guards in support, was now to continue the drive on Calcar. In preparation the Canadians and the Scots Guards came up to Bedburg that afternoon.

That day nothing of note happened on the Seaforth's front.

Five miles away to the southward the 43rd and 53rd Divisions were closing on the northern and north-eastern approaches to Goch against stubborn opposition.

17th February dawned misty, but the weather gradually cleared. Moving south out of Bedburg by the Udem road, the Canadians and the Tank Scots Guards wheeled left to the southward of the Esels-Berg, to advance east past the H.L.I.'s position soon after mid-day. Two days of bitter and intensive fighting were to follow in and around the terminal covert south of Moyland, while the 46th Brigade and the H.L.I. kept the ring. When the Tank Scots Guards went out to rest on the night of 18th February, the enemy paratroopers were still resisting ferociously.

That morning Lieutenant-Colonel Remington Hobbs had sent the reserve company of the Cameronians to relieve the Glasgow Highlanders (less "A" Company), astride the sunken lane in the wood to the

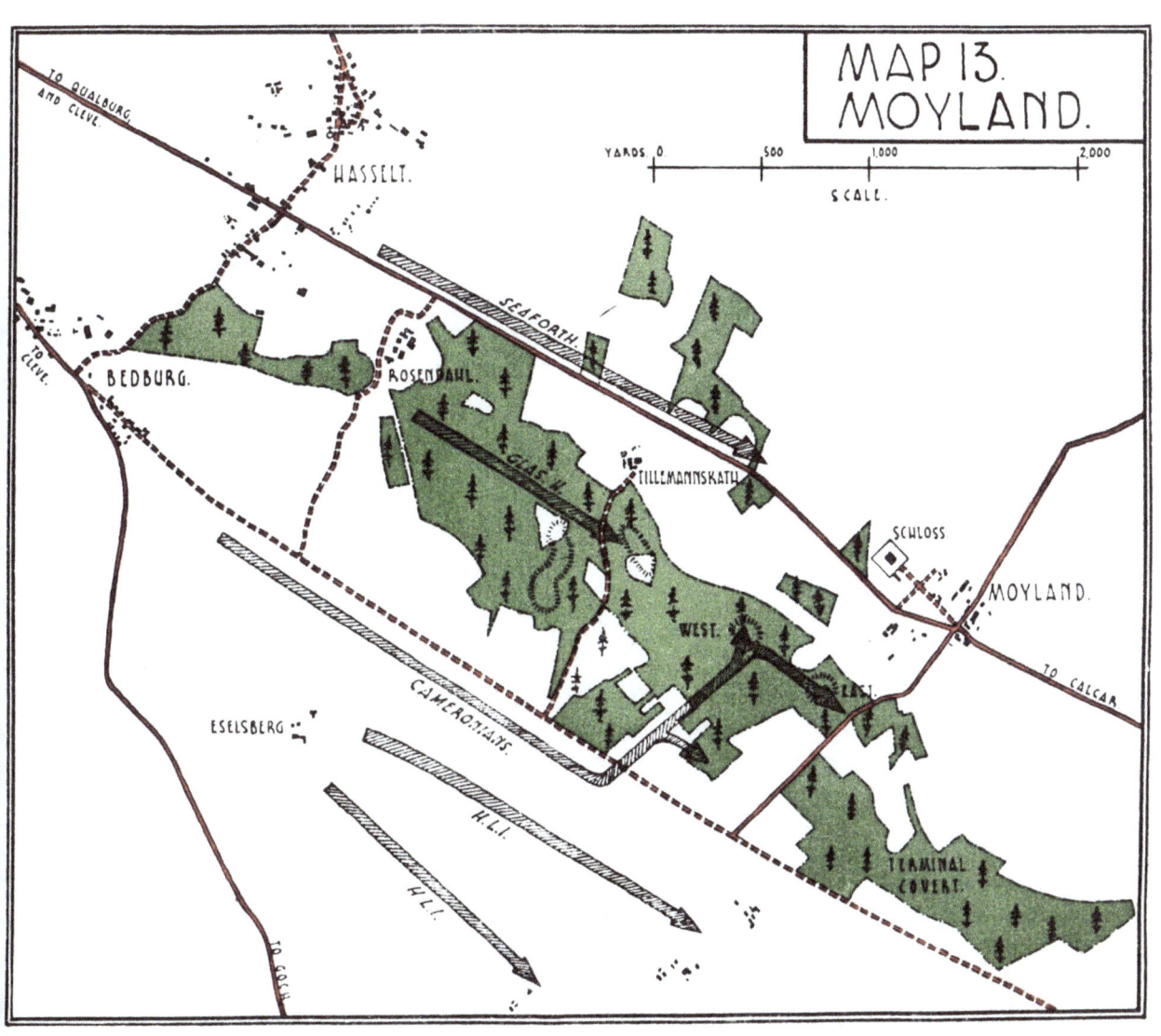

westward. Thereupon the Glasgow Highlanders pulled out to a concentration area to the southward, where they stood to at thirty minutes' notice, and where also Lieutenant-Colonel Baker-Baker briefed his company commanders for their impending attack on Schloss Moyland. The briefing was somewhat unusual in that the owner of the Schloss was there to take an enthusiastic interest in the plans for its destruction. He was Captain Van Moyland, a member of a Dutch Commando unit, who, having forty-eight hours' leave due, had come up to view the battle on a busman's holiday. His intimate knowledge of the ground was invaluable. A.G.R.A.s, tanks, Typhoons—all might rain destruction on his home for all he cared, if only the assaulting troops would rescue for him his precious pair of shot-guns. Later, the Canadians' slow progress led to the postponement of the Glasgow Highlanders' attack till the next day.

That night Lieutenant-Colonel Hunt put in " B " Company of the Seaforth against the small wood that lies astride the main Calcar road five hundred yards north-east of Tillemanskath. This wood had long been a menace to the Seaforth's security. The whole of the Corps artillery supported the attack. After an initial check " B " Company not only took the wood but also pushed a platoon on to the next patch of cover within two hundred yards of the grounds of the Schloss Moyland itself.

The 46th Brigade's bitter battle for Moyland was drawing to an end at last—though the long-drawn-out agony of shelling, exposure, sleeplessness, cold, and hunger was to continue for a day or two longer. Next day " B " Company of the Cameronians was again to be heavily counter-attacked on East Knoll, whereupon " D " was to come up in support and the two remnants were to amalgamate to form one weak company. Before they could get their new slit-trenches dug, however, they were to be in the thick of yet another counter-attack supported by a hurricane of fire.

The Glasgow Highlanders, too, were to stand to again next day, but the Canadians were to meet with another check in the terminal covert, and this was to lead to the final cancellation of the Glasgow Highlanders' assault on the Schloss. On the night of 18th February the Glasgow Highlanders were to pull out for what proved to be an extremely brief rest at Cleve. They were to be followed on 19th February by the rest of the 46th Brigade and the H.L.I.—dead tired, unshaven, unwashed, hungry and thirsty, but still full of fight. All

17th Feb. were to agree that it had been the worst experience they had endured since the campaign began. As a captured German Order showed, the enemy regarded the main axis Cleve-Calcar as the key to the defence of the Rhineland. This fact accounts for the unprecedented weight of artillery and mortar-fire which the enemy had concentrated on the axis, and also for the ferocious resistance of the German paratroopers. Moreover, since so much of the fighting took place in woods, the air-burst effect of the enemy's fire was unusually deadly. In the woods, too, wireless was wholly unreliable, while cable was being perpetually cut, so runners became the only sure means of keeping touch. But above all there were the mud and the floods, though the weather itself was fine at last.

We now come to a new phase in the operations—the capture of Goch. It was on 17th February that the Divisional Commander issued his orders to the 44th Brigade for the assault on Goch. It is a town of about ten thousand inhabitants on the River Niers, and the Germans had turned it into a pivot of their defence system. Round it they dug two anti-tank ditches, an inner and an outer, and in it they had put a garrison consisting of odd battle groups of the 2nd, 7th, and 8th Parachute Divisions and of the 180th and 190th Infantry Divisions—all of which, however, had already taken a pretty severe beating in the preceding fighting. On to Goch were now closing the 53rd and 43rd Divisions from the north and north-east, and the 51st Division from the south-west.

The plan was this. During the night of the 17th the 214th Brigade of the 43rd Division was to reconnoitre the crossing-places in the outer ditch on the 44th Brigade's proposed front of attack to the eastward of the Goch-Cleve railway. Starting at 11 A.M. next day, the 51st Division was to clear that part of Goch which lies south of the River Niers. In the afternoon the 44th Brigade was to come up from Cleve by Kangaroo and to take Goch north of the Niers by a Blerick operation, which was to begin at 3 P.M. Meanwhile the 53rd Division was to maintain its position on the right of the 44th Brigade, between the Goch-Cleve railway and the River Niers.

18th Feb. During the night of the 17th the 214th Brigade took and held nine crossing-places over the outer ditch at a radius of about two thousand five hundred yards from the centre of Goch. The 214th Brigade also sent a fighting patrol to the near anti-tank ditch, which

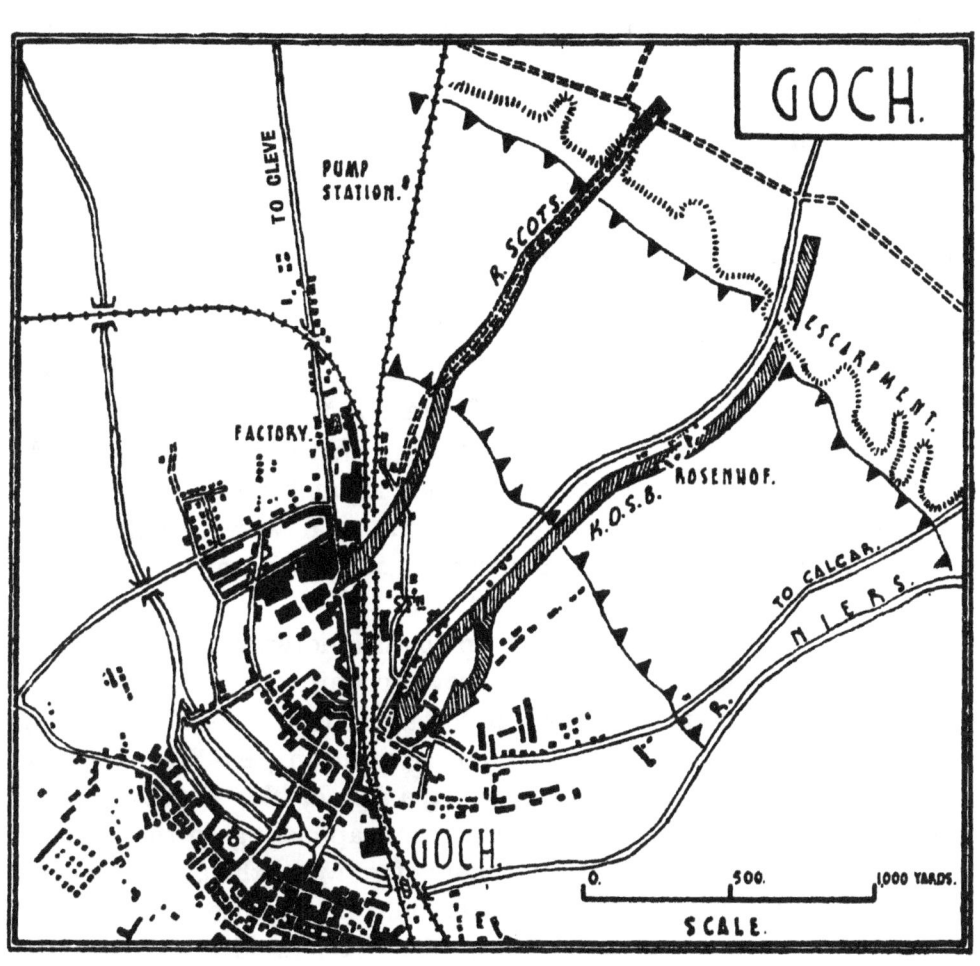

18th Feb. took twenty prisoners and came back with a report that the place was only weakly held.

Next morning the 44th Brigade moved out from Cleve in Kangaroos to a forward assembly area near Pfalzdorf, where it was joined by the Tank Grenadiers and the " Funnies " of the Armoured Breaching Force. According to plan the assault was to go in at 3 P.M. First, the Armoured Breaching Force would clear lanes from the outer to the inner ditch and would bridge the ditch. Then the 44th Brigade would assault in Kangaroos, with two battalions up—right, the Royal Scots; left, the K.O.S.B. The Royal Scots were to have as their axis the track which runs south from Stadenhof to cut the outer ditch at crossing No. 1, six hundred yards east of the pump station on the railway. The K.O.S.B. were to have as their axis the third-class road that cuts the outer ditch at crossing No. 4, eight hundred yards farther east. There was to be massive artillery support, which would include Mattresses. When they had entered the town, both battalions were to capture a number of self-contained key positions, each with a company group, and were to hold these during darkness. When daylight came, companies were to join up and the battalions were to clear the town.

While his troops were moving up to their forward assembly area Brigadier Cumming-Bruce himself drove forward along the left-hand or eastern axis in his armoured car to have a look at Goch. Passing over No. 4 crossing in the outer ditch he went on past Rosenhof and almost to the inner ditch without seeing a sign of life. It looked very much as if the enemy garrison, seeing the trap closing on them north and south, had decided to call it a day before worse things befell them —a theory to which the 43rd Division's intelligence reports lent support. Brigadier Cumming-Bruce, therefore, decided to rush the place then and there—if he could.

So back in the forward assembly area, about 11 A.M., the Royal Scots, the leading battalion of the Brigade, got an order to send a company straight into Goch along the Brigade axis—along, that is, the left-hand or K.O.S.B.'s axis. About 1.15 P.M. " A " Company of the Royal Scots in its Kangaroos duly arrived at No. 4 crossing on the outer ditch, to advance thence with a troop of Grenadiers in front and another troop behind. Major M'Queen, the company commander, did not know what he would find at the inner ditch—a crossing practicable for his Kangaroos or only for his infantry on foot—or, failing an immediate crossing of either sort, a situation which would allow him to cover from the near bank the laying of a bridge by the " Funnies " who were following in rear.

18th Feb.

Nothing happened till the leading tank had almost reached the inner ditch. Then something hit it—probably a Bazooka or Panzerfaust, whereupon a second tank in rear got ditched. The leading platoon of the Royal Scots promptly dismounted, and, after taking twenty prisoners from houses on the near side, reached the road-crossing, where they found the bridge blown but the ditch itself passable on foot where its banks had subsided. So they crossed the ditch successfully in face of some frontal and flanking spandau-fire and established a small bridgehead on the far bank. The platoons in rear, however, found the ditch wide of the road-crossing to be too deep and sheer to cross: it was about twenty-five feet wide by ten feet deep. Moreover, they were getting a number of casualties, for spandau-fire was increasing and mortars and an S.P. had opened up. About 2.15 P.M. Brigadier Cumming-Bruce saw that his *coup de main* was not " on," whereupon he ordered Lieutenant-Colonel Pearson to revert to the original plan—with the modification that " A " Company of the Royal Scots would stay where it was astride the ditch, to cover the laying of the A.V.R.E. bridge and the advance of the K.O.S.B. on this left-hand axis.

About this time two bridge-laying A.V.R.E.s lurched forward under the covering fire of the Grenadiers. So high were their bridges that they had great difficulty in passing under the trees on either side of the road. The first A.V.R.E. deposited its bridge, but its release mechanism then jammed so it could not part company. The second A.V.R.E. itself slid in the ditch. For the time being, therefore, the ditch on the left-hand axis remained unbridged.

Shortly after 3 P.M., in resumption of the original plan, the Royal Scots (less " A " Company), travelling by their own right-hand axis, reached the edge of the escarpment overlooking Goch. There was a thick mist which reduced the accuracy of the German mortar-fire. The troop of Grenadiers on ahead had found the bridge on this axis seemingly intact, so the leading tank had proceeded to cross it. The bridge, however, was not all it seemed, for it promptly collapsed, depositing the tank in the ditch. The Grenadiers soon pulled it out, however, and whistled up one of their own bridge-laying tanks. At the second attempt it laid its bridge successfully. A little

18th Feb.

after 5 P.M. the Royal Scots, still in their Kangaroos, crossed the bridge, preceded by the tanks. Enemy fire was now pretty heavy, particularly from a group of houses on the left flank. After clearing this group of houses, "B" Company, the leading company of the Royal Scots, went on under heavy and incessant mortar-fire, which caused a number of casualties, particularly in company headquarters, to clear the extensive factory area between the Goch-Cleve railway and the Goch-Cleve road. The Grenadiers gave covering fire from the east side of the railway. By 7.30 P.M. "B" Company had completed this job of clearing all the large and scattered buildings and had taken a few prisoners. It then concentrated once more on the factory, which it had originally cleared. Here it remained very isolated until "D" Company passed through about 10 P.M. to work its way across the quadrangle beyond. On the farther side "D" met the enemy in strength, and there were exchanges of fire at very close quarters throughout the night. Nevertheless both companies had taken up firm positions in the heart of the enemy fortress, and the subsequent collapse of enemy resistance was due to this.

The tanks, which had perforce been left behind short of the waterlogged meadows, in pitch darkness clambered up the railway embankment and followed the Royal Scots into the town, a manœuvre which contributed largely to the success of the Royal Scots' operation.

Meanwhile, soon after 3 P.M. that afternoon, the K.O.S.B. had followed the Royal Scots out of the forward assembly area. The K.O.S.B. took the left-hand axis; the Armoured Breaching Force was on ahead. On nearing the inner ditch, "D" Company, the leading company, came under spandau and mortar-fire, and word came back from the Grenadiers that both the A.V.R.E. bridges here on the K.O.S.B.'s lane had failed, as we have seen, and that the crumbling banks were useless as bridge foundations. Major Jackson, who was commanding the K.O.S.B. in Lieutenant-Colonel Richardson's absence on leave, at once sent for fascines to fill the gap. He then went on himself in his Kangaroo—a most unpleasant journey—to see Major Elliott of "D" Company, who was out of wireless touch. Together they made a plan, though, owing to the recent rain, the condition of the ground was terrible and manœuvre was going to be most difficult. After dark "D" Company was to attack on foot

ASSAULT ON GOCH BY 44TH LOWLAND INFANTRY BRIGADE
(Drawing by Captain Bryan de Grineau. Reproduced by courtesy of 'The Illustrated London News')

through "A" Company of the Royal Scots, already at the crossing. 18th Feb. The rest of the K.O.S.B. (less "B" Company) were to follow "D" across; "B" Company was to go round by the left to cross the ditch farther east.

This plan made, Major Jackson returned to his headquarters, and almost immediately Major Jack Elliott was hit by a burst of spandau-fire and died soon after. So the plan hung fire. By 7.30 P.M. "D" Company on the main axis and "B" Company on the left had both been held up north of the ditch. Nothing daunted, Major Jackson set to work to make yet a third plan.

By 11.30 P.M. the crossing on this axis had been made practicable. After a short, sharp artillery concentration "D" Company, in its Kangaroos, rushed the crossing in fog and darkness—a most gallant action made possible by a magnificent piece of driving on the part of the Kangaroo drivers. In the first group of houses the enemy opened up with Panzerfaust and hit three of the Kangaroos. Dismounting, "D" Company cleared these houses and then consolidated a tight bridgehead—ready to exploit at first light. Here they joined up with the forward platoons of "A" of the Royal Scots, which had been isolated on the farther bank.

On the left, meanwhile, "B" Company of the K.O.S.B. had been fighting its way along a trench system which led south-east from Rosenhof towards its objective, the bridge—still standing—on the main Calcar-Goch road where it crossed the inner ditch. "B" found this trench system held by a detachment of the Flieger Ausbild Battalion 45, and a fierce grenade-slinging match followed. In the course of it, Sergeant Telfer's platoon took fourteen casualties, but they gave better than they got, for they bombed out the opposing paratroopers. For his fine leadership here Sergeant Telfer was to get the D.C.M. So "B" reached the bridge, stormed across it, and occupied the first houses beyond. Here two isolated platoons held on till morning, despite the counter-attacks and close-range fire of the paratroopers all around them.

So ended the fighting of 18th February—with the Royal Scots well across on the right-hand axis and the K.O.S.B. established in two small bridgeheads on the left. Coming up from the south-west the 51st Division had attacked at 11 P.M. according to plan, and had been driving east all day south of the Niers—across the 44th Brigade's front.

19th Feb.

Early next morning "D" Company of the Royal Scots, with the help of a troop of Grenadiers, finished the clearance of the factory area beyond the railway most successfully. As the tanks hotted up each house in turn, the enemy's morale began to crack. Soon there were white rags waving from every doorway. "D" Company's bag amounted to 4 killed and over 230 prisoners at a cost of 1 killed and 5 wounded. About 7 A.M. Lieutenant-Colonel Pearson held an "O" Group and gave his companies their orders for the further clearing operations. "A" Company of the Royal Scots on the left-hand axis he ordered to rejoin in Goch.

On the left-hand or main axis "A" Company of the K.O.S.B. had passed through "D" Company's bridgehead at 6 A.M. and had gone on into the centre of Goch. "D" they found in high spirits—with some 30 prisoners taken at a cost of only 1 killed and 7 wounded. Before light, too, a group of tanks had arrived in support of "B" Company of the K.O.S.B. in their bridgehead, still farther east on the main Calcar-Goch road. At the first few rounds from the tanks, 25 paratroopers in the houses surrounding the bridgehead surrendered precipitately.

There still remained the area to be cleared between "A" and "B" Companies of the K.O.S.B. and extending down to the Niers. About noon Major Jackson put "C" Company into this gap, supported by the troop of the Grenadiers which had now entered by the bridge on the Calcar road. Working very closely with the tanks and taking cover behind their hulls, the Borderers cleared the houses down to the river.

While the Royal Scots and the K.O.S.B. had been busy in Goch, the R.S.F. had spent a most unpleasant night under incessant shelling and mortaring outside the town. About 7 A.M., as the R.S.F. moved up behind the K.O.S.B. on the left and into the area of north-eastern Goch allotted to them, the enemy fire swelled in a new crescendo and casualties were fairly heavy, among them Major Harrison, the acting commanding officer of the R.S.F.

The R.S.F. found the opposition patchy, and they took about a hundred prisoners. For nearly twenty-four hours the 51st Division, coming in from the west, had been busy clearing the district of Goch which lies south of the Niers. By 10.30 A.M. the R.S.F. and the 7th Black Watch of the 153rd Brigade had made visual contact across the Niers. By dark the R.S.F. had cleared their areas save for a few enemy posts on the north bank near the blown bridges in the centre of the town. Fire from the south bank was still severe.

By 6 P.M. the 44th Brigade generally had cleared Goch down to the Niers and had taken 600 prisoners, among them nearly the whole of the 190th Fusiliers, who had just arrived post-haste from Venlo on their bicycles. For the rest the enemy had withdrawn southward across the Niers. Of the Grenadiers only the squadron accompanying the Royal Scots on the right-hand axis and the troop which had come in on the extreme left by the Calcar road had been able to enter the town: the crossing on the K.O.S.B. axis, which the R.S.F. also used, had proved impassable to Churchills. In their absence Wasps had been most effective during the mopping-up.

During the day the 71st Brigade of the 53rd Division came up on the right into the district of Northern Goch which lies between the Niers and the Goch-Cleve road, and collected a large number of prisoners who had been engaged and cut off by the Royal Scots.

Back in Cleve the Glasgow Highlanders had come under the 227th Brigade in replacement of the H.L.I., who were still under the 46th Brigade. That day, after the Glasgow Highlanders had been out at rest only twenty-four hours, Brigadier Colville held an "O" Group at 227th Brigade Headquarters, at which he issued orders to his commanding officers and company commanders for an attack next day through the 214th Brigade (43rd Division) to take Buchholt, a village on the east bank of the Niers about two and three-quarter miles east of Goch in the direction of Udem. Kangaroos were to be provided for two companies per battalion. The balance of the infantry would ride on the tanks of the three supporting squadrons of the Coldstream. A troop of Crocodiles would be also in support.

Next morning the 227th Brigade Group moved early to a forward assembly area near the Forst Cleve, whence the two forward battalions —right, the Glasgow Highlanders; left, the Argylls—went to their forming-up places near Imigshof. The Gordons were in reserve. At 10 A.M. the Glasgow Highlanders and the Argylls passed their start-line, the Goch-Calcar road, in their Kangaroos. About two thousand yards ahead across the undulating ground they could see the line of trees and buildings on the skyline that marked the position of Buchholt. The Glasgow Highlanders' objective extended from the wooded escarp-

19th Feb.

20th Feb.

20th Feb.

ment overlooking the Schloss Calbeck on the right to the southern half of Buchholt on the left; the Argylls' objective extended from the northern half of Buchholt to Bremershof. Still farther to the left the 129th Brigade (43rd Division) was attacking simultaneously on Holbenboom, but without armour or Kangaroos, so its progress was likely to be slow.

On the right the attack went smoothly, though the enemy's fire was very heavy. By 1 P.M. the Glasgow Highlanders had taken all their objectives, and with them some 150 prisoners for a loss of about 50 men. They consolidated under intense fire, which grew even heavier towards evening. The enemy had evidently realised that he would have to go back across the Rhine, and he was firing off all the ammunition in the Siegfried Line dumps before he went. Here at Buchholt the going was so deep that carriers failed completely to bring up food and water. Eventually Brigade Headquarters had to release a Kangaroo for the purpose.

The Argylls on the left meanwhile had had some trouble with direction-keeping in the smoke of the shelling and of burning farms. The Kangaroos lost their way in consequence. The Germans, however, showed little fight, so the Argylls were able to sort themselves out without interference. They went on to take their objective and with it 194 prisoners—but the Germans had missed an ideal chance for a counter-attack.

The Gordons then went through with the task of clearing the woods round the Schloss Calbeck down to the Goch-Udem railway and establishing a bridgehead over the stream immediately beyond. The boggy tracks and rides through the woods they found intersected by wide ditches and blocked by craters and fallen trees. All the tanks of their accompanying troop of Coldstream soon got bogged, but by dint of laying two tank-bridges some did get through later. The Gordons took the Schloss after their Wasps had set part of it on fire. Battalion tactical headquarters struggled through to it, with one Kangaroo which carried the rear link. By this time shelling was extremely heavy, coming from east, west, and south. By nightfall "A" Company had crossed the railway and had established a small bridgehead over the stream beyond. Here it was up against fierce resistance and under heavy shell-fire. Meanwhile "D" Company had cleared the wood south-east of the Schloss.

In Goch north of the Niers the enemy's fire was still fierce and the

44th Brigade still had some snipers to deal with. During the day 20th Feb. Brigadier Cumming-Bruce himself crossed the Niers to attend a conference in a cellar with Brigadier Sinclair of the 153rd Brigade. This was a notable reunion, for Brigadier Sinclair had commanded the 2nd Gordons in the Division until after the battle of Caumont, and Brigadier Cumming-Bruce had commanded 153rd Brigade during the break-out from Normandy, when he was Commanding Officer of the 1st Gordons. The 153rd Brigade was still meeting stubborn resistance in the southern quarter of Goch.

On 21st February the R.S.F. passed under command of the 227th 21st Feb. Brigade on their relief in Goch by the 2nd Battalion the Monmouthshire Regiment. The rôle of the R.S.F. was to attack through the Gordons south of the Schloss Calbeck and to extend their bridgehead across the Goch-Wesel railway and the stream immediately to the southward of it. This bridgehead, which the 46th Brigade was to use as its forming-up place next day, was to include the bridge over the stream, and also the Schloss Kalbeck—not to be confused with Calbeck—a large building which stood to the right of the road, between the railway and the stream.

That morning Lieutenant-Colonel Ian Mackenzie withdrew the R.S.F. from Goch and concentrated them on the escarpment to the north-east, where all ranks had a hot meal, while he himself reported to Brigadier Colville for orders. After a quick reconnaissance Lieutenant-Colonel Mackenzie returned to hold an " O " Group, while his battalion moved off about 6 P.M., with " A " Company leading, to join the 227th Brigade.

While " A " Company of the R.S.F. formed up north of the stream and behind " A " Company of the Gordons, the guns put down twenty minutes' preparation. Then at 8 P.M. " A " Company of the R.S.F. rushed across the bridge in the darkness and pushed on to the cross-roads a hundred yards beyond. The remaining companies followed through, but in their attempt to extend the bridgehead they met fierce resistance from both small-arms and mortars and had many casualties. Wasps then came up and met with some success till they ran into S.P. guns and mines, when two of them were quickly knocked out. Lieutenant-Colonel Mackenzie saw that he would have to wait till next morning to extend his bridgehead with the help of tanks, so he ordered his companies to dig in where they were.

266   THE FIFTEENTH SCOTTISH DIVISION

21st Feb.   Enemy shelling became more violent during the night—some of it short-range shelling by tanks and S.P.s which could be heard moving in the wood close by. A troop of S.P. A.Tk. guns came up as a very welcome support.

That afternoon Brigadier Villiers had held his 46th Brigade " O " Group at the headquarters of the 227th Brigade, at which he had explained his plan for the 46th Brigade's attack next day through the R.S.F.'s bridgehead. Once more his chief anxiety was the getting of his troops to the start-line; after that, he felt, things would be comparatively simple. He had the Glasgow Highlanders under his command once more on their relief at Buchholt by the H.L.I. Their fight at Buchholt under the 227th Brigade had come so soon after their ordeal in the Moyland woods that he was particularly anxious to rest them in the forthcoming action.

That evening the 214th Brigade (43rd Division), farther east towards Udem, came temporarily under command of the 15th Scottish Division.

Back in the south-eastern quarter of Goch the 51st Division was still meeting fierce resistance. Not till next day was the last of this resistance crushed. The 44th Brigade was able to help materially by observation and fire from the K.O.S.B.'s sector across the Niers.

22nd Feb.   At 6 A.M. next morning Lieutenant-Colonel Mackenzie gave out his orders for the enlargement of the bridgehead to his company commanders of the R.S.F., the squadron commander of the Coldstream, and the troop of S.P.'s. " B " Company, on the right front, was to start the operation at 7 A.M. As " B " Company commander was giving out his orders in his turn, however, the enemy, who had been reinforced by a company of paratroopers in the night, counter-attacked his company heavily, killing one officer and the C.S.M. and inflicting a number of other casualties. In the resulting confusion the troop of tanks went forward unaware that the orders to advance had never reached the infantry. After they had shot up the houses of Hooesaat on the right front for fifteen minutes or so the tanks withdrew again behind the infantry. Thus the plan had failed to get going. Instead, the enemy continued to press in fiercely on the R.S.F., who were holding their ground with great difficulty.

On learning the position, Brigadier Colville ordered the R.S.F. to hold their bridgehead at all costs until the 46th Brigade could come through later in the day. Lieutenant-Colonel Mackenzie ordered his companies to dig-in in a tight hedgehog round the cross-roads immediately south of the bridge, with tanks and S.P.s within the perimeter. There they settled down to endure what turned out to be a day of the most intense shell and mortar-fire they had ever experienced.

22nd Feb.

The Gordons, too, were having a very rough passage that morning. The enemy now had the Schloss Calbeck taped. One salvo had set four Bren carriers alight, one of which was loaded with Bangalore torpedoes. The resulting explosion nearly collapsed the headquarters cellar and knocked out the rear link. The enemy were still in the Schloss Kalbeck over the way and in the woods all round the R.S.F., and they had also overflowed northwards into the woods on the Gordons' side of the Goch-Wesel railway line. Major R. Henderson, who was temporarily in command, sent "B" and "C" Companies to clear the woods on his front down to the railway, and so to consolidate what was now to become the Divisional axis up to the R.S.F. But here, too, just as the two companies were forming up, the enemy counter-attacked fiercely and threw them into considerable confusion. Recovering themselves rapidly, however, the companies attacked and by mid-day had reached the railway. Soon after, Major Henderson put in another attack by a company and a troop of tanks against the strip of wood which runs along the railway farther east. As the company reached the strip, it was counter-attacked and thrown back. Some of the tanks hung on, however, and the company rallied and took the strip at the second time of asking. In all this fighting the Gordons' gunner-adviser, Major G. C. Campbell, carrying his 22-set on his back, gave invaluable help in breaking up counter-attacks when the F.O.O.'s 18-sets had failed.

The 46th Brigade, less the Glasgow Highlanders, set out that morning on its approach march from Cleve, with the Cameronians in the lead riding on the Scots Guards' tanks. After their brief rest the Cameronians and the Seaforth were already like fresh troops. In the new situation the 46th Brigade's first task was to fight for room to deploy beyond the stream. Brigadier Villiers' amended plan, therefore, was to send the Cameronians across the bridge and through the R.S.F. to get elbow-room for the Seaforth, who would follow.

The Cameronians moved up through the grounds of the Schloss Calbeck and into the woods beyond, under extremely heavy fire. By now the Schloss itself was a sorry sight, its ruins in flames and its courtyards packed with a grotesque array of vehicles, almost all of

22nd Feb. them wrecked. The cellars, however, still gave welcome shelter to several headquarters and R.A.P.s. Beyond were the Gordons, still fighting fiercely, as we have seen, to keep the Divisional axis open.

Beginning about 2 P.M. Lieutenant-Colonel Remington Hobbs passed three companies of the Cameronians over the bridge one after another. Passing through the R.S.F. at the cross-roads, the Cameronians cleared the wood south of the bridge against surprisingly light opposition, though they continued to get casualties from the unabating fire. The Seaforth followed with another squadron of Scots Guards, to clear the adjoining wood to the eastward against rather severe opposition.

Both battalions were now fully committed, and the enemy were still in the houses of Hooesaat between the Cameronians' right and the Niers. Reluctantly, Brigadier Villiers ordered a company of the Glasgow Highlanders to clear Hooesaat. This the company did with only a few casualties from shelling, for the houses were only lightly held. Later, the rest of the Glasgow Highlanders followed over the bridge to relieve the R.S.F., who then reverted to the 44th Brigade. So ended the 46th Brigade's very successful action. In all, the Brigade had taken about a hundred prisoners.

Meanwhile the 44th Brigade had been placed under orders to attack through the 46th Brigade next day, and Brigadier Cumming-Bruce and his commanding officers had been busy making very careful plans accordingly. The 53rd Division was about to advance south from Goch on to Weeze along the west bank of the Niers. The object of the 44th Brigade's attack was to occupy the high ground on the east bank that overlooks the approaches to Weeze on the west bank, and so to secure the 53rd Division's flank during its attack.

23rd Feb. First thing next morning the Gordons completed their task of consolidating the Divisional axis by putting in a successful company attack on the Schloss Kalbeck itself, supported by a squadron of the Scots Guards. Soon after, the 44th Brigade, accompanied by Tank Grenadiers, came up to continue the attack southward for another two thousand yards or so on to the high ground which overlooks Rottum. Brigadier Cumming-Bruce's plan was to attack on a two-battalion front—right, the K.O.S.B.; left, the Royal Scots—each supported by a squadron of the Grenadiers. No Kangaroos were available. The Brigade axis and inter-battalion dividing line was the road that runs south past Fasanenkath.

The Royal Scots were in the lead and they crossed the bridge first and went on to a forming-up place in the woods in the Seaforth's area. The K.O.S.B. followed to a forming-up place in the woods in the Cameronians' area. The enemy shelling and mortaring was, if possible, heavier than ever.

23rd Feb.

"D" Company of the Royal Scots passed the start-line on time and advanced on the first objective—a fortified house in Saarbrockshof and the woods west of it. A 20-mm. firing from the K.O.S.B.'s front pinned one platoon at once, but the other two pushed on and, after the tanks had shot up the fortified house with H.E. and Besa fire, rushed it. Forty Germans surrendered, and there were six dead.

The K.O.S.B. were delayed and reached their start-line late. Captain Shaw, their F.O.O., extended the artillery programme, however, to cover their two-company attack across the five hundred yards of open to their first objective, the houses of Fasanenkath. These they reached successfully, taking two S.P.s and a number of prisoners.

The pause on the first objective enabled the K.O.S.B. and the Royal Scots to start in step again on their advance to the final objective, the extensive stretch of woodland about a thousand yards square that loomed ahead of them.

On the left "B" and "C" Companies of the Royal Scots passed through "D" in the area of Saarbrockshof at 11 A.M. and advanced straight into the woodland on the east side of the Brigade axis. In the maze of rides they found direction-keeping extremely difficult, so much so that "A" Company, the reserve company, at one stage found itself in the lead. The Royal Scots met no ground opposition other than from an S.P. which fired two rounds and then surrendered. Sorting themselves out under a ceaseless rain of shells and mortar-bombs, "B" and "C" Companies resumed the lead and reached the farther edge of the wood, where they consolidated, with "A" Company echeloned behind them in the wood and "D" still back at Saarbrockshof. Later, on relief by the R.S.F., "D" Company moved up to help "A" to watch the left or eastern flank, which in this continuous woodland was about as blind and open to infiltration as it well could be.

Presently, out in front, two S.P.s appeared along a road coming from the east and approached "B" Company's area under the white flag. Arrived at very short range, they opened fire, inflicting eleven

23rd Feb. casualties, and then withdrew before they could be dealt with. For forty-eight more unpleasant hours the Royal Scots were to remain in this most uneasy position in the woods, under ceaseless mortaring, shelling, and sniping. Here the Luftwaffe, too, singled them out for one of its now rare bombing attacks.

On the right the K.O.S.B., too, had started at 11 A.M. They had to begin their advance by crossing an expanse of open before they could reach the near edge of the woodland. Here they came under enfilade fire from the Germans in Host on the far bank of the Niers. So effective was the barrage, however, and so close did the leading tanks and infantry keep to it that the Germans on the K.O.S.B.'s own front had no time to man their weapons. Indeed the artillery fire caused many of them—men of the Battalion Graefing—to abandon some excellent entrenchments and to surrender without a fight. Farther on in the wood the K.O.S.B. suffered much from the enemy's tree-bursts, particularly deadly as these always are, and Major Malone of " A " Company was killed. In the dense cover the tanks gave magnificent support in difficult conditions. By 3.30 P.M. the K.O.S.B. had reached the southern edge of the wood, their final objective, where they cleared some emplacements with grenades and took more prisoners. Here the K.O.S.B. consolidated. In the houses about three hundred yards farther south they located elements of the 901st Panzer Grenadier Regiment with S.P. guns. Everything seemed to point to an immediate counter-attack—and, as always in woodland, the K.O.S.B.'s wireless was refusing to work.

Major Jackson promptly sent patrols into the loop of the Niers on the right front. On learning that the tiny villages of Heishof and Vasenhof were empty, he occupied these with the K.O.S.B.'s dismounted carrier platoon. From the high ground close by there was perfect observation over the 53rd Division's intended line of advance on the far bank, from Host through Rottum and almost to Weeze. Here on the high ground the Intelligence Section and Captain Shaw, R.A., both established their O.P.s. Thus by evening the 44th Brigade had completed its allotted task of securing what would be the 53rd Division's left flank in its forthcoming advance. The Lowlanders had taken a total of 150 prisoners and 8 S.P.s.

Far away to the southward great events had now begun. Ever since the opening days of " Veritable " the weather had been fine and the ground had been drying. By 23rd February General Simpson's Ninth

U.S. Army was at last able to put in its complementary attack across the Roer, so long delayed. By this time the prolonged and gruelling fighting on the First Canadian Army's front had sucked in all the German reserves. A screen of nothing more than two German Divisions was all that was now left to face the Ninth U.S. Army. In consequence the American offensive went apace. Within a week the Ninth U.S. Army was to penetrate to the Rhine; by 3rd March it was to link up with the 53rd Division at Geldern; by 10th March the last battered remnants of the enemy's forces were to be thrown back across the Rhine—the end of the war would be in sight.

23rd Feb.

Next day the First Canadian Army switched the weight of its army artillery from the 30th Corps' front to that of the 2nd Canadian Corps, in preparation for the closing phase of the battle—the Canadian's Operation "Blockbuster" directed on Xanten and Wesel, which was to begin on 26th February.

24th Feb.

On the 15th Scottish Division's right flank that morning the 158th Brigade of the 53rd Division began its drive from Goch through Host on Rottum. It was the 44th Brigade's anxious task to hold the vitally important salient on the opposite bank, with the 46th Brigade backing up in a counter-attack rôle behind. The enemy's anxiously awaited counter-attack did not materialise, however.

The observation from the O.P.s on the Heishof-Vasenhof spur in the K.O.S.B.'s area was magnificent, and, by an odd chance, the frequency of the K.O.S.B. rear link to 44th Brigade turned out to be almost exactly the same as the frequency of the leading tanks of the 53rd Division. So Major Jackson promptly put himself on to the 53rd Divisional net and fed in much precious information about enemy movements on the 53rd Division's axis of advance. Also, despite the fact that the K.O.S.B. had been given a very comprehensive "no firing" area on the 53rd Division's front, their Brens, mortars, and supporting guns were able to engage many excellent targets with perfect safety—and to the great surprise and consternation of the enemy. Later, at Rottum, the 71st Brigade went through the 158th, whereupon the battle passed on southward out of sight towards Weeze.

The relief of the 15th Scottish Division was now approaching. The 3rd Division had come up from the Second Army on the Maas to join the 30th Corps, and on the night of 24th February the 1st K.O.S.B. of the

24th Feb. 9th Brigade (3rd Division) relieved the H.L.I. and the Argylls in the Buchholt area. Thereupon both these battalions went out to Goch. The 46th Brigade, too, was able to thin out at last, so the Glasgow Highlanders went back to Nijmegen.

25th and 26th Feb. On the next night the 9th Brigade completed the relief of the 227th Brigade, while the 8th Brigade (3rd Division) relieved the 44th Brigade and 46th Brigade. This, as it turned out, was to be the final parting of the 44th Brigade and the Grenadiers. They had trained together in England and they had fought together in many battles. The bond of mutual respect and affection between them had grown strong indeed.

At 1 A.M. on 26th February operational command passed to the 3rd Division, and the 15th Scottish Division began its move by motor transport to the Tilburg area and to the fourteen days' rest that it had earned so well. Divisional Headquarters went to Boxtel; the 44th Brigade to Vught and thence to Turnhout two days later; the 46th and 227th Brigades to Tilburg. The twelve days of Operation " Veritable " cannot be better summed up than in the words of the ' 46th Brigade History ' :—

" We had been told to fight ourselves to a standstill and we had done so. The limit of human endurance is an unknown quantity and can only be gauged by experiment. We had very nearly reached this limit in Operation ' Veritable.' "

At the end of the operation the Division received the following congratulatory messages :—

From 30th Corps Commander to 15th Scottish Infantry Division Commander :—

" Requested convey to you General Crerar's (Commander of First Canadian Army) admiration of the manner in which your Division has carried out its important responsibilities during the last fortnight of your heavy fighting. The Division has more than maintained its very fine fighting record."

From Major-General C. M. Barber, 15th Scottish Infantry Division :—

" The Divisional Commander is proud to add his personal congratulations to all ranks of the Division on their magnificent achievements since 8th

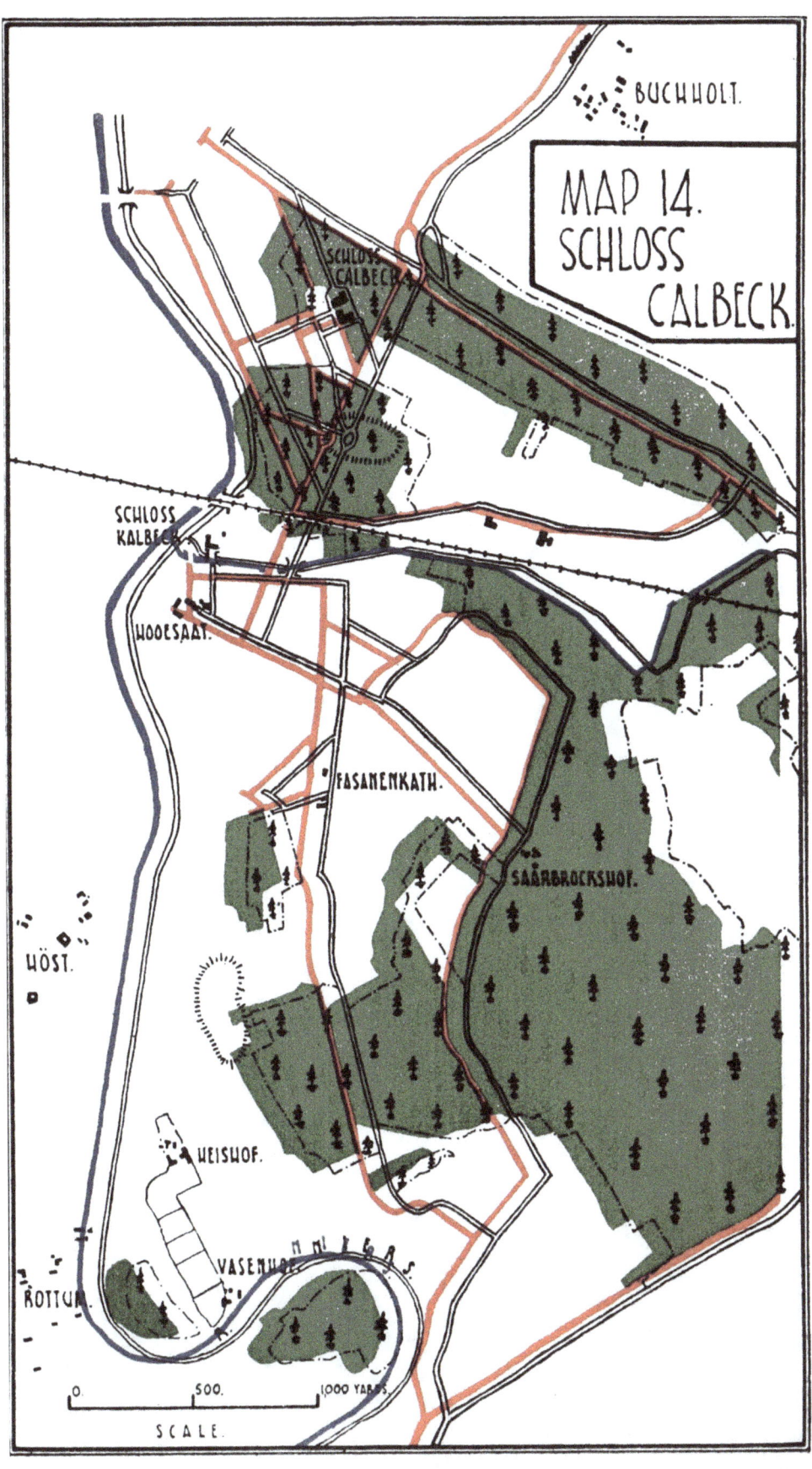

MASSED PIPES AND DRUMS PLAYING "RETREAT" IN TILBURG, 4TH MARCH 1945

February. Everything they set out to do they have accomplished, and, by their deeds, they have enhanced the already high traditions of 15th Scottish Infantry Division. No one could have a prouder command, and I salute you all on your great deeds."

<small>25th and 26th Feb.</small>

At Tilburg there was the invariable homecoming and welcome which always awaited the 15th Scottish Division. A Divisional social centre, the Red Lion Club, had now been opened, and the townsfolk vied with each other to ensure that it should lack nothing. The fourteen days' interlude that followed was one of the most pleasant in the campaign. There was no work after 3 P.M.; an extensive programme of entertainments was laid on locally; every officer and man had forty-eight hours' leave in Brussels. Turn-out very soon returned to normal—in time for a series of inspections by the Divisional Commander. Drafts arrived and were quickly absorbed. Soon the Division was ready for its next great adventure—the crossing of the Rhine.

CHAPTER IX.

THE RHINE CROSSING.

7th to 21st March.

AFTER an energetic week or so of refitting, accompanied by festivities of all sorts, the 15th Scottish Division moved from the Tilburg area down into Belgium to renew its acquaintance with the Maas in the neighbourhood of Roermond. As early as the end of January Montgomery had pulled out the 12th Corps Headquarters into reserve and had set it to study the technique of river-crossing on the Maas as part of his long-term planning for the crossing of the Rhine. On 7th March the 15th Scottish Division passed under command of the 12th Corps, and the planning for Exercise " Buffalo," a practice crossing over the Maas, began.

Next day the 8th Corps, which was to hold the front during the preparatory stages, took over on the Rhine between Wesel and Emmerich. On the same day the 30th Corps reverted from the First Canadian Army to the Second Army, and the Second Army opened its roadhead between the Maas and the Rhine. The great build-up had begun. In the next fortnight no less than 30,000 tons of R.E. stores, 60,000 tons of ammunition, and 28,000 tons of miscellaneous stores were to reach Second Army's roadhead.

On 9th March Montgomery issued his orders for 21st Army Group's crossing of the Rhine north of the Ruhr. The Ninth U.S. Army on the right and the Second Army on the left were to cross between Rheinberg and Rees. The initial objective was to be the communication centre of Wesel, but the bridgehead was to be deep enough to serve as forming-up place for the subsequent drive eastward and north-eastward. In the Second Army the assault was to be delivered by two corps : right, the 12th Corps, and left, the 30th Corps. As the preparations proceeded, the 52nd Lowland Division under 12th Corps was to take over the Corps front on the Rhine from the 8th Corps. When all was ready, the 12th Corps' night assault, Operation " Plunder," was to be delivered through the 52nd Lowland Division by the 1st Commando Brigade on the right directed on Wesel, and by the 15th Scottish Division on the left directed on Bislich and Mehr, while the 30th Corps' night assault was to be delivered by the 51st Highland Division directed on Rees. At the same time the Ninth U.S. Army would cross farther up-stream at Rheinberg. Next day the 18th U.S. Airborne Corps (right, the 17th U.S. Airborne Division; left, the 6th British Airborne Division) would land on the 15th Scottish Division's front in the area of the Diersfordter Wald and Hamminkeln, to silence the enemy's guns and to secure the crossings over the Issel. Montgomery set 24th March as the target date.

The crossing of the Rhine was to be the culminating operation of the whole campaign, comparable in magnitude with that of D Day. The two brigades of the 15th Scottish Division selected for the assault were the 44th and the 227th, and these two brigades were detailed accordingly to carry out two full-scale practice crossings of the Maas: the first, a daylight exercise on 14th March; the second, a night exercise on 15th March.

Under command for this exercise the 15th Scottish Division had the following formations and units, which were to remain under it till it crossed the Rhine: the 4th Armoured Brigade, of which the 44th Royal Tanks were equipped with D.D. Tanks (Shermans), fitted with water-wings and propellers which enabled them to swim under their own power; the 11th Army Group R.E. (A.G.R.E.); an S.P. Anti-Tank Battery; and a "Bank Group," composed of signals, medical, recovery, and traffic control sub-units grouped round the 5th Royal Berkshire. For the exercise, as for the real crossing, two squadrons of the Royal Dragoons and about fifty officers from Reinforcement Holding Units were given to the Royal Berkshire in addition. The Bank Group thus disposed of about a hundred officers—enough to allow of an officer at every small control-post. This Bank Group was to function in much the same way as a Beach Group and to control the forward passage of troops, vehicles, and stores across the river obstacle.

In support, the Division had the "Funnies" of the 33rd Armoured Brigade. Besides the usual Flails, Crocodiles, and Kangaroos, there were here two regiments, the 11th Royal Tanks and the East Riding Yeomanry, equipped with Buffaloes or L.V.T.s—large amphibious vehicles these, capable of carrying twenty-eight men or one small vehicle (carrier or jeep) and its team. The 11th Royal Tanks were to lift the assaulting battalions of the 44th Brigade, the East Riding

7th to 21st March.

Yeomanry those of the 227th. To each assaulting company were allotted six L.V.T.s (one troop). Besides its own men, the company had to fit in a miscellaneous assortment of machine-gunners, signallers, stretcher-bearers, Bank Control personnel for the far bank, F.O.O. parties, R.E. reconnaissance parties, R.E. bridging and raft-making parties, and the like. In addition, each assaulting battalion was allotted twelve L.V.T.s (two troops) for essential vehicles—6-pounders, wireless carriers, medical jeeps—of which it might pre-load eleven. For headquarters at every level from Division down to company the preparation of L.V.T. loading tables was a nightmare, not only before the exercise but also before the real crossing.

The day exercise of 14th March was carried out in brilliant sunshine. All went well save that the steepness of the farther bank defeated many of the L.V.T.s, which were meant to clamber ashore and deposit their loads well inland. The night exercise, on the other hand, was carried out in the worst possible conditions of fog and darkness. Much went wrong in consequence, but the snags that had been revealed were duly dealt with after the post-mortem. The only serious mishap occurred when an L.V.T. of the East Riding Yeomanry overturned and its driver and co-driver were drowned.

Simultaneously with these practice crossings the planning of the actual crossings began. Where the Divisional reconnaissance parties had to work between Wesel and Rees, the Rhine winds through a flat, rather featureless plain, five to ten miles wide. The river itself in March is normally four to five hundred yards in width, with a $3\frac{1}{2}$-knot current. The winter floods had made the water-level abnormally high, but, thanks to the spell of marvellous weather which had now set in, the water was falling daily and the country was drying out fast.

An important feature of the plain is the system of dykes to prevent flooding. Near the river-bank there are low " summer dykes," designed to contain any ordinary rise of water; these summer dykes are not troublesome obstacles. A few hundred yards inland, however, one finds much more formidable " winter dykes " or " bunds," designed to contain the extraordinary floods which sometimes sweep down in winter or early spring. Up to seventy feet thick at the base and twenty feet high, these bunds could rarely be crossed by L.V.T.s. Between the summer and winter dykes the ground, or " flood-bed " as it is called, is flat, open water-meadow, rather like the Dutch polders. When the Rhine rises to cover this flood-bed, its width increases to about twelve hundred yards. On the east bank the enemy had honeycombed the whole system of dykes with his weapon-pits.

7th to 21st March.

The meanders or old beds of the Rhine are a no less important feature of the plain. On what was to be the 15th Scottish Division's front there was in particular a continuous water-obstacle which encompassed the plain on the enemy bank, starting at Bislich in the south, whence the Bislicher Ley or water-channel runs eastward to Diersfordt village, then curving northward along the far edge of the plain to the southern end of the Lange Renne lake. There the chain of lakes—the Lange Renne, the Bellinghoven Meer, and the Haganer Meer—take up the running northward to the Sonsfeld Forest, whence another ley leads westward to the Alter or old Rhine, where it joins the new at Rees. This continuous water-obstacle made of the plain an island, from which the 15th Scottish Division would have to force a second crossing after it had crossed the Rhine itself.

Across the plain from Xanten are visible, three or four miles away, the tree-tops of the Diersfordter Wald, a large forest of mixed pine and beech, which stands, as it were, on the rim of the saucer beyond the curve of the Bislicher Ley. Here in the Diersfordter Wald, where the ground rises nearly a hundred feet above the plain, was the enemy's O.P. and gun area, and here the 18th Airborne Corps was to drop. A few miles still farther on beyond the Diersfordter Wald yet another water-obstacle flowed parallel with the Rhine: it was the River Issel, certain crossings of which the airborne troops were to seize.

This, then, was the setting in which the Divisional Commander made his plan for Operation " Torchlight," as the 15th Scottish Division's share in 12th Corps' Operation " Plunder " was called. On the right the 44th Brigade, supported by the 11th Royal Tanks (L.V.T.s), was to capture the area Schüttwick-Loh-Bislich, while on the left the 227th Brigade, supported by the East Riding Yeomanry (L.V.T.s), was to capture the area Haffen-Mehr. These two assaulting brigades were then to clear the intervals between their objectives up to their own boundaries. The 44th Brigade was responsible also for joining up with the 6th Airborne Division and the 17th U.S. Airborne Division.

In reserve for the assault was the 46th Brigade, with the D.D. tanks of the 44th Royal Tanks (4th Armoured Brigade) in support. The 46th Brigade was to cross the Rhine in the ferry wave and to assemble on the far side. It was then to establish itself in the area east of the Haganer Meer and on the high ground south-east of the

7th to 21st March

Sonsfeld Forest. Thus to reach its objectives the 46th Brigade would have to cross the chain of lakes, preferably by the bridge over the narrow neck of the Bellinghoven Meer north-east of Mehr, which bridge thus assumed great importance.

Meanwhile the 4th Armoured Brigade was to hold ready a mobile striking force of which the basis was to be an armoured regiment and a motor battalion, together with a squadron of Kangaroos for picking up a battalion of the 44th Brigade. This mobile striking force, which was to have high priority on the Class 50/60 rafts, had the task of seizing the Wissmann bridge over the Issel west of Dingen. This bridge was outside the area of the airborne troops. In certain circumstances the 44th Brigade might be used to seize the Wissmann bridge instead of or in conjunction with the mobile striking force.

While the planning continued, units reconnoitred their marshalling areas and the routes thence to their crossing-places. The marshalling areas chosen were large stretches of woodland accessible by metalled road and far enough back to be out of enemy observation and defensive fire. The 44th Brigade's marshalling area was to be in " Railway Wood," about two and a half miles due west of Xanten; the 227th Brigade's in the Hoch Wald, a couple of miles west of Vynen; the 46th Brigade's in the Tuschun Wald, immediately south of the Hoch Wald. In these marshalling areas the units of the " assault wave " were to marry up with their L.V.T.s, pre-load on D Day, and then move straight up to their crossing-places and cross at H-hour without a pause. Routes for the L.V.T.s, both up and down, were to be lighted by concealed lighting on posts put up by the Bank Group. Units of the " ferry wave," on the other hand, which was to follow the assault wave, were to march up from their marshalling areas to L.V.T. or storm-boat " waiting areas " near the proposed ferry sites.

Lack of cover along the bank, combined with " Monty's smoke-screen "—the stupendous fifty-mile screen built up by countless canisters that from 16th March onwards poured forth their smoke day after day to cover the concentration—made satisfactory reconnaissance of the crossing-places almost impossible. In fact, only the Argylls could get near enough to their crossing-place by Vynen for the close-up so necessary in the choosing of suitable landing-places for L.V.T.s: for the rest, commanders and staff had to look from afar during brief interludes in the smoke-screen. Fortunately, however, there were not only a plentiful supply of air photographs, but also an outfit of most

THE RHINE CROSSING

remarkable models, made of " Sorbo " rubber or similar composition, which showed the country in faithful detail down to the last telegraph post. Platoon commanders and even drivers and section leaders were all able to see the model at least once and to get a clear picture of the topography.

As to the nature of the opposition which the 15th Scottish Division was likely to meet : facing the 21st Army Group was Blaskowitz's Army Group " H." Of that Army Group the 1st Parachute Army held the front Essen-Emmerich with four Parachute Divisions and three Infantry Divisions forward and with the 116th Panzer and the 15th Panzer Grenadier Divisions and one Infantry Division in immediate reserve. Opposite the 44th Brigade's crossing-place at Xanten were elements of the 84th Infantry Division, which the 15th Scottish Division had already written off once in the Siegfried Line. Opposite the 227th Brigade's crossing-place at Wardt and Vynen were elements of the 7th Parachute Division, which was to prove a much tougher proposition.

By this time Kesselring, who had succeeded Rundstedt as German Commander-in-Chief in the West, was having to pay the price of Rundstedt's offensive in the Ardennes and of the subsequent prolonged and bitter fighting west of the Rhine. He lacked the troops to hold the Rhine securely. Moreover, Kesselring's task had been made far harder by Hodges and his First U.S. Army, who had "bounced" the Remagen bridge on 7th March. By 23rd March the Remegen bridgehead beyond the Rhine was thirty miles wide by nine miles deep —a running sore which was fast draining the enemy's failing strength.

As 24th March approached, the rolling, wooded country between the Maas and the Rhine became a scene of unbelievable activity. The few available roads were choked with slowly moving traffic—guns, tanks, bridging equipment, rafts, boats, ammunition, men, material of every sort. The whole teeming concentration was shrouded by " Monty's smoke-screen." Behind this screen was carried out the vast programme of dumping of artillery ammunition. The gun areas had to be very far forward on the plain in the direction of Xanten, Wardt, and Vynen, in order to obtain the longest possible range beyond the Rhine. In consequence the dumping was difficult to hide.

As may be imagined, the Second Army and 12th Corps had a job to handle this traffic, which during the week before 24th March amounted to nearly 40,000 tanks and vehicles of all sorts coming up for the battle alone. For traffic control during the subsequent move across

7th to 21st March.

7th to 21st March.

the Rhine, 12th Corps made the 15th Scottish Division responsible and put the Bank Control Organisation under the Divisional Commander. On the night of 21st March Divisional Headquarters moved up to a farmhouse centrally placed on the lateral road that runs north and south along the eastern edge of the Balberger Wald and the Hoch Wald, and which thus passed close by the marshalling areas. Here at Divisional Headquarters the 1st Royal Berkshire set up Headquarters, Bank Control.

On the same night the two L.V.T. regiments moved up into their respective marshalling areas, where they were to have twenty-four hours spare for maintenance before they were joined by the infantry brigades of the assault wave, the 44th and the 227th, on the night of 22nd March.

22nd March.

The two assault brigades set up their headquarters at Lüttingen and Vynen respectively, with their R.E. advisers and company headquarters, Bank Units, alongside them. These combined headquarters were termed Right and Left Crossing Control.

On the night of 22nd March, too, the 46th Brigade went into its marshalling area and the artillery deployed—very far forward on the plain, as I have already mentioned. Every back garden and shed and barn was hiding its quota of guns. A change of wind had blown the smoke across the gun area in a pea-soup fog. Many of the gunners were extremely sick in consequence. The glorious weather still continued, but dust and smoke were suffocating.

The job of the Bank Group was twofold: to ensure that units or parts of them crossed in accordance with priorities laid down by Division and to prevent piling up near the bridges or ferries. The chain of responsibility was this. Divisional Headquarters gave Bank Control the priority of all serials. Bank Control passed these priorities to Crossing Control, who was responsible for calling up the serials from marshalling areas to vehicle waiting areas, or to armour waiting areas in the case of tanks, whence serials were fed forward to one of six traffic control points on the river-bank for loading on to craft or ferries. As soon as possible there was to be established on the far bank a Forward Control Headquarters, which would direct serials to forward assembly areas.

This whole business of priorities was further complicated by the fact that, from the evening of D Day, there would be the " land tails " of the 18th Airborne Corps, amounting to 5000 vehicles of all types, to be put over in accordance with Airborne Corps' priorities.

22nd March.

The Bank Group had wireless inter-communication with buried cable in addition on the near bank. From start to finish the organisation was to work with perfect smoothness. At any stage the officer commanding Royal Berkshire was able to give the Divisional Commander instant information as to the precise " form " at the crossings.

No less fundamental to the success of Operation " Torchlight " was the engineer plan, on which the actual crossings depended. Here, too, the 12th Corps made the Commander, 15th Scottish Division, responsible. To help him to establish and maintain routes across the river, the Divisional Commander had under him Colonel R. Foster, commanding the 11th Army Group R.E. (A.G.R.E.), whose Group consisted of no less than seven headquarters R.E., of different types, together with the equivalent of twenty-three field companies R.E., one bridging company R.C.A.S.C., and detachments of R.A.S.C. transport and Royal Pioneer Corps labour—all additional to the 15th Scottish Divisional Engineers. There were, too, some R.N. parties and an Assault Regiment R.E. in support.

Colonel Foster's task was to establish and maintain the following: two L.V.T. ferries (sites only), two storm-boat ferries, four Class 9 raft ferries, one Class 50/60 ferry, one D.U.K.W. ferry, one Class 9 bridge (folding-boat equipment), one Class 12 Bailey pontoon bridge, one Class 40 Bailey pontoon bridge (tactical), and, later, one Class 40 all-weather pontoon bridge (high level). He had also to establish a Class 40 route on the corps' main axis through Xanten, together with a variety of subsidiary routes; and he had to provide boom protection both above and below the bridging sites.

The Commander of the 100th Anti-Aircraft Brigade undertook the military protection of this R.E. work.

Colonel Foster established a dump of 5000 tons of R.E. stores on wheels at Kavalaer, fed from the Second Army dump at Goch. Only assault equipment was dumped forward before D Day, in carefully concealed hides.

Montgomery set such store by the airborne operation that he was prepared to wait five days for the proper sort of weather. On 23rd March, however, he got the favourable weather forecast that he wanted, and he gave the word " Go." All heard with tense excitement that afternoon

23rd March.

23rd March. that 12th Corps' Operation "Plunder" would begin that evening as planned. At 5 P.M. the 30th Corps' counter-battery programme opened on the left; an hour later the 12th Corps' guns took up the tale.

In accordance with the Second Army's assault programme, the 51st Highland Division of the 30th Corps led off on the left at 9 P.M. with a two-brigade assault on Rees. An hour later the 1st Commando Brigade on the right of the 12th Corps assaulted at Wesel.

Meanwhile in each of the two assaulting brigades of the 15th Scottish Division the two forward battalions were boarding their L.V.T.s in their marshalling areas in readiness to advance straight to their crossing-places and to cross on time at their H-hour, fixed for 2 A.M. next morning, 24th March. At the same time the reserve battalions of the two assaulting brigades and the reserve brigade itself were getting ready to move up to L.V.T. or storm-boat waiting areas in readiness to cross in the ferries when these began to ply. The Seaforth were to cross behind the 44th Brigade; the Cameronians and the Glasgow Highlanders behind the 227th Brigade. Presently the order to move off reached the waiting troops.

Of the five assaulting infantry brigades that night four were purely Scottish, while in the two assaulting divisions were represented every regiment of Scottish infantry. In the words of the 44th Lowland Brigade's History, "Surely throughout her long martial history Scotland has never seen a day like this."

The actors in that night's drama are never likely to forget it. The flash and thud of the bursting bombs in nearby Wesel; the coming of the good news that the Commandos and the leading battalions of the 51st Division were safely over; the earth-shaking crash at 11.30 P.M. as the 700 guns of the 15th Scottish Divisional Artillery Group spoke in the opening salvo of the softening bombardment; the start of the Divisional "Pepperpot" at 1 A.M. to swell the din in a mad crescendo and to criss-cross the darkness with the vivid red of anti-aircraft and anti-tank and machine-gun tracer; the rushing, rending crash of the Mattresses; the luminous trails of the Buffalo columns curving towards the river like giant serpents—these are some among the memories. The enemy's answering fire was feeble; clearly he was in no shape to riposte to such a weight of metal.

24th March. The 44th Brigade was to attack astride Bislich, with the R.S.F. and the Royal Scots up, each with three companies in their first flight.

BUFFALOES CROSSING THE RHINE

On the west bank the Engineers had breached the bund at the last 24th March. moment, so that the L.V.T.s had no difficulty in making their way down to the river's edge. Exactly at 2 A.M. the first of them crawled down the bank and put to sea. Soon they were lost in the wilderness of water, which looked so infinitely vast when viewed from a Buffalo in mid-stream. Not a Buffalo was knocked out by the enemy fire, and all reached their chosen landing-places. Thanks to the thorough reconnaissance, most of these turned out to be practicable. The R.S.F.'s objective was the bund immediately in front of Bislich, and, despite some casualties from Schumines and an unfortunate incident with two short shells that knocked out nearly half of two of "D" Company's platoons, they took it with the utmost dash and speed. By 4 A.M. the R.S.F. had consolidated along the bund from Loh, through the western outskirts of Bislich, and had contacted the Royal Scots on their left. They had also taken a large number of prisoners.

The Royal Scots, also attacking on a three-company front, made an equally faultless crossing and reached the bund farther north without serious resistance. Here they, too, had consolidated by first light.

By 3 A.M. the L.V.T.s had returned and were beginning to ferry over the vehicles. A few minutes later Brigadier Cumming-Bruce ordered the K.O.S.B. to cross in their storm-boats. By 4 A.M. they had crossed without a casualty. By that time the river-bank had been thoroughly cleared of all enemy snipers and machine-gunners, so the Engineers were able to get on with their bridge-building and the Seaforth and the D.D. tanks were able to cross.

It dawned fine and clear, with a slight mist. To quote the 44th Brigade History once more :—

"The scene at the river was like Henley or the Thames at Oxford in 'Eights Week'; the banks were crowded with men and vehicles ... The storm-boats, rafts and Buffaloes plied backwards and forwards with their loads, every moment landing more stuff on the east bank; and the D.D. tanks, like strange canvas boxes, dived into the water and swam slowly across, emerged on the far bank, shook themselves, deflated, and then miraculously appeared as Sherman tanks again."

At first light "A" and "B" Companies of the K.O.S.B. went through the R.S.F. on the bund and on into Bislich, where they met some resistance from the 1062 Grenadier Regiment. By 7 A.M.,

24th March. however, they were firmly established in Bislich. "C" and "D" Companies then went through in their turn to reach Schüttwick before 10 A.M.

About the same time "B" and "D" Companies of the Royal Scots, with the support of a squadron of D.D. tanks, pushed on five hundred yards or so to occupy the villages of Vissel and Jöckern, taking a number of prisoners. This rapid progress on the 44th Brigade front was of supreme importance, since it would be the task of the 44th Brigade to link up with the airborne troops as soon as possible after these latter had landed.

As ten o'clock approached our guns fell silent and all eyes turned westward: it was the hour appointed for the 18th Corps' great airborne landing. Sure enough, a few minutes before the hour the cry went round, "They're here," and there they were, coming in from the west, a multitude of four-engined bombers, Dakotas, and gliders, flying low and glittering in the sun. It was a crowning manifestation of triumphant air-power. Exactly at 10 A.M. the first parachute drop over the Diersfordter Wald began, and for three hours thereafter the procession of 1700 aircraft and 1400 gliders continued. Hard on the tail of this procession there roared over a re-supply mission of 250 Liberators, flying at only about eighty feet. Despite the heavy anti-Flak bombardment that had preceded the drop, Flak remained heavy throughout and accounted for about 70 aircraft and 50 gliders. The black, oily clouds of smoke rising skywards were a grim reminder of the price to be paid for victory.

With the landing of the airborne troops the enemy artillery fire began to slacken. Soon there was only an occasional shell coming over. The 44th Brigade's first task was to get wireless touch with the airborne troops. By noon the K.O.S.B. had got through successfully on the special set allocated to them for the purpose. Then came the link-up on the ground.

About noon Lieutenant-Colonel Richardson had sent out a patrol of the K.O.S.B. to contact the airborne troops at the prearranged meeting-point a mile or so to the east. Meanwhile "C" Company of the K.O.S.B., who were consolidating in Schüttwick, could see in front of them many parties of retreating Germans. At first they engaged these with their Brens. Later, however, the company commander sent out Captain Carey with his carrier to round up a party. After putting many stragglers in the bag, the carrier joined up with the patrol and then went on alone to the contact point. There at the road junction south of Diersfordt, at 2.45 P.M., Captain Carey saw two figures emerge from the wood to greet him. They were American parachutists.

24th March.

Less than half an hour later the R.S.F. also contacted the 17th U.S. Airborne Division to the eastward of Loh. Finally, about 3.20 P.M., it fell to the Royal Scots to make contact with the 5th Parachute Brigade of the 6th Airborne Division. At about 12.45 P.M. Lieutenant-Colonel Pearson had sent out the Royal Scots' carrier platoon from Feldwick to push north-east through Jöckern and to capture the bridge over the Bislicher Ley, where it runs along the south-west edge of the Diersfordter Wald. Beyond the bridge the patrol expected to contact the 6th Airborne Division. After capturing about forty prisoners, together with two 155-mm. guns and two mortars, the carrier patrol pushed on, driving a pack of stragglers streaming before them, to reach the bridge. There they found that the paratroopers had forestalled them by about five minutes. The ground in front of the bridge was littered with the bodies of those stragglers who had failed to make their getaway.

Thus within little more than five hours of the first parachute drop the 44th Brigade had made a treble link-up with both of the Airborne Divisions. At nightfall the K.O.S.B. moved north to Bergen in the Royal Scots area, in readiness to move east at first light. 44th Brigade Headquarters was now in Bislich. Already the 44th Brigade had taken over 1000 prisoners, with a loss of less than 100 casualties. It had been a great day.

Meanwhile on the 227th Brigade front things had not been going so smoothly. On the right the H.L.I. went in on a two-company front opposite Wolffskath; on the left the Argylls on a three-company front opposite Hübsch. The leading flights of both battalions entered the water on time at 2 A.M. and crossed the river without difficulty, encountering little or no enemy fire. It was when they reached the farther bank that their troubles began.

According to Lieutenant-Colonel Bramwell Davis's plan the right-hand company of the H.L.I., "C," should have cleared Wolffskath and then advanced inland along the bund to Overkamp, while "A" Company on the left should have cleared westward along the other bund that runs parallel to the river close to its edge. When "A" Company had reached the junction point with the Argylls it was to have pushed inland and cleared Ree, where it would have found itself abreast of "C" in Overkamp.

Unfortunately, however, the L.V.T.s got off their course and both companies were landed up-stream of their own areas. In consequence, "A" Company had to take on the clearing of Wolffskath instead of "C," while the riverside bund—which, it turned out, was manned by a parachute battalion—remained uncleared. Confused and bitter fighting followed, in which "A" Company lost all its officers. C.S.M. John Wright at once took command; he was afterwards awarded the D.C.M. for his cool handling of "A" Company.

"C" Company had also pushed down-stream to Wolffskath, where it was promptly pinned by 20-mm. and L.M.G. fire, losing all its officers but one. Most of the tracer was coming from the houses at Bettenhof, about a thousand yards inland from Wolffskath: clearly Bettenhof had to be cleared. The F.O.O.'s wireless was "out," but "C" Company's 18-set was still working and it passed the F.O.O.'s call for fire on Bettenhof.

Meanwhile "B" and "D" Companies in the second flight had also arrived, but they too had been landed wrongly. As the plan finally emerged from a highly confused situation, "B" took on the clearing of the riverside bund, while "D" formed up behind "C" to the eastward of the north-south bund that led to Overkamp.

It was at this stage of the fight that the guns answered the call for fire on Bettenhof. Down came the concentration exactly where it was wanted, whereupon "C" and "D" Companies—totalling together much less than one company's strength—went in in open order. They took Bettenhof together with forty-four prisoners, and there in the southern portion of Overkamp they dug in.

To return now to "B" on the riverside bund. In front of "B" there were, it turned out, no less than twelve spandau positions manned by paratroopers who meant to fight. Steadily and methodically "B," under Major D. A. Beatson-Hird, who had commanded it in every action since D Day, dealt with each position in turn. Lieutenant Farmer and Sergeant Scanlon were afterwards decorated for the parts they played in this series of very gallant actions. At the sluice-gate on the riverside bund "B" Company linked up at last with the Argylls, who had cleared their section of the bund up to the sluice-gates as a preliminary to taking Lohr.

Meanwhile Battalion Headquarters of the H.L.I. and the carrier platoon, who had pushed some three hundred yards inland, had found 24th March. themselves under fire at close quarters from all sides and had been forced to withdraw to Wolffskath at dawn. During this retirement the complete O.P. party of the 131st Field Regiment, R.A., was ambushed and wiped out. Among the killed was Major J. Oliver, who had been gunner-adviser to the H.L.I. throughout the whole campaign.

By about 9 A.M. the situation in the H.L.I.'s area was sufficiently in hand to allow the battalion assault echelons of transport to cross and the R.E. to start bridging. In this bitter fight, in which they had met and worsted a complete parachute battalion which was fighting with all its accustomed courage, the H.L.I. had lost three officers killed and four wounded, fourteen other ranks killed and seventy wounded. They had good reason to look back with pride on their Rhine crossing.

On the left of the 227th Brigade the Argylls had assaulted with "D," "B," and "A" Companies up in the first flight. According to Lieutenant-Colonel Russell Morgan's plan, "D" was to have landed on the east side of the Hübsch inlet and to have gone straight for Hübsch and Lohr, where they would have been in touch with the H.L.I. in Ree, while "B" and "A" Companies were to have landed west of the inlet and to have pushed north, astride the bund, towards Wayerhof, in preparation for an attack on Haffen from the west.

Unfortunately, five out of "D" Company's six L.V.T.s found it impossible to land at the eastern corner of the inlet, so they put their loads ashore on the west side. Thus "D" Company had a mile's march round the inlet before they could tackle Hübsch, so all hope of surprise was lost. Outside Hübsch "D" were held in close fighting by paratroopers, who were in strength along the reverse side of the bund and in the scrub to the southward. By first light "C" Company arrived, having crossed in the second flight. "D" and "C" Companies together then cleared Hübsch, losing a lot of men. Meanwhile "B" and "A" Companies had pushed north without waiting for Hübsch to be cleared. After a stiff fight "A" Company took Hoverhof, north-west of Haffen. "B" Company, farther east, beat off a two-company counter-attack with the help of most effective defensive fire put down by the F.O.O., and took ninety prisoners. Thus dawn found "B" and "A" Companies closely engaged with the enemy and separated by some two thousand five hundred yards from "D" and "C" in Hübsch. Battalion Headquarters was betwixt and between at Dornemardt.

24th March.

Meanwhile at 6.15 A.M. Brigadier Colville had ordered the Gordons in brigade reserve to send a company to reinforce the Argylls. According to the original plan the Gordons were to have crossed by storm-boat ferry into the H.L.I. sector. These new orders involved "A" Company of the Gordons in a twelve hundred yards trip down-stream by storm-boat, throughout which it had to run the gauntlet of the enemy posts in Lohr and along the bund. In the outcome "A" Company lost an officer and three men killed, ten men wounded, and a number of boats sunk.

The remnants of "A" Company of the Gordons joined "C" and "D" Companies of the Argylls at Hübsch. Here the situation was this. Any movement in Hübsch drew heavy fire from Lohr. Yet till Lohr was cleared it would be impossible for the Engineers to begin bridging or for the two waiting battalions of the 46th Brigade to cross.

Lieutenant-Colonel Russell Morgan came up to Hübsch and, having discussed things with Major Graham Graham of "C" Company, gave him what was left of "D" Company, together with a platoon of medium machine-guns, two sections of 3-inch mortars, and "A" Company of the Gordons for fire support, and told him to clear Lohr.

The attack had to go in across open fields, but, owing to the fact that the airborne operation was now about to begin, no artillery plan could be laid on. First, "C" Company of the Argylls cleared the bund from Hübsch towards Lohr in face of fierce resistance. Then, a little later, "D" Company of the Argylls attacked Lohr itself, only to be pinned in the group of houses some four hundred yards short of it. Soon after, however, "A" Company of the Gordons, who had now joined in, took another group of houses on the right, some four hundred yards to the south. At that the resistance in Lohr collapsed, some of the paratroopers withdrawing on Haffen, the others surrendering. These latter included a formidable outfit of women snipers in uniform, whom the Jocks regarded with some awe. It was at this moment that two D.D. tanks arrived in Lohr to report "Lohr cleared, found only one German."

The arrival of these tanks had come about in this wise. On the 227th Brigade front it was not till afternoon that, after several attempts, the Cameronians and the Glasgow Highlanders were able at last to carry out their storm-boat crossing. Meanwhile, about 10 A.M., the Divisional Commander had ordered the Seaforth and a squadron of D.D. tanks—both of whom, it will be remembered, had crossed early

2ND GORDON HIGHLANDERS CROSSING THE RHINE FLOODBANK

[*To face p.* 289

on the 44th Brigade front—to clear the riverside bund between the 44th Brigade and the H.L.I., and, that done, between the H.L.I. and the Argylls, and so break the deadlock on the 227th Brigade front. On the first part of their journey the Seaforth met no enemy, but they ran into a large extent of flooded country round Bergen, where they had great difficulty in finding a route for their tanks and other vehicles. It was some considerable time, therefore, before the Seaforth contacted the H.L.I. in Wolffskath. "A" Company of the Seaforth, supported by tanks, then attacked Sandenhof, which is a northerly extension of Lohr. When the tanks reached Lohr, however, they found the enemy already gone—hence the message aforesaid. A little earlier, so the Argylls and the Gordons were ready to assure them, they would have found enemy in plenty.

The rest of the Gordons now crossed without incident, followed by the Cameronians and the Glasgow Highlanders. Soon after 5 P.M. that afternoon the Gordons passed through the Argylls to westward of Haffen. Haffen is divided into two separate halves, east and west. That evening "B" and "C" Companies of the Gordons took most of the western half with the bayonet, capturing seventy-one prisoners, but the enemy hung on doggedly in the northern outskirts. Bad luck still pursued "A" Company of the Gordons, who, caught in the open by mortar-fire, lost all their remaining officers wounded.

To return now to the Seaforth: at about 1 P.M. they had set out from Wolffskath, most of them riding on the D.D. tanks of their supporting squadron of the 44th Royal Tanks, and had pushed inland through the H.L.I. in Overkamp, heading for Mehr. "A" Company from Lohr had rejoined *en route*. After a sharp fight the Seaforth cleared Mehr. Half a mile on to the north-east lay the bridge over the Bellinghoven Meer, which is the narrow neck between the two long lakes, the Lange Renne and the Hagener Meer. This bridge was the Seaforth's main objective. Patrols, however, soon found that the bridge area was strongly held, and the enemy too was patrolling vigorously.

At about 2.30 P.M. Brigadier Villiers saw all battalion commanders of the 46th Brigade at Ree on the east bank. The Glasgow Highlanders he ordered to concentrate in Bellinghoven, the Cameronians in Haffen, whence they were to advance north-east. All three battalions he ordered to patrol vigorously to find crossings over the chain of water obstacles, the Seaforth in the bridge area, the Glasgow Highlanders near Belling-

24th March. hoven itself, the Cameronians north of the Hagener Meer. Acting on these orders the Cameronians took the eastern half of Haffen at about 6 P.M.—that is, about the time when the Gordons were taking the western half. Half a mile north-east of Haffen, however, the Cameronians ran into stiff resistance, and in the end none of Brigadier Villiers's battalions was able to find a crossing-place that evening.

At the close of this first day's fighting the three infantry brigades of the Division were disposed as follows: of the 44th Brigade, the Royal Scots and the K.O.S.B. were in and around Bergen, with the R.S.F. farther south; of the 46th Brigade, the Cameronians were in contact with the enemy north of Haffen, the Glasgow Highlanders were in reserve in Haffen, the Seaforth were fighting hard round Mehr; of the 227th Brigade, the H.L.I. were in Overkamp and Ree, the Gordons were in Haffen, the Argylls with their forward companies in close touch with the enemy between Haffen and the Rhine to the westward. On the 46th Brigade and 227th Brigade fronts the 7th Parachute Division was still resisting fiercely.

On the right the 1st Commando Brigade was still heavily engaged in Wesel; on the left the 51st Division was meeting fierce opposition in Rees.

The Engineers had had their Class 9 rafts working on the 44th Brigade front by 6.30 A.M. that morning, on the 227th Brigade front by soon after mid-day. The Class 50/60 rafts near Wardt were working by 6.30 P.M. The Class 9 F.B.E. bridge, also near Wardt, opened that night at 11 P.M., but was damaged soon after and put out of action for half a day.

25th March. That night the Seaforth in Mehr were heavily counter-attacked. "C" Company was in the eastern outskirts of Mehr, facing the bridge, with "D" Company in depth behind it and "A" and "B" Companies farther north. About midnight two parties of paratroopers, each about sixty strong and led by English-speaking officers, broke into Mehr. Spandau-fire streamed down the streets; bazooka bombs crashed through roofs; confusion reigned. For a time indeed these paratroopers held complete control of the village and were all round "C" Company Headquarters. It happened that Captain Whitton of 531st Field Battery was "Troop F.O.O." with "C" Company that night. His wireless had failed, so the company commander sent him back to Battalion Headquarters to report the position. Diving out of a back window, Captain Whitton and his party made a break for

Battalion Headquarters, which itself was now under close-range fire. There he found Lieutenant-Colonel Hunt and Major Wingate, the gunner-adviser. Appreciating that the Seaforth in and around Mehr were mostly under cover, whereas the Germans were out in the streets and gardens, they decided to bring down defensive fire actually on Mehr itself. The first " stonk " caught the Germans in the open, whereupon they rushed for shelter—many of them into the very house in the cellars in which " C " Company Headquarters had taken refuge. When the fire lifted, however, out came the Germans again. This was exactly what Major Wingate had been counting on. Down came another " stonk," killing and wounding many more. By that time the Germans had had a bellyful, so they withdrew—only to lose more of their number by the fire of the medium artillery which had been put down on the bridge area. By daylight on the 25th the situation had been restored, but the Seaforth, too, had lost heavily in this fighting.

25th March.

The orders for the 44th Brigade next morning were to push some ten miles north-eastward and seize the Wissmann bridge over the River Issel west of Dingen. It was a vitally important mission, for this bridge would soon be urgently needed for the break-out from the bridgehead.

At 7.30 A.M. the K.O.S.B., who were to be in the lead, set out from Bergen with two of their companies riding on the tanks of the 3/4th County of London Yeomanry (the Sharpshooters of the 4th Armoured Brigade), the other two companies marching. With the vanguard there were Major Meredith, the F.O.O., and a troop of S.P. A.Tk. guns; behind followed the Royal Scots. The R.S.F. were to picket the brigade axis in rear. Back on the Rhine the 181st Field Regiment was to complete its crossing by raft that afternoon—the first field regiment to cross.

Their way took the K.O.S.B. across the bridge over the Bislicher Ley, where the Royal Scots and our paratroops had met the day before, and on through the area beyond, which was held by our 5th Parachute Brigade. According to the original plan the K.O.S.B. were to have passed the cross-roads on the Haldern-Wesel road that lies about twelve hundred yards due east of the bridge over the Bellinghoven Meer, which the Seaforth were approaching from the west. As this route was not yet open, however, the K.O.S.B. branched off farther south by a rough track through the Diersfordter Wald. Enemy shelling had set the undergrowth on fire; the smoke

25th March. was choking; ammunition was going up in all directions. It was an exciting march.

The 44th Brigade was now passing through the rear area of the German 7th Parachute Division, and the first contact came at the railway line, where enemy shelling was heavy. Through the woods beyond, the K.O.S.B. and their tanks fought their way northward another two thousand yards to reach the road from Mehr to Hamminkeln by about 4 P.M. From this road to the Autobahn to the north-east was a fifteen hundred yard bound over dead-open country commanded by enemy S.P.s, which had already stopped three of the Yeomanry's tanks. Till dark that bound was not " on." Beyond the Autobahn was another bound of two thousand yards to the Issel bridge, over much closer country dotted with farms. Lieutenant-Colonel Richardson decided that, having secured the line of the Autobahn as soon after dark as possible, the K.O.S.B. would fight their way on silently by alternate companies through the farm zone. The need for speed was now all the greater since news had just come in that the 116th Panzer Division from army reserve had appeared beyond the Issel to the south-east.

At dark the K.O.S.B. carrier platoon darted forward to the Autobahn, which they found to be still very much in the making. Soon after, the leading company crossed the Autobahn to begin the silent attack. The first two or three farms fell without resistance. But presently, when the Borderers had advanced three-quarters of a mile or so and had committed three rifle companies, the enemy, now fully alive to what was going on, began to fight back strongly. Lieutenant-Colonel Richardson decided, therefore, to postpone his final assault on the bridge till the early hours in order to give the enemy time to settle down and so reintroduce some element of surprise. The hour he fixed was 4.30 A.M. The K.O.S.B. set to work to prepare accordingly, with the Royal Scots holding a firm base behind them. Their goal, the bridge over the Issel, was now only eight hundred yards away. The 44th Brigade's advance that day into the heart of the enemy territory was one of their finest achievements of the whole campaign.

Next we come to the 46th Brigade. Soon after daylight Brigadier Villiers had held an " O " Group at the headquarters of the Seaforth at Mehr. A frontal attack to capture the all-important bridge over the Bellinghoven Meer seemed suicidal. Brigadier Villiers decided, therefore, to send the Glasgow Highlanders round south of the Lange Renne to drive north through the woodland on its eastern shore. For this operation the Argylls were under command of the 46th Brigade. At the same time the Seaforth were to close on the bridge from the west as opportunity offered, while the Cameronians were to continue to push north-east from Haffen.

Leaving Haffen about noon the Glasgow Highlanders reached a point about a mile to the east of the southern end of the Lange Renne about 3.30 P.M., where they formed up behind the front held by Brigadier James Hill's 5th Parachute Brigade. After a check at the start-line, where one company came under heavy small-arms fire, the Glasgow Highlanders adjusted their fire plan and then cleared a firm base in the wood from which to start the main operation.

Meanwhile the Argylls, too, had started about noon, after a hurried relief of " B " Company by the Gordons north-west of Haffen. " A " Company in the same area, which was also due for relief, had to be left behind: it was so closely engaged that it took a company attack by the Gordons to extricate it after dark. After a hasty dinner in Hübsch, the Argylls (less " A " Company) pushed east in choking dust on their forced march of five miles or so round the southern end of the Lange Renne to join forces with the Glasgow Highlanders.

The Argylls on the right and the Glasgow Highlanders on the left then swept north through the woods, coming on countless dugouts and trench systems, but meeting little opposition. In the growing dusk, direction-keeping was extremely difficult. After nightfall the Glasgow Highlanders cleared the houses immediately east of the bridge, where they took many prisoners. More important still, they here linked up with the Seaforth, who had approached from the west, so the 46th Brigade had won its bridge. Unfortunately, however, the bridge had been too far demolished to take vehicles, so all night long the A.Tk. guns and vehicles of the Glasgow Highlanders and the Argylls had to journey round by the circuitous route south of the Lange Renne to join their battalions. For the night the Glasgow Highlanders consolidated along the east edge of the wood at the eastern end of the bridge; the Argylls consolidated round Kapenhof, about half a mile to the north-east.

It had been a successful but very exhausting day, and it was to be followed by an anxious night, during which there was to be no sleep for anyone. The woods were full of Germans, most of them

25th March. spoiling for a fight, who managed more than once to break into both battalion areas—to be thrown out only after close fighting. To enliven matters further, two phosphorous bombs dropped on Kapenhof, setting it alight, and all night long streams of tracer flecked the darkness.

West of the lakes in the area north-east of Haffen the Cameronians had been kept busy throughout the day by two determined counter-attacks, both of which they held. In the evening the Cameronians attacked in their turn. After half-an-hour's artillery bombardment " D " and " B " Companies went in at 8 P.M. and soon took their objectives, the little villages of Brukshof and Wisshof, which the forward companies had been unable to reach the day before. In Wisshof " D " Company took sixty-five prisoners.

That night the Cameronians sent an officers' patrol north into Sonsfeld Forest in the hope of getting in touch with the 51st Highland Division. The patrol never returned.

In the 227th Brigade area 25th March was the day of mopping up and reorganisation. The Gordons remained in the area between Haffen and the Rhine, the H.L.I. round Overkamp. That night the H.L.I. moved north-east to relieve the Seaforth and the Cameronians in front of Mehr and Haffen respectively.

The 157th Brigade of the 52nd Lowland Division had now crossed into the bridgehead and had come under command of the 15th Scottish Division. Its rôle was to relieve the 6th Air Landing Brigade round Hamminkeln.

By 4.30 P.M. that day the Class 40 Bailey pontoon bridge at Xanten was open—that is, only 38½ hours after H-hour as opposed to the 70 hours estimated. This achievement was due to the speed with which the 44th Brigade had established its bridgehead no less than to the fine work of the sappers.

26th March. For the 44th Brigade on the banks of the Issel 26th March was to be a day of strenuous fighting, which began early. It was the enemy who took the initiative. As the K.O.S.B. were preparing for their dawn attack on the Issel bridge the enemy at battalion strength savagely counter-attacked the two forward companies, " B " and " C." As ill-luck would have it, Battalion Headquarters and " D " Company happened at that moment to be on the move, so for once the enemy—who turned out to be a fresh battalion just arrived from Bocholt—caught the K.O.S.B. off balance. " D " Company managed to disengage and to take up a defensive position, but "C" Company had to fight it out where they stood in the open and, after they had expended all their ammunition and grenades, were overrun. The R.A.P., too, was captured after the stretcher-bearers had laboured heroically to get most of the wounded away. The climax of the night's drama was the stand made by No. 12 Platoon in the corner of an orchard, and in particular by Private Howe and his section, who were wiped out to a man. Next morning Private Howe was found with his lifeless fingers still gripping his Bren gun and with ninety-eight dead Germans around him. That stand broke the counter-attack. By 6.30 A.M. the whole of the 3/4th County of London Yeomanry had arrived in support of the K.O.S.B., and things were again in hand.

Indeed most of the fight seemed to have gone out of the enemy, for, when "D" Company made a local attack soon after, they took 132 prisoners very easily, and also recovered the K.O.S.B. wounded, whom the Germans had left behind in the care of a captured stretcher-bearer. In this night's fighting the K.O.S.B. had lost one officer and seventy men, mostly from "C" Company. They remained where they were throughout the day to reorganise and to form a firm base for the assault on the bridge. About mid-day ten enemy tanks appeared to the north-west, but were driven off by gun-fire. An enemy S.P. gun made periodical appearances from some farm buildings five hundred yards north-west of the Issel bridge and destroyed two armoured cars of the 15th Divisional Reconnaissance Regiment which were trying to feel their way along the road towards the bridge.

During the morning some Kangaroos arrived, whereupon Brigadier Cumming-Bruce made a plan to force a crossing of the Issel—the bridge over which, he had now ascertained, had been destroyed. The Issel is a small, sluggish, weedy river, eight to ten yards wide; it will stop tanks but not infantry. The R.S.F. were to carry out the assault. Having approached the Issel in the Kangaroos, they were to dismount, wade across, and win a bridgehead large enough to permit of the building of a bridge. Meanwhile the Royal Scots were to push a mile or two northward astride the unfinished Autobahn to give left flank protection.

Lieutenant-Colonel Mackenzie put in his attack about 4 P.M. "D" Company of the R.S.F. led off in Kangaroos, supported by two troops of tanks and a troop of Crocodiles. Its task was to clear the enemy position on the near or west bank and to establish a firm base there.

26th March. "D" took its first objective, together with some prisoners, without great difficulty. Beyond, however, it came under very heavy small-arms fire and mortar-fire from both front and flanks. At the same time enemy S.P.s opened up on the tanks and held up their further advance. The tanks moved out to the flanks, where they rounded up nearly seventy prisoners, but it was not till the Crocodiles arrived to burn the second objective that "D" was able to get on and to establish its firm base. Even then there were a lot of enemy still about on the west bank, as Sergeant Urie, the medical sergeant, was to discover later that evening after the crossing had been won. On his way up to the bridge site Sergeant Urie took the wrong turning and soon found himself a prisoner. However, victory was in the air, and he quickly persuaded his captors—to the tune of forty-five—to come in and surrender. To the astonishment of all beholders he presently arrived in "D" Company's lines bearing a large white flag and with his prisoners trailing behind him. In all, "D" Company collected 160 prisoners that evening for the loss of one killed and six wounded.

"A," "B," and "C" Companies then passed through "D" in their Kangaroos and ran down under heavy mortar and machine-gun fire to de-bus on the river-bank. Four enemy 20-mm. guns were firing viciously from the farther side and knocked out the leading Kangaroo. Down on the bank the Fusiliers found themselves in the middle of what proved to be still an enemy position. Some of the enemy fired; more waved white flags. Leaving rear parties to deal with both persuasions, the Fusiliers charged for the river in a single line, firing as they went, and slid down the steep bank into three feet of water to wade across. Finding no cover under the farther bank, they had to clamber out and, still under fire from both sides of the river, charge on straight for the guns. By 10 P.M. they had taken all their objectives and with them over 200 more prisoners, at the cost of about 12 killed and 50 wounded. To quote the '44th Brigade History' once more: "This brilliant operation, which showed magnificent courage and skill, must take its place amongst the very finest feats of this well-tried battalion." Brigadier Cumming-Bruce now sent up a company of the Royal Scots to reinforce the R.S.F. during the consolidation of the bridgehead.

Now that the bridgehead had been won, there remained the bridge to be built. If these forward companies of the R.S.F. were to have the support they might need to meet a dawn counter-attack, this 26th March. bridge must go up that night. The forward move of the heavy bridging lorries presented a real problem. At 6 P.M. that evening the long spell of perfect weather had ended in a thunderstorm, which had promptly turned the cross-country routes used by the 44th Brigade into impassable quagmires. The only possible alternative was the main road that runs north from Hamminkeln, now in the area of the 157th Brigade. The trouble was that this road was commanded by the east or enemy bank of the Issel, to which it runs parallel. Moreover, the enemy had certainly had posts actually on the road itself during the day. None the less, Brigadier Cumming-Bruce decided that he must accept the risk. Shortly before midnight he ordered the K.O.S.B. to send their carrier platoon south to meet the bridging train at a rendezvous north of Hamminkeln. Off went the carriers with all the stealth they could muster. Brushing aside the enemy they met along the road, they reached the rendezvous soon after 2 A.M.; soon the convoy was roaring back up the road with a Bren gunner on top of every lorry. It was a triumph. By 6 A.M. on 27th March the bridge was built.

We must now return to the Royal Scots who, it will be remembered, had gone north on the morning of the 26th to hold a position astride the Autobahn. In the afternoon Brigadier Cumming-Bruce ordered the Royal Scots (less " C " Company, now in the bridgehead) to make a further advance north-east to give left-flank protection to the R.S.F. almost up to the west bank of the Issel. Lieutenant-Colonel Pearson put in " B " and " D " Companies to take the first group of farms, which they did successfully at nightfall. The very effective 25-pounder bombardment, however, had set " D " Company's farm ablaze, so " D " had to consolidate silhouetted against the burning buildings and giving a perfect target to a very active enemy. The lesson they learned that evening was that, on such occasions, the fire plan could well include a smoke-screen to cover the consolidation.

" A " Company, supported by a troop of the Yeomanry's Shermans, next went through to take the farm buildings called Heisterhof, which lie about three-quarters of a mile due west of the bridge. At first all went well. Before 8 P.M. " A " were digging in around Heisterhof. They were not to be left in peace for long, however. Out here on the Issel the 44th Brigade lay right across the enemy's communications, and the Royal Scots were on the 44th Brigade's open flank. The

26th March. enemy were determined to break through. Just to the left or west of Heisterhof, not more than two hundred yards away, lay a similar group of farm buildings amongst the trees. Very soon from the direction of these buildings the enemy began to close on Heisterhof. Creeping along the ditches, they used their bazookas with deadly effect against the Royal Scots, who were clearly visible as they wielded their picks and shovels in the moonlight. " A " Company lost a lot of men, and every officer other than the company commander.

Regardless of the bazooka fire, the Yeomanry's Shermans moved out in front and used their Bezas with great effect. They were powerless, however, to stop the enemy from getting into the buildings of Heisterhof itself. It was a very ugly situation. If at that moment the enemy behind could have reinforced this success, " A " Company would have had a poor chance of survival. It was the guns that intervened to stop the flow of enemy reinforcements. Using " A " Company's 46-set when his own 19-set had failed, the F.O.O. brought down defensive fire all round as close as safety limits would allow, repeatedly stonking the other farm though it was only two hundred yards away. The flow of enemy reinforcements into Heisterhof dried up. That was the Royal Scots' chance to clear out the intruders, and they made the most of it. The outstanding performance of the ensuing dog-fight was put up by Corporal Mallon, acting platoon commander, who, wounded and having lost his Sten gun, went in with fists and feet.

Though Heisterhof was now cleared, the fighting still went on unabated. Anxiety was not over. By 11 P.M. " A " Company had fired all its 2-inch mortar-bombs and nearly all its small-arms ammunition. In the nick of time a Weasel with a stout-hearted driver arrived, bringing ammunition reserves. Later, about 2 A.M., a troop of S.P. guns came up to replace the Shermans, which had done magnificent work. It was after that that things began to quieten down at last. " A " Company spent the rest of the night digging themselves a strong defensive position. At dawn on 27th March the guns scattered some enemy who were seen forming up for a counter-attack.

Next we come to the 46th Brigade. Brigadier Villiers's orders for 26th March were to advance towards Sonsfeld Forest, which lies southeast of Haldern. It was there that the 15th Scottish Division was to link up with the 51st Division, which latter had now taken Rees. Brigadier Villiers was to use as his axis the main road Wesel-Haldern.

This road was not yet clear, however. His first task, therefore, was 26th March. to get more elbow-room in his bridgehead to the eastward of the Bellinghoven Meer. To this end Brigadier Villiers ordered the Glasgow Highlanders on the right and the Seaforth on the left to attack eastward at first light to a depth of half a mile or so. The Glasgow Highlanders and the Seaforth were to pass south and north respectively of the Argylls round Kapenhof.

The Glasgow Highlanders met strong resistance in some farm buildings on their right, but took these with the help of Wasps, and a large number of prisoners with them. The right-hand company of the Seaforth, supported by two troops of Crocodiles, also reached its objective quickly and took over 150 prisoners. The left-hand company got into difficulties, however, so the Crocodiles were switched to this front. By that time the Crocodiles were out of fuel and were reduced to only one troop of three tanks. Acting as fighting tanks, these three not only shot the Seaforth on to their objective, but also went on with the Cameronians when the latter passed through.

After a preliminary move at 2 P.M. the Cameronians attacked northward at 4.30 P.M. through the left-hand company of the Seaforth and occupied their objectives north of Mehr by dark.

As soon as the Glasgow Highlanders and the Seaforth had passed them by at Kapenhof that morning, the Argylls had been able to relax somewhat after fifty-six hours of fighting and marching with very little sleep. They were to remain in the Kapenhof area for the next forty-eight hours.

By midnight the 53rd Division and the 7th Armoured Division had concentrated in the 12th Corps' bridgehead, ready for the break-out north-eastward. In consequence, Brigadier Villiers received orders late that evening that the Glasgow Highlanders were to take over from the 2nd K.R.R.C. (4th Armoured Brigade) about one mile east of Mehrhoo next morning and were to act as flank-guard to the armour. Enemy morale was cracking at last, though the process was not to be apparent on the 46th Brigade's front for a day or two yet.

In the 227th Brigade's area to the westward of the string of lakes the H.L.I. that day had extended their front east to include Bellinghoven, from which the enemy had already withdrawn. Back at Haffen the Gordons had now mopped up all the surrounding farms, and, pushing north, had made contact at last with the 5/7th Gordons of the 153rd Brigade (51st Division), about a mile and a half south-

26th March. east of Rees, thus linking up the bridgeheads of the 15th and 51st Divisions.

By 9 A.M. that morning the Class 12 Bailey pontoon bridge had opened at Hübsch nearly on time. It bridged both the Rhine and the Hübsch inlet, and its length totalled close on two thousand feet. Of all his programme Colonel Foster had now only the all-weather Class 40 bridge left to build.

Contemplating its achievement, 15th Scottish Division was fully conscious of the immense debt of gratitude which it owed, not only to its A.G.R.E. but also to its two faithful regiments of Buffaloes and to the Bank Group, whose united efforts had all been indispensable to success.

27th March. Out on the Issel next morning the R.S.F. and the Royal Scots were both still closely engaged, but no counter-attack developed against the bridgehead. By now companies were all very weak and the men, who had been fighting with little or no sleep for four days, were almost at the limits of exhaustion. To hold the bridgehead for another twenty-four hours was vitally important, for the 7th Armoured Division and the 53rd Division were now passing through to the southward and their way must be kept open. The final hunt was up.

At 5.30 P.M. the enemy made their last and desperate effort against the bridgehead, which was still held by three companies of the R.S.F. and " C " Company of the Royal Scots. At the outset the R.S.F. were hard pressed, for the enemy penetrated into the woods on the east bank, which formed part of the bridgehead itself. Brigadier Cumming-Bruce moved up two companies of the K.O.S.B. in support, however, and the R.S.F. stood firm. By 10 P.M. they had cleared the woods and the danger was over.

A little later the 53rd Division attacked northward, east of the Issel, and occupied Dingen. The 44th Brigade's task was then ended. For the next week the Brigade was to remain in the Hamminkeln area, whilst the hunt swept on towards Osnabruck and Munster.

The Lowlanders had had the luck of the draw on the 24th when they found themselves opposed by the 84th Division instead of the 7th Parachute Division. They had made the most of their luck. They had crossed the Rhine and had cleared the far bank so quickly that the R.E. had been able to build the Xanten bridge in record time. And they had linked up with both Airborne Divisions within five hours of their landing. After that they, too, had met the enemy paratroops. Yet they had pushed far out into the enemy territory to relieve the 6th Airborne Division and to establish their Issel bridgehead; they had held this pivot against all-comers till the break-out was complete; they had taken 2000 prisoners. For the 44th Brigade the past four days had been indeed a fitting climax to the campaign. *27th March.*

Next we come to the 46th Brigade farther west. The Glasgow Highlanders that morning took over from the 2nd Battalion K.R.R.C. east of Mehrhoo as ordered. Patrolling north-west towards the Wittenhorst woods, which are the easterly extension of the Sonsfeld Forest, they ran into an enemy position within a thousand yards. Against this position Lieutenant-Colonel Baker-Baker put in a two-company attack about noon, supported by artillery and Crocodiles. At the same time he sent a third company to try to work round the left flank. The two companies in the main attack reached their objectives, only to be pinned by intense fire from 88-mm.s and 20-mm. multi-barrelled flak guns at close range. The flanking company was also held up with its leading platoons pinned by fire. Lieutenant-Colonel Baker-Baker then put in his reserve company under cover of smoke, but as night fell it was counter-attacked and driven back. Thus at the end of the day the Glasgow Highlanders found themselves with all four companies committed and two of them pinned on their ground. Things might have been awkward. However, after a particularly vicious final bombardment by every gun and mortar he had got, the enemy quietened down.

Meanwhile the Cameronians farther west had also been pushing north on a more or less parallel course towards the Wittenhorst woods. Here they, too, bumped the enemy in strength in a village which formed a westerly extension of the defensive position opposite the Glasgow Highlanders. Having put in a company attack against this village which failed to take it, Lieutenant-Colonel Remington Hobbs decided to wait for tanks before he renewed the attack. The only tanks then with the 46th Brigade were the Crocodiles, which were supporting the Glasgow Highlanders a mile or so farther east, so it was not till 7.15 P.M. that the attack could go in. Again the Crocodiles had almost no flame left, but they shot the Cameronians on to their objective none the less. Brigadier Villiers then moved up the Seaforth into reserve in the gap between the Cameronians and the Glasgow Highlanders.

27th March.

The 46th Brigade, with the Argylls still under command, was ordered that evening to carry out a new attack next day. All were now dog-tired, but protests were unavailing. For this attack the 6th H.L.I. of the 157th Brigade (52nd Division) were to come under command of the 46th Brigade, while the Cameronians were to pass under command of the 227th Brigade.

During the day the 157th Brigade (less the 6th H.L.I.) left Hamminkeln and Ringenberg to join the 7th Armoured Division.

28th March.

The 46th Brigade's task on 28th March was to clear the Wittenhorst woods east of the Sonsfeld Forest up to the line of the road that runs due east from Haldern to Bocholt. Brigadier Villiers's plan was to put in the Seaforth first of all, to clear the enemy salient which still separated the Glasgow Highlanders and the Cameronians and where the enemy still had some sort of defence. The Seaforth went in supported by the two faithful troops of Crocodiles and under a short but intense barrage.

Here it was that for the first time since the 46th Brigade had crossed the Rhine the enemy on its front packed up without fighting. The Seaforth took fifty parachutists, tired, hungry, and dispirited, without themselves suffering a single casualty. White flags were hanging from all the farms, and the countryside was strewn with abandoned equipment. Both sides had been under almost unendurable strain, but it was that redoubtable body of men, the 7th Parachute Division, that first reached breaking-point.

In the next phase the 6th H.L.I. on the right and the Argylls on the left were to go through to clear the woods. Enemy resistance was likely to be almost nil, so 46th Brigade Headquarters cancelled the programme of artillery support. The 6th H.L.I. and the Argylls carried out their sweep through the woods without finding any enemy. As the Argylls were nearing the lateral road which was their objective, however, they were heavily stonked for twenty minutes by the guns probably of another Division engaged on another fire plan, and lost some men. Such needless losses are always particularly hard to bear, but in the vast convolutions of the battlefield human error can never be altogether eliminated. The 6th H.L.I. and the Argylls dug in on the general line of the lateral road.

Meanwhile, farther west, the Divisional Reconnaissance Regiment had relieved the 227th Brigade (less the Argylls), which had then

THE RHINE CROSSING

moved east across the Bellinghoven Meer and into the Cameronians' 28th March. area. At 2 P.M. the H.L.I. on the right and the Gordons on the left advanced north-west through the Cameronians, the Gordons with their left on the main road Wesel-Haldern. Neither battalion met any enemy, but both found large numbers of mines, which caused some casualties. They consolidated on the high ground somewhat short of and overlooking the eastern edge of the Sonsfeld Forest.

So ended that operation unique in war, the crossing of the Rhine. All who took part in it will ever recall the crossing with pride. It had marked the penetration of the last great rampart of Hitler's Reich. Already the Guards Armoured Division, the 7th and 11th Armoured Divisions, the 6th Airborne Division—accompanied now by those good companions of the 15th Scottish Division, the 6th Guards Armoured Brigade—and the Americans, all were pouring through the breach into the doomed fortress. Final victory was very near. Yet there was little feeling of elation—rather a feeling of intense exasperation that the enemy should be so perverse as still to fight on.

For the five or six days that followed, the 15th Scottish Division 29th March rested and refitted in the bridgehead which it had done so much to to 2nd April. win. Seldom has rest been more welcome or better deserved. Units received and absorbed their drafts in readiness for the " Swan " which was to follow.

On the afternoon of 29th March the weather broke; thereupon the Divisional Commander gave the word to abandon tactical layouts and to find shelter in farms. Current policy enjoined non-fraternisation and no consideration for the Germans in the matter of billets. Since every house was already packed far beyond capacity with refugees from the much-bombed Rhineland and from Eastern Germany, where fear of the Russians reigned supreme, the billeting order was difficult to carry out. The British soldier has traditions of mercy of which he cannot rid himself at the word of command.

The 15th Scottish Division received the following congratulatory message from the Divisional Commander for the part it had played in Operation " Plunder " :—

" I am extremely proud to be able to pass on to all ranks the following messages received from Lieutenant-General Sir Miles Dempsey, K.C.B., D.S.O., M.C., Commander, Second Army, and from Lieutenant-General N. M.

29th March to 2nd April. Ritchie, C.B., C.B.E., D.S.O., M.C., Commander, 12th Corps, and I direct that these messages be read out to all ranks on parade:—

'From Lieutenant-General Sir Miles Dempsey, K.C.B., D.S.O., M.C., Commander, Second Army:—

'The Battle of the Rhine has now been won, and the break-out from the bridgehead is well under way.

'Your Division was one of two which carried out the assault crossing of the river.

'You defeated the enemy on the other side and made possible all that followed.

'A great achievement.

'I send you and the Division my very sincere congratulations.

'I am sure you are all very proud of what you have done.'

'From Lieutenant-General N. M. Ritchie, C.B., C.B.E., D.S.O., M.C., Commander, 12th Corps:—

'Now that you are out of the immediate battle, I feel that I must write and congratulate the Division on the great achievement of forcing the crossings of the Rhine.

'No one pretends that this was an easy job; it was a mighty difficult one. That the operation was so successful was due entirely to the fighting qualities of the Division. Personally I am tremendously proud to have been able to take part in this venture, but much more so that the operation was carried out by a formation from our own country. Will you pass on to all those under you how highly we all think of you in this corps? I am afraid that I have often asked you to carry out very hard jobs. You have never failed. The present operations, I hope, may well develop into a pretty liquid party, so that I hope before long you will be up in the forefront again.

'It is a great memory to me to know that the two crossings over the Seine and the Rhine have been carried out by your Division for the 12th Corps.

'I send you my very best congratulations on a difficult task magnificently performed.'

"No praise could be higher than these, and I am indeed proud to have the honour of commanding such a fine Division. I thank one and all for their fine fighting qualities which have carried us through all the hard times we have had from the Normandy beaches to the Rhine.

(Signed) C. M. BARBER,
Major-General Commanding 15th Scottish Infantry Division."

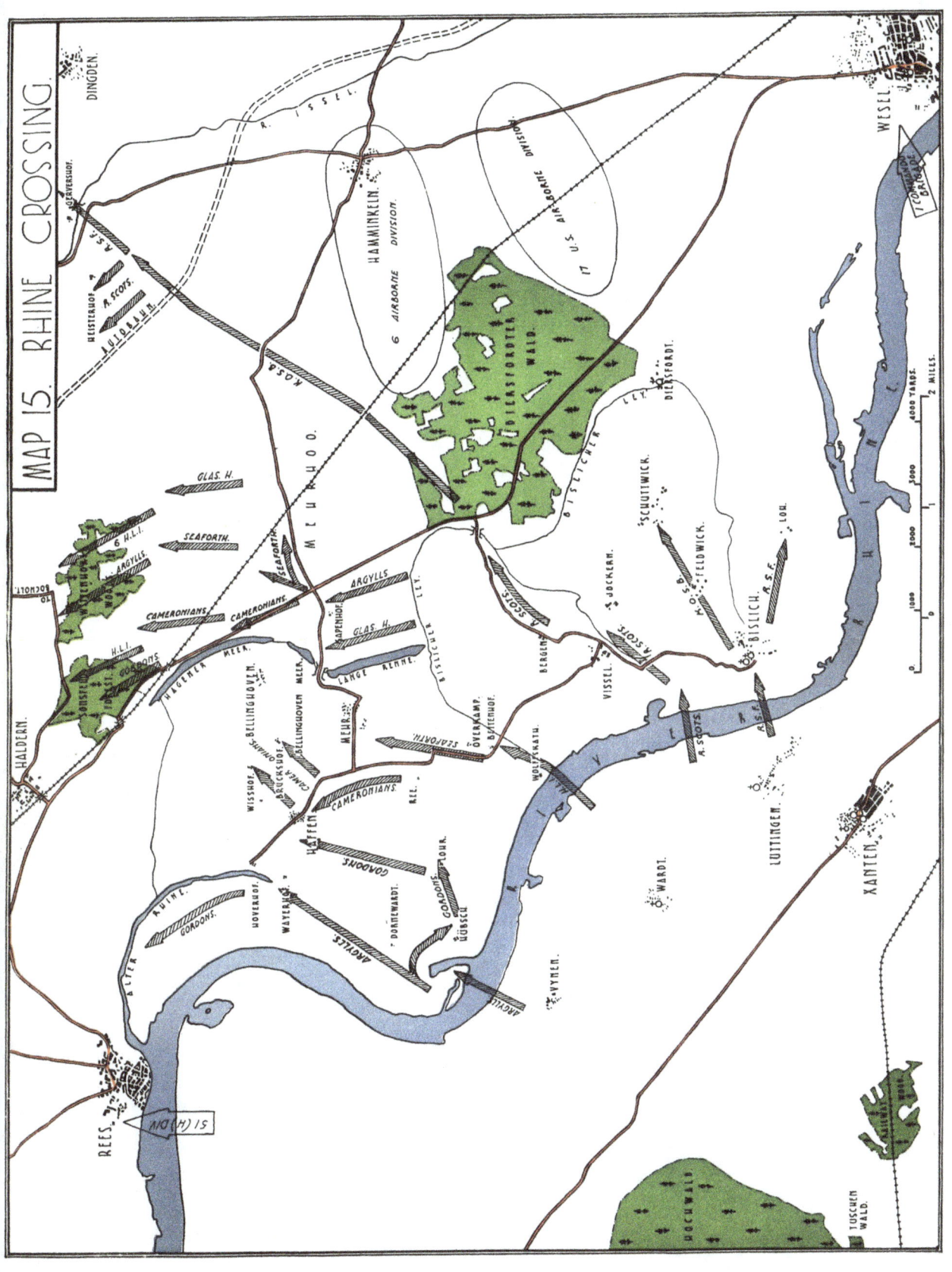

CHAPTER X.

THE ADVANCE TO THE ELBE.

THE 21st Army Group advanced from the Rhine bridgehead towards the Elbe on a three-corps front. On the right was the 8th Corps, directed on Osnabruck, Celle, and Uelzen; in the centre, the 12th Corps, directed on Luneburg; on the left, the 30th Corps, directed on Bremen and Hamburg. 27th March to 2nd April.

It is with the 8th Corps that we are mainly concerned. When it set out from the bridgehead, the 8th Corps consisted of the 11th Armoured Division (now equipped with Comet tanks, the newest cruisers), the 6th Airborne Division with the 4th Tank Grenadiers of the 6th Guards Armoured Brigade under command, and the 1st Commando Brigade.

The 8th Corps made very rapid progress. By 3rd April the leading troops of the 6th Airborne Division had reached Osnabruck, eighty miles from the Rhine; the 11th Armoured Division had taken a bridgehead over the Dortmund Ems Canal opposite Ibbenburen, which lies north-west of Osnabruck. This bridgehead, where the enemy were resisting stubbornly, the 11th Armoured Division was now handing over to the 7th Armoured Division of the 12th Corps on their left. 3rd April.

That day the 15th Scottish Division, which had been resting in the bridgehead, was called forward. According to the original plan, the 15th Scottish Division was to have come under the 12th Corps with the task of relieving the 7th Armoured Division in the Ibbenburen bridgehead, where the going was proving so difficult. The 227th Brigade moved up by motor transport that day to a concentration area about eight miles west of Ibbenburen, and the 46th Brigade to an area east of Bocholt. The Army Commander, however, ultimately decided to exploit success instead. Before the 15th Scottish Division could carry out any reconnaissances in the Ibbenburen bridgehead, its

3rd April.	orders were changed and it found itself placed under the 8th Corps farther south, where the front was more fluid.
4th to 7th April.	Next day, 4th April, the 44th Brigade moved up into the area south of the 227th Brigade; and on 6th and 7th April the 15th Scottish Division, with the 6th Guards Armoured Brigade (less the 4th Tank Grenadiers) under command once more, moved forward into the area north of Minden. The Division had completed its concentration by midnight on 7th April: it was still well behind the front.

In many ways this advance from the Rhine to the Elbe was to be reminiscent of the advance from the Seine. There were these differences, however: whereas the French and the Belgians had given our troops an unforgettable welcome, here the Germans sullenly ignored them. Indeed the only welcome here came from the displaced persons and released prisoners of all nationalities and in their countless thousands, who as they trudged along—the luckier of them pushing their worldly goods on perambulators or wheel-barrows—would wave a greeting to passing columns.

It was these D.P.s who created the real problems of military government. Despite all instructions to stay "put," one and all they left their camps as soon as these were liberated—the west-bound D.P.s pushing west with the blind purpose of ants, the east-bound merely milling around aimlessly. This exodus produced near-chaos. How to keep the roads clear; how to feed these D.P.s; how to prevent looting and to preserve law and order generally—these were the problems to be solved, but, with the staff and detachments available, military government itself could not begin to handle them. Inevitably, therefore, units and formations had to undertake many of these jobs, and these used up a great deal of man-power, transport, and supplies. In comparison with these D.P. problems, those created by the Germans themselves—disciplined by generations of regimentation—were as nothing. The Germans did as they were bid by their burgomasters, and the much-advertised werewolves proved a myth.

Throughout these moves from the Rhine to the Elbe the weather remained excellent. As the distance that separated corps from army engineer and supply dumps grew daily greater the strain on transport resources increased. T.C.V.s, therefore, were rarely available. Brigade groups sometimes moved with borrowed transport. More often the infantry travelled some on the tanks attached to the group and the rest distributed over the group transport.

In anticipation of the 15th Scottish Division's taking over the lead from the 6th Airborne Division, which had already spearheaded the corps so fast and so far, the 15th Scottish Reconnaissance Regiment was now under command of the 6th Airborne Division, which was already well across the Weser. Operating in front of the 5th Parachute Brigade, the Reconnaissance Regiment made a brilliant advance on 7th April and seized a bridge intact over the River Leine at Bordenau.

Next morning, 8th April, a squadron of the Reconnaissance Regiment, working south, seized another bridge over the Leine at Ricklingen. Knowing that there was still an enemy force west of the Ricklingen bridge, the squadron commander sited his only A.Tk. gun facing west. Sure enough, about 2 P.M. enemy infantry mounted on a Tiger and two Panther tanks tried to break out eastward over the bridge. The squadron beat off the attack, killing twenty Germans, and later handed the bridge over still intact to the 13th U.S. Corps.

Meanwhile the 11th Armoured Division on the left was still back on the Weser, where it had been held up temporarily by stiff enemy resistance. That day the 15th Scottish Divisional Engineers were placed under command of the 11th Armoured Division to build a Class 40 bridge over the Weser about twenty miles down-stream—that is, north—of Minden.

On 10th April the 15th Scottish Division was ordered to concentrate forward between the Weser and the Leine. The Second Army was now changing direction north-east. Next day the 15th Scottish Division was to advance through the 6th Airborne Division and to occupy Celle and then Uelzen.

That day the 13th U.S. Corps took Hanover.

On 11th April the 15th Scottish Division took over the running from the 6th Airborne Division on the right of the 8th Corps. The 15th Scottish Division went through with two brigades up: on the right the 46th Brigade, supported by the Tank Coldstream; on the left the 227th Brigade, supported by the Tank Scots Guards. Thus the old partnership between the Division and the 6th Guards Brigade

11th April. had been renewed, though the continued absence of the 4th Tank Grenadier Guards—the 44th Brigade's old partners—was sadly felt. The 46th and 227th Brigades were both directed on Celle, which the former was to approach from the south by way of Wunstorf and Grosse Burgwedel, the latter from the south-west by way of Neustadt, Mellendorf, and Fuhrberg. The Divisional Reconnaissance Regiment, which had now reverted under command, went ahead, covering the whole front.

After a hot and tiring march of about sixty miles by way of the northern outskirts of Hanover, the Cameronians at last overtook the Reconnaissance Regiment, who had met the enemy in the wood athwart the main axis at the level-crossing of Ehlershausen, some six miles south of Celle. At 7.30 P.M. two companies of the Cameronians, with their supporting squadron of the Coldstream, attacked astride the road and through the wood. The enemy, who turned out to be a bunch of fifty or more young officer cadets fighting with the courage of despair, resisted fiercely, making admirable use of their bazookas in the thick cover. They had soon knocked out the two leading tanks. After dark the right-hand company of the Cameronians fought its way to its objective, but the left-hand company got hung up. Here, then, were these two companies closely engaged with an aggressive enemy in darkness and thick woodland. There were all the makings of a thoroughly uncomfortable night. Lieutenant-Colonel Remington Hobbs brought up his two reserve companies, readjusted his dispositions, and sent back his tanks, and the Cameronians consolidated as best they could.

Meanwhile the 227th Brigade farther north was advancing by way of Neustadt, with the Gordons supported by a squadron of Scots Guards as advanced guard. Ahead lay unsearched country, so progress was slow and there were many checks, especially at broken bridges, in the later stages of the advance. By dark the Gordons had reached the line of the canal about two miles south-west of Celle, where they were engaged with a miscellaneous assortment of enemy detachments hastily recruited from battle and cadet schools, convalescent homes, and the like. The main obstacle that barred the Gordons' way was an enormous crater which would take some time to bridge. According to prisoners' stories, Celle itself was full of hospitals but empty of troops. The rest of the 227th Brigade Group spent a hot and stuffy night parked in the woods farther west, which had been set alight by the tanks.

THE ADVANCE TO THE ELBE

Early next morning, 12th April, the enemy withdrew from the Cameronians' front after blowing up every bridge in the countryside. On the 46th Brigade's axis no bridging material was available, so there was no means of getting the tanks and vehicles across the numerous streams and canal tributaries ahead. In consequence the 46th Brigade was switched on to the main Divisional axis, and followed the 227th Brigade into Celle, where it spent the night.

On the main Divisional axis, meanwhile, the H.L.I. had gone through the Gordons before dawn on 12th April to clear Celle and to force a crossing of the Aller. The two forward companies passed through Celle and crossed the Aller by assault-boat without trouble. By dawn three companies were holding a bridgehead on the east bank. The R.E. at once began to build a Class 40 bridge, which they finished by midnight that night.

All the bridges at Celle had been blown. The Scots Guards Reconnaissance Troop, however, with a platoon of Gordons aboard, raced off to Altencelle, a couple of miles up-stream to the south-east, to ascertain whether or not the two bridges there—over the Aller and over the canal beyond—were still standing. Sure enough they were, though they turned out to be rickety wooden affairs that might collapse at any moment. Following behind, the Gordons and the Argylls, accompanied by the tanks and group transport, crossed the Aller successfully. The canal bridge beyond, however, collapsed almost at once, so there were soon some eight hundred assorted vehicles piled up between the two bridges. When at last the R.E. were able to build a Bailey bridge over the canal the jam got sorted out, and the 227th Brigade moved on a mile or two to halt for the night echeloned along the main axis that led north-east towards Uelzen.

In Celle the 15th Scottish Division came upon a small but truly horrible concentration camp, a Belsen in microcosm, in which there were a few hundred dead and dying. The citizens of Celle expressed a bland ignorance of the horrors that had been going on in their midst. Colonel F. M. Richardson, A.D.M.S. of the Division, however, took appropriate steps to bring the truth home to them. He saw to it not only that the citizens of Celle themselves removed the corpses, but also that they provided medical attention, linen, and supplies for those victims who had survived.

Seven miles down-stream, near the Winsen bridge, was the concentration camp of Belsen itself, for the handing over of which negotiations

12th April. were now in progress between Headquarters 8th Corps and the Wehrmacht. Till these negotiations were completed, the 11th Armoured Division could not use the Winsen crossing. Some seventeen miles still farther down the Aller, the 11th Armoured Division was fighting for a bridgehead which would permit of its bridging the Aller on its main axis. Thus the 15th Scottish Division across the Aller at Celle now found itself out of touch with the 11th Armoured Division on its left. Moreover, between it and the 11th Armoured Division there was a large extent of unsearched country. By this time, too, the Wehrmacht had managed to organise a number of battle-groups—flying columns consisting of a few tanks, S.P. guns, and lorry-loads of Panzer Grenadiers—which were roaming the country full of fight. It was no time to neglect protective measures.

13th April. Next day was Friday, 13th April—ominous combination. The 15th Scottish Division's orders were to take Uelzen. The 227th Brigade again formed the advanced guard, with the H.L.I. in the lead.

At 8 A.M. the H.L.I. left Celle, their rifle companies as far as possible riding on the tanks of the supporting squadron of Scots Guards. Behind them came Brigadier Colville's tactical headquarters, accompanied by the commanding officers of his supporting arms; behind that again stretched the rest of the Brigade Group over some seven miles of road. The column first ran into trouble about seven miles out of Celle, where it was brought to a halt by a blown bridge. After half an hour reconnaissance parties found an alternative route, and the column made a detour through the forest to rejoin the main road at Eschede, ten miles out of Celle, from the south. All this time small parties of German prisoners, mainly youths from disorganised G.A.F. units, were being brought in.

Only a few miles on from Eschede the H.L.I. were brought to a halt once more by a twenty-foot crater across the road, in a bog where a diversion was impossible. The enemy had the crater covered by two S.P. guns and small-arms fire. After further delay the H.L.I. drove off the covering party, whereupon the two S.P. guns trundled off down the road. By this time it was clear to all that these S.P.s were covering a demolition group which was moving only a mile or two ahead of the 227th Brigade.

After the Scots Guards had laid a tank-bridge across this crater the column resumed its advance. But not for long; soon the leading

10TH HIGHLAND LIGHT INFANTRY CARRIED BY TANKS OF 3RD SCOTS GUARDS DURING ADVANCE TO UELZEN

(Standing by Staff car are: Brigadier E. C. Colville, D.S.O., Commander, 227th Brigade, and Lieutenant-Colonel C. I. H. Dunbar, D.S.O., Commander, 3rd Scots Guards)

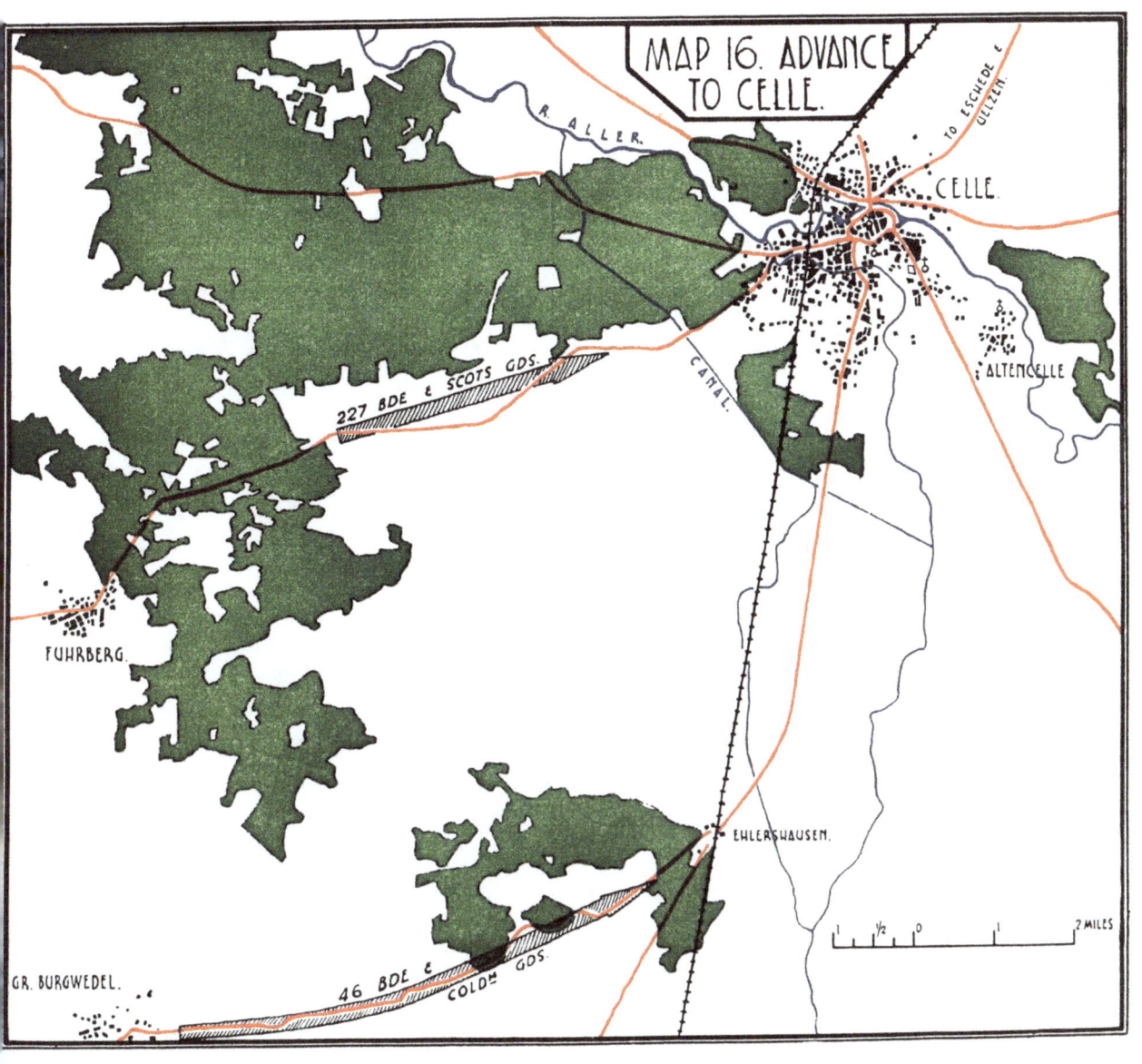

tanks reported another crater—the largest yet, which would, in the expert opinion of the officer commanding 20th Field Company, need a forty-foot Bailey bridge. This crater, too, the enemy had covered by small-arms and bazooka-fire. Nor was that all: presently a time-bomb exploded in the road, destroying an R.E. vehicle and wounding eleven of the R.E. reconnaissance party. A search revealed eight more of these time-bombs, so Lieutenant-Colonel Bramwell Davis had the area cordoned off and sent out reconnaissance parties to find a detour by the north.

13th April.

At 6 P.M. the column set off once more on its northerly detour through the forest, with the intention of joining the main axis at a cross-roads some eight miles on from Eschede. Up to this point progress had averaged only two miles per hour, but Friday, the 13th, had not yet exhausted its repertoire. Presently, as it began to grow dusk and the H.L.I. were approaching the cross-roads from the north where they would have rejoined the main axis, they found their way barred by yet another crater as big as any yet. Moreover ominous explosions "off" told of still further craters to come.

At this point Brigadier Colville, who had come forward to the head of the column, made a very bold decision. The main axis, he decided, was finished for the time being at least. But there was an alternative route to Uelzen—a track through the forest that runs more or less parallel to the main axis and two or three miles to the left of it. This track rejoined the main axis at Holdenstedt, some fourteen miles on and only about a couple of miles short of Uelzen. A night approach by this track might not only by-pass the enemy's demolitions, but also take him completely by surprise. True, the intervening forest might conceal a whole hornets' nest of battle-groups, to whose attack the 227th Brigade—moving by night and in column of route—must be terribly vulnerable. Still, it was a good gamble. Brigadier Colville decided to risk it. He ordered the column to be prepared to move off along the track at 1 A.M. next morning. Meanwhile it was to park in a ride in the forest, which most fortunately was wide enough to take the eight hundred vehicles of the Brigade Group treble-banked and yet leave room for petrol and ammunition supply. There for the moment we must leave it.

Throughout 13th April the 46th Brigade had been following the 227th Brigade along the main axis. The 46th Brigade's task was to mop up on either side of the axis on a very broad front. The brigade

13th April. was advancing in three battalion groups, each containing tanks. Right of the road moved the Glasgow Highlanders forward and the Cameronians in reserve; left of the road moved the Seaforth. The Reconnaissance Regiment covered the front. Only Brigade Tactical Headquarters might use the main axis itself. In consequence there was great difficulty in finding routes fit for wheels, and the 46th Brigade ended the day—throughout which mopping-up operations had gone on more or less continuously—with the three battalion groups widely separated and out of touch with brigade on account of the interference caused by the woods.

14th April. We return now to the 227th Brigade Group parked in its ride in the forest. Friday, the 13th, had been left behind at last. At 1 A.M. next morning, 14th April, the column moved off once more into the unknown, with the H.L.I. again in the lead. As guides, two reputed members of the German Resistance had been enlisted. It was a dark night, lit only by faint moonlight, but searchlights had arrived to give the enterprise a send-off without which it would have been all but impossible. Though the track was no better than a poor third-class, the leading vehicles set a cracking pace. To keep touch, those behind had to go flat-out, with branches whipping the faces of the vehicle commanders as they peered out through the dust. Yet there were few vehicles that went astray—a sufficient testimony to the high standard of driving. The Jocks perched on the tanks had a wild ride—in imminent danger of suffering the fate of Absalom and with their feet toasting nicely on the red-hot engine-plates.

With their "whips out" the H.L.I. raced through a series of small villages, shooting up one enemy staff car and a number of other vehicles by the way. Their passing left the enemy in these villages so scared and bewildered that for the most part they surrendered meekly at daylight to those who came behind. The total pick-up after the night approach amounted to about eight hundred.

Shortly before dawn the H.L.I. approached Holdenstedt, where they were to rejoin the main axis. The climax of the night's advance had arrived. Flares and Verey lights were going up ahead and small-arms fire had become pretty general. Clearly the element of surprise which stood the column in such good stead so far could no longer be counted on. On went the column none the less through Holdenstedt as dawn was breaking and along the main road to Uelzen.

The 227th Brigade was certainly sticking its neck out. On the 14th April. right the 15th Scottish Division was now out of touch with the 13th U.S. Corps; on the left the 11th Armoured Division was some twenty miles back at Winsen on the Aller.

Not only had surprise been lost, but Uelzen, as soon became apparent, was one of those communication centres which, in their endeavour to gain time to prepare a defence line on the Elbe, the German command meant to hold even at the cost of committing some of its few remaining reserves of Panzer Grenadiers. Here in Uelzen, as the H.L.I. were soon to find, there were fresh troops from Denmark, newly arrived and unbroken by defeat. As still in column they hurtled down the main road past the level-crossing, the H.L.I. ran straight into a flak site on the left of the road that the enemy was in the act of manning. Unfortunately, a burning ammunition lorry, blocking the road, here delayed matters. The enemy reacted viciously, telescoping the H.L.I. and breaking up the advanced guard into several parts. S.P. multi-barreled flak guns cruised alongside, destroying nearly all the H.L.I.'s transport at short range, while enemy infantry infiltrated through the wood on the right and took a number of prisoners. In face of this attack the H.L.I. fought a series of confused and more or less isolated actions, in which the Churchills and the section of the 131st Field Regiment—firing over open sights—played prominent parts.

Meanwhile the rest of the 227th Brigade column had halted about Holdenstedt. At 9.30 A.M. Brigadier Colville sent up the Argylls to clear the wood on the right of the road, into which the enemy had infiltrated, and also another squadron of the Scots Guards to protect the rear of the H.L.I. At that, pressure on the H.L.I. relaxed and they were able to re-form and re-organise. They had lost heavily, "S" Company in particular having only one officer left. The day passed with the H.L.I. in close contact with the enemy.

Brigadier Colville's plan for that night was this: the H.L.I., starting soon after midnight, were to take the suburb of Veerssen on the southerly outskirts of Uelzen, while the Gordons were to come down the main road and clear Uelzen itself; the Argylls meanwhile would continue to protect the right flank. The R.S.F. were to be under Brigadier Colville's command and were to protect the rear of the 227th Brigade. The 44th Brigade had moved north along the main

14th April. axis throughout the day, finding its way still much obstructed by demolitions and time-bombs.

Farther south, throughout 14th April, the 46th Brigade continued its approach to Uelzen, mopping up astride the Divisional main axis. On the right of the road the Glasgow Highlanders and a troop of the Reconnaissance Regiment surprised a column of a couple of hundred Germans in the act of withdrawing. After killing a few, they took the rest prisoners.

That night the Glasgow Highlanders halted in the village of Stadensen, six miles south-east of Holdenstedt. Realising that his battalion was out on its own and that there might be enemy battle-groups in the offing, Lieutenant-Colonel Baker-Baker wisely decided to form a perimeter camp, with his rifle companies at the four corners and with his tanks, artillery, mortars, machine-guns, and transport parked in the centre. The squadron of the Reconnaissance Regiment which had been covering his front went into harbour at Nettelkamp, about a mile to the north-east. Shortly before midnight the Glasgow Highlanders heard sounds of firing coming from the direction of Nettelkamp.

15th April. At 12.30 A.M. on 15th April the H.L.I. resumed their advance into Veerssen, on the southern outskirts of Uelzen. From the start they met savage opposition. The enemy counter-attacked and broke up the H.L.I.'s right forward company, which ceased for a time to be an entity, though its several parts continued to fight on stoutly. The enemy had plenty of machine-guns and S.P. guns admirably sited to command every approach. These formed the framework of a defence which was completed by squads of determined infantrymen armed with bazookas or machine carbines. In these conditions the Scots Guards' Churchills could not advance. The close-packed battle resolved itself into a house-to-house struggle at point-blank range. Lieutenant-Colonel Bramwell Davis was wounded and was replaced by Major Noble. By daylight the H.L.I. had won a foothold in Veerssen, but no more.

Meanwhile the Gordons on the right had attacked up the road on a one-company front into the houses and gardens on the southern outskirts of Uelzen itself. There they fared no better than the H.L.I., and their forward company was soon held up by more S.P.s, supported by spandau and bazooka teams, before it had advanced far beyond the level-crossing. Both H.L.I. and Gordons spent 15th April with their forward troops pinned by fire and unable to make progress. They had taken about two hundred prisoners.

15th April.

We must now return to the Glasgow Highlanders, whom we left in laager at Stadensen at midnight on 14th-15th April. The sounds of firing in the direction of Nettelkamp soon died away. In fact, as afterwards became known, the squadron of the Reconnaissance Regiment in harbour at Nettelkamp had been overrun. In their battalion group that night the Glasgow Highlanders had a lot of 3-ton lorries attached to them, besides their own transport—not to mention the squadron of Coldstream, an S.P. 17-pounder troop of the 91st Anti-Tank Regiment, the Headquarters of the 190th Field Regiment and the 529th and 530th Field Batteries, and a platoon of Engineers. All this mass of vehicles was parked hugger-mugger in the streets and alleys of Stadensen. It was not till about 4 A.M. that the fighting at Stadensen itself began, when both companies at the eastern side of the perimeter reported simultaneously that they were under fire and that they could hear the noise of track vehicles " off." Immediately after, enemy infantry riding on armoured half-tracks and supported by S.P. guns overran the forward platoons of both companies and came crashing into the village. A wild and terrible mêlée followed, in which the enemy S.P.s set most of the houses of Stadensen alight—and these in turn set fire to the Glasgow Highlanders' transport. Lieutenant-Colonel Baker-Baker hurried round his companies and gave them the encouragement which was all they needed to make them fight it out where they stood. On his return to battalion headquarters he found that an enemy S.P., which had penetrated into the courtyard, was in the act of blowing away his signal-office at point-blank range.

To the smoke and flames of the houses was soon added the blast of explosives as piles of German ammunition went up, followed by several ammunition trucks. In this confusion the crews of tanks and guns had a frantic struggle to hold the flames at bay till they could extricate themselves and get into action. Here Major J. H. M. Stephenson of the 530th Field Battery showed leadership of the finest order. First he shot a German officer with his revolver; next he knocked out two German half-tracks with a P.I.A.T.; and finally he manned a 25-pounder with success in an anti-tank rôle. He was to get a Military Cross for his night's work. Guns and tanks at

15th April. last succeeded in taking up positions to cover the main road-junctions, and the Glasgow Highlanders, fighting back stubbornly, managed to stop further infiltration. The dreadful ordeal continued, however, till after dawn, when the enemy began to withdraw. Now it was our turn. The two field batteries were in action south-west of Stadensen, with an O.P. manned. These two batteries, the S.P. troop of the 91st Anti-Tank Regiment, the Churchills, and the Glasgow Highlanders' 6-pounders all took their toll. The enemy left behind him twelve S.P. guns and ten armoured half-tracks destroyed, besides very many killed and prisoners.

From these last and from marked maps captured it was learnt that the battle-group which had carried out this attack belonged to the Panzer Division Clausewitz, a newly created formation which had orders to break through southward and join up with the German forces encircled in the Harz Mountains. The battle-group had approached Stadensen not by the roads—which, according to the book, the Glasgow Highlanders were covering—but across country. To this fact the enemy's initial success was largely due.

For their part the Glasgow Highlanders had lost seven killed and forty-seven wounded and missing. Fire had played havoc among their transport, their losses in vehicles amounting to twenty-two carriers, ten half-tracks, and thirty-one miscellaneous vehicles, besides two 17-pounder guns. Stadensen itself was a ruin, and casualties among the villagers had been very heavy. But for the unshakable resolution of all concerned when the attack came, the enemy would certainly have overrun the battalion-group.

The Glasgow Highlanders spent the day reorganising in Stadensen. The Cameronians moved up to Nettelkamp, which they occupied without resistance, taking eighty prisoners. On the left the Seaforth were still in contact with the enemy west of the main axis.

That evening the 6th Air Landing Brigade of the 6th Airborne Division relieved the 46th Brigade, which was now to take over from the 227th Brigade outside Uelzen. The Glasgow Highlanders were extremely short of equipment and transport, but Ordnance performed miracles of replacement. It was at this stage that the 44th Brigade came into the picture once more. On the morning of 15th April the 44th Brigade struck north-east from the main road to pass across the front of the Glasgow Highlanders in Stadensen. It was the beginning of the 44th Brigade's move round Uelzen by the right which was to

THE ADVANCE TO THE ELBE

break the deadlock. The R.S.F. took Haligsdorf after a sharp fight, and by evening the K.O.S.B. had gone through to take Hambrock in the south-eastern outskirts of Uelzen, where "D" Company took sixty-three prisoners and eight 20-mm. guns after a brilliant assault. *15th April.*

In the early hours of 16th April the Cameronians moved up to Veerssen to relieve the H.L.I., whom they found holding on somewhat precariously to a small and irregularly shaped island divided from the enemy only by the width of a street. At the same time the Glasgow Highlanders in 46th Brigade reserve took over from the Gordons, who were near the level-crossing. The Seaforth remained back beside the railway line, some four miles south-west of Uelzen. *16th April.*

As the lovely summer-like day was breaking, the H.L.I. and the Gordons pulled out to the 227th Brigade's rest-area, a couple of miles south of Uelzen. There the Argylls joined them, for the 44th Brigade's move round the right flank had made their watch to the eastward superfluous.

During the day the 44th Brigade improved its position on the south-eastern outskirts, where the R.S.F. came up on the right of the K.O.S.B. in Hambrock. In both the 44th and the 46th Brigades snipers were active and had many successes.

On the morning of 17th April the Divisional Commander held an "O" Group, at which he gave out his plan for the assault on Uelzen and the subsequent advance to the Elbe. The 44th Brigade on the right and the 46th Brigade on the left were to assault in the early hours of 18th April. *17th April.*

Meanwhile, however, developments had taken place on the 44th Brigade front which were to alter these plans. Early that morning a carrier section of the K.O.S.B., which was carrying out a reconnaissance in front of Hambrock, boldly charged straight into the German position on the initiative of Sergeant White, the section commander. Though there was some shooting, a number of Germans decided to surrender, and the section secured a footing in the position. Lieutenant-Colonel Richardson, who had witnessed this incident, was quick to order the supporting rifle company of the K.O.S.B. to exploit this success. By 7 P.M., after a hard day of impromptu fighting, the K.O.S.B. had three companies firmly established in the south-eastern section of Uelzen. That night No. 7 platoon of the K.O.S.B. under Sergeant Lee stormed and took the important bridge over the River Ilmenau in the centre of the town.

In view of the K.O.S.B.'s progress, the Divisional Commander decided in the course of the day to put in the 46th Brigade that evening instead of the next morning, as he had originally planned. Brigadier Villiers had detailed the Seaforth for this attack. In the evening, when they were already in their forming-up place waiting to begin, there came another change of plan: the Seaforth's attack was cancelled. The reason was this: about 5 P.M. the Cameronians had found that, for the first time since they had entered their congested bridgehead in Veerssen, they were able to send out patrols, and that moreover the enemy was now surrendering fairly freely. Thereupon Lieutenant-Colonel Remington Hobbs had ordered a company to follow up the patrols. It was on learning of this state of affairs that Brigadier Villiers cancelled the artillery programme in support of the Seaforth, sent their squadron of Coldstream to support the Cameronians, and reallocated to the Cameronians the Seaforth's objective. The Cameronians advanced accordingly, and by daylight on 18th April three of their companies had taken the whole of Veerssen for a loss of only four killed and nine wounded. They then sent patrols on into Uelzen itself.

On 17th April the 6th Airborne Division, by-passing Uelzen to the east, and the 11th Armoured Division, by-passing to the west, had linked up about three miles beyond it to the north-east. Uelzen had been encircled: a fact which no doubt had contributed to the enemy's weakening defence.

Next day the 44th Brigade's attack began at 4 A.M. Opposition was light. By 7 A.M. the K.O.S.B., with the R.S.F. and the Royal Scots supporting them on their right, had cleared all Uelzen east of the River Ilmenau.

West of the Ilmenau, however, the 46th Brigade had a more difficult job. After a heavy bombardment the attack began at 6 A.M. On the right were the Glasgow Highlanders, who got off to an unlucky start; on the left the Seaforth. Covered by the infantry, the tanks worked their way down the middle of the streets, raking the houses with their 6-pounders and Bezas. Tank versus S.P. duels went on all day long. The infantry went forward slowly, methodically searching every house, usually after their accompanying tanks had shot it up

THE ADVANCE TO THE ELBE

as a precaution against snipers. The tracer had its inevitable effect and soon most of the town was on fire. At about 3 P.M. the Cameronians went through the Glasgow Highlanders and finished the job, clearing up to the northern outskirts of the town. There the Cameronians had the satisfaction of liberating a prisoner-of-war camp which contained some of the men of the original 51st Highland Division taken at St Valery. To the very end the enemy infantry and S.P.s kept up their stubborn resistance.

18th April.

That afternoon the 11th Armoured Division, coming up from the south-west, occupied Luneburg, twenty miles due north of Uelzen and almost on the banks of the Elbe. The Corps Commander's intention was to close the rest of the 8th Corps northward on to the Elbe as quickly as possible.

At 6 A.M. next morning the 227th Brigade moved north from the ruins of Uelzen, heading for the Elbe. Enemy jet aircraft were much in evidence. In this particular line the enemy was now ahead both in performance and in production. The Argylls were in the lead. Their way took them across the Luneburg heath, leaving Luneburg itself some eight miles away on their left hand. Ahead, the 11th Armoured Division had now reached the Elbe.

19th April.

It was a long and tedious march with many checks. At the end of the day the Argylls had reached Hittbergen, the H.L.I. Scharnebeck, and the Gordons Barum—all on the southern bank facing Lauenburg, and a mile or two back from the river's edge. Here the 227th Brigade relieved the 29th Armoured Brigade (11th Armoured Division). The railway bridge opposite Lauenburg was in the Argylls' sector; the enemy had blown its two middle spans when the leading troops of the 29th Armoured Brigade were already within two hundred yards of it. Along the river's edge itself, at Artlenburg and elsewhere, the enemy still held positions on the southern bank. After dark the H.L.I. moved up to Lüdershausen to cover the bridging of the stream immediately south of that village.

During the day the 44th and 46th Brigades concentrated respectively about three and ten miles north of Uelzen.

Next day, 20th April, the 46th Brigade made an "advance-to-contact" move directed on the Elbe at Bleckede to the eastward of the 227th Brigade's sector. The Cameronians formed the advanced guard.

20th April.

20th April. They found Bleckede strongly held and were preparing to attack it when the Divisional boundary was moved west, with the result that Bleckede was transferred to the 5th Division, newly arrived from Italy, which had come up now on the right of the 8th Corps. Strangely enough, it then fell to the 2nd Cameronians of the 5th Division to carry out this attack. So the 9th Battalion had the novel experience of seeing the 2nd Battalion pass through them. Later the 9th were to learn with great regret of the heavy casualties that the 2nd had suffered in the taking of Bleckede.

During 20th April the H.L.I. had been preparing an attack on the enemy strong-point at Artlenburg. Just before midnight two companies attacked under a considerable artillery bombardment. After a short fight, the policemen who formed the garrison decided to surrender and came trooping in to the number of nearly two hundred. A third company of the H.L.I. then went through to clear the nearby village of Avendorf. The bend of the river between Bleckede and Lauenburg was now clear.

21st April. Next day, 21st April, the 46th Brigade on the right closed up to the Elbe, west of Bleckede: the 227th Brigade, farther west, did not move. The 8th Corps had completed its march of 103 miles from Rhine to Elbe in fourteen days. The two brigades were to remain in these positions for the next week or so while the preparations for the crossing of the Elbe—a river nearly as large as the Rhine—were completed. At Neetze the 46th Brigade made an unusual capture— a circus, to wit. The management was prevailed on to give two performances, to the great satisfaction of the troops. During this period all villagers were evacuated from the area between the Neetze Canal and the Elbe. As usual, the enemy had the advantage of position; our bank of the Elbe was low and marshy and completely overlooked by the cliffs on the northern bank. Occasionally the enemy used the advantage this observation gave him to fire a few shells. For the rest, it was pleasant, unspoilt country. In the intervals between "O" Groups the chief amusements were boating and fishing on the canals and backwaters—sad to tell, it was explosives that caught most of the fish.

Meanwhile the 44th Brigade was closing up steadily on the Elbe. By 25th April it was concentrated in Luneburg.

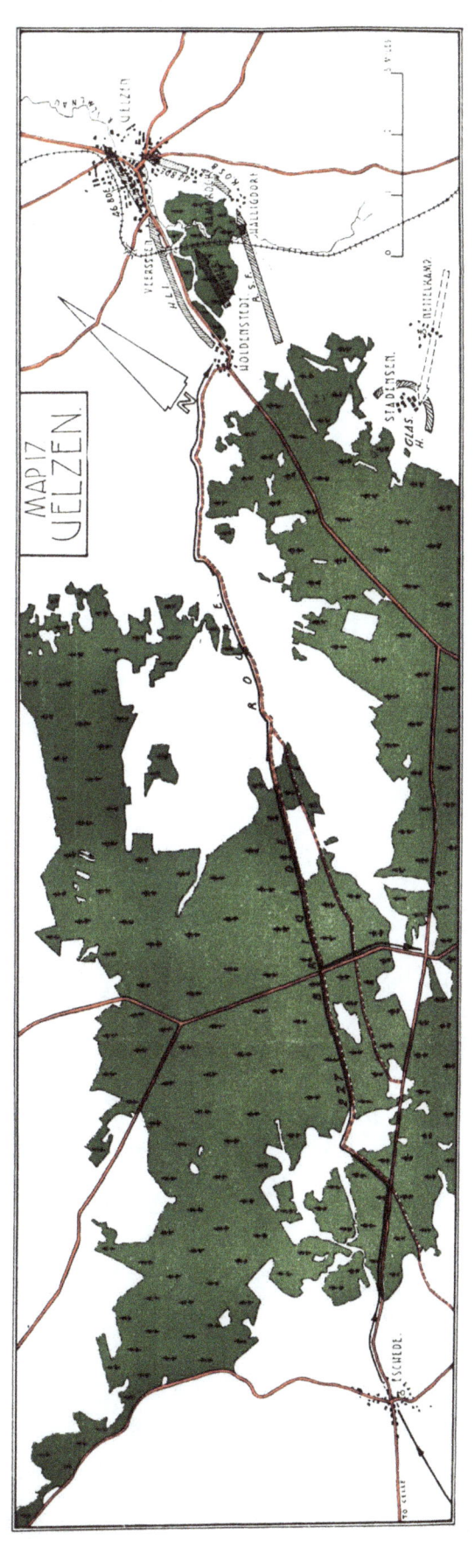

CHAPTER XI.

THE ELBE CROSSING AND THE FINAL ADVANCE TO THE BALTIC.

ABOUT mid-April General Eisenhower ordered the 21st Army Group to advance to the Baltic as quickly as possible. His object was to intercept the mass of fugitives which was pouring westward out of Mecklenburg before the Red Army and to seal off Schleswig-Holstein and Denmark. Montgomery issued his instructions accordingly. The 8th Corps was to cross the Elbe in the vicinity of Lauenburg and was to establish a bridgehead fifteen miles wide by eight miles deep. Having established its bridgehead, the 8th Corps was then to break out northeastward and to take Lubeck, while the 12th Corps—following through the 8th Corps' bridgehead—was to swing west and take Hamburg. In conjunction with this Operation "Enterprise," which was to be the 21st Army Group's last great operation in North-West Europe, the 18th U.S. Airborne Corps, again under Montgomery's command, was to force a crossing of the Elbe on the right of the 8th Corps with the task of protecting the 21st Army Group's right flank during its advance to the Baltic.

19th to 28th April.

To the 15th Scottish Division was to fall the honour of spearheading the 8th Corps' assault. To its assaults across Seine and Rhine, the 15th Scottish Division would thus add a third great crossing—that of the Elbe. It was a unique honour, since no other Division would have been in the forefront of all three of these historic crossings.

As early as 19th April the Divisional Commander had discussed with the Corps Commander whether or not to "rush" the Elbe by storm-boat on the nights of 19th and 20th April before the defences had had time to crystallise. Reluctantly they had come to the conclusion that an impromptu crossing of this sort was not "on." So, with Divisional Headquarters now at Scharnebek, planning began on the basis that the assault on the Elbe must be a fairly deliberate affair which could not take place before 27th April.

19th to 28th April.

Indeed, the assault here was going to be in many ways more difficult than that across the Rhine. In the reach to the westward of the Elbe-Trave Canal, where the 15th Scottish Division would have to cross it, the Elbe in April is a river some three hundred yards or more in width, with a current of one and a half to two knots. Its two banks are completely different in character. On the south bank—which was the British bank—the country is flat, marshy, and intersected by canals, ditches, and old beds of the river. There is here a system of flood-dykes or bunds very similar to that on the Rhine. To a depth of a couple of miles or so from the river's edge the country is bare save for the scattered villages, though farther back towards Neetze and Luneburg large and frequent woods begin. Leading forward to the river there are only two main roads—that from Scharnebek to the Lauenburg railway-bridge and that from Luneburg to Artlenburg; the ground between is bogland, so these two roads were the only approaches which would take Buffaloes (L.V.T.s) and heavy bridging lorries.

The north bank, on the other hand, rises steeply from the water's edge in a hundred-foot bound so sheer as to amount almost to a cliff. The steepness of this cliff was going to make the north-bank exits for L.V.T.s and other traffic extremely difficult. On what was the Division's right front the cliff is crowned by the houses of Lauenburg; on what was the Division's left front opposite Artlenburg the cliff is clothed by the dense Grünhof pine forest. Behind the rim of the cliff a plateau stretches back in a medley of hill and valley, effectually screened to view from the south. From his vantage-points here on the high north bank the enemy enjoyed perfect observation over the south bank to a depth of at least six miles. In consequence no movement of vehicles north of the Neetze Canal could be allowed in the 15th Scottish Divisional area by daylight.

The 15th Scottish Division would have to reckon with the equivalent of about eight or nine enemy battalions—a very mixed bunch who were holding down to the water's edge and were supported by about a hundred guns, mostly flak. The German Command was bent on holding the Elbe as long as possible in order to keep the westward passage across the Elbe-Trave Canal open to the fleeing multitudes behind.

Under command for the crossing the 15th Scottish Division was to have the 1st Commando Brigade, under Brigadier Mills Roberts, the Royals—who were to act as the nucleus of the Bank Group—the

RIVER ELBE AT ARTLENBURG

4th Tank Coldstream, the 146th Battery of the 63rd S.P. Anti-Tank 19th to 28th April. Regiment, and the 11th A.G.R.E., which last, together with the Divisional Engineers, would amount to the equivalent of fifteen field companies. In support the Division was to have the L.V.T.s of the 11th Royal Tanks and of the 77th Squadron Assault R.E., the D.D. Tanks of a squadron of the Staffordshire Yeomanry, and a platoon of storm-boats and another of D.U.K.W.s. Guns taking part in the artillery programme would amount to ten field, one mountain, four medium, and two heavy regiments R.A.

According to the plan as it finally took shape, the 15th Scottish Division would assault on a two-brigade front at 2 A.M. on 29th April. On the right the 1st Commando Brigade was to cross a little to the westward of Hohnstorf and was to take Lauenburg from the rear; on the left the 44th Brigade was to assault simultaneously astride Artlenburg and to secure a bridgehead about two thousand five hundred yards wide and one thousand five hundred yards deep, which would include Schnakenbek. The 46th Brigade was then to go through the 1st Commando Brigade, and the 227th Brigade through the 44th Brigade, whereafter the 15th Scottish Division was to expand the bridgehead progressively up to the Corps' limits. It would thus prepare the way for the break-out of the 11th Armoured Division. Such was the plan on to which Colonel R. Foster, the Commander of the 11th A.G.R.E., had now to hang his vitally important engineer preparations, by the success or failure of which the whole operation would stand or fall.

Among his multifarious tasks Colonel Foster had to provide the following crossings: suitable L.V.T. and D.D. tank crossing-places, with approaches, entries, and exits; a D.U.K.W. crossing; two storm-boat ferries, each twelve-boat; a Class 9 raft ferry of four rafts and a Class 9 bridge of folding-boat equipment, both at Lauenburg; a Class 40 raft ferry of four rafts and a Class 40 Bailey pontoon-bridge, both at Artlenburg, with a Class 40 road forward thence through Schnakenbek and Juliusburg to Schwarzenbek. On the right the Class 9 rafts were to be working within four hours, and the Class 9 F.B.E. bridge within fifteen hours, of the capture of Lauenburg; on the left the Class 40 rafts were to be working within four hours, and the Class 40 Bailey bridge within thirty hours, of the initial assault. In addition, Colonel Foster had to provide boom protection above and below the crossing-places and to arrange for the cutting of the bunds on the south bank for the L.V.T.s and the D.D. tanks just before

19th to 28th April.

H-hour, for mine clearance and the construction of exits on the north bank, and for the maintenance of the main corps axis.

Colonel Foster asked for special reconnaissances of the crossing-places, and these the Royal Naval Commando carried out. Unfortunately the moon was bright and the enemy were alert, so our swimmers could not reach the actual sites of the exits on the north bank. They brought back useful information, however, about strength of current and depth of water and slope of bottom on the far side.

Clearly one of the main difficulties which would arise soon after H-hour would be growing congestion in Artlenburg. There was only one approach road to Artlenburg, which is a small town with narrow side-streets, set in gardens and woods. Yet, as soon as the two forward battalions of the 44th Brigade had crossed there, two L.V.T. ferries would have to start plying, and work would have to begin on four Class 40 rafts and on the Class 40 bridge—all to be built against time. The need for carefully organised Bank Control and traffic circuits and for an effective system of priorities was sufficiently obvious.

Briefly, the system of control adopted was this. Bank Control, organised by the Royals, was at Divisional Headquarters at Scharnebek, on the lateral road adjoining the two main forward routes. Well forward on each of these routes there was a Crossing Control—Right Crossing Control situated a little south of Hohnstorf, Left Crossing Control a little south of Artlenburg. On each, too, there was a marshalling area well back on the Neetze Canal, where tree cover was available. In these rear marshalling areas troops and vehicles destined for the initial assault were to be preloaded in their L.V.T.s. After the initial assault, vehicles were to be called up from these marshalling areas according to the priorities allotted them by Divisional Headquarters. Vehicles other than bridging lorries would go to Vehicle Waiting Areas (V.W.A.s) well forward on both routes, whence they would be fed forward by Crossing Control to L.V.T. Loading Areas (L.V.T.L.A.s), as L.V.T.s returning from the ferries arrived there to pick them up. Bridging lorries would go straight to Bridge Marshalling Harbours (B.M.H.s), situated as near as possible to the bridging sites.

During the week's pause which preceded the assault crossing, reconnaissance parties from all battalions visited the sites where they would have to cross and made careful examinations of the opposite bank. According to the drill, these parties had to reach the bank before dawn and to remain concealed throughout the day, withdrawing after dark.

It was so peaceful by the riverside and so perfect was the weather that it was hard to associate the idyllic scene with war. All ranks, too, made a thorough study of air photographs, both oblique and vertical. These careful preparations were a most necessary preliminary to a night assault into such steep and intricate country as that facing the 15th Scottish Division on the north bank of the Elbe.

19th to 28th April.

The enemy was far from aggressive. The ferrymen still plied their trade, ferrying passengers to our bank—and charging them twenty pfennigs. Soldiers came down to wash their mess-tins in full view of our O.P.s. On the road between Lauenburg and Boizenburg German staff cars sped to and fro in care-free abandon—till they got shot up for their pains. The climax was reached when an officer of the Commando Brigade sent a German across to tell the garrison of Lauenburg that he himself would cross next day to negotiate their surrender and got a reply that he would be received. Next day the officer set out in a storm-boat complete with white flag, but, alas for the dignity of the occasion, the engine conked out in mid-stream. Thereupon a German rescue party towed him in. He interviewed a series of German commanders of ascending magnitude, but all pled lack of authority to negotiate. After that, breathing threatenings and slaughter, the officer returned to his own bank, bringing back with him a very clear picture of the German defences and of the lie of the land on the other side.

By D−1 all was ready. Late on the afternoon of Saturday, 28th April, the 44th Brigade moved up in troop-carrying vehicles from its concentration area at Luneburg to the left-hand marshalling area in the square wood by Brietlingen. There the 44th Brigade was joined by the Argylls, who were under its command for the crossing. In the marshalling areas the men had a last hot meal and then got some sleep, albeit somewhat disturbed by sounds of sporadic shelling and mortaring down by the river. About 11 P.M. the two forward battalions, the R.S.F. and the Royal Scots, paraded and filed off to board their L.V.T.s of the 11th Royal Tanks in the marshalling area. Scarcely were all aboard—with thoughts of snatching a bit more sleep—when the counter-battery bombardment opened at midnight. Several batteries were sited in and around the marshalling area, and their noise was shattering: all hope of sleep vanished. Soon the deep boom of the heavies, the thump of the mediums, the wicked crack of the 25-pounders, all merged into one monotonous roar, which would wax

19th to 28th April.

in volume as the guns engaged each new target, to wane again as they switched on to the next.

By this time the rear battalions, the K.O.S.B. and the Argylls, were also standing by to march up to the Rear Battalion Waiting Areas (R.B.W.A.s) by Artlenburg, in readiness to board their L.V.T.s in due course in the L.V.T.L.A.s nearby. For the last time in this war the waiting infantry watched the flashes of the bursting shells of a great bombardment and the crimson glow of many newly kindled fires.

Over in the right-hand marshalling area meanwhile, one and a half miles east of Scharnebek, the 1st Commando Brigade, with the Seaforth under command, had been following more or less the same ritual as the 44th Brigade. Here, too, the two leading Commando battalions were now ready to move off in their L.V.T.s; while the Seaforth and a third Commando battalion were ready to march to the L.V.T.L.A.s near Hohnstorf. The Engineers had now blown the two intervening bunds under cover of the noise of the bombardment and had cleared a passage for the L.V.T.s with their bulldozers.

So ended D−1, 28th April.

29th April.

About 12.50 A.M. next morning, as the roar of the guns swelled in a new crescendo to mark the opening of the preliminary or "softening" bombardment, forward battalions got the order to move from the marshalling areas. At the same time rear battalions began their march to the R.B.W.A.s.

Forward in Artlenburg those who waited the arrival of the assault wave saw strange sights that night. The sky was densely overcast: so much so that the whole programme of air support for next morning had been cancelled. Yet so bright was the Movement Light of the many searchlights that slanted their diffused beams into the clouds from positions in rear that onlookers could stand unseen in the shadows of Artlenburg with nothing but the waters of the Elbe, molten and gleaming, between them and the enemy.

The bombardment was awe-inspiring—but not so much for its incessant noise, which after a time almost ceased to be noticeable, as for its strangely theatrical effects. There, barely four hundred yards away, a bleak cliff as high as the cliff at Rottingdean was being pulverised before the onlookers' eyes. Over it there played in fantastic pattern a

ELBE CROSSING AND FINAL ADVANCE TO BALTIC

29th April.

myriad stabs and flashes of orange flame that took shape and died the same instant like forked lightning. Here and there distinct and separate shell-bursts made antic play among the trees, tossing up balls of fire like Roman candles, while overhead the Bofors tracer passed in diagonal streams, reflected crimson in the water. Presently the one small house on the far shore took fire and glowed like a Chinese lantern till it burst into flames. So elemental was the force of this bombardment that those who watched it could not but ask themselves uneasily what their own reactions would have been, had they been subjected to a like test.

As 2 A.M. drew near, the air was filled with a droning roar as of approaching heavy aircraft, and out of Artlenburg's main street one by one emerged the Buffaloes, immense and black, to turn alternatively right and left in the shadow. The R.S.F. were to cross a short way up-stream of the Artlenburg ferry; the Royal Scots a short way down-stream of it. Having reached their respective crossing-places, the Buffaloes turned again, lumbered down the grassy bank towards the river, and—exactly at 2 A.M.—took to the water with great splashes like a school of hippopotami. Almost at the same moment the artillery fire lifted from the opposing foreshore on to the cliff summit above. As the first flight crossed, only an occasional burst of enemy L.M.G. fire came to spray the water. The heavy Brownings mounted on the L.V.T.s chattered in answer. A minute or two later the L.V.T.s were clambering out to disgorge their loads on the hundred yards or more of rocky but fairly level foreshore at the bottom of the cliff. At once the L.V.T.s returned to pick up the K.O.S.B. and the Argylls, while the R.S.F. and the Royal Scots, having assembled below the cliff, went on to scale its steep and sandy slopes and to establish themselves on the rim of the plateau above. By this time the enemy was waking up. Though his resistance was pretty shaky, some mortar-bombs were coming over, and long-range shelling of the crossing was growing more and more accurate and heavy.

About 3.30 A.M. the Argylls and the K.O.S.B. crossed in their turn. Both battalions selected for their forward assembly areas the large quarry in the cliff face up-stream of the ferry. By the worst of ill-fortune the enemy guns, firing down the river at long range, found the mouth of this quarry just as three companies of the Argylls were assembling in it. In these few minutes the Argylls lost nine men

29th April.
killed and over forty wounded. While the K.O.S.B. made a detour up-stream below the cliff to approach Schnakenbek up the forest-track from the south-east, the Argylls went straight on to take over the close protection of the bridgehead from the R.S.F., who then pushed eastward to link up with the 1st Commando Brigade. By 8 A.M. the K.O.S.B. had cleared Schnakenbek, capturing its discouraged garrison of Green Police; while the Royal Scots were pushing northward across the plateau, taking many prisoners as they went. Everywhere opposition was slight and patchy.

Near Hohnstorf meanwhile the forward battalions of the 1st Commando Brigade had also crossed successfully at 2 A.M. and had gone into Lauenburg from the north. About 3.20 A.M. the Seaforth followed. Pushing farther inland, the Seaforth met no enemy. By 6 A.M. they were established on the two hills that command both main roads, about two thousand yards north of Lauenburg. Less than an hour later the Commandos had cleared Lauenburg itself and had captured the bridge intact on the main road leading eastward from it over the Elbe-Trave Canal.

Next it was the turn of the rear brigades. First, let us follow the fortunes of the 46th Brigade on the right. Between midnight and 4 A.M. the Cameronians and the Glasgow Highlanders had marched from their concentration areas to the R.B.W.A.s at Hittbergen, whence they had moved on almost immediately to the L.V.T.L.A.s at Hohnstorf. By 5 A.M. they had begun to cross the Elbe. At that time only occasional shells were falling. Within an hour both battalions were safe in their forward assembly areas on the north bank. By 9.30 A.M., thanks to the fine work of the sappers in clearing sunken roads blocked by tree-trunks and other blocked exits from the river, first priority vehicles, such as command post and company vehicles, were beginning to arrive. Soon after, both battalions "advanced-to-contact" in a northerly direction. The Cameronians on the right passed through the Seaforth on their twin hills and advanced on Basedow, whereupon the Seaforth reverted under command and came into 46th Brigade reserve. The Glasgow Highlanders on the left advanced on Krüzen and Lütau. During the advance most of the essential transport of the Brigade joined up, as did also the squadron of Staffordshire Yeomanry (D.D. tanks), two troops of which were allotted to the support of each forward battalion. By evening the Cameronians had reached Basedow, where they consolidated for the night with

ELBE CROSSING AND FINAL ADVANCE TO BALTIC

their right flank resting on the Elbe-Trave Canal. They had taken 240 prisoners at a cost of 2 killed and 5 wounded. On the left the Glasgow Highlanders had captured the twin hills of Heid-Berg and Hunger-Berg, about two thousand yards short of Lütau, after a sharp fight. There they, too, consolidated for the night.

29th April.

We come now to the 227th Brigade on the left. In the early hours the H.L.I. and the Gordons had moved up to the R.B.W.A.s near Artlenburg *en route* for the L.V.T.L.A.s. Already Altenburg itself was becoming highly congested. The first bridge serial for the Class 40 bridge had just arrived: that serial alone represented seventy vehicles. It was about 7 A.M. when both battalions began to cross. By this time the enemy was shelling the crossing and the exit track up the ravine on the far side with great accuracy: his long-range railway guns had got both taped. Before they could reach their forward assembly area in the woods on the north bank the Gordons had a number of casualties, but the H.L.I. were luckier. Through all this turmoil the Engineers and the L.V.T. ferries worked on undismayed. By 10 A.M., when the 227th Brigade began its advance, both forward battalions had already received nearly all their essential vehicles.

In the process of expanding the 15th Scottish Division's bridgehead, the 227th Brigade had the task of pushing out on the left, while the 44th Brigade pushed out in the centre and the 46th Brigade on the right. The 227th Brigade's ultimate objective was Geesthacht, six miles down-stream from the Artlenburg crossing. In the first phase of this advance the Gordons were now to push north-west along the main road that runs across the plateau parallel to the river and about a mile from it. Their job was to take Tesperhude, about half-way to Geesthacht, and then to clear the Grünhof Forest between Tesperhude and Artlenburg. On the Gordons' right the H.L.I. were to conform farther inland. The Argylls, now back under command, were in 227th Brigade reserve, with the task of going through the H.L.I. and taking Grünhof village as soon as the Gordons had taken Tesperhude.

When the Gordons set out, enemy shells were passing overhead in an almost continuous stream, to burst around the Class 40 bridging site in the river-bed below. Down there things were very unpleasant, and the 7th Army Troops Engineers were losing both men and equipment apace, yet their work never faltered. About 1 P.M. the Luftwaffe arrived to add to the trials of the sappers. Approaching under cloud cover, about a dozen enemy jet-aircraft suddenly appeared, flying so

29th April. low that they passed beneath onlookers on the cliff. They attacked with bombs and cannon, killing eight and wounding twenty-two of the 8th Corps Troops Engineers who were busy on the Class 9 F.B.E. bridge, and doing a lot of damage to the immediate bridge-approaches. Several more times before nightfall the Luftwaffe returned to the attack on the bridge sites, each time leaving a trail of killed or wounded. The behaviour of the sappers in face of these attacks won the intense admiration of all beholders.

In the course of the afternoon the Gordons took Tesperhude after overcoming some stiffish resistance. They then mopped up the Grünhof Forest, which was full of Germans, taking 400 prisoners and killing many more. Here Major G. C. Campbell, who had been gunner-adviser to the Gordons throughout the whole campaign, was severely wounded. The H.L.I. meanwhile had occupied its objectives, two desolate hills lying inland and to the north-east of Tesperhude. The weather had broken. There the H.L.I. spent a wet and wretched night without a house in sight. The Argylls moved up behind the H.L.I.

At 11 P.M., in pouring rain, the Argylls passed through the H.L.I. to attack Grünhof. Their objective was an arms factory in the village. Before the Argylls could reach the factory, however, the Gordons from Tesperhude had occupied it.

It remains to describe the doings of the 44th Brigade in the centre. By evening the Royal Scots were established in Krukow, where they were in touch with the H.L.I. on their left; the R.S.F. were in Juliusburg, where they were in touch with the Glasgow Highlanders on their right. And late that night the K.O.S.B. occupied Gulzow out in front. Thus at the close of D Day the 15th Scottish Division held a more or less solid bridgehead from the Elbe-Trave Canal at Basedow to the Rhine at Tesperhude. Thirteen enemy aircraft, mostly fighter-bombers, had been shot down and over 1400 prisoners taken. The Division was well over the last fence.

Despite grievous interruptions the Engineers had all but maintained their own exacting schedule. At 10 P.M. the position was this: the two Class 40 rafts were working and had ferried over thirty-five tanks; the Class 9 ferry had been open since 2 P.M. and had put across ninety-three vehicles; the Class 9 F.B.E. bridge had been open to traffic for nearly two hours; the Class 40 bridge was expected to be opened by noon next day. Well might Colonel Foster survey his men's handiwork with satisfaction.

ELBE CROSSING AND FINAL ADVANCE TO BALTIC

30th April.

On the morning of 30th April it was to fall to the lot of the Cameronians in Basedow to meet the last heavy and sustained counter-attack of the campaign.

The night before, the Cameronians had dug in with "D" Company on the right by the Elbe-Trave Canal, "C" Company in the centre covering the direct approaches from Dalldorf, "B" Company on the left astride the main Dalldorf-Lauenburg road, and "A" Company in depth behind "B." According to plan, the Seaforth were to have gone through "A" and "B" Companies of the Cameronians at 5.30 A.M. on 30th April and to have taken Dalldorf, which was the 46th Brigade's objective.

About 8 P.M. the night before, Lieutenant-Colonel Remington Hobbs had sent out his carrier platoon to reconnoitre the road to Dalldorf. The platoon had returned at last light to report that it had seen no enemy. At midnight an officers' patrol set out on foot to see whether or not Dalldorf was clear. The patrol returned about 3 A.M. after meeting a platoon of the enemy south of Dalldorf. A third patrol went out at 4.15 A.M., but returned at once, bringing the news that it had met the enemy approaching apparently in battalion strength and only about five hundred yards away. Sure enough, while the patrol commander was making his report, the attack began. At once the guns put down defensive fire.

At first the pressure was heaviest on "D" Company over by the canal and on "C" Company north of Basedow. The enemy attacked most resolutely, closing in on the Cameronians' forward platoons, bazooka-ing their slit-trenches, digging in within a few yards of their foremost localities, and trying repeatedly to infiltrate into Basedow and round the right flank. For four or five hours it was a ding-dong fight at close quarters, in which the Cameronians fired an unprecedented quantity of ammunition—particularly of 2-inch mortar-bombs and small-arms ammunition. About 5.20 A.M. the enemy extended his attack to "B" Company astride the main road on the left, and he soon got a firm hold on a small wood on "B" Company's left front. The Cameronians were widely extended, and they had their work cut out to stop infiltration.

All this time the Seaforth, with the squadron of the Staffordshire Yeomanry in support, were formed up on the road behind Basedow in readiness to attack north. About 7 A.M. Brigadier Villiers sent up the Yeomanry to help the Cameronians, whereupon the tanks soon

30th April. eased the pressure on "C" and "D" Companies. None the less the enemy kept up his attacks till 11 A.M. Even then he showed no signs of withdrawing, but held his front strongly, threatening both flanks of the Cameronians. According to prisoners' reports, the attacking force consisted of about four companies, each about 120 strong.

The Seaforth were still awaiting an opportunity to advance through "A" and "B" Companies of the Cameronians and to take the wooded hill, two thousand yards to the northward, known as Zucker Holz. The enemy, however, was firmly established in the small wood on "B" Company's immediate front, where he had resisted all attempts to eject him. After discussing the position with the two commanding officers, Lieutenant-Colonels Hunt and Remington Hobbs, Brigadier Villiers decided that, until this small wood had been cleared, the Seaforth could not attack Zucker Holz. He therefore made a new plan, according to which the Seaforth relieved "A" Company of the Cameronians and took over responsibility for the main road, whereupon "A" Company of the Cameronians moved over to the right to reinforce "D" Company on the canal. That done, Brigadier Villiers ordered two companies of the Seaforth to attack and clear the small and troublesome wood. There were about 70 Germans in it, and they resisted these two Seaforth's companies for four hours. At the finish the Seaforth had killed 30 or more and had taken 35 prisoners. Only 4 Germans escaped, and these were captured later by the Cameronians.

So ended the fight round Basedow. The Cameronians had held all their positions in face of heavy attack, had killed 40 Germans, and had taken 142 prisoners. It had been a good day—and a fitting end to the serious work of the campaign. In the evening the 15th Brigade of the 5th Division passed through and took Dalldorf. The 15th Brigade was temporarily under command of the 6th Airborne Division, which had been passing over the Class 9 bridge at Lauenburg since mid-day.

Over on the 46th Brigade's left-hand axis meanwhile the Glasgow Highlanders had made an early advance from the Heid-Berg and the Hunger-Berg northward on Lütau. After some trouble with snipers, they entered Lütau and cleared it, killing a lot of Germans and taking 100 prisoners. And there the Glasgow Highlanders were ordered to remain while the 1st Commando Brigade went through in the late afternoon.

Next we come to the 44th Brigade in the centre. The R.S.F. had spent the night in Juliusburg, the Royal Scots in Krukow, the K.O.S.B. in Gulzow. Early on 30th April the 15th Scottish Division Reconnaissance Regiment passed through, heading for Schwarzenbek. The R.S.F. and the Royal Scots followed on two different axes. The R.S.F. on the right reached Schwarzenbek, on the boundary of the Corps' bridgehead, by 4 P.M. They were nearly three days ahead of schedule. The Royal Scots on the left met some enemy S.P.s in Kollow which delayed them somewhat. They arrived about an hour later. The K.O.S.B. also went through Kollow to patrol the great stretch of woodland on the west flank, the Gülzower Holz, where they took a number of prisoners and found two 12-inch guns destroyed and abandoned by the Germans.

On the left, too, it was much the same state of affairs: the 227th Brigade spent the day expanding the bridgehead against crumbling resistance. After halting for a few wet and uncomfortable hours the H.L.I. had moved forward again at 1.30 that morning to occupy two more hill-features on the right of the Argylls. At first light the Argylls relieved the Gordons in the factory at Grünhof, which "D" Company of the Gordons had occupied in the early hours. "D" Company had been out betimes to clear the wooded heights to the westward of the Tesperhude Gorge. For the rest, the Gordons had spent a quiet and comparatively dry night in Tesperhude. Early in the morning they made an unusual catch in the shallows by Tesperhude —to wit, two German "frogmen" in full aquatic order who had swum up-stream intent on blowing the Artlenburg bridge. An onlooker among the Jocks was heard to observe, "Thon wull be what they ca' the 'herrin' folk'" (*herrenvolk*).

By this time there were unmistakable signs that the enemy was throwing in his hand. The German Command had opened negotiations over the civil telephone with Brigadier Colville for the surrender of Geesthacht, where there was a store of V-1 fuel—and reputedly another of poison gas, capable of devastating the whole countryside. Meanwhile the 227th Brigade pushed on. Evening found the H.L.I. in Wiershop, the Argylls in Krummel, the Gordons in Hamwarde, where the last-named had arrived riding on the tanks of the Coldstream, who had now crossed into the bridgehead.

At the bridges 30th April was a much easier day, for our fighter cover was now effective and enemy shelling was only intermittent.

30th April. At 9 A.M. the 8th Corps Troops Engineers captured yet another frogman close to the Class 9 F.B.E. bridge at Lauenburg. At noon the Class 40 bridge at Artlenburg opened as anticipated. By evening the 15th Scottish Division was for all intents and purposes across complete, and the 11th Armoured Division and the 6th Airborne Division began to pour into the bridgehead in their turn. At this stage the 11th A.G.R.E. reverted to Corps command.

About the same time the Luftwaffe reappeared, but without much success. Enemy shelling was still a factor to be reckoned with, however. That evening, for instance, "A" Echelon of the Gordons, together with a number of R.E. trucks loaded with explosives, was parked in an assembly area just over the Class 40 bridge when the area was heavily shelled and many vehicles set on fire. Thereupon Captain and Quartermaster W. G. Lewis of the Gordons at once took charge of the salvage work and himself drove several vehicles to safety out of the flames. For his very gallant conduct he was afterwards awarded the Military Cross.

1st May. On 1st May the 15th Scottish Division got orders for 2nd May to clear the Sachsenwald, which is the very extensive forest lying northeast of Hamburg and beginning three or four miles north of Geesthacht. The Division was to sweep the forest from east to west with the 44th Brigade on the right, the 46th Brigade in the centre, and the 227th Brigade on the left. During 1st May these three brigades were busy positioning themselves for this drive.

The 46th Brigade side-stepped left to concentration areas round Gulzow, where it was out of touch with the enemy. The 44th Brigade remained in and around Schwarzenbek, with the K.O.S.B. at Brunstdorf to the south.

On the 227th Brigade front the negotiations had ended satisfactorily. The Germans evacuated Geesthacht according to agreement at noon. The 158th Brigade of the 53rd Division, which had entered the bridgehead by the Class 40 bridge and come temporarily under the 15th Scottish Division, then occupied Geesthacht, where the 12th Corps was now to bridge the Elbe for its advance on Hamburg. The Gordons remained in Hamwarde; the H.L.I. occupied Worth before noon; the Argylls moved round the north of Geesthacht in the afternoon into billets on the road leading north towards the Sachsenwald.

Meanwhile at first light the 11th Armoured Division had begun its break-out from the 8th Corps' bridgehead. The 159th Brigade advanced from Schwarzenbek north-westward through the eastern extremity of the Sachsenwald; the 29th Armoured Brigade advanced north directed on Lubeck. Meanwhile the 5th Division farther east had entered the bridgehead by the Class 9 bridge, and, concentrating behind the 6th Airborne Division, had resumed command of the 15th Infantry Brigade. The 5th Division's task was to advance northward along the Elbe-Trave Canal directed on Molln. At the same time the 6th Airborne Division had struck eastward across the Elbe-Trave Canal to link up with the 82nd U.S. Airborne Division, which had now crossed the Elbe about Bleckede.

1st May.

At 8 A.M. on 2nd May the 15th Scottish Division began its westward drive through the Sachsenwald. The drive, which lasted till evening, produced a lot of prisoners at a negligible cost. On the right the K.O.S.B. made notable captures in the persons of the Prince and Princess von Bismarck, whom they found sheltering in the Schloss of Friedrichsruh. In the centre the 46th Brigade, advancing on a three-battalion front, took about three hundred prisoners.

2nd May.

On the left the 227th Brigade met more resistance. In Hohenhern at the start the H.L.I. had a sharp fight with some marine cadets from the flak school at Hamburg. Again at the end of the day, when they had emerged from the forest, the H.L.I. met determined resistance round Neu Bornsen, their final objective. They spent the night in a tight perimeter round Neu Bornsen cross-roads.

Farther south the Argylls advanced along the main Geesthacht-Bergedorf road, with Bornsen as their objective. Here the marine cadets, manning their 20-mm. flak guns, were again very much to the fore and full of fight, while our own guns, having outrun their ammunition supplies, were unable to give their usual support. In consequence the Argylls had some difficult fighting on the steep, cliff-like and thickly wooded hill above the road. By noon, however, white flags were beginning to appear. The news had spread that Hitler was dead, and the Wehrmacht was left with little more to fight for.

On the main road where the side road from Fahrendorf joins it, the cadets were manning a road-block on the front of the Argylls. Soon senior German officers by ones and twos were clambering over this road-block eager to discuss terms. These emissaries the Argylls

2nd May. duly blindfolded and packed off to 227th Brigade Headquarters, where the Divisional Commander had arrived to be at hand in case of a worth-while offer of surrender. Finally, no less a personage than Chief of Staff of Army Group Blumentritt agreed to go off to 8th Corps Headquarters with the Divisional Commander to arrange preliminaries of surrender. The cadets helped to remove the road-block, and off went the German Chief of Staff in his own car. Most of the cadets then decided to surrender, but a few picked up their weapons again and made off sullenly down the road towards Hamburg. The Argylls went on to spend the night in Bornsen.

On all sides that day great events were happening: the 6th Airborne Division reached the Baltic coast and met the Red Army; the 5th Division was advancing north along the western shore of the Ratzeburger See; the 11th Armoured Division entered Lubeck; Hamburg surrendered to Major-General L. O. Lyne, whose 7th Armoured Division had crossed the Elbe at Geesthacht; the German forces in Italy laid down their arms.

3rd May. On 3rd May the 15th Scottish Division, having handed over to the 53rd Division of the 12th Corps on the direct route to Hamburg, moved a short way north-westward from the Sachsenwald into concentration areas to the north-east of Hamburg. The 44th Brigade, now on the left, found itself on the high ridge overlooking the city, whose chimneys and spires were plain to see some five miles away. But Hamburg had now surrendered and the 12th Corps was already entering it.

Here north of the Elbe the whole land was alive with disbanded Wehrmacht and homeless refugees flying before both Russians and British. Nearly all seemed to be heading for Hamburg. Towards this imagined sanctuary an endless stream of human flotsam was pouring along every road: Luftwaffe, Panzer Grenadiers, Marines, infantry, gunners—dirty and dejected, they came trudging by in their thousands, or trundling along on farm-carts or in ramshackle buses, the whole sorry multitude of them to be herded into the prisoners' cages that awaited them. Such was the bitter end of the once all-conquering Wehrmacht—though so far as the 15th Scottish Division was concerned that end still lacked official confirmation.

Meanwhile, however, Montgomery back in Luneburg was carrying on peace negotiations with Von Keitel which would soon end the war in North-West Europe.

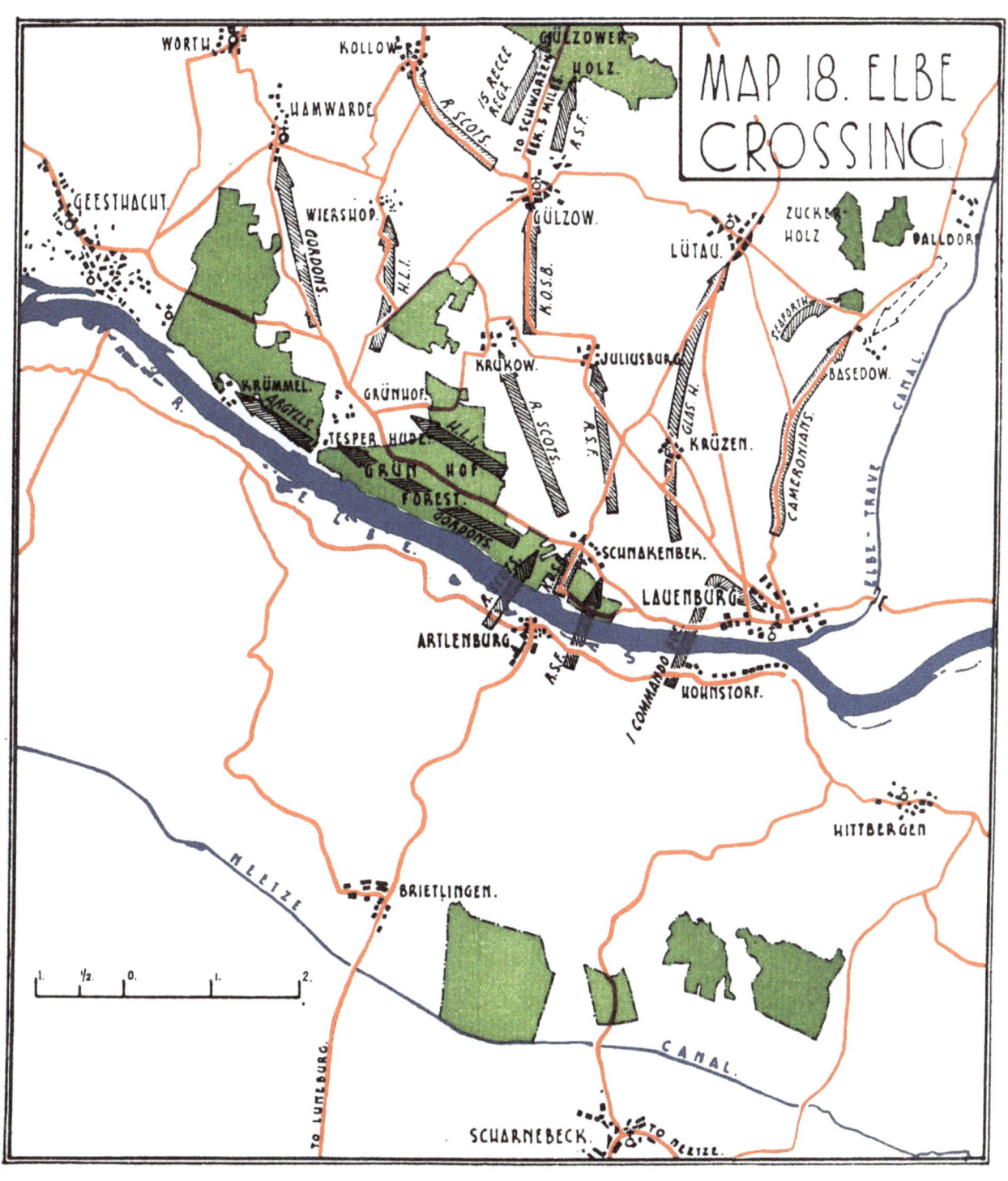

ELBE CROSSING AND FINAL ADVANCE TO BALTIC

On 4th May the 15th Scottish Division moved once more in the direction of Lubeck. The 46th Brigade halted in the Sprenze area, the 44th Brigade round Bargteheide, the 227th Brigade round Ahrensburg. It was a pleasant countryside unspoilt by war, and the Division settled itself in comfortably. That evening definite news came at last. At 6.20 P.M. Montgomery signed an agreement whereby the capitulation of all German forces in the North-West, other than those immediately opposed to the Russians, would be effective from 8 A.M. next day, 5th May. At that hour all hostilities were to cease. At once the B.B.C. spread the news. Most units heard the announcement that same evening; those who did not, heard it early on 5th May. The war was over.

On 6th May, a spring day in a lovely countryside, thanksgiving services were held throughout the Division, at which were read a message of congratulation from H.M. The King and an address by the Divisional Commander. The work of the Division had been well and truly done. Yet there were no feelings of triumph or exultation—only thankfulness. All thoughts turned to the long and painful journey that had led to victory, and to the many who had fallen by the way.

CHAPTER XII.

DISSOLUTION.

VE DAY found the Division just north of the Hamburg-Lubeck Autobahn, with the rôle of protecting the left flank of the 11th Armoured Division. The 44th Brigade was in Bargteheide and Delingsdorf; the 227th Brigade in Ahrensburg; the 46th Brigade around Trittau; Divisional Headquarters at Hammoor; while the 15th Scottish Divisional Reconnaissance Regiment, with the 1st S.A.S. Regiment in support, was feeling out towards Forst Segeberg.

The Divisional Commander at once summoned his Brigadiers to an unorthodox " O " Group at Divisional Headquarters to celebrate the end of the campaign. An infantry brigade was required immediately to support the small naval detachment which was to take the surrender of the German Navy in Kiel. The infantry brigade commanders thus assembled drew lots out of a hat, and the lot fell upon the 46th Brigade.

The days that followed produced problems which would have been beyond solution by the Directing Staff of any earthly Staff College. The 15th Scottish had to provide for the feeding and staging, not only of the 8th Parachute Division and the 5th Flak Division whose surrenders they had accepted, but also of the countless P.O.W.s from other allied sources who were passing through the Divisional area *en route* for the Oldenburg Peninsula north of Lubeck, where they were to be collected. Moreover, there were allied ex-P.O.W.s and displaced persons of every nationality and by the thousand, all of whom had to be looked after and controlled.

On 8th May the last action of the campaign was fought in Forst Segeberg. This action was a purely German affair. There in the forest an S.S. unit, which had refused to surrender, had been standing at bay. So the Wehrmacht was told off to clean up the forest. A ring was marked out which had to be kept clear of British troops and within which the Wehrmacht had the 8th Corps' permission to do battle. The Wehrmacht duly cleared the forest from east to west, while the 15th Scottish Divisional Reconnaissance Regiment found stops to round up any S.S. who might try to break out to the north-east.

The adventures of the 46th Brigade in Kiel are typical of those days. When Brigadier Villiers reached Kiel on 6th May he found that the incredibly detailed intelligence dossier which he had been given was quite out of date. The dossier had been corrected with meticulous accuracy up to 15th April, but subsequently the Allied Air Forces had flattened the place. In the resulting chaos of ruins and rubble the 46th Brigade had the greatest difficulty in finding billets that would provide even roofs over their heads. Indeed, the F.O.I.C., Admiral Baillie-Grohman, who had come to take the surrender of the German fleet, had to be content with a concrete air-raid shelter for his headquarters.

The first step was to round up the mob of German soldiers, sailors, and airmen who were roaming the streets of Kiel in their thousands. Naval ratings were sent to one large barracks, airmen of the G.A.F. to another, soldiers to a third. The German commandant of the naval barracks soon began to complain loudly that his barracks were overcrowded. When Brigadier Villiers went to investigate he found that, though most of the blocks and the barrack square were certainly packed to capacity, in one of the blocks there were only two or three men per room. That block, the commandant explained, was allotted to U-boat men—and he dared not ask them to put themselves out. Brigadier Villiers did not share his scruples.

Against all orders, refugees were crowding into Kiel, many of them in boats which put in to discharge their loads of starving humanity. On the third day of occupation the climax was reached: a convoy from the Russian zone bringing 150,000 refugees—many of them gravely ill—was signalled as approaching Kiel. Fortunately the Corps Commander, Lieutenant-General Sir Evelyn Barker, happened to be visiting Kiel at the time. He at once undertook to send up senior representatives of the Services with a large pool of rations. First, the sick were disembarked from the holds and taken to hospital. This was no easy job, for the decks were so crowded that it was almost impossible to remove the hatches, while the atmosphere down in the holds, packed with sick and those suffering from gangrenous wounds, was terrible. Later, the able-bodied were disembarked on a large expanse of open ground on the far side of the harbour, where a camp was formed to receive them.

On the same day a formation of large four-engined German bombers caused quite a stir by flying low over Kiel. " Come ye in peace or come ye in war ? " The question was on every lip. However, the bombers landed peacefully enough—to discharge an astonishing load of passengers, partly G.A.F. and partly civilian. These were more refugees seeking deliverance from the fury of the Russians.

About 10th May ten German destroyers came in to surrender. Their upper decks were packed with fleeing humanity, each destroyer having over two hundred soldiers aboard besides her crew. They put in after dark, but the N.O.I.C. insisted that all aboard must be disembarked at once to obviate any risk of scuttling. The only available escort consisted of one squadron of the Reconnaissance Regiment and a party of Cameronians. These duly shepherded their flock, some four thousand strong, through the darkness to the P.O.W. camp three miles away.

Duties in Kiel were very heavy: the men of the 46th Brigade were getting only one night in three in bed. After the Brigade had been in occupation for about ten days, however, the C.C.R.A. was ordered to take over. Gunner regiments soon began to arrive, and these lightened the duties. It was not till early June, however, that the 46th Brigade was relieved of the last of its duties in Kiel. On the last Sunday in May, before they went, the Cameronians held their annual Conventicle. A year before they had held this Conventicle at Hove, in Sussex : it had been a full year.

So much for the 46th Brigade. Meanwhile the 44th Brigade had taken over Kreis Segeberg and the Divisional Artillery Kreis Stormarn, while the 227th Brigade had taken over Lubeck. Divisional Headquarters was in Ahrensburg. There were innumerable guards to be found on V.P.s, dumps, and P.O.W. camps, and everyone else who could be spared was out scouring the countryside for arms or visiting outlying villages to hold curfew checks. There was plenty to do. At the same time there were also amusements in plenty—sailing, boating, bathing, games of all sorts on excellent sports-grounds, E.N.S.A. shows and cinemas. And gradually order grew out of chaos.

On 9th June the Division (less the Divisional Artillery and the 227th Brigade, but with the 106th Anti-Aircraft Brigade under command) moved to the Russian frontier zone to relieve the 5th Division. The Divisional Artillery stopped in Lauenburg, the 227th Brigade in Lubeck. For the rest, the Division was now disposed as follows: Divisional Headquarters and the 44th Brigade in and around Schwerin; the 46th Brigade in and around Wismar; the 106th Brigade in and around Ludwigslust.

Here the Division found itself in clover. It was delightful country, the billets were good, the barracks were of the excellent German type. The weather could not have been better, and guard duties were now lighter. Strawberries were so plentiful that "Strawberry Points" were opened, to ensure that all got a fair share. There was good sailing and boating, and an excellent Opera in Schwerin. "A" Mess was suitably housed in the extremely comfortable palace of the Duke of Mecklenburg and Schwerin, on the shore of the Schwerin See.

At higher levels Scotsmen and Russians quickly made contact and exchanged hospitality. The Scotsmen took a little time to get acclimatised to vodka, but they noted with relief that the Russians went no less warily with the whisky. At lower levels, however, things were much stickier. One football match was brought off, in which a company team of the Royal Scots comfortably defeated a battalion team of the Russians, but there contacts pretty well ceased.

On 16th June Lieutenant-General Sir Miles Dempsey, Commander of the Second Army, paid his farewell visit to the Division. He inspected the 46th Brigade on Wismar airfield and the 44th Brigade in front of the Opera House in Schwerin, where there was a great turnout of the populace. After luncheon he visited the gunners at Molln and the 227th Brigade in Lubeck. The 10th H.L.I. provided a Guard of Honour at Lubeck airport when he left.

Towards the end of June there were rumours of an impending withdrawal behind the Yalta demarcation line. Sure enough, on the night of 29th June, orders reached Divisional Headquarters that the Division was to hand over to the Russians on 1st July and to get back behind the line, which here ran along the eastern border of Kreis Lubeck and Lauenburg. In this Operation "Comma," as it was called, about three Russian Divisions were to take over from the three Brigades of the 15th Scottish. The operation went off smoothly enough despite the fact that, in one instance, the Russian main bodies that marched in had no connection whatever with the reconnaissance parties which had preceded them. The populace, who had been warned of the impending bouleversement only on the previous afternoon, behaved with exemplary obedience and stoicism.

The exodus of the British forces was a remarkable sight. The procession of tank transporters bearing yachts and motor-boats had to be seen to be believed. The 44th Brigade went back to Kreis Segeberg, the 46th Brigade to Kreis Stormarn, Divisional Headquarters to Ahrensburg. Since these were to be final locations, all necessary steps were taken to ensure comfort. All parted with regret with their good friends of the 106th Anti-Aircraft Brigade, who now went off to Hamburg.

On 10th July Field-Marshal Montgomery honoured the Division with a visit and addressed all of its Brigades.

Many familiar faces now began to disappear under the release scheme. Those who had served longest with the Division and to whom it owed the most were the first to go. The Gordons were the first unit to leave; in August they left for the M.E.F., and were replaced later by the 6th Seaforth from the 5th Division. So general was the lawlessness at this time of the large number of D.P.s the Division had to look after, that guard duties tended to increase. For the rest, life was uneventful.

On 15th September the Division held its final Games in Lubeck. Everyone in the Rhine Army who had ever served in the Division seemed to be there. And there, too, and specially welcome, were Colonel Harry Clark, on tour from Home Forces, and Brigadier "Bosun" Hilton, over from Oslo. The 44th Brigade repeated their pre-D-Day performances and carried off the honours for the third time. Many wondered why Tossing the Caber did not figure in the programme—till it was whispered that the 1st Middlesex had won that event in one of the Brigade Championships.

In October, with the disbanding of the 190th Field Regiment and the 119th Light Anti-Aircraft Regiment, came the beginning of the end of a great Division. December saw the 131st and 181st Field Regiments go; in January the 6th K.O.S.B., the 10th H.L.I., and the 6th and 7th Seaforth followed.

Next it was the turn of the Headquarters of the 44th and 46th Brigades to disband. At the same time the 102nd Anti-Tank Regiment and the 1st Middlesex left to join the Guards Division, the 2nd Argylls to join the 51st Highland Division. By the end of March 1946 the remaining battalions, the 8th Royal Scots, the 6th R.S.F., the

9th Cameronians, and the 2nd Glasgow Highlanders were all in process of disbandment.

On 10th April 1946 the 15th Scottish Division, worthy reincarnation of its famous predecessor of the 1914-18 War, came to an end, after a life of seven years all but five months in this its second avatar. Those who served in it cherish none but the proudest memories—memories of a very happy family—memories of those great days of 1944-45 when the Red Lion Rampant in the pride of his strength stormed through North-West Europe in the van of our victorious armies from Normandy to the Elbe.

APPENDICES

APPENDIX A.

COMPILED FROM ARMY FORM W 5251—CASUALTIES OF UNITS BY BATTLES.

BATTLES.	ODON. 27th June to 2nd July 1944.						GAVRUS. 15th to 19th July 1944.					
	Officers.			Other Ranks.			Officers.			Other Ranks.		
	K.	W.	M.	K.	W.	M.	K.	W.	M.	K.	W.	M.
H.Q. 15th (S.) Inf. Div.												
H.Q. 15th (S.) Inf. Div., D. and E. Pl.											4	
H.Q. 44th (L.) Inf. Bde.											1	
H.Q. 44th (L.) Inf. Bde., D. and E. Pl.												
8th Royal Scots	2	9	1	33	197	70	2	5		17	121	7
6th R.S.F.	3	9	2	23	110	95		5		16	59	3
6th K.O.S.B.	3	5		17	100	41	1	5	1	11	110	2
44th (L.) Inf. Bde. L.A.D.												
H.Q. 46th (H.) Inf. Bde.		1			1							
H.Q. 46th (H.) Inf. Bde., D. and E. Pl.												
9th Cameronians	2	10	2	24	163	154		2		1	10	
2nd Glasgow Highlanders	3	8		15	130	68		5		12	80	17
7th Seaforth	3	7		40	235	26	2	1		8	4	
46th (H.) Inf. Bde. L.A.D.		1			1							
H.Q. 227th (H.) Inf. Bde.	1	1			1		1					
H.Q. 227th (H.) Inf. Bde., D. and E. Pl.												
10th H.L.I.	3	9	1	31	161	113	1	1	1	7	57	5
2nd Gordons	3	8	2	17	96	189	1	3			62	2
2nd A. and S. H.	1	12		28	176	28	1	2		4	58	15
227th Bde. L.A.D.												
H.Q. R.A.		1										
131st Field Regt.	1	3		2	12			1		4	19	
181st Field Regt.	1	1			3	1		1			15	
190th Field Regt.	1				5			1		1	2	
119th L.A.A. Regt.	1	1		4	5			1			3	
97th Anti-Tank Regt.		1		3	46					4	23	
102nd (N.H.) Anti-Tank Regt.												
H.Q. R.E.												
20th Field Coy.	1	1		1	19					2	12	
278th Field Coy.	1			10	18						2	
279th Field Coy.											14	
624th Field Park Coy.												
15th (S.) Recce. Regt.		1		1	7			1		3	12	
1st Middlesex	1	1		4	42			1		3	67	3
Signals					3			2	1		4	3
H.Q. R.A.S.C.												
62nd Coy. R.A.S.C. (Inf. Bde.)												
399th Coy. R.A.S.C. (Inf. Bde.)												
283rd Coy. R.A.S.C. (Inf. Bde.)												
284th Coy. R.A.S.C. (Div. Troops)												
193rd Field Ambulance					11							
194th Field Ambulance		1						1		1	18	
153rd Field Ambulance				4	3							
22nd F.D.S.						1						
23rd F.D.S.												
40th Field Hyg. Sec.												
H.Q. R.E.M.E.												
44th (L.) Inf. Bde. Workshops												
46th (H.) Inf. Bde. Workshops												
227th (H.) Inf. Bde. Workshops												
Provost Coy.					2					3	3	
Counter Mortar Staff												
39th F.S. Sec.												
TOTAL	31	91	8	257	1547	786	9	38	3	97	760	57

FIFTEENTH SCOTTISH DIVISION

BATTLES.	CAUMONT. 30th July to 5th Aug. 1944.						ESTREY. 6th to 10th Aug. 1944.					
	Officers.			Other Ranks.			Officers.			Other Ranks.		
	K.	W.	M.	K.	W.	M.	K.	W.	M.	K.	W.	M.
H.Q. 15th (S.) Inf. Div.		2			1							
H.Q. 15th (S.) Inf. Div., D. and E. Pl.												
H.Q. 44th (L.) Inf. Bde.												
H.Q. 44th (L.) Inf. Bde., D. and E. Pl.												
8th Royal Scots				1	2			1			9	
6th R.S.F.		2		8	26	3		3		14	63	31
6th K.O.S.B.	1	2		11	37	4	1	5	1	19	104	19
44th (L.) Inf. Bde. L.A.D.												
H.Q. 46th (H.) Inf. Bde.												
H.Q. 46th (H.) Inf. Bde., D. and E. Pl.												
9th Cameronians	1	2		12	46	16		5		12	67	25
2nd Glasgow Highlanders		6		9	32			6		11	65	5
7th Seaforth		5		4	36		1	4		7	52	18
46th (H.) Inf. Bde. L.A.D.												
H.Q. 227th (H.) Inf. Bde.												
H.Q. 227th (H.) Inf. Bde., D. and E. Pl.					1							
10th H.L.I.		2		6	52		1	7	1	9	124	6
2nd Gordons		2		10	84	9	1	6		11	102	21
2nd A. and S. H.		3		3	23		1	4		16	73	9
227th Bde. L.A.D.						2						
H.Q. R.A.												
131st Field Regt.					6						1	
181st Field Regt.		1			3						3	
190th Field Regt.		1			7						2	
119th L.A.A. Regt.		1		4	10							
97th Anti-Tank Regt.					16			1			11	1
102nd (N.H.) Anti-Tank Regt.												
H.Q. R.E.	1											
20th Field Coy.					6						2	
278th Field Coy.					1							
279th Field Coy.		1			2						1	
624th Field Park Coy.												
15th (S.) Recce. Regt.	1	1		3	24	2				3	11	2
1st Middlesex				3	24		1			6	27	2
Signals					5						1	
H.Q. R.A.S.C.												
62nd Coy. R.A.S.C. (Inf. Bde.)												
399th Coy. R.A.S.C. (Inf. Bde.)												
283rd Coy. R.A.S.C. (Inf. Bde.)												
284th Coy. R.A.S.C. (Div. Troops)					1						1	
193rd Field Ambulance			1	3	6	1						
194th Field Ambulance												1
153rd Field Ambulance										1	10	
22nd F.D.S.												
23rd F.D.S.												
40th Field Hyg. Sec.												
H.Q. R.E.M.E.												
44th (L.) Inf. Bde. Workshops												
46th (H.) Inf. Bde. Workshops												
227th (H.) Inf. Bde. Workshops												
Provost Coy.					1							
Counter Mortar Staff												
39th F.S. Sec.												
TOTAL	4	31	1	77	452	37	6	42	2	109	729	140

APPENDIX A

BATTLES.	RIVER SEINE. 27th to 28th Aug. 1944.						COUTRAI. 6th to 9th Sept. 1944.					
	Officers.			Other Ranks.			Officers.			Other Ranks.		
	K.	W.	M.	K.	W.	M.	K.	W.	M.	K.	W.	M.
H.Q. 15th (S.) Inf. Div.												
H.Q. 15th (S.) Inf. Div., D. and E. Pl.												
H.Q. 44th (L.) Inf. Bde.												
H.Q. 44th (L.) Inf. Bde., D. and E. Pl.												
8th Royal Scots												
6th R.S.F.		1		2	4	3				2	8	
6th K.O.S.B.												
44th (L.) Inf. Bde. L.A.D.												
H.Q. 46th (H.) Inf. Bde.												1
H.Q. 46th (H.) Inf. Bde., D. and E. Pl.												
9th Cameronians		1			2		1			13	25	
2nd Glasgow Highlanders										1	9	3
7th Seaforth								1		11	19	
46th (H.) Inf. Bde. L.A.D.												
H.Q. 227th (H.) Inf. Bde.												
H.Q. 227th (H.) Inf. Bde., D. and E. Pl.												
10th H.L.I.				1	15							
2nd Gordons	2	1	1	5	45	30						
2nd A. and S. H.		1		1	4							1
227th Bde. L.A.D.												
H.Q. R.A.												
131st Field Regt.												
181st Field Regt.												
190th Field Regt.												
119th L.A.A. Regt.												
97th Anti-Tank Regt.												
102nd (N.H.) Anti-Tank Regt.												
H.Q. R.E.												
20th Field Coy.		1		1	9	9						
278th Field Coy.	1				3							
279th Field Coy.					4							
624th Field Park Coy.												
15th (S.) Recce. Regt.					1			2		5	10	6
1st Middlesex					1							
Signals												
H.Q. R.A.S.C.												
62nd Coy. R.A.S.C. (Inf. Bde.)												
399th Coy. R.A.S.C. (Inf. Bde.)												
283rd Coy. R.A.S.C. (Inf. Bde.)												
284th Coy. R.A.S.C. (Div. Troops)												
193rd Field Ambulance												
194th Field Ambulance												
153rd Field Ambulance					1							
22nd F.D.S.												
23rd F.D.S.												
40th Field Hyg. Sec.												
H.Q. R.E.M.E.												
44th (L.) Inf. Bde. Workshops												
46th (H.) Inf. Bde. Workshops												
227th (H.) Inf. Bde. Workshops												
Provost Coy.												
Counter Mortar Staff												
39th F.S. Sec.												
TOTAL	3	5	1	10	89	42	1	3		32	71	11

FIFTEENTH SCOTTISH DIVISION

BATTLES.	GHEEL. 13th to 21st Sept. 1944.						BEST. 22nd Sept. to 2nd Oct. 1944.					
	Officers.			Other Ranks.			Officers.			Other Ranks.		
	K.	W.	M.	K.	W.	M.	K.	W.	M.	K.	W.	M.
H.Q. 15th (S.) Inf. Div.												
H.Q. 15th (S.) Inf. Div., D. and E. Pl.												
H.Q. 44th (L.) Inf. Bde.												
H.Q. 44th (L.) Inf. Bde., D. and E. Pl.												
8th Royal Scots	3	5	3	28	129	50	1	3		7	54	5
6th R.S.F.	2	4	1	16	100	49		1		5	13	
6th K.O.S.B.	3	5		10	102	46	1	3	1	19	78	64
44th (L.) Inf. Bde. L.A.D.												
H.Q. 46th (H.) Inf. Bde.												
H.Q. 46th (H.) Inf. Bde., D. and E. Pl.												
9th Cameronians		3		7	7		2	1		15	54	7
2nd Glasgow Highlanders		2		13	67	2		8	1	11	70	102
7th Seaforth	1				2			6	2	14	85	30
46th (H.) Inf. Bde. L.A.D.												
H.Q. 227th (H.) Inf. Bde.											1	
H.Q. 227th (H.) Inf. Bde., D. and E. Pl.												
10th H.L.I.		1		5	31			2		3	25	
2nd Gordons	1	3		7	49	1	2	4	1	25	54	63
2nd A. and S. H.	1	5		9	48		2	1		4	20	1
227th Bde. L.A.D.												
H.Q. R.A.												
131st Field Regt.		3			2					1	5	
181st Field Regt.		1		3	8	1					3	
190th Field Regt.					4		1				2	
119th L.A.A. Regt.										1	2	
97th Anti-Tank Regt.					3		1	1		2	6	
102nd (N.H.) Anti-Tank Regt.												
H.Q. R.E.		1										
20th Field Coy.		1			3							
278th Field Coy.		1			5							
279th Field Coy.				2	29						5	
624th Field Park Coy.												
15th (S.) Recce. Regt.					6	2				2	11	1
1st Middlesex		1		1	12			1			8	1
Signals						1				1	1	
H.Q. R.A.S.C.												
62nd Coy. R.A.S.C. (Inf. Bde.)												
399th Coy. R.A.S.C. (Inf. Bde.)												
283rd Coy. R.A.S.C. (Inf. Bde.)						1						
284th Coy. R.A.S.C. (Div. Troops)												
193rd Field Ambulance												
194th Field Ambulance		1										
153rd Field Ambulance						1						
22nd F.D.S.												
23rd F.D.S.												
40th Field Hyg. Sec.												
H.Q. R.E.M.E.												
44th (L.) Inf. Bde. Workshops												
46th (H.) Inf. Bde. Workshops												
227th (H.) Inf. Bde. Workshops												
Provost Coy.												
Counter Mortar Staff												
39th F.S. Sec.												
TOTAL	11	37	4	101	607	154	10	31	5	110	495	274

APPENDIX A

BATTLES.	TILBURG. 20th to 27th Oct. 1944.						MEIJEL. 29th Oct. to 15th Nov. 1944.					
	Officers.			Other Ranks.			Officers.			Other Ranks.		
	K.	W.	M.	K.	W.	M.	K.	W.	M.	K.	W.	M.
H.Q. 15th (S.) Inf. Div.											3	
H.Q. 15th (S.) Inf. Div., D. and E. Pl.								1			1	
H.Q. 44th (L.) Inf. Bde.												
H.Q. 44th (L.) Inf. Bde., D. and E. Pl.												
8th Royal Scots					2			6		11	74	5
6th R.S.F.		1		2	3			1		13	80	2
6th K.O.S.B.		1		2				5		16	113	4
44th (L.) Inf. Bde. L.A.D.												
H.Q. 46th (H.) Inf. Bde.												
H.Q. 46th (H.) Inf. Bde., D. and E. Pl.												
9th Cameronians	1	1		2	15	12	1	2		14	51	17
2nd Glasgow Highlanders	1	1			13	1		3		11	45	2
7th Seaforth	1	3		3	36		2	2		15	39	1
46th (H.) Inf. Bde. L.A.D.												
H.Q. 227th (H.) Inf. Bde.												
H.Q. 227th (H.) Inf. Bde., D. and E. Pl.												
10th H.L.I.				1	10			1		7	16	1
2nd Gordons				1			1	2		8	33	1
2nd A. and S. H.					3			1		4	32	12
227th Bde. L.A.D.												
H.Q. R.A.												
131st Field Regt.		1		2	5		1			1	1	
181st Field Regt.								1			3	
190th Field Regt.					1		1			1	4	
119th L.A.A. Regt.				2	2						1	
97th Anti-Tank Regt.		1		2	3					6	9	
102nd (N.H.) Anti-Tank Regt.												
H.Q. R.E.												
20th Field Coy.								1		2	8	
278th Field Coy.					4							
279th Field Coy.										4	7	
624th Field Park Coy.												
15th (S.) Recce. Regt.		1		2	17					3	8	3
1st Middlesex					2	2		1		2	19	
Signals								1			5	
H.Q. R.A.S.C.												
62nd Coy. R.A.S.C. (Inf. Bde.)												
399th Coy. R.A.S.C. (Inf. Bde.)												
283rd Coy. R.A.S.C. (Inf. Bde.)												
284th Coy. R.A.S.C. (Div. Troops)												
193rd Field Ambulance												
194th Field Ambulance												
153rd Field Ambulance												
22nd F.D.S.												
23rd F.D.S.												
40th Field Hyg. Sec.												
H.Q. R.E.M.E.										1	3	
44th (L.) Inf. Bde. Workshops												
46th (H.) Inf. Bde. Workshops												
227th (H.) Inf. Bde. Workshops										2		
Provost Coy.												
Counter Mortar Staff												
39th F.S. Sec.												
Total	3	10		19	116	15	6	28		121	555	48

FIFTEENTH SCOTTISH DIVISION

BATTLES.	BLERICK. 3rd to 4th Dec. 1944.						SIEGFRIED LINE. 8th to 25th Feb. 1945.					
	Officers.			Other Ranks.			Officers.			Other Ranks.		
	K.	W.	M.	K.	W.	M.	K.	W.	M.	K.	W.	M.
H.Q. 15th (S.) Inf. Div.										1	1	
H.Q. 15th (S.) Inf. Div., D. and E. Pl.												
H.Q. 44th (L.) Inf. Bde.											1	
H.Q. 44th (L.) Inf. Bde., D. and E. Pl.											1	
8th Royal Scots		3		5	23	3		2		17	105	24
6th R.S.F.				1	7	4	1	6		8	69	23
6th K.O.S.B.		1		5	2	3	3	6		14	110	2
44th (L.) Inf. Bde. L.A.D.												
H.Q. 46th (H.) Inf. Bde.												
H.Q. 46th (H.) Inf. Bde., D. and E. Pl.												
9th Cameronians	1			1	5	2		6		35	117	51
2nd Glasgow Highlanders		1		2	8			5		19	135	50
7th Seaforth	1			4	7		4	6		44	129	19
46th (H.) Inf. Bde. L.A.D.												
H.Q. 227th (H.) Inf. Bde.												
H.Q. 227th (H.) Inf. Bde., D. and E. Pl.												
10th H.L.I.							1	4	1	29	88	20
2nd Gordons							2	5		16	87	6
2nd A. and S. H.							1	6		14	116	19
227th Bde. L.A.D.												
H.Q. R.A.												
131st Field Regt.										5	8	
181st Field Regt.					4					1	5	
190th Field Regt.							1					
119th L.A.A. Regt.	1				8					1	1	
97th Anti-Tank Regt.												
102nd (N.H.) Anti-Tank Regt.												
H.Q. R.E.												
20th Field Coy.					1			1			1	
278th Field Coy.					1						1	
279th Field Coy.		1			6						2	
624th Field Park Coy.												
15th (S.) Recce. Regt.		1			1			1		3	17	
1st Middlesex				1	4		3			6	23	
Signals										1	7	
H.Q. R.A.S.C.												
62nd Coy. R.A.S.C. (Inf. Bde.)												
399th Coy. R.A.S.C. (Inf. Bde.)												
283rd Coy. R.A.S.C. (Inf. Bde.)												
284th Coy. R.A.S.C. (Div. Troops)												
193rd Field Ambulance											1	
194th Field Ambulance					1						1	
153rd Field Ambulance												
22nd F.D.S.												
23rd F.D.S.												
40th Field Hyg. Sec.												
H.Q. R.E.M.E.												
44th (L.) Inf. Bde. Workshops												
46th (H.) Inf. Bde. Workshops												
227th (H.) Inf. Bde. Workshops												
Provost Coy.								1				
Counter Mortar Staff											1	
39th F.S. Sec.												
TOTAL	3	7		19	78	12	16	51	1	216	1031	214

APPENDIX A

BATTLES.	RIVER RHINE. 24th to 30th Mar. 1945.						ADVANCE TO RIVER ELBE. 9th to 24th April 1945.					
	Officers.			Other Ranks.			Officers.			Other Ranks.		
	K.	W.	M.	K.	W.	M.	K.	W.	M.	K.	W.	M.
H.Q. 15th (S.) Inf. Div.												
H.Q. 15th (S.) Inf. Div., D. and E. Pl.												
H.Q. 44th (L.) Inf. Bde.												
H.Q. 44th (L.) Inf. Bde., D. and E. Pl.												
8th Royal Scots	1	5		14	67	17				1	8	
6th R.S.F.		3		12	69	3		1		2	8	
6th K.O.S.B.	1	1		16	83	21		1		1	15	6
44th (L.) Inf. Bde. L.A.D.												
H.Q. 46th (H.) Inf. Bde.												
H.Q. 46th (H.) Inf. Bde., D. and E. Pl.												
9th Cameronians	1	4	1	13	69	18	1	5		3	15	4
2nd Glasgow Highlanders	1			5	48	6	3	3		6	34	22
7th Seaforth	2	4		13	71	23		3		2	26	
46th (H.) Inf. Bde. L.A.D.												
H.Q. 227th (H.) Inf. Bde.												
H.Q. 227th (H.) Inf. Bde., D. and E. Pl.												
10th H.L.I.	3	4		12	72	2		3	1	15	80	32
2nd Gordons	2	7		7	42	3		1		5	32	16
2nd A. and S. H.	1	2		18	65	16				1	11	1
227th Bde. L.A.D.												
H.Q. R.A.												
131st Field Regt.	1			3	4			1		1	15	4
181st Field Regt.		2		2	1	1				1	3	
190th Field Regt.					6					1	4	
119th L.A.A. Regt.												
97th Anti-Tank Regt.												
102nd (N.H.) Anti-Tank Regt.				1	6						4	1
H.Q. R.E.												
20th Field Coy.		1			3						15	
278th Field Coy.										2	4	9
279th Field Coy.		1										
624th Field Park Coy.												
15th (S.) Recce. Regt.				2	2	3	1	6	1	8	33	50
1st Middlesex		1		2	16						8	
Signals											1	
H.Q. R.A.S.C.												
62nd Coy. R.A.S.C. (Inf. Bde.)												
399th Coy. R.A.S.C. (Inf. Bde.)												
283rd Coy. R.A.S.C. (Inf. Bde.)												
284th Coy. R.A.S.C. (Div. Troops)												
193rd Field Ambulance												
194th Field Ambulance												
153rd Field Ambulance												
22nd F.D.S.												
23rd F.D.S.												
40th Field Hyg. Sec.												
H.Q. R.E.M.E.												
44th (L.) Inf. Bde. Workshops												
46th (H.) Inf. Bde. Workshops												
227th (H.) Inf. Bde. Workshops											2	
Provost Coy.				2	6							
Counter Mortar Staff												
39th F.S. Sec.												
Total	13	35	1	122	630	113	5	24	2	49	318	145

354 THE FIFTEENTH SCOTTISH DIVISION

BATTLES.	RIVER ELBE. 29th April to 6th May 1945.					
	Officers.			Other Ranks.		
	K.	W.	M.	K.	W.	M.
H.Q. 15th (S.) Inf. Div.						
H.Q. 15th (S.) Inf. Div., D. and E. Pl.						
H.Q. 44th (L.) Inf. Bde.						
H.Q. 44th (L.) Inf. Bde., D. and E. Pl.						
8th Royal Scots	2			4	28	7
6th R.S.F.				3	15	1
6th K.O.S.B.				2	4	
44th (L.) Inf. Bde. L.A.D.						
H.Q. 46th (H.) Inf. Bde.						
H.Q. 46th (H.) Inf. Bde., D. and E. Pl.						
9th Cameronians		4		12	24	
2nd Glasgow Highlanders				6	18	1
7th Seaforth		2		7	23	
46th (H.) Inf. Bde. L.A.D.						
H.Q. 227th (H.) Inf. Bde.						
H.Q. 227th (H.) Inf. Bde., D. and E. Pl.						
10th H.L.I.		1		5	13	4
2nd Gordons				6	28	1
2nd A. and S. H.	1			9	59	3
227th Bde. L.A.D.						
H.Q. R.A.						
131st Field Regt.		1			1	
181st Field Regt.		1			4	
190th Field Regt.						
119th L.A.A. Regt.						
97th Anti-Tank Regt.						
102nd (N.H.) Anti-Tank Regt.						
H.Q. R.E.		1				
20th Field Coy.					12	
278th Field Coy.						
279th Field Coy.						
624th Field Park Coy.						
15th (S.) Recce. Regt.		1			4	
1st Middlesex					2	
Signals					1	
H.Q. R.A.S.C.						
62nd Coy. R.A.S.C. (Inf. Bde.)						
399th Coy. R.A.S.C. (Inf. Bde.)				1		
283rd Coy. R.A.S.C. (Inf. Bde.)						
284th Coy. R.A.S.C. (Div. Troops)				1		
193rd Field Ambulance						
194th Field Ambulance						
153rd Field Ambulance						
22nd F.D.S.						
23rd F.D.S.						
40th Field Hyg. Sec.						
H.Q. R.E.M.E.						
44th (L.) Inf. Bde. Workshops						
46th (H.) Inf. Bde. Workshops						
227th (H.) Inf. Bde. Workshops						
Provost Coy.						
Counter Mortar Staff					2	
39th F.S. Sec.						
TOTAL	3	11		56	238	17

GRAND TOTAL:—

	K.	W.	M.
Officers	124	444	28
Other Ranks	1395	7716	2065
	1519	8160	2093 = 11,772

APPENDIX B.

COMMANDERS, FIFTEENTH SCOTTISH DIVISION
As at Assuming Command.

Major-General R. Le Fanu, D.S.O., M.C.	28th Aug. 1939 to 22nd Aug. 1940
Major-General R. C. Money, M.C.	23rd Aug. 1940 to 31st Jan. 1941
Major-General Sir Oliver W. H. Leese, Bt., C.B.E., D.S.O.	1st Feb. 1941 to 16th June 1941
Major-General A. F. P. Christison, M.C.	17th June 1941 to 13th May 1942
Major-General D. C. Bullen-Smith, M.C.	14th May 1942 to 26th Aug. 1943
Major-General G. H. A. MacMillan, C.B.E., D.S.O., M.C.	27th Aug. 1943 to 2nd Aug. 1944
Major-General C. M. Barber, D.S.O.	3rd Aug. 1944 to disbandment

G.S.O.s 1, FIFTEENTH SCOTTISH DIVISION
As on Assuming Appointment.

Brigadier H. M. Dendy, D.S.O., M.C.	14th Sept. 1939 to 5th July 1940
Lieutenant-Colonel M. B. Dowse (R.W.F.)	6th July 1940 to 11th Jan. 1941
Lieutenant-Colonel G. R. Bradshaw (R.A.)	12th Jan. 1941 to 22nd May 1941
Lieutenant-Colonel E. L. Bols (King's)	23rd May 1941 to 14th Feb. 1942
Lieutenant-Colonel D. H. Haugh, M.C. (Seaforth)	15th Feb. 1942 to 12th Dec. 1942
Lieutenant-Colonel E. B. Smith, M.C. (R.A.)	13th Dec. 1942 to 25th May 1943
Lieutenant-Colonel J. N. D. Tyler, M.C. (R.A.)	26th May 1943 to 14th Jan. 1945
Lieutenant-Colonel J. M. Hailey, D.S.O. (R.A.)	15th Jan. 1945 to 18th April 1945
Lieutenant-Colonel W. A. Stevenson, D.S.O. (Camerons)	19th April 1945 to 7th Nov. 1945

A.A. AND Q.M.G.s, FIFTEENTH SCOTTISH DIVISION
As on Assuming Appointment.

Colonel H. F. Grant-Suttie, D.S.O., M.C.	14th Sept. 1939 to 10th Feb. 1940
Lieutenant-Colonel E. T. L. Gurdon, M.C. (Black Watch)	11th Feb. 1940 to 28th June 1940
Lieutenant-Colonel J. D. Milne (Royal Scots)	29th June 1940 to 13th Mar. 1941
Lieutenant-Colonel J. G. Nicholson (Buffs)	14th Mar. 1941 to 5th Mar. 1942
Lieutenant-Colonel T. G. Robinson (Glasgow Highlanders)	6th Mar. 1942 to 6th Aug. 1942
Lieutenant-Colonel H. C. L. Kingsford-Lethbridge (R.F.)	7th Aug. 1942 to 3rd Feb. 1945
Lieutenant-Colonel A. M. Man (Middlesex)	4th Feb. 1945 to 14th Dec. 1945

LIST OF COMMANDERS
As on Assuming Appointment.

(* Denotes in Command on D Day.)

R.A.C.
    15th Scottish Reconnaissance Regiment.
        Lieutenant-Colonel J. A. Grant-Peterkin.*
        Lieutenant-Colonel K. C. C. Smith.

C.R.A.
    Brigadier J. Scott.
    Brigadier C. T. Beckett, M.C.
    Brigadier R. Hilton, D.F.C., M.C.*
    Brigadier L. Bolton, D.S.O.

    131st Field Regiment.
        Lieutenant-Colonel R. A. P. R. Kidston, T.D.
        Lieutenant-Colonel J. M. Hailey.*
        Lieutenant-Colonel J. N. D. Tyler, O.B.E., M.C.

    181st Field Regiment.
        Lieutenant-Colonel E. O. Herbert, D.S.O.
        Lieutenant-Colonel A. C. E. Devereux.*
        Lieutenant-Colonel R. B. W. Bethell.
        Lieutenant-Colonel T. P. Keene.

    190th Field Regiment.
        Lieutenant-Colonel R. J. Streatfield.*

    119th L.A.A. Regiment.
        Lieutenant-Colonel J. F. Young.*

    97th Anti-Tank Regiment.
        Lieutenant-Colonel J. N. D. Tyler, M.C.
        Lieutenant-Colonel P. L. Graham, M.C.
        Lieutenant-Colonel K. L. Beddington.*
        Lieutenant-Colonel P. R. Henderson.

    102nd (N.H.) Anti-Tank Regiment.
        Lieutenant-Colonel R. W. Jelf, O.B.E.

Royal Engineers.
    C.R.E.
        Lieutenant-Colonel J. F. Gibson, M.C., T.D.
        Lieutenant-Colonel M. R. Caldwell.
        Lieutenant-Colonel R. K. Millar.*

Royal Signals.
    Lieutenant-Colonel V. D. Warren, M.B.E., T.D.
    Lieutenant-Colonel F. C. Seeley.*

H.Q. 44th Lowland Infantry Brigade.
    Brigadier B. C. Lake.
    Brigadier J. A. Campbell, D.S.O.
    Brigadier H. D. K. Money, D.S.O.*
    Brigadier J. C. Cockburn, M.B.E.
    Brigadier The Hon. H. C. H. T. Cumming-Bruce, D.S.O.

8th Battalion The Royal Scots.
    Lieutenant-Colonel J. E. M. Richard, T.D., O.B.E.
    Lieutenant-Colonel D. R. G. Cameron, M.B.E.
    Lieutenant-Colonel R. Delacombe, M.B.E.*
    Lieutenant-Colonel P. R. Lane Joynt.
    Lieutenant-Colonel B. A. Pearson.

6th Battalion The Royal Scots Fusiliers.
    Lieutenant-Colonel The Lord Rowallan, M.C.
    Lieutenant-Colonel N. Macleod.
    Lieutenant-Colonel C. R. Buchanan.*
    Lieutenant-Colonel I. Mackenzie.

6th Battalion The King's Own Scottish Borderers.
    Lieutenant-Colonel The Lord Napier and Ettrick, M.C.
    Lieutenant-Colonel J. G. Shillington.*
    Lieutenant-Colonel C. W. P. Richardson.

H.Q. 46th Highland Infantry Brigade.
    Brigadier H. J. D. Clark, M.C.
    Brigadier C. M. Barber, D.S.O.*
    Brigadier R. M. Villiers.

9th Battalion Cameronians (Scottish Rifles).
    Lieutenant-Colonel R. I. F. Gordon.
    Lieutenant-Colonel H. D. K. Money, D.S.O.
    Lieutenant-Colonel H. H. Storey, M.C.
    Lieutenant-Colonel R. M. Villiers.*
    Lieutenant-Colonel Sir Edward M. A. Bradford.
    Lieutenant-Colonel E. Remington Hobbs.

2nd Battalion Glasgow Highlanders.
    Lieutenant-Colonel T. G. Robinson.
    Lieutenant-Colonel G. Laird.
    Lieutenant-Colonel P. U. Campbell.*
    Lieutenant-Colonel H. C. Baker-Baker, D.S.O., M.B.E.

APPENDIX B

7th Battalion Seaforth Highlanders.
  Lieutenant-Colonel G. Borthwick.
  Lieutenant-Colonel D. H. Haugh, M.C.
  Lieutenant-Colonel E. H. G. Grant, M.C.*
  Lieutenant-Colonel D. Robertson.
  Lieutenant-Colonel P. M. Hunt.

H.Q. 227th Highland Infantry Brigade.
  Brigadier J. R. Mackintosh-Walker, M.C.*
  Brigadier E. C. Colville.

10th Battalion Highland Light Infantry.
  Lieutenant-Colonel L. Morrison, T.D.
  Lieutenant-Colonel F. A. Hawkins, M.C.
  Lieutenant-Colonel T. W. Hamilton.
  Lieutenant-Colonel R. G. Collingwood.
  Lieutenant-Colonel J. D. S. Young, D.S.O., M.C.*
  Lieutenant-Colonel D. R. Morgan.
  Lieutenant-Colonel H. P. Mackley, O.B.E.
  Lieutenant-Colonel R. A. Bramwell-Davis.

2nd Battalion Gordon Highlanders.
  Lieutenant-Colonel E. C. Colville.*
  Lieutenant-Colonel J. R. Sinclair.
  Lieutenant-Colonel R. W. de Winton, D.S.O.

2nd Battalion Argyll and Sutherland Highlanders.
  Lieutenant-Colonel J. W. Tweedie.*
  Lieutenant-Colonel D. R. Morgan, M.C.

1st Battalion The Middlesex Regiment Divisional Machine Gun Battalion.
  Lieutenant-Colonel J. P. Hall.*
  Lieutenant-Colonel A. N. W. Kidston.

6th Guards Tank Brigade.
  Brigade Command.
  Brigadier G. L. Verney, M.V.O.*

4th Tank Grenadier Guards.
  Lieutenant-Colonel H. R. H. Davies.*

4th Tank Coldstream Guards.
  Lieutenant-Colonel N. W. Gwatkin, M.V.O.

3rd Tank Scots Guards.
  Lieutenant-Colonel The Hon. H. K. M. Kindersley, M.C.

SERVICES.

Chaplains.
  Rev. G. Kerr M'Kay, T.D., M.A.
  Rev. A. M. M'Pherson, M.B.E.
  Rev. J. A. Williamson.
  Rev. W. M. Maxwell, D.D.*
  Rev. A. W. Sawyer, M.C.

R.A.S.C.
  Lieutenant-Colonel E. Doolan, M.C.
  Lieutenant-Colonel G. A. Bond.
  Lieutenant-Colonel C. J. Midmer.
  Lieutenant-Colonel M. G. Hallowes.
  Lieutenant-Colonel B. L. Percival.
  Lieutenant-Colonel K. M. Whitworth.*

Medical.
  Colonel J. Gibson, D.S.O.
  Colonel R. Murphy.
  Colonel J. C. M'Grath, M.C.
  Colonel D. L. Kerr.*
  Colonel F. M. Richardson, D.S.O.

193rd Field Ambulance.
  Major A. Bingham.
  Lieutenant-Colonel J. A. Crawford.
  Lieutenant-Colonel F. W. A. Warren, T.D.*

194th Field Ambulance.
  Lieutenant-Colonel B. B. Macfarlane.*
  Lieutenant-Colonel W. M. Oxley.

153rd Field Ambulance.
  Lieutenant-Colonel D. Campbell.*
  Lieutenant-Colonel W. A. M. Scott.
  Lieutenant-Colonel C. B. R. Pollock.

22nd Field Dressing Station.
  Major A. M. George, M.C.*

23rd Field Dressing Station.
  Major I. B. Rees Roberts.*

40th Field Hygienic Section.
  Major P. J. H. Clarke.*
  Major D. S. Buchanan.

R.A.O.C.
  Lieutenant-Colonel F. W. S. Walker, O.B.E.*

R.E.M.E.
  Lieutenant-Colonel S. J. Cox.
  Lieutenant-Colonel R. H. H. Gardiner.*

A.P.M.s.
  Captain Stewart.
  Captain M. Bell.
  Captain U. J. Breese.
  Captain R. Digby Clarke.
  Major J. E. Smart.
  Major M. C. Chittock.*
  Major A. B. Cooper.

UNITS WHICH SERVED PART TIME ONLY IN FIFTEENTH DIVISION BEFORE D DAY.

H.Q., 45th Infantry Brigade.
    Brigadier D. S. Davidson, D.S.O., M.C.
    Brigadier J. D. Russell, D.S.O., M.C.

R.A.
    129th Field Regiment.
        Lieutenant-Colonel A. S. Hardie.
        Lieutenant-Colonel A. N. Skinner, M.V.O.
        Lieutenant-Colonel J. H. de Robeck, M.B.E.

    130th Field Regiment.
        Lieutenant-Colonel H. Mathie, M.C., T.D.
        Lieutenant-Colonel A. N. Skinner, M.V.O.
        Lieutenant-Colonel S. Simmons.
        Lieutenant-Colonel R. G. Price.

R.E.
    280th Field Company.
        Major S. Reilly.
        Major K. W. Hancock.
        Major S. R. C. Shaw.

    281st Field Company.
        Captain M. H. Beard.
        Captain J. W. Robinson.
        Major T. L. Coffin.

Infantry.
    4th Northumberland Fusiliers.
        Lieutenant-Colonel E. H. D. Grimley.

    7th K.O.S.B.
        Lieutenant-Colonel The Earl of Galloway.
        Lieutenant-Colonel L. F. Machin, M.C.

    10th Cameronians.
        Lieutenant-Colonel D. G. Moncrieffe-Wright, M.C.
        Lieutenant-Colonel E. K. G. Sixsmith.

    10th Black Watch.
        Lieutenant-Colonel H. K. Purvis-Russell-Montgomery, O.B.E.

    11th H.L.I.
        Lieutenant-Colonel H. K. de R. Channer.

    4th Cameron Highlanders.
        Lieutenant-Colonel I. E. Begg, M.B.E.

    7th Cameron Highlanders.
        Lieutenant-Colonel R. P. Haig.

    11th Argyll and Sutherland Highlanders.
        Lieutenant-Colonel E. L. P. Slaytor.

APPENDIX C.

FIFTEENTH SCOTTISH INFANTRY DIVISION ORDER OF BATTLE.

SEPTEMBER 1939–OCTOBER 1941.

H.Q. 15th Scottish Infantry Division.
  H.Q. 44th Lowland Infantry Brigade.
    8th Royal Scots.
    6th K.O.S.B.
    7th K.O.S.B.
  H.Q. 45th Lowland Infantry Brigade.
    6th R.S.F.
    9th Cameronians.
    10th Cameronians.
  H.Q. 46th Highland Infantry Brigade.
    10th H.L.I.
    11th H.L.I.
    2nd Glasgow Highlanders.
  Machine Gun Battalion.
    1/7th Middlesex.
  R.A.
    129th Field Regiment.
    130th Field Regiment.
    131st Field Regiment.
    64th Anti-Tank Regiment.

R.E.
  278th Field Company.
  279th Field Company.
  280th Field Company.
  281st Field Park Company.

Signals.
  15th Scottish Division Signals.

R.A.S.C.
  282nd Company.
  283rd Company.
  284th Company.

R.A.M.C.
  193rd Field Ambulance.
  194th Field Ambulance.
  195th Field Ambulance.
  40th Field Hygienic Section.

NOTE.

Whilst in Suffolk in 1940-41, 37th Independent Infantry Brigade were under command. 6th R.S.F. left the Division in December 1939 for Northern Command. They later proceeded to B.E.F. and fought with 51st Highland Division, being evacuated via Cherbourg.

DECEMBER 1941.

H.Q. 15th Scottish Infantry Division.
  H.Q. 44th Lowland Infantry Brigade.
    8th Royal Scots.
    6th K.O.S.B.
    7th K.O.S.B.
  H.Q. 45th Lowland Infantry Brigade.
    6th R.S.F.
    9th Cameronians.
    10th Cameronians.
  H.Q. 46th Highland Infantry Brigade.
    2nd Glasgow Highlanders.
    7th Seaforth Highlanders.
    7th Cameron Highlanders.
  Reconnaissance.
    One Independent Squadron.

R.A.
  129th Field Regiment.
  131st Field Regiment.
  64th Anti-Tank Regiment.

R.E.
  278th Field Company.
  279th Field Company.

Signals.
  15th Scottish Division Signals.

R.A.S.C.
  283rd Company.
  284th Company.

R.A.M.C.
  193rd Field Ambulance.
  194th Field Ambulance.

NOTES ON CHANGES.

Infantry.
    6th R.S.F. rejoined the Division after Dunkirk.
    10th H.L.I. left November 1941 for Shetlands.
    11th H.L.I. left November 1941 for conversion to R.A.C.
    7th Seaforth Highlanders arrived from Shetland.
    7th Cameron Highlanders arrived from Wick.

M.G.
    1/7th Middlesex moved to 51st Highland Infantry Division.

R.A.
    130th Field Regiment left for India, October 1941.

R.E.
    280th Field Company and 281st Field Park Company left November 1941.

R.A.S.C.
    282nd Company left October 1941.

R.A.M.C.
    195th Field Ambulance left November 1941.

JANUARY 1943.

H.Q. 15th Scottish Infantry Division.
  H.Q. 6th Guards Tank Brigade.
    4th Grenadier Guards.
    4th Coldstream Guards.
    3rd Scots Guards.

  H.Q. 44th Lowland Infantry Brigade.
    8th Royal Scots.
    6th R.S.F.
    6th K.O.S.B.

  H.Q. 46th Highland Infantry Brigade.
    9th Cameronians.
    2nd Glasgow Highlanders.
    7th Seaforth Highlanders.

Reconnaissance.
  One Independent Squadron.

Support Battalion.
  4th Northumberland Fusiliers.

R.A.
  131st Field Regiment.
  97th Anti-Tank Regiment.

R.E.
  278th Field Company.
  279th Field Company.

Signals.
  15th Scottish Division Signals.

R.A.S.C.
  283rd Company.
  284th Company.

R.A.M.C.
  193rd Field Ambulance.
  194th Field Ambulance.

NOTES.

There were many changes during 1942 owing to redistribution of units and the impending conversion to a mixed Division.

  Infantry.
    44th Brigade.
      7th K.O.S.B. left in November 1942 for Airborne Forces and were replaced by 6th R.S.F.

APPENDIX C

45th Brigade.

Sent 6th R.S.F. to 44th Brigade and 9th Cameronians to 46th Brigade. 45th Brigade Headquarters, with 10th Cameronians, 10th Black Watch from 46th Brigade and 11th Argyll and Sutherland Highlanders (who replaced 7th K.O.S.B.), left for 80th Reserve Division.

46th Brigade.

7th Camerons were converted to 5th Scottish Parachute Regiment in March 1942 and were replaced by 4th Cameron Highlanders *ex* West Indies. 4th Camerons left in October 1942 for Shetland and were replaced by 10th Black Watch, who shortly afterwards joined 45th Infantry Brigade and were replaced by 9th Cameronians.

R.A.

129th Field Regiment left for India in June 1942. 64th Anti-Tank Regiment left in August 1942 and were replaced by 97th Anti-Tank Regiment.

26TH JUNE 1944.

H.Q. 15th Scottish Infantry Division.

H.Q. 44th Lowland Infantry Brigade.
  8th Royal Scots.
  6th R.S.F.
  6th K.O.S.B.

H.Q. 46th Highland Infantry Brigade.
  9th Cameronians.
  2nd Glasgow Highlanders.
  7th Seaforth Highlanders.

H.Q. 227th Highland Infantry Brigade.
  10th H.L.I.
  2nd Gordon Highlanders.
  2nd Argyll and Sutherland Highlanders.

Reconnaissance.
  15th Scottish Reconnaissance Regiment.

Machine Gun Battalion.
  1st Middlesex.

R.A.
  131st Field Regiment.
  181st Field Regiment.
  190th Field Regiment.
  97th Anti-Tank Regiment.
  119th L.A.A. Regiment.

R.E.
  20th Field Company.
  278th Field Company.
  279th Field Company.
  624th Field Park Company.

Signals.
  15th Scottish Division Signals.

R.A.S.C.
  62nd Company.
  283rd Company.
  284th Company.
  399th Company.

R.A.M.C.
  153rd Field Ambulance.
  193rd Field Ambulance.
  194th Field Ambulance.
  40th Field Hygienic Section.
  22nd Field Dressing Station.
  23rd Field Dressing Station.

Ordnance.
  15th Ordnance Field Park.
  305th M.L. and B.U.

R.E.M.E.
  44th Lowland Infantry Brigade Workshops.
  46th Highland Infantry Brigade Workshops.
  227th Highland Infantry Brigade Workshops.
  15th Infantry Troops Workshops.

Pro.
  15th Scottish Division Provost Coy. R.C.M.P.

F.S.
  39th F.S. Section.

NOTES.

In May 1943 the Division was mobilised as an Infantry Division, and in place of 6th Guards Tank Brigade received in July 227th Highland Infantry Brigade. The Independent Reconnaissance Squadron was expanded into 15th Scottish Reconnaissance Regiment.

M.G.

    4th Northumberland Fusiliers left Division in September 1943 and were replaced by 1st Middlesex.

R.A.

    181st Field Regiment joined July 1943.
    190th Field Regiment joined May 1943.

R.E.

    20th Field Company joined July 1943.
    624th Field Park Company joined January 1943.

R.A.S.C.

    62nd Company joined July 1943.
    399th Company joined July 1943.

R.A.M.C.

    153rd Field Ambulance joined July 1943.
    20th and 22nd F.D.S. joined August 1943.

Ordnance.

    These units joined July 1943.

R.E.M.E.

    Formed and joined July/August 1943.

F.S.

    39th F.S. Section joined July 1943.

This Order of Battle survived the period of operations except—

    (i) 97th Anti-Tank Regiment were disbanded November 1944 and replaced by 102nd (Northumberland Hussars) Anti-Tank Regiment *ex* 50th Division.

    (ii) 22nd F.D.S. transferred to 8th Corps Troops, March 1945.

APPENDIX D.

SOME STATISTICS.

R.E.

(a) Numbers of Bridges built.

278th Field Company R.E.	23
279th Field Company R.E.	19
20th Field Company R.E.	20
624th Field Park Company R.E.	1
Total	63

(b) Longest Bridge built.

278th Field Company R.E.—170-ft. Bailey, consisting of 130 ft. double-single on Bailey piers with 20 ft. single-single at each end. Constructed over the Wilhelmina Canal, near Best, on 27th September 1944.

279th Field Company R.E.—380-ft. floating Bailey, consisting of 2 × 110 ft. triple-single landing-bays, 2 × 40 ft. double-single-end floating-bays, and 2 × 40 ft. double-single floating-bays. Constructed over the River Weser at Schlusselburg, between Minden and Nienburg, in 14 hours on 8th April 1945.

20th Field Company R.E.—314-ft. Bailey, consisting of 180 ft. triple-double on 2 × 40 ft. Bailey piers with 67 ft. triple-single approach spans at either end. Constructed over canal between Weert and Roermond in January 1945 (known as "Red Lion" Bridge).

624th Field Park Company R.E.—110-ft. Bailey, triple-single. Constructed at Oirschot, near Tilburg, Holland, in November 1944. This is probably one of the few instances of a Division Field Park Company having constructed a tactical bridge during operations.

(c) Quickest Time.

278th Field Company R.E.—60-ft. double-single Bailey was constructed in 2½ hours in the Horst area, Holland, on 25th November 1944.

279th Field Company R.E.—60-ft. double-single Bailey was constructed in 1 hour 50 minutes at Hammilkeln, near Bocholt, Germany, on 27th March 1945.

20th Field Company R.E.—70-ft. double-single Bailey was constructed in 1¾ hours over crater during advance from Celle to Uelzen in April 1945.

(d) Other notes.

The first major bridge to be built by the Division R.E. during the campaign was built by 279th Field Company R.E. on 15th August 1944. This was a 200-ft. folding-boat bridge built in 11¼ hours over the River Orne, France.

Royal Signals.

(a) General Note *re* Traffic.

On an average day approximately 250 messages would be handled in t Divisional Headquarters Signal Office, but this figure was considerabl increased during operations. Peak traffic under operation conditio reached 800 to 900 messages of all types, and in periods before maj attacks when wireless silence was in force, D.R. Section would themselv clear 400 messages in a day. In battle, clearance of traffic by line w often extremely difficult, and messages would be cleared by wireless a D.R., the latter providing a vital source of information to the Sign master by keeping him briefed with the latest information regardi moves, new locations, and route conditions.

(b) During the North-West Europe campaign some 7800 miles of Signal cal were laid in the Division—4000 miles by Royal Signals linesmen and 38 miles by regimental signallers in battalions and regiments.

(c) Miscellaneous Information.

Replacement wireless sets were issued in large numbers, and in all 823 se of all types were replaced in the Division.

R.A.S.C.

Total number of miles run 5,781,20

Loads carried.

(a) Ammunition.

(i) No record of tonnages of small-arms ammunition was maintained.

(ii) 25-pounder.

Number of rounds handled 825,6
Tonnage 12,3
Equivalent 3-ton loads 4,1

(b) Petrol (from June 1944 to 11th May 1945).

Gallons issued 3,500,0
Equivalent tons 17,5
Equivalent 3-ton loads 5,8

(c) Supplies.

Rations issued during period of operations . . . 8,050,0
Equivalent tonnage 7,18
Equivalent 3-ton loads 2,3

R.E.M.E.

	Vehicles recovered.	Vehicles repaired.
L.A.D.s	5500	8800
Workshops	450	4260

APPENDIX E.

HONOURS AND AWARDS.

C.B.	2
C.B.E.	1
Bar to D.S.O.	10
D.S.O.	31
O.B.E.	8
M.B.E.	28
Bar to M.C.	3
M.C.	141
D.C.M.	21
Bar to M.M.	1
M.M.	212
B.E.M.	12
French Croix de Guerre	41
U.S. D.S.C.	1
U.S. Silver Star	1
U.S. Bronze Star	3
Belgian Decorations	32
Mentions in Despatches	554
Commander-in-Chief's Certificates	288

INDEX

N.B.—French names of places beginning with Le, La, or Les are entered under the initial letter of the second word. Thus for Le Havre, see under Havre, Le.

Aa, River, 176.
Aart, 131, 134-6, 138, 140-7, 148, 149, 150, 159.
Abbeville, 119.
Acht, 157.
Achterbosch, 145.
Achterste Hees, 210, 211.
Achterste Steeg, 208, 210.
Adjutant General's Branch, the, 24.
Ahrensburg, 337, 338, 340, 342.
Alamein, El, 229.
Albert Canal, the, 124, 125, 127, 129, 130, 131, 140, 146.
Alencon, 58, 102.
Aller, River, 309, 310, 313.
Altencelle, 309.
Alter Rhine, the, 243, 277.
Amaye-sur-Orne, 106.
Amerika, 192, 208, 211, 212.
Amiens, 113, 119.
Andé, 115, 116.
Andelys, Les, 109, 117.
Antwerp, 111, 120, 121, 125, 127, 128, 172, 173.
Arclais, 93-4, 95.
Ardennes, the, 279.
Argentan, 102, 105.
Argyll and Sutherland Highlanders, 2nd—*At home,* 17; *in the Battle of the Odon Crossings,* 37, 39-41, 42-3; *in the Battle of Gavrus,* 45, 49-50, 52-3, 55, 71-2, 74; *in the Break-out at Caumont,* 85-6, 87, 88-9, 90, 96; *in the Battle of Estrey,* 99, 100-1, 101-2, 103; *at the Crossing of the Seine,* 109, 112, 115, 116; *in the Battle of Courtrai,* 119-20, 123, 124; *in the Battle of Gheel,* 132, 140, 143-4, 145; *in the Battle of Best,* 163, 165, 166; *in the Battle of Tilburg,* 173-4; *in the Battle of Meijel,* 191, 200, 205, 207; *in the Battle of Blerick,* 209, 211, 212, 213; *forcing the Siegfried Line,* 234-5, 236, 241-2, 244, 246, 263, 264, 272; *crossing the Rhine,* 278, 285, 286, 287, 288, 289, 290, 293, 299, 302; *in the advance to the Elbe,* 309, 313, 317, 319; *in the Elbe Crossing,* 325, 326, 327-8, 329, 330, 333, 334, 335-6; *leaves the Division,* 342.
Armies—
First Airborne, 129.
First Canadian, 96, 102, 105, 109, 113, 121, 128, 220, 224, 241, 250, 253, 271, 272, 274.
First U.S., 30, 58, 77, 78, 90, 113, 120, 121, 173, 241, 279.
Second British, 29, 30, 55, 57, 58, 59, 60, 65, 80, 106, 109-10, 111, 113, 120, 121, 184, 186, 200, 224, 271, 274, 279, 281, 282, 307.
Third U.S., 101.
Eighth British, 20.
Ninth U.S., 224, 241, 270-1, 274.
Armoured Breaching Force, the, 218, 236, 238, 258, 260.
Army Groups—
12th U.S., 102, 205.
21st, 21, 30, 57, 129, 172, 173, 185, 188, 274, 279, 305, 321; 2nd Echelon, 20.
Arnhem, 120, 129, 156, 159, 164.
Arras, 113.
Artlenburg, 319, 320, 322, 323, 324, 326, 327, 329, 333, 334.
Artois, 121.
Asten, 184, 186, 188, 189, 190, 191, 192, 202, 204, 205, 206, 213, 214.
Au Cornu, 96, 98, 102, 105.
Audenarde, 122, 124, 125.
Auf den Heovel, 233.
Aunay-sur-Odon, 80, 96.
Avelgham, 124.

INDEX

Avendorf, 320.
Avranches, 90, 101.
"Ayr" route, 208, 209, 210, 211, 212.

Baarlo, 220, 222.
Baggaley, Captain, 221.
Bailey Bridges, 131, 135, 281, 294, 300, 309, 311, 323, 363.
Baillie-Grohman, Admiral, 339.
Bain, Captain and Quartermaster, 45.
Bakel, 170, 173, 175.
Baker-Baker, Lieutenant-Colonel H. C., 249, 255, 301, 314, 315, 356.
Balberger Wald, the, 280.
Baltic, the, v, 321, 336.
"Bank Control," 280, 324.
"Bank Group," the, 275, 278, 280, 281, 300, 322.
Barber, Brigadier C. M., 11, 26, 43, 45, 49, 78, 88, 91, 94; (Major-General), ix, 96, 107, 168, 272, 304, 355, 356.
Bargteheide, 337, 338.
Barker, Lieutenant-General Sir Evelyn, 220, 339.
Baron, 46, 54, 60, 61, 66, 67-8, 69, 70, 71, 72.
Barum, 319.
Basedow, 328, 330, 331-2.
Bassée, La, 120, 121.
Bata Shoe Factory, Best, 157.
"Battle for the Bonnet," 15.
Battle of Britain, 10.
Battles in North-West Europe—
    Best, 149-70.
    Blerick, 208-19.
    Caumont, v, 21, 80-107.
    Courtrai, 119-28.
    Elbe, advance to, 305-20.
    Elbe Crossing, the, 321-34.
    Estrey, 97-105.
    Gavrus, 43-73.
    Gheel, 129-48.
    Maas River, the, 220-3.
    Meijel, 185-207.
    Odon Crossings, the, 31-42.
    Rhine Crossing, the, 274-304.
    "Scottish Corridor," 34-55.
    Seine Crossing, the, 108-18.
    Siegfried Line, 324-73.
    Tilburg, 171-84.
Bazoches, 108, 109.
Beatson-Hird, Major D. A., 286.
Beaumont le Roger, 112.
Beckett, Brigadier C. T., 9, 356.
Bedburg, 240, 245, 247, 248, 254.
Beek, 246, 247.

Beek, Major Leoringen van, 201.
Beeringen, 125, 127, 140.
Belgium, 111, 119-52, 274.
Belisha, Rt. Hon. Hore, 1.
Bellinghoven, 289, 299.
Bellinghoven Meer, the, 277, 278, 289, 291, 292, 299, 303.
Belsen Camp, 309.
Beny Bocage, Le, 59, 79, 80, 90, 91, 92, 93, 95.
Bergedorf, 335.
Bergen, 285, 289, 290, 291.
Beringen, 206, 207, 208, 210.
Bernaville, 119, 120.
Bernay, 111.
Best, 149-70, 173, 174, 175, 176, 178.
Bethune, 120, 121.
Bettenhof, 286.
Biest, 181, 183.
Bingley, Major (Glasgow Highlanders), 64.
Binnemeinde, 132.
Bislich, 275, 277, 282, 283, 284, 285.
Bislicher Ley, the, 277, 285, 291.
Bismarck, Prince and Princess von, 335.
Black Watch, 7th, 262.
Blair, Major (Seaforth), 91.
Blair, Sergeant (Glasgow Highlanders), 74.
Blaskowitz, General, 279.
Bleckede, 319-20, 335.
Blerick, 208, 214-19, 256.
Blericksche Bergen, 218.
Blitterswijk, 213.
Blumentritt, Chief of Staff, 336.
Bocholt, 294, 302, 305.
Boekel, 170.
Boersteeg, 232.
Bois des Monts, the, 97, 98, 104.
Bois du Homme, the, 81, 83, 86, 87, 89, 90, 91, 92, 93, 106.
Bois Halbout, 108, 109.
Boizenburg, 325.
Bolton, Brigadier Lyndon, 50, 61.
Bombardment Division, 9th U.S., 231.
Bon Repos, Le, 67, 68, 69, 70, 72, 74.
Bordenau, 307.
Bornsen, 335, 336.
Boschkant, 166.
Bossuyt, 124, 125.
Bougy, 49, 65, 67, 69, 72-3, 77.
Bourg, Le, 85.
Bourg Leopold, 136.
Boxtel, 145, 151, 155, 156, 163, 166, 173, 174, 175, 272.
Bradford, Lieutenant-Colonel Sir E. M. A., 116, 160, 177, 178, 182, 190, 196, 356.
Bradley, General, 58, 59, 78, 80.

Bramwell-Davis, Lieutenant-Colonel R. A., 253, 285, 311, 357.
Branden Berg, the, 234.
Brander, Major (Seaforth), 98.
Breda, 173, 225.
Bremen, 305.
Bremershof, 264.
Bresserberg, 239, 240.
Bretteville l'Orgueilleuse, 31, 33.
Bretteville-sur-Laize, 30, 50.
Bretteville-sur-Odon, 61, 63.
Brettevillette, 73.
Brietlingen, 325.
Brigades—
  1st Commando, 274, 282, 290, 305, 322, 323, 325, 326, 328, 332.
  4th Armoured, 46, 47, 50, 110, 118, 119, 120, 124, 125, 181, 192, 275, 278.
  4th Canadian Infantry, 64.
  5th Parachute, 285, 291, 293, 307.
  6th Air Landing, 294, 316.
  6th Guards Tank, ix, 16, 17, 18, 20, 24, 81, 106, 107, 154, 172, 173, 174, 175, 183, 184, 188, 229, 240, 303, 305, 306, 307.
  7th Canadian, 246, 254.
  8th British, 272.
  8th Canadian, 30, 61, 63.
  9th, 272.
  15th Infantry, 332, 335.
  22nd Armoured, 119, 162.
  29th Armoured, 39, 40, 41, 45, 46, 319, 335.
  31st Tank, 24, 31, 54, 215.
  32nd Guards Infantry, 51.
  33rd Armoured, 275.
  34th Tank, 65, 66, 76, 117.
  37th Independent Infantry, 11, 359.
  44th Lowland—*At home*, 3, 4, 5, 6, 7, 11, 14, 16, 18, 20, 22, 24, 26; *in the Battle of the Odon Crossings*, 31, 35, 36, 39, 42; *at Gavrus*, 44, 46, 52, 54, 55, 60-1, 64, 66, 68-9, 72, 73, 76, 77, 78, 79; *in the break-out at Caumont*, 80, 86, 87, 90, 93, 94-5, 96; *at Estrey*, 101, 102, 104, 105; *at the crossing of the Seine*, 111, 113, 114, 115, 116, 117; *at Courtrai*, 120, 121, 122, 123, 124, 125; *at Gheel*, 129, 130, 131, 132, 136, 138, 140, 141, 142, 143, 144, 145, 147; *in the Battle of Best*, 152, 155, 156, 159, 162, 163, 166, 168, 169, 170; *of Tilburg*, 173, 174, 175, 178, 181, 183; *of Meijel*, 188, 189, 190, 197, 199, 201, 202, 204, 205, 206; *of Blerick*, 210, 211, 212, 213, 214, 216, 219, 220, 223; *forcing the Siegfried Line*, 226, 229, 236, 237, 238, 239, 240, 241, 242, 243, 246, 256, 258, 261, 263, 266, 268, 270, 271, 272; *crossing the Rhine*, 275, 277, 278, 279, 280, 282, 285, 289, 290, 291, 292, 294, 297, 300, 301; *in the advance to the Elbe*, 306, 307, 308, 313, 316-17, 318, 319; *crossing the Elbe*, 323, 325, 329, 330, 333, 334, 336, 337; *after end of hostilities*, 338, 340, 341; *disbanded*, 342.
  45th Infantry, 3, 4, 5, 6, 7, 11, 16.
  46th (H.L.I.)—*At home*, 3, 4, 5, 7, 9, 11, 13, 14, 18, 22, 25; *at the Odon Crossings*, 31, 32, 34-5, 37, 38-9, 41, 42; *at Gavrus*, 46, 48-9, 52, 54, 60, 61-2, 64, 66, 76, 77, 78, 79; *in the break-out at Caumont*, 80, 83, 86-7, 89, 90, 93, 94, 95, 96; *at the Battle of Estrey*, 97, 101, 102, 105, 106; *crossing the Seine*, 108, 109, 110, 112, 114, 116, 117; *at the Battle of Courtrai*, 119, 121, 122, 123, 124, 125, 128; *of Gheel*, 129-30, 131, 141, 143, 144, 147; *of Best*, 150, 152, 155, 158, 164, 169, 170; *of Tilburg*, 172, 174, 175, 181; *of Meijel*, 189, 190, 191, 194-5, 198, 199, 201; *of Blerick*, 210, 211, 212, 213, 214, 219, 220-1, 223; *forcing the Siegfried Line*, 226, 229, 231, 236, 237, 239, 240, 243, 244, 245, 246, 252, 253, 254, 255, 263, 265, 266, 267, 268, 271, 272; *crossing the Rhine*, 277, 278, 280, 289, 290, 292-3, 298, 299, 301, 302; *advancing to the Elbe*, 305, 308, 309, 311-12, 314, 316, 317, 318, 319, 320; *crossing the Elbe*, 323, 328, 329, 332, 334, 335, 337; *after hostilities*, 338-40, 341; *disbanded*, 342.
  69th, 130.
  70th Infantry, 54.
  71st Infantry, 55, 60, 65, 73, 77, 124, 149, 150, 263, 271.
  106th Anti-Aircraft, 340, 341.
  129th, 36, 46, 47, 51, 60, 62, 241, 242, 243, 244, 245, 246, 248, 264.
  130th, 51, 60, 62, 247, 248.
  131st, 124, 125, 126, 128, 144, 147, 163, 168, 169, 173.
  146th, 213, 214.
  151st, 129.
  152nd, 170, 173, 174, 205, 207.
  153rd, 170, 262, 265, 299.
  154th, 170.
  157th, 294, 297, 303.

158th, 55, 60, 65, 66, 74, 75, 76, 125, 168-9, 221, 271, 334.
159th, 42, 45, 46, 50-1, 52, 54, 105, 335.
160th, 52, 54, 60, 64, 65, 76, 77, 108, 125, 220.
176th, 78.
214th, 38, 39, 51, 58, 60, 66, 77, 241, 244, 256, 263, 264.
227th Highland—*At home*, 17, 18; *at the Odon Crossings*, 31, 32, 37, 39-41, 42; *at Gavrus*, 46, 49, 52, 53, 55, 60, 66, 67, 68-70, 71, 74, 76, 77, 79; *in the break-out at Caumont*, 80, 82-3, 87, 92, 96, 97; *at Estrey*, 98-9; *crossing the Seine*, 110, 112, 113, 114, 115, 116, 117; *at the Battle of Courtrai*, 120, 121, 123, 124, 125; *of Gheel*, 129, 130, 132, 142, 143, 147; *of Best*, 150, 156, 159, 162, 163, 165, 166, 169, 170; *of Tilburg*, 173, 174, 175, 178, 183, 184; *of Meijel*, 186, 187, 190, 191, 192, 198, 200, 201, 202, 204, 205; *of Blerick*, 209, 211-12, 213, 214, 220, 223; *forcing the Siegfried Line*, 226, 229, 231, 233, 234, 237, 239, 240, 242, 243, 246, 263, 266, 272; *crossing the Rhine*, 275, 276, 277, 278, 279, 280, 282, 285, 287, 288, 290, 299, 302; *advancing to the Elbe*, 306, 308, 310, 311, 312-13, 316, 317, 319, 320; *crossing the Elbe*, 323, 329, 333, 334, 337; *after hostilities*, 338, 340, 341.
231st, 140.
Briggs, Major (Glasgow Highlanders), 160.
Brimoy, 93.
Briquesard brook, 82, 85, 86.
British Expeditionary Force, the, 5, 8.
Broekhoven, 181, 182.
Broekhuizervorst, 212, 213, 214.
Brown, Major-General Lloyd D., 21.
Brukshof, 294.
Brunstdorf, 334.
Brussels, 120, 220, 273.
Bruyère, La, 97.
Buchan, John, 20.
Buchanan, Lieutenant-Colonel C. R., 103, 356.
Bucholt, 263-4, 266, 272.
Buggenum, 221.
Bullen-Smith, Major-General D. C., 15, 17, 355.
Byude, La, 45.

Caen, v, 30, 35, 36, 58, 59, 65, 78, 79, 82, 91, 96, 105, 108.
Cahagnes, 81, 83, 84, 90.

Cahier, 65, 76, 78.
Calbeck, the Schloss, 264, 265, 267-8.
Calcar, 231, 240, 245, 246, 252, 254, 255, 256, 261.
Cameron Highlanders, 4th, 14; 5th, 207; 7th, 14.
Cameronians, 2nd, 320.
Cameronians, 9th—*At home*, 14; *at the Odon Crossings*, 31, 34-5, 41, 42; *at the Battle of Gavrus*, 43, 44, 46, 48, 52, 62, 63-4, 76; *of Caumont*, 82, 83-4, 85, 87, 90, 91-2, 93, 94, 95; *of Estrey*, 97, 98; *crossing the Seine*, 116, 117; *at the Battle of Courtrai*, 121, 122, 124, 125; *of Gheel*, 130, 131, 136, 144; *of Best*, 150, 157, 158, 160, 163, 164, 165, 168, 169, 170; *of Tilburg*, 174, 175, 176, 177-8, 182-3; *of Meijel*, 189-90, 194-5, 196-7, 198, 199, 200, 207; *of Blerick and the Maas*, 209, 211, 213, 214; *forcing the Siegfried Line*, 231, 233-4, 235, 246, 247-8, 249, 250, 252, 253-4, 255, 267-8, 269; *crossing the Rhine*, 282, 288, 289, 290, 293, 294, 301, 302, 303; *advancing to the Elbe*, 308, 309, 312, 316, 317, 318, 319; *crossing the Elbe*, 328, 331-2; *after hostilities*, 340; *disbanded*, 343.
Campbell, Brigadier J. A., 7, 356.
Campbell, Lieutenant-Colonel P. U., 68, 74, 88, 126, 154-5, 160, 356.
Campbell, Major G. C., 267, 330.
Canadian Armoured Personnel Carrier Regiment, 1st, 229, 236.
Canadian Rocket Projector Unit, 1st, 215.
Canal de Ghent, 126.
"Canloan" Scheme, 23.
Canteloup, 99.
Carey, Captain (K.O.S.B.), 284-5.
Carpiquet airfield, 33, 36, 38, 58, 60.
Carruthers, Captain (Cameronians), 196.
Catheolles, 92, 93, 94.
Caumont, v, 35, 36, 78, 79, 80, 81, 82-4, 87, 89, 90, 106, 223.
Caverie, La, 96, 97, 98, 99, 101, 103, 104.
Celle, 305, 307, 308, 309.
Chambois, 109.
Charentenne, River, 111.
Château des Buspins, 116.
Cherbourg, 30, 58.
Cheux, 32, 33, 35, 37, 38, 39, 42, 44, 45, 48, 49, 51, 52, 66.
Chichester, the Bishop of, 24.
Christison, Major-General A. F. P., 11, 15, 355.
Churchill, Rt. Hon. Winston, 23.

INDEX

Clark, Brigadier Harry, xi, 11; (Colonel), 23, 25, 26, 109, 342, 356.
Clark, Major (Cameronians), 84.
Cleve, 225, 227, 228, 229, 231, 235, 238, 239, 240, 241, 242, 243, 244, 245, 246, 247, 250, 255, 256, 258, 263, 267.
Clever-Berg, 241, 242, 244.
Clyde, the, 5.
Cockburn, Brigadier J. C., 80, 93, 94, 123, 136, 142, 163, 166, 167, 175, 178, 181, 182, 188, 189, 190, 194, 199, 201, 356.
Codmet, Le, 97.
Coldstream Guards, 4th (Tank), 83, 86, 87, 88, 90, 91, 92, 97, 98, 183, 193, 194, 195, 197, 205, 227, 231, 232, 237, 240, 245, 248, 251, 263, 264, 266, 307, 308, 318, 323, 333.
Colleville, 38, 39, 40, 41, 42, 43, 44, 45, 49, 50, 51, 52, 53, 61, 66.
Colville, Lieutenant-Colonel E. C., 38, 39; (Brigadier), 112, 115, 140, 163, 166, 186, 187, 191, 241, 263, 266, 288, 310, 313, 333, 357.
Combat Commands " A " and " R " (U.S.), 202, 205.
Conches, 113.
Condé, 80.
Confirmation Schools, 20, 22, 24.
Cornwall, Major (R.A.), 53.
Corps—
 1st, 16, 17, 30, 31, 58, 59, 65, 78, 170, 184.
 2nd Canadian, 65, 79, 119, 253, 271.
 5th U.S., 80, 91, 95, 96-7, 108.
 7th U.S., 59.
 8th, 17, 19, 20, 21, 29, 30, 54, 57, 58, 65, 78, 80, 81, 89, 91, 93, 96, 106, 109, 129, 170, 172, 173, 183, 185, 186, 187, 189, 200, 201, 205, 207, 208, 220, 305, 306, 307, 310, 319, 320, 321, 339.
 9th, 14, 15.
 11th, 7, 10.
 12th, 65, 77, 105, 109, 110, 111, 113, 118, 119, 120, 121, 128, 129, 131, 143, 146, 150, 170, 173, 200, 205, 208, 209, 212, 213, 220, 274, 279-80, 281, 282, 299, 305, 334, 336.
 13th U.S., 307, 313.
 15th U.S., 105, 109.
 18th U.S. Airborne, 275, 277, 281, 284, 321.
 19th U.S., 59, 96, 109, 111, 113.
 30th, 30, 38, 54, 60, 66, 73, 77, 78, 80, 81, 82, 91, 96, 109, 111, 112, 119, 120, 127, 129, 143, 145, 149, 150, 155, 159, 163, 164, 166, 170, 200, 220, 221, 223, 224, 225, 228, 271, 272, 274, 275, 282, 305.
Counter-mortar organisation, 61, 104.
County of London Yeomanry, 3/4th, 130, 131, 132, 291, 292, 297-8.
Courtrai, 121, 122, 123-4, 125.
Courtrai-Bossuyt Canal, 122, 123, 124.
Couverville, 116, 117.
Crerar, Lieutenant-General, 224, 272.
Croix des Filandriers, 66, 68.
" Crossing Control," 280, 324.
" Crossing Sweepers," the, 40.
Cumming-Bruce, Brigadier Hon. H. C. T., 210, 214, 215-16, 218, 239, 242, 243, 258, 259, 265, 268, 283, 295, 296, 300, 356.
Cunis, Captain J. S., 123-4.

Dalldorf, 331.
Dampierre, 81.
Danvou, 96.
Davies, C.S.M., D.C.M. (Argylls), 165.
Davies, Major J. C., 63, 177, 180, 190-1, 194.
Davis, Sapper (279th Field Company), 135.
Deerlyk, 123.
Delacombe, Lieutenant-Colonel R., 72, 73, 356.
Delingsford, 338.
Dempsey, Lieutenant-General Sir Miles, v, 29, 30, 56, 57, 58, 59, 78, 80, 106, 120, 173, 303-4, 341.
Denmark, 321.
Deurne, 172, 184, 189, 192, 194, 201, 212.
Deurne Canal, 183, 185, 186, 188, 192, 195, 196, 199, 206, 207.
De Winton, Lieutenant-Colonel R. W., 112, 244, 357.
Deynse, 121, 125.
" Diamond Wood," 199, 201, 202, 204, 205.
Diersfordt, 277, 285.
Diersfordter Wald, the, 275, 277, 284, 285, 291.
Diest, 128.
Dingen, 278, 291, 300.
Dinther, 173, 175.
Displaced persons, problem of, 306, 338, 342.
Divisions—
 1st Airborne, 155, 164.
 2nd Canadian, 64, 65, 228, 237.
 2nd London, 7.
 3rd British, 31, 93, 104, 172, 185, 188, 208, 212, 213, 271, 272.

3rd Canadian, 30, 31, 32, 58, 60, 65, 228, 236, 242, 246, 253.
4th Canadian Armoured, 111, 113.
5th British, 320, 335, 336, 341.
5th U.S., 78, 79.
6th British Airborne, 223, 275, 277, 285, 301, 303, 305, 306, 316, 318, 332, 334, 335, 336.
7th British Armoured, 118, 119, 120, 121, 122, 124, 125, 140, 144, 146, 147, 150, 156, 168, 173, 182, 184, 299, 300, 302, 303, 305, 336.
7th U.S. Armoured, 172, 183-4, 185, 187, 189, 192, 202.
9th Armoured, 21.
9th Highland, 13.
11th Armoured, 21, 32, 40, 42, 43, 44, 45, 46, 50, 81, 86, 88, 89, 90, 91, 92, 93, 95, 96, 105, 117, 119, 120, 124, 188, 208, 211, 212, 213, 214, 303, 305, 307, 310, 313, 318, 319, 323, 334, 338.
15th Scottish. *See under* Fifteenth.
17th U.S. Airborne, 275, 277, 285.
28th U.S. Infantry, 21.
30th U.S., 102.
38th Infantry, 21.
42nd, 11.
43rd Wessex, 17, 36, 38, 46, 51, 58, 60, 61, 62, 66, 67, 81, 82, 87, 88, 89, 90, 92, 93, 95, 96, 97, 101, 104, 111, 112, 117, 155, 229, 240, 241, 243, 245, 247, 254, 256, 258, 263, 264.
47th Infantry, 21.
49th West Riding, 30, 34, 38, 42, 45, 54, 60, 73, 209, 212, 213.
50th, 82, 125, 127, 129, 140.
51st Highland, 13, 15, 17, 30, 112, 170, 173, 174, 180, 205, 206, 207, 209, 220, 228, 250, 256, 262, 266, 275, 282, 290, 294, 298, 300, 319, 342.
52nd Lowland, 1, 2, 3, 4, 5, 159, 274, 294.
53rd Welsh, 51, 52, 55, 60, 61, 64, 65, 73, 76, 77, 108, 109, 118, 119, 120, 121, 124, 127, 143, 145, 146, 147, 149, 150, 168, 173, 174, 175, 220, 221, 228, 233, 240, 250, 254, 256, 263, 268, 270, 271, 299, 300, 336.
59th, 13, 73, 75, 78.
61st, 17.
79th Armoured, 31, 32, 154, 182.
80th, 16.
82nd U.S. Airborne, 159.
102nd U.S. Airborne, 149.
Also see under Bombardment, Guards Armoured, *and* Polish.

Dommel, River, 149, 162, 165, 166, 167, 168, 169, 174.
Donck (near Moll), 130, 132, 140.
Donck (near Meijel), 206, 207.
Donderdonk, 164, 166, 168, 173, 175.
Donsbreuggen, 228, 239, 241, 242, 243, 244, 246.
Dornemardt, 287.
Dorsets, 4th, 62.
Dortmund, 305.
Drabich-Waechter, General-Lieutenant Von, 89.
Dragoons, 22nd, 215, 229.
Drew, Major-General James, 2.
Drome, River, 80, 87.
Drouet, 95.
Druerie, La, 98.
Dumfries, 5.
Dunkirk, 170.
Dusseldorf, 224.
Dutch Resistance, the, 171, 175.

Earlston, 4.
"East Knoll," 250, 253, 255.
East Lancashire Regiment, 1st, 76.
East Riding Yeomanry, 275, 277.
East Yorkshire Regiment, 1st, 188.
Eastern Command, 7.
Ecuis, 117.
Eerde, 168.
Ehlershausen, 308.
Eikelenbosch, 212.
Eindhoven, 142, 146, 149, 151, 155, 159, 163, 226.
Eisenhower, General, 24, 105, 321.
Elbe, River, 305-37, 322.
Elbe-Trave Canal, the, 322, 328, 329, 330, 331, 335.
Elbeuf, 111.
Elizabeth, H.M. Queen, 23.
Elizabeth, H.R.H. Princess, 23.
Elliott, Major (K.O.S.B.), 260-1.
Elsenhof, 234-5.
Elst, 156.
Emanville, 112.
Emmerich, 227, 229, 240, 244, 274, 279.
Ems, 305.
Escaut, River, 121, 122, 123, 124, 125.
Eschede, 310, 311.
Esels-Berg, the, 247, 252, 254.
Esperance, 239.
Essen, 279.
Esquay, 46, 52, 66, 67, 68, 71, 72, 74, 75, 77, 96, 105.
Estry, 92, 96, 97, 99-100, 101, 102, 103, 104, 105.

INDEX

Eterville, 60, 61, 62, 64, 108, 192.
Evans, Private Albert (Glasgow Highlanders), 127.
Evrechy, 46, 65, 67, 69, 70, 71, 72, 75, 77, 96, 105, 108, 192.
Evreux, 59, 109.
Exercises for the Crossing of the Rhine, 275-6.
Exercises, Training, 10.
 "Blackrock," 19.
 "Brasso," 17, 18.
 "Buffalo," 274.
 "Cheviot," 15.
 "Clansman," 20-1.
 "Eagle," 21-2.
 "Gallop," 132.
 "Glaxo," 19.
 "Heretic," 19.
 "Oyster 1," 19.
 "Oyster 2," 22.
 "Tally-ho," 21.
 "Tatler," 22.
 "Tatler 2," 25.

Fahrendorf, 335.
Falaise, 59, 77, 79, 96, 101, 102, 104, 105, 108, 109, 110.
Farmer, Lieutenant (H.L.I.), 286.
Fasanenkath, 268.
Ferguson, Major (Argylls), 109.
Ferme de Mondeville, 65, 67, 71, 75.
Ferriere au Doyen, La, 88, 90, 91, 92.
Feuguerolles, 105.
Fife and Forfar Yeomanry, 1st, 215; 2nd, 39, 41, 42.
Fifteenth Scottish Division—*Begotten of 52nd Lowland Division, 1-2; and of the old 15th, 2; its sign, "O," 2, 9-10; its Commanders, 2, 9, 10, 11, 15, 17, 94, 355; Scotland to Wiltshire, 6; to Essex, 7; inspected by H.M. the King, 9, 23; reverted to "Lower Establishment," 13-16; loses 45th Brigade, 16; to Yorkshire, 17; to Sussex, 23; crosses to Normandy, 27-8; in the Crossings of the Odon, 29-77; and the break-out from Caumont, 80-102; spearheads crossing of Seine, 108; and of Rhine, 274; and of Elbe, 321; praised by higher authority, 57, 106-7, 303-4; and by Field-Marshal Montgomery, 222-3.*
Fifteenth Scottish Division—
 Artillery, 340, 341.
 Battle School, 19.
 Casualties, 56, 347-54.
 Games, 11, 25, 26-7, 342.
 Headquarters, xi, 3, 4, 7, 14, 18, 23, 26, 27, 31, 120, 226, 245, 247, 250, 272, 280, 321, 324, 338, 340, 341, 342.
 Honours and Awards, 365.
 Order of Battle, 359-62.
Flers, 104.
Fleury, 119.
Fontaine Étoupefour, 62.
Fontainebleu, 110.
Fontenay-le-Pesnil, 38.
Forêt du Lyons, 120.
Formerie, 120.
Forst Segeberg, 338-9.
Forth Defences, the, 5.
44th Brigade History, The, 216, 282, 283, 296.
46th Brigade History, The, 272.
"Forward Control," 280.
Foster, Colonel R., 281, 300, 323-4, 330.
Fouquerie, La, 83.
Frasselt, 227, 228, 234, 235, 236, 238.
Fratershoef, 167, 168, 169.
Free French Infantry, 117, 119, 121.
Fretteville, 116.
Frevent, 121.
Friedrichsruh, 335.
Fuhrberg, 308.
"Funnies," 31, 102, 104, 182, 225, 231, 234, 237, 258, 259.
Fyfe, Major Alan, 40, 101.

Gaillon, 113.
Galashiels, 4, 5.
Galet, 91.
Galgensteeg, 233, 235.
Gardiner, Lieutenant-Colonel R. H. H., 26, 357.
Gasthuishoef, 166-7.
Gaule, La, 32, 36.
Gavere, 125.
Gavrus, 42-3, 45, 46, 47, 49, 51, 52, 53, 60, 61, 67, 69, 72-3.
Geesthacht, 329, 333, 334, 336.
Geldern, 224, 227, 271.
Gemert, 170, 175.
Gennep, 172, 227, 228.
George VI., H.M. King, 9, 23, 337.
German formations—
 Army Group "B," 220, 223.
 Army Group "H," 279.
 Ausbild Regiment, 95.
 Battalion Graefing, 270.
 Flieger Ausbild Battalion, 261.
 Hermann Goering Training Regiment, 136, 137, 138.
 Hermann Parachute Regiment, 185.

INDEX

Hitler Youth Division, 33.
Hubner Parachute Regiment, 185, 195.
Panzer Division Clausewitz, 316.
Panzer Lehr, the, 29, 59.
1st Panzer Division, 46, 55, 59, 77.
1st Parachute Army, 136, 142, 150, 279.
2nd S.S. Panzer Corps, 50, 59.
2nd S.S. Panzer Division, 42, 45, 52, 55.
2nd Parachute Division, 256.
5th Flak Division, 338.
6th Parachute Division, 243.
7th Parachute Division, 240, 256, 279, 290, 292, 300, 302.
8th Parachute Division, 256, 338.
9th S.S. Panzer Division, 46, 47, 49, 50, 51, 55, 66, 77, 93, 95, 96, 99, 186.
10th S.S. Panzer Division, 52, 55, 66, 77, 93.
12th S.S. Division, 29, 33, 36, 42, 45-6, 55, 77.
15th Army, 58, 96, 150.
15th Panzer Grenadier Division, 186, 246, 279.
16th G.A.F. Division, 59, 129.
19th S.S. Panzer Division, 50.
19th S.S. Panzer Grenadiers, 47.
21st Panzer Division, 29, 36, 46, 55, 59, 91, 92.
21st Panzer Grenadier Regiment, 66, 93.
22nd Panzer Grenadier Regiment, 66.
47th Panzer Corps, 185, 186, 195.
51st and 53rd Air Force Regiments, 136.
84th Infantry Division, 228, 279, 300.
116th Panzer Division, 246, 279, 292.
125th Panzer Grenadier Regiment, 92.
180th Infantry Division, 256.
190th Fusiliers, 263.
190th Infantry Division, 256.
276th Infantry Division, 59.
277th Infantry Division, 59.
326th Division, 79, 82, 89.
344th Division, 185.
752nd Grenadier Regiment, 85.
901st Panzer Grenadier Regiment, 270.
1062nd Grenadier Regiment, 283.
Gheel, 125, 127, 128, 129-48, 156, 219.
Ghent, 121, 124, 125, 126, 128.
Ginn, Major Sam (R.A.), 219.
Glasgow, 5.
Glasgow Highlanders, 2nd—*At the Odon Crossings*, 31, 35, 41, 42; *at the Battle of Gavrus*, 43, 44, 45, 46, 48, 49, 63-4, 66, 67-8, 73-4, 75, 76; *of Caumont*, 87, 90, 93, 95; *of Estrey*, 97-8; *crossing the Seine*, 116, 117; *in the Battle of Courtrai*, 121, 122, 123, 124, 125-9; *of Gheel*, 132, 136, 138, 141, 142, 143; *of Best*, 152, 153-5, 156, 157-8, 159-62, 166; *of Tilburg*, 175, 176, 177, 178, 179-81, 182, 183; *of Meijel*, 190-1, 193-4, 197, 198, 199, 200; *of Blerick and the Maas*, 210, 211, 213, 214, 216; *forcing the Siegfried Line*, 231, 232-3, 246, 247, 248-50, 251, 252, 254-5, 263-4, 266, 267, 268, 272; *crossing the Rhine*, 282, 288, 289, 290, 293, 299, 301, 302; *advancing to the Elbe*, 312, 314, 315-16, 317, 318, 319; *crossing the Elbe*, 328, 329, 330, 332; *disbanded*, 343.
Goch, 227, 228, 229, 231, 241, 254, 256-63, 264, 265, 266, 267, 268, 271, 272, 281.
Goirle, 181, 223.
Gordon Highlanders, 2nd—*At home*, 17; *at the Odon Crossings*, 37-8, 40-1, 42; *at the Battle of Gavrus*, 45, 46, 49, 51, 52, 55, 68-70, 71, 72, 73, 74, 76; *of Caumont*, 83, 84-5, 88, 96; *of Estrey*, 99-100, 101; *crossing the Seine*, 112, 115, 116; *at the Battle of Gheel*, 132, 140, 144, 145; *of Best*, 163, 165, 166, 170; *of Tilburg*, 173; *of Meijel*, 191, 205; *of Blerick and the Maas*, 209, 211, 212, 213, 214; *forcing the Siegfried Line*, 236, 238, 241, 242, 244, 246, 263, 264, 267, 268; *crossing the Rhine*, 288, 289, 290, 293, 299, 303; *advancing to the Elbe*, 308, 309, 314-15, 317, 319; *crossing the Elbe*, 329, 330, 334; *leaves for the Middle East*, 342.
Gordon Highlanders, 5/7th, 299.
Gourney, 71, 97, 104, 119, 120.
Graham, Major Graham, 288.
Grainville, 30, 37, 39, 41, 42, 43, 44, 45, 46, 47, 48, 49, 51, 52, 55, 60, 76, 78, 134.
Grammont, 223.
Grand Rocherolles, 116.
Grant, Lieutenant-Colonel E. H. G., 43, 44, 98, 357.
Grant, Major Iain, 23.
Grave, 225, 226.
Green, C.S.M., D.C.M. (Argylls), 234.
Green Howards, the, 130.
Grenadier Guards, 1st and 2nd, 94.
Grenadier Guards, 4th (Tank), 83, 85, 87, 88, 90, 92, 94, 95, 99-100, 102, 104, 175, 181, 182, 193, 194, 197-8, 199, 201, 202-4, 205, 236, 239, 244, 258, 260, 262, 263, 268, 272, 305, 306, 308.
Groesbeek, 232, 237.
Groot Bridge, De, 127, 129, 142.
Groote Stroom, 175.

Grosse Burgwedel, 308.
Grubbenvorst, 214, 220, 221, 222.
Grünhof, 329, 330, 333.
Grünhof forest, the, 322, 329, 330.
Guards Armoured Division, 11, 19, 21, 24, 51, 81, 90, 92, 93, 96, 101, 104, 117, 120, 124, 125, 127, 129, 142, 229, 303.
Guigne, River, 66, 75.
Gulzow, 330, 333, 334.
Gulzower Holz, the, 333.

Haelen, 221.
Haffen, 277, 287, 288, 289, 290, 293, 294, 299.
Hagan, Dr E. J., 22, 222.
Haganer Meer, the, 277, 289, 290.
Haies, Les, 94.
Hailey, Lieutenant-Colonel J. M., 69, 187, 355.
Haldern, 291, 298, 302, 303.
Haligsdorf, 317.
Halluin, 122, 123.
Hambrock, 317.
Hamburg, 305, 334, 335, 336, 338.
Hamilton, 5.
Hamminkeln, 275, 292, 294, 297, 300, 302.
Hammoor, 338.
Hamwarde, 333, 334.
Hanover, 307, 308.
Harding, Lieutenant-General John, 20.
Harlebeke, 125.
Harrison, Major (R.S.F.), 242, 262.
Harrison, Major (Seaforth), 91.
Harz Mountains, 316.
Hasselt, 245, 246, 247, 249.
Hasselt Branch Canal, 140, 143.
Hau, 244.
Haus Kreuzfuhrt, 232, 233.
Haut du Bosq, Le, 32, 33, 35, 37, 38, 39, 44, 46, 48, 51, 54, 60, 61, 77.
Havre, Le, 121.
Hawick, 4, 5.
Heeze, 186.
Heid-Berg, 329, 332.
Heishof, 270, 271.
Heisterhof, 297-8.
Heitrak, 192, 199.
Hekkens, 227, 228, 250.
Helden, 220.
Helena Canal, 206, 207, 209.
Helenaveen, 186, 208, 209, 210.
Helmond, 170-2, 174, 184, 185, 186, 189, 192, 205, 212.
Henderson, Major R. (Gordon Highlanders), 267.
Henderson, Major (Seaforth), 249.

Hendrik, Major (Cameronians), 196.
Herenthals, 130, 143.
Herqueville, 115.
s'Hertogenbosch, 145, 150, 156, 173, 174, 175, 177, 326.
Hervieux, 86, 87, 88.
Hesdin, 121.
Hettsteeg, 232.
Hettsteeghof, 234, 235.
Heusden, 187, 191, 200, 212.
Highland Light Infantry, 6th, 302.
Highland Light Infantry, 10th—*At home*, 13, 17; *at the Battle of Odon*, 37, 42; *of Gavrus*, 44, 45, 46, 49, 50, 51, 55, 71-2; *of Caumont*, 85, 86, 87, 96; *of Estrey*, 99, 100, 101, 103; *crossing the Seine*, 112, 115, 116, 117; *at the Battle of Courtrai*, 120, 124; *of Gheel*, 132, 140, 144, 145-6; *of Best*, 156, 159, 163, 165, 166, 168, 170; *of Tilburg*, 173; *of Meijel*, 191, 198, 204, 205, 206, 207; *of Blerick and the Maas*, 209, 210, 212, 213; *forcing the Siegfried Line*, 234, 235-6, 238, 244, 246, 252, 253, 254, 255, 266, 272; *crossing the Rhine*, 285-7, 289, 303; *advancing to the Elbe*, 309, 310-11, 312-13, 314, 317, 319, 320; *crossing the Elbe*, 329, 330, 333, 334, 335; *after hostilities*, 341; *disbanded*, 342.
Highland Light Infantry, 11th, 13.
Hill, Brigadier James, 293.
Hill 208: 99, 101.
Hill 238/244: 92, 93.
Hilton, Brigadier R., 14, 26, 41-2, 342, 356.
Hingst-Berg, the, 236, 239.
History of the K.O.S.B., 221.
Hitler, Adolph, 6, 303, 335.
Hittbergen, 319, 328.
Hobbs, Lieutenant-Colonel Remington, 233, 250-1, 253, 254, 268, 301, 308, 318, 331, 332, 356.
Hoch Wald, the, 228, 278, 280.
Hodges, General (U.S.), 279.
Hoelke, 163.
Hof, 206.
Hohenhern, 335.
Hohnstorf, 323, 324, 326, 328.
Holben boom, 264.
Holdenstedt, 311, 312, 313, 314.
Holland, 153.
Home Forces, G.H.Q., 21.
Hooesaat, 266, 268.
Hooge Hof, 232, 234.
Hoogebrug bridge, 186, 195, 197, 199, 207, 208, 209.

Horrocks, Lieutenant-General, 146, 225.
Horst, 209, 211, 212, 213.
Host, 270, 271.
Household Cavalry Regiment, 2nd, 81, 92, 229.
Hout Blerick, 212.
Houthuizen, 213.
Houville, 117.
Hoverhof, 287.
Howe, Private (K.O.S.B.), 295.
Hubsch, 285, 287, 288, 293, 300.
Hunger-Berg, 329, 332.
Hunt, Lieutenant-Colonel P. M., 116, 152, 164, 245, 250, 255, 291, 332, 357.
Hunter, Major A. D. N., 242.
Hussars, 8th, 169; 14/18th, 188, 189.
Hutten, 192, 197, 199.

Ibbenburen, 305.
L'Ile du Bac, 115.
Ilmenau, River, 318.
Imigshof, 263.
Inns of Court Regiment, 20, 81, 89, 90.
Intelligence Corps, 270.
    39th Field Security Section, 16.
Irish Guards, 142.
Irish Guards, 2nd (Armoured), 92.
Issel, River, 275, 277, 278, 291, 292, 294, 295, 297, 300, 301.
Italy, 336.

Jackson, Major (K.O.S.B.), 260-1, 262, 270, 271.
Jarvis, Dr, 20.
Jedburgh, 4, 5.
Jöckern, 284, 285.
Johnstone, 5.
Joynt, Major P. R. Lane, 73.
Juliusburg, 323, 330, 333.
Jurques, 90.

Kalbeck, the Schloss, 265, 267, 268.
Kapenhof, 293-4, 299.
Kastenaar, 212.
Kavalaer, 281.
Keitel, General Von, 336.
Kenneth, Major (Argylls), 109.
Kerkhove, 123, 125.
Kerr, Colonel D. L., 26.
Kessel, 220.
Kesselring, Marshal, 279.
Kiekberg, 227.
Kiel, 338, 339-40.
Killemanskath, 252.
Kilmarnock, 5.

Kilsyth, 5.
King's Own Scottish Borderers, 1st, 272.
King's Own Scottish Borderers, 6th—
At home, 24; *at the Battle of the Odon Crossings*, 36; *of Gavrus*, 44, 45, 47-8, 54, 55, 60, 68-70, 72, 73, 75, 76, 77; *in the break-out at Caumont*, 80, 92, 94-5; *at the Battle of Estrey*, 102-3, 104; *of the Seine Crossing*, 116, 117; *of Courtrai*, 122, 123, 125; *of Gheel*, 130, 131, 132-4, 138, 141, 143, 144, 145; *of Best*, 155, 156, 157, 159, 162, 163, 166-7, 168, 170; *of Tilburg*, 178, 181, 182; *of Meijel*, 189, 190, 194, 195, 197, 198, 199, 200-1, 204, 205-6, 207; *of Blerick and the Maas*, 210, 216, 219; *forcing the Siegfried Line*, 237, 238, 239, 240, 242, 243, 244, 258-63, 266, 268, 269-70, 271; *crossing the Rhine*, 283, 284, 285, 290, 291-2, 294-5, 297, 300; *advancing to the Elbe*, 317-18; *crossing the Elbe*, 326, 327-8, 330, 332, 334, 335; *disbanded*, 342.
King's Royal Rifle Corps, 2nd, 299.
Kingsford-Lethbridge, Lieutenant-Colonel, 26, 355.
Kirkintilloch, 5.
Kleine Heitrak, 197, 199.
Klinkenberg, 234.
Kluge, General Von, 59, 105.
Knaresborough, Bishop of, 20, 22.
Knight, Brigadier, 215, 218.
Kollow, 333.
Konigsheide, 238.
Kranenburg, 227, 228, 229, 233, 234, 235, 236, 237, 238, 240, 246, 247.
Kreis Segeburg, 340, 342.
Kreis Stormarn, 340, 342.
Kremsel, 166.
Krukow, 330, 333.
Krummel, 333.
Krüzen, 328.

Lambie, Major (Glasgow Highlanders), 64.
Lange Renne lake, the, 277, 289, 293.
Lassy, 96, 98, 100.
Lauder, Sir Harry, 4.
Lauenburg, 319, 320, 321, 322, 323, 325, 331, 332, 334, 341.
Lauwe, 123.
Lawton, Captain C. G., xi.
Laycock, Lieutenant-Colonel (Commandos), 9.
Lee, Sergeant (K.O.S.B.), 318.
Leensel, 190, 191, 194, 197.
Leese, Major-General Sir Oliver, 10-11.

Le Fanu, Major-General R., 2, 9, 355.
Leine, River, 307.
Lewis, Captain and Quartermaster, M.C., 334.
Liege, 220.
Liemde, 165, 174.
Lierre, 127.
Liesel, 186, 188, 189, 192, 193, 194, 195, 196, 197, 198, 201, 208.
Lieu Mondant, Le, 85.
Lille, 121, 122, 124.
Lion Rampant (*Divisional Sign*), 9-10, 224, 225, 243.
Lipperloo, 128.
Lisle, Captain, M.C. (Cameronians), 196.
Lloyd, Lieutenant, M.C. (Middlesex Regiment), 193-4.
Local Defence Volunteers, 8.
Lochore, Major John, 52.
Loges, Les, 83, 86, 90.
Loh, 277, 285.
Lohr, 286, 287, 288, 289.
Lommel, 143, 145, 146, 149, 150.
Londe, Le, 117.
London District, 7.
Lookout Tower, 241, 242.
Loon, 194, 195.
Loonsche Bann, the, 196.
Loos, 38, 121.
Lorrimer, Corporal (Glasgow Highlanders), 64.
Lothians and Border Yeomanry, 81.
Lottum, 213.
Lountain, Lieutenant (K.O.S.B.), 132.
Louviers, 109, 111, 112, 113, 114, 115.
Louvigny, 63, 64.
Lubeck, 335, 336, 337, 338, 340, 341, 342.
Lubertsche Straat, 232.
Lüdershausen, 319.
Ludwigslust, 341.
Luftwaffe, the, 270, 329-30, 334, 336.
Luneburg, 305, 319, 320, 322, 325.
Lutain Wood, 82, 84-5.
Lütau, 328, 332.
Luttingen, 280.
Lyne, Major-General L. O., 336.
"Lys Force," the, 121-2.
Lys River, 121, 122, 123, 124, 125.

Maas, River, 129, 149, 172, 173, 185, 200, 206, 207, 208-23, 224, 227, 271, 274, 275, 279.
Maasbree, 219.
Maat, De, 143, 149.
Machelen, 125.
M'Elwee, Major (Argylls), 53.

Mackenzie, Major Ian, 103; (Lieutenant-Colonel), 163, 175, 182, 265, 266, 295, 356.
Mackintosh-Walker, Brigadier R., 17, 26, 49, 53, 69, 357.
Mackley, Lieutenant-Colonel H. P., 124, 198, 357.
M'Laren, Sergeant (Glasgow Highlanders), 127.
Macleod, Pipe-Major, 23.
MacMillan, Major-General G. H. A., 15, 17, 25, 26, 31, 46, 56, 75, 94, 107, 355.
Maconochie, Lieutenant (K.O.S.B.), 205-6.
M'Queen, Major (Royal Scots), 258.
M'Queen, Sergeant (K.O.S.B.), 132.
Mair, Major M'Kenzie, 91.
Maizet, 65, 74, 108.
Malden, 250.
Malines, 127, 128, 129, 130.
Mallon, Corporal (Royal Scots), 298.
Malone, Major (K.O.S.B.), 270.
Maltot, 60, 62, 77, 108.
Mancelliere, La, 92, 96.
Mann, Major J. P., 244.
Manoir, Le, 42, 45.
Mans, Le, 58.
Marcelet, 36, 38, 48.
Mariahoeve bridge, 206, 207, 208.
Marman, Major J. F., 27.
Martin, Lieutenant-General H. G. (*the Author*), vii, ix, xi.
Mary, H.R.H. Princess, 24.
Massy, Lieutenant-General H. R. S., 7.
Materborn, 228, 232, 239, 240, 241, 242, 243, 244, 245, 246.
"Mattresses," 215, 218, 235, 252, 258, 282.
Mecklenburg, 321.
Mecklenburg and Schwerin, Duke of, 341.
Meerhout, 132.
Mehr, 275, 277, 278, 289, 290-1, 292, 294, 299.
Mehrloo, 299, 301.
Meijel, 184-207, 208, 210, 219.
Mellendorf, 308.
Melrose, 4, 5.
Mélun, 110.
Menin, 121, 122, 123.
Meredith, Captain (R.A.), 70; (Major), 291.
Merrifield, Major (H.L.I.), 236.
Merzplas, 223.
Mesnil, Le, 63.
Mesnil Andé, Le, 115, 116.
Mesnil Patry, Le, 32, 33, 36, 42, 51, 52, 76.
Meuse, River, 220.

Meuse-Escaut Junction Canal, the, 127, 129, 130, 131, 132, 136, 140, 143, 146, 149, 150, 159.
Middlesex Regiment, 1st, 18, 24, 31, 53, 61, 67, 102, 157, 193-4, 342; 1/7th, 9, 13.
Miebord, 66, 67.
Milheeze, 170.
Millar, C.S.M., M.C. (K.O.S.B.), 103.
Millar, Lieutenant-Colonel R. K., 26, 130-1, 356.
Millar, Major (Glasgow Highlanders), 160.
Minden, 306, 307.
Ministry of Labour, the, 4.
Missy, 78.
Moergestel, 176, 177, 178, 179, 182, 183.
Moll, 130, 132, 140, 152.
Molln, 335, 341.
Monceaux, 52, 78.
Mondrainville, 40, 42, 43, 46, 48, 49, 51, 52, 53, 55, 60, 68, 76.
Money, Brigadier Douglas, 25-6, 36, 47, 73, 80, 356.
Money, Major-General R. C., 9, 11, 355.
Monmouthshires, 2nd, 73, 76.
Monnai, 110.
Montamy, 93, 96.
Montchamps, 93, 95, 96, 101, 102.
Montcharival, 93, 94, 95, 96.
Montgomery, Field-Marshal Viscount, 21, 24, 29, 55, 57, 58, 59, 65, 77, 78, 80, 109, 120, 128, 148, 164, 172, 184, 185, 200, 220, 222-3, 224, 234, 274, 275, 281, 321, 336, 337, 342.
"Monty's Smoke-screen," 278, 279.
Mook, 225, 226, 227, 228.
"Moon" route, 110, 112.
Moostdijk, 199, 200, 204, 205.
Moreton, Major (Argylls), 101.
Morgan, Major D. Russell, 53, 85; (Lieutenant-Colonel), 100, 115, 120, 287, 288, 357.
Morichesse les Mares, La, 84, 87, 88, 89.
Mortain, 101, 102, 104, 105.
Moscrun, 124.
Motor Coach Company No. 20, 15.
Motte, La, 95.
Mouen, 45, 46, 51, 60, 62, 66.
"Movement Light," 66-7, 69, 71, 74-5, 229, 236, 326.
Moyland, 246, 250, 253, 254, 255, 266.
Moyland, Captain van, 255.
Moyland, the Schloss, 250, 254, 255.
Muc stream, 33, 36.
Muids, 114, 116.
Munster, 300.

Naastebest, 151, 158, 163, 174, 175.
Namur, 121.
Nazareth, 125.
Nebelwerfer rockets, 35, 99.
Nederbeke, 123.
Nederijksche woods, the, 232, 234, 236.
Neerkant, 199, 205, 207, 210.
Neetze, 320, 324.
Neth, River, 141.
Nettelkamp, 314, 315, 316.
Neu Bornsen, 335.
Neubourg, Le, 111-12, 113, 114.
Neustadt, 308.
Nichol, Pipe-Major, 23.
Nicholson, Brigadier C., 7.
Niers, River, 256, 261, 262-3, 264, 266, 268, 270.
Nijmegen, 145, 149, 164, 172, 200, 213, 224, 225, 226, 227, 228, 229, 236, 237, 240, 245, 247, 272.
Noble, Major (H.L.I.), 314.
Noorder Canal, 183, 185, 186, 192, 202, 206, 207.
Normandy, 27-110.
Normandy to the Baltic, 55.
Norrey-en-Bessin, 32, 33, 55.
Northamptonshire Yeomanry, 2nd, 35, 44.
Northumberland Fusiliers, 4th, 16, 18.
Norway Expeditionary Force, 6.
Noyers, 46, 48, 54, 66, 73, 75, 117.
Nutterden, 228, 232, 236, 238, 239, 240, 241, 242, 245, 246, 247.

O'Connor, Lieutenant-General Sir Richard, 21, 50, 57, 65, 81, 106, 220.
Odon, River, 30, 37-77, 215, 222.
Oelen, 140.
Oerschot, 150, 151, 157, 174, 175, 176, 178, 182.
Oistersijk, 176-7, 178, 179-81, 182.
Oldenburg Peninsula, the, 338.
Oliver, Major John, 198, 287.
Olland, 174.
Operations—
 "Blockbuster," 271.
 "Bluecoat," 60, 80, 81, 89, 106.
 "Box," 145.
 "Charnwood," 59.
 "Comma," 341.
 "Enterprise," 321.
 "Epsom," 28, 31, 38, 40, 42, 60.
 "Flood," 142, 143.
 "Greenline," 60, 64, 67, 77, 78.
 "Haggis," 170.
 "Jupiter," 60, 61, 64.

INDEX

"Market Garden," 129, 131, 140, 142-3, 146, 164.
"Pheasant," 173, 174.
"Plunder," 274, 277, 282, 303.
"Swan," 303.
"Torchlight," 277, 281.
"Veritable," 223, 224, 225, 231, 270, 272.
"Windsor," 59.
Orbec, 111.
Orleans, 58.
Orne, River, 30, 40, 59, 61-3, 65, 69, 78, 97, 105, 108.
Osnabruck, 300, 305.
Ospel, 186, 205.
Oss, 173.
Ottersum, 250.
Overkamp, 285-6, 289, 290, 294.
Oxfordshire and Buckinghamshire Light Infantry, 1st, 150, 157.

Panningen, 207.
Parachute Regiments (U.S.)—
    501st, 149.
    502nd, 166.
    506th, 149, 157, 162.
Paris, 58, 112, 117.
Pas de Calais, the, 58, 111.
Path of the Lion, The, xi.
Patton, General, 110.
Pearson, Lieutenant-Colonel B. A., 259, 262, 285, 297, 356.
"Peel" of Holland, the, 185, 204, 205, 207.
Periers, 59.
Petit Roncherolles, 116, 117.
Pfalzdorf, 258.
Picardy, 121.
Pierre du Fresnes, 90.
Pike, Major (Grenadier Guards), 238.
Pinçon, Mont, 59, 79, 96, 97, 101.
Piping Society, Divisional, 23.
Point de l'Arche, 113.
Point 112: 40, 50, 51, 60, 61, 62, 66, 67, 68, 71, 74, 105, 108.
Point 113: 50, 51, 60, 67, 69, 70, 72, 73, 74, 75, 105.
Point 226: 83, 86, 88.
Point 361: 81, 87.
Polish Armoured Division, the, 109.
Polish Brigade, the, 159.
Pont Soffrey, La, 97.
Portjoie, 113, 114.
Poses, 113.
Poyel, 130.

Princess Irene (Dutch) Brigade, 181, 182.
Provost Corps, 113, 118.

Qualburg, 245, 246.
Quaremont, 124.
Quarry Hill, 81, 83, 87, 88, 89, 90, 91, 92, 93, 96.
Queen's Royal West Surrey Regiment, 1/7th, 124; 5th, 126; 6th, 126, 127.
Quinn, Lieutenant (Glasgow Highlanders), 64.

"Railway Wood," 278.
Ratzeburger See, the, 336.
Rauray, 34, 38, 42, 48, 54, 60, 73.
Reconnaissance Regiment, 11th, 35, 44.
Reconnaissance Regiment, 15th Scottish—*At home*, 9, 16; *in the Battle of Gavrus*, 48, 67; *of Caumont*, 89, 90, 91, 92, 93, 96; *of Estrey*, 104; *of the Seine Crossing*, 114-15, 117; *of Courtrai*, 119, 121, 122, 123, 125; *of Gheel*, 130, 132, 138, 140, 143, 144, 145; *of Best*, 155, 156, 162, 166; *of Tilburg*, 175, 176, 178; *of Meijel*, 199, 201; *of Blerick and the Maas*, 210, 211, 212, 214, 219; *of the Siegfried Line*, 240, 244, 245; *crossing the Rhine*, 295, 302; *the Elbe*, 307, 308, 312, 314, 333; *after hostilities*, 338, 340.
Reconnaissance Regiment, 49th, 34.
Recussonniere, La, 86.
Red Lion Club, the, 273.
Ree, 286, 287, 289, 290.
Rees, 274, 275, 276, 277, 282, 290, 298, 300.
Regimental Groups (U.S.), 10th and 11th, 79.
Reichswald forest, 172, 225, 227, 228, 233, 234, 239, 240, 250.
Reinforcement Group, 105th, 24.
Reinforcements, 1st, 24.
Remagen bridge, the, 279.
Renault, Monsieur, 119.
Repas, Le, 79.
Rethy, 131, 132, 134, 143.
Rheinberg, 274, 275.
Rhine, River, 128, 129, 149, 224, 227, 228, 229, 271, 273, 274-304, 305, 321, 330.
Rhineland, the, 200, 220, 223, 224-73.
Richardson, Colonel F. M., 309, 357.
Richardson, Major C. W. P., 72; (Lieutenant-Colonel), 77, 134, 166, 239, 260, 284, 292, 317, 356.
Ricklingen, 307.
Rifle Brigade, 8th, 40, 90.

Ringenberg, 302.
Rinkveld, 190, 194.
Risle, River, 111, 112.
Ritchie, Lieutenant-General Neil, 65, 73, 114, 146, 218, 304.
Roberts, Brigadier Mills, 322.
Roberts, Major-General G. B. P., 188.
Robertson, Lieutenant-Colonel D., 98, 357.
Robinson, Major H. C., 165.
Rocrenil, 63.
Roer, River, 224.
Roermond, 172, 221, 224, 227, 274.
Roggel, 221.
Roggelsche, 204, 207.
Rollo, Captain (K.O.S.B.), 54; (Major), 134.
Rommel, Marshal, 29, 80.
Rooth, 216, 219.
Rosendahl, 248, 249.
Rosenhof, 258.
Rotterdam, 225.
Rottum, 270, 271.
Rouen, 111, 117.
Roulers, 121.
Royal Air Force, 10, 32, 110, 132, 231.
Royal Armoured Corps—
    7th Royal Tank Regiment, 31, 42, 49.
    9th Royal Tank Regiment, 31, 37-8, 42, 44.
    11th Royal Tank Regiment, 275, 277, 323, 325.
    44th Royal Tank Regiment, 46, 275, 277, 289.
    49th Armoured Personnel Carrier Regiment, 215, 229, 236.
    101st Regiment, 229.
    107th Regiment, 215.
    147th Regiment, 117.
    153rd Regiment, 72.
    157th Regiment, 67.
Royal Army Medical Corps, 147.
    20th Field Dressing Station, 16.
    22nd Field Dressing Station, 16.
    153rd Field Ambulance, 16.
Royal Army Ordnance Corps—
    15th Divisional Field Park, 16.
    305th Mobile Laundry, 16, 22.
Royal Army Service Corps, 281.
    62nd Company, 16, 226.
    399th Company, 16.
    535th Guards Company, 24.
Royal Artillery—
    A.G.R.A.s, 215, 225.
    25th Field Regiment, 187, 188.
    56th Medium Regiment, 8.
    64th Anti-Tank Regiment, 3, 5, 14.
    91st Anti-Tank Regiment, 47, 80, 90, 315, 316.
    97th Anti-Tank Regiment, 16, 48, 53, 102, 103.
    100th Anti-Aircraft Brigade, 281.
    119th Light Anti-Aircraft Regiment, 16.
    129th Field Regiment, 5, 14.
    130th Field Regiment, 5.
    131st Field Regiment, 7, 11, 14, 31, 53, 72, 132, 144-5, 186-8, 287, 313, 342.
    146th Anti-Tank Battery, 323.
    177th Battery, 123.
    181st Field Regiment, 16, 31, 54, 70, 123, 142, 145, 291, 342.
    190th Field Regiment, 16, 31, 315, 342.
    319th Field Battery, 132.
    529th Field Battery, 315.
    530th Field Battery, 315.
    531st Field Battery, 32, 48, 219.
Royal Berkshire Regiment, 5th, 275, 280, 281.
Royal Dragoons, 1st, 118, 121, 122, 123, 275, 322, 324.
Royal Electrical and Mechanical Engineers, 211, 212, 364.
    15th Division Workshops, 16.
Royal Engineers, 22, 31, 67, 113, 115, 116, 118, 127, 134, 140, 147-8, 152, 156, 175, 178, 207, 208, 211, 212, 276, 281, 290, 300, 309, 311, 326, 330, 363.
    A.V.R.E.s, 236, 237-8, 259, 260.
    6th Assault Regiment, 229.
    7th Army Troops, 329.
    8th Corps Troops, 330, 334.
    11th A.G.R.E.s, 275, 281, 323, 334.
    20th Field Company, 16, 130, 145-6, 311, 363.
    77th Assault Squadron, 323.
    81st Assault Regiment, 215.
    208th Field Company, 131.
    278th Field Company, 14, 130, 143, 145, 363.
    279th Field Company, 14, 130, 134-6, 141, 147, 148, 363.
    624th Field Park Company, 16, 363.
Royal Inniskilling Dragoon Guards, 5th, 162-3.
Royal Naval Commando, the, 324.
Royal Pioneer Corps, 281.
Royal Scots, 8th—*At home*, 8, 27; *at the Battle of the Odon Crossings*, 31, 36; *of Gavrus*, 44, 47, 48, 60, 64, 72, 73; *of Caumont*, 90, 91, 92, 94-5; *of Estrey*, 104, 105; *of the Siene Crossings*, 111, 115; *of Courtrai*, 123, 125; *of Gheel*,

130, 131, 134, 136, 137-8, 142, 144, 145; *of Best*, 159, 162, 163, 166, 167-8, 170; *of Tilburg*, 173, 174, 175, 178, 181; *of Meijel*, 190, 194, 197-8, 199, 201, 204, 205; *of Blerick and the Maas*, 210, 216, 218; *of the Siegfried Line*, 239, 240, 242, 243, 244, 258-63, 268, 269-70; *of the Rhine Crossings*, 282, 283, 284, 285, 290, 291, 292, 295, 296, 297-8, 300; *of the Elbe*, 318, 325, 327, 328, 330, 332; *after hostilities*, 341; *disbanded*, 342.

Royal Scots Fusiliers, 6th—*At home*, 5, 14; *at the Battle of the Odon Crossings*, 31, 35-6, 41; *of Gavrus*, 47, 54, 60; *of Caumont*, 94, 95; *of Estrey*, 102, 103, 104; *of the Seine Crossings*, 115, 117; *of Courtrai*, 123, 125; *of Gheel*, 136, 137-8, 141, 143, 144, 145; *of Best*, 159, 162, 163, 165, 166, 167, 168; *of Tilburg*, 175, 178, 181-2, 184; *of Meijel*, 190, 191, 193, 194, 195, 196, 197, 199, 201, 204, 205, 206; *of Blerick and the Maas*, 210, 216, 218; *of the Siegfried Line*, 238-9, 242-3, 244, 262-3, 265, 266, 267, 268, 269; *of the Rhine Crossings*, 282, 283, 285, 290, 291, 295-7, 300; *of the advance to the Elbe*, 313, 317, 318; *of the Elbe Crossings*, 325, 327, 328, 330, 332; *disbanded*, 342.

Royal Scots Greys, 119.
Royal Signals, 364.
Royal Ulster Rifles, 2nd, 213.
Royal Welch Fusiliers, 7th, 75, 76.
Rubaix, 124.
Ruhr, the, 224, 274.
Rundstedt, General Von, 58, 59, 149, 164, 183, 184, 200, 220, 223, 226, 279.
Russell, Brigadier J., 16, 358.

Saarbrockshof, 269.
Sachsenwald, the, 334, 335, 336.
S.A.S. Regiment, 1st, 338.
St Boswells, 4.
St Denis, 125.
St Gabriel, 31.
St Genois, 124.
St Jean le Blanc, 96.
St Lô, 59, 77, 79, 80.
St Martin, 89, 90, 91, 92, 93.
St Martin des Besaces, 83, 95.
St Mauvieu, 33, 36, 41, 42, 46, 51.
St Oedenrode, 149, 151, 159, 163, 164, 165, 166, 173.
St Paul de Vernay, 78.
St Pierre du Vauvray, 112, 114, 115, 116, 117, 119.

St Pierre Tarentaine, 93, 105.
St Pol, 113, 120, 121, 123, 124.
Ste Croix-Grand-Tonne, 64, 65.
Sandenhof, 289.
Scanlon, Sergeant (H.L.I.), 286.
Schans, 201, 204.
Scharnebek, 319, 321, 322, 324, 326.
Scheldrode, 125.
Scheldt, River, 121, 126, 172, 173, 184, 185.
Schelm, 201, 202, 205.
Schijndel, 168, 169, 173, 174.
Schleswig-Holstein, 321.
Schnakenbek, 323, 328.
Schottheide, 238.
Schüttwick, 277, 284.
Schwarzenbek, 323, 333, 334, 335.
Schwerin, 341.
Scotland the Brave, Divisional March, 27.
Scots Guards, 3rd (Tank), 83, 86, 87, 89, 92, 96, 99, 100, 172, 176, 178, 179, 187, 200, 205, 212, 231, 234, 235, 236, 238, 241, 242, 244, 254, 267, 268, 307, 308, 309, 310, 313, 314.
Scott, Brigadier John, 3, 9, 356.
Scott, Captain (H.L.I.), 39.
"Scottish Corridor," the, 38, 45, 51, 55, 58.
Seaforth Highlanders, 6th, 342.

Seaforth Highlanders, 7th—*At home*, 14; *in the Battle of the Odon Crossings*, 35, 38-9, 41, 42; *of Gavrus*, 43, 46, 48, 52, 53, 63, 64, 76; *of Caumont*, 87, 88, 90, 93, 95; *of Estrey*, 98, 103; *of the Seine Crossings*, 116, 117; *of Courtrai*, 122, 123, 124, 125; *of Gheel*, 132, 144; *of Best*, 151, 152, 156, 157, 158-9, 163, 164-5, 167, 169; *of Tilburg*, 175, 176-7, 178, 179, 180, 181, 182, 183, 184; *of Meijel*, 190, 194, 195, 196, 197, 198; *of Blerick and the Maas*, 210, 211, 213, 214, 219; *forcing the Siegfried Line*, 240, 243, 245, 246, 247, 249-50, 251-2, 254, 255, 267, 268, 269; *crossing the Rhine*, 282, 288, 289, 290-1, 294, 299, 301, 302; *advancing to the Elbe*, 312, 316, 317, 318; *crossing the Elbe*, 326, 328, 331-2; *disbanded*, 342.

Secqueville-en-Bessin, 55, 64, 65.
Seeley, Lieutenant-Colonel Frank, 26, 356.
Seine, River, 58, 108-18, 306, 321.
Selkirk, 4, 5.
Senneville, 117.
Sept Vents, 82, 84, 85, 88.
Sevenum, 208, 209, 210, 211.

Shaw, Captain (R.A.), 270.
Shearer, Major (Cameronians), 84.
Shillington, Lieutenant-Colonel J. G., 54, 72, 356.
Short History of the 15th Scottish Division in the 1914-18 War, 20.
Shropshire Light Infantry, 4th, 45.
Siegfried Line, the, 173, 225, 227-8, 229, 236, 238, 264, 279.
Simpson, General (U.S.), 270.
Sinclair, Major J. R., 50, 72 ; (Lieutenant-Colonel), 85, 99, 100, 112 ; (Brigadier), 170, 265, 357.
"Skye" route, 208, 209, 210, 211.
Slot, 191, 193, 194, 195, 197, 198, 199.
Sluis, 145.
Smith, Lieutenant-Colonel A. W. A., 197.
Somerset Light Infantry, 7th, 39.
Somme, River, 38, 119, 120, 121.
Sonsfeld Forest, the, 277, 278, 294, 301, 302, 303.
Soulevre, River, 89, 90, 93, 94, 95.
Spoordonk, 175.
Sprenze area, the, 337.
Stadenhof, 258.
Stadensen, 314, 315-16.
Staff College, the, 72, 338.
Staffordshire Yeomanry, 323, 328, 331.
"Star" route, 110, 111, 120.
Steenweg, 155, 156, 157, 166, 174.
Stephenson, Major J. H. M., M.C., 315.
Stern-Berg, the, 242, 243.
Stewart, Lieutenant-Colonel J., 20.
Stewart, Major (R.A.), 186-7.
Stokers Horst, 202.
Stoppel-Berg, the, 240.
Student, General, 136.
Sullivan, Captain (R.S.F.), 242, 244.
"Sun" route, 110, 112.
Sussex, 23-4.
Swolgen, 212.

"Tam-o'-Shanters," *Divisional Concert Party*, 4, 23.
Telfer, Sergeant, D.C.M. (K.O.S.B.), 261.
Territorial Army duplicated, 1.
Tesperhude, 329, 330, 333.
Tessel, 45.
Theil, Le, 99.
Thielt, 121.
Thomson, Captain H. R., 167.
Thuit, Le, 116, 117.
Thury Harcourt, 59, 65, 108.
Tienraij, 212, 213.
Tilburg, 173-84, 188, 189, 223, 224, 225, 272-3, 274.
Tillemanskath, 248, 249, 255.
Tinchebray, 80, 93.
Tirlemont, 121.
Tortigni, 90, 91.
Tourcoing, 124.
Tourmanville, 37, 39, 40, 42, 45, 51, 52, 53, 60, 61, 68, 69, 72.
Tourneur, Le, 90, 92, 93.
Tourville, 37, 38, 40, 42, 45, 46, 49, 52, 55, 60.
Trette Poux, 63.
Trittau, 338.
Trun, 110.
Turnhout, 131, 134, 136, 138, 141, 143, 145, 146, 149, 159, 272.
Tuschun Wald, the, 278.
Tuthees, 233.
Tweedie, Lieutenant-Colonel J., 39, 40, 42-3, 53, 71, 101, 109, 357.
Tyler, Lieutenant-Colonel Desmond, 26, 355, 356.
Tyneside Scottish, the, 54.

Udem, 231, 254, 263, 264, 266.
Uden, 155.
Uelzen, 305, 307, 309, 310, 311, 312, 313, 314, 316, 317, 318-19.
Uitwaterings Canal, 206, 207.
Urie, Sergeant (R.S.F.), 296.
Utrecht, 225.

Vacherie, La, 117.
Vacquerie, La, 79.
Vallée, La, 86.
Valtru, Le, 43-4, 46, 48, 49, 51, 52, 53.
Vasenhof, 270, 271.
Vassy, 92, 93, 99, 100, 101.
"V-bombs," 28, 111, 121, 124, 225.
Veerssen, 313, 314, 317, 318.
Veghel, 149, 155, 163, 173.
Veldhoven, 150.
Venables, 114.
Vendes, 73.
Venlo, 185, 192, 208, 212, 214, 219, 263.
Venraij, 172, 185, 208.
Verney, Brigadier G. L., 18, 81, 86, 87, 357.
Verson, 58, 60, 63, 66.
Vieruitersten, 199.
Villains, Les, 72.
Ville Dieu, 90.
Villeneuve, 84.
Villers Bocage, 58, 66, 80, 92, 96, 105.
Villiers, Lieutenant-Colonel R. M., 41, 62, 63, 84, 94 ; (Brigadier), xi, 98, 108, 116, 122, 156, 158, 175, 177, 178, 182, 189, 190, 195, 199, 207, 211, 245, 246, 247,

INDEX

250, 252, 266, 267, 268, 289, 290, 293, 298-9, 301, 318, 331, 332, 339, 356.
Vimoutiers, 110.
Vire, 80, 83, 89, 90, 93, 95, 96-7, 103, 104, 105.
Vissel, 284.
Vleut, 159, 162, 163, 166, 173, 175.
Voordelonk, 190.
Voorste Stroom, the, 176-7, 179.
Vorst, 210, 211.
Vught, 272.
Vynen, 278, 279, 280.

Walker, Lieutenant-Colonel F. W. S., 26, 357.
Waller, Major, M.C. (Middlesex Regiment), 157.
Wardt, 279, 290.
Waters, Major (K.O.S.B.), 104.
"Weasels," 209, 211, 298.
Weert, 172.
Weeze, 231, 268, 270, 271.
Wehrmacht, the, 310, 335, 336, 338-9.
Welfare Fund, Divisional, 23.
Welsh Guards, 24, 94, 95.
Wesel, 228, 229, 265, 267, 271, 274, 275, 276, 282, 290, 291, 298, 303.
Weser, River, 307.
Wessem, 208.
Wessem Canal, 172, 185, 192, 206.
"West Knoll," 250-1, 253.
Weyelghem, 123.
"White" Brigade of Belgium, 123.
White, Sergeant (K.O.S.B.), 317.
Whitton, Captain (R.A.), 290-1.
Whitworth, Lieutenant-Colonel K., 26.
Wiershop, 333.
Wilhelmina Canal, 149, 150, 151, 153, 159, 162, 163, 177.
Willems Waart Canal, 149, 162, 173.
Wingate, Major (R.A.), 291.
Winsen bridge, the, 309, 310, 313.
Wismar, 341.
Wisshof, 294.
Wissmann bridge, the, 278, 291.
Wittenhorst Woods, the, 301, 302.
Wolffskrath, 285, 286, 289.
Wolfs-Berg, the, 236, 239.
Wood, Lieutenant-Colonel (R.A.C.), 72.
Wood, Lieutenant, M.C. (K.O.S.B.), 197.
Wood, Major P. T. (R.E.), 135, 140, 141.
Wood, Private (K.O.S.B.), 205-6.
Worth, 334.
Wright, C.S.M. John, D.C.M., 286.
Wunstorf, 308.
Wyatt, Brigadier R. S. P., 11.
Wyler, 227, 228, 235, 237, 240, 241, 243, 247.

Xanten, 224, 228, 271, 277, 278, 279, 281, 294, 300.

Yalta demarcation line, the, 341.
Young, Captain (K.O.S.B.), 104.
Young, Lieutenant-Colonel J. D. S., 37, 50, 61, 71, 85, 357.
Ypres, 122.

Zandpol, 236.
Zittaart, 132.
Zon, 149, 150, 151, 162, 166, 167.
Zonsche wood, 151, 152, 155.
Zonsche Steeg, 157.
Zucker Holz, 332.
Zuid Willems Vaart Canal, 202.
Zulte, 125.
Zyfflich, 236.

www.ingramcontent.com/pod-product-compliance
Lightning Source LLC
Chambersburg PA
CBHW080753300426
44114CB00020B/2717